AUTOMOTIVE ELECTRONICS HANDBOOK

Related McGraw-Hill Books of Interest

Handbooks

Avallone and Baumeister • MARK'S STANDARD HANDBOOK FOR MECHANICAL ENGINEERS
Benson • AUDIO ENGINEERING HANDBOOK
Brady • MATERIALS HANDBOOK
Chen • COMPUTER ENGINEERING HANDBOOK
Considine • PROCESS/INDUSTRIAL INSTRUMENTS AND CONTROL HANDBOOK
Coombs • PRINTED CIRCUITS HANDBOOK
Coombs • ELECTRONIC INSTRUMENT HANDBOOK
Di Giacomo • DIGITAL BUS HANDBOOK
Fink and Beaty • STANDARD HANDBOOK FOR ELECTRICAL ENGINEERS
Fink and Christiansen • ELECTRONICS ENGINEERS' HANDBOOK
Ganic • McGRAW-HILL HANDBOOK OF ESSENTIAL ENGINEERING INFORMATION
Harper • ELECTRONIC PACKAGING AND INTERCONNECTION HANDBOOK
Harper and Sampson • ELECTRONIC MATERIALS AND PROCESSES HANDBOOK
Hicks • STANDARD HANDBOOK OF ENGINEERING CALCULATIONS
Hodson • MAYNARD'S INDUSTRIAL ENGINEERING HANDBOOK
Johnson • ANTENNA ENGINEERING HANDBOOK
Juran and Gryna • JURAN'S QUALITY CONTROL HANDBOOK
Kaufman and Seidman • HANDBOOK OF ELECTRONICS CALCULATIONS
Lenk • McGRAW-HILL ELECTRONIC TESTING HANDBOOK
Lenk • LENK'S DIGITAL HANDBOOK
Mason • SWITCH ENGINEERING HANDBOOK
Schwartz • COMPOSITE MATERIALS HANDBOOK
Townsend • DUDLEY'S GEAR HANDBOOK
Tuma • ENGINEERING MATHEMATICS HANDBOOK
Waynant • ELECTRO-OPTICS HANDBOOK
Woodson • HUMAN FACTORS DESIGN HANDBOOK

Other

Boswell • SUBCONTRACTING ELECTRONICS
Gieck • ENGINEERING FORMULAS
Ginsberg • PRINTED CIRCUIT BOARD DESIGN
Johnson • ISO 9000
Lenk • McGRAW-HILL CIRCUIT ENCYCLOPEDIA AND TROUBLESHOOTING GUIDE,
   VOLS. 1 AND 2
Lubben • JUST-IN-TIME MANUFACTURING
Markus and Sclater • McGRAW-HILL ELECTRONICS DICTIONARY
Saylor • TQM FIELD MANUAL
Soin • TOTAL QUALITY CONTROL ESSENTIALS
Whitaker • ELECTRONIC DISPLAYS
Young • ROARK'S FORMULAS FOR STRESS AND STRAIN

*To order or to receive additional information on these or any other
McGraw-Hill titles, please call 1-800-822-8158 in the United States.
In other countries, please contact your local McGraw-Hill office.*

BC14BCZ

AUTOMOTIVE ELECTRONICS HANDBOOK

Ronald K. Jurgen Editor in Chief

McGraw-Hill, Inc.

New York   San Francisco   Washington, D.C.   Auckland   Bogotá
Caracas   Lisbon   London   Madrid   Mexico City   Milan
Montreal   New Delhi   San Juan   Singapore
Sydney   Tokyo   Toronto

Library of Congress Cataloging-in-Publication Data

Automotive electronics handbook / Ronald Jurgen, editor in chief.
    p.   cm.
    Includes index.
    ISBN 0-07-033189-8
    1. Automobiles—Electronic equipment.   I. Jurgen, Ronald K.
TL272.5.A982   1994
629.25'49—dc   94-39724
                                                  CIP

3 4 5 6 7 8 9 0   AGM/AGM   9 0 9 8 7 6 5

ISBN 0-07-033189-8

The sponsoring editor for this book was Stephen S. Chapman, the editing supervisor was Virginia Carroll, and the production supervisor was Suzanne W. B. Rapcavage. It was set in Times Roman by North Market Street Graphics.

Printed and bound by Arcata Graphics/Martinsburg.

McGraw-Hill books are available at special quantity discounts to use as premiums and sales promotions, or for use in corporate training programs. For more information, please write to the Director of Special Sales, McGraw-Hill, Inc., 11 West 19th Street, New York, NY 10011. Or contact your local bookstore.

This book is printed on acid-free paper.

This book is dedicated to Robert H. Lewis and to the memories of Douglas R. Jurgen and Marion Schappel.

CONTENTS

Part 4   Displays and Information Systems

Part 5   Safety, Convenience, Entertainment, and Other Systems

CONTRIBUTORS

Robert E. Bicking   *Honeywell, Micro Switch Division* (CHAP. 4)

Tracy Blake   *Arizona State University* (CHAP. 30)

David S. Boehmer   *Intel Corporation* (CHAP. 11)

Werner Brehm   *Robert Bosch GmbH* (CHAP. 13)

Wolfgang Bremer   *Robert Bosch GmbH* (CHAP. 22)

Wolfgang Bullmer   *Robert Bosch GmbH* (CHAP. 13)

Jerry L. Cage   *Allied Signal, Inc.* (CHAP. 15)

Tom Chrapkiewicz   *Philips Semiconductor* (CHAP. 25)

Armin Czinczel   *Robert Bosch GmbH* (CHAP. 16)

Jeffrey N. Denenberg   *Noise Cancellation Technologies, Inc.* (CHAP. 31)

William C. Dunn   *Motorola Semiconductor Products* (CHAP. 7)

Randy Frank   *Motorola Semiconductor Products* (CHAPS. 2, 5, 32)

Robert L. French   *R. L. French & Associates* (CHAP. 29)

Frieder Heintz   *Robert Bosch GmbH* (CHAP. 22)

Gary C. Hirschlieb   *Robert Bosch GmbH* (CHAP. 12)

Raymond S. Hobbs   *Arizona Public Service Company* (CHAP. 30)

Gerhard Hötzel   *Robert Bosch GmbH* (CHAP. 6)

Robert Hugel   *Robert Bosch GmbH* (CHAP. 22)

Ronald K. Jurgen   *Editor* (CHAPS. 1, 20, 21)

George G. Karady   *Arizona State Univeristy* (CHAP. 30)

Donald B. Karner   *Electric Transportation Application* (CHAP. 30)

Shinichi Kato   *Nissan Motor Co., Ltd.* (CHAP. 24)

Bernhard K. Mattes   *Robert Bosch GmbH* (CHAP. 23)

Fred Miesterfeld   *Chrysler Corporation* (CHAP. 26)

Salim Momin   *Motorola Semiconductor Products* (CHAP. 32)

James P. Muccioli   *JASTECH* (CHAPS. 27, 28)

Klaus Müller   *Robert Bosch GmbH* (CHAP. 10)

Kurt Neuffer   *Robert Bosch GmbH* (CHAP. 13)

Harald Neumann   *Robert Bosch GmbH* (CHAP. 6)

Paul Nickson   *Analog Devices, Inc.* (CHAP. 3)

Johann Riegel   *Robert Bosch GmbH* (CHAP. 6)

Makoto Sato   *Honda R&D Co., Ltd.* (CHAP. 18)

Gottfried Schiller   *Robert Bosch GmbH* (CHAP. 12)

Shari Stottler   *Robert Bosch GmbH* (CHAP. 12)

Richard Valentine   *Motorola Inc.* (CHAPS. 14, 19)

Helmut Weyl   *Robert Bosch GmbH* (CHAP. 6)

Hans-Martin Wiedenmann   *Robert Bosch GmbH* (CHAP. 6)

William G. Wolber   *Cummins Electronics Co., Inc.* (CHAPS. 8, 9)

Akatsu Yohsuke   *Nissan Motor Co., Ltd.* (CHAP. 17)

PREFACE

Automotive electronics as we know it today encompasses a wide variety of devices and systems. Key to them all, and those yet to come, is the ability to sense and measure accurately automotive parameters. Equally important at the output is the ability to initiate control actions accurately in response to commands. In other words, sensors and actuators are the heart of any automotive electronics application. That is why they have been placed first in this handbook where they are described in technical depth. In other chapters, application-specific discussions of sensors and actuators can be found.

The importance of sensors and actuators cannot be overemphasized. The future growth of automotive electronics is arguably more dependent on sufficiently accurate and low-cost sensors and actuators than on computers, controls, displays, and other technologies. Yet it is those nonsensor, nonactuator technologies that are to many engineers the more "glamorous" and exciting areas of automotive electronics.

In the section on control systems, a key in-depth chapter deals with automotive microcontrollers. Without them, all of the controls described in the chapters that follow in that section—engine, transmission, cruise, braking, traction, suspension, steering, lighting, windshield wipers, air conditioner/heater—would not be possible. Those controls, of course, are key to car operation and they have made cars over the years more drivable, safe, and reliable.

Displays, trip computers, and on- and off-board diagnostics are described in another section, as are systems for passenger safety and convenience, antitheft, entertainment, and multiplex wiring. Displays and trip computers enable the driver to readily obtain valuable information about the car's operation and anticipated trip time. On- and off-board diagnostics have of necessity become highly sophisticated to keep up with highly sophisticated electronic controls. Passenger safety and convenience items and antitheft devices add much to the feeling of security and pleasure in owning an automobile. Entertainment products are what got automotive electronics started and they continue to be in high demand by car buyers. And multiplex wiring, off to a modest start in production cars, holds great promise for the future in reducing the cumbersome wiring harnesses presently used.

The section on electromagnetic interference and compatibility emphasizes that interference from a variety of sources, if not carefully taken into account early on, can raise havoc with what otherwise would be elegant automotive electronic designs. And automotive systems themselves, if not properly designed, can cause interference both inside and outside the automobile.

In the final section on emerging technologies, some key newer areas are presented:

- Navigation aids and intelligent vehicle-highway systems are of high interest worldwide since they hold promise to alleviate many of vehicle-caused problems and frustrations in our society.

- While it may be argued that electric vehicles are not an emerging technology, since they have been around for many years, it certainly is true that they have yet to come into their own in any really meaningful way.

- Electronic noise cancellation is getting increasing attention from automobile designers seeking an edge over their competitors.

The final chapter on future vehicle electronics is an umbrella discussion that runs the gamut of trends in future automotive electronics hardware and software. It identifies potential technology developments and trends for future systems.

Nearly every chapter contains its own glossary of terms. This approach, rather than one overall unified glossary, has the advantage of allowing terms to be defined in a more application-specific manner—in the context of the subject of each chapter. It should also be noted that there has been no attempt in this handbook to cover, except peripherally, purely mechanical and electrical devices and systems. To do so would have restricted the number of pages available for automotive electronics discussions.

Finally, the editor would like to thank all contributors to the handbook and particularly two individuals: Otto Holzinger of Robert Bosch GmbH in Stuttgart, Germany and Randy Frank of Motorola Semiconductor Products in Phoenix, Arizona. Holzinger organized the many contributions to this handbook from his company. Frank, in addition to contributing two chapters himself and cocontributing a third, organized the other contributions from Motorola. Without their help, this handbook would not have been possible.

Ronald K. Jurgen

AUTOMOTIVE ELECTRONICS HANDBOOK

P · A · R · T · 1

INTRODUCTION

CHAPTER 1
INTRODUCTION

Ronald K. Jurgen
Editor

1.1 THE DAWN OF A NEW ERA

In today's world of sophisticated automotive electronics, it is easy to forget how far the technology has come in a relatively short time. In the early 1970s, other than radios and tape players, the only standard electronic components and systems on most automobiles were alternator diodes and voltage regulators.[1] By the fall of 1974, "there were twelve electronic systems available, none of which were across the board standard production items. . . . The twelve electronic systems or subsystems were: alternator diodes, voltage regulators, electronic fuel injection, electronic controlled ignition, intermittent windshield wipers, cruise control, wheel lock control, traction control, headlamp control, climate control, digital clocks, and air bag crash sensors."[1]

1.1.1 Car Makers and the Electronics Industry: Friendly Adversaries

In the early days of automotive electronics, the automotive industry and the electronics industry were often at odds. Carmakers needed inexpensive components and systems that would operate reliably in the extremely harsh automotive environment. The electronics industry, on the other hand, used to producing high-quality but expensive parts and systems for the military, was skeptical about its ability to produce the components the automobile industry wanted at the prices they demanded. But both industries realized that electronics could provide the capability to solve automotive problems that defied conventional mechanical or electromechanical approaches.

Some of the leading electronics engineers who worked in the automotive industry—as well as their counterparts in the electronics industry—realized that this existing friendly adversarial relationship had to be converted to a mutual effort to find cost-effective and reliable solutions to urgent automotive problems.

Thus it was in 1973 that Trevor Jones (then with General Motors), Joseph Ziomek (then with Ford), Ted Schaller (Allen Bradley), Jerry Rivard (then with Bendix), Oliver McCarter (General Motors), and William Saunders (Society of Automotive Engineers), proposed that a new conference be held in 1974.[1] Dubbed Convergence to signify the coming together of the two industries, the first conference was successful and, sponsored alternately by the Society of Automotive Engineers and the Institute of Electrical and Electronics Engineers, it has been held successfully every other year ever since.

1.1.2   The United States Government Forces the Issue

One of the major problems facing the automotive industry at the time of the first Convergence conference was upcoming stricter government-mandated exhaust emissions controls. When the United States government first mandated emissions standards for all United States cars, car makers met the challenge through the use of catalytic converters for hydrocarbon and carbon monoxide emissions and exhaust gas recirculation techniques for nitrogen oxides emissions. But they knew that in 1981, when the standards would be tightened from the previous limit of 2.0 grams per mile to 1.0 gram per mile, those approaches would no longer in themselves be sufficient. A new approach was necessary and it involved use of a three-way catalyst for all three emissions together with a closed-loop, engine control system.[2]

Tighter emissions control solved one problem but created another—fuel economy. The two seemed to be mutually exclusive. Charles M. Heinen and Eldred W. Beckman, writing in *IEEE Spectrum* in 1977,[3] said, "The simple truth is that there is very direct interaction between emissions and fuel economy. Probably the clearest example of that interaction is the fact that automobiles equipped to meet California's tight emissions control regulations have consistently demonstrated about 10 percent poorer fuel economy than have comparable cars equipped to meet the less stringent Federal U.S. standards." As a result of this interdependence, emissions and fuel economy measures tended to be compromises. Greater fuel economies could be achieved if emissions levels were not a problem.

1.2   THE MICROCOMPUTER TAKES CENTER STAGE

The microcomputer, introduced in 1971, had yet to make major inroads in automobiles. But it became increasingly obvious that it was the key to meeting government exhaust emission and fuel economy demands while also providing car buyers with cars that performed well. Meeting these needs necessitated precise engine control in such areas as the air/fuel ratio and idle speed.

1.2.1   Early Applications of Microcomputers

One of the first microcomputer applications in cars was an advanced ignition system built by Delco-Remy for the 1977 Oldsmobile Toronado. Called the MISAR (microprocessed sensing and automatic regulation) system, it controlled spark timing precisely no matter what load and speed conditions prevailed while meeting emissions control requirements and providing good driveability. Input signals from sensors provided data on crankshaft position, manifold vacuum, coolant temperature, and reference timing.[4] The microprocessor used had a capacity of 10,240 bits.

Early applications such as the MISAR paved the ground for what would later become the prolific use of microcomputers in cars. Once reliable microcomputers met the cost restraints of carmakers, there was no end in sight to microcomputer applications in cars. In the late 1970s, total engine control with microcomputers became widespread and, as time went on, use of microcomputers spread to other controls for transmission, braking, traction, suspension, steering, lighting, air conditioning, and so forth.

1.2.2   The Bells and Whistles Period

There was also a time in the early 1980s when carmakers, heady with success with microcomputers in other areas, went through a period of electronic overkill. Notable in this regard were voice commands and warnings that tended to wear out their welcome quickly with car drivers and elaborate and flashy information displays that also turned off many car buyers. It was a period of doing things with microcomputers because they could be done rather than doing them because they were needed.

That overindulgent microcomputer period quickly waned as car buyers made their feelings known. Voice commands were all but totally abandoned and displays were made less garish. There was even a return to analog displays for speedometers, for example, albeit electronically based rather than the old mechanical or electromechanical system. Carmakers returned to using microcomputers in truly functional ways to answer real needs.

1.3 LOOKING TO THE FUTURE

The future for automotive electronics is bright. Electronic solutions have proven to be reliable over time and have enabled carmakers to solve problems otherwise unsolvable. But what does the future hold? Some predictions for the future have been discussed in the following pages by contributors.

1.3.1 Contributors' Predictions

Although there have been many significant automotive electronics advances over the years, the end is certainly not in sight. The final chapter in this handbook describes many upcoming advances in detail. Authors Frank and Momin, for example, state that a likely future scenario "will be a combination of centralization and distributed intelligence where the centralization would be based along the lines of body, chassis and safety, powertrain, and audio/entertainment and communications. Within these centralized systems would be distributed intelligence based on multiplex wiring with smart sensors, switch decoders, and smart actuators all controlled by a central intelligence."

Here are additional selected future developments cited by contributors in other chapters:

- Expansion of the air bag system to include side impact protection (Dunn, Chap. 7)
- Magnetic transistors and diodes that can be directly integrated with signal conditioning circuits (Dunn, Chap. 7)
- Electronic switched stop lamps involving a rate-of-closure detector system to determine if the vehicle's speed is safe for objects ahead of it. If the closure rate is unsafe, the stop lights could be activated to alert trailing drivers to a pending accident (Valentine, Chap. 14)
- The integration of watchdog and failsafe functions onto a microcontroller (Boehmer, Chap. 11)
- Microcontrollers that operate at frequencies of 24 MHz or 32 MHz to allow more code to be executed in the same amount of time (Boehmer, Chap. 11)
- In the mid-90s, cars will have twice the electronic content of today's cars but will be easier to manufacture because there will be half the number of modules due to feature content integration. The data network interconnecting the modules will reduce the size and number of cables and cut the number of circuits by 50 percent (Miesterfeld, Chap. 26)
- A move from switching units to stepped operation actuators and the substitution of continuous for discrete time control (Müller, Chap. 10)
- Electrorheological and magnetorheological fluid actuators (Müller, Chap. 10)
- Micromechanical valves as actuators for converting low control power as in regulating the flow of fluids in hydraulic or pneumatic systems (Müller, Chap. 10)

REFERENCES

1. Trevor O. Jones, "Convergence—past and future," *Proceedings,* 1992 International Congress on Transportation Electronics (Convergence), P-260, Society of Automotive Engineers, Inc., Warrendale, Pa., Oct. 1992, pp. 1–3.

2. George W. Niepoth, and Stonestreet, Stephen P., "Closed-loop engine control," *IEEE Spectrum,* Nov. 1977, pp. 52–55.

3. Charles M. Heiner, and Beckman, Eldred W., "Balancing clean air against good mileage," *IEEE Spectrum,* Nov. 1977, pp. 46–50.

4. Trevor O. Jones, "Automotive electronics I: smaller and better," *IEEE Spectrum,* Nov. 1977, pp. 34–35.

P · A · R · T · 2

SENSORS AND ACTUATORS

CHAPTER 2
PRESSURE SENSORS

Randy Frank
Technical Marketing Manager
Motorola Semiconductor Products

2.1 AUTOMOTIVE PRESSURE MEASUREMENTS

Various pressure measurements are required in both the development and usage of vehicles to optimize performance, determine safe operation, assure conformance to government regulations, and advise the driver. These sensors monitor vehicle functions, provide information to control systems, and measure parameters for indication to the driver. The sensors can also provide data log information for diagnostic purposes.

Depending on the parameter being measured, different units for indicating pressure will be used. Since pressure is force per unit area, basic units are pounds per square inch (psi) or kilograms per square centimeter. For example, tire pressure is usually indicated in psi. Manifold pressure is typically specified in kiloPascals (kPa). A Pascal, which is the international unit (SI or Systems Internationale) for pressure, is equal to 1 Newton per meter^2 or $1 \text{ kg} \cdot \text{m}^{-1} \cdot \text{s}^{-2}$. Other common units of pressure measurement include: inches, feet, or centimeters of water; millibars or bars, inches, or millimeters of mercury (Hg), and torr. The conversion constants as defined per international convention are indicated in Table 2.1.

Pressure can be measured by a number of devices that provide a predictable variation when pressure is applied. Sensors used on vehicles range from mechanical devices—with position movement when pressure is applied—to a rubber or elastomer diaphragm, to semiconductor-based silicon pressure sensors. Various pressure-sensing techniques are explained in Sec. 2.3.

The type of pressure measurement that is made can be divided into five basic areas which are independent of the technology used for the measurement: gage, absolute, differential, liquid level, and pressure switch.

2.1.1 Gage Pressure Measurements

The silicon pressure sensor technology explained in Sec. 2.3.5 is used to visualize the difference between gage, absolute, and differential pressure (refer to Fig. 2.1). For gage pressure measurements, the pressure is applied to the top of a (silicon) diaphragm (Fig. 2.1), creating a positive output. The opposite (back) side of the diaphragm is exposed to atmospheric pressure. Gage vacuum is a special case of gage pressure. For gage vacuum measurements, vacuum is applied to the back side of the diaphragm resulting in a positive output signal. Gage and gage vacuum are single-sided pressure measurements. Gage pressure is frequently indicated by psig.

TABLE 2.1   Pressure Unit Conversion Constants

(Most commonly used per international conventions)

	psi*	In H₂O†	In Hg‡	K Pascal	Millibar	cm H₂O§	mm Hg¶
psi*	1.000	27.680	2.036	6.8947	68.947	70.308	51.715
In H₂O†	3.6127×10^{-2}	1.000	7.3554×10^{-2}	0.2491	2.491	2.5400	1.8683
In Hg‡	0.4912	13.596	1.000	3.3864	33.864	34.532	25.400
K Pascal	0.14504	4.0147	0.2953	1.000	10.000	10.1973	7.5006
Millibar	0/01450	0.40147	0.02953	0.100	1.000	1.01973	0.75006
cm H₂O§	1.4223×10^{-2}	0.3937	2.8958×10^{-2}	0.09806	0.9806	1.000	0.7355
mm Hg¶	1.9337×10^{-2}	0.53525	3.9370×10^{-2}	0.13332	1.3332	1.3595	1.000

* PSI = pounds per square inch
† At 39 °F
‡ At 32 °F
§ At 4 °C
¶ At 0 °C

2.1.2   Absolute Pressure Measurements

An absolute pressure measurement is made with respect to a fixed (usually a vacuum) reference sealed within the sensor (Fig. 2.1). For a 100-kPa-rated absolute unit, the diaphragm is fully deflected with standard atmospheric pressure. Application of a vacuum restores the diaphragm to its undeflected (flat) position. The result is a high-level output with no vacuum applied and a low-level signal at full vacuum unless the zero is established at the full-scale deflection of the diaphragm. Pressure can also be applied to absolute units with appropriately designed diaphragms to withstand the additional applied stress. Absolute pressure is frequently indicated by psia.

2.1.3   Differential Pressure Measurements

Differential or Delta-P measurements are also shown in Fig. 2.1. The higher pressure is applied to the top of the diaphragm and the lower pressure, possibly a reference pressure, is applied to the opposite side. The diaphragm's deflection is a result of the pressure difference.

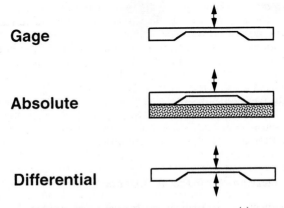

FIGURE 2.1 Types of pressure measurements: (*a*) gage, (*b*) absolute, and (*c*) differential.

Typically, the pressure differential is only a small percentage of the total line pressure and a system fault can expose one side of the sensor to the full line pressure. This must be taken into account when choosing the sensor and determining the rated pressure range that will be required. Differential pressure is frequently indicated by psid.

2.1.4 Liquid Level Measurements

The height of a column of liquid can be measured by a pressure sensor. The term *head* is frequently used in hydraulics to denote pressure. Measurements of inches or feet of water and centimeters of mercury are direct indications of the effect of pressure on liquid level. Other liquid levels are dependent on their specific weight and can be calculated by $h = (P_L - P_H)/w$, where $(P_L - P_L)$ is the pressure differential caused by the height of the fluid column and w is the specific weight of the liquid. The vapor pressure in a sealed enclosure will have an effect on the measurement of liquid height. Returning the reference side of a differential pressure sensor to the top of the enclosure will compensate for vapor pressure.

2.1.5 Pressure Switch

A pressure switch is typically achieved by mounting an electric contact on a diaphragm (rubber or any elastic material). The application of sufficient pressure (or vacuum) on one side of the diaphragm causes the movable contact to meet a stationary contact and close the circuit.

A pressure switch can also be achieved by any of the previously described techniques merely by establishing a reference threshold voltage that is calibrated to indicate the point that the pressure changes from an acceptable to unacceptable (or low to high) level. Once the threshold voltage is achieved, additional electronic circuits can be used to produce an electronic switch that can control loads such as an indicator lamp.

2.2 AUTOMOTIVE APPLICATIONS FOR PRESSURE SENSORS

Automotive requirements for pressure measurements range from the basic—oil pressure—to the sophisticated—air pressure differential from one side of the vehicle to the other. This section elaborates on the various possibilities for pressure measurements that exist either in the development, laboratory, or pilot phases of the vehicle, to actual volume production. Table 2.2 lists a number of potential pressure measurements versus vehicle systems and provides an indication of the pressure range and type of measurement.

Automotive specification and testing guidelines have been developed and published by the Society of Automotive Engineers (SAE) specifically for manifold absolute pressure (MAP) sensors. These documents are intended to assist in establishing test methods and specifications for other sensors. Other SAE documents that may apply to sensors are summarized in Table 2.3.

The packaging and testing requirements for automotive sensors can represent 50 to 80 percent of the sensor cost and over 90 percent of the warranty and in-service problems. The pressure-sensing applications that are presented in the following sections will include packaging requirements that are of particular concern.

2.2.1 Existing Applications for Pressure Sensors

A late twentieth century production vehicle is likely to have a number of pressure sensors for measurements such as manifold pressure and engine oil pressure, and has the potential for

TABLE 2.2 Pressure Sensing Requirements for Various Vehicle Systems

System	Parameter	Pressure range	Type
Engine control	Manifold absolute pressure	100 kPa	Absolute
	Turbo boost pressure	200 kPa	Absolute
	Barometric pressure (altitude)	100 kPa	Absolute
	EGR pressure	7.5 psi	Gage
	Fuel pressure	15 psi—450 kPa	Gage
	Fuel vapor pressure	15 in H_2O	Gage
	Mass air flow		Differential
	Combustion pressure	100 Bar, 16.7 Mpa	Differential
	Exhaust gas pressure	100 kPa	Gage
	Secondary air pressure	100 kPa	Gage
Elect transmission	Transmission oil pressure	80 psi	Gage
(continuously variable	Vacuum modulation	100 kPa	Absolute
transmission)			
Idle speed control	AC clutch sensor/switch	300–500 psi	Absolute*
	Power steering pressure	500 psi	Absolute*
Elect power steering	Hydraulic pressure	500 psi	Absolute*
(also elect assisted)			
Antiskid brakes/	Brake pressure	500 psi	Absolute*
traction control	Fluid level	12 in H_2O	Gage
Air bags	Bag pressure	7.5 psi	Gage
Suspension	Pneumatic spring pressure	1 MPa	Absolute*
Security/keyless entry	Passenger compartment pressure	100 kPa	Absolute
HVAC (climate control)	Air flow (PC) Compressor pressure	300–500 psi	Absolute*
Driver information	Oil pressure	80 psi	Gage
	Fuel level	15 in H_2O	Gage
	Oil level	15 in H_2O	Gage
	Coolant pressure	200 kPa	Gage
	Coolant level	24 in H_2O	Gage
	Windshield washer level	12 in H_2O	Gage
	Transmission oil level	12 in H_2O	Gage
	Tire pressure	50 psi	Gage/absolute
	Battery fluid level	1–2 in below	Optical
Memory seat	Lumbar pressure	7.5 psi	Gage
Multiplex/diagnostics	Multiple usage of sensors		

* Gage measurement but absolute sensors used for failsafe

TABLE 2.3 SAE Specifications That Effect Pressure Sensors

Recommended environmental practices for electronic equipment design	SAE J1211
Performance levels and methods of measurement of electromagnetic radiation from vehicles and devices	SAEJ551
Performance levels and methods of measurement of EMR from vehicles and devices (narrowband RF)	SAEJ1816
Electromagnetic susceptibility procedures for vehicle components (except aircraft)	SAE J1113
Vehicle electromagnetic radiated susceptibility testing using a large TEM cell	SAE J1407
Open-field whole-vehicle radiated susceptibility 10 kHz–18 GHz, electric field	SAE J1338
Class B data communication network interface	SAE J1850
Diagnostic acronyms, terms, and definitions for electrical/electronic components	SAE J1930
Failure mode severity classification	SAE J1812
Guide to manifold absolute pressure transducer representative test method	SAE J1346
Guide to manifold absolute pressure transducer representative specification	SAE J1347

several other pressure measurements. Tighter emissions control and improved efficiency may necessitate further sensor use in future systems.

Manifold, Barometric and Turbo Boost Pressure.   Manifold absolute pressure (MAP) is used as an input to fuel and ignition control in internal combustion engine control systems. The speed-density system that uses the MAP sensor has been preferred over mass air flow (MAF) control because it's less expensive, but stricter emission standards are causing more manufacturers to use mass air flow for future models.

Higher resolution from 32-bit engine controllers, with greater analog-to-digital (A/D) conversion capability and higher operating frequencies, will provide greater accuracy for a given MAP sensor during the critical transitions of the engine cycle. As shown in Fig. 2.2, previous changes from 8-bit to 16-bit controllers have resulted in a two-time improvement in resolution in the digital conversion for the intake manifold pressure. The 8-bit control unit performed the A/D conversion on a 4-ms timer interrupt in order to maintain a balance with other controls, with the resulting 1.1-ms lag time (worst case) during periods of overlapping interrupts. The 16-bit microcontroller performs the A/D conversion every 2 ms, which reduces the lag time to 0.3 ms. The actual system improvements that can result from using the higher performing microcontrol units is a result of other factors such as more precise and faster control of fuel injectors and sparkplugs, and additional and/or more accurate sensors and control algorithms.

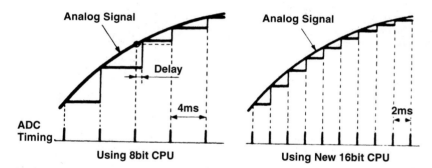

FIGURE 2.2   Effect of A-D on pressure measurements.

The MAP error band is also being tightened with a goal of 1 percent accuracy over the entire automotive temperature range. Existing specifications allow tolerances to increase as shown by the bowtie specification in Fig. 2.3 with associated multiplier(s).

The need for barometric pressure is often desirable in MAF systems to provide altitude information to the engine control computer. The barometric pressure range is typically from 60 to 115 kpA with accuracy on the order of 1.5 percent over the operating pressure range. The error band tolerance increases by a temperature multiplier of up to 2× outside the 0 to 85 °C range. MAP and barometric pressure sensors are frequently mounted inside control modules making the mounting technique a key consideration for manufacturability. The increased usage of surface mount technology, and the need to reduce space so that additional features can be included in control modules are factors that will affect next-generation sensor designs.

A typical turbocharger can provide boost pressure in the range of 80 kPa over the naturally aspirated internal combustion engine. This increases the maximum rating for the sensor to 200 kPa absolute, but other requirements are scaled appropriately.

MPX4100 • MPX4101 SERIES

Transfer Function

Nominal Transfer Value: $V_{out} = V_S (0.01059 \times P - 0.1518)$
$+/- (\text{Pressure Error} \times \text{Temp. Mult.} \times 0.01059 \times V_S)$
$V_S = 5.1 \text{ V} \pm 5\% \ P_{in} \text{ kPa}$

Temperature Error Multiplier

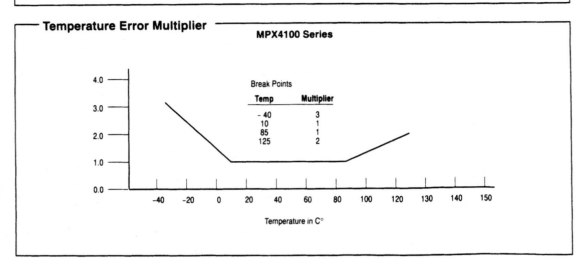

Pressure Error Band

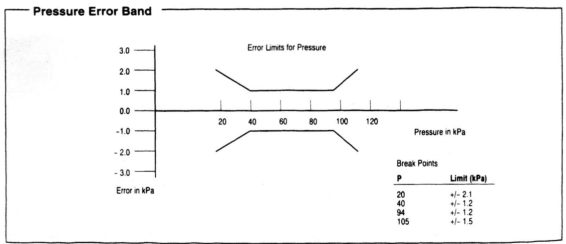

FIGURE 2.3   Error band for MAP sensor.

Oil Pressure.   Oil pressure on automobiles has traditionally been measured by the deflection of a rubber diaphragm which closes a set of contacts (switch) providing a lamp indication with low oil pressure or moves a potentiometer to provide an analog signal for a gage.

A replacement for the conventional electromechanical oil pressure sending unit is an electronic device such as the one designed by Chrysler's Acustar Division. In addition to a silicon piezoresistive pressure sensor, the unit contains transient protection circuitry, signal amplification for the sensor output, and output drivers for both an electromagnetic gauge and a fuel pump. The FET output drivers are capable of handling 10 A based on the heat dissipated though a heatsink that is integral to the sensor package.

The unit utilizes a supply voltage from 9 to 16 V and operates over a media temperature range of −40 to +150 °C. The overall accuracy is ±3.25 percent with linearity ≤ ±0.25 percent over the entire operating pressure range of 200 psi. The switch point for the low pressure indication is 4 psi ± 1.5 psi.

The sensor package was specially designed for easy assembly. The housing interfaces to the sensor with an extremely reliable O-ring seal that can withstand a burst pressure over 400 psi. Special materials were used for both the package and the protective gel that covers the sensor, which allow it to survive qualification tests with over 1 million pressure cycles, including portions conducted at high temperatures. This exceeds the number of cycles that can be achieved with traditional diaphragm-driven potentiometers that have been used for providing the indication of oil pressure. The sensor has been designed for a 10-year/100,000-mile life that could be required for future vehicle warranties.

Media Compatibility in Automotive Measurements.   Pressure sensors frequently have to interface with an environment that is more demanding than other electronic components. For example, the measurement of engine oil pressure, transmission oil pressure, fuel pressure, and so on, or fluid level (oil, gas, coolant, etc.) requires the sensor package to be exposed to one or more fluids that are detrimental to the operation of semiconductor circuitry. Each of these media interface problems is addressed separately, depending on the application. Automotive cost requirements usually limit the usage of stainless steel as the isolation technique. Instead, more cost-effective protective polymers and chemically tolerant plastic and rubber materials have been developed for sensor packages.

2.2.2 New Applications for Pressure Sensing

The list of potential applications for sensing pressure in the automobile includes several new applications. These measurements are frequently made during the development of new vehicle systems. Their actual use on the vehicle is determined by factors such as cost, legislated requirements, need for diagnostics, and value added to the system. Applications in this section will identify areas of concern, range of pressure measurement, and factors that affect the usage of a pressure sensor.

Transmission Oil Pressure and Brake Pressure.   Transmission pressure is required as an input in computer-controlled transmission shift points. This pressure can be measured with sensors similar to those developed for engine oil pressure.

Pressure in a hydraulic system, such as the master cylinder of an antilock brake system (ABS), is much higher than transmission oil pressure typically requiring a sensor with minimum rating of 500 psig. Pressures in other locations in the ABS system can be lower. The dynamic pressures in brake tubing can be of interest during the development phase of passenger vehicles and may be of interest in heavy duty commercial vehicles. These pressures can be below 150 psig.

The ABS system controls front and rear tire slip. Tradeoffs that exist in developing an ABS system for a particular vehicle include stopping deceleration to achieve the shortest possible stopping distance versus more steering control. Increased yaw stability can be obtained by reducing the deceleration rate of the rear wheels. The addition of traction control to the system improves stability during acceleration and provides independent control of each wheel during a variety of driving maneuvers for improved vehicle performance.

Passenger vehicles may have a single pressure sensor to monitor the pressure in the hydraulic system. One system, General Motors' ABS-VI, provides information on the brake pressure by detecting the current going to motors in the system. For the ABS-VI system, a pressure sensor is not required to provide optimum brake pressure at each wheel. However, other systems rely on the rate of brake application and release to control lockup. Commercial vehicles may have several sensors for sensing brake pressures. Sensors close to brake cylinders report the actual pressure, which is compared to the reference value stored in the control unit.

Tire Pressure. The continuous monitoring of tire pressure offers increased fuel economy and safety to passenger cars or commercial vehicles. Underinflated tires create excessive rolling friction and therefore decrease fuel economy. Overinflated tires have excessive stress that can result in failure during operation. Improperly inflated, either over- or underinflated, tires have uneven wear patterns which decrease tire life. Available tire pressure systems consist of a tire pressure sensor (or switch) at each wheel, wheel speed indicator, temperature sensor, a radio frequency transmitter, electronic receiver/controller, and a display unit. The dashboard display provides an indication to the driver that the tires are improperly inflated. Tire pressure increases with temperature approximately 1.5 psi for every 10 °C of tire air temperature rise, so the system must provide correction for this effect. Abrupt increases in temperature and pressure can be sensed by these systems and provide a warning of eminent tire failure providing an additional safety factor.

Another tire pressure system utilizes a separate hand-held reader to easily verify the proper tire inflation when the vehicle is stationary. Yet another commercial vehicle system for trucks with dual tires operates while the vehicle is stationary and employs a visual indication for the driver that adequate pressure exists. This system provides a single fill point for the dual tires, maintains equal pressure under normal conditions, and provides an isolation valve in the event that a blowout or slow leak develops in one tire.

EGR Pressure. EGR (exhaust gas recirculation) back pressure and a pressure differential exist across the EGR valve used to control NO_x emissions in the engine control system. The valve is modulated by a vacuum which lifts a pintle from its seated position to allow exhaust gas to be recirculated. A change in vacuum pressure from 50 to 90 mm Hg is sufficient to fully open the valve, and a pressure differential across the valve of 200 mm Hg is typical. Pressure measurements are made during the development phase to determine system operating characteristics. However, a position sensor is typically used to measure the EGR valve's position and control NO_x emissions during normal vehicle operation.

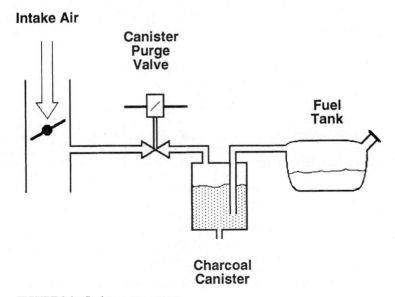

FIGURE 2.4 Canister purge system.

Fuel Rail and Vapor Pressure.   Evaporative emissions that occur when the engine is off are currently stored in an activated charcoal canister of about 850 to 1500 cc until the engine is running, as shown in Fig. 2.4. The vapors are then consumed by the combustion chamber and catalytic converter. One implementation of on-board vapor containment of refueling hydrocarbons (on-board refueling vapor recovery or ORVR) would require refueling canisters on the vehicle that could be three to four times the volume of existing canisters. If leaks need to be detected in this system, a diagnostic pressure sensor may be required.

One approach to fuel routing, employed in the 5.9-liter Dodge Magnum engine, is to mount the fuel filter and pressure regulator at the fuel tank. The fuel pump is mounted inside the tank. Therefore, since only a fuel supply line to the fuel rail and a line to the evaporative canister are necessary, the fuel return line is eliminated. This system maintains lower fuel tank temperatures, resulting in lower evaporative emissions.

Monitors required for on-board diagnostic (OBD) systems per California Air Resources Board's (CARB's) OBDII legislation were originally targeted to be phased in between model year 1994 and model year 1996. A Bosch fuel injection system with on-board diagnostics is shown in Fig. 2.5 that identifies a differential air pressure sensor for tank vapor pressure.

Overpressure Occurrences.   Fuel supply pressures in automobile fuel injection systems normally operate at pressures below 75 psi; however, fuel pumps develop pressures up to 3200 psi to open injectors. Pressure spikes can be reflected back through the fuel supply system that measure up to 300 psi during each fuel injection pulse.

Overpressure created by backfire can also apply a positive pressure of 75 psi and higher to the intake manifold absolute pressure sensor. Techniques used to prevent failure from over-

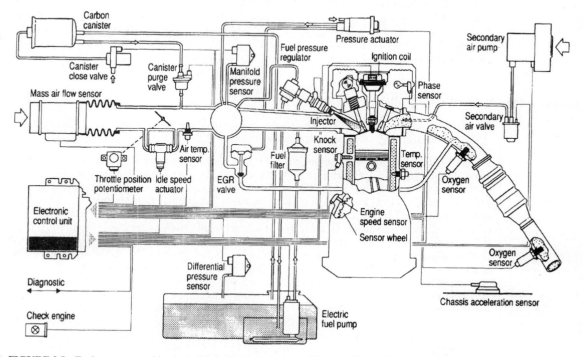

FIGURE 2.5   Fuel vapor control in electronic fuel injection system. (*Courtesy Robert Bosch, GMBh*)

pressure include overpressure stop built into the transducer, mechanical pulse filtering, and a sensor designed to operate within the overpressure range.

Mechanical stops have been a traditional protection technique for mechanical pressure sensors. This is possible where the amount of diaphragm deflection is large. Silicon pressure sensors have a modulus of elasticity that is the same as steel (30×10^6 psi) and a yield strength (180,000 to 300,000 psi) that is higher than steel, allowing high overpressure without diaphragm damage. However, the sensor package itself must be designed to handle the maximum pressure safely.

Snubbing, or mechanical filtering, is commonly used for static pressure measurements. A small diameter tube reduces the dynamic variation in applied pressure. If dynamic measurements are desired, the ac component of the desired signal may also be attenuated.

Increasing the diaphragm thickness of the sensor to safely handle the full range of pressure within normal operating range will also result in a lower sensitivity.

Alternate Fuel and Alternate Engine Implications to Pressure.   Legislation that requires a percentage of the vehicles sold in California to be LEV (low emissions vehicles) and even ZEV (zero emissions vehicles) is increasing the demand for alternate fuel and electric vehicles. Among the alternate fuel vehicles, CNG (compressed natural gas) and hydrogen cells most likely would require sensors for pressure measurements. CNG is pressurized at 3000 psi and the distribution system includes pressure regulators, a transducer, valves, and idle air solenoids. Before the natural gas enters the engine, a regulator reduces the fuel pressure to near atmospheric pressure. Sensing may be required in both low- and high-pressure portions of the system. Development of alternative engines, such as the two-stroke engine for vehicle applications, will utilize electronics for control functions similar to four-cycle engines. However, the range and necessity for pressure measurements will differ from four-cycle engines. The pressure range for direct fuel injection is considerably higher for a two-stroke engine. The need to control the oil pump may necessitate pressure sensing in two-stroke systems as well.

Hydrogen fuel cells are another potential source of energy for use in electric vehicles. In one design, the proton-exchange membrane (PEM) design, a turbocompressor is used to pressurize the system and maintain hydration of the membrane. A pressure of at least three atmospheres (0.3 MPa) is required to remove the water. This pressure or the pressure drop across the membrane may need to be monitored during operation.

2.2.3   Other Applications for Pressure Sensors

Pressure sensors can be used on vehicles for measuring flow through pressure differential, or delta-P, measurements and for determining liquid level.

Delta-P (Flow-Sensing) Measurements.   Applications on the vehicle for flow sensing include mass air flow; heating compartment flow; oil, fuel, and cooling liquid flow; and vehicle flow in an air stream. Mass air flow is typically accomplished by hot-wire anemometer or Karman vortex flow meters which do not use pressure-sensing techniques. Other vehicle flow requirements, including the pressure drop across the air filter, could be sensed and monitored by a differential pressure sensor. In addition to requirements such as media compatibility (Sec. 2.2.1), the lower-level signals require higher-sensitivity pressure sensors and/or additional amplification and must tolerate faults that could apply full line pressure to only one side of the sensor.

One of the more interesting applications of differential pressure measurements applied to flow analysis is the flow of the vehicle itself relative to crosswinds. A rear-wheel steering system developed by Daimler-Benz uses two pressure sensors to measure the pressure caused by wind on the vehicle's sides. An electronic control unit analyzes the pressure difference and inputs from other sensors, and alters the rear-wheel setting according to the wind strength. The system that measures the crosswinds directly is faster than yaw sensors, which are reactive and measure the change in attitude and direction of the vehicle.

Other laboratory measurements of airflow and crosswind force have also been made by Daimler-Benz that utilize 10 differential pressure gages with a range of ±3700 kPa. All pressure sensors were connected to a single pressure vessel to have a common reference. The reference pressure was measured by a 100-kPa absolute pressure sensor. The measurements were used to determine aerodynamic forces and moments and to compensate for wind effects in an active steering system.

Fluid Level Sensing.   Various liquid levels can be measured in a vehicle, as shown in Table 2.4. All of these requirements, except fuel level, could be satisfied by a switch that simply detects that a predefined minimum level of liquid has been reached so that a driver indication can be provided. This can be accomplished by directly illuminating a dash lamp or through a microcontroller in a body computer which activates an output driver.

TABLE 2.4   Liquid Level Measurements

Level	Type	Range
Engine oil	Switch	38.1 cm of water
Transmission oil	Switch	30.5 cm of water
Coolant	Switch	61 cm of water
Windshield washer fluid	Switch	30.5 cm of water
Battery	Refraction switch	5.1 cm below reference
Power steering fluid	Switch	7.6 cm below reference
Brake fluid	Switch	30.5 cm of water
Fuel	Sensor and switch	38.1 cm of water

Sensing the fuel level has traditionally been performed by a float to sense the fluid level and a variable resistor with the wiper arm connected to the float. Configuration for the sensor depends upon the specific tank for which it was designed, necessitating a unique sensor for each vehicle. Manufacturers with several different vehicle models have the additional impetus to replace the existing techniques with a nonwearing, more accurate, self-calibrating electronic alternative. However, media compatibility for fuel level is among the harshest requirements for a pressure sensor. In addition to gasoline, oxygenated fuels containing ethanol, methanol, benzene, MTBE, engine additives, and even sour gas must be tolerated by the sensor. Nonintrusive differential sensors isolate the liquid from the sensor interface but must still tolerate fuel vapors. Also, the sloshing of the fuel in a vehicle's tank requires a time amplitude filter to smooth out the indication provided to the driver.

2.2.4   Combustion Pressure

The direct measurement of combustion pressure is being investigated for detecting misfire to meet CARB OBDII requirements. The high pressure (≥ 16 MPa) and temperature ranges combined with other environment factors make the design of a pressure sensor for this application extremely expensive. As a result, other techniques are being developed as alternatives to direct pressure measurement. These technologies include optical, fiberoptics measuring luminous emissions from combustion, and noncontact torque sensors. Section 2.3.7 explains a fiber optic technique.

The operation of the reciprocating-piston, internal combustion engine is represented by a constant volume process and the engine power cycle is analyzed by using pressure-versus-volume and pressure-versus-crank angle diagrams. To obtain these measurements in a laboratory environment a number of techniques have been developed. Direct (in-cylinder) pressure measurements have been performed with small diameter piezoresistive sensors placed in (or near) the sparkplug and piezoelectric washers placed under the spark plug. A high natural frequency is required for these sensors based on the dynamic measurement involved in the combustion process. Indirect measurements with shaft torque and optical phase shift are additional possibilities. The need to determine misfire due to component failure during vehicle operation is part of OBDII requirements. A sensor used on production vehicles will be required to survive the high pressure and temperature environment for the life of the vehicle, which could be 100,000 miles and 10 years. It must also have no need for periodic zeroing or calibration and be available at a low cost.

2.2.5 Other Pressure Measurements

An adaptive suspension system (see Chap. 17) can be accomplished with an air pressure controlled shock absorber damping, such as Mitsubishi's Active-ECS (Electronically Controlled Suspension). This system has two air pumps and nine solenoids that regulate air pressure based on inputs from sensors including an air pressure sensor in the rear of the vehicle that measures the passenger and cargo load. The driver can select soft, medium, or hard suspension. Another system utilizes an air reservoir charged to a pressure of 1 Mpa by a compressor. A pressure switch monitors when the pressure drops below 760 kPa to recharge the reservoir. Air springs operate at 300 kPa unloaded and at 600 kPa in the rear when fully loaded.

HVAC (heating, ventilating, and air conditioning) changes are occurring as manufacturers are required to convert from refrigerant CFC-12 to alternatives such as HFC-134a. The theoretical performance of these two refrigerants will mean about a 6 percent loss in efficiency, compressor discharge pressure that is 175 kPa higher, and a discharge temperature that is about 8 °C lower. Measuring the compressor discharge pressure (almost 1900 kPa for the HFC-134a system) is desirable for electric load control as vehicles add more requirements to the 12-V charging system. Also, the effect on engine performance and fuel economy when the A/C is used could make the refrigerant pressure sensor a standard vehicle sensor in the future. An absolute sensor used to measure gage pressure of the refrigerant provides a deadhead effect to prevent refrigerant loss in the event of a sensing diaphragm failure.

The measurement of the pressure developed when the air bag is inflated is part of the evaluation, qualification, and lot acceptance criteria of air bag inflating techniques. Time-to-peak pressure and peak tank pressure measurements require measurements in the tens of milliseconds range. Inflated bag pressures are in the range of 100 kPa or less. Hybrid inflators use a stored inert gas, such as argon, in place of sodium-azide propellant that requires a squib for ignition. The hybrid uses a pressure sensor to monitor the status of the stored gas.

Special heavy duty/commercial truck measurements require pressure measurements that are quite different from those made on passenger cars. Accumulator-type fuel injection systems for direct injection diesel engines have fuel pressurized to 20 to 100 MPa in the accumulator by a high-pressure pump. The accumulator pressure is monitored in this approach to reduce particulates. Another method to reduce diesel particulates utilizes a ceramic fiber as a filter in a canister. A pressure sensor monitors the backpressure and allows the full filter to be regenerated by burning off the accumulated particulates in the filter. A heater element in the trap has power supplied from the power-switching module. A temperature approaching 1300 °F (700 °C) is reached inside the filter cartridge to incinerate the particles.

Lumbar support systems utilize a pressurized system with a pressure sensor (≤ 7.5 psig) as the feedback element controlling the air pump to provide additional support to the driver's lower back in luxury vehicles. Pressure-sensitive grids have been used in the development process to automatically measure up to 3600 contact points for visual display and weight distribution analysis.

2.2.6 Partial Pressure Measurements

The oxygen (or lambda-) sensor in engine control systems is a chemical sensor that utilizes partial pressures to provide a feedback signal for the closed-loop control system. Lambda is defined as the actual air/fuel ratio divided by the stoichiometric (14.6) fuel ratio. The operation of the oxygen sensor is defined by the Nernst equation: $U_L = RT/4F \cdot \ln(P_{O2}''/P_{O2}')$, where U_L is the unloaded output voltage of the sensor, R is the universal gas constant, T is the absolute temperature, F is the Faraday constant, P_{O2}'' is the oxygen partial pressure of the air (about 2.9 psi), and P_{O2}' is the equilibrium partial pressure of the oxygen in the exhaust gases. Equilibrium occurs due to the catalytic activity of the platinum electrodes used to coat the inside and outside of the Y_2O_3 stabilized ZrO_2 ceramic electrode. The oxygen partial pressure changes by a factor of 10^7 at 900°C (or 10^{19} at 500°C) when the exhaust gas changes from a reducing environment (lambda = 0.999) to an oxidizing environment (lambda = 1.001).

2.3   TECHNOLOGIES FOR SENSING PRESSURE

A number of technologies have been used for on-vehicle measurements of static and dynamic pressure: diaphragm-potentiometer, linear variable differential transformer (LVDT), aneroid, silicon or ceramic capacitive, piezoresistive strain gage, piezoelectric ceramic or film, and optical phase shift (combustion pressure). Recent advances in sensing have focused on transducers that provide an electric signal easily interfaced to microcontrollers. Mechanical devices are frequently used in the laboratory for calibration and component development or on the vehicle during the development phase of the vehicle systems. Common mechanical devices include the Bourdon tube, bellows, diaphragms, deadweight gage, and manometer.

The Bourdon tube is a curved or twisted, flattened tube with one end closed that acts as a force collector. When pressure is applied at the open end, the tube tends to straighten and the resulting motion is used as an indication of the applied pressure.

The bellows, or pressure capsule, is a chamber that expands with applied pressure. Absolute pressure can be measured by sealing a reference pressure (e.g., vacuum) inside a closed unit and applying pressure to the outside. The movement of the chamber is proportional to the applied pressure.

Diaphragms are the most common force collector used in modern pressure sensors. The diaphragm material can be rubber, elastomer, stainless steel, silicon, ceramic, or even sapphire. Diaphragm shapes are circular or square and can be supported or clamped around their periphery.

A deadweight tester or piston gage can withstand extreme pressure changes and high overpressure occurrences. The piston is sealed in a cylinder using O-ring or Teflon seals. Pressure on the piston causes a deflection that can be measured by position-sensing techniques. Precision weights allow calibration for high-accuracy measurements. The deadweight tester is one of the few pressure-sensing techniques that measures pressure in terms of its fundamental units—force and area. Errors associated with the measurement are air-bouyancy corrections, gravity error, surface tension, fluidhead, and thermal expansivity. These errors are normally small but should be taken into account when high accuracy is required.

The manometer is used both as a pressure-measuring instrument and a standard for calibrating other instruments. Its simplicity and inherent accuracy result from it being the measurement of the height(s) of a column of liquid. Three basic types of manometers are the U-tube, well (cistern), and slant-tube.

Other measurement devices including McLeod, Pirani, Alphatron, and thermocouple gages which can measure vacuum in the range of 10^{-5} mm Hg.

Sensing techniques that provide a transducer for conversion from mechanical to electrical units include resistive, LVDT, capacitive, piezoresistive, and piezoelectric.

2.3.1   Potentiometric Pressure Sensors

Prior to electronic engine control systems, carburetor dashpots and distributor vacuum advance units used the distance that a rubber diaphragm traveled when pressure was applied as a mechanical indication of pressure. A diaphragm which moves a potentiometer (resistor with a sliding element or wiper) provides an electric signal that can be applied to a remote gage such as an oil pressure gage. Potentiometric sensors inherently have some level of noise and wear associated with their operation due to the contact of the wiper to the resistive element. Stiction or static friction is also a potential concern with these devices, especially if control of ≤0.5 percent of the total resistance is required. The finite resolution of wirewound potentiometers is overcome by the use of newer thin-film plastic resistor designs.

2.3.2 Linear Variable Differential Transformer

One of the earliest pressure inputs for engine control systems was provided by the LVDT pressure sensor. The principle of operation is demonstrated in Fig. 2.6. An LVDT pressure sensor consists of a primary winding and two secondary windings positioned on a movable cylindrical core. The core is attached to a force collector which provides differential coupling from the primary to the secondaries resulting in a position output that is proportional to pressure.

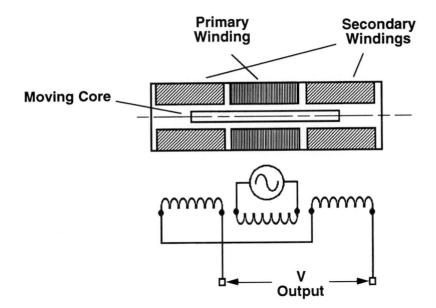

FIGURE 2.6   LVDT pressure sensor.

An alternating current is used to energize the primary winding, which results in a voltage being induced in each of the secondary windings. The windings are connected in series opposing, so the equal but opposite output of each winding tends to cancel (except for a small residual voltage called the null voltage). A pressure applied to a Bourdon tube or diaphragm causes the core to be displaced from its null position and the coupling between the primary and each of the secondaries is no longer equal. The resulting output varies linearly within the design range of the transducer and has a phase change of 180° from one side of the null position to the other. Since the core and coil structures are not in physical contact, essentially frictionless movement occurs.

Electronic devices necessary to signal condition the output of an LVDT consist of an oscillator for the supply voltage, circuitry to transform the constant voltage to a constant current, an amplifier with high input impedance for the output, a synchronous demodulator, and a filter with characteristics designed for quasistatic or dynamic measurements.

2.3.3 Aneroid Diaphragms

Another early design for sensing automotive manifold pressure consisted of dual sealed aneroid diaphragms. The diaphragms were bonded and sealed with a vacuum inside each unit to a metallized conductive ring on opposite sides of a ceramic substrate. The substrate served as the fixed plates of two separate capacitors. Manifold vacuum was applied to one chamber and the second served as a reference for compensating and signal conditioning that minimized common mode errors due to vibration and shock.

2.3.4 Capacitive Pressure Sensors

Capacitive pressure sensors have one plate that is connected to a force collector (usually a diaphragm), and the distance between the plates varies as a result of the applied pressure. The nominal capacitance is $C = Ae/d$, where A is the area of the plate, e is the permittivity, and d is the distance between the plates. Two common capacitive pressure sensors used in automotive applications are based on silicon and ceramic capacitors.

Silicon.   A silicon capacitive absolute pressure (SCAP)-sensing element is shown in Fig. 2.7. The micromachined silicon diaphragm with controlled cavity depth is anodically bonded to a Pyrex® glass substrate. Feedthrough holes are drilled in the glass to provide a precise connection to the capacitor plates inside the unit. The glass substrate is metallized using thin-film deposition techniques. Photolithography is used to define the electrode configuration. After attaching the top silicon wafer to the glass substrate, the drilled holes are solder-sealed under vacuum to provide a capacitive-sensing element with an internal vacuum reference and solder bumps for direct mounting to a circuit board or ceramic substrate. The value of the capacitor changes linearly from approximately 32 to 39 pF with applied pressure from 17 to 105 kPa. The capacitive element is 6.7 mm × 6.7 mm and has a low-temperature coefficient of capacitance (−30 to 80 ppm/°C), good linearity (≈1.4 percent), fast response time (≈1 ms), and no

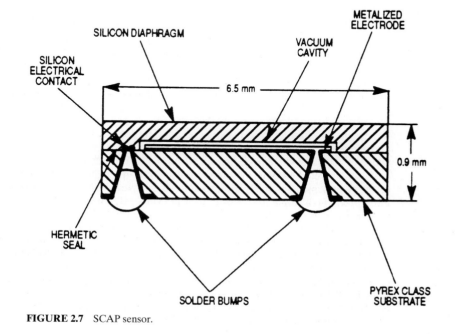

FIGURE 2.7 SCAP sensor.

exposed bond wires. The output of the sensor is typically signal-conditioned to provide a frequency variation with applied pressure for easy interface to microcontrollers.

Surface micromachining and bulk micromachined silicon-on-silicon techniques (see Sec. 2.3.5) have also been used to build silicon capacitive pressure sensors. These approaches also address the addition of signal-conditioning electronics on the same silicon structure.

Ceramic.   The ability to make thin diaphragms from ceramic material combined with thin-film deposition to provide metal plates and connections has been used to manufacture ceramic pressure sensors. Their operation and signal-conditioning requirements are similar to the silicon capacitive sensor described in Sec. 2.3.4.

2.3.5   Piezoresistive Strain Gage

Strain-gage pressure sensors convert the change in resistance in four (sometimes in two) arms of a Wheatstone bridge. The change in the resistance of a material when it is mechanically stressed is called piezoresistivity.

The open-circuit voltage of an unbalanced Wheatstone bridge is given by $V_O = \mathbf{E}[(R1*R3 - R2*R4)/(R1 + R2)(R3 + R4)]$, where V_O is the output voltage, $\mathbf{E}$ is the applied voltage, and $R1$ through $R4$ are the resistive elements of the bridge. Additional variable resistive elements are typically added to adjust for zero-offset and sensitivity, and to provide temperature compensation.

Different approaches to piezoresistive strain gages range from traditional bonded and unbonded to the newest integrated silicon pressure sensors.

Bonded and Unbonded Strain Gages.   The bonded resistance strain-gage pressure sensor consists of a filament-wire or foil, metallic or semiconductor, bulk material or deposited film bonded to the surface of a diaphragm. Pressure applied to the diaphragm produces a change in the dimension of the diaphragm and, consequently, in the length of the gage, and, therefore, a change in its resistance ($R = \rho \, L/A$). The change per unit length is called strain. The sensitivity of a strain gage is indicated by gage factor

$$GF = \Delta R/R \div \Delta L/L = 1 + 2\mu + \Delta\rho/\rho \div \Delta L/L \tag{2.1}$$

Foil strain gages have a negligible piezoresistive effect and their gage factor is usually between 2 and 3.

When a pressure sensor is used for measuring an applied force it is called a load cell.

Integrated Silicon Pressure Sensors.   The GF for a strain gage is improved considerably (to about 150) by using a silicon strain gage. In addition to the conventional Wheatstone bridge, silicon processing techniques, and the relative size of piezoresistive elements in silicon enable the design of a unique piezoresistive sensor. The sensor signal can be provided from a single piezoresistive element located at a 45° angle in the center of the edge of a square diaphragm which provides an extremely linear measurement. The offset voltage and full scale span of the basic sensing element vary with temperature, but in a highly predictable manner. In addition to the basic sensing element, an interactively laser-trimmed four-stage network has also been integrated into a single monolithic structure (Fig. 2.8). The size of the silicon die, including the diaphragm, sensing element, and signal-conditioning electronics, is only 0.135 in by 0.145 in. The die is attached to the six-terminal package through the use of a stress-isolating layer of RTV (room temperature vulcanizing) silicone. This approach allows a minimum of external components for amplification to provide a usable output signal.

Two silicon wafers are used to produce the absolute piezoresistive silicon pressure sensor (Fig. 2.9). The top wafer is etched until a thin, square diaphragm, approximately one mil in thickness, is achieved. The square area is extremely reproducible as is the 54.7° angle of the cavity wall based on the characteristics of bulk micromachined silicon. The top wafer is

FIGURE 2.8 Silicon pressure sensor with integrated electronics. *(Courtesy Motorola, Inc.)*

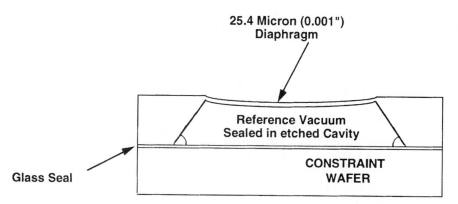

FIGURE 2.9 Cross section of piezoresistive silicon pressure sensor for measuring absolute pressure.

attached to a support wafer by a glass frit to provide a structure which is isolated from mounting stresses.

The bulk micromachining process used to form the diaphragm and the etched cavity in the majority of silicon pressure sensors is a chemical etching process that allows a thin (0.001-in) mechanical structure—the diaphragm—to be precisely etched from a silicon wafer that is approximately 0.015 in thick. Hundreds of sensors can be formed simultaneously on a 4-in (100-mm) diameter silicon wafer, and several wafers can be batch-processed to yield thousands of sensors in a single lot. Silicon pressure sensors can also be achieved by using surface micromachining techniques. In these sensors, a layer of sacrificial material (usually an oxide) is grown on top of a silicon wafer, and material such as polysilicon is then deposited on the sacrificial layer and patterned to achieve a particular structure. The sacrificial material is removed by a chemical etchant. Both bulk and surface micromachining techniques can be combined with semiconductor processing techniques to provide additional circuitry on the same monolithic structure. A number of new terms are used relative to silicon pressure sensors that are defined in the glossary to this section.

Both bulk and surface micromachining, discussed previously, are performed at the wafer level. A polysilicon thin-film sensor that consists of a thin film of silicon that is doped with boron and vapor-deposited over a stainless steel diaphragm is shown in Fig. 2.10. A thin deposited layer of silicon dioxide insulates the silicon from the stainless steel diaphragm. Silicon nitride is used to cover the strain-sensitive elements. Silicon-on-insulated-stainless-steel (SOISS) sensors are not formed using silicon wafer techniques, but they use batch-processing techniques and are inherently suited for harsh environments.

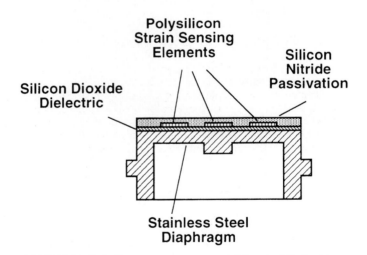

FIGURE 2.10   Polysilicon pressure sensor on stainless steel diaphragm.

2.3.6 Piezoelectric Pressure Sensors

A piezoelectric sensor produces a change in electric charge when a force is applied across the face of a crystal or piezoelectric film. The inherent ability to sense vibration and the necessity for high-impedance circuitry are taken into account in the design of modern piezocrystal sensors. Transducers are constructed with rigid multiple plates and a cultured-quartz sensing element, which contains an integral accelerometer to minimize vibration sensitivity and suppress resonances. A typical unit also contains a built-in microelectronic amplifier to transform the high-impedance electrostatic charge output from the crystals into a low-impedance voltage signal. Units made in stainless steel housings have an invar diaphragm laser welded to seal the

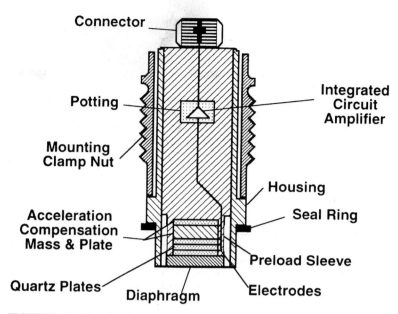

FIGURE 2.11   Piezoelectric pressure sensor.

sensing elements inside the package. Figure 2.11 shows the cross section of a piezoelectric pressure sensor.

More recently, piezo film sensors, which produce an output voltage when they are deflected, provide a very inexpensive method for pressure measurements. One approach has the piezo film cemented to a metallic dimple substrate with the dimple pointed toward the high-pressure source. As the pressure rises, a point is reached when the dimple snaps in the opposite direction and the movement is sufficient for the piezo film to generate a transient voltage.

Surface micromachining techniques have also been combined with piezoelectric thin-film materials, such as zinc oxide, to produce a semiconductor piezoelectric pressure sensor.

2.3.7   Fiber Optic Combustion Pressure Sensor

For extremely high pressure, or pressure measurements at high temperatures, different pressure measurement techniques are used. Figure 2.12 shows an alternative to traditional pressure-sensing techniques that is being developed to sense production vehicles' combustion

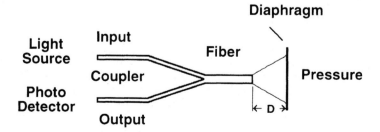

FIGURE 2.12   Fiber optic combustion pressure sensor.

pressure. The fiber optic pressure sensor can withstand temperatures (up to 550 °C) that are well above the normal range for piezoelectric sensors. Furthermore, the design has a normal pressure range of 0 to 1000 psi and overrange capability of 3000 psi.

The sensor's operation is the result of a light source input to an optical fiber coupler and a photodetector at the receiving end of the coupler. Light exits the optical fiber as a diverging cone which illuminates a diaphragm. The maximum angle is determined by an aperture. The amount of light that is returned to the sensor fiber after it is reflected from the diaphragm depends upon the gap D between the fiber and the diaphragm. The diaphragm can be sized to allow the sensor to be integrated into a spark plug for easy access to the combustion pressure of each cylinder. Accuracy within 5 percent has been demonstrated within the 550 °C operating temperature range.

2.3.8 Pressure Switch

A pressure switch can be simpler and more cost effective than a pressure sensor for an application that only requires detecting a single pressure level. Sufficient motion of the force-collecting diaphragm (e.g., elastomer, Kapton®, fluorosilicon) allows a spring to be compressed and a set of contacts to be closed in a traditional mechanical switch. The design of the contacts may allow several amperes to be switched.

Converting the output of any of the electric sensors in Sec. 2.3 to a threshold-sensing level requires additional circuits, including an electronic switch, such as a power FET, to conduct the current. The sensor can have multiple switch points depending on the amount of additional circuitry that is provided.

2.3.9 Pressure Valves/Regulators

Pressure is frequently controlled in automotive applications by pressure regulators or valves. The actuation of these mechanisms can be a result of applied pressure to a mechanical structure such as an integral piston or relief valve held closed by a spring force, or an electric signal generated from a sensor and subsequent activation of a solenoid, which opens a valve or moves a pintle in an orifice to change the pressure. The thermostat in the engine cooling system allows flow based on a minimum temperature being achieved. It must operate independently of the pressure variations in the cooling system. A common solution is an expansion-element thermostat which actuates a valve to redirect the flow of coolant into a radiator bypass line when the control temperature is reached.

Extremely small and precise silicon-based regulators, and even pumps, are possible using micromachining techniques. Figure 2.13 shows a silicon Fluistor™ (or fluidic transistor) microvalve that is approximately 5.5 mm by 6.5 mm by 2 mm. The valve is actually a thermopneumatic actuator which accepts an electric input. The cavity is etched in the middle silicon chip by bulk micromachining described in Sec. 2.3.4 and filled with a control liquid. When the liquid is heated, the silicon diaphragm moves outward over the valve seat. This approach has demonstrated a dynamic range of 100,000:1 controlling gas flows from 4 μlpm to 4 lpm at a pressure of 20 psid.

The microvalve combined with a pressure sensor and electronic feedback loop provides a solid state pressure regulator. It has potential for usage in both gas and liquid flow control applications on future vehicles. The integration of EGR and idle-air control (IAC) has already been accomplished in a somewhat conventional (patented) manner. A feedback-controlled valve with two inlets and a single outlet orifice eliminate stepper motor programming in the engine controller and only one calibration curve is needed for both EGR and IAC functions. The combination of this approach to control systems and newly developed technologies, such as the silicon microvalve, will allow additional advances in vehicle performance, efficiency, and control.

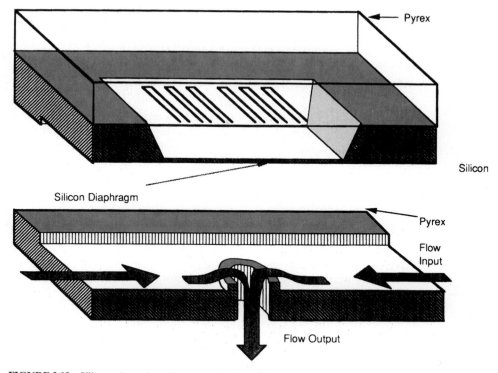

FIGURE 2.13   Silicon microvalve. *(Courtesy of Redwood MicroSystems, Inc.)*

2.4   FUTURE PRESSURE-SENSING DEVELOPMENTS

The different types of pressure measurements, different technologies for measuring pressure, and potential pressure measurements in automotive applications have been explained in this chapter. In addition, alternatives to making pressure measurements, such as indirect sensing and the use of pressure regulators, have been discussed. The use of semiconductor technology applied to sensing applications is producing sensors with inherently more decision and diagnostic capability that can communicate bidirectionally with host microcomputers in complex systems. The desire to directly produce a signal that is compatible with microcomputers rather than requiring analog signals to be converted to digital format through A/D converters is spurring development activity that could affect future automobile systems. Furthermore, recently developed fuzzy logic and neural network approaches to control systems and multiplexing of sensor outputs for use in several systems will make previously cost-prohibitive sensing applications a reality.

Increased and recently initiated sensing activity from industrial organizations such as SAE, the American National Standards Institute (ANSI), and the Institute of Electrical and Electronics Engineers (IEEE) should provide a greater level of understanding, common terminology, and improved specifications and test procedures for the numerous approaches that can be taken to sense pressure in automotive applications.

All trademarks are the property of their respective owners.

GLOSSARY

Altimetric pressure transducer   A barometric pressure transducer used to determine altitude from the pressure-altitude profile.

Diaphragm   The membrane of material that remains after etching a cavity into the silicon sensing chip. Changes in input pressure cause the diaphragm to deflect.

Error band   The band of maximum deviations of the output values from a specified reference line or curve due to those causes attributable to the sensor. Usually expressed as "±% of full-scale output." The error band should be specified as applicable over at least two calibration cycles so as to include repeatability and verified accordingly.

Linearity error   The maximum deviation of the output from a straight-line relationship with pressure over the operating pressure range. The type of straight-line relationship (end-point, least-square approximation, etc.) should be specified.

Operating pressure range   The range of pressures between minimum and maximum pressures at which the output will meet the specified operating characteristics.

Overpressure   The maximum specified pressure that may be applied to the sensing element of a sensor without causing a permanent change in the output characteristics.

Piezoresistance   A resistive element that changes resistance relative to the applied stress it experiences (e.g., strain gauge).

Pressure error   The maximum difference between the true pressure and the pressure inferred from the output for any pressure in the operating pressure range.

Pressure sensor   A device that converts an input pressure into an electric output.

Ratiometric (ratiometricity error)   At a given supply voltage, sensor output is a proportion of that supply voltage. Ratiometricity error is the change in this proportion resulting from any change to the supply voltage. Usually expressed as a percent of full-scale output.

Response time   The time required for the incremental change in the output to go from 10 to 90 percent of its final value when subjected to a specified step change in pressure.

Temperature error   The maximum change in output at any pressure in the operating pressure range when the temperature is changed over a specified temperature range.

BIBLIOGRAPHY

"Acustar Electronic Oil Pressure Sensor," *Automotive Industries,* March 1993, pp. 26–29.

Budd, John W., "A Look at Pressure Transducers," *Sensors,* July 1990, pp. 10–15.

Doeblin, Ernest O., *Measurement Systems Application and Design,* McGraw-Hill, New York, 1975.

He, Gang, and Marek T. Wlodarczyk, "Spark Plug-Integrated Fiber Optic Combustion Pressure Sensor," *Proceedings of Sensors Expo,* Chicago, Sept. 29–Oct. 1, 1992, pp. 211–216.

Holt, Daniel J., "ABS Testing," *Automotive Engineering,* March 1993, pp. 26–29.

Keebler, Jack, "Automakers, gas refiners debate vapor control units," *Automotive News,* Oct. 14, 1991, p. 39.

Lynch, Terrence, "Integrated Valve Meters EGR and Idle Air," *Design News,* Feb. 22, 1993, pp. 159–160.

Motorola Pressure Sensor Device Data Book, Q1/93, Phoenix, Ariz.

Norton, Harry N., "Transducers and Sensors," *Electronic Handbook,* McGraw-Hill, New York.

PCB Electronics, Inc., comments in "Piezoelectric Pressure Transducers," *Measurements & Control,* Oct. 1990, pp. 20–222.

Sawyer, Christopher A., "On-Board Diagnostics," *Automotive Industries,* May 1992, p. 57.

Siuru, Jr., William D., "Sensing Tire Pressure on the Move," *Sensors,* July 1990, pp. 16–19.

Tran, Van Truan, "Wind Forces and Moments," *Automotive Engineering,* April 1990, pp. 35–38.

ABOUT THE AUTHOR

Randy Frank is a Technical Marketing Manager for Motorola's Semiconductor Products Sector in Phoenix, Arizona. He has a BSEE, MSEE, and MBA from Wayne State University in Detroit, Michigan, and over 25 years' experience in automotive and control systems engineering. For the past 10 years he has been involved with semiconductor sensors, power transistors, and smart power ICs.

CHAPTER 3
LINEAR AND ANGLE POSITION SENSORS

Paul Nickson
Product Line Manager
Analog Devices, Inc.,
Transport & Industrial Products Division

3.1 INTRODUCTION

Position sensors of one form or another are an integral and necessary part of the modern automobile. Position sensors range in technology from the ubiquitous microswitch warning to the driver of a door ajar to linear variable differential transformers (LVDTs) used in sophisticated active suspension systems. Whether as monitors or as critical parts of safety systems, market and legislative pressures for longer warranties and lower emissions are opening avenues for a wide range of sensing technologies to find a place in the modern automobile.

The automotive systems designer must take into account many factors when choosing the appropriate technology for an application. Each sensor type has its own vocabulary, and it is important when making comparisons to understand how a figure of merit for one sensor relates to that of another. It is equally important to understand how the choice of output signal format, whether digital or analog, can affect the resolution of measurement and subsequently the performance or stability of an automotive system.

The purpose of this chapter is to give an overview of position sensor technologies currently used and available for use in automobiles and to compare their characteristics and suitability for particular applications. Consideration is given to the interfacing requirements of each type of sensor with an emphasis on the advantages and disadvantages of each method as they apply in the automotive environment. Where appropriate, descriptions of applications of the various sensor types in automobile applications are given. Other available technologies and technologies in development which have desirable characteristics for automotive applications are also discussed.

3.2 CLASSIFICATION OF SENSORS

Sensors may be classified in many different ways. From the perspective of a system designer, the basic questions are: What kind of information does the sensor provide and how is the sensor used? For the purposes of this discussion, a position sensor is defined as an electromechanical device that translates position information into electric signals. Sensors can be grouped into two basic categories.

3.2.1   Incremental or Absolute

Position information can be presented in two different ways. Incremental position sensors measure position as the distance from an arbitrary index or zero. Alternatively, position information may be provided that gives an unambiguous or absolute measure of the distance from a well-defined index.

Incremental sensors usually rely on some method of pulse counting. One pulse in the sequence is designed to be wider or of opposite polarity than the others so that it may be used as a nominal zero. A typical optical angle encoder consists of a glass disk marked with a number of equally spaced radial opaque lines and transparent gaps. The disk is illuminated on one side and a light sensor and associated electronics on the other side detect the passage of dark lines and gaps and generate corresponding electric pulses. Dedicated electronics built into the sensor or a remote microcontroller can be used to count the pulses. A zero is established by detecting the wider pulse, known as *North Marker* in optical encoder terminology, and then resetting the pulse counter. The advantage of this data format is that few wires are required to carry the information. Typically, four or five wires would be required depending on the exact details of the format (see Sec. 3.3.2). The biggest disadvantage of incremental sensors is that at power-up the system has no position information and requires a mechanical indexing cycle to find the marker pulse. Another disadvantage is that the system is prone to the effects of noise, which may lead to erroneous counts.

In contrast, absolute position sensors produce an unambiguous output at power-up. Each position or angle has a unique value. The output may be a voltage or frequency or other analog of the input position. Potentiometers are often used in applications requiring this characteristic. Many absolute position sensors have binary digital outputs. The digital formats vary depending on the construction of the sensor. Some optical encoders use Gray code to avoid ambiguities at code transitions. Other sensors, such as resolvers, do not directly produce a digital output but are almost always used with an analog-to-digital converter that may output in parallel or serial form one of the common formats—for example, two's complement or offset binary.

3.2.2   Contact or Proximity

Position sensors are designed to detect the position of components of mechanical systems by either being directly coupled by some shaft or linkage, as in the case of potentiometers or optical encoders, or by some noncontact or proximity means. Environmental issues are often a key influence in the choice of sensor for a given application. High levels of vibration, particularly in small engine applications, may cause rapid wear of the conductive track of a throttle-position-measuring potentiometer. Dirt and dust usually exclude optical sensors from underhood applications due to rapid degradation of the optical path.

The most common form of proximity sensors are based on various methods of magnetic field detection. A device based on magnetic field sensing principles may be more easily isolated from the destructive effects of the harsh environment encountered in many automotive applications.

3.3   POSITION SENSOR TECHNOLOGIES

3.3.1   Microswitches

The simplest form of contact sensor is a switch. Contact position sensors may be as simple as the microswitches that operate anything from brake lights to courtesy lights in the automobile. Many applications of microswitches in position sensing are as limit switches, usually

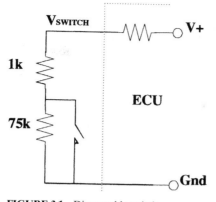

FIGURE 3.1 Diagnosable switch.

wired to limit or warn of the extent of travel of a mechanical component by disconnecting power to an electric motor or by operating an indicator lamp. In some cases, for safety reasons, it is desirable to be able to detect fault conditions that would make the switch inoperable. In some applications, it is possible to connect the switch as shown in Fig. 3.1. In this case, a diagnostic circuit measuring the voltage, V_{SWITCH}, can differentiate between the normal conditions of switch open or closed and can also determine if the switch is disconnected or if V_{SWITCH} is shorted to either power supply.

An undesirable characteristic of switches is that the contacts may bounce on closing. If it is important in the application that the first switching edge is detected, then a simple switch-debouncing logic that rejects noisy signals can be used. If a microcontroller is used to monitor the switch output, then debouncing can be accomplished by software means. This may be a better solution in applications subject to shock or heavy vibration, which may cause occasional false switching. In these cases, a microcontroller can be configured to poll the switch over some period of time and report switch closure only if a number of consecutive readings are the same.

3.3.2 Optical

Optical angle encoders for incremental shaft angular position measurement are constructed of a disk with a series of transparent and opaque equally spaced sectors. The disk can be made of glass for precision applications. Mylar film and metal disks offer high and medium resolutions, respectively, at low cost. The encoder disk is illuminated on one side and light sensors on the other side detect the passage of light and dark sectors as the disk is rotated. (Low-resolution versions such as the Hewlett-Packard HRPG series use an alternative reflective technology.) Most encoders have two sets of light sources and detectors offset by half the width of a sector. Figure 3.2 shows the relationship between the outputs of the light sensors as the encoder is rotated. This format is often referred to as "A quad B," since the signals are in quadrature. The passage of one pair of light and dark sectors over a detector is referred to variously as one cycle, one count, one line or 360 electrical degrees (°e). Encoder resolutions range from around 16 counts per revolution (CPR) for low-cost applications to over 6000 CPR for precision position control systems. Most encoders also include a third signal for use as an index or reference pulse. The index, or North marker as it is sometimes called, occurs once per revolution. The pulse width is usually equal to 90 °e.[1]

Four separate states, each of 90 °e, can be derived from the A and B outputs using integrated circuits available from a number of vendors. This allows a resolution of four times the number of lines on the encoder disk to be achieved. These ICs also determine the direction of rotation of the encoder by observing which output leads the other. By convention for clockwise rotation, the low-to-high transition of A leads the low-to-high transition of B. Control circuitry can be added to improve noise immunity by only allowing valid next states to be counted.

Incremental angle encoder accuracy specifications fall into two categories. The angular position accuracy is the difference between the actual shaft angle and the angle indicated by the encoder. This error is normally expressed in degrees or minutes of arc. The second category includes specifications for the symmetry and repeatability of individual cycles; these are usually

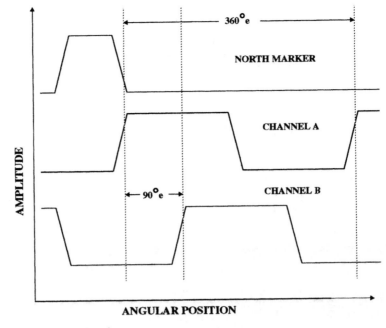

FIGURE 3.2 Encoder outputs.

expressed in electrical degrees. Typical characteristics are detailed in Fig. 3.3 and Table 3.1 Errors are caused by eccentricity and axial play of the code wheel and manufacturing defects in the lithography or etching of the code wheel. Modular encoders consisting of a light source and sensor head are available which use a collimated light source and an array of integrated photodiodes to minimize the effects of these error sources. Differential connection of the photodiodes ensures insensitivity to errors caused by light source variability due to environmental or other factors. A further source of error can occur if the encoder is rotated at high enough speeds that the rise and fall time of the digital outputs significantly affects the pulse width. The light sensor bandwidth usually determines the maximum rotational speed of the sensor. Typical bandwidths are below 100 kHz, which would limit the speed of a 100-CPR encoder to 1000 rpm.

Linear incremental optical encoders are available from many vendors. These allow direct measurement of linear motion. Modular sensor/emitter heads are available that can be used in these applications. The technology is basically the same as incremental angle encoders and the terminology used to describe specifications is the same as for angle encoders. Linear encoders are described in terms of their count density or resolution in counts per mm or mm

TABLE 3.1 Incremental Encoder Specifications

	Minimum	Typical	Maximum	Units
Position error		10	40	min of arc
Cycle error		3	10	°e
Pulse-width error		7	30	°e
Phase error		2	15	°e
State-width error		5	30	°e
Index pulse width	60	90	120	°e

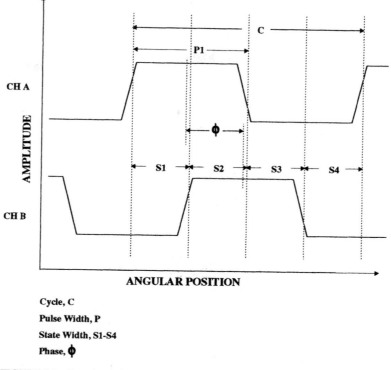

Cycle, C
Pulse Width, P
State Width, S1-S4
Phase, ϕ

FIGURE 3.3   Encoder definitions.

per count. Line counts range up to approximately 8 per mm, allowing an ultimate linear resolution of around 30 μm.

If it is important to have an unambiguous measure of position as soon as power is applied to a system, then an absolute encoder must be used. Absolute optical encoders are manufactured with resolutions from one part in 2^6 to one part in 2^{16}. The data format can be binary, binary-coded decimal (BCD), or Gray code. An absolute angle encoder is divided into equal sectors which are arranged so that adjacent sectors contain consecutive digital words. The binary bits of each word form N concentric tracks on the encoder disk, where N is the digital word length. N sets of light sources and photodiodes detect the parallel word representing the input shaft angle.

Absolute optical encoders often use Gray code to eliminate code transition errors. In a natural binary sequence between zero and full scale on the disk, all the bits of the digital word change state together. Any misalignment of the code wheel and the light sensors, or sensor-to-sensor misalignment, will cause false codes to be generated. This could be disastrous for a position control system since a misread code could indicate an angle up to 180° away from the correct angle. Gray coding eliminates this problem. Gray code is a unit distance code; consecutive codes differ by only one binary bit. If a code transition is misread, the largest error will be one least significant bit of the digital word.

3.3.3 Potentiometric

Potentiometers are widely used as position sensors in automotive applications such as throttle and accelerator pedal position measurement. The automotive industry increasingly demands low-cost mechanically and electrically rugged sensors to provide control or measurement of position in the modern automobile. This has resulted in the development of potentiometers that are capable of operational life far in excess of the life of the average car, and in some cases capable of continuous rotational speeds of above 1000 rpm for more than 1000 hours.[2]

Potentiometers can be constructed using a wire-wound track. The resolution of these potentiometers is determined by the number of turns of wire used to wind the track. The resolution of rotary wire-wound potentiometers is often quoted as the number of turns per degree and can be anywhere between 1 (1° per turn) and 7 (8.5 arcmin per turn). The track resistance is proportional to the number of turns used and can be in the range of 10 ohms to 100 kilohms, with a tolerance of approximately 5 percent. Wire-wound potentiometers have advantages where low-value variable resistors are required but do not excel in linearity, resolution, or rotational life which can be as low as 10^5 revolutions. Potentiometers for position-sensing applications are constructed using a resistive track of conductive material, usually a graphite and carbon black doped plastic, and a collector track molded on some supporting substrate. A drive shaft or pushrod draws precious metal multifingered wipers along the tracks. Wiper damping is usually included to make the potentiometer insensitive to vibration. Potentiometers of this type are manufactured with a range of resistance from around 500 ohms to 20 kilohms with a tolerance of 10 to 20 percent (Table 3.2). Potentiometers of this type are capable of excellent linearity and very high resolution.

TABLE 3.2 Potentiometer Specifications

Parameter	Minimum	Maximum
Electrical travel	90°, 10 mm	360, 3000
Nominal resistance	500 ohms	20 kilohms
Resistance tolerance	10%	20%
Resistance temperature coefficient (TC)		500 ppm/°C
TC of V_{out} in voltage divider mode		5 ppm/°C
Linearity error	0.01%	1%

Potentiometric sensors are used as voltage dividers. A reference voltage is applied across the resistive element and the wiper voltage is used as an absolute measure of the position of the actuator. Linear potentiometers are available in a wide range of lengths from 10 mm to 300 cm. Rotary potentiometers are usually restricted to 355° of useful range due to the dead band created by the track-end contacts. Some versions are available with true 360° operation. These use multiple wipers and dedicated electronics to eliminate the dead band.

All potentiometers are ratiometric sensors. That is, the wiper voltage at a given position is some fraction of the reference voltage applied across the resistive track. If the reference voltage is varied, the potentiometer output remains in the same ratio to the reference voltage. Sensor potentiometers, when properly terminated, maintain ratiometric operation over a wide range of temperatures with temperature coefficients typically less than 5 parts per million (ppm) per degree centigrade. Without special signal processing, ratiometricity is compromised at the end of the electrical travel of a potentiometer by the change in resistivity of the track as it joins the end contact and by any parasitic external resistance in series with the track. Figure 3.4 shows the effective limitations on the potentiometer at its endpoints.

Ratiometricity is a very desirable characteristic for a sensor that is used with comparators or analog-to-digital converters. For example, if the same reference voltage that powers the sensor is used as the reference for an analog-to-digital converter, then the measurement system will be insensitive to the absolute value of the reference voltage. A given shaft angle will always be reported as the same digital code. In most automotive control systems, analog-to-digital converters (usually on board a microcontroller) use the regulated 5-V engine controller

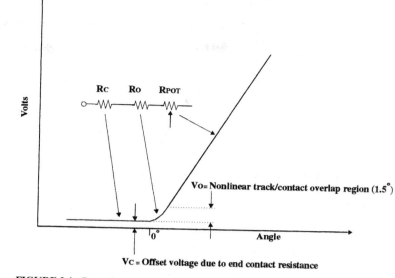

FIGURE 3.4   Potentiometer endpoint nonlinearity.

(ECU) power supply as reference to avoid the additional cost of a separate voltage reference chip. It is desirable that the same voltage, perhaps buffered to isolate the control module from accidental shorts, is used as reference by any ratiometric sensors in the automobile.

Potentiometers are subject to a number of sources of error, of which linearity is the most important. The linearity error is the difference between the actual transfer function of the potentiometer and the ideal transfer function (output voltage change versus mechanical travel) as a percentage of the applied reference voltage. Linearity specifications between 0.03 and 1 percent are available, with sensor cost inversely proportional to linearity. Microlinearity can be an important indicator of the suitability of the potentiometer for use in accurate control systems where large changes in the local gradient of the transfer function may cause instability. Ratiometricity, linearity, and offset errors can be caused by improperly loading the wiper of the potentiometer. The maximum error is at the center of travel of the wiper. If the load is a constant current, such as the input current of a buffer amplifier, a voltage will be developed across R_{EXT} that will cause an offset error at the extremes of travel of the wiper and an additional linearity error at the center of travel. Sensor potentiometers are usually specified with some maximum wiper current (100 nA, typically) to eliminate these errors. Plastic track potentiometers are capable of resolutions better than 0.001 percent of travel. This is primarily limited by the homogeneity of the resistive track material and hysteresis caused by limitations in the mechanical construction of the potentiometer related to bearings, wiper stiffness, and coefficient of friction of the track.

Plastic track sensor potentiometers are capable of operational life in excess of 10^7 revolutions for a rotary sensor or 10^7 strokes for a linear sensor. Unfortunately, no universal standards are available defining test conditions, and these may vary from vendor to vendor. Generally, two types of test are carried out. Dither testing simulates conditions which may exist in control applications or areas with high levels of vibration. The wiper is moved over a small proportion of the travel, say 1 or 2°, at a test frequency of 100 Hz. Information about contact resistance and local gradient changes in the potentiometer transfer function can be gathered rapidly using this technique. A change in gradient (ohms/percent of travel) relative to the mean gradient of the potentiometer can be equated to a change in loop gain in a control system. Sensitive systems may become unstable at worn points in the potentiometer track due to relative gradient errors.

A second method of potentiometer reliability testing is to repeatedly move the wiper at around 10 Hz over a large proportion of the available range. An excursion from 0 to 50 percent of the available travel will result in the maximum change in linearity error over a large number of cycles, since only one-half of the track is subject to wear. The criteria for failure of a potentiometer will be very application-specific and may, for example, be a doubling in linearity error. It is important to work with the potentiometer vendors to understand how their specifications can be extrapolated to make a prediction of operational life.

3.3.4 Magnetic

By far the largest category of position sensors relies on electromagnetic induction principles. This group of sensors can be broken into subgroups depending on the details of the employment of the phenomenon. Other sensors in this category rely on materials with magnetoresistive or magnetostrictive properties. Electromagnetic sensors have a number of advantages over other technologies. In general, this class of sensors measures or responds to changes in the relative position of components in a magnetic circuit. The components are always separated by an air gap and are not subject to friction wear. In many cases, it is possible to construct rugged sensors that are insensitive to the harshest automotive environments.

Variable Reluctance.   The reluctance of a magnetic circuit determines the magnetomotive force (amp turns) required to produce a flux of a given value.[3] Variable reluctance devices operate by sensing changes in the reluctance within a magnetic circuit. In most cases, the reluctance change is caused by a change in the length of an air gap. The change in reluctance causes a change in the magnetic flux which induces a voltage in an output signal coil. The voltage induced is typically a bipolar pulse shape whose amplitude is proportional to the rate of change of flux (Faraday's law).

$$V = \left(\frac{d\Phi}{dt} \right) \tag{3.1}$$

This sensor technology cannot be used at zero speed since, if the rate of change of flux is zero, then the output will be zero.

In automotive applications, variable reluctance sensors are used to detect the position and speed of rotating toothed or slotted wheels in crank-, cam-, and wheel-monitoring applications. An easily magnetized or "soft" magnetic core or bobbin wound with a sense coil is magnetized by a strong permanent magnet such as samarium cobalt (Sm_2Co_{17}). The sense end of the core is placed in close proximity to a toothed gear wheel. The flux change that occurs when a tooth edge passes the sensor causes a voltage to be induced in the coil. Remote signal-conditioning electronics associated with the ECU are used to amplify the signal and produce a signal that a microcontroller can interpret as a position increment. An alternative construction[4] uses a coaxial pole piece to improve the magnetic circuit. This construction is particularly suited to sensing holes or apertures in a sense wheel. Sensors that detect slots and are positioned in close proximity to the target with a small air gap work at low reluctance and are less likely to be disturbed by interfering fields than sensors configured to detect teeth at a low mark space ratio.

Variable reluctance sensors are prone to a number of sources of error. Vibrations or resonance sometimes exacerbated by the attractive forces between the sensor and the target can seriously degrade the signal-to-noise ratio of the device. The sensors' target is usually a rotating ferromagnetic wheel or gear. Eddy currents will be generated by the movement of the wheel in the magnetic field of the sensor. This may lead to false readings from the sensor. In some refinements of variable reluctance sensors, the holes or apertures in the wheel are filled with an electrically conductive nonmagnetic material to homogenize eddy currents.[4]

Significant advantages of variable reluctance sensors in the automotive environment are their simple rugged construction and low cost. Additionally, they have a wide operating temperature range and require only two wires for operation. Variable reluctance sensors can also be used as variable inductance sensors by exciting the sense coil with alternating current and employing inductance-measuring means in the signal-conditioning electronics.

Hall Effect.   Electric current is carried through the motion of electric charge. If a conductor is moved through a magnetic field with velocity v, the charges in the conductor will experience a force (Lorentz force) in a direction perpendicular to both the direction of motion and the magnetic field. This gives rise to an electric field of strength:

$$\mathbf{E} = v\mathbf{B}$$
(3.2)

The charges will move and a surface charge will develop on the conductor until an electrostatic field forms which counterbalances the electric field due to motion, $v\mathbf{B}$. A voltage due to the movement of charge can be detected with a voltmeter. The voltage is proportional to the field $\mathbf{B}$ and the velocity and length of the conductor. The result of this effect in thin films of material was first described by Hall over 100 years ago. When he passed current through a rectangle of gold foil in the presence of a magnetic field perpendicular to the plane of the foil, a voltage could be measured across the other axis of the foil.

Devices can be constructed using semiconductor materials which can utilize this effect to detect the strength of magnetic fields. Figure 3.5 illustrates the construction and operation of a silicon Hall effect device. A voltage is amplified across one axis of a thin block of high-resistivity n-type epitaxial material. In the presence of the field $\mathbf{B}$, charges move in the direction of the arrow. A voltage directly proportional to $\mathbf{B}$, the current density in the silicon and the Hall coefficient (scattering factor) can be measured at the point shown. The sensitivity is low and amplification is required to render a useful signal. For example, with a current of 10 mA flowing in an n-type silicon epitaxial layer 1 μm thick with a doping level of $10^{15}/cm^3$ and a field of 100 mT, a voltage difference of approximately 30 mV will be measured at 25 °C. Offsets caused by resistivity gradients, piezoelectric effects from packaging stress, and contact misalignment can amount to 10 mT or more. Layout techniques, such as cross-coupled structures to minimize the effects of resistivity gradients, can significantly improve offsets. Careful alignment of the Hall cell layout with crystal axes can mitigate piezoelectric effects. Silicon Hall effect devices are insensitive to magnetoresistive effects as the field strengths encountered in most applications have good linearity with errors of <0.1 percent for fields from 0 to >100 mT.[5]

The Hall voltage is strongly temperature dependent and, with constant current bias, is proportional to the magnetic field, the bias current, the carrier concentration, the scattering factor, and a constant G, which is a function of the geometry of the device.

$$VH = GI\mathbf{B} \left(\frac{r}{qnt} \right)$$
(3.3)

A typical silicon Hall device will exhibit a temperature coefficient of the Hall voltage of approximately 1000 ppm/°C under these bias conditions. The temperature dependence can be reduced with a current source, the temperature coefficient of which is designed to compensate for the Hall voltage TC. In this way, the sensitivity of a Hall effect device can be controlled within 1 or 2 percent over the range of temperatures normally encountered in automotive wheel position and speed applications. The temperature coefficient of the compensated device can be matched to the magnetic circuit if necessary; a typical requirement might be to provide a residual TC of 200 ppm/°C to compensate for the TC of a Sm_2Co_{17} magnet.

Hall effect devices can be constructed from semiconductor materials other than silicon—for example, gallium arsenide (GaAs). GaAs offers higher carrier mobility and some promise for higher temperature operation than silicon. Silicon has the advantage of low cost and the availability of integrated circuit processing techniques that can be used to integrate Hall effect devices with sophisticated signal conditioning. Dielectrically isolated silicon processes,

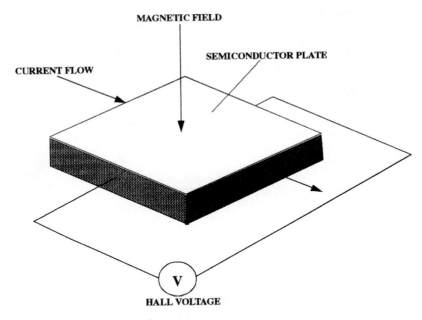

FIGURE 3.5 Hall effect device.

combining integrated circuit techniques with low leakage device isolation, can equal or better the high temperature performance of GaAs.

Hall effect integrated circuits are best categorized in terms of their output characteristics. Analog output devices are usually designed to provide a voltage output that is proportional to the applied magnetic field and also to the power supply voltage. An output ratiometric to the supply allows the device to be easily interfaced to analog-to-digital converters. Analog output devices can be used to construct noncontact absolute position transducers, where the Hall effect device measures a varying field which is designed to be proportional to an angle or linear position. Sensors such as these have no wearing parts other than bearings and can have significant reliability advantages over potentiometers in applications such as throttle-position measurement applications.

Digital output devices are used to construct limit switches or incremental position sensors. The Hall device can be designed to detect homopolar or bipolar fields. Important specifications for digital output devices are operate and release points and the differential between them. The operate point is the maximum field that must be applied to turn the output ON; where ON may be a current-sourcing or current-sinking function. The release point is the minimum field that will guarantee that the sensor is OFF. The differential is the difference between the actual operate and release points. The differential is built in to provide some hysteresis or noise margin to prevent false triggering, particularly at low rates of change of field. The differential may be considerably smaller than the difference between the specified operate and release points. Unipolar devices are specified with operate and release points of the same sign. Bipolar devices are specified with a positive operate point and a negative release point. A caution here is that some devices specified as bipolar do not always require a change of phase of field to operate and release; truly bipolar devices always do.

High-performance Hall effect ICs employ various circuit techniques to improve sensitivity.[6,7] Differential Hall sensors designed for use as gear wheel position sensors use two Hall cells ideally separated by half the gear tooth pitch. This kind of sensor is capable of detecting small changes in unipolar fields. Differential sensors produce an output pulse whose width depends on the rate at which the gear tooth passes the sensor. At very low and very high speeds a very small mark space ratio output results. At high speeds, the timing of the output will be delayed from the mechanical event by a significant proportion of the tooth pitch. A second method is to use a filter circuit to determine the average value of an alternating field and then detect variations from the average value. This method also eliminates any offset that the sensor may have. This method more accurately tracks the mechanical stimulus. A disadvantage is that the filtering function imposes a lower limit on the speed that can be tracked. The devices detailed in Refs. 6 and 7 have lower limits of around 4 Hz. An additional limitation is that the sensor may fail to operate with a high mark space ratio stimulus since the average value of the input will be close to the value of the longest part of the cycle.

A typical Hall sensor application is shown in Fig. 3.6. The Hall device is assembled into a probe with a biasing magnet. The Hall device orientation will depend on its mode of operation, whether unipolar or bipolar. In all cases, the device is sensitive to fields perpendicular to the plane of the silicon surface. Figure 3.6 also compares output waveforms of the Hall sensor configurations discussed earlier as they would appear in this application.

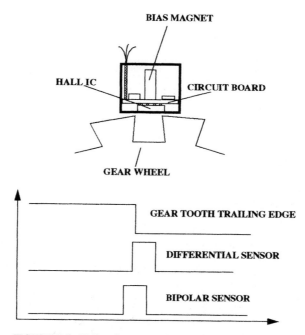

FIGURE 3.6   Hall probe gear position sensor.

Inductive Angle Transducers.   Synchro resolvers, or simply resolvers, are absolute angle transducers. Due mainly to their construction, modern brushless resolvers offer the most rugged, reliable, and highest-resolution solution to angle sensing. Resolvers are often considered a high-cost transducer for automotive applications due to the high labor content in the production of most variants. Some designs[8] provide a cost-effective solution by employing sensing and output windings that can be produced on conventional armature-winding machines. Resolvers can be obtained either fully enclosed or as "pancake" devices, with the stator and rotor supplied separated to facilitate over shaft mounting. Resolvers are often referred to by their size. This is the diameter of the case of the device in inches, rounded up to the nearest 10th, and multiplied by 10. For example, a size 11 resolver will be a fraction less than 1.1 in in diameter. Resolver accuracies are specified in arc min. Typical values for accuracy lie in the range 7 arcmin, with more or less accurate versions available from some vendors.[9]

Resolvers are basically rotating transformers. The construction of a typical device and the output waveforms for a 360° rotation are shown in Fig. 3.7. An alternating voltage connected to the reference input provides primary excitation. The range of frequencies used can be 400 to 20 kHz depending on the construction of the resolver; most resolvers are optimized for the 2 to 5 kHz frequency range. The reference signal is coupled to the rotor via a transformer mounted at one end of the rotor shaft. A second rotor winding couples to two orthogonally oriented stator windings. The stator coils are wound so that as the rotor shaft rotates, the amplitudes of the outputs of the stator windings vary as sine and cosine of the shaft angle relative to some zero.

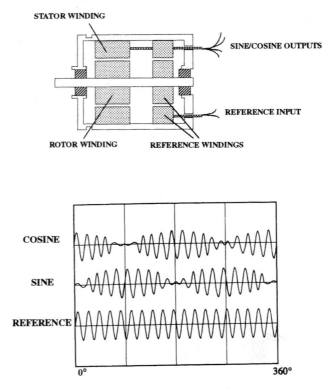

FIGURE 3.7   Resolver construction and output format.

By far, the most economical way of decoding the output of a resolver is to use an IC resolver-to-digital converter (R to D). A functional block diagram of a typical converter is shown in Fig. 3.8. The sine and cosine amplitude-modulated input signals from the resolver representing a shaft angle θ are multiplied by the cosine and sine, respectively, of the current value ϕ of the up/down counter. The resulting signals are subtracted giving:

$$V\mathbf{E} = A \sin(\omega t) \sin(\theta - \phi) \tag{3.4}$$

where $A \sin(\omega t)$ represents the reference carrier.

This signal is synchronously demodulated and an integrator and voltage-controlled oscillator form a closed loop with the counter/multiplier, which seeks to null $\sin(\theta - \phi)$. When the

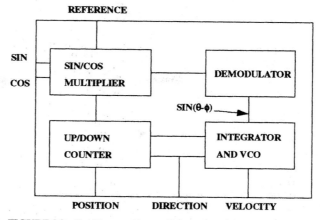

FIGURE 3.8   Tracking resolver-to-digital converter.

null is achieved, the counter value represents the resolver shaft angle within the rated accuracy of the converter. IC R-to-D converters are available that provide parallel or serial digital outputs with resolutions of from 10 to 16 bits and accuracies from 2 to 30 arcmin. Versions are available[10] that emulate standard optical encoder outputs for applications where absolute position measurement is not required but the environment is too harsh for an optical encoder. The system described is a type 2 servo loop which is characterized by zero position and velocity error (not including the limitations of the amplifiers in the IC). R-to-D converters of this type also provide a signal proportional to the angular speed of the resolver from zero to some upper limit, typically 1000 s of rpm, depending on the converter characteristics.

Inductive potential dividers are another class of transducers that are available in many variants.[11,12] A good example is the *rotary variable transformer* or ROVAT.[12] This device comprises a single coil wound on a circular ferromagnetic stator with a number of teeth wound as alternate polarity poles. The stator is excited with an AC signal of around 20 kHz. A rotor with a semicircular conductive screen on its inside surface encircles the stator. The screen reduces the flux linkage between the rotor and stator and the inductance of the screened portion of the stator is reduced, reducing the voltage drop across this portion of the stator. The voltage measured at a central tap on the stator is linearly proportional to the angle of the rotor. Further taps at 90° and 270° from the nominal zero allow a waveform to be measured with amplitude in quadrature with the signal measured at the center point. This allows a 360° absolute angle transducer to be realized, using decoding techniques similar to those which will be described later for the LVDT.

Inductive Linear Displacement Sensors.   Shading ring or short-circuit ring sensors are absolute displacement sensors consisting of an E-shaped core with a winding on the central leg of the E. The winding is excited with high-frequency alternating current. An electrically conductive ring of Al or Cu is allowed to slide, maintaining an air gap along the central leg. The ring is attached to the mechanical component, whose position is to be measured. The ring is equivalent to a short-circuited secondary turn in a transformer. The ring has a shading effect, preventing any flux coupling between the legs of the core from its position along the central leg of the core to the open ends of the core (Fig. 3.9).[13] An inductance change can be measured at the terminals of the excitation coil. These sensors are usually used in a potential divider configuration with a reference inductance of similar construction to the main sensor connected in series with the main sensor. A reference alternating voltage is applied across the series-connected reference and sensor inductances, forming an inductive potential divider. The output is then proportional to the ratio of the inductances. This renders the sensor insensitive to tem-

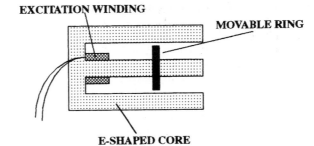

FIGURE 3.9   SCR sensor construction.

perature variations and allows easy adjustment of offsets. Signal-processing electronics can be used to rectify and filter the output and transmit the result to a remote control unit. An alternative construction is to replace the movable ring with an angled channel which can move, relative to the E-shaped core, in a plane perpendicular to the core. Again, the inductance of the sensor is proportional to the linear movement of the angled channel.

Another form of absolute linear displacement sensor is the linear variable differential transformer or LVDT.[14] LVDTs are rugged and reliable and capable of working in harsh environments. Suitable automotive applications include mounting inside hydraulic cylinders in suspension control systems.

LVDTs are constructed from a primary excitation coil positioned centrally on a cylindrical hollow former. Two identical secondary coils are positioned on either side of the primary. The coils have a common core which is free to move within the cylindrical former (Fig. 3.10). The secondaries are normally connected in series, with opposing phases such that with the core centrally positioned and coupling equally to each secondary, the voltage at the node common to both coils will be zero. With this connection, as the core is moved from one extreme of travel through the center to the other extreme, the output signal will vary from a maximum value in phase with the excitation through zero to a maximum value in antiphase with the excitation.

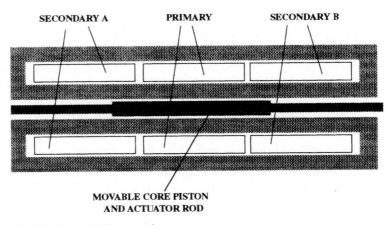

FIGURE 3.10   LVDT construction.

LVDTs are designed to give a linear output within some tolerance, typically ±0.25 percent, over a specified proportion of the available stroke length. The distribution of turns on the secondary coils is carefully arranged to maximize linearity over the widest possible range. LVDTs are available that maintain good linearity with stroke lengths from ±0.05 to ±10 in.

LVDTs operate with effective transformer ratios of between 10:1 to 2:1. The range of primary excitation frequencies can be from 20 Hz to 20 kHz, depending on the construction of the device. Most LVDTs are optimized for the 2- to 5-kHz frequency range. The output signal from an LVDT can be decoded in several different ways and a number of analog and digital integrated circuit solutions exist for this purpose.[15] An example of a typical connection scheme using an LVDT-to-digital converter is shown in Fig. 3.11. In this example, it is assumed that the sum of the voltages across the series-connected secondaries $V_A + V_B$ is a constant over the range of displacements of interest. The majority of LVDTs in production meet this criterion; for those that do not, an additional nonlinearity will result. The IC decodes the function $(V_A - V_B)/(V_A + V_B)$ over the range $[(V_A - V_B)] \leq (V_A + V_B)/2$ into a 13-bit digital word that can be accessed via a three-wire serial interface. Additional bits indicate null and over or under range for signals outside the linear range. The ratiometric decoding scheme described here is insensitive to primary-to-secondary phase shifts, temperature, and any residual null voltage that the transducer may have due to stray capacitive coupling.

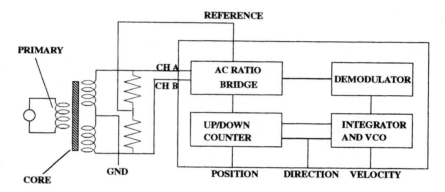

FIGURE 3.11   Tracking LVDT-to-digital converter.

Analog methods of decoding utilize the same basic algorithm as the converter already described. An analog decoder senses the secondary output voltages and evaluates the ratiometric function introduced earlier. The decoder output is filtered and amplified to produce an output voltage proportional to the position of the movable core.

Magnetoresistive.   An interesting group of sensors utilize the property of some FeNi alloys such that their resistivity is strongly affected by the presence of a magnetic field. The magnetoresistive effects of one of the useful alloys, Permalloy, which is 81 percent nickel and 19 percent iron, enables sensitive magnetic field sensors with full-scale fields of 5 mT to be built. The variation in resistance is around 2.5 percent for a field of this magnitude. The resistance decreases with increasing field strength; the relationship between field strength and resistance is very nonlinear, approximating a cosine-squared function. Using thin films of Permalloy deposited on a silicon substrate allows signal-conditioning electronics to be integrated with the sensor. Despite the nonlinearity of the phenomenon, accurate linear sensors can be constructed by using the sensor in a bridge arrangement together with flux nulling means, such as a servo-driven coil surrounding the sensor, to effectively operate the sensor at constant resistance. An alternative construction uses opposing "barber pole" thin-film elements.[16] An element is composed of a rectangular thin film of Permalloy overlaid with a series of shorting stripes of aluminum at 45° to the long axis. Two series-connected elements, which are mirror images of each other (reflected about the long axis), form a potential divider. Magnetoresistive sensors generally exhibit high sensitivity, but this leaves them prone to interference from unwanted fields and, therefore, they are unsuitable for some applications.

Magnetostrictive.   Magnetostriction is a property of materials that respond to a change of magnetic flux by developing an elastic deformation of their crystal structure. Magnetostrictive linear displacement sensors utilize this phenomenon by launching a compression wave down a cylindrical waveguide using electromagnetic means, usually a current pulse. The waveguide passes through a movable permanent magnet ring at some distance from a receiver site. The compression wave generated at the magnet position travels to the receiver site at approximately 2800 m/s where it causes a change of flux and generates a voltage pulse in a sense coil. The time of flight of the pulse can be measured to determine the distance of the movable ring magnet down the wire. Transducers with stroke lengths in excess of 7.5 m are available that use this technique.

3.3.5 Other Technologies

A number of other technologies can be applied to position-sensing problems, limited only by engineering ingenuity. Some, like capacitive-sensing techniques, are not tolerant of the automotive environment due to sensitivity to humidity, vibration, or temperature or pressure extremes. Others, like resolvers of traditional construction, are sufficiently rugged but prohibitively expensive unless low-cost manufacturing techniques can be found. Occasionally, a nonobvious method finds a niche. An example is a fuel-level sensor disclosed by workers at Bosch,[17] which, in principle, could be applied as a position sensor. The device operates by exciting a metal rod with acoustic waves such that it resonates. One end of the rod is immersed in the fuel. The resonant frequency is a function of the depth of immersion and the fuel level can be determined by suitable electronics.

A significant influence in the selection of technologies for automotive use is the mandatory inclusion of safety systems. Microwave or laser-ranging techniques can be applied to anti-collision systems to anticipate obstacles at nighttime or in poor-visibility driving conditions. These will be a ubiquitous component of automobiles in years to come.

3.4 INTERFACING SENSORS TO CONTROL SYSTEMS

All sensors, whether they have digital or analog outputs, provide measurement of real-world phenomena that are then interpreted by another system to either indicate a value, a warning, or close a control loop. It is vitally important that the integrity of the data is maintained by the proper choice of interface.

Cost and reliability in automotive systems are primary drivers in the choice of interface. For a given performance, the sensor that requires the fewer connections will always be selected. In some cases, such as LVDTs where the basic sensor requires 5 or 6 wires, it may be advantageous to locate the signal-conditioning electronics with the sensor and communicate the processed data to a remote controller via a simple serial interface. Interfacing incremental or serial binary data to a microcontroller is straightforward. In the case of incremental data, typically the mechanical system being monitored is moved until some limit or index is detected. Knowledge of the absolute position of the mechanical component is then known. A counter or register can be set to an initial nonzero value or reset to zero. As the motion is detected, pulses from the incremental sensor can be counted and stored as a measure of position. The indexing cycle must be performed each time power is applied. Binary serial data can be read into a register and used directly with no further processing.

Analog-to-digital converters (ADCs) require some special considerations to optimize performance. Not least of these is grounding. In most applications, chassis ground returns cannot be used. Modern automobiles may have voltage drops of 1 V or more between the chassis at the ECU and the sensor site, due to return currents from electric equipment. This voltage is likely to be noisy with many transients and will certainly upset all but the crudest sensors.

Previous sections have discussed the advantages of ratiometric sensors that can use the same reference as the converter. The advantage is that a least-significant bit of the ADC is always a fixed percentage of the sensor span. This eliminates gain, offset, and temperature errors that may occur if separate references are used. Resolution and gain accuracy of a system can be further optimized by making certain that the span of the sensor output uses all of the available input span of the converter. Many ADCs include on board a microcontroller and use switch capacitor techniques to acquire the analog input values. These present a transient load to the sensor once or twice per conversion cycle. Some sensor outputs, particularly sensors with buffer amplifiers, require isolation from this transient to achieve rated accuracy. A simple technique is to use a simple RC filter on the output of the sensor. This limits the transient current that the sensor output sees and shunts the ADC input with a capacitor.

GLOSSARY

Absolute output sensor   The sensor output is an unambiguous measure of position and is valid when power is applied.

Arcminute   An angular measure. There are 60 arcminutes in 1 degree of arc.

Incremental sensor   The sensor indicates changes in position. An additional position reference, such as a limit switch, is often used with this type of sensor.

Linearity error   The amount by which the sensor output differs from an ideal characteristic. Usually expressed in percent.

Ratiometric output sensor   An input stimulus causes the output to be a fraction of a reference voltage.

REFERENCES

1. Hewlett-Packard, *Optoelectronics Designers Guide,* San Jose, Calif., 1991–1992.
2. Novatechnik Position Sensor Data, Ostfildern, Germany, 1992.
3. P. Hammond, *Electromagnetism for Engineers,* Pergamon Press Ltd., Oxford, England, 1965.
4. Roland K. Kolter, European Patent Application EP 0 019 530 A1, Applicant Bendix, 1980.
5. Henry P. Baltes, and Popovic, Radivoje S., "Integrated magnetic field sensors," *Proceedings of the IEEE* vol. 74, no. 8, Aug. 1986, pp. 1107–1132.
6. Hartmut Jasberg, "Differential Hall IC for gear-tooth sensing," *Sensors and Actuators,* A21–A23, 1990, pp. 737–742.
7. AD22150 Data Sheet, Analog Devices, Norwood, Mass.
8. Charles S. Smith, U.S. Patent 4 962 331, Assigned to Servo-Tek Products Co. Inc., Hawthorne, N.J., 1990.
9. Clifton Precision, Analog Components Data, Clifton Heights, Pa.
10. AD2S90 Data Sheet, Analog Devices, Norwood, Mass.
11. Novatechnik Angle Sensor Data, Ostfildern, Germany, 1993.

12. Donald L. Hore, and Flowerdew, Peter M., "Developments in inductive analog transducers for 360° rotation or tilt and for linear displacement," *IEE International Conference,* No. 285, 1988.

13. E. Zabler, and Heintz, F., "Shading-ring sensors as versatile position and angle sensors in motor vehicles," *Sensors and Actuators* **3**, 1982/3, pp. 315–326.

14. *Schaevitz Linear and Angular Displacement Transducers Catalog,* Pennsauken, N.J.

15. AD2S93 and AD598 Data Sheets, Analog Devices, Norwood, Mass.

16. F. Heintz and Zabler, E., "Application possibilities and future chances of 'smart' sensors in the motor vehicle," *SAE Technical Paper Series* #890304.

17. E. Zabler, "Universal low-cost fuel-level sensor," Robert Bosch GmbH, Ettingen, Germany.

ABOUT THE AUTHOR

Paul Nickson is product line manager for Analog Devices' Sensor and Automotive Group in Wilmington, Mass. He has BSc Honours in Electronic and Electrical Engineering from the University of Birmingham, England and 16 years' experience in integrated circuit design. For the past five years, he has focused on silicon sensors and sensor signal conditioning.

CHAPTER 4
FLOW SENSORS

Robert E. Bicking
Senior Engineering Fellow
Honeywell, Micro Switch Division

4.1 INTRODUCTION

Measurement of flow rate is important to optimize the performance of several key engine control subsystems. Mass air flow sensors are replacing the indirect calculation of intake mass air flow for improved performance, driveability, and economy. New requirements for on-board diagnostics are opening new applications for flow sensing in the automobile.

If the parameter to be measured is a gaseous mass flow as opposed to a volume flow, this further focuses the sensing technology selection since only a few technologies inherently measure mass flow. For liquid flow, either a mass flow or volumetric flow approach may be used since the density of a liquid changes only a small amount with atmospheric pressure and temperature.

This chapter is intended to give the reader an understanding of where and why flow sensors are being specified for use in engine control systems and an understanding of the trade-offs among alternative technologies in particular applications.

4.2 AUTOMOTIVE APPLICATIONS OF FLOW SENSORS

4.2.1 Intake Air Mass Flow

Electronic fuel injection has almost universally replaced the carburetor in the auto engine. This is because it provides better performance and is the only way to meet government mandated emissions standards. To do fuel injection, the mass flow rate of air going into the engine must be determined. There are two competing approaches to determining the mass air flow rate. The first, *speed density,* calculates the mass flow rate by measuring engine speed (RPM), intake air temperature (T_a) and intake manifold pressure (P). The per-cylinder nominal displacement (V) is known, as is the gas constant of air (R_a). The engine's volumetric efficiency (η) may be modeled as a function of speed. Then, the mass flow rate ($\dot{m}_a$) is calculated as follows:

$$\dot{m}_a = \frac{(\text{RPM } V \, \eta \, P)}{(R_a T_a)} \tag{4.1}$$

4.1

By using a mass flow sensor, this calculation is eliminated and $\dot{m}_a$ is measured directly. The advantages of using a direct measurement include better accuracy under dynamic conditions because the manifold pressure changes more slowly than the mass flow rate. Also, no assumptions are made about engine displacement or volumetric efficiency, both of which affect the speed density calculation. Volumetric efficiency can change as the intake system becomes contaminated. Mass air flow sensors are presently being used on roughly 20 percent of the cars sold in the United States. They are not more widely used because they cost more than the pressure sensor needed to do the speed-density calculation. The largest drawback to using a mass flow sensor is that a wide dynamic range sensor is needed since the mass flow rate can change over a 100-to-1 range from idle to full throttle, whereas the manifold pressure only changes over a 5-to-1 range. Other important factors in sensor selection include resistance to contamination and particulate damage, accuracy, ability to measure reverse flow, and sensitivity to upstream and downstream ducting.

Fuel is injected to each cylinder on a sequential basis for optimum performance. This requires using the crankshaft sensor and camshaft sensor outputs to time the injection of fuel into the intake manifold at the proper point on the intake stroke. The fuel injector is fed with a constant pressure and is pulse-width modulated to control the amount of fuel injected. The calculation of the mass rate ($\dot{m}_f$) of fuel injected follows:

$$\dot{m}_f = \dot{m}_a \, \lambda \tag{4.2}$$

where $\dot{m}_a$ = mass air flow rate
λ = stoichiometric air/fuel ratio

4.2.2 Potential or Future Applications of Flow Sensors

Fuel Flow for Gas Mileage Measurement. Driver information systems that predict range and gas mileage need to know the amount of fuel flow. As seen from the preceding discussion of mass air flow measurement, the fuel flow is calculated from the air flow so that this data is already in the engine control computer. By simply summing the injector "on" time over a revolution or multiple revolutions, the fuel flow is known.

Alternatively, the fuel flow can be measured by taking the difference between the fuel coming into the fuel rail and that being returned. This approach could be subject to substantial error, however, due to the fact that these flows are purposely much larger than the net flow into the engine so that the fuel rail will be maintained at a constant pressure. Future fuel-handling systems may simplify the measurement by eliminating the return line and simply modulating the fuel pressure pump to maintain constant pressure. Then, the measured flow would be simply that flow going into the engine.

Exhaust Gas Recirculation Flow. Exhaust gas recirculation (EGR) is performed to reduce the emission of nitrous oxides (NO_x) by cooling the combustion process. If the EGR valve begins to clog or only partially opens, its flow will be reduced and emissions will increase. In the near future, OBDII legislation will require cars to have on-board diagnostics capable of determining when an emissions-related failure (such as that just described) occurs. Measurement of the flow is one way to diagnose a faulty EGR valve. Another way would be the use of an NO_x sensor to measure the emissions. However, no low-cost NO_x sensors have yet been developed.

Secondary Air Pump Flow. The secondary air pump is used to reduce the emissions of carbon monoxide (CO) and hydrocarbons (HC). Measurement of its flow rate is an approach to verifying that it is operating properly and doing its part to reduce emissions. Another way, of course, would be to directly measure the emissions of HC and CO in the exhaust. To date, however, there is no low-cost real-time means to do that. A way to verify air pump operation without using any additional sensors is to command the air pump full-on when the fuel injection is slightly rich of stoichiometry. The oxygen sensor output should switch from rich to lean if the air pump is operating properly.

Fuel Flow for Fuel-Air Ratio Feedback Control.   Present engine control systems treat the fuel flow as a dependent variable, measuring the intake air flow and then operating the fuel injectors to meter the proper amount of fuel into the engine. This tacitly assumes that each of the injectors is precisely calibrated so that a given "on" time provides a given amount of fuel. Fuel injectors typically use a needle valve in an orifice to meter the fuel. The orifice area is proportional to the square of the diameter so that the fuel flow error will be proportional to two times the diameter tolerance. By measuring the fuel flow, the accuracy of fuel injection could be improved. Table 4.1 summarizes the performance requirements by application.

TABLE 4.1

Application	Measurement type	Range, kg/h	Accuracy, %
Intake air	Mass	10–1000	±4
Fuel flow	Mass/vol.	1–66	±10
EGR flow	Mass	30–100	±10
Air pump flow	Vol.	50	±20
Fuel flow	Mass/vol.	1–66	±4

4.3   BASIC CLASSIFICATION OF FLOW SENSORS

4.3.1   Energy Additive or Energy Extractive

Flowing fluid possesses energy, both potential and kinetic. One approach to flow measurement extracts energy from the flow. Alternately, energy may be added to the flow and its effect observed. The energy-additive approach typically is nonintrusive, so the act of measuring doesn't affect the flow. As might be expected, flowmeter selection involves a number of factors, as will be discussed later.

4.3.2   Measurement of Mass Flow or Volume Flow

Intake air measurement requires that the mass of air flowing into the engine be measured. This favors a mass-flow approach, since, otherwise, pressure and air temperature must be measured to calculate the mass flow from the volume flow. The mass flow rate ($\dot{m}_a$) is calculated as follows:

$$\dot{m}_a = \dot{V}_a \, \rho \tag{4.3}$$

where ρ = air density
$\dot{V}_a$ = volumetric flow rate

The density, in turn, is calculated as follows:

$$\rho = \frac{P}{ZR_aT_a} \tag{4.4}$$

where P = air pressure
Z = compressibility factor
R_a = gas constant for air
T_a = air temperature

4.4 APPLICABLE FLOW MEASUREMENT TECHNOLOGIES

4.4.1 Gaseous Flow

Vane. The vane simply consists of a vane or paddle which is located in the flow duct and is restrained by a spring so that it blocks the duct with no flow. The deflection of the vane is thus proportional to flow. This deflection is read out by a potentiometer. The largest drawback of a vane sensor is that it increases the pressure drop in the intake tract, reducing the volumetric efficiency of the engine. This approach was used in the earliest engine control systems and is being replaced by technologies such as hot-wire air flow sensors which offer much lower pressure drop.

Thermal. This is the favored approach and is used in all engines currently being manufactured that employ direct measurement of the intake air mass. Depending on design details, it provides a nearly direct measurement of the mass flow and thus simplifies the engine control strategy. A variety of designs exists, from the straightforward hot-wire air flow sensor to more complex schemes. The basic idea is to heat a fine wire, and then as the gas flows past the wire, convection removes heat. The amount of heat removed can be measured with an electronic circuit and is proportional to mass air flow rate as the following equation shows:

$$\Delta P \cong \Delta T \, [C_t + (2\pi d C_v \dot{m}_a)^{1/2}]* \tag{4.5}$$

where ΔP = change in electric power due to a given flow rate
$\quad \Delta T$ = temperature difference between air and sensor
$\quad C_t$ = thermal conductivity of air
$\quad d$ = diameter of hot wire
$\quad C_v$ = thermal capacity of air
$\quad \dot{m}_a$ = mass flow rate of air

Note that the first term of the equation isn't proportional to flow rate. Either this needs to be modeled and removed or the change in ambient air temperature needs to be minimized to accurately measure mass flow rate. A hot-wire air flow sensor and its control circuit is shown in Fig. 4.1. Control circuits typically either supply constant power to the heated element or

---

* From Joseph P. DeCarlo, *Fundamentals of Flow Measurement,* Instrument Society of America, 1984, pp. 173 and 176.

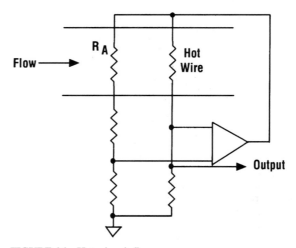

FIGURE 4.1 Hot-wire air flow sensor.

operate it at a constant temperature delta above the ambient temperature. The latter is shown in Fig. 4.2 and is preferred because it simplifies temperature compensation.

One of the problems with the hot-wire sensor is that fine dust particles may pass through the air filter and, under full-throttle conditions, can impact the hot wire with sufficient force to break it. Particulate build-up is also a source of error and has been alleviated by placing the heated element in a bypass channel or by incorporating a burn-off cycle at power-on. Most of the development in hot-wire sensors has been to ruggedize them to withstand the automotive environment and to desensitize them to upstream and downstream flow anomalies. Figure 4.2 is an example of a bypass design for a hot-element mass air flow sensor. It uses a platinum wire wound on a ceramic mandrel and coated with glass as the sensing element. It is located in a bypass channel away from the main flow to reduce the likelihood of particulate contamination. The bypass exits into the main channel through slots which are intended to desensitize it to backflows and backfires.

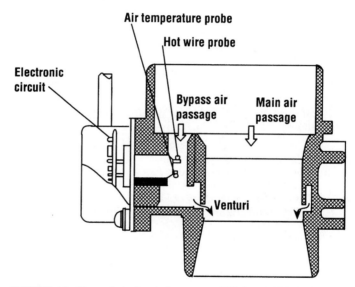

FIGURE 4.2 Bypass hot-wire air flow sensor. *(U.S. Patent 4,264,961)*

Backflow can occur in engines with four or fewer cylinders at low speed. It is most desirable for the sensor to measure the backflow, but most either don't measure it at all or rectify it, which makes the measured flow appear larger than it really is. This error is compensated by measuring the backflow on an engine and then using software to remove the nominal error. One of the issues with bypass designs is that upstream ducting of the air may affect measurement accuracy. A bend just ahead of the sensor will cause the air to move toward the outside of the bend and, depending on where the bypass is located, it may read either too low or too high. This effect is minimized by placing a screen or honeycomb in the sensor to straighten the flow.

Micromachined air flow sensors have been available commercially for several years and efforts are underway to adapt them to automotive applications. Their primary advantages include the low cost of the sensing element due to batch fabrication; excellent performance over temperature due to the close proximity of the heated and reference elements; the ability to measure reverse flows; low operating power due to the small size of the heated element; and fast response, again due to the small size of the heated element. Because of the use of integrated circuit manufacturing techniques, it is no more difficult to include additional resistors on the sensor chip than to simply replicate a hot wire. A calorimetric flow sensor may be constructed by separating the heater and sensor functions as shown in Fig. 4.3. The advantage

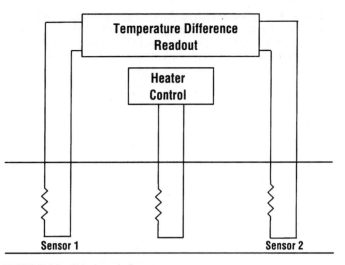

FIGURE 4.3   Calorimetric flow sensor.

of a calorimetric flow sensor is that it does measure the mass flow rate as the following equation shows:

$$\Delta P = \dot{m}_a C_p \, \Delta T* \tag{4.6}$$

where ΔP = change in power due to a given mass flow rate
$\dot{m}_a$ = mass air flow rate
C_p = thermal capacity of air
ΔT = temperature difference between air and sensor

One of the issues with microstructure sensors is protection from damage due to particle impact and preventing build-up of contamination. This requires clever packaging.

Table 4.2 compares the main types of thermal mass air flow sensors.

Differential Pressure.   A simple way to measure volumetric flow is to place an obstruction in a flow channel and measure the differential pressure drop across it. The flow is proportional to the square root of the differential pressure. This only works well for narrow flow ranges because to operate over a given flow range, the pressure sensor must operate over the square of that range. For the automotive intake flow range of 100 to 1, a pressure sensor with a range of 10,000 to 1 is required, which is not achievable except at high cost. An important advantage of this approach is that it is resistant to contamination, since the pressure sensor merely needs

---

* From "Fundamentals of Flow Measurement," Joseph P. Decarlo, Instrument Society of America, 1984, pp. 173 and 176.

TABLE 4.2

Type	Effect of contamination	Meas. rev. flow	Affected by ducting	Power used
Hot Wire	High*	Rectifies	Low	Medium
Hot RTD Bypass	Low	Ignores	High	High
Micro RTD	Low	Yes	Low	Low

* Burn-off cycle used to alleviate.

to sense the pressure difference across the flow restriction (in the case of an orifice plate or venturi). The differential pressure approach could be suitable for some low-accuracy or low dynamic range applications such as EGR valve flow. Venturis (Fig. 4.4), flow restrictions (Fig. 4.5), and pitot tubes (Fig. 4.6) all operate on the same principle.

4.4.2 Liquid Flow

Differential Pressure.   The preceding discussion on differential pressure sensing applies equally to liquid flows.

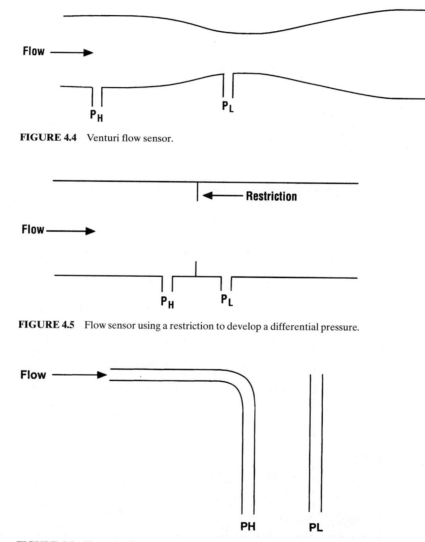

FIGURE 4.4   Venturi flow sensor.

FIGURE 4.5   Flow sensor using a restriction to develop a differential pressure.

FIGURE 4.6   Pitot tube flow sensor.

Turbine. A turbine blade placed in a flow channel can offer low restriction to flow, and by counting the speed of rotation it can also measure flow. It is analogous to the vane described previously except that it is more subject to wear since it is revolving, not merely deflecting. Use of a noncontacting means of counting revolutions (such as a Hall effect sensor) is recommended. This approach is well-suited to measurement of fuel flow.

Vortex Shedding. Oscillations may be induced in a fluid by placing an obstruction in the flow stream. The oscillations may be measured thermally, by pressure changes or using ultrasonics. This approach doesn't work well at low flow rates due to instability in the vortex shedding mechanism, so it is not suited to wide dynamic range applications such as intake air measurement. An example of a vortex shedding flow sensor is shown in Fig. 4.7.

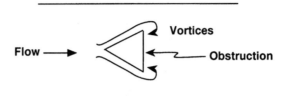

FIGURE 4.7   Vortex shedding flow sensor.

Other Technologies. There are a number of other technologies which are not well-suited to automotive applications, primarily due to cost considerations. A variety of flow sensors has been developed for industrial applications where performance is paramount and cost is secondary. These include the use of ultrasonics, gyroscopic effects, ionization of gases, and so on. These will not be discussed herein. Information on these technologies is given in the books by DeCarlo and Norton. See the list of suggestions for further reading.

GLOSSARY

Backflow   The flow of air out of the intake system of an engine. This occurs at low speeds in engines containing only a few cylinders when all intake valves are closed at once.

Exhaust gas recirculation   A process in which exhaust gases (containing primarily nitrogen) are returned to the intake system to reduce emissions by lowering the combustion temperature.

Micromachining   Formation of very small three-dimensional structures in a semiconductor material.

Speed density   A method of calculating the intake mass air flow rate by measuring engine speed and air density.

Stoichiometry   The air-to-fuel ratio at which all the oxygen is consumed during combustion.

Volumetric efficiency   The volume flow rate of air into the intake system divided by the volume rate of piston displacement.

BIBLIOGRAPHY

Adler, Ulrich, *Automobile Electric/Electronic Systems,* Robert Bosch, Stuttgart, 1988.

DeCarlo, Joseph P., *Fundamentals of Flow Measurement,* Instrument Society of America, Research Triangle Park, 1984.

Heywood, John B., *Internal Combustion Engine Fundamentals,* McGraw-Hill, New York, 1988.

Norton, Harry N., *Handbook of Transducers,* Prentice Hall, Englewood Cliffs, N.J., 1989.

ABOUT THE AUTHOR

Robert E. Bicking received the B.E.E. and M.S.E.E. degrees from the University of Minnesota and has been involved with sensors nearly all of his 32 years in engineering. He is currently involved with the development of new automotive sensors at the Micro Switch division of Honeywell. He has been awarded three U.S. patents and is the author of over 24 technical papers. He is a member of the I.S.A., I.E.E.E., and S.A.E.

CHAPTER 5
TEMPERATURE, HEAT, AND HUMIDITY SENSORS

Randy Frank
Motorola Semiconductor Products

5.1   TEMPERATURE, HEAT, AND HUMIDITY

Temperature sensing and taking into account the effect of temperature on the performance and reliability of automotive components, and therefore the systems that contain these components, is one of the more important aspects of vehicle design. The heat sources that are present on modern automobiles range from the engine itself to catalytic converters, losses in power conversion (e.g. the alternator), and specific heat-generating devices such as heated windshields, seats, and mirrors. Humidity adds to the effect that temperature has on the reliability of components and also impacts vehicle performance and passenger comfort.

5.1.1   Temperature—the Effect of Heat

The temperature of a body or substance is (1) its potential of heat flow, (2) a measure of the mean kinetic energy of its molecules, and (3) its thermal state with reference to its ability to transfer heat to other bodies or substances.

Temperature affects every aspect of automobiles, from the performance of the engine and various vehicle systems to the comfort of the driver and passengers. The wide range of worldwide vehicle operating temperatures (from −60° to +57 °C) and the subsequent localized electronic module temperature ambients underhood (from −40 to +125 °C) and in the passenger compartments (from −40 to +85 °C) affect both the performance and reliability of electronic components. The viscosity of lubricating and cooling fluids is also affected by the wide temperature variations that must be tolerated. Even paint, fabric, plastics, rubber, and other organic and inorganic materials must be designed to survive the environmental extremes of temperature and humidity. Sensing the temperature of these components is essential during vehicle development.

5.1.2   Conduction, Convection, and Radiation

Heat energy is transferred with corresponding temperature changes by conduction, convection, and/or radiation. Conduction occurs by diffusion through solid material or in stationary liquids or gases; convection involves the movement of a liquid or gas between two points, and radiation occurs through electromagnetic waves.

5.1.3   Heat Sources in Vehicles

In addition to the temperature rise that can be generated by sunlight on the metal and glass that form the body of the vehicle, there are several heat-generating devices in a vehicle as shown in Table 5.1. The foremost heat source is the engine in internal combustion engine equipped vehicles. This causes the engine compartment to generally be classified as a +125 °C ambient for electronic components, although considerably higher temperatures are reached within the combustion chamber ($\geq$1000 °C) or on the engine block.

The catalytic converter used to reduce unburnt hydrocarbons and carbon monoxide emissions has a peak catalyst efficiency around 450 °C, minimum operating temperature around 350 °C, and high temperature operation in the area of 1000 °C.

Tire flexure and friction generated between the tires and the road surface are major sources of heat. Moreover, heat is generated by friction between any moving components of a vehicle. Gears and bearings in transmissions, rear axle, and pumps are most notable for generating a significant temperature rise. Brake surfaces also create high temperatures when the brakes are applied.

Even though they do not generate heat, in the process of reducing the temperature of other components, heat exchangers—such as coolant or transmission radiators for the passenger compartment heater and their associated plumbing and electronic heat sinks—have considerably higher than ambient temperatures.

Electric heating elements, including heated back light, windshield, windshield wiper, mirrors, and seats, increase the temperature to improve visibility and driver comfort. Heated windshield wipers can be maintained at 15 °C even when outside temperatures are around −40 °C. In some cases, temperatures in the area of 350 °C are produced by supplemental heating elements for components such as the catalytic converter, the oxygen sensor, and some advanced electric vehicle batteries.

The windings of electric components such as the starter motor, heater motor, alternator, and solenoids are a source of heat and high temperatures, especially in continuously moving, heavily loaded units like the alternator. The resistance in the windings as well as resistance in semiconductor components like alternator rectifiers and power transistors creates a power loss proportional to the square of the current being conducted ($P = I^2R$). In semiconductors, the change in temperature is related to the power dissipated through the thermal resistance.

$$\Delta T = R_\theta P \tag{5.1}$$

where R_θ = thermal resistance in °C/W
ΔT = temperature difference in °C (frequently $T_{\text{junction}} - T_{\text{case}}$)
P = power in watts

TABLE 5.1   Heat Sources in Vehicles

General category	Example	Max. temperature °C
Engine	Combustion/ignition process	>1000
Catalytic converter	Chemical reaction	>1000
Road/tire friction	Tires	<100
Brakes	Disk/drum	250
Mechanical motion (gears, bearings)	Transmission/rear axle/air pump/power steering pump	200
Heat exchangers	Radiator (coolant, transmission), heater, heatsink	>175
Electric heaters	Windshield, backlight, seats, mirrors	Ta + 25
Electric windings	Motors, alternator, solenoids	<155 (Class F)
Resistors	Ballast resistor	150
Lamps	Headlamps, tail lamps, dash lamps	125
Power transistors	Ignition driver, voltage regulator	Up to 200
Electric vehicle battery	Sodium sulfur	300

Lamps have a significant inrush current (10 · steady state) and a high steady state value which generate high temperatures as well.

Temperature at various locations in the vehicle are shown in Table 5.2.

TABLE 5.2 Temperature at Various Vehicle Locations

Location	Temperature, °C			Humidity		
	Low	High	Slew Rate	High	Low	Frost
Underhood—Engine						
Exhaust manifold	−40	+649	−7 °C/min	95% at 38 °C	0	Yes
Intake manifold	−40	+121	−7 °C/min	95% at 38 °C	0	Yes
Underhood—Dash Panel						
Normal	−40	+121	Open	95% at 38 °C		
Extreme	−40	+141	Open	80% at 66 °C		
Chassis						
Isolated	−40	+85	NA	98% at 38 °C	0	Yes
Near heat source	−40	+121	NA	80% at 66 °C	0	Yes
At drive train temperature	−40	+177	NA	80% at 66 °C	0	Yes

5.1.4 Effect of Humidity

Humidity affects the comfort of the drivers and the passengers as well as the performance of the engine and impacts the reliability of vehicle components. The primary measurement for humidity is relative humidity RH, the ratio of water partial pressure to saturation pressure. Other measurements include dew point (temperature); specific humidity (mixing ratio); the mass of water per unit mass of dry gas; and volume ratio, the parts of water vapor per million parts of air. The dew point is a direct measure of vapor pressure and absolute humidity. Humidity is the water vapor in gas. Water in a solid or liquid is called moisture. High humidity and low dew point can lead to increased moisture content which can affect the operation of vehicle fluids such as fuel and brake fluid and impact solid surfaces like the windshield or brake linings.

5.1.5 Reliability Implications to Electronic Components

The effect of temperature on electronic components was recognized as "one of the most severe environments generally encountered on the automobile." Warm-up time of engine liquids and local ambient temperatures are as high as several tens of minutes, especially in cold weather. A recommended practice, SAE J1211, was published in November 1978 that still serves as a guideline to developing environmental design goals for electronic equipment, especially in the area of temperature variations within various vehicle locations.

Temperature affects the performance and expected life of electronic components. Mechanical stress created by different coefficients of thermal expansion can cause failures in thermal cycling test (air-to-air) or thermal shock (water-to-water) transitions.

The failure of electronic components also occurs because the mechanical durability, solder strength, or glass transition of plastic mold compound is exceeded. Electrical properties including thermal runaway in bipolar transistors and loss of gate control in MOS-gated (Sec. 5.4.6) devices also directly cause failure due to temperature extremes.

The typical failure rate for a semiconductor component can be expressed by the Arhennius equation:

$$\lambda = A \cdot \exp \frac{\theta}{kT} \tag{5.2}$$

where λ = failure rate
      A = constant
   exp = 2.72
     θ = activation energy
     k = Boltzmann's constant
       $8.62 \cdot 10^{-5}$ eV/°K
    T = temperature in °K

The failure rate of semiconductor components typically doubles for every 10 to 15 °C increase in operating temperature. However, increased testing and design improvements have minimized the failures due to specific failure mechanisms. Semiconductor components manufactured in the 90s are orders of magnitude more reliable than those first used in vehicles in the 60s. However, their response time is considerably faster than vehicle liquids and local ambients. For example, the transient thermal response, $r(t) \, R\theta_{JC}$, which is a reduced level of the thermal resistance (Sec. 5.1.4) based on the transistor operating in a switching mode and being off for a period of time, approaches the dc level within a second. Excessive temperatures can be generated quickly and must be detected within milliseconds to prevent failure.

Accelerated life testing is performed at elevated temperatures to determine the reliability of electronic components and obtain the maximum amount of information in the minimum amount of time. The actual failure mechanisms are a result of the component design and environment in which they operate. Life testing seeks to identify areas that are vulnerable in a particular design and provides minimum acceptable criteria for qualification.

The activation energy is directly proportional to the degree of influence that temperature has on the chemical reaction rate. Temperature acceleration factors for a particular failure mechanism can be expressed as the ratio of the failure rates at two different levels of stress:

$$F_a = \exp\left(\frac{\theta}{k}\right) \cdot \frac{1}{T_r - 1/T_t} \tag{5.3}$$

where F_a = acceleration factor
    θ = activation energy
    k = Boltzmann's constant, $8.62 \cdot 10^{-5}$ eV/°K
    T_r = junction temperature in °K at the rated ambient temperature
    T_t = junction temperature in °K at the life test ambient temperature

To determine a component's ability to withstand the adverse effects of temperature and humidity extremes to which the vehicle is exposed, a number of reliability stress tests are included in the qualification procedure. These tests include:

- *High-temperature Storage Life* is performed to accelerate failure mechanisms which are thermally activated through extreme temperatures.

  Typical test conditions: T_a = 70 to 200 °C, no bias, time = 24 to 5000 h

- *Temperature Cycling* (air-to-air) evaluates the ability of a device to withstand both exposure to temperature extremes and transition between temperature extremes. This test also exposes excessive thermal mismatch between materials.

  Typical test conditions: T_a = −65 to 200 °C, cycle = 10 to 4000 (1000 most common)

- *Thermal Shock* (liquid-to-liquid) testing evaluates the ability of the device to withstand both exposure to extreme temperature and sudden transitions between temperature extremes. This testing also exposes extreme thermal mismatch between materials.

  Typical test conditions: T_a = 0 to 100 °C, cycle = 20 to 300 (100 most common)

- *H^3TRB* (high-humidity, high-temperature reverse bias) is an environmental test designed to measure the moisture resistance of plastic encapsulated devices. A bias is applied to accelerate corrosive effects on internal components of semiconductors.

  Typical test conditions: T_a = 85 to 95 °C, RH = 85 to 95%, bias = 80 to 100% of max rating, time = 96 to 1750 h

- *Autoclave* (or pressure cooker) testing is performed to measure device resistance to moisture penetration and resulting galvanic corrosion. This is a highly accelerated and destructive test.
  Typical test conditions: $T_a = 121$ °C, RH = 100%, $p = 1$ atmosphere, time = 24 to 96 h
- *Moisture Resistance* testing evaluates the moisture resistance of components under tropical environments.
  Typical test conditions: $T_a = -10$ to 65 °C, RH = 80 to 98%, time = 24 h/cycle, cycle = 10

In addition, a number of high-temperature tests under different biasing conditions are also performed for semiconductor devices, including high-temperature forward bias, high-temperature reverse bias, and high-temperature gate bias.

5.2   AUTOMOTIVE TEMPERATURE MEASUREMENTS

Numerous temperature measurements are made during the development of the vehicle to ensure the proper operation of systems and components. Some measurements are included in the control system strategy or as diagnostics for production vehicles. A list of the potential temperature and humidity measurements that can be made and may be incorporated in future systems is shown in Table 5.3. The technique used to measure temperature may vary from development to production mode, from one vehicle manufacturer to another and even from system to system within a given vehicle manufacturer. The choice in technology for production sensors depends upon performance, reliability, and cost. For development vehicles, cost is not a major concern, but availability of test probes, compatibility with readout equipment, and ease of use are additional factors that should be taken into consideration.

Common vehicle temperature measurements will be explained in the remainder of this section.

5.2.1   Measuring Liquid Temperatures

A number of liquid temperatures are measured during vehicle development, especially under high vehicle ambient temperatures and severe driving conditions, such as trailer towing up steep grades and stop-and-go Phoenix traffic during summer months. These include coolant, engine oil, transmission oil, fuel, power steering, brake, and battery electrolyte. Monitoring coolant temperature is common in engine control systems in production vehicles. Engine and transmission oil temperature are being evaluated for future monitoring. Racing vehicles frequently monitor oil and fuel temperature in addition to coolant temperature to achieve peak performance. Sensing fuel temperature may be required to meet future emissions standards. A latent heat cooling system has been developed that uses a temperature sensor to control the engine under various operating conditions. The system employs control valves that control the flow of vaporized coolant based on temperature in a manifold connected to the top of the combustion chamber.

Mounting location, fluid contacting the sensor, and packaging are critical concerns for liquid temperature sensors. Upper temperature limits are typically around 150 to 200 °C and operation down to –40 °C is usually required.

Battery temperature measurements in vehicle development use glass thermometers or glass-shielded thermocouple probes to protect the sensor from the corrosive electrolyte.

5.2.2   Battery Temperature

Maintaining the proper state of charge in the vehicle's battery is essential for obtaining adequate cranking rpm during starting and for ensuring optimum battery life. The charge accep-

TABLE 5.3   Sensing Requirements versus Vehicle Systems

System	Parameter
Engine control	Air charge (intake air) temperature Engine coolant temperature Intake air humidity Ambient temperature Fuel temperature
HVAC (climate control)	Humidity in passenger compartment (PC) Temperature (PC) Outside air temperature
Electronic transmission (continuously variable transmission)	Transmission oil temperature
Driver information (body computer inputs)	Coolant temperature Ambient air temperature Temperature (PC) Tire surface temperature Rain sensor Windshield moisture Sun sensor Battery temperature
Multiplex/diagnostics Cruise control Idle speed control Memory seat Navigation	Multiple usage of sensors
Antiskid brakes	Brake fluid temperature
Traction control/ABS	Brake moisture sensor
Air bags	
Suspension	
Electronic power steering	Power steering fluid temperature (also electric assisted)
Four-wheel steering Security and keyless entry	

tance curves of lead-acid batteries require that the charging voltage be modified for temperature. A higher voltage is required at lower temperatures. Cold temperatures also place the most difficult requirements on the battery because the viscosity of engine oil is low and the load on the cranking system is very high.

Compensation circuitry in the voltage regulator in the charging system is designed to provide a voltage that is within an acceptable range over the entire vehicle operating temperature range as shown in Fig. 5.1. Semiconductor sensing techniques (Sec. 5.4.6) are used in this approach. The most desirable location for the voltage regulator is close to the battery. However, some systems integrate the regulator inside the alternator and provide a temperature environment that can be considerably different from the battery. The temperature of the battery can also vary by several degrees from cells closest to the engine to those further away from the engine. The overall mass of the battery prevents these temperatures from changing very quickly. However, a failed voltage regulator that applies full voltage to the alternator can easily cause excessive battery temperatures to be generated.

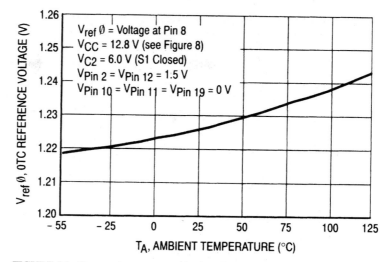

FIGURE 5.1 Temperature compensation in voltage regulator.

Batteries for electric vehicles (EVs) may require maintaining a specified high-temperature operating range. Sodium sulfur cells can store four times the energy of lead acid cells, but the battery's operating temperature must be kept within 300 to 350 °C. Solid oxide fuel cells operate at 1000 °C. If higher-temperature batteries are adopted for use in EV systems, sensing the battery temperature could be part of the diagnostic and fault detection.

5.2.3 Air Temperature Measurements

Air is measured for ambient temperature, passenger compartment temperature, and inlet air on production vehicles. For development purposes, a number of location ambients are always evaluated as potential mounting locations for electronic components. Upper temperature ranges are lower than liquid measurements, with 85 or 125 °C being common upper limits.

5.2.4 Catalyst Temperature

Measuring catalyst temperature during vehicle development has been performed since the earliest implementation of these devices. Concern for excessive temperatures in nearby vehicle locations meant that a number of measurements were made. However, the converter must be at a minimum temperature, usually above 350 °C, to be effective. Tougher exhaust emission standards are spurring manufacturers to utilize the converter sooner after the vehicle is started. Techniques are being pursued that would decrease the warm-up time for the catalyst to increase its effectiveness in controlling emissions. One technique involves heating the catalyst briefly by igniting a measured mixture of fuel and air in an afterburner ahead of the catalyst. Another technique utilizes electric heating to reduce the warm-up time. The power required for this approach would require an excessive power drain from the vehicle's power system. A linear temperature sensor has been developed to measure the temperature across the catalyst. A thermistor (see Sec. 5.4.1) is inserted diagonally inside the converter. A range of resistance has been evaluated and a time constant of about 2 s has been achieved. For fault condition monitoring, the sensor is able to detect a localized hot spot inside the catalyst and may prove to be able to detect misfire as part of future on-board diagnostic equipment required by the California Air Resources Board or the federal Environmental Protection Agency.

The temperature of exhaust gases increases rapidly under severe operating conditions such as continuous high speed or insufficient octane rating. One company has monitored their efforts at controlling the engine's operating temperature by locating a temperature sensor in the exhaust manifold. If the sensor detects an exhaust gas temperature rise above an established limit, a computer sends a command to inject extra fuel into the combustion chamber to cool the engine. Since exhaust gas temperatures can reach 1000 °C, a specially designed magnesium oxide thermocouple in a metal tube is used to sense the temperature (see Sec. 5.4.2). This approach may also be used in the future to reduce catalyst warm-up time.

5.2.5   Oxygen Sensor

The oxygen sensor used as the feedback element in closed-loop engine control systems generates a signal based on the difference in the oxygen concentration from inside the exhaust gas and ambient. As shown in the Nernst equation:

$$V_S = RT/4F \ln (P_a/P_g) \tag{5.4}$$

where V_S = the generated output voltage
$\quad P_a$ = oxygen partial pressure of the air
$\quad P_g$ = oxygen equilibrium pressure
$\quad R$ = gas constant
$\quad F$ = Faraday's constant
$\quad T$ = absolute temperature of the sensor

In addition to being affected by temperature, the oxygen sensor requires a minimum temperature to operate properly and provide a closed-loop control system. Typically, this minimum temperature is $\geq$450 °C. To reduce the oxygen sensor's warm-up time, heaters are added. A heated oxygen sensor achieves operating temperature much sooner than an unheated unit and allows closed-loop operation to be initiated. Monitoring temperature during engine and vehicle development is part of control strategy and component development.

5.2.6   Tire Temperature Sensing

Sensing the temperature within the tire is part of the pressure measurement and fault detection provided by tire pressure measuring and automatic adjustment systems. In a system like the one developed by Michelin (Fig. 5.2) that is used on Peugot's experimental sports car, the Proxima, both a pressure and temperature sensor are located on each wheel. A circular antenna and a transceiver allow these signals to be sent to an electronic processing module. An air compressor attempts to maintain desired tire pressure under normal conditions. If the pressure-temperature indications go above 85 °C, the system recommends speeds be held below 240 km/h (148 m/h). For temperatures above 90 °C, the limit is 160 km/h and for 95 °C, the limit is 80 km/h. For temperatures in excess of 100 °C, the system recommends stopping the vehicle.

5.2.7   Fault Detection for Electronic Components

As indicated in Sec. 5.1.6, temperature can cause reliability failures from several mechanisms in electronic systems. Therefore, detecting excessive temperature and designing system strategies to account for excessive temperatures can minimize improper operation and catastrophic failures.

Sensing for fault conditions, like a short circuit, is an integral part of power ICs or smart power transistors. The ability to obtain temperature sensors in mixed Bipolar-CMOS-DMOS semiconductor processes provides protection and diagnostics as part of the features of smart power ICs, like Motorola's SMARTMOS™ products. The primary function of the power IC is to provide a microcontroller-to-load interface for solenoids, lamps, and motors. It is a definite

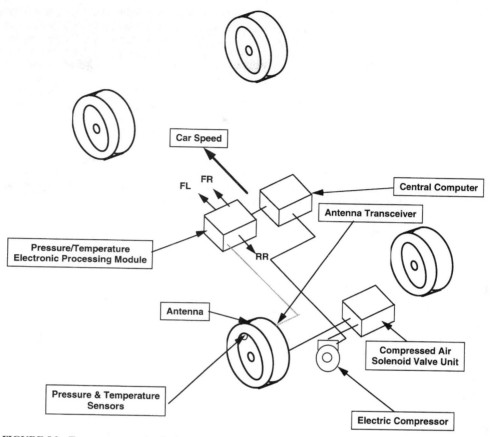

FIGURE 5.2   Temperature sensing in tire pressure control.

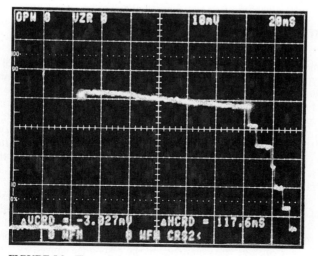

FIGURE 5.3   Thermal shutdown of six outputs of smart power IC.

advantage in multiple-output devices, to sense the junction temperature of each device, provide status input to the microcontroller and, if necessary, shut down a particular unit that has a fault condition. The sequential independent shutdown of six output drivers with a short applied across each unit's load is shown in Fig. 5.3. The action that is taken based on sensing a fault condition can vary depending on the control system. Sensing excessive temperature in a power device may mean that the device can turn itself off to prevent failure in one case and in another situation, a fault signal provides a warning but no action is taken. The remaining portion of the system is allowed to function normally. With the fault conditions supplied to the MCU, an orderly system shutdown can be implemented.

5.2.8   Mass Air Flow Sensor

The generalized model of a transducer is shown in Fig. 5.4. In addition to the desired input, undesired environment effects, like temperature and, to a lesser extent, humidity, are factors that affect the performance and accuracy of the transducer and must be taken into account during the design of the transducer.

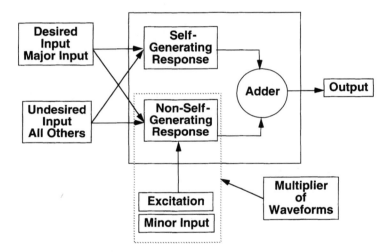

FIGURE 5.4   Generalized model of a transducer.

In the case of mass air flow sensing, temperature effects are used as part of the measurement process. A typical approach for mass air flow involves a hot-wire anemometer with a platinum wire as the sense elements, as shown in Fig. 5.5. The air temperature probe detects the temperature of the air flowing into the combustion process. The hot-wire probe is heated by current supplied from a power transistor. The difference in temperature between the probes is detected as a difference in electrical resistance. The electronic circuitry regulates the heating current to the hot-wire probe to keep the temperature difference constant at any flow rate (Fig. 5.6). The current required is proportional to the air flow rate. One of the main issues in this type of sensor is the response time. Improvements which reduce the response time from 50 to 30 ms have been made in recently developed units.

A microbridge silicon mass air flow sensor has been developed that utilizes temperature-resistive films laminated within a thick film of dielectric material and micromachined cavity as shown in Fig. 5.7. The resistors are suspended over the etched cavity, which also provides thermal isolation for the heater and sensing resistor. Heat is transferred from one resistor to the other as the result of flow. The imbalance in the resistance caused by the heat transfer

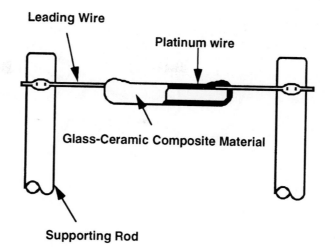

FIGURE 5.5   Probe for hot-wire anemometer mass air flow sensor.

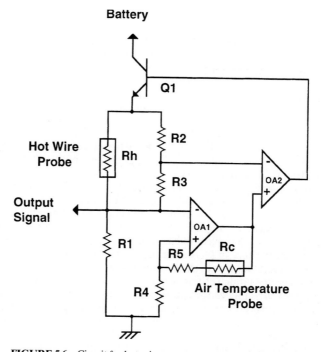

FIGURE 5.6   Circuit for hot-wire anemometer mass air flow sensor.

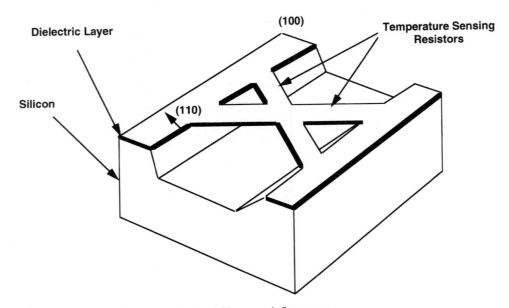

FIGURE 5.7   Temperature sensor in microbridge mass air flow sensor.

is directly proportional to the flow. The small size of the resistors allows fast response time (≤3 ms) and high sensitivity to flow. The device has also been found to be useful as a differential or absolute temperature sensor.

5.2.9   Temperature Measurements in New Systems

As new vehicle systems are developed or existing systems are modified to provide improved performance, or meet legislated or customer demands, new applications for temperature sensors will occur. An example of two systems, air bags and thermo accumulator, is provided.

In inflatable restraint systems, the air bag is inflated based on the ignition of a gas generant. In this system, an igniter receives an electric impulse, passes it through to a heating filament, and actuates a small pyrotechnic charge to ignite the gas generant, which produces nearly pure nitrogen gas to inflate the bag. The initial temperature is high but the nitrogen gas cools rapidly, so a fully deployed bag is only slightly above room temperature. Measuring the temperatures that occur during this event is part of the development activity.

A heat battery, or thermoaccumulator, can store the latent heat from a previously driven vehicle for up to three days at an ambient temperature of –29 °C. The accumulator is made of salt-based crystals which change from solid to liquid form above 78 °C. Heat provided by this device has proven to reduce the emissions which are generated during the first 20 s of the federal emissions test procedure. The unit also has potential application in passenger compartment heating.

5.3   *HUMIDITY SENSING AND VEHICLE PERFORMANCE*

Correlation of a number of vehicle tests requires that the humidity be monitored. Variations in humidity can explain variations that occur in test results.

Significant, repeatable, and controllable results may lead to humidity sensing being part of future engine control systems and passenger compartment comfort control systems.

Some sensors, such as rain (and/or windshield moisture) or sun sensors, are already being used on some vehicles to control wiper blade and fan controls.

5.3.1 Engine Performance

Injecting water to cool the intake charge and prevent premature detonation is a technique that has been used in high-compression ($\geq$10:1) engines. The cooling effect from evaporation reduces the operating temperature.

An increase in inlet air humidity has been shown to reduce the nitric oxide emissions. Condensation in the gas tank can add a considerable amount of moisture to the fuel. Measuring the actual amount of humidity or moisture present during development tests is useful to identify all variables that can affect performance.

5.3.2 Passenger Compartment Comfort

A traditional passenger temperature control system shown in Fig. 5.8 uses only temperature as the indication for the system to open or close blend doors in the HVAC (heater, ventilating, and air conditioning) system. Laboratory evaluations monitor the HVAC systems' effectiveness under known and controlled humidity conditions. A fuzzy logic system combining temperature and humidity sensing has been investigated by researchers for home use. In this case, additional humidity is available to speed up the effect of adding heat. In a vehicle application, the blower speed could be adjusted based on the presence of humidity or an alternate strategy could be developed which uses less energy from the vehicle to make the driver and passengers comfortable.

The development of new test techniques frequently involves either the development of new sensors or novel use of existing sensors. A sweat impulse test developed at Volkswagen AG allows researchers to evaluate the ability of a seat to direct sweat away from its surface.

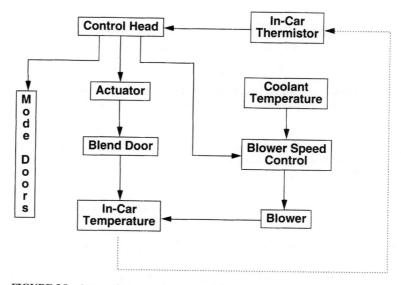

FIGURE 5.8   Automatic temperature control diagram.

As part of the measurement process, a platinum RTD (Sec. 5.4.5) and a capacitive humidity sensor provide data. In excessive sweating situations, the fabric is unable to absorb sufficient moisture, so it is passed to the surrounding environment as increased humidity.

5.3.3 Brake Moisture Sensing

Brake fluids are hygroscopic and, therefore, absorb moisture. Sufficient moisture lowers the boiling point of the brake fluid, and eventually vaporizes the fluid resulting in loss of stopping power. A meter has been developed that can be inserted into the master cylinder reservoir and measure the boiling point of the brake fluid. A heating element boils a sample of the brake fluid. A microcontroller calculates the actual boiling point by the initial temperature reading, temperature drop, and time between cooling and boiling. This approach may be applicable to other vehicle fluids that can be checked during maintenance procedures.

5.4 SENSORS FOR TEMPERATURE

Several different sensing techniques are used in production vehicles and during vehicle development to provide the temperature measurements. Table 5.4 shows a list of these techniques and the temperature range that is typical for this approach. Characteristics of temperature-sensing devices that allow a designer to determine if the approach will meet development or production requirements are explored in this section. In addition to the operating temperature range, linearity, response time, packaging, reliability, and cost are factors that must be considered. Temperature sensors can be as simple as thermal expansion devices, such as mercury or alcohol thermometers, or as complex as infrared sensors used in night vision systems. Common sensors and some recent additions to temperature sensing are covered in this section. Other sensor techniques, including the temperature-generating characteristics of quartz and temperature-sensing reed switches, are also possible but not covered.

5.4.1 Thermistors

Thermistors have found broad application acceptance in several vehicle systems that require temperature sensing from the coolant system to control the engine. The thermistor is a special

TABLE 5.4   Temperature Sensing Techniques versus Operating Range

Sensing technique	Temperature range, °C	Usage: Production (P) Development (D) Future (F)
Thermistor	0 to 500	P
Thermocouple	−200 to +3000	D
Bimetallic switch	−50 to +400 (650)	P
Potentiometer temperature sensor	−40 to +125	P
Platinum wire resistor (RTD)	−200 to +850 (−40 to +200)	D (P)
Semiconductor (junction)	−40 to +200	P
Thermostat (pressure spring)	−50 to +500	P
Fiber optic temperature sensor	+1800	D/F
Temperature indicator	+40 to +1350	D
Infrared	>Ta	F
Liquid thermometer	−200 to +1000	D

class of resistance temperature sensor (Sec. 5.4.5) based on semiconductor type materials that exhibit a wide range of temperature coefficients. The resistivity depends upon the material used to form the thermistor. Both negative (NTC) and positive temperature coefficient (PTC) devices can be produced. Commercially available thermistor forms are beads, probes, disks, and rods. The characteristics of thermistor output are shown in Fig. 5.9. The exact relationship between temperature and resistance depends on the material used for the sensor, but the general form of the output can be expressed by the equation

$$R = R_O \cdot e^{\beta}(1/T - 1/T_O) \tag{5.5}$$

where R = resistance at temperature T in ohms
R_O = resistance at temperature T_O in ohms
e = base of natural log
T, T_O = absolute temperature in K
β = indicator of shape of NTC curve

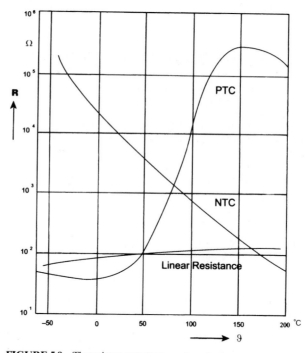

FIGURE 5.9   Thermistor output versus temperature.

This accounts for the high degree of nonlinearity in the output. However, the thermistor's nonlinearity can either be tolerated in many automotive applications, or corrected by an MCU or by circuit techniques. In the case of the water temperature indicator, for example, the thermistor's resistance is matched to a normal operating point on the gage; thus, the nonlinearity during conditions that generate higher temperature is not a problem.

Thermistors have a usable temperature range from −250 to +650 °C. Recent developments in automotive thermistors have focused on techniques to reduce cost and improve the manufacturability and reliability.

5.4.2 Thermocouples

Thermocouples are used frequently during the development phase of the vehicle because of their low cost, the broad range of temperature measurements that are possible from a single thermocouple such as iron-constantan, ease of extending the range through other materials, ease in obtaining a variety of form factors (especially small shapes), ease in forming the thermocouple, and ease in interfacing to temperature-recording equipment. The thermocouple type, wire size, and construction are factors that allow different units to be used from −250 to +1700 °C.

A thermocouple is formed by a pair of dissimilar conductors connected at one end. A voltage output E, proportional to the difference in temperature T_1 and T_2, is the basis of thermoelectric temperature measurements, also known as the Seebeck effect.

Thermocouple junctions can be formed by welding, soldering, or pressing materials together. Measurements can be made very easily; however, the highest accuracy is obtained by taking into account a number of factors, including reference junction considerations and a number (five) of laws that govern thermocouple behavior. Common types and their operating characteristics are shown in Table 5.5.

TABLE 5.5   Common Thermocouples and Application Factors

ISA code	Conductor Positive	Conductor Negative	Temperature Range, °C	Standard error Limit, °C	Seebeck Coefficient, μV/°C
E*	Chromel	Constantan	0 to +316	±2	62
J*	Iron	Constantan	0 to +277	±2	51
T*	Copper	Constantan	−59 to +93	±1	40
K*	Chromel	Alumel	0 to +277	±2	40
N*	Nicrosil	Nisil	0 to +277	±2	38
S*	Platinum[†]	Platinum	0 to +538	±3	7
R*	Platinum[‡]	Platinum	0 to +538	±3	7

* Other temperature ranges and error limits are available.
[†] 10% Rhodium.
[‡] 13% Rhodium.

5.4.3 Bimetallic Switch

A bimetallic temperature switch uses two metal strips with different coefficients of linear expansion that are welded together. Increasing temperature causes the strips to warp predictably. A switch point can be established by an initial calibration that indicates that a critical temperature has been reached and provides an input to an electronic control unit or a lamp indication. Switch types can be disk or cantilever construction. The use of switches does not require analog-to-digital conversion in control systems with microcontrollers, but provides limited information (only above or below a desired operating point) about the system. Early engine control systems used a disk switch in the air cleaner to indicate operation below 13 °C and a cantilever design in the engine coolant to indicate temperature above 71 °C.

5.4.4 Potentiometer Temperature Sensor

A bimetallic actuator can be combined with a high-resolution potentiometer to provide a temperature sensor for automotive applications. The linear movement of the bimetallic stack is transmitted by a stainless steel tube and measured as a distance by a conductive plastic film potentiometer providing a linear indication of temperatures up to 650 °C. The time constant for the sensor is approximately 70 s.

5.4.5   RTDs

A resistive temperature detector, or RTD, made of platinum is the highest inherent accuracy temperature sensor. The RTD has an output that varies with temperature based on the following equation:

$$RTD = R_O \cdot (1 + A \cdot T + B \cdot T^2) \tag{5.6}$$

where RTD = value of RTD at 0 °C in ohms and is 100 Ω for Pt100 and 200 Ω for Pt200
    A = detector constant = $3.908 \cdot 10^{-3}$ (°C^{-1}) for Pt100
    B = detector constant = $-5.802 \cdot 10^{-7}$ (°C^{-2}) for Pt100
    T = temperature in °C

A constant current is applied to the RTD to obtain a voltage output over the range from −200 to +850 °C. Linearity can be within 3.6 percent for a range of 0 to 850 °C.

Other metals like nickel, nickel-iron alloy, copper, and aluminum can also be used for the RTDs. In addition to wire-wound RTDs, thin-film techniques also allow an RTD to be applied to a substrate, such as ceramic or silicon.

5.4.6   Semiconductor Techniques

Several semiconductor parameters vary linearly over the operating temperature range. As shown in Fig. 5.10, the gate threshold voltage of a power MOSFET changes from 1.17 to 0.69 times its 25 °C value when the temperature increases from −40 to 150 °C. Also, the breakdown voltage of the power MOSFET varies from 0.9 to 1.18 times its value at 25 °C over the same −40 to 150 °C temperature range (Fig. 5.10). These relationships are frequently used to determine the critical temperature (junction temperature) of semiconductor components in actual circuit operation. External package-level temperature measurements can be several degrees different than the junction temperature, especially during rapid, high-energy switching events. The actual junction temperature and the resulting effect on semiconductor parameters must be taken into account for the proper application of semiconductor devices. Semiconductors can be used for sensing temperature within their operating temperature range.

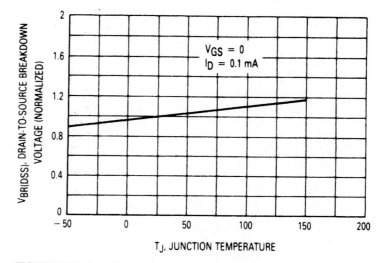

FIGURE 5.10   Breakdown voltage versus temperature.

The most commonly referenced transistor temperature measurement is the V_{BE} relationship to temperature. A silicon temperature sensor that utilizes this effect has a nominal output of 730 mV at −40 °C and an output of 300 mV at 150 °C. The linearity of this device is shown in Fig. 5.11. The total accuracy is within ±3.0 mV including nonlinearity which is typically within ±1 °C in the range of −40 to 150 °C. The readings are made with a constant (collector) current of 0.1 mA passing through the device to minimize the effect of self-heating of the junction.

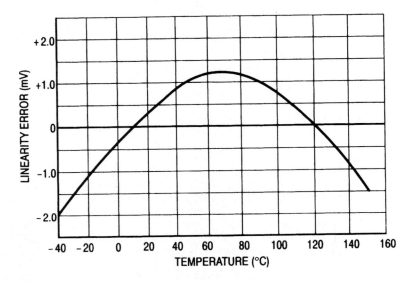

FIGURE 5.11   Linearity of silicon temperature sensor.

The linear relationship of the V_{BE} of a transistor to temperature provides a considerable improvement in accuracy over a thermistor. However, the limited operating range of semiconductor temperature sensors (−40 to 150 °C) has limited their application in vehicles. To be cost-effective in automotive applications, semiconductor sensing is usually incorporated with other sensing or interface devices.

An RTD (Sec. 5.4.5) with an aluminum metal film has been integrated with a semiconductor process to provide a temperature sensor that can directly drive the analog-to-digital input in a microcontroller unit (MCU). The sensor has better than ±2 percent accuracy over a −50 to 150 °C temperature range. On-chip linearization techniques avoid look-up table linearization by the MCU.

Another integrated semiconductor temperature sensor uses the fact that two identical transistors operating at a constant ratio of collector current densities r results in the difference in base-emitter voltages being $(kT) \cdot (\ln r)$. Both Boltzman's constant k and the charge of an electron q are constant, so the resulting voltage is directly proportional to absolute temperature. The voltage is then converted to a current by low-temperature coefficient thin-film resistors.

Polysilicon diodes and resistors can be produced as part of a power MOSFET semiconductor manufacturing process and used as temperature-sensing elements to determine the junction temperature of the device. The thermal sensing that is performed by the polysilicon elements is a significant improvement over power device temperature sensing that is performed by an external temperature-sensing element. An extreme thermal gradient exists between the maximum junction temperature at the top (active area) of the power device and the remote point which is able to be measured by a thermistor or thermocouple. Placing the thermal-sensing element inside the package improves the measurement process considerably.

By sensing with poly resistors or diodes, the sensor can be located close to the center of the power device near the source bond pads where the current density is the highest and, consequently, the highest die temperature occurs. The thermal conductivity of the oxide that separates the polysilicon diodes from the power device is two orders of magnitude less than that of silicon. However, because the layer is thin, the polysilicon element offers an accurate indication of the actual peak junction temperature.

A very low on-resistance power FET that incorporates a temperature sensing diode is shown in Fig. 5.12. The power device achieves an on-resistance of 5 milliohms (including packaging resistance) at 25 °C utilizing a production power FET process. The power FET process was chosen instead of a power IC process because a large die size was required to meet the power dissipation requirements of a very cost sensitive application. A minor modification (the addition of a single masking layer) to a production power FET process allows both sensing and protection features to be integrated. Devices that are produced using the SMARTDISCRETE technology, as this approach is called by Motorola, are one way to provide more cost-effective, smart power semiconductors, especially for high-current or low on-resistance power applications.

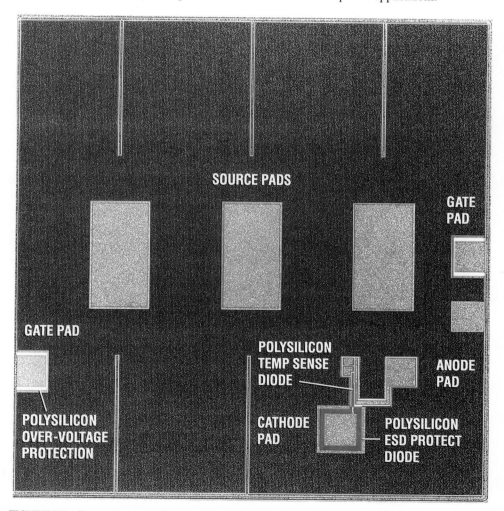

FIGURE 5.12 Temperature sensor integrated in power MOSFET. *(Die photomicrograph Courtesy Motorola Inc.)*

An accurate indication of the maximum die temperature is obtained by monitoring the output voltage when a constant current is passed through the integrated polysilicon diode(s). A number of diodes are actually provided in the design. A single diode has a temperature coefficient of 1.90 mV/°C. Two or more diodes can be placed in series if a larger output is desired. For greater accuracy, the diodes can be trimmed during wafer-level testing by blowing fusible links made from polysilicon. The response time of the diodes is less than 100 μs which has allowed the device to withstand a direct short across an automobile battery with external circuitry providing shutdown prior to device failure. The sensing capability also allows the output device to provide an indication (with additional external circuitry) if the heatsinking is not proper when the unit is installed in a module or if a change occurs in the application which would ultimately cause a failure.

A smart power IC, like Motorola's SMARTMOS™ process, can have multiple power drivers integrated on a single monolithic piece of silicon. Each of these drivers can have a temperature sensor integrated to determine the proper operating status and shut off only a specific driver if a fault occurs. The temperature sensor is basically a band gap reference. In this case, two diodes' junctions are biased with different current densities. Circuitry in the smart power IC process establishes a voltage reference and a trip point.

5.4.7 Thermostat (Mechanical Temperature Sensing)

The earliest method of temperature regulation used in vehicles is still in use today—the thermostat. The expansion element usually activates a valve which redirects the flow of coolant into a radiator bypass line when a specific temperature is reached.

5.4.8 Fiber Optic Temperature Sensors

High-temperature sensors capable of operating up to 1800 °C have been developed using optical fibers. The response time of the sensor is on the order of 500 ms and the accuracy is within ±0.5 percent. The noncontact sensor uses a single optical fiber that has an outside diameter of 0.5 to 1.0 mm. The probe structure is critical to the sensor's sensitivity and the distance coefficient that relates the detection surface area to the distance at which the probe will be placed for measurement.

A sapphire fiber optic sensor has been developed to measure high temperatures such as those found near the tip of a spark plug during combustion. The sensor can withstand temperatures up to 4000 °C and has an accuracy of 0.2 percent at 1000 °C. The sensor has been used to identify knock and to characterize flame front propagation.

5.4.9 Temperature Indicators

Temperature-indicating materials have been developed with melting points that can be calibrated to ±1 °C. When the temperature of the device is exceeded, a phase change occurs and the material changes color. The material is available in paint, patch, pellet, and applicator stick form. Temperature ranges from 38 to 1371 °C are available. This kind of indication is useful during the development phase of automotive components to verify that a critical design temperature has not been exceeded.

5.4.10 Infrared Temperature Sensing

Blackbody emittance is the basis for infrared (IR) thermometry. Objects at temperatures above −273 °C emit radiant energy in an amount proportional to the fourth power of their temperature. An IR sensor consists of collecting optics, lenses, and/or fiber optics, spectral filtering, and a detector as the front end. The primary characteristic of the optics is the field of view (FOV) which allows a specific target to be measured at a prescribed distance.

Infrared sensors have been used extensively for noncontact temperature measurements in process control. In automobiles, infrared sensors use temperature variations to produce a monochrome image in night vision systems. Board-level temperature testing also utilizes IR-sensing techniques to identify hot spots and potential failure points.

5.4.11 Thermal Actuators/Thermal Cooling

Chemical sensors like the oxygen sensor described in Sec. 5.2.6 require a minimum operating temperature to be effective. Semiconductor technology allows platinum and silicon heaters and temperature sensors to be produced on a thin diaphragm, or window, etched into a silicon substrate. Temperatures can be produced in the window which exceed 1200 °C, while the supporting rim of silicon remains essentially at room temperature. This ability may allow fast-response sensors to be developed for vehicle applications.

Other silicon development activity using micromachining techniques may allow heat pipes and silicon-level heatsinks to remove heat more effectively from rapidly switching semiconductor devices.

5.5 HUMIDITY SENSORS

Humidity sensors are used extensively during vehicle and component development, especially in determining the ability to withstand humidity and temperature cycling tests. Engine performance can be affected by humidity. A sensor that can pass rigorous automotive qualification tests and meet the desired specifications and cost criteria would provide additional input for the engine control system. In a less rugged application, HVAC systems may benefit from the input from humidity sensors. Humidity sensors are not used on production vehicles at the present time. However, some potential techniques that are used in development and nonautomotive applications are described in this section.

Techniques to measure humidity are listed in Table 5.6. Most of these are actually laboratory instruments. The most well known approach to humidity measurements is the use of wet bulb and dry bulb thermomometer readings interpreted through the use of a psychrometric chart which relates all basic humidity readings. The effect of humidity on polymers and the use of semiconductor-processing techniques has created actual sensors that do not require the constant calibration, have less drift, improved reliability, and potentially can achieve automotive cost objectives. Three sensing techniques that have potential for future vehicle use are capacitive, resistive, and oxidized porous silicon.

5.5.1 Capacitive Humidity Sensors

A thin-film polymer capacitive-type relative humidity sensor can be produced by using semiconductor technology. The dielectric constant of the polymer thin film changes linearly with changes in atmospheric relative humidity. A desirable feature, in addition to long-term stability and operation to 180 °C, is fast wet-up/dry-down performance.

A temperature sensor can easily be added to the RH sensor, which increases the operating range and the functionality.

TABLE 5.6   Techniques for Measuring Humidity/Moisture

Principle	Type measurement
Gravimetric hygrometer	Instrument
Pressure-humidity generator	Instrument
Wet bulb/dry bulb (psychrometer)	Instrument
Hair element	Instrument
Electric conductivity	Instrument
Dew cell	Instrument
Chilled mirror	Instrument
Karl Fisher titration	Instrument
Electrolytic	Instrument
Lithium chloride	Instrument
Capacitance hygropolymer	Production sensor
Bulk polymer (resistance)	Production sensor
Thin-film polymer (capacitance)	Production sensor
Gold/aluminum oxide	Production sensor
Oxidized porous silicon (OPS)	Experimental sensor

5.5.2 Resistive Humidity Sensors

Both surface and bulk polymer resistance sensors have been developed for measuring relative humidity. In bulk polymer film units, mobile ions are released from the molecular structure with increased humidity levels resulting in orders-of-magitude change in resistance over the operating range. Diode temperature compensation is used to improve accuracy over the temperature range. With an ac excitation at 1 kHz, a change from 10 to 100 percent RH produces a corresponding resistance variation from $2 \cdot 10^7$ to $2 \cdot 10^3$ ohms.

5.5.3 Oxidized Porous Silicon

A capacitive-type sensor has been developed that uses oxidized porous silicon (OPS) as a moisture-absorbing dielectric between the electrodes of the capacitor. An electrolysis process is used to create a thin porous layer on the top of a silicon wafer. The silicon is converted to OPS by a high-temperature treatment in either oxygen or steam. Metal electrodes are deposited on the top and back of the OPS to complete the capacitive structure.

When water vapor contacts the sensor, it permeates through the porous structure between the electrodes. The response of a typical sensor increases 800 percent when exposed to an RH change from 1 to 40 percent. Since semiconductor techniques are used in the manufacturing process, the potential to integrate signal conditioning and other sensors may provide an attractive solution for future vehicle sensing requirements.

5.6 CONCLUSIONS

Several factors are influencing the temperature-sensing requirements for future vehicles. The ultra-efficient vehicle will operate at higher temperatures and utilize brake energy-recovery. Both of these aspects will increase the temperature environment for other vehicle components.

The requirements for sensors in future vehicle systems include improved performance (sensitivity) and reliability in spite of operating at higher temperatures, lower cost, space and weight reduction, greater functionality including diagnostics and self-test, and ease of interfacing with an MCU for adaptive control and interchangeability. The capability of semiconductor technology to provide sensing information for failure detection provides a means for increased reliability in several vehicle subsystems.

All trademarks are the property of their respective owners.

GLOSSARY

Accuracy   A comparison of the actual output signal of a device to the true value of the input. The various errors (such as linearity, hysteresis, repeatability, and temperature shift) attributing to the accuracy of a device are usually expressed as a percent of full-scale output (FSO).

Maximum operating temperature   The maximum body temperature at which the thermistor will operate for an extended period of time with acceptable stability of its characteristics. This temperature is the result of the internal or external heating, or both, and should not exceed the maximum value specified.

Negative temperature coefficient (NTC)   An NTC thermistor is one in which the zero-power resistance decreases with an increase in temperature.

Operating temperature range   The range of temperature between minimum and maximum temperature at which the output will meet the specified operating characteristics.

Self-generating   Providing an output signal without applied excitation, such as a thermoelectric transducer.

Self-heating   Internal heating resulting from electric energy dissipated within the unit.

Storage temperature range   The range of temperature between minimum and maximum which can be applied without causing the sensor (unit) to fail to meet the specified operating characteristics.

Temperature coefficient of full-scale span   The percent change in the full-scale span per unit change in temperature relative to the full-scale span at a specified temperature.

Temperature hysteresis   The difference in output at any temperature in the operating temperature range when the temperature is approached from the minimum operating temperature and when approached from the maximum operating temperature with zero input applied.

Thermal time constant   The thermal time constant is the time required for a thermistor to change to 63.2 percent of the total difference between its initial and final body temperature when subjected to a step function change in temperature under zero-power conditions.

Transfer function   A mathematical, graphical, or tabular statement of the influence which a system or element has on the output compared at the input and output terminals.

BIBLIOGRAPHY

Automotive Electronics Reliability Handbook, SAE, Warrendale, Pa., 1987.
Automotive Handbook, Robert Bosch GmbH, 1986.

BR923/D Discrete and Special Technologies Group Reliability Audit Report 1Q90, Motorola Semiconductor Products Sector, Phoenix, Ariz.

Collings, N., W. Cai, T. Ma, and D. Ball, "A linear catalyst temperature sensor for exhaust gas ignition (EGI) and on board diagnostics of misfire and catalyst efficiency," SAE SP-957, *U.S. and European Automotive Technology Emissions Technology,* International Congress and Exposition, Detroit, March 1–5, 1993.

De Vera, D., T. Glennon, A. A. Kenny, M. A. H. Khan, and M. Mayer, "An automotive case study," *Quality Progress,* June 1988, pp. 35–38.

Dosher, J., "Smart and active sensors," *Proceedings of Sensors Expo West,* 1991, pp. 103C-1–6.

Hao, T., E. F. Malinowski, and C-C. Liu, "High temperature fiber optic sensor for industrial applications," *Proceedings of Sensors Expo West,* San Jose, Calif., March 2–4, 1993, pp. 227–228.

Norton, Harry N., "Section 10—Transducers and Sensors," in D. G. Fink and D. Christiansen (eds.), *Electronics Engineers' Handbook* (3d ed.), McGraw-Hill, New York, 1989.

Pressure Sensor Device Data, Motorola Semiconductor Products Sector, Phoenix, Ariz., 1993.

Recommended Environmental Practices for Electronic Equipment Design, SAE J1211, Warrendale, Pa., Nov. 1978.

Temming, J., "Measuring seat comfort," *Automotive Engineering,* July 1993, pp. 25–30.

CHAPTER 6
EXHAUST GAS SENSORS

H.-M. Wiedenmann, G. Hötzel,
H. Neumann, J. Riegel, and H. Weyl
Robert Bosch GmbH
Lambda Oxygen Sensor Development

6.1 BASIC CONCEPTS

6.1.1 Combustion

The sole products of complete fuel combustion are the nontoxic substances carbon dioxide and water:

$$C_mH_n + \left(m + \frac{n}{4}\right)O_2 \rightarrow m\,CO_2 + \frac{n}{2}\,H_2O \tag{6.1}$$

The theoretical air requirement for this process is 14.7 kg air for each kilogram of fuel; this corresponds to approximately 10 m^3 air per liter of fuel. The air/fuel ratio is defined as stoichiometric when the engine is supplied with the exact quantity of air required for complete combustion.

6.1.2 Definition of Normalized air/fuel Ratio Lambda

The mixture ratio is defined by the normalized air/fuel ratio lambda (λ):

$$\lambda = \frac{\text{current air-fuel ratio}}{\text{stoichiometric air-fuel ratio}} \tag{6.2}$$

Because the conditions within the engine do not correspond to the absolute ideal required for perfect combustion, a number of products of incomplete combustion occur, even if a stoichiometric air/fuel ratio ($\lambda = 1$) is maintained. Thus, the CO_2 and H_2O are joined by CO, H_2, and HC (hydrocarbons C_xH_y) along with corresponding amounts of not reacted (free) oxygen. The water-gas equilibrium defines the ratio of CO to H_2. At high combustion temperatures, the N_2 and O_2 in the air supply form nitrous oxides such as NO, NO_2, N_2O (generic designation: NO_x).

6.1.3 Composition of Untreated Exhaust Gas

The composition of the exhaust gases entering the catalytic converter (untreated or raw emissions) varies according to the quality of combustion and, even more importantly, as a function of the normalized air/fuel ratio lambda (λ) (Fig. 6.1). Rich mixtures (lambda < 1, excess fuel) produce high concentrations of CO, H_2, and HC, while lean mixtures (lambda > 1, excess oxygen) generate higher levels of NO_x and free oxygen. The lower combustion-chamber temperatures associated with mixture ratios of lambda > 1.2 result in reductions in NO_x concentrations accompanied by increased HC concentrations. Maximum emissions of CO_2 (greenhouse gas) occur at a slightly lean mixture (lambda $\approx$ 1.1).

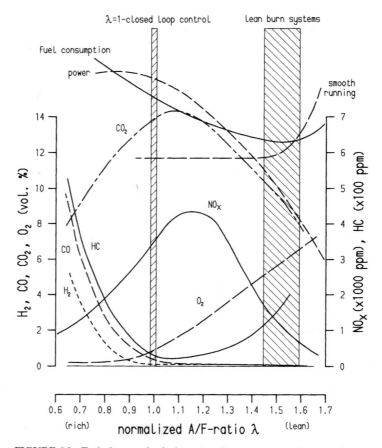

FIGURE 6.1 Typical curves for fuel consumption, power, smoothness, and composition of raw exhaust gases relative to lambda in a spark-ignition engine.

6.1.4 Lambda Closed-Loop Control: Design Concepts

Lambda Control Ranges.   The main elements considered in defining the range of the lambda closed-loop control system (Table 6.1) are engine design, emission limits, fuel consumption, and the requirements for performance and smooth running.

Treatment of Exhaust Gases.   Catalytic treatment of exhaust gases is essential for achieving compliance with the stringent current United States emission standards (Table 6.2). In the catalytic process, CO, H_2, and HC are oxidized to form CO_2 and H_2O, while the constituents of

TABLE 6.1 Lambda Control Ranges

	Lambda = 1—spark ignition engine	Lean-burn concept	Lean-mix concept	Diesel engine
Lambda-control range	Lambda = 1 ± < 0.005	1.4–1.7	1.4–1.7 and lambda = 1	1.1–7
Target	Opt. catalytic aftertreatment	Fuel economy low CO, HC, (NO$_x$)*	Improved fuel economy within allowable emission	Reduced emissions particles and NO$_x$
Lambda sensors	Lambda = 1 sensor	Lean A-F sensor	Wide-range A-F sensor	Lean A-F sensor
Exhaust gas aftertreatment	Three-way-catalyst (TWC)	Oxi-cat NO$_x$-cat*	TWC NO$_x$-cat*	Particle filter* NO$_x$-cat*
Control concepts	Conventional or continuous	Continuous	Lean: continuous lambda = 1: conventional	Full-load and EGR-control
Series production	Discont. control	—	Yes	—

* Not available yet.

TWC: three-way-catalyst; Oxi-cat: oxidation-catalyst; NO$_x$-cat: NO$_x$-reduction-catalyst.

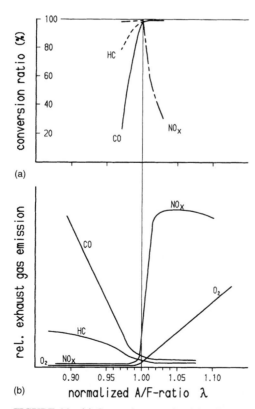

(a)

(b)

FIGURE 6.2 (a) Conversion rates for CO, NO$_x$, and HC in a new three-way catalytic converter; (b) typical curve for exhaust-gas composition downstream from a new three-way catalytic converter.

NO$_x$ are reduced to N$_2$ and O$_2$. A three-way catalytic converter TWC (selective catalytic converter) and closed-loop control system featuring a lambda sensor are essential elements in achieving adequate reductions in all three pollutants (Fig. 6.2). The engine must be operated within a narrow range of $|\Delta\lambda| <$ 0.005 at lambda = 1.

Oxidation catalysts are sometimes employed to reduce CO and HC emissions from lean-burn and diesel engines. Meanwhile, NO$_x$ reduction catalysts and particle filters are being developed for future applications (Table 6.1).

Lambda Closed-Loop Control. Lambda closed-loop control is incorporated in the engine's electronic control system. The control system regulates lambda upstream from the catalytic converter with the aid of an oxygen sensor. System lag results in relatively long control-response delays, especially at low rpm. For this reason, the system must incorporate a pilot-control function capable of adjusting the mixture to the desired lambda with the highest possible degree of precision. This arrangement makes it possible to avoid excessive control deviations and harmful emission peaks of the kind that lead to high emission levels and reduced vehicle performance.

Conventional Closed-Loop Lambda Control. The closed-loop control concept pre-

TABLE 6.2   Summary of Emission Levels for Spark-Ignition Engines
(Status: July 1992)

	Start of sale	Exhaust emission limits			HC + NO$_x$	Unit	Remarks	
		HC	CO	NO$_x$				
California	MY 1993	0.25	3.4	0.4	—	g/mile		
	MY 1994	0.125	3.4	0.2	—	g/mile	TLEV 10 %	% of fleet,
	MY 1997	0.075	3.4	0.2	—	g/mile	LEV 25 %	stepwise
	MY 1997	0.04	1.7	0.2	—	g/mile	ULEV 2 %	increase
	MY 1998	0.0	0.0	0.0	—	g/mile	ZEV 2 %	
USA (Fed.)	MY 1983	0.41	3.4	1.0	—	g/mile		
	MY 1994	0.25	3.4	0.4	—	g/mile		
	MY 2003	0.125	1.7	0.2	—	g/mile	on need	
Japan	4/1981	0.25	2.1	0.25	—	g/km	10-mode	
EG	1992	—	2.72	—	0.97	g/km	MVEG I	
	10/1996	0.15	2.1	0.3	—	g/km	MVEG II	proposal parliament
		—	2.2	—	0.5	g/km		proposal commission
	1996	—	1.5	—	0.2	g/km	MVEG III	proposal Germany

TLEV: Transitional Low-Emission Vehicles
ULEV: Ultra Low-Emission Vehicles
LEV: Low-Emission Vehicles
ZEV: Zero-Emission Vehicles
MVEG: Motor Vehicle Emission Group

sently in use in spark-ignition engines is based on 2-point lambda = 1 control (Fig. 6.3) with the mixture composition oscillating around the optimum lambda. When the exhaust mixture shifts from rich to lean, the voltage from a lambda = 1 probe drops from approximately 800 mV (lambda < 1) to approximately 100 mV (lambda > 1), with a steep signal change (lambda jump) occurring at lambda = 1 (Sec. 6.2.1). Once the signal from the sensor crosses beyond the specified threshold value (e.g., 450 mV), the system responds by progressively leaning out the mixture until the probe signal drops below this border again. Once this process is completed, the system reverts to graduated mixture enrichment. Depending upon the system lag, the subsequent control-oscillation rate will lie in the 0.5 . . . 5 Hz range, with an amplitude of $\Delta\lambda = \pm 0.01$ ... 0.05 relative to the median lambda. During the lean-operation period, the catalytic converter stores oxygen for release during the rich-mixture phases. This arrangement ensures high conversion rates despite the control oscillations. Preferably an algorithm with proportional plus integral characteristics (PI controller) is used. Variations in system lag and integrator pitch affect the amplitude and the frequency of the oscillations. The proportional factors have to be adapted. Because load and rpm have a major effect on system lag, control parameters are defined and stored in a load/rpm control map.

Continuous Lambda = 1 Control.   A continuous lambda = 1 control can be employed to achieve substantially smaller control deviations, providing attendant reductions in emissions, especially when used with aged catalytic converters. An oxygen sensor with a roughly linear or linearized lambda characteristic curve is required for this arrangement (Secs. 6.2.5 and 6.2.6).

6.1.5   On-Board Diagnosis (OBD II)

From the 1994 model year onward, on-board devices capable of monitoring the operation of all emission-relevant vehicle components will be required in the United States. Pollutant emission sensors (see Sec. 6.6) to measure levels of CO, NO$_x$, and HC emissions downstream from the catalytic converter represent an ideal means of monitoring the performance of both converter and oxygen sensor. Unfortunately, there are still no sensors of this type suitable for

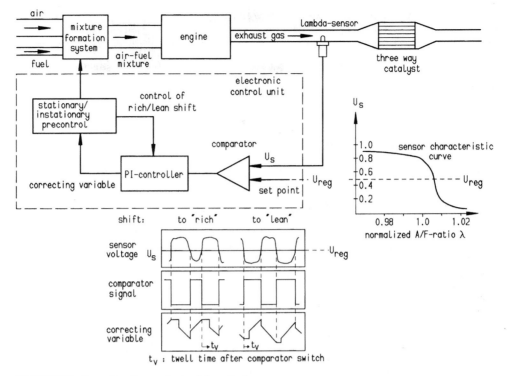

FIGURE 6.3   Operating diagram for lambda control.

use in the engine's exhaust stream. As an alternative, there exist concepts that employ a second oxygen sensor behind the catalytic converter to detect aging in the converter and/or the lambda sensor.

6.2   PRINCIPLES OF EXHAUST GAS SENSORS FOR LAMBDA CONTROL

6.2.1   Lambda = 1 Sensor: Nernst Type (ZrO₂)

Sensing Mechanism.   In principle, the lambda sensor operates as a solid-electrolyte galvanic oxygen-concentration cell (Fig. 6.4). A ceramic element consisting of zirconium dioxide and yttrium oxide is employed as a gas-impermeable solid electrolyte. This mixed oxide is an almost perfect conductor of oxygen ions over a wide temperature range (Sec. 6.3). The solid electrolyte is designed to separate the exhaust gas from the reference atmosphere. Both sides feature catalytically active platinum electrodes. At the inner electrode (air; $pO_2'' \sim 0.21$ bar), the electron reaction

$$O_2 + 4e^- \rightarrow 2\,O^{2-} \tag{6.3}$$

incorporates oxygen ions in the electrolyte. These migrate to the outer electrode (exhaust gas; pO_2' variable $< pO_2''$), where the counterreaction occurs at the three-phase boundary (electrolyte-platinum-gas). A counteractive electrical field is created, and an electrical voltage U_s corresponding to the partial-pressure ratio is generated in accordance with the Nernst equation:

$$U_s = \frac{RT}{4F} \ln \frac{pO_2''}{pO_2'} \tag{6.4}$$

where R = general gas constant
F = Faraday's constant
T = absolute temperature
pO_2 = partial pressure of oxygen

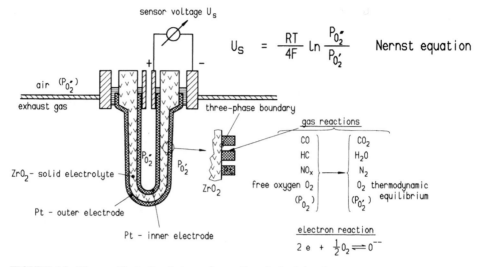

FIGURE 6.4 Diagram illustrating design and operation of a lambda = 1 sensor.

Catalytic Process.   Measurements of oxygen content can only serve as the basis for unambiguous conclusions regarding the lambda of the exhaust gas when a state of thermodynamic gas equilibrium is established at the catalytically active electrodes on the oxygen sensor (residual oxygen). The absolute concentrations of the individual components in the engine's exhaust gases fluctuate across a wide range in accordance with the instantaneous operating conditions (warm-up, acceleration, steady-state operation, deceleration). The oxygen sensor must thus be capable of converting the gas mixture that it receives into a state of complete thermodynamic equilibrium. The resulting requirements are a high level of catalytic activity at the electrode and a protective layer capable of limiting the gas quantity. Should it prove impossible to achieve thermodynamic equilibrium at the electrode, the sensor's lambda signal will be erroneous.

Characteristic Curve.   The concentration of residual oxygen fluctuates exponentially (by several orders of 10) in the vicinity of a stoichiometric air/fuel mixture (lambda = 1). In accordance with Eq. (6.4), this leads to massive variations in sensor voltage (lambda = 1 jump) with the characteristic lambda curve (Fig. 6.5).

Reference Atmosphere.   Ambient air is the most commonly used O_2 reference. Alternatives include a metal-metal oxide mixture or a pumped reference medium. With this method, an O_2 reference pumping current is superimposed on the voltage measurement to generate an approximately constant O_2 partial pressure at the encapsulated reference electrode.

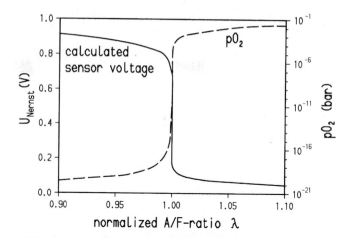

FIGURE 6.5   Equilibrium partial pressure of oxygen pO_2 and resulting curve for Nernst voltage at ≈ 700 °C relative to the normalized air-fuel ratio lambda.

6.2.2   Lambda $= 1$ Sensor: Semiconductor Type

Sensing Mechanism.   Oxidic semiconductors such as TiO_2 and $SrTiO_3$ rapidly achieve equilibrium with the oxygen partial pressure in the surrounding gas phase at relatively low temperatures. Changes in the partial pressure of the adjacent oxygen produce variations in the oxygen vacancy concentration of the material (TiO_{2-x} respectively $SrTiO_{3-x}$), thereby modifying its volume conductivity.

$$R_T = A \; pO_2{}^n \exp\left(\frac{E}{kT}\right) \tag{6.5}$$

where $R_T =$ semiconductor resistance
   $A =$ constant
   $E =$ activation energy
   $k =$ Boltzmann constant
   $T =$ absolute temperature
   $n \approx 1/4$.

This effect, which is exploited to determine lambda, is also superposed by the conductivity's temperature dependence. Electrical resistance and sensor response times are both inversely proportional to temperature, as equilibrium is achieved more rapidly through diffusion in the oxygen vacancies.

Design.   The ability to dispense with an O_2 reference allows an extremely simple design featuring an integrated heater. The porous semiconductor thick-film layer is generally positioned and sintered onto a planar Al_2O_3 substrate between two electrodes. Thin-film layers are also being developed as an alternative.

Characteristic Curve.   At lambda $= 1$, the sensor layer displays an extreme change in conductivity due to the large pO_2 variation (see Sec. 6.2.1 and Fig. 6.5). When new, TiO_2 sensors provide essentially the same response as ZrO_2-based lambda $= 1$ probes. Variations in the rates of increase for lean and rich resistance and for response time occur over its lifetime, with the emission-control system undergoing a significant shift toward lean.

Principles of Operation.   A voltage is applied to the TiO_2 resistor R_T and a serial reference resistor. The voltage drop at the serial resistor depends on R_T, respectively on lambda. In a three-pole version, the applied voltage is taken from the heater voltage; for the four-pole version (insulated ground) a separate supply is employed. Temperature compensation may be required, depending upon the specific application.

6.2.3   Lean A/F Sensor: Nernst Type

Sensing Mechanism.   It is always possible to employ a potentiometric lambda = 1 sensor (Sec. 6.2.1) as a lean A/F sensor by using the flat part of the Nernst voltage curve (Sec. 6.4 and Fig. 6.5) to derive the values at lambda > 1. The diminutive characteristic sensor voltages in this lambda range ($U_S < 65$ mV at lambda > 1.05) mean that stringent requirements for consistency must be met. Minute voltage deviations of just a few mV are sufficient to produce substantial errors in lambda.

Design.   For this reason, special sensors must be employed in applications in which quantitative determination of lambda > 1.05 is required. To this end, special electrode manufacturing techniques are used to enhance catalytic activity, while a power heater (18 W) is used in conjunction with a protection tube featuring a lower gas-flow rate to provide a more constant ceramic temperature.

Principles of Operation.   A high-output input amplifier is required for measurement of the low voltage levels associated with lean exhaust gases. In vehicle testing, lambda control has proven effective when used together with a classical mixture regulator. Even alternating operation (lambda = 1 and lean) with a sensor in the same vehicle is possible. Depending upon accuracy requirements, lean operation is possible in a range extending to lambda ≈ 1.5.

Nonautomotive Applications.   Lambda-controlled operation can be employed to maintain narrow tolerances and to limit drift in oil- and gas-fired units; the benefits include low fuel consumption, enhanced safety, and lower emissions. The use of sensors in stationary power plants—for instance, in central heating plants—is particularly interesting as a potential means of dealing with fluctuations in the calorific content of the fuel.

6.2.4   Lean A/F Sensor: Limiting-Current Type

Sensing Mechanism.   An external electrical voltage is applied to two electrodes on a heated ZrO_2 electrolyte to pump O_2 ions from the cathode to the anode (electrochemical O_2 pumping cell) (Fig. 6.6a). When a diffusion barrier impedes the flow of O_2 molecules from the exhaust gas to the cathode, the result is current saturation beyond a certain pumping voltage threshold (limiting current condition). Because the resulting limiting current I_1 is roughly proportional to the exhaust gas' oxygen concentration c_{O2}

$$I_1 = 4FD \, \frac{Q}{L} \, c_{O2} \tag{6.6}$$

where F = Faraday's constant
$\quad D$ = diffusion coefficient
$\quad Q$ = effective diffusion cross section
$\quad L$ = effective diffusion length

Design.   Figure 6.6b provides a schematic illustration of this sensor type featuring planar technology and an integrated electric heater element.

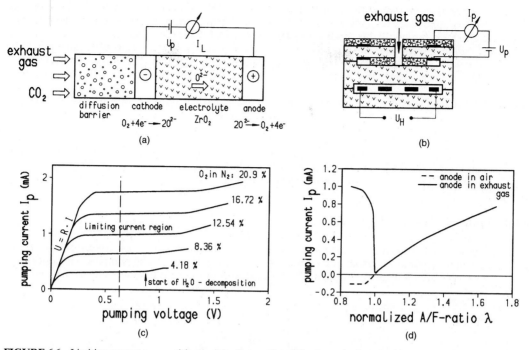

FIGURE 6.6 Limiting current sensor: (*a*) principle of operation; (*b*) schematic diagram; (*c*) current/voltage characteristics; (*d*) response curve as function of lambda.

Characteristic Curve.   Figure 6.6*c* shows the current-voltage pattern for a limiting current sensor at various O_2 concentrations. If, at a constant pumping voltage, the pumping current is entered above lambda instead of c_{O2}, the resulting curve will correspond to Fig. 6.6*d*. In lean exhaust gas, the signal drops in response to reductions in lambda as indicated in Eq. (6.7), but below lambda = 1 there is a radical surge. This response pattern is at variance with the basic theory, and can be explained as the result of decomposition effects at the cathode. As a result, this sensor is only suitable for use in lean gases. Depending upon the design of the diffusion barrier (pore radius to free path length for the gas molecules, according to the proportion of gas phases to Knudsen diffusion), various relationships are observed between pumping current (measurement signal) and exhaust pressure and sensor temperature.

Principles of Operation.   Depending on the accuracy requirements, a stable operating temperature in the range 600 to 800 °C is needed. Pumping voltages must always be selected to satisfy the conditions for limiting current. In addition, this limiting current has to be calibrated due to the manufacture scattering of the diffusion gap.

6.2.5   Wide-Range A/F Sensor: Single-Cell

Design and Operation.   When the anode of a limiting current sensor of the type described in Sec. 6.2.4 is exposed to reference air instead of to the exhaust gas, the total voltage U_S at the probe will be the sum of the effective pumping voltage U_P and a superimposed Nernst voltage U_N.

$$U_S = U_P + U_N \tag{6.7}$$

In operation, holding U_S to, as an example, 500 mV will produce a positive pumping voltage in lean exhaust gases ($U_N < 500$ mV); the diffusion limits the rate at which O_2 is pumped from the cathode to the anode. At lambda = 1 ($U_N \approx 500$ mV), the pumping voltage and, with it, the pumping current drop toward zero. In rich exhaust gas ($U_N > 500$ mV), the effective pumping voltage U_P becomes negative, causing oxygen to be pumped from the reference air electrode to the exhaust gas electrode ($I_P < 0$), where it reacts with the rich gas components CO, H_2, and HC.

Characteristic Curve.   The pumping current displays a uniform upward trend between mildly rich and extremely lean lambda values (Fig. 6.6*d*).

Applications.   This type of sensor is in series production as a thimble-type design for lean-mix concepts. In this application, operation as a limiting current sensor is restricted to lean conditions; during operation at lambda = 1, the pumping voltage is switched off and the Nernst voltage serves as the control signal.

6.2.6   Wide-Range A/F Sensor: Dual-Cell

Design.   Skillful combination of a limiting-current sensor with a Nernst concentration cell on a single substrate will produce a dual-cell wide-range A/F sensor. The pumping and concentration cells are made of ZrO_2. Each cell is coated with two porous platinum electrodes, and they

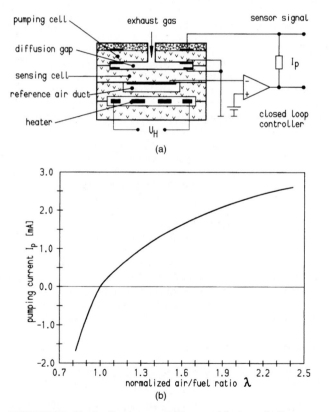

FIGURE 6.7   Dual-cell wide-range A-F sensor: (*a*) schematic diagram; (*b*) response curve as function of lambda ($T_{gas} \approx 400$ °C, $P_H \approx 12$ W).

are arranged with a measurement gap of approximately 10 to 50 μm in height between them. A gas-intake opening in the solid electrolyte connects this measurement gap to the exhaust gas while the gap is serving as a diffusion barrier to control limiting current (Fig. 6.7).

Operation Mode.   An electronic circuit regulates the current applied to the pumping cell to maintain a constant gas composition (for instance, lambda = 1) in the measurement gap. This corresponds to a Nernst-cell voltage of $U_N \approx 450$ mV. If the exhaust gas is lean, the pumping cell drives the oxygen outward from the measurement gap. If the exhaust gas is rich, the flow direction is reversed and oxygen from the surrounding exhaust gas (e.g., from decomposition of CO_2 and H_2O) is pumped into the measurement gap.

Characteristic Curve.   The pumping current is proportional to the oxygen concentration (or oxygen requirement). With the attendant electronic control circuitry, an unambiguous, linear signal increase over a wide lambda range of 0.7 < lambda < infinite (air) can be obtained if the current is calibrated due to the manufacture scattering (Fig. 6.7). The integrated heating element provides an operating temperature in excess of 600 °C.

6.3   TECHNOLOGY OF CERAMIC EXHAUST GAS SENSORS

6.3.1   ZrO$_2$-based Sensors

The zirconium dioxide used to manufacture oxygen sensors is not pure; instead, the solid electrolyte consists of a mixed oxide, ZrO_2/Y_2O_3. The Y_2O_3 concentration used for actual applications lies in the 4 to 5 mol% range. This level is commensurate with optimum sensor operation in the important properties of ion conductivity, thermal stability, and mechanical strength.

Ion Conductivity.   The substitution of trivalent yttrium ions for quadrivalent zirconium ions leads to the formation of oxygen vacancies through which the oxygen ions can move. Initially, the increases in ion conductivity are roughly proportional to the rise in Y_2O_3 content, as they are accompanied by a simultaneous rise in the number of oxygen vacancies. This pattern is observed with yttrium as well as with other bi- and trivalent alkaline earth metals, at least until a certain level of defect concentration is reached. Beyond this limit, the mutual influence of the vacancies reaches such levels that any further increases in defect concentration are accompanied by reductions in ion conductivity. The maximum is obtained at approximately 9 to 10 mol% Y_2O_3.

Phase Composition and Mechanical Stability.   At room temperature, zirconium dioxide is monocline. It becomes tetragonal (metastable) above 1200 °C, and assumes a cubic form beyond 2370 °C. Yttrium doping can be employed to partially or completely stabilize the tetragonal and cubic modification, even at room temperature (PSZ—partially stabilized zirconium; FSZ—fully stabilized zirconium, above approximately 10 mol%, with certain manufacturing processes 7 to 8 mol% Y_2O_3). ZrO_2, with an essentially monocline structure, does not display sufficient resistance to temperature fluctuations for application in automotive exhaust systems—the changes in the geometry of the individual crystallites which accompany the phase transition lead to fatigue symptoms in the ceramic material. At the same time, the cubic phase does not possess the physical strength required to resist the physical shocks and thermal stresses. However, good mechanical characteristics can be obtained by using partially stabilized ceramic materials, with maximum strength being achieved within the range of 2 to 4 mol% Y_2O_3.

Manufacture of Partially Stabilized ZrO$_2$ Ceramics.   The most common procedure consists of mixing and grinding the ZrO_2 and Y_2O_3 together (mixed oxide). The differences in the length of the diffusion paths—the two oxides are located adjacently as separate powder particles—do not generally produce a completely homogeneous distribution of yttrium in the ZrO_2. Thus, both fully stabilized cubic crystallites and tetragonal crystallites can be formed during the sintering process. During the phase transition to monocline ZrO_2 that takes place during cooling, the latter provoke internal tension, causing the ceramic material to harden. Certain combinations of yttrium concentration and manufacturing techniques can be employed to obtain exclusively tetragonal crystallites, which remain stable even after cooling (TSZ—tetragonal stabilized zirconia). Due to the absence of a phase transition within the temperature range associated with the intended application, stabilized tetragonal zirconium dioxide displays a virtually constant coefficient of thermal expansion. Both of the partially stabilized ZrO_2 ceramics described here are used in the manufacture of oxygen sensors.

6.3.2 Thimble-Type Sensors

Shaping.   The ceramic base (Fig. 6.4) is shaped in the usual manner with dry pressing of granulated ZrO_2 and subsequent grinding of the compact material.

Electrodes.   The application of the gas-permeable platinum electrodes is one of the most critical processes in the manufacture of oxygen sensors. A basic distinction is made between two different procedures:
   Thin-Film Process.   In this process, a thin microporous platinum layer (electrode thickness < 1 μm) is applied to the previously sintered base using one of three methods: thermal evaporation, sputtering, or chemical deposition with subsequent thermal treatment.
   Thick-Film Process.   In this process, a (for example) platinum-cermet layer (mixture of noble metal and ceramic phase) is printed onto the unsintered base (electrode thickness 5 to 10 μm).
   As far as actual operation is concerned, the salient difference between the two processes resides in the fact that the three-phase boundary required for the conversion of oxygen (common border of platinum, zirconia, and gas phase) remains restricted to the surface of the base when thin-film electrodes are used. In contrast, the use of thick-film cermet electrodes with a ceramic phase of ZrO_2 results in a substantially larger border area along with enhanced high-temperature adhesion.

Protective Layer.   As the outer electrode is exposed to the exhaust gases, a suitable protective layer, combining the requisite porosity with optimal adhesive properties, is essential to ensure the long-term stability of the oxygen sensor. In the conventional plasma or flame-spraying process, a porous layer 50 to 300 μm in thickness (e.g., magnesium spinel) is applied to the sintered and electrodes-equipped base. A cofiring technique with ZrO_2-based protective layers or a combination of both processes is being employed in the production of a new generation of oxygen sensors with enhanced long-term stability.
   Well-defined porosity levels must be maintained to ensure satisfactory operation. With cofired protective layers, the required porosity level can be obtained by using organic pore-forming substances, which are burned out during sintering, or by adding a second, sinter-inactive ceramic phase, such as Al_2O_3. Porous protective layers also provide a diffusion barrier for the exhaust-gas molecules before they reach the electrodes. These layers thus exercise a determining influence on the sensor's control characteristics because the components of the exhaust gas which exhibit various diffusion coefficients are not in a state of thermodynamic equilibrium (see Sec. 6.4). This effect can be partially neutralized through defined pigmentation in the protective layers, which not only display catalytic characteristics, but can also inhibit contamination.

6.3.3 Planar Oxygen Sensors

The planar oxygen sensor derives its designation from the fact that, as opposed to the thimble-type sensor, its design arranges all operating layers in plain, consecutive surfaces. The technology applied in their manufacture is quite similar to the multilayer technology employed to produce ceramic multilayer capacitors and high-density electronic circuit boards (e.g., MCM—multichip modules).

Manufacture of Ceramic Green Sheet. First, an organic binder phase is added to the ZrO_2 powder in a tape-casting process to produce ceramic substrate layers.

Printing on the Ceramic Green Sheet. A screen-printing process (thick-film process) is employed to attach the individual function groups, e.g., galvanic cell, pumping cell, reference-air duct and heater (see also Sec. 6.2) to the green tape in the desired layer sequence. Several printed layers are generally required for each side of the tape; these layers can also consist of various inorganic materials.

Lamination. A number of screen-printed substrates can be stacked and laminated (bonded in a process combining temperature and pressure) to form composite structures representing virtually any desired level of complexity. A simplified version of a lambda = 1 sensor in planar technology is illustrated in Fig. 6.8.

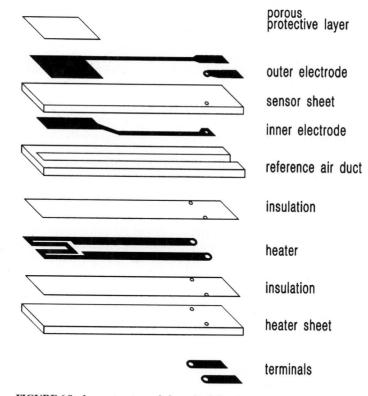

porous
protective layer

outer electrode

sensor sheet

inner electrode

reference air duct

insulation

heater

insulation

heater sheet

terminals

FIGURE 6.8 Layer structure of planar lambda = 1 sensor.

Advantages of Planar Technology. The application of surface-design technology also provides an additional advantage by making it possible to combine a number of individual elements on a single substrate for subsequent separation (multiple application) and sintering to form monolithic sensors with integrated heating elements. The coefficients of thermal expansion of the ZrO_2, cermet, and insulation layers must be precisely matched to ensure that the resulting ceramic elements display adequate thermal and mechanical stability.

Sensor elements manufactured with this new technology offer a number of advantages: the integration of heater and sensor provides a single unit with a lower total thermal mass, allowing substantial reductions in the continuous heating requirement (30 to 40 percent of that required with a thimble-type sensor), shorter delay between activation and readiness for active control, and smaller sensor dimensions. These characteristics make the unit ideal for meeting the demands of the modern motor vehicle (reductions in energy requirements, weight and space savings, and more stringent emission requirements). In addition, planar technology is an essential factor in obtaining complicated operating abilities such as those found in the dual-cell wide-range A/F sensor (see Sec. 6.2.6).

6.3.4 Al_2O_3-based Sensors

Sensors for oxygen and other exhaust gases which employ variations in the conductivity of the sensor material (TiO_2, SnO_2, etc.) to detect changes in the gas concentration are usually designed as planar sensors. The preferred substrate material is Al_2O_3. As the combinations of functions (e.g., heater, electrodes, etc.) are essentially those required with planar ZrO_2 sensors, the manufacturing techniques are also quite similar. Al_2O_3 provides advantages in the form of lower material costs and a simplified internal structure, made possible by the fact that Al_2O_3 maintains its good insulation properties at high temperatures. A disadvantage, particularly in terms of long-term stability, is the difficulty with sintering and sensor-material adhesion, as cofiring technology cannot be employed for this procedure.

6.3.5 Construction

Figure 6.9 shows completely assembled a heated thimble sensor and a planar lambda sensor. Although similar in external appearance—the planar sensor is somewhat shorter and narrower—the two units differ substantially in their respective internal structures. The differences are largely a result of the fact that heater and sensor in the heated thimble-type sensor are two separate components requiring assembly and electrical contact. Various ceramic support components are incorporated to enhance structural integrity and to ensure an impermeable seal between the reference air and the exhaust gases while also providing a degree of impact protection for the sensor unit. On the exhaust-gas side, the sensor elements receive both physical and thermal protection from a protection tube. Due to its basic design configuration, the planar sensor element does not share the rotational symmetry of its thimble-type counterpart. Thus, it must be installed in a specific position; the protection tube features a partial double wall to facilitate orientation. The offset inlet openings provide a uniform flow of exhaust gases past the measurement electrode, regardless of its position relative to the exhaust-gas stream. Thermal insulation from the exhaust gases is also improved.

Although unheated thimble-type sensors are still on the market, they are becoming less important due to the increasing demands for precision of emission control systems.

6.4 FACTORS AFFECTING THE CONTROL CHARACTERISTICS OF LAMBDA = 1 SENSORS

6.4.1 Factors Affecting the Static Curve

Due to the porous protective layer around the electrode, the steep voltage change in the sensor's characteristic curve does not occur at precisely lambda = 1; instead, it is displaced a small

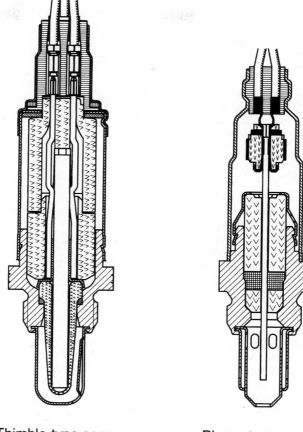

Thimble-type sensor   Planar-type sensor

FIGURE 6.9   Construction of thimble-type and planar-type oxygen sensors.

amount into the lean range. The lower the porosity of the protective layer, the greater the diffusion of H_2 relative to O_2 toward the electrode. This phenomenon induces changes in the lambda value at the electrode relative to the lambda of the exhaust gas, the electrode detects richer exhaust gas and the lambda characteristic curve is displaced into the lean range.

Lean Shift.   The lean shift is caused by exhaust-gas residue, such as oil ash and SiO_2, which partially plug the pores of the protective layer, and by reductions in sensor temperature.

Rich Shift.   Fractures and flake-off of the protective layer lead to reductions in response times and shift the static characteristic curve toward rich. Electrode deactivation, especially due to lead contamination, will produce a flatter static response curve, as free, unconverted oxygen will also be detected. This effect also displaces the switchpoint threshold toward a lower lambda. A similar effect occurs when the reference atmosphere is contaminated (Chemical Shift Down, or CSD), for instance, with exhaust gases or water. Figure 6.10 shows typical characteristic curves for these conditions.

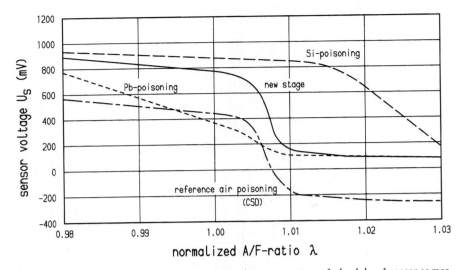

FIGURE 6.10   Effects of contamination on the static response curve of a lambda = 1 sensor as measured at laboratory test stand at $T_{gas} \approx 350\,°C$.

6.4.2 Factors Affecting Sensor Dynamics and Control State

Factors.   The control state (adjusted lambda) depends upon a number of factors. These include static sensor characteristics, sensor dynamics and asymmetry in sensor response times (switching times), t_{rs} (rich to switchpoint) during the surge from rich to lean, and t_{ls} (lean to switchpoint) during the jump from lean to rich. The sensor switching times t_{rs} and t_{ls} are strongly influenced by the configuration of the protection tube, the protective layer, and the sensor's temperature. Without the protection tube, switching times of less than 10 ms have been measured for ZrO_2 sensors with $T_{ceramic} \approx 900\,°C$. However, such rapid response times are neither necessary nor desirable with many of the systems presently in use.

Response Times.   An increase in response time that is not accompanied by a variation in the differential between t_{rs} and t_{ls} results in worse emissions with a constant control state due to the fact that the control amplitude increases while the conversion rate of the catalytic converter is reduced (see sec. 6.1.4 and Fig. 6.2).

Asymmetry.   An asymmetrical increase in the response times t_{rs} and t_{ls} will also affect the control state due to the lambda shift.
    Lean Shift.   A pronounced increase in t_{rs} leads to a displacement toward lean. This can occur for any of several reasons. The dwell time in the rich exhaust gas is determined by control frequency and amplitude, and affects t_{rs} through the adsorption of CO and HC. Should the protective layer be obstructed (for instance, by oil ash), or should the sensor temperature drop, t_{rs} will generally rise more than t_{ls}.
    Rich Shift.   In contrast, a more pronounced rise in t_{ls} will lead to a displacement toward the rich range. The conversion rate of the electrode and the protective layer exercise a major influence on t_{ls}. Lead deposits diminish catalytic activity, causing t_{ls} to rise without exercising any substantive effect on t_{rs}.

Temperature.   As a general rule, the susceptibility to sensor contamination is inversely proportional to electrode temperature. The factors determining the temperature of the ceramic material are the heater, the gas temperature, the gas flow rate (rpm, load), and the protection tube. Depending upon the installation location, the ceramic temperature generally lies between 350 and 1000 °C for exhaust temperatures ranging between 150 and 900 °C. The flow velocity of the gas varies between 2 m/s at idle, 40 m/s at moderate rpm and load, and up to 80 m/s under full load. The influence exercised by gas temperature and the protection tube can be seen in Fig. 6.11. The ceramic temperature has a major effect on the controlled lambda. A protection tube providing a lower gas flow (see Fig. 6.11: 1 hole/4 flaps) and a higher heater

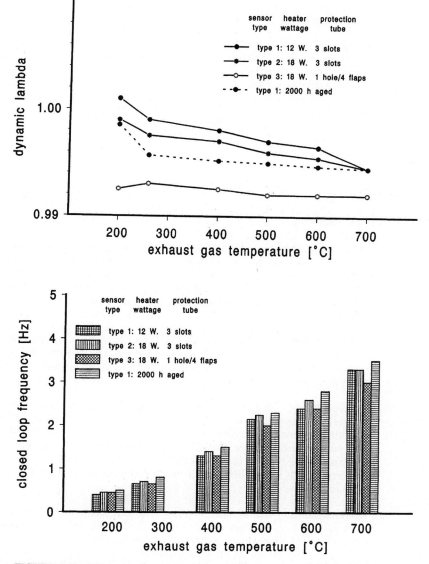

FIGURE 6.11   Effects of exhaust-gas temperature (rpm) on dynamic lambda and control frequency.

power (18 W) will lead to higher ceramic temperatures with enhanced temperature consistency relative to exhaust temperature. This measure is employed to obtain a more stable controlled lambda. The lambda value displays a moderate rich shift compared to that obtained with a more open tube (see Fig. 6.11: 3 slots) and 12 W heater power.

System Lag.   System lag is dependent on the sensor's installation position (0.2 to 2 m downstream from the exhaust manifold, with approx. 1 meter downstream from the exhaust valve being typical) and the gas velocity as determined by load, rpm, and the exhaust pipe diameter. It can be up to 500 ms at idle, and drops down to delays as low as 20 ms at full load. The sensor (protection tube, heater power) is of secondary significance (Fig. 6.11). The influence of sensor response times (t_{rs}, t_{ls}) on the control state increases as a function of their share of the total system lag.

tv Shift.   The cumulative effect of all extraneous influences is a slight lean control state of the lambda = 1 sensor. Electronic compensation for the lean shift is available in the form of an asymmetrical control-oscillation pattern (see Sec. 6.1.4). This is provided either by means of a switching delay after the sensor surge (tv shift, Fig. 6.3), through variations in the controller's surge amplitude, and/or via asymmetrical ramp slope. Those parameters for the electronic lambda displacement which vary according to load and rpm can be stored as a program map in the electronic control unit (ECU). This method can be employed for lambda corrections up to $|\Delta\lambda| \leq 0.015$.

6.5 APPLICATIONS

6.5.1 Operating Conditions

Environmental Factors.   Table 6.3 provides a summary of the types and magnitudes of the major stress factors affecting the sensor. Beyond the actual function of the sensor itself, optimal selection and precise mixture of all applied materials (ceramics, metals, synthetics) are essential factors in obtaining the thermal, mechanical, and chemical characteristics needed to achieve the obligatory extended service life of over 100,000 miles.

Sensor Installation Location.   Because it is of determining significance for both external influences and control function, correct sensor location is a critical factor in calibrating the performance of the total lambda-control system. The sensor must be far enough from the exhaust valves to ensure that it monitors representative exhaust gases for all cylinders, but near enough to hold system lag to acceptable levels. Both factors affect emissions.

Thermal Stress.   Thermal stresses at the sensor stem from the high-potential exhaust-gas temperatures as well as from the temperature gradients that occur. Exhaust temperature is essentially a function of engine speed, and can reach a maximum of 1000 °C at the sensor on high-performance engines. The most extreme temperature gradients at the sensor occur during hard driving directly in the wake of a warm start at which the exhaust system and the sensor have already cooled off. These conditions can produce exhaust-gas temperature gradients of up to 500 K/s.

Thermal Shock.   In the warm-up phase following a cold start, condensation on the pipe walls can cause the ceramic material to crack once the electric heater warms it beyond the critical temperature of approximately 300 °C. Accumulations of condensation can be largely avoided by locating the sensor as close as possible to the engine to provide rapid heating of the upstream exhaust pipe. Depending upon the specific vehicle, a time delay for switching on the sensor heater may be required.

TABLE 6.3 Overview of Stress Factors for Exhaust Gas Sensors

Mechanical stress	Stress caused by environmental conditions	Thermal stress	Stress caused by exposition to exhaust gas
Vibrational stress (<1300 m/s²) by engine vibration (<5 kHz) by pulsation of the exhaust gas (< ±300 mbar) by ambient wind (cable, <10 Hz)	Splash water, gush of water (in case containing NaCl, CaCl₂, MgCl₂)	Exhaust gas temperature (150 °C ... 1000 °C)	Exhaust gas composition ch between lambda = 0.85 (fuel load enrichment) and lambda infinite (overrun fuel)
Stone impact (<1.5 Nm)	Dust (organic, inorganic origin) Oil, dirt undercarriage protection	Exhaust gas temperature gradients at cold start (<500 K/s) at overrun fuel cutoff (<200 K/s)	Catalyst poisoning from fuel additives: permissible lead content: <0.013 g/l sulfur content: <0.1 % Br-, Cl-compounds
Installation/removal (torque about 50 Nm when assembled)	Fluctuation of the electrical supply system (9 ... 15 V)	Temperature increase after engine stalling (<300 °C at cable outlet)	
Wire pull test (>70 N)	EMC (<200 V/m)		Oil ash (Ca-, P-, S-, Zn-compounds up to 1 kg within ~60000)
Handling (shock load up to 1000 g)	Variation of climatic conditions (−40 °C ... +50 °C, 10 ... 100% rel. humidity)	Radiant heat (may require corresponding protective measures)	Miscellaneous corrosion products (e.g., Fe-oxides)
			Condensation water

Mechanical Stresses. The main sources of mechanical stress on the sensor are vibration, exhaust-gas pulsation, stone impact, and cable tension (Table 6.3).

Sealing. The cable outlet of the sensor must be sealed to prevent water splash from penetrating to its interior and distorting the reference air (see Sec. 6.4.1 and Fig. 6.10). At the same time, the sealing element must be flexible enough to absorb the accelerative forces associated with vibration as well as any tensile forces transmitted through the cable.

6.5.2 Emission Certification

It would be impossible for a vehicle equipped only with an unregulated catalytic converter and lacking an oxygen sensor to achieve compliance with the American emission standards. When a regulated catalytic converter is used together with an oxygen sensor, emissions remain well below the limits. Even after vehicle mileage corresponding to more than 100,000 miles, the sensor limits emission increases to a minimum (Fig. 6.12). The introduction of a new system must be accompanied by precise calibration of the engine-control system to match the production tolerances and aging characteristics which affect the sensor's control response. The considerable effects that temperature and aging exercise on the catalytic converter must also be considered.

Durability Tests

Life Cycle. To determine aging behavior, the sensors undergo a standard durability test in the exhaust-gas stream of a test engine. The test cycle is designed to simulate combined urban and rural operation, and has been adopted by many automobile manufacturers as a standard program. The mean average speed is approximately 100 km/h for a midrange car. All newly developed products must withstand 2000 h (more than 100,000 miles) operation in this program without failure.

Hot Durability Testing. In a substantially more demanding test, essentially consisting of simulated full-load operation, the sensors must survive at least 1000 h (roughly 100,000 miles). The main stress factors for the sensors in these tests are thermal exposure (exhaust-gas temperatures reaching 950 °C, housing temperatures up to 650 °C), exhaust gas loads, and vibration.

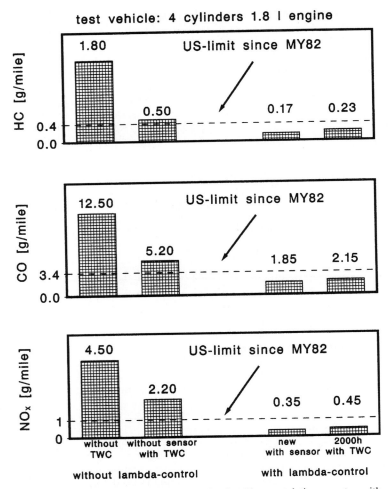

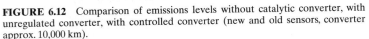

FIGURE 6.12 Comparison of emissions levels without catalytic converter, with unregulated converter, with controlled converter (new and old sensors, converter approx. 10,000 km).

Durability Testing of Contamination Resistance.   Short durability tests featuring higher levels of Pb, Si, and oil are employed to determine the sensor's resistance to contamination damage.

6.6 SENSOR PRINCIPLES FOR OTHER EXHAUST GAS COMPONENTS

Sensors capable of monitoring the levels of the regulated toxic exhaust substances—CO, NO_x, and HC—would be desirable as elements of the On-Board Diagnosis systems (OBD I and OBD II) specified by the California Air Resources Board. Due to the extreme operating conditions, only a few of the many tested configurations have a chance to be used in engine-exhaust gas.

6.6.1 Mixed-Potential Sensors

Sensing Mechanism. If reduced catalytic activity prevents gas equilibrium from being achieved at the electrode of a galvanic ZrO_2 cell, competing reactions can occur. These, in turn, prevent a state of reduction/oxidation equilibrium in the oxygen, and lead to the formation of a mixed potential. This potential is determined by electrode activity, temperature, and gas composition. It is difficult to design manufacturing techniques that can consistently produce electrodes capable of maintaining specific, defined rates of catalytic activity over extended periods of time. Every change in electrode activity (for instance, due to aging) leads to a variation in mixed potential. Pt electrodes give rise to a mixed potential at very low temperatures, with extended response delays relative to lambda sensors. Other electrode materials with lower rates of catalytic activity continue to provide a mixed potential at higher temperatures, making it possible to achieve response times < 1 s.

Selectivity. Careful selection of electrode materials, operating temperature, and selective precatalyzation layers offers opportunities for improving selectivity.

Operation Mode. Because the effect is temperature-sensitive, a constant sensor temperature must be regulated in the range of 300 to 600 °C, depending upon the individual application.

6.6.2 Semiconductor Gas Sensors

Sensing Mechanism
   Ceramic and Thick-Film Layers.   On the surface of nonstoichiometric metal oxides such as SnO_2, TiO_2, In_2O_3, and Fe_2O_3 (*n*-type semiconductors), oxygen is absorbed and dissociated in air at high temperatures and is bonded to the crystal lattice. This leads to the formation of a thin depletion layer at the crystallite surface with a resultant arch in the potential curve. This phenomenon produces reductions in surface conductivity and higher intercrystalline resistance at the boundaries between two crystallites; this is the major factor determining the total resistance of the polycrystalline metal oxide. Oxidation gases such as CO, H_2, and C_xH_y, which react with surface oxygen, increase the density of charge carriers in the boundary layer and reduce the potential barrier. Reduction gases, such as NO_x and SO_x raise the potential barrier and, with it, the surface/intercrystalline resistance.
   Thin-Film Layers.   Compared to porous polycrystalline materials, thin-film layers display only limited numbers of crystalline boundaries at the layer surface for reaction with the exhaust gases. The depletion-layer barrier makes up a substantial proportion of the layer thickness on thin-film devices, meaning that changes in charge-carrier density within the barrier layer due to adsorbed gases will also result in substantial variations in the total resistance.

Selectivity. Selected doping materials and temperatures can be employed to achieve selectivity for CO, HC, or NO_x. The resistance of metal-oxide semiconductors is always a function of the partial pressure of the O_2.

Specific Influences of Exhaust Gas. Engine exhaust gas with minimal, highly variable O_2 partial pressures is characterized by a high level of O_2 cross-axis sensitivity. Within the lambda = 1 to lambda < 1 operating range, an irreversible long-term change in sensor resistance leading to disintegration of the metal oxide is also possible. High operating temperatures are conducive to the diffusion of oxygen vacancies and doping materials. When amplified by sintering effects, these lead to resistance drift and attenuated sensor response.

Standard operating temperatures for metal-oxide gas sensors range from 100 to 500 °C, with up to 600 °C being seen in some restricted applications. With SnO_2, a high level of selectivity for, for example, CO can be achieved at temperatures as low as the 100 to 200 °C range. However, the response times can be measured in minutes. At higher temperatures, in the 300 to 550 °C range, response times of less than 1 s can be obtained, but with reduced selectivity.

6.6.3 Catalytic Gas Sensors

Sensing Mechanism.   The catalytic gas sensor is essentially a temperature sensor featuring a catalytically active surface. An exothermic reaction (basically an oxidation reaction in air) at the catalytically active surface causes the temperature of the sensor to rise. The increase in temperature is proportional to the concentration of an oxidation gas in an excess-oxygen atmosphere. A temperature sensor of the same basic design—but without the catalytic response—is employed to enhance sensitivity and to provide temperature compensation by means of differential-signal evaluation. Materials employed for the temperature sensor include coiled Pt wire, Pt thin-film and thick-film layers, transistors, and NTC and PTC thermistors.

Operating Conditions.   Catalytic gas sensors are relatively insensitive and can be employed in a range >1000 ppm. Excess oxygen is required to monitor concentrations. Due to the sensitivity to flow rate, these units are generally operated in flowheads with diffusion limiters. Measurement and reference sensors must be exposed to the same flow conditions, with no mutual thermal influences. Symmetrical configurations in pellet form are thus preferred over planar shapes. Operating temperatures for commercial sensors are in the 500 to 600 °C range, but extension to higher temperatures is possible. The requirement for long-term stability in the catalytic converter is the limiting factor governing the operating temperature. Catalytic gas sensors are not selective, instead providing a summing signal for all combustion gases. Thus catalytic sensors for application in exhaust gases are restricted to monitoring the state of the catalytic converter.

BIBLIOGRAPHY

Arndt, J., "Ceramics and Oxides," in W. Göpel, J. Hesse, and J. N. Zemel (eds.), *Sensors—Fundamentals and General Aspects,* vol. 1, S.252 ff, VCH Verlagsgesellschaft, Weinheim, 1989.

Barnes, G. J., R. L. Klimisch, and B. B. Krieger, "Equilibrium Considerations in Catalytic Emission Control," SAE Paper 730200, *SAE National Automobile Engineering Meeting,* Detroit, Jan. 1973.

Bosch, *Automotive Electric/Electronic Systems,* VDI, Düsseldorf, May 1987.

Bosch, *Automotive Handbook,* VDI-Verlag, Düsseldorf, 1986.

Duecker, H., K.-H. Friese, and W.-D. Haecker, "Ceramic Aspects of the Bosch Lambda-Sensor," SAE Paper 750223, *SAE National Automobile Engineering Meeting,* Detroit, 1975.

Gruber, H. U., and H. M. Wiedenmann, "Three Years Field Experience with the Lambda-Sensor in Automotive Control Systems," SAE Paper 800017, *SAE National Automobile Engineering Meeting,* Detroit, Feb. 1980.

Moseley, P. T., and B. C. Tofield (eds.), *Solid State Gas Sensors,* Adam Hilger, Bristol and Philadelphia, 1987.

Saji, K., "Characteristics of Limiting Current-Type Oxygen Sensor," *J. Electrochem. Soc.: Electrochem. Science and Technology,* vol. 134, no. 10, 1987, pp. 534–542.

Saji, K., H. Kondo, T. Takeuchi, and I. Igarashi, "EMF Characteristics of Zirconia Oxygen Sensor in Nonequilibrium Gas Mixtures Containing Combustible Gas and Oxygen," *Proc. 1st Sensor Symposium,* Tsukuba, Japan, June 1981, pp. 103–107.

Soejima, S., and S. Mase, "Multi-Layered Zirconia Oxygen Sensor for Lean Burn Engine Application," SAE Paper 850378, *SAE National Automobile Engineering Meeting,* Detroit, 1985.

Takami, A., "Development of Titania Heated Exhaust-Gas Oxygen Sensor," *Ceramic Bulletin,* vol. 67, no. 12, 1988, pp. 1956–1960.

Wiedenmann, H. M., "Characteristics of Oxygen Sensors for Lean Exhaust Gas," *VDI Berichte* 578, S.129–151, VDI-Verlag, Düsseldorf, 1985.

ABOUT THE AUTHORS

HANS-MARTIN WIEDENMANN studied physics and meterology in Tübingen and Munich, where he received his Ph.D. in Physics in 1969. He joined Bosch in 1970 and is now senior manager for the development of lambda oxygen sensors.

GERHARD HÖTZEL studied chemistry in Konstanz and received his Ph.D. in 1986 at the University of Stuttgart. At Bosch, he is responsible for physical bases and measurement techniques for lambda oxygen sensors.

HARALD NEUMANN studied solid-state electronics in Aachen where he received a Ph.D. in 1988. Since that time, at Bosch he has been responsible for the technology of planar-type ceramic sensors.

JOHANN RIEGEL studied electrical engineering in Karlsruhe and received a Ph.D. in 1989. At Bosch he is responsible for the investigation of planar-type ceramic sensors.

HELMUT WEYL studied mechanical engineering in Darmstadt and was graduated from there in 1966. He has been with Bosch since 1968 and is now responsible for proving lambda oxygen sensors.

CHAPTER 7
SPEED AND ACCELERATION SENSORS

William C. Dunn
Motorola Inc.
Semiconductor Products Sector

7.1 INTRODUCTION

In the automotive arena, speed and acceleration sensors are used in a wide variety of applications, from improving engine performance through safety to helping to provide creature comforts.

Speed sensing can be divided into rotational and linear applications. Rotational speed sensing has two major application areas: engine speed monitoring to enhance engine control, and performance and antilock breaking and traction control systems for improved road handling and safety. Linear sensing can be used for ground-speed monitoring for vehicle control, obstacle detection, and crash avoidance. Acceleration sensors are used in air bag deployment, ride control, antilock brake, traction, and inertial navigation systems.

In most cases, there are a number of different sensor types available for a specific monitoring function. However, the choice of sensor for a specific application can be difficult to make. The selection may be determined by the familiarity of the system's designer with the sensor. On the other hand, the output from one sensor can be used for several applications, and the individual requirements of each application may eventually determine the sensor to be used.

Electronics and electronic sensors are making rapid inroads into the automotive market. In order to analyze the large amounts of sensor data needed for low emissions and efficient engine control, it is necessary to process the information using microcontrollers (MCUs), which can operate at high speeds and in real time. Sensors that can convert information directly into a digital format for MCU compatibility have a distinct advantage over an analog output format. Digital signals are also supply-line voltage-insensitive, virtually unaffected by noise, and have better resolution than can be obtained with analog signals. If the addition of an analog-to-digital converter (on or off the MCU) is required for compatibility, the system cost is increased. The accuracy of the control system is only as good as the integrity of the sensor data supplied to the MCU. Hence, the importance of the performance of the sensor.

This chapter concentrates on speed and acceleration, and therefore does not go into all the other different types of applications for which many of these sensors can be used in the automobile.

7.2   *SPEED-SENSING DEVICES*

In automotive applications, the environment must be taken into consideration. The sensing must be accurate, the devices must be rugged and reliable, and they must function in the presence of oil, grease, dirt, and inclement weather conditions. These requirements have severely limited the use of a number of otherwise practical alternatives, such as optical sensors and contact sensing.

In the area of rotational speed monitoring, the most practical devices use magnetic field sensing. These sensors are Hall effect devices, variable reluctance (VR), and magnetoresistive or magnetic resistance element (MRE) devices. Both the Hall effect and VR devices have been widely used and have a proven track record. The MRE device has only recently come into its own with improved technology and provides a viable alternative to the Hall effect device. The MRE device has a higher sensitivity and a wider operating temperature range than the Hall effect device.

For the measurement of ground speed and object detection, optical, radar, laser, infrared, and ultrasonics have been explored. Linear sensing devices typically use the Doppler effect for speed sensing and pulse modulation for distance measuring. These devices are used for object detection in blind spots when reversing or changing lanes, and in such applications as collision avoidance systems.

7.2.1   Variable Reluctance Devices

Variable reluctance devices are in effect small ac generators with an output voltage proportional to speed, but they are limited in applications where zero speed sensing is required. The operating frequency range of the VR device is from about 10 Hz to 50 kHz. It is insensitive to mechanical stress and has a wide temperature operating range from −40 to 190 °C. The supply voltage and offset drift will depend upon the control electronics. The VR device, originally designed around existing automotive electromechanical systems, was adapted for electronic control. The ferrous metal in the VR system is designed for maximum output voltage at low rpm (revolutions per minute), to get as close as possible to zero speed sensing without generating excessive voltages at maximum rpm (up to 150 V). This device gives a linear output voltage with frequency. Most systems use MCUs for data processing, so the VR device needs an analog-to-digital (A/D) converter to generate a digital signal for compatibility with the MCU. Although the VR device itself is inexpensive, the extra costs for data conversion may eventually lead to its demise in many automotive applications.

7.2.2   Hall Effect Devices

The Hall effect exists when a current flowing in a carrier experiencing a magnetic field perpendicular to the direction of current flow results in the current being deflected perpendicular to the field and to the direction of the current. The Hall effect is shown in Fig. 7.1. A current I_c flowing through the device between terminals 1 and 2 will produce a potential VH between terminals 3 and 4, when a magnetic field **B** is applied perpendicular to the device. The potential VH is determined by the strength of the magnetic field and the current flowing. Hall effect devices can be manufactured with indium, gallium arsenide, or silicon. A comparison of their properties is given in Table 7.1.

As can be seen, silicon is the most sensitive material. It is compatible with ICs and has a wide operating temperature range. The Hall effect device is well known both in industry and in the automotive arena for rotational and position-sensing applications. However, recent developments in Hall sensing devices, such as differential sensing and integration, have given improved sensor characteristics, which may result in greater potential in automotive applications.

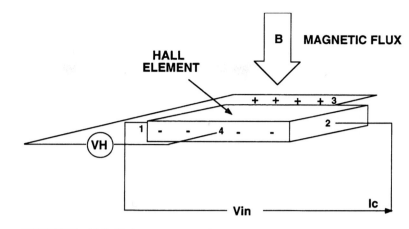

FIGURE 7.1   Hall effect.

The Hall effect device is very versatile, flexible in use, easy to package, and can be used for zero speed sensing (it can give an output when there is no rotation). Hall devices give a frequency output that is proportional to speed, making them compatible with MCUs. The Hall device is normally configured as a bridge to minimize temperature effects and to increase the sensitivity of the sensor.

A typical Hall effect sensor configuration with waveforms is shown in Fig. 7.2. The teeth of the ferrous wheel concentrate the magnetic flux when the teeth come into close proximity to the Hall sensor and magnet. The output from the sensor is a sinusoidal waveform, whose frequency is the rpm of the ferrous wheel multiplied by the number of teeth on the wheel. The resolution of the system depends on the number of teeth in the wheel (typically 20).

7.2.3 Magnetoresistive Devices

The magnetoresistive effect is the property of a current-carrying ferromagnetic material to change its resistivity in the presence of an external magnetic field. For example, a ferromagnetic (permalloy) element (an alloy containing 20 percent iron and 80 percent nickel) will change its resistivity by 2 to 3 percent when it experiences a 90° rotation in a magnetic field.[1] The resistivity value rises to a maximum when the direction of current and magnetic field are coincident, and is a minimum when the fields are perpendicular to each other. This relationship is shown in Fig. 7.3. This attribute is known as the Anisotropic Magneto Resistive Effect. The resistance R of an element is related to the angle q between the current and the magnetic field directions by the expression:

$$R = R_{\parallel} \cos^2 q + R_l \sin^2 q \qquad (7.1)$$

TABLE 7.1   Comparison of Properties of Hall Effect Materials

Material	Operating temp. °C	Supply voltage	Sensitivity @ 1 kA/m	Frequency range
Indium	−40 to 100	1V	7 mV	0 to 1 MHz
GaAs	−40 to 150	5 V	1.2 mV	0 to 1 MHz
Si (with conditioning)	−40 to 150	12 V	94 mV	0 to 100 kHz

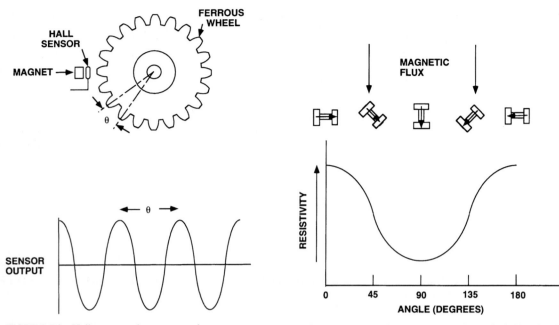

FIGURE 7.2   Hall sensor and output waveforms.

FIGURE 7.3   Relationship between magnetic field and resistivity change in MRE devices.

where $R_\parallel$ is the resistance when the current and the magnetic field directions are parallel and R_l is the resistance when the current and the magnetic field directions are perpendicular.

MRE devices give an output when stationary, which make them suitable for zero speed sensing. MRE devices also give an output frequency that is proportional to speed, making for ease of interfacing with an MCU. For good sensitivity and to minimize temperature effects, a bridge configuration is normally used. In an MRE sensor, aluminum strips can be put across the permalloy element to linearize the device. This configuration is shown in Fig. 7.4 together with a typical MRE characteristic. The low-resistance aluminum stripes cause the current to flow at 45° in the permalloy element, which biases the element into a linear operating region.

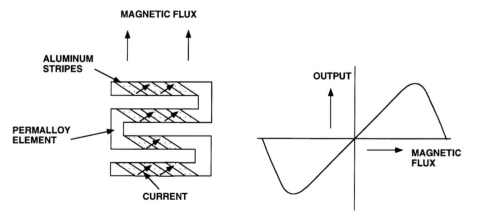

FIGURE 7.4   Use of permalloy strip for linearization in MRE devices.

Integrated MRE devices can typically operate from –40 to 150 °C, over a supply voltage range of 8 to 16 V, and at frequencies from 0 to 1 MHz. In comparing the MRE sensor to a Hall effect device, the MRE has a higher sensitivity, is less prone to mechanical stress, has a wider operating frequency range, has the potential of being more cost effective, gives better linearity, and is more reproducible. However, it is more sensitive to external magnetic fields. Table 7.2 shows a comparison of rotational sensing devices.

TABLE 7.2   Comparison of Sensing Devices

Sensor type	Operating temperature (°C)	Sensitivity 1 kA/m (mV)	Frequency range	Mechanical stress
Hall effect	–40 to 150	90	0 to 100 kHz	High
MRE	–40 to 150	140	0 to 1 MHz	Low
VR	–40 to 190		1 to 50 kHz	None
Magnetic transistor	–40 to 150	250	0 to 500 kHz	Low

It should be noted that Hall effect and MRE devices have many applications in the automobile outside of rotational speed sensing, such as position sensing, fuel-level sensing, and active suspension. The magnetic transistor is showing potential in rotational speed sensing and position-sensing applications, and may eventually be another viable contender to the Hall effect device in the automotive market.

7.2.4   Ultrasonic Devices

Ultrasonic devices can be used to measure distance, ground speed, and as a proximity detector. To give direction and beam shape, the signals are transmitted and received via specially configured horns and orifices. The transmitter and receiver horns are similar in shape, but are normally separate to accommodate different characteristics. The ultrasonic devices are made from PZT crystal-oriented piezoelectric material ($PbZrO_3$—$PbTiO_3$).

For the measurement of distance or object detection, a pulse of ultrasonic energy is transmitted and the time is measured for the reflected pulse to return to the receiver. The frequency of the transmitted ultrasonic waves are typically about 40 kHz and travel with a velocity of 340 m/s at 15 °C. This velocity changes with temperature and pressure. However, these parameters can be measured and corrections made if high accuracy is required. The repetition frequency and power requirements depend on the distance to be measured. To measure speed, the distance variation with time can be measured and the velocity calculated. A more common method is to use the Doppler effect, which is a change in the transmitted frequency as detected by the receiver due to motion of the target (or, in this case, the motion of the transmitter and receiver).

7.2.5   Optical and Radio Frequency Devices

Optical devices are still being used for rotational speed sensing. They are normally light-emitting diodes (LEDs) with optical sensors. Figure 7.5 shows a typical optical sensor system. An optical sensor detects light from an LED through a series of slits cut into the rotating disc, so that the output from the sensor is a pulse train whose frequency is equal to the rpm of the disc multiplied by the number of slits. The higher the number of slits in the disc, the smaller the angle of rotation that can be measured. The optical sensor can be a single photodiode or a photodiode array as shown. This array gives a more accurate determination of the position of the slit, resulting in higher resolution of the position of the disc.

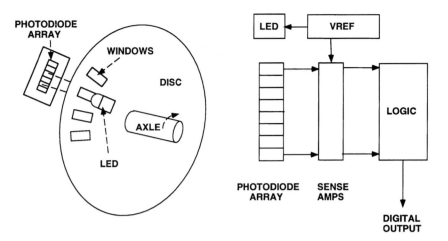

FIGURE 7.5   Optical sensor.

Optical and radio frequency (RF) devices are used for object detection, linear approach speed, and distance measurements in crash avoidance systems where distances greater than about 10 m are involved. These devices use the same principles as the ultrasonic devices. Optical devices normally use lasers or infrared devices for the transmitting source and optical sensors for the receivers. RF devices use gallium arsenide or Gunn devices to obtain the power and high frequency (about 100 GHz) required in the transmitter. The high operating frequency is set to a large extent by the need for a small antenna. These applications are under development and are discussed in Sec. 7.7.2.

7.3   *AUTOMOTIVE APPLICATIONS FOR SPEED SENSING*

There are several applications for rotational speed sensing. First it is necessary to monitor engine speed. This information is used for transmission control, engine control, cruise control, and possibly for a tachometer. Electronics and electronic sensing in the automobile were brought about by the need for higher-efficiency engines, better fuel economy, increased power and performance, and lower emissions. Second, wheel speed sensing is required for use in transmissions, cruise control, speedometers, antilock brake systems (ABS), traction control (ASR), variable ratio power steering assist, four-wheel steering, and possibly in inertial navigation and air bag deployment applications.

Linear speed sensing can be used to measure the ground speed. This measurement also has the possibly of use in ABS, ASR, and inertial navigation. Similar types of sensors can be used in crash avoidance, proximity, and obstacle detection applications.

7.3.1   Rotational Applications

The high timing accuracy that can be obtained with fuel injection systems and replacement of points by sensors have made cost-effective engine control and low maintenance a reality. Adjustment of the stoichiometric ratio of air to fuel, accurate ignition timing, and oxygen sensors in the exhaust system, have vastly improved engine performance and greatly reduced emissions over widely varying operating conditions. The two important factors in engine control are the engine speed in rpm and the crank angle. These signals are used by the engine control MCU for determination of fuel injection and ignition timing. The engine rpm measurement range is from 50 to (say) 8000 rpm. A resolution of about 10 rpm is required for an accuracy of about 0.2 percent. For injection and ignition control in a six-cylinder engine, the interval between combustion at maximum rpm is 2.5 ms, so that this time sets the injection period. In practice, a crank angle accuracy of between 1 and 2 degrees per revolution is required. Newer systems with sequential fuel injection, may also require information on TDC (top dead center) for each cylinder to determine the timing. With the low frequencies involved in this application, either Hall effect or MRE devices can be used for monitoring both the engine rpm and crank angle.

Vehicle speed measurements are in the range 0 to 180 km/h (120 mph) and digital displays must have an accuracy of 1 km/h. Some systems have a mechanical pickoff from the drive shaft, which can then use optical sensors for the measurement of road speed. However, newer systems have a pickoff located directly on the drive shaft, which makes optical devices less practical. It is preferred to eliminate the remote sensing via mechanical coupling to save the cost of the associated mechanical components, seals, maintenance, and so on. One method of pickoff is a ring magnet with between 4 and 20 magnetic poles (depending on the required resolution). Figure 7.6 shows such a system using an MRE sensing device. The magnetic flux changes are sensed by an MRE bridge sensor when the magnet disc is rotating. The bridge is supplied from a voltage reference circuit, and its output is amplified and shaped to give a frequency output that is proportional to shaft rotation speed. A ferrous toothed wheel pickoff with magnet and flux concentrator can also be used (see Fig. 7.2). Vehicle speed sensing can be performed with Hall effect, MRE, or VR devices. The number of pulses P per second from the detector are counted to measure speed S, from the following relationship:

$$P = N \times S \times K \tag{7.2}$$

where N = the number of magnetic poles on ring magnet or wheel teeth
    K = a constant determined by axle ratio and wheel size

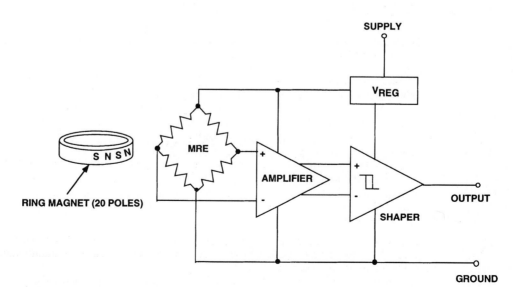

FIGURE 7.6   MRE speed-sensing module.

The resolution in vehicle speed is then:

$$\frac{P}{S} = N \times K \tag{7.3}$$

The typical system requirements are an operating temperature of −40 to 120 °C, rotational speed detection of 5 to 3000 rpm (1000 p/s), and a duty cycle ratio of 50 ± 10%.

In applications such as ABS, ASR, and four-wheel steering, additional speed sensors are attached to all four wheels so that the slip differential between the wheels can be measured. VR devices have been used and are very cost effective in this application. But the cost of other devices is dropping and as they become cost effective, they are being designed into new systems. In electronic transmission applications, information from the road and engine speed sensors, as well as torque data and throttle position are required for the MCU to select the optimum gear ratio. Electronic control can ensure smooth transition between gear ratios. Transmissions using electronic control are also smaller than conventional automatic transmissions, thus enabling more gear ratios for better performance, higher torque, efficiency, and acceleration.

Cruise control systems require information from the road and engine speed sensors to control the throttle position, and possibly the optimum selection of transmission ratios. Variable ratio assisted power steering also requires information from the wheel speed sensors for adjustment of the steering ratios for ease of turning at low speeds and good road control at high speeds. If automatic tire pressure adjustment becomes a reality, this system may also require information from the wheel speed sensors.

Another application for rotational speed sensing is to control the speed of the radiator cooling fan. The speed of the fan is determined by the coolant temperature. Hall effect devices (MRE can also be used) have been used to monitor the position of the armature and speed of the cooling fan motor. The motor controller uses this information to modulate the power to the motor through a three-phase bridge driving circuit for the control of the fan motor speed.

7.3.2 Linear Applications

Under linear applications are the detection of obstacles close to the vehicle, crash avoidance, distance of the chassis relative to the ground for ride control, measurement of ground speed for ABS, ASR, and inertial navigation. Ultrasonic devices are normally used for short distance measurements (<10 m) and RF devices for long distance measurements (see Sec. 7.6.2). For the measurement of objects from 0.5 to 2 m using ultrasonics, a pulse repetition rate of about 15 Hz is used. The reflected pulses take from 3 to 12 ms to return. The return time T is given by

$$L = C \times \frac{T}{2} \text{ (m)} \tag{7.4}$$

where L = distance to target
C = the transmission speed [given by $C = 331 + 0.6\,t$ (m/sec)]
T = temperature (at 15 °C), the speed of ultrasonic waves is 340 m/s.

In the case of chassis-to-ground measurements for ride control and ground speed measurements, the distance to be measured is from 15 to 50 cm and a higher pulse repetition rate can be used (up to 50 Hz). In this case, the reflected pulse takes from 0.9 to 3 ms to return. For ride control applications, an accelerometer has an advantage over distance measurement, in that it is unaffected by varying distance measurements over rough terrain.

7.4 ACCELERATION SENSING DEVICES

Acceleration sensors vary widely in their construction and operation. In applications such as crash sensors for air bag deployment, mechanical devices (simple mechanical switches) have been developed and are in use. Mechanical switches are normally located at the point of impact in the crash zone. With the development of micromachined devices, solid state analog accelerometers have been designed for air bag applications. The analog accelerometers are centrally placed on the automotive frame. These devices can be very cost effective when compared to mechanical switches and are rapidly replacing the electromechanical devices. Silicon micromachined sensors provide a higher degree of functionality, can be programmed, have high reliability, have excellent device-to-device uniformity, and can be integrated with memory circuits to create a more accurate sensor. Additional features such as self-test and diagnostics are also available.

7.4.1 Mechanical Sensing Devices

Mechanical switches are simple make-break devices. Figure 7.7 shows the cross section of a Breed type of switch or sensor. The device contains a spring, a metal ball, and electric contacts in a tube. On impact, the inertia in the ball causes it to move against the retaining force of the spring and closes the electric contacts at the end of travel. An alternative to this device is the one shown in Fig. 7.8. It consists of a cylindrical mass wound in a flat spring. The seismic mass

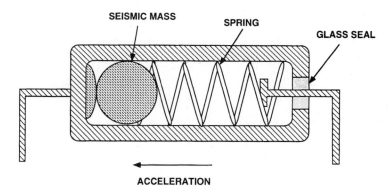

FIGURE 7.7 Cross section of mechanical sensor.

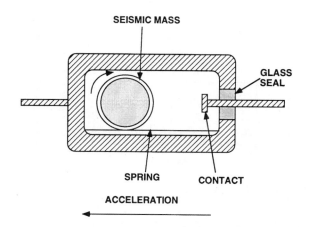

FIGURE 7.8 Cross section of mechanical switch.

rolls on impact against the spring tension, and again makes electrical contact at the end of travel. The machining tolerances on these devices are high and give wide variations in the acceleration trigger point.

7.4.2 Piezoelectric Sensing Devices

Piezoelectric devices consist of a layer of piezoelectric material (such as quartz) sandwiched between a mounting plate and a seismic mass. Electric connections are made to both sides of the piezoelectric material. The cross section of such a device is shown in Fig. 7.9. Piezoelectric material has the unique property that when a force or pressure is applied to opposite faces of the material, an electrical charge is produced. This charge can be amplified to give an output voltage that is proportional to the applied force. Piezoelectric devices can be effective in some applications, but are not suitable for sensing zero- or low-frequency acceleration, that is <5 Hz due to offset and temperature problems (pyroelectric effect). Piezoelectric sensors have a high Q, low damping, and a very high output impedance. Self-test features are also difficult to implement. The main advantages of piezoelectric devices are their wide operating temperature range (up to 300 °C), and high operating frequency (100 kHz).

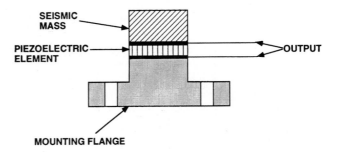

FIGURE 7.9 Cross section of a piezoelectric accelerometer.

Figure 7.10 shows a typical signal-conditioning circuit[2] and the trimming network used with piezoelectric sensors. The output from the sensor is fed to a charge amplifier, which converts the charge generated by the sensor into a voltage proportional to the charge. The circuit

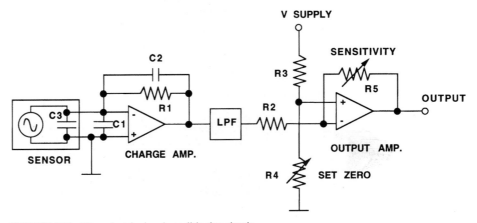

FIGURE 7.10 Piezoelectric signal-conditioning circuit.

is a modified virtual ground voltage amplifier. Feedback via capacitor C2 and resistor R1 is used to maintain the input at a virtual ground potential. This type of circuit minimizes the effect of stray or ground capacitance C1. The output voltage from the amplifier is fed via a low-pass filter (LPF) to an output amplifier, where it is trimmed for offset by R4 and sensitivity by R5. In system development, the sensitivity is set by the piezoelectric material used. Higher-sensitivity materials however, exhibit higher sensitivity to temperature variations.

7.4.3 Piezoresistive Sensing Devices

The property of some materials to change their resistivity when exposed to stress is called the piezoresistive effect. In silicon, the sensing resistors can be either P or N type doped regions, which can be very sensitive to strain. The resistors are also sensitive to temperature, so that the strain gauge is normally designed as a bridge configuration to minimize temperature effects and to obtain higher sensitivities (see also Chap. 2). In order to maintain good linearity, the operating temperature of piezoresistive devices is limited to about 100 °C. The nonlinearity is caused by excessive junction leakage current at high temperatures. Higher operating temperatures have been obtained using oxide-isolated strain gages (up to 175 °C). An uncompensated strain gauge has a typical error of 3 percent over the operating temperature range –20 to 80 °C. This error can be reduced with a compensating resistor, and still further reduced to about 0.5 percent by the use of thermistors, over an improved operating temperature range of –40 to 110 °C.

Piezoresistive sensing can be used with bulk micromachined accelerometers. Such a device is shown in Fig. 7.11. The strain-sensing elements are diffused into the suspension arms. These elements can then detect strain in the arms caused by acceleration forces on the seismic mass.

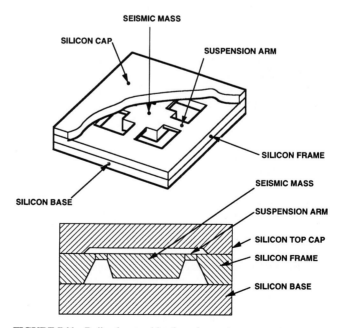

FIGURE 7.11   Bulk micromachined accelerometer.

7.4.4   Capacitive Sensing Devices

When used with micromachined structures as shown in Figs. 7.11 and 7.12, differential capacitive sensing has a number of attractive features when compared to other methods of sensing: easily implemented self-test, temperature insensitivity, and smaller size. In addition, comparing capacitive sensing to piezoelectric sensing reveals that capacitive sensing has the advantages of dc and low-frequency operation and well-controlled damping. When compared to piezoresistive sensing; differential capacitive sensing has the advantage of a wider operating temperature range and requires less complex trimming. Capacitive sensing has one other major advantage over other sensing methods in that it can be used in closed-loop servo systems. In these systems, voltages can be applied to the capacitive plates to produce electrostatic forces, which will balance the forces on the seismic mass due to acceleration. The main advantage of closed-loop operation is to make the sensor to a large extent independent of process variations. Signal-conditioning circuits can be designed to detect changes in capacitance of <0.1 fF, so that plate capacitances in the range of 200 to 400 fF can be used. The small spacing between capacitor plates in micromachining technology (2 μ) enables practical acceleration sensors as small as 500 μ × 500 μ. When designing capacitive sensors, care must be taken to ensure that the sensing voltages are properly balanced to minimize offsets due to electrostatic forces. These forces can also be produced by internal noise sources. The attributes of capacitive sensing are a linear response, operation over wide temperature ranges (−40 to 150 °C), and a frequency response from dc to about 2 kHz.

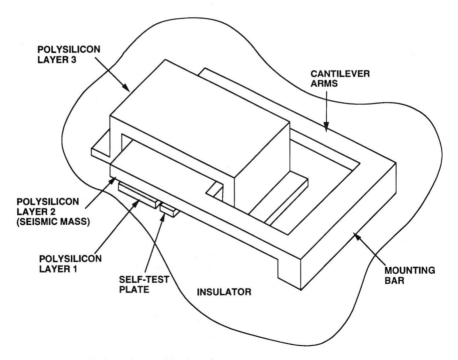

FIGURE 7.12   Surface micromachined accelerometer.

Micromachined Structures.   There are a variety of types of micromachined structures that can be used in accelerometers. These structures fall into two technologies: bulk micromachined structures and surface micromachined structures. Bulk micromachined devices are structures etched out of silicon wafers. Figure 7.11 shows the cross section of a bulk micromachined device consisting of three layers of silicon bonded together. The center layer is shaped to form a seismic mass suspended by four arms[3] (a cantilever structure has also been designed with two suspension arms[4]). When acted upon by acceleration forces, the seismic mass moves between the top and bottom plates. In this case, the movement can be sensed using piezoresistive elements diffused into the suspension arms, or differential capacitive sensing can be used between the seismic mass and the upper and lower silicon plates. The top and bottom plates can also be made of glass with metalized areas to form the top and bottom capacitors. Such devices have been designed to operate from the high g range (>1000 g), down to sensors with resolution in the μg range. Closed-loop control techniques are normally used in these lower g ranges.

The surface micromachined device shown in Fig. 7.12 is built using layers of polysilicon and sacrificial glass, which are alternately deposited and shaped. In this case, three layers of polysilicon and two layers of sacrificial glass were used. After deposition of the third polysilicon layer, the sacrificial glass is etched away leaving the freestanding structure as shown. A number of etch holes are normally placed in the second and third layer of polysilicon to speed up the etch process. These etch holes are also used to control the squeeze film damping and bandwidth of the device. The seismic mass of the second-layer polysilicon in these devices is of the order of 5×10^{-10} kg. A second plate under the middle polysilicon can be used for self-test. This function is achieved by applying a voltage to the self-test plate, which in turn will produce an electrostatic force on the center polysilicon plate causing it to deflect. This deflection will simulate an external acceleration force. An alternative to the polysilicon and glass structure is nickel with sacrificial copper.[5]

Differential capacitive sensing is used with all of these structures. Both bulk and surface micromachined devices have a very rugged construction. These devices use squeeze film damping to control bandwidth and to ensure critical damping of the resonant frequency (about 2 kHz for bulk and 10 kHz for surface micromachined devices). Film damping also ensures high resistance to shock in the sensing direction. In the directions perpendicular to the sensitive axes, the devices are rugged by construction with low cross-axis sensitivity (<3 percent). An accelerometer designed to sense a few g will typically have a shock tolerance of well over 5000 g. As already noted, surface micromachined devices that have been developed for air bag deployment have analog outputs. These devices normally operate from a 5-V supply, have a bandwidth of about 1 kHz and a sensitivity of 40 mV per g, giving a full-scale output with ±50 g input. Both open- and closed-loop techniques have been used for sensing. In comparing bulk and surface micromachined devices, the bulk structure is larger, using crystal-oriented etching with end stops, which require extra diffusions; whereas, the surface micromachined device uses isotropic etching (masking) with different materials acting as end stops. Surface structures have the potential for easier integration and use a simpler less costly process, but do require annealing.

Open-Loop Sensing.   Open-loop signal-conditioning circuits amplify and convert the capacitance changes into a voltage. Such a CMOS circuit using switched capacitor techniques is shown in Fig. 7.13. The circuit contains a virtual ground amplifier to minimize the effect of stray capacitance. The positive input of the amplifier is referenced to a voltage of $V_{REF}/2$, when switch S2 is closed the amplifier has unity gain, and the voltage on the middle plate of the sensor is set to $V_{REF}/2$. After S2 is opened, S1 is switched so that any differences between sensor capacitors C_1 and C_2 produces a charge at the negative input of the amplifier. This charge produces a voltage (V_{out}) at the output of the integrating amplifier. The output voltage of the amplifier is given by

$$V_{out} = V_{REF} \frac{C_1 - C_2}{C_3} \tag{7.5}$$

where C_1 and C_2 are the sensor capacitances
  C_3 is the integrator capacitance

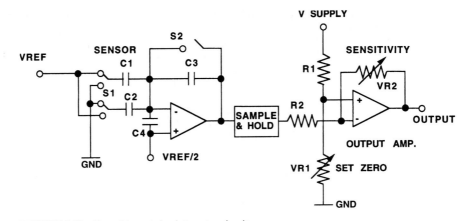

FIGURE 7.13 Capacitive sensing integrator circuit.

If the reference voltage is made proportional to the supply voltage, a ratiometric output is obtained. That is, the system gain is proportional to the supply voltage. This is a requirement in some systems to facilitate the design of the A/D converter.

A block diagram of the system is shown in Fig. 7.14. The system contains an internal oscillator, voltage reference, amplifier, sample and hold, switched capacitor filter, trim network, and output buffer. The output voltage in such a circuit is proportional to the capacitance change. This change is proportional to 1/displacement, or 1/acceleration, giving rise to some nonlinearities. However, the displacement is small compared to the spacing between the plates, so that the output voltage approximates to acceleration, giving less than 3 percent nonlinearity. The filter is used for noise reduction and to set the bandwidth for specific applications. Trimming is used to set the zero operating point and sensitivity of the system.

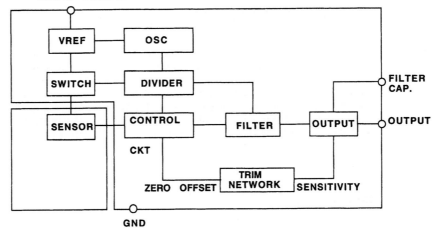

FIGURE 7.14 Signal-conditioning block diagram.

An alternate circuit with improved linearity is shown in Fig. 7.15. In this case, the output voltage is fed back to the input of the integrator, forming a bridge circuit. The feedback also sets the amplitude of the driving voltage across the sensing capacitors, so that it is proportional to their displacement. This also balances the electrostatic forces on the middle plate.

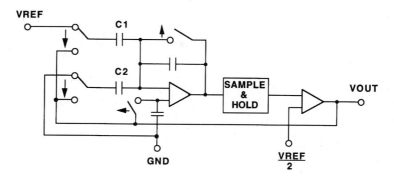

FIGURE 7.15   Linearized circuit schematic.

In this case

$$V_{\text{out}} = \frac{(C_1 - C_2)}{(C_1 + C_2)} \frac{V_{\text{REF}}}{2} \tag{7.6}$$

where

$$C_1 \propto 1/d_1$$
$$C_2 \propto 1/d_2$$
$$d_1 + d_2 = K \text{ (constant)}$$

so that

$$V_{\text{out}} = V_{\text{in}} \frac{(d_1 - d_2)}{K} \tag{7.7}$$

showing that, in this case, V_{out} is proportional to displacement and acceleration giving improved linearity (<1 percent nonlinearity).

Closed-Loop Sensing.   An alternative to the open-loop sensing circuit is the closed-loop sensing circuit, which can be configured to give an analog or digital output. Figure 7.16a shows the balanced electrostatic forces exerted on a seismic mass by upper and lower capacitor plates, which are at voltages of $+V$ and $-V$. If the seismic mass experiences a force due to acceleration, and a voltage δV is applied to the middle plate to generate enough electrostatic force to counterbalance the acceleration force, then the forces are as shown in Fig. 7.16b.

That is

$$m \times a = \frac{C(V + \delta V)^2}{2d} - \frac{C(V - \delta V)^2}{2d} \tag{7.8}$$

from which

$$m \times a = 2 C \times V \times \frac{\delta V}{d} \tag{7.9}$$

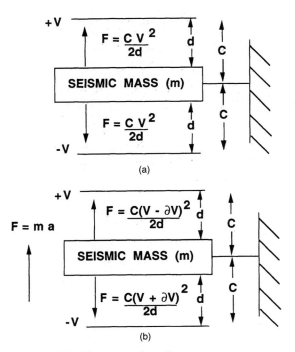

FIGURE 7.16 Electrostatic force diagram.

This shows that an acceleration force can be balanced by a linear voltage applied to the center plate. This voltage can be amplified to give a linear output voltage proportional to acceleration.[6]

In a micromachined structure, the electrostatic force produced by a δV of about 1 V can counterbalance the force produced by an acceleration of 50 g on the seismic mass. Figure 7.17 shows a block diagram of the analog closed-loop system. The top and bottom plates are dc-biased by the resistor divider network consisting of R1, R2, and R3. The ac antiphase signals used for sensing the position of the center plate are fed to the top and bottom sensor plates via the capacitors (C1, C2) from the control logic. The analog output voltage from the filter is feedback to the positive input of the integrator. When the integrator is clocked into the unity gain phase, the feedback voltage is applied to the center plate of the sensor. The electrostatic forces produced on the center plate by the differential voltage between the top and bottom plates, and the feedback voltage on the center plate, will force the center plate back to its normalized position as given in Eq. (7.9). Other methods that have been used for closed-loop operation are pulse width modulation (PWM), and delta sigma modulation (DSM).

The block diagram and waveforms of a PWM system are shown in Fig. 7.18. In this case, the center plate is held at a fixed voltage (0). The output of the integrator is amplified and converted into a PWM signal (VP), this signal and the inverted signal (VPN) are fed to the top and bottom plates of the sensor. The leading edges of the VP and VPN signals are used to sense the position of the middle plate. The electrostatic force generated by the voltage × time differential between the middle plate and the top and bottom plates, will act on the middle plate to counterbalance the forces on the plate due to acceleration. With zero acceleration, the PWM signal has a 50 percent duty cycle, so that the resulting electrostatic forces on the seismic mass are zero. The transfer function of the PWM system is given by

$$\text{Duty cycle} = \frac{\text{Acc} \times g \times d}{C \times V_{\text{REF}}^2} \tag{7.10}$$

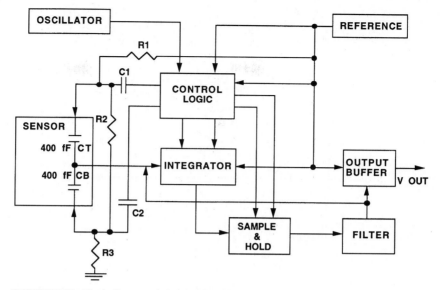

FIGURE 7.17   Block diagram of analog closed-loop system.

where g = gravitational constant
  d = plate spacing
  C = plate capacitance

The output can either be the PWM digital signal, or an analog output (obtained by feeding the PWM signal through a low pass filter).

Figure 7.19 shows the block diagram and waveforms of a DSM system. In this case, the middle plate is held at VF (volts). As can be seen, transient edges of the plate-drive waveforms are used for sensing the position of the center plate. The output from the integrator is fed to a comparator, whose output is then clocked into a latch where it sets up a "1" or a "0" (high or low) depending on the output from the integrator. The output from the latch is used to apply a voltage V_{REF} to the appropriate top or bottom capacitor plate, so that the electrostatic forces generated by the voltage V_{REF} − VF will maintain the center plate in its no-load position. The one-bit serial data stream from the latch can be fed directly to the MCU, or fed via a decimator circuit (which will convert the data into an 8-bit word) to the MCU. Alternatively, an LPF can be used to convert the data into an analog output. Bipolar or CMOS circuits can be used for signal conditioning. However, CMOS signal conditioning has the following advantages: a very high input impedance, good switching characteristics, low power requirements, small size, compatibility with MCU processes with the prospect of future integration, switched capacitor filters are available for noise reduction and bandwidth control, and EPROM technology is available for trimming (see Fig. 7.14). BiMOS circuits have also been used for signal conditioning.[6] In the BiMOS circuits, thin-film resistors are used to enable laser trimming of the zero offset and voltage reference; external capacitors and resistors are used for filtering and gain control.

Single vs. Multichip Control Circuits.   The processing of sensors is not completely compatible with IC fabrication. Consequently, for the integration of sensors and ICs, a number of additional steps are required, which can have a detrimental effect on yields. The question then arises as to which is the most cost effective: a sensor die plus a control die with the additional cost of assembly, or a monolithic approach.

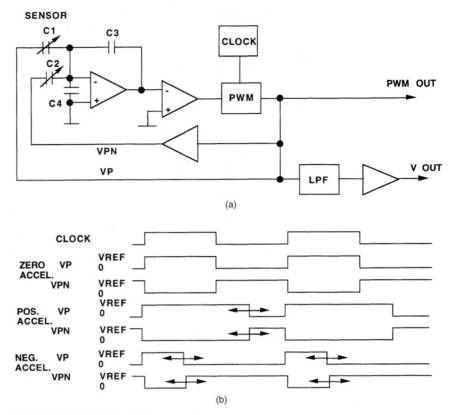

FIGURE 7.18   PWM block diagram.

In the case of micromachined devices, there are a number of advantages to using the dual-chip approach, such as flexibility, in that one type of sensor can be interfaced with a number of different types of control die, or several types of sensors can be interfaced with one type of control die. This provides a variety of input and output options. The control die and sensor can be developed simultaneously, minimizing development time. Problem solving is made easier, and the processing for both die can be optimized for performance. With the two-die approach, the sensor can also be capped and sealed during processing in a clean room atmosphere, thus eliminating contaminants and particles for good longevity. In the monolithic approach, this is not the case. In the monolithic approach, changes required to improve one section can affect the other section, which may then require additional changes in that section. The main disadvantage of the dual-chip approach is the introduction of parasitic capacitances. However, these can be addressed by existing control circuit design techniques.

7.5   AUTOMOTIVE APPLICATIONS FOR ACCELEROMETERS

Accelerometers have a wide variety of uses in the automobile. The initial application is as a crash sensor for air bag deployment. This application is normally associated with head-on collisions, but can also be applied to rear-end impact collisions to prevent rebound impact between the passengers and the windshield. An extension of this application is the use of

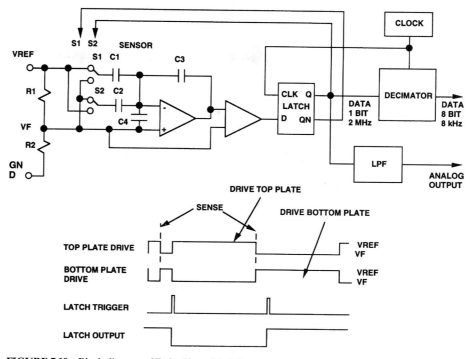

FIGURE 7.19 Block diagram of Delta Sigma Modulator.

accelerometers for the detection of side impact. This application will require additional air bags to the side of the occupants. Other low *g* linear accelerometers are being developed for ride control, ABS, traction, and inertial navigation applications.

Solid state acceleration sensors have special mounting requirements that are different from normal integrated circuits. These are to ensure that acceleration forces are transmitted to the sensor package. An advantage of the solid state device is self-test features for diagnostics. In acceleration applications, the devices are required to operate over the temperature range −40 to 85 °C (125 °C under the hood), and to withstand >2000 *g* shock. Other similar devices that have application in the automotive arena are vibration devices.

7.5.1 Air Bag Deployment Application

Crash sensors that use mechanical switches (sensors) are typically located some 40 cm from the point of impact, which necessitates the use of multiple sensors (normally 3 to 5 sensors are used in multipoint sensing) for crash sensing and air bag deployment. These devices are velocity change detectors, and are calibrated to make contact when the change of velocity in the passenger compartment is at least 20 km/h, this being the velocity change at which the front seat occupants will strike the windshield.

A centrally located analog sensor can be used as a crash sensor (single point). In the case of a centrally located accelerometer, the g level to be sensed is lower than that of a point-of-impact device. However, only one device is required to monitor the crash signature. This signature will vary with different types of chassis and different types of impacts. Consequently, an MCU is used to monitor the output of the accelerometer to determine if a crash has occurred. The typical output of a centrally located accelerometer during a 48 km/h crash is shown in Fig. 7.20. Deceleration of the vehicle and occupant displacement are also shown. At 48 km/h, the sensor has 20 ms to detect the crash and trigger the air bag. This results in inflation of the air bag 50 ms after impact, at which time the occupant has moved about 18 cm or approximately halfway to the windshield and at the contact point with the inflated air bag. During the initial 20 ms, deceleration can reach 20 g, but the average is about 5 g when the air bag is triggered. The centrally located accelerometer can take one of several forms: a piezo-electric sensor, a piezoresistive device, or a capacitive sensor.

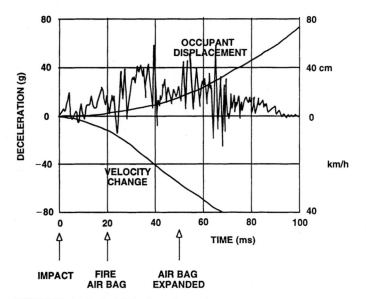

FIGURE 7.20   Typical 48 km/h crash waveform.

The centrally located accelerometer has a number of performance advantages over its mechanical counterpart. These are the reduction in the number of sensors and required buss-ing, which makes the centrally located system much more cost effective. There is an improve-ment in sensing and signal-processing accuracy with the single-point sensing accelerometer over the mechanical sensor. This gives a better-defined trigger point and overall improved performance across different chassis types. Capacitive sensors appear to have the edge in this application, because they have the potential of being cost effective, meet the requirements of the application, and have self-test features plus diagnostics available. In this application, a typ-ical accelerometer specification is ±50 g full-scale output, accuracy ±5 percent over tempera-ture, bandwidth dc to 750 Hz, and cross-axis sensitivity <3 percent. During impact, the crash sensor can also be used for seat belt locking.

7.5.2 Ride Control Application

In ride control systems, the leaf or coil springs located on the axles are replaced by four *wheel stations,* which form an active suspension. Each wheel station contains an oil-filled cylinder with a piston to set the distance of the frame above the axles and to isolate the frame from axle vibration. This is achieved using a servo feedback system. When a vehicle with conven-tional suspension encounters a foreign object on the highway, the load on the wheel increases as it moves up to negotiate the obstacle. This load increase makes the vehicle rise up. With a fully active suspension, the increase in load is detected and a servo valve is opened to transfer the necessary amount of oil from the appropriate cylinder to a storage container. Conse-quently, the load exerted on the chassis by each wheel is maintained at its specific level and the chassis remains at its static level. After the object has been traversed, oil is pumped back into the cylinder to reestablish the static load conditions.

An alternative to the active suspension is the adaptive suspension system. In this case, information from the front wheels is gathered and used to predict road conditions for the control of the rear wheels. The advantage over the fully active suspension is one of cost, as the number of acceleration sensors is halved. During cornering, oil is also pumped into the outside wheel cylinders to minimize roll angle.[7]

A combination of sensors is used for active suspension. These are accelerometers, wheel speed sensors, chassis-to-ground sensing, and piston-level sensing in the suspension system. The low g accelerometers used on the axles of the four wheels to detect the load changes on the wheels have the following specifications: ± 2 g full-scale, accuracy ± 5 percent over temperature, bandwidth dc to 10 Hz, and cross-axis sensitivity <3 percent. The acceleration information and data from the wheel speed sensors is used to provide the information necessary for the MCU to operate the servo control valves. Hall effect, MRE, and opto sensors have been used for monitoring the level of the pistons in the wheel stations cylinders.

7.5.3 Vibration Applications

Lean-burn engines are being developed for improved emission levels and for better fuel economy (10 to 15 percent improvement). NO_x emissions are greatly reduced to meet federal standards. Lean-burn engines use high stoichiometric ratios; 20:1 and higher are necessary. At these ratios, combustion becomes unstable and torque fluctuations large. Consequently, antiknock and vibration sensors are required to supply the information necessary to the MCU, so that it can adjust the injected fuel amount and ignition timing for stability over widely varying conditions.

There are two types of solid state sensors that can be used in this application: piezoelectric devices and capacitively coupled vibration sensors. A typical vibration sensor contains a number of fingers of varying length which vibrate at their resonant frequencies when those frequencies are encountered. The resonance is capacitively coupled to the sensing circuit, and the outputs as shown are obtained. Optical sensors have also been used as antiknock sensors. In this case, the ignition spectrum is monitored for the detection of misfiring or knocking. Vibration sensors can also be used for vibration monitoring in maintenance applications.

7.5.4 Antilock Brake System Applications

In antilock brake systems, speed sensors are attached to all wheels to determine wheel rotation speed and slip differential between wheels. VR devices, as well as Hall effect and MRE devices, can be used in this application, as zero speed sensing is not required. VR devices have been used and shown to be cost effective in this application, but Hall effect and MRE devices are now being designed into these systems. Pressure sensors are used to monitor brake fluid pressure, and an accelerometer or ground-speed sensor can be used to provide information on changes in the vehicular speed. Brake pedal position and brake fluid pressure information are also required for control. All of this information is fed to an MCU, which processes the data and adjusts the brake fluid pressure to each wheel for optimum braking. Many of the elements of the ABS system can be used for the detection of lateral slippage on high-speed cornering, and can be used for traction and the direction of power to the wheels. Traction control applies in particular to slippery surfaces and with four-wheel-drive vehicles. Additional information over that used in ABS systems is required by the MCU for ASR applications, such as engine speed and throttle angle. In this application, servo feedback to the throttle may also be necessary.

A more cost-effective, but less accurate, system for ABS and ASR is the adaptive control system in which accelerometers are normally used to measure deceleration when braking, and acceleration when the throttle is opened. If skidding occurs during braking, the brake pressure is reduced and adjusted for maximum deceleration, or the throttle adjusted for maximum traction. Typical specifications for the accelerometer required in this application are: ±1 g full-scale output, accuracy ±5 percent over temperature, bandwidth 0.5 to 50 Hz, and cross-axis sensitivity <3 percent.

7.6   NEW SENSING DEVICES

New cost-effective sensors are continually being developed. The technology and cost are often pushed by the application and volume requirements of the automotive industry and federal mandates. Today's silicon sensors and control electronics are limited in operating temperature to 150 °C to ensure long life of the devices. This operational temperature is adequate for most applications, but higher temperature operation may be required for sensors mounted in the engine compartment. The limit on the operating temperature of silicon devices can be extended to between 200 and 250 °C by the use of special isolation techniques such as dielectric isolation (this operating temperature applies to surface micromachined devices). For higher-temperature operation, alternative materials such as GaAs or SiC are being developed, but the cost of these devices limits their use at present.

A list of semiconductor conductor materials and maximum practical operating temperatures is given in Table 7.3. Higher operating temperatures have been reported but with poor longevity.

TABLE 7.3   Device Operating Temperatures

Material	Maximum practical operating temperature, °C
Si	150
Si (dielectric iso.)	250
GaAs	300
AlGaAs	350
GaP	400
SiC	500

7.6.1   New Rotational Speed-Sensing Devices

A number of new devices are being investigated to detect magnetic fields. These are flux gate, Weigand effect, magnetic transistor, and magnetic diode. The magnetic transistor at present is showing the most promise. The device operates on a similar principle to the Hall effect device. That is, the current division between split collectors (bipolar) or split drains (MOS) can be changed by a magnetic field. This current differential can then be detected and amplified to give an output voltage proportional to magnetic field strength. These devices can use either majority or minority carriers, and can be either vertical or lateral bipolar or MOS devices. The magnetic transistor has the potential of higher sensitivity than the Hall effect device.

Figure 7.21 shows the cross section of a lateral PNP magnetic transistor. The current from each collector is equal until a magnetic field is applied perpendicular to the surface of the device. The magnetic field causes an imbalance of current between the two collectors. Sensitivities with this type of structure have been reported as being an order of magnitude greater than in the Hall effect device.[8] Magnetic transistors and diodes can be directly integrated with the signal-conditioning circuits, which could make them very cost effective in future applications. A comparison of the magnetic transistor to other practical devices is given in Table 7.2.

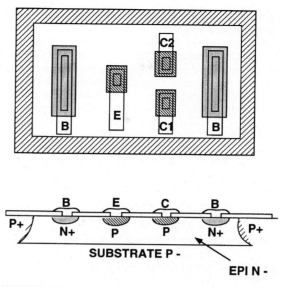

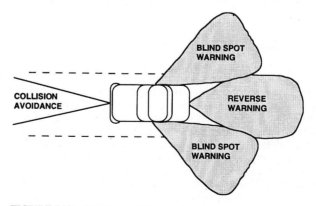

FIGURE 7.21   Cross section of a field-assisted PNP magnetic transistor.

7.6.2   New Linear Speed-Sensing Devices

A number of different sensing technologies can be used for distance, object detection, and approach speed measurements. Shown in Fig. 7.22 are the areas covered by blind-spot, rear, and forward-looking sensors. Ultrasonics, infrared, laser, and microwaves (radar) can be used in the detection of objects behind vehicles and in the blind areas. From a practical standpoint, no technology has come to the forefront. However, with new innovations in technology the situation may change very rapidly. Ultrasonics and infrared sensors are cost effective but degrade with inclement weather conditions such as ice, rain, snow, and the accumulation of road grime. Infrared devices are also color-sensitive, in that the sensitivity to shiny black objects is very low compared to other colors. Microwave devices appear to have the edge

FIGURE 7.22   Collision-avoidance patterns.

when considering environmental conditions,[9] but are expensive, and radar can be affected by false return signals and clutter.

For the detection of obstacles and vehicles in front of a vehicle, the choice is between laser and microwaves due to the distances involved (up to 90 m). Microwaves have the disadvantage of high cost and large antenna size when considering available devices in the 60 GHz range. Frequencies greater than 100 GHz are preferred for acceptable antenna size. However, collision avoidance radar in the 76/77-GHz band has been developed in Europe. Collision avoidance radar in the 77, 94, and 144 GHz is being considered in the United States. A typical system uses a 38.5-GHz VCO (voltage controlled oscillator) with frequency-doubling to obtain about 40 mW of power at 77 GHz. A frequency-modulated continuous wave or pulse-modulated system can be used. The system uses GaAs devices to meet the frequency and power requirements. Lasers can be cost effective in this application, but also have their drawbacks: degradation of performance by fog, reflections from other light sources (sun, etc.), build-up of road grime on sensor surfaces, and poor reflecting surfaces at laser frequencies, such as grimy and shiny black surfaces.

7.6.3 New Inertial and Acceleration-Sensing Devices

Recent developments in solid state technology have made possible very small cost-effective devices to sense angular rotation. The implementation of one such gyroscopic device is shown in Fig. 7.23. This device is fabricated on a silicon substrate using surface micromachining techniques. In this case, three layers of polysilicon are used, with the first and third layers being fixed and the second layer free to vibrate about its center. The center is held in position by four spring arms attached to four mounting posts as shown. This device can sense rotation about the X and Y axes and sense acceleration in the direction of the Z axis. The center layer of polysilicon, driven by electrostatic forces, vibrates about the Z axis. These forces are produced by voltages applied between the fixed comb fingers and the comb fingers of the second polysilicon. Capacitor plates as shown are formed between the first and third polysilicon on the X and Y axes, and the second layer of polysilicon. Differential capacitive sensing techniques can then be used to sense any displacement of the vibrating disc caused by angular rotation. For example, if angular rotation takes place about the X axis, Coriolis forces produce a deflection of the disc about the Y axis. This deflection can be detected by the capacitor plates on the X axis. The sensing of the three functions is achieved by using a common sensing circuit that alternatively senses the X rotation, Y rotation, and acceleration. The gyroscope is designed to have a resolution of <10 degrees per hour for angular rate measurements, and an acceleration resolution of 0.5 mg.

7.7 FUTURE APPLICATIONS

New applications to increase creature comfort and safety are constantly being developed, but their rate of introduction will depend on the cost effectiveness of the technology, demand, and government mandates. Other concerns of automotive manufacturers are size, weight, power requirements, and adverse effects on styling and appearance. Many of the new sensor technologies are in their infancy, and thus are not yet cost effective on medium- and low-priced automobiles, but are being made available as options on luxury cars.

7.7.1 Future Rotational Speed-Sensing Applications

A future application for speed-sensing devices will be in continuously variable transmissions. In this application, engine and wheel speed, as well as torque, will be measured, and the infor-

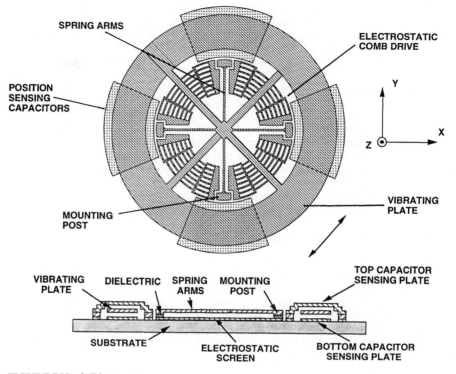

FIGURE 7.23   Solid state gyroscope.

mation processed by an MCU to optimize transmission ratios for engine performance and efficiency. All-wheel steering is also under development, and requires speed-sensing information, in addition to steering, front-, and rear-wheel angle position data for processing and control.

7.7.2   Future Linear Speed-Sensing Applications

Another application that has been developed is the use of speed- and distance-measuring devices for collision avoidance. These devices fall into three categories: near-obstacle detection (rear), blind-spot detection, and semiautomatic frontal object detection and control[9] (see Fig. 7.22).

Near-obstacle detection is used to prevent accidents during reversing. Blind-spot detection is used to prevent accidents due to careless lane changing, and when backing out of a driveway, garage, or alley into traffic. The semiautomatic frontal detection is a long-range system. The distance and closing speed between vehicles, or between a vehicle and a fixed object, can be measured and the speed adjusted as necessary to avoid a collision,[10] or the driver can be warned of impending danger. An addition to this is to monitor road surface conditions for friction—for example, dry roads compared to wet or icy roads—and also to use this information to adjust approach speeds and distance. Without collision avoidance, road condition monitoring can be used to caution vehicle operators. Collision avoidance systems can be used to minimize collisions, or can be used to operate protection systems before an unavoidable collision happens to protect the automobile passengers. In this case, vehicles closing at or approaching an obstacle at 80 km/h will be less than 7 m apart before a collision-is-imminent determination can be made. This gives 200 ms decision-making time for the system MCU. This is, however, long compared to today's air bag deployment systems, which have 20 ms decision-making time after the event. In the future, an idealistic system may be a combination of the two systems.

7.7.3   Future Acceleration Applications

One of the future applications being considered is the expansion of the air bag system to include side impact protection. The sensor used for crash sensing is unidirectional, so that it can only detect forward impact. A similar sensor, mounted perpendicular to the air bag sensor, can be added to the system to detect side impact and to deploy protection for the passengers. This device will typically require a 250-g accelerometer. Another application for accelerometers is to detect slippage during cornering in advanced steering systems. These systems will employ a low-g accelerometer (1–2 g).

7.7.4   Inertial Navigation Applications

A number of inertial navigation systems are being developed for short- and long-range travel. Long-range inertial navigation systems normally obtain their location by using a triangulation method. This method references three navigation satellites with known locations in fixed orbits. However, there are certain conditions under which contact with all three satellites is lost. This occurs when the vehicle is in the shadow of tall buildings or high hills, and triangulation is not possible. Under these conditions, the guidance system has to rely on such devices as gyroscopes, which sense angular rotation or change in direction, and/or monitor vehicular motion relative to the road.

Short-range inertial navigation systems or inertial measurement units (IMU) rely to a large extent on high-accuracy accelerometers and gyroscopes. A typical accelerometer specification for this application is: ±2-g full-scale output, accuracy 0.5 percent over temperature, bandwidth dc to 20 Hz, and a cross-axis sensitivity <0.5 percent. A centrally located IMU can be expanded to cover other applications such as suspension, ABS, ASR, and working with crash avoidance sensors. This may be the way to handle cost-effective system design in the future. The IMU can also be designed to provide location data for intelligent vehicle highway systems. These systems (Prometheus,[11] Amtics[12]) improve travel efficiency and reduce fuel consumption and pollution by selecting the optimum route to a given destination. The route is chosen to avoid traffic congestion, road construction, and accidents (see Chap. 29).

7.8   SUMMARY

In this chapter, a number of speed-sensing devices, both rotary and linear, have been described, together with potential applications. VR, MRE, Hall effect, and opto devices (possibly magnetic transistor in future applications) can be used in rotational applications for engine control, transmission, and wheel speed sensing. Of these devices, Hall effect, VR, and opto have been widely used. With the tendency for direct pickoff, optical devices may become impractical. MRE devices are being designed in and will become a serious contender to the Hall effect device. In linear applications for crash avoidance, microwave devices have the edge over performance and optical devices in terms of cost. However, as the cost of microwave devices declines, they could become cost effective. For blind-area alert and reversing obstacle detection, ultrasonics and infrared devices are cost effective, but performance degrades during inclement weather.

The accelerometer has possibly the greatest potential for applications in the automobile. These applications range from crash sensing, ride control, ABS, and ASR to IMU systems. Accelerometers needed will range in sensitivities from 50 *g* in crash sensing to 1 *g* in the IMU. Advances in technology are providing a number of new sensors that are showing potential, such as the magneto transistor and the micromachined gyroscope. To summarize, Figs. 7.24 and 7.25 show the types of sensors used in specific applications, and the technologies used for specific sensors. As can be seen, one type of sensor can be used in a number of applications. In applications where a sensor output is shared, care must be taken to ensure that a failure in one system does not disable the sensor or other systems. Because of the similarities in several of the systems and the use of shared sensors, the greatest potential for cost-effective system design is a single control system. The IMU shows great potential to be the controller for ride control, ABS, ASR, four-wheel-drive, and steering applications. The rate of introduction of new sensors and systems will depend on federal mandates, customer demand, and the need to improve engine fuel efficiency and to reduce emissions.

GLOSSARY

Adaptive suspension A suspension system that monitors motion of the front wheels and adjusts the suspension of the rear axle accordingly.

Arntics Acronym for Advanced Mobile Traffic Information and Communication System.

ASR (traction) A system to prevent wheel spin on slippery surfaces, to give maximum traction and acceleration.

Sensor \ Application	Air Bag Deployment	Ride Control	ABS	Engine Control	Transmission	4 Wheel Drive	All Wheel Stearing	Engine Vibrarion	Cruise Control	Seat Belts	Power Steering Assist	Traction (ASR)	Collision Avoidance	Obstacle Detection	Inertial Navigation
Speed Rotation	USED	USED	USED	USED	USED	USED	USED		USED		USED	USED			
Speed Linear			MAY BE USED		MAY BE USED				MAY BE USED		MAY BE USED	MAY BE USED	MAY BE USED	MAY BE USED	MAY BE USED
Acceleration	USED	USED	USED	USED						USED		USED			USED
Vibration								USED							
Angular Rotation															USED

USED MAY BE USED

FIGURE 7.24 Sensor applications.

Measurand / Sensing Technique	Mechanical	Piezoelectric	Piezoresistive	Capacitive	Optical	Infrared	Radar	Laser	Ultrasonic	Hall Effect	Variable Reluctance	Magnetoresistive
Speed Rotation					▨					▨	▨	▨
Speed Linear						▨	▨	▨	▨			
Acceleration	▨	▨	▨	▨								
Vibration		▨		▨								
Angular Rotation				▨								

FIGURE 7.25 Sensor technologies.

Coriolis forces   Forces exerted by a spinning body to oppose any motion at right angles to the axle.

Crash signature   Shock waveform projected through a chassis during a collision.

Inertial navigation   Guidance system giving accurate location.

IMU (inertial measurement unit)   System used for guidance between two locations indicates road hazards and delays.

Lean burn   Engine with high compression ratios and high air-to-fuel ratios for increased efficiency and low emissions.

Micromachining   Manufacturing technology for micromechanical structures using chemical etching techniques.

NO$_x$ Chemical symbol for oxides of nitrogen.

Prometheus   Acronym for PROgraM for a European Traffic with Highest Efficiency and Unprecedented Safety.

Switched capacitor filter   Technique for switching capacitors to simulate high-value resistors for low-frequency filters to minimize size.

REFERENCES

1. Osamu Ina, Yoshimi Yoshino, and Makio Lida, "Recent Intelligent Sensor Technology in Japan," S.A.E. paper 891709, 1989.
2. D. E. Bergfried, Mattes, B., and Rutz, R., "Electronic Crash Sensors for Restraint Systems," *Proceedings of the International Congress on Transportation Electronics,* Detroit, Oct. 1990, pp. 169–177.

3. E. Peeters, Vergote, S., Puers, B., and Sansen, W., "A Highly Symmetrical Capacitive Microaccelerometer with Single Degree of Freedom Response," *Tranducers 91,* 1991, pp. 97–103.

4. J. T. Suminto, "A Simple High Performance Piezoresistive Accelerometer," *Transducers 91,* 1991, pp. 104–107.

5. J. C. Cole, "A New Capacitive Technology for Low-Cost Accelerometer Applications," *Sensors Expo. International,* 1989.

6. T. A. Core, Tsang, W. K., and Sherman, S. J., "Fabrication Technology for an Integrated Surface-Micromachined Sensor," *Solid State Technology,* Oct. 1993, pp. 39–47.

7. H. Wallentowitz, "Scope for the Integration of Powertrain and Chassis Control Systems: Traction Control—All Wheel Drive—Active Suspension," *Proceedings of the International Conference on Transportation Electronics,* S.A.E. paper 901168, 1990.

8. H. Kaneko, Muro, H., and French, P. J., "Optimization of Bipolar Magneto-Transistors," *Micro Systems Technologies 90,* 1990, pp. 599–604.

9. L. Raffaelli, Stewart, E., Borelli, J., and Quimby, R., "Monolithic Components for 77 GHz Automotive Collision Avoidance Radars," *Proceedings Sensors Expo,* 1993, pp. 261–268.

10. S. Aono, "Electronic Applications for Enhancing Automotive Safety," *Proceedings of the International Conference on Transportation Electronics,* SAE 901137, 1990, pp. 179–186.

11. J. Hellaker, "Prometheus-Strategy," *Proceedings of the International Congress Transportation Electronics,* SAE 901139, 1990, pp. 195–200.

12. H. Okamoto, and Hase, M., "The Progress of Amtics-Advanced Mobile Traffic Information and Communication System," *Proceedings of the International Congress Transportation Electronics,* SAE 901142, 1990, pp. 217–224.

ABOUT THE AUTHOR

William C. Dunn is a member of the technical staff in the Advanced Custom Technologies group at Motorola's Semiconductor Product Sector in Phoenix, Arizona. He has over 30 years' experience in circuit design and systems engineering. For the past 15 years he has been involved in the development of semiconductor sensors, smart power devices, and control systems for the automotive market. Prior to joining Motorola, he worked for several large corporations in the United Kingdom and United States, has written over 30 papers, and has over 30 patents issued and pending on mechanical sensor structures, semiconductor technology, and circuit design.

CHAPTER 8
ENGINE KNOCK SENSORS

William G. Wolber
Executive Engineer
Cummins Electronics Co., Inc.

8.1 INTRODUCTION

Knock is a phenomenon characterized by undesirable structural vibration and noise generation and is peculiar to spark-ignited engines. Knock is undesirable both from a customer acceptance standpoint and also because severe knock can cause engine damage. The terms *ping* (light, barely observable knock) and *predetonation* (knock caused by ignition of the charge slightly before the full ignition of the flame front by the spark plug) are also commonly used in the industry, and not always with precision.

Historically, knock became an important engine phenomenon in the 1930s. In their search for performance improvements, designers of spark-ignited engines increased compression ratios beyond the capabilities of the gasoline formulations available to provide smooth, knock-free combustion. The discovery of gasoline additives such as tetraethyl lead, which improve the stability of the combustion process primarily by decreasing burn rate, permitted the fuel suppliers to provide a range of fuel knock properties at the pump to match with the range of engine requirements. As a result, by 1950, knock was not regarded as a significant engine performance limiting parameter since the car company could specify what fuel should be selected, ranging from "regular" to "super premium" grades. A blending fuel pump was even provided by one fuel company which allowed the operator of the vehicle to select exactly what grade of fuel he or she wished to use from a selection of six grades.

In the late 1960s, the situation began to change drastically. In response to public concern about air quality and health, legislation on automotive emissions became a new constraint on automotive engine design, first in the United States and more recently worldwide. The use of fuel additives to improve gasoline knock characteristics fell into disfavor for two reasons:

• Many of the better additives resulted in combustion products not desirable in the air. For example, most lead compounds are toxic at low levels to human and animal life.

• As engine designers strove to provide lower engine emissions, the use of the three-way catalytic converter cleanup device in the exhaust system became nearly universal. Unfortunately, most good fuel additives that improve knock characteristics poison the catalyst of the converter, rendering it ineffective. Also, many engine controls began to make use of the oxygen sensor feedback control loop. The catalyst on the oxygen sensor also is poisoned by the better additives.

This situation led to gradually more stringent federal regulation of the fuel industry, a trend which, in the end, legislated fuels with knock-improving additives completely off the market, so that by the mid 1980s, all spark-ignited automobile engines in the United States were being operated using lead-free gasoline. Of course, as leaded gasoline disappeared, the knock phenomenon returned. The auto industry knew what to do—lower compression ratios—but this step alone has accompanying negative consequences, such as lower fuel economy. Thus, the situation was one driven by the need to optimize between several principal goals: emission regulations, fuel supply characteristics, fuel economy goals, customer acceptability, and vehicle performance.

8.2   THE KNOCK PHENOMENON

8.2.1   Definition

Spark-ignited engine knock has been defined as "an undesirable mode of combustion that originates spontaneously and sporadically in the engine, producing sharp pressure pulses associated with a vibratory movement of the charge and the characteristic sound from which the phenomenon derives its name."[1] This definition at once conveys some of the difficulties of measuring the phenomenon and devising engine controls to minimize it. First, the ultimate standard is the reaction of the human to the vibration felt or the sound heard as a result of the knock. An attempt to measure the cause of the phenomenon leads one to the difficult problem of observing pressure waves in the cylinder. In fact, over the years these difficulties led the industry to devise an experimental comparison measurement technique which measured the octane rating of the *fuel,* not of the engine.

8.2.2   Laboratory Measurements

The CFR Engine.   The basic comparison method which evolved for rating fuel knock quality involved the use of a simple, single-cylinder, spark-ignited engine called the CFR engine, and a pure hydrocarbon fuel—100 percent isooctane. Researchers discovered that they could reproduce knock phenomenon, laboratory to laboratory, by running this engine under specified conditions with this fuel.

Gasoline Octane Rating.   A system of rating the knock characteristics of fuels, called the octane rating, was developed based on a comparison of the CFR engine performance with the test fuel compared to pure isooctane. On this scale, osooctane has an octane rating of 100; passenger car engine fuels ranged from the high 70s for "regular" to the high 90s for "super premium." (Fuel formulations with an octane rating over 100 were possible but were used mainly for aircraft engines.)

As the industry strove to put knock on a solid engineering basis, methods of measuring the resulting phenomena on the CFR engine, and commercial engines as well, were developed. The parameter on which the industry standardized was "jerk," the third-time derivative of engine block displacement. Scales evolved for comparing the relative knock performance of fuels and of engines based on the output of this kind of sensor. Much work was also done to correlate jerk sensor measurements with cylinder pressure phenomena.

The fundamental resonant frequency of the knock-generated pressure signal is dependent on engine cylinder geometry and the speed of sound in the charge gas. The structural vibration characteristics of the engine block that are excited by the fundamental knock event are determined by the engine block transfer function. Testing conducted on one cylinder of a six-cylinder spark-ignited engine demonstrates that high-frequency structural vibration components are good indicators of knock, despite the relatively low frequency high-pressure excitation event.[2] Structural vibration induced by mechanical events, such as valves opening and closing, introduces noise that can be confused with knock-induced vibrations. Careful signal analysis is required to overcome a sometimes poor signal-to-noise ratio.

The reverberation resonance of the cylinder typically lies in the range between 2 and 12 kHz. A useful rough estimate of the knock frequency for a given engine cylinder geometry is given by Draper's equation[3]:

$$\text{fr} = \frac{\text{Pmn} \times C}{\pi B} \tag{8.1}$$

where fr is the knock resonant frequency
Pmn is a vibration mode constant
C is the velocity of sound in the gas in the cylinder
and B is the radius of the cylinder

Using this equation, assuming that the average gas temperature is 2000 K so that C is 900 m/s, the first circumferential mode resonant frequency is estimated at 5.75 kHz for a cylinder of 10-cm bore.

As better cylinder pressure sensors have become available, cylinder pressure wave measurements, along with signal analysis techniques for deriving a knock rating number, have supplemented jerk measurements in the laboratory. The most popular signal analysis approach is to declare the maximum amplitude or peak-to-peak value of the bandpass filtered pressure data as a knock number, usually referred to as *knock intensity*.

Other ways of describing knock level are the root-mean square, mean square, or integral of the absolute value of the bandpass pressure oscillations during the knocking portions of the cycle. The spectral power of the pressure transformed into the frequency domain has been used for measurement. Derivative-based methods have also been established, based on rapid changes of cylinder pressure during the knock phenomenon, using the first, second, and third derivatives of the cylinder pressure history.

8.2.3 On-Board Knock Control

Improved Fuel Economy by Lowering Engine Compression Ratio. As engine control using microcomputers became established in the late 1970s and early 1980s for gasoline passenger car engines, and the octane rating of the fuels available for them dropped below 90, the automotive industry responded by lowering engine compression ratios. However, some of these smaller engines were equipped with turbochargers to recover some of the lost performance at wide open throttle. It was found that these engines could experience destructive high-speed knock at maximum speed and power. Not only were the knock reverberations in the cylinder large, but they were modulating a high base pressure wave. This could occur because the extra boost pressure from the turbocharger permits additional fuel to be metered to the engine without violating emissions restrictions on the control, since the amount of oxygen available to react with the fuel is greater. This could result in knock wave peaks exceeding the cylinder head pressure limit, as well as excessive vibration of the entire engine.

The knock occurring at wide open throttle had to be decreased, but retaining the additional power from the turbocharger at part throttle was very desirable. The electronic control was available to modulate the amount of fuel injected during the dangerous engine state; however, a means of sensing engine knock on-board in real time was needed. The sensors used are described in Sec. 8.3. The control operates by sensing that knock is over the permissible limit, and then reduces it either by retarding ignition timing or by opening a wastegate valve on the boosted manifold pressure.

Improved Fuel Economy by Raising Compression Ratio. Following the successful implementation of knock limit control on turbocharged engines, considerable experimentation was carried out to assess whether or not there is value in applying knock limit control to naturally aspirated spark-ignited engines. It was determined that if the engine knock was always kept less than an empirically determined limit for that type of engine and stored in the microcomputer control memory, then the knock level would not be objectionable even to the more critical car operators. Moreover, this could be accomplished while raising the compression ratio one full number—for example, from 8:1 to 9:1. If used to improve fuel economy, this change results in a 3 percent improvement in the corporate average fleet economy (CAFE) rating for that model/engine combination. At today's CAFE values, this is close to a one-mile-per-gallon improvement.

CAFE values are extremely important to a passenger car original equipment manufacturer (OEM). The larger, heavier luxury cars cannot achieve as low a CAFE value as the smaller, lighter cars. However, the larger cars are more profitable to produce. Thus, the mix of cars produced by an OEM can depend on just how close his CAFE results are coming to the mandated value. A way of improving fuel economy without downsizing, adding significant cost, or losing performance is very valuable.

Starting in the early 1980s, more and more passenger cars had a knock limit control and increased compression ratio. Such a change is usually scheduled at a time when the engine design and the tooling to make the engine are changing for other reasons. By 1990, 25 to 30 percent of the naturally aspirated passenger car engines produced in the United States (and all of the turbocharged engines) featured knock limit control.

8.2.4 Measurement and Control System Considerations

In addition to the problem of developing a suitable on-board sensor for knock, once the parameter to use had been selected, a number of other considerations had to be settled in effecting a satisfactory control. It was already pointed out that engine knock can be reduced either by retarding spark timing or by opening a manifold boost wastegate valve. In the United States, the candidate engines already had electronic control of spark timing, so that all that was needed to implement the knock control was an easily added change in the timing command in the control microcomputer. However, many control strategies exist for processing the knock signal. Perhaps the most elaborate of these was implemented on the first turbocharged engine knock limit control:

- The vibration frequency of the knock is specific to the engine model but lies between 2 and 12 kHz for passenger car engines. The sensor used was mechanically bandpass-tuned to match this characteristic with a Q of about 2.

- The major knock reverberations for a given cylinder occur during a time window that starts shortly after the cylinder reaches top dead center and ends 60 to 90 crank-angle degrees later. The control opened a signal gate to allow the knock signal to pass through and be averaged only when the engine was in these time windows.

- To prevent engine damage, whenever the knock signature exceeded the limit value, the control very rapidly retarded ignition by as much as 10 crank-angle degrees so that the engine would not be in severe knock even for the next few cylinder events. Then the control would very slowly advance the timing until the process repeated. This resulted in somewhat less than best engine performance but assured a comfortable margin of safety for the engine.

- The knock threshold limit in the control was modulated to increase with engine speed so as to compensate for greater noise background at high engine speed.

8.3 TECHNOLOGIES FOR SENSING KNOCK

A number of different parameters have been selected for measuring knock in real time on board, and sensors have been developed for this purpose. It must be recognized that these sensors measure the magnitude of a consequential parameter driven by the knock, rather than the knock phenomenon itself. The overall effectiveness of the control is therefore determined not only by the intrinsic performance and stability of the sensor and control, but also by how robust the chain of causality is between the knock phenomenon and the parameter measured.

8.3.1   Jerk Sensors

Naturally enough, the first turbocharged engine knock limit control used a jerk sensor, a productionized version of the kind of sensor used for laboratory CFR engine testing. An exploded view of this sensor is shown in Fig. 8.1.

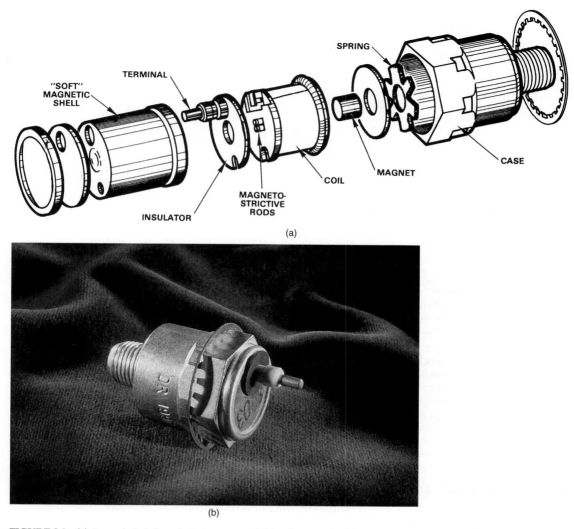

FIGURE 8.1   (*a*) An exploded view of a jerk sensor, and (*b*) a photograph of the sensor.

Referring to the exploded view, it must be understood that when the sensor is fully assembled, the spider spring is preloaded, and all parts of the sensor except the coil cover are in compression. The nickel alloy magnetostrictive rods are biased mechanically in lengthwise compression and magnetically by the field impressed through the rods from the permanent magnet, returning through the ferromagnetic soft iron coil cover. The nickel alloy rods are the highest reluctance element in this magnetic circuit, and are in magnetic saturation.

The vibrations which are picked up and transmitted from the engine block through the mounting stud appear in the nickel alloy rods. These rods are of such a length that they comprise a broad passband mechanically resonant element. The compressive mechanical bias is sufficiently strong that the compression and rarefraction waves picked up are never large enough to take the rods out of net compression. The waves present in the rods therefore linearly modulate the magnetic reluctance of the magnetic circuit.

The many-turn coil wound around the magnetostrictive rods generates a voltage proportional to the rate of change of the magnetic flux; the flux, in turn, is inversely proportional to the magnetic reluctance of the rods. Since the vibrations picked up are already due to accelerations from the knock reverberations transmitted through the engine block, the voltage from the coil represents the third-time derivative of displacement, or jerk.

The vibration signal from a knocking engine is present virtually everywhere on the engine block, with signals from all cylinders superimposed. For passenger car engines, which rarely have more than eight cylinders, the major part of the knock signatures from the successive cylinder events are not superimposed in time, but rather consecutive without overlap. The time delay due to the distance from the cylinder to the sensor is always much less than 1 ms, whereas the cylinder-to-cylinder time is 2.5 ms even for an eight-cylinder engine at 6000 rpm.

However, the *absolute amplitude* of the knock signal does vary from location to location on the block. There is no best place to mount the sensor; rather, a site with a strong amplitude should be selected for a given engine model, and the sensor should always be mounted at that point on that engine model. The knock threshold is experimentally determined on that engine model with the sensor mounted at that location.

The method used for processing the knock signal and effecting control was described in Sec. 8.2.4. As time has gone on, the knock signal processing has tended to become simpler, although in the 1990s this may be changing. Time windows and mechanically resonant sensors have largely disappeared, and much of the filtering is now done digitally.

8.3.2 Accelerometer Sensors

The magnetostrictive jerk sensor, while satisfactory in performance, has too many parts to be a low-cost solution to measuring knock on board. Moreover, its mechanical assembly is not simple. In an effort to achieve lower-cost solutions, the industry found that the second-time derivative of displacement—acceleration—could be measured and used to implement a satisfactory knock control. The drawback to using an accelerometer compared to a jerk sensor is that it does not yield as good a signal-to-noise ratio; however, by using appropriate filtering, a good control signal can be achieved.

The first accelerometers used were mechanically bandpass-tuned, and some still are. However, in the 1990s, the trend has been to broadband sensors, again used with much electronic filtering. This has the advantage that one sensor model can be used for all engines, with the engine-specific frequency filtering characteristics built into the electronics module, which has to be engine-specific anyway. If the crucial filtering features are provided digitally, they can be installed as part of the engine-specific software.

Piezoelectric Accelerometer.   Certain crystals of a specific cut or orientation possess the property that, when stressed, they produce a corresponding voltage. If such a crystal is loaded with a mass and spring, vibrations entering the assembly squeeze and pull the crystal with respect to the mass, and result in a signal which is a measure of the acceleration of the body to which the assembly is attached. These signals can be substantial in size but appear electrically to be sourced at a high (capacitive) driving point impedance. Thus, care has to be taken to ensure that capacitively coupled noise does not contaminate the signal.

There are a variety of single crystals which exhibit the piezoelectric effect, but silicon is not one of them. Efforts to devise a silicon micromachined accelerometer were stymied for a long time by this fact, but a solution will be described below. Single crystal quartz is the material which was used in the single-crystal piezoelectric accelerometers.

In some cases, it is possible to use the mass of the piezoelectric element itself as the mass, and to combine the spring with one of the crystal electrodes. In such a design, the only parts are a spring, a contact, the crystal, and the housing.

Piezoceramic Accelerometer. Another type of piezoelectric element is the piezoceramic device. Piezoceramics are not single crystals. They can be fired into just about any shape, just like a ceramic insulator or a vase. By impressing a high voltage across electrodes on the ceramic while the material is at a high temperature—above its Curie temperature—and then gradually lowering the temperature, the piezoceramic becomes *poled,* or piezoelectric across the electrodes.

The best piezoceramics tend to belong to the lead-zirconate-titanate (PZT) family. These materials have a Curie temperature from 250 to 500 °C. If the sensor ever gets above its Curie temperature, its poling becomes degraded, and its calibration is no longer valid. However, these engine block-mounted sensors will not experience temperatures higher than about 125 to 150 °C, even during hot soak, so they can be used for the knock sensor.

Single-crystal piezoelectric accelerometers also have a Curie temperature, but it is typically much higher than for the piezoceramics. Quartz, for example, has a Curie temperature over 600 °C.

Because the piezoceramic materials can be molded into any shape, handled roughly, sawn and machined, coated with thick-film metallic electrodes, and so on, they lend themselves to easy, low-cost mass production. As a result, they have become pretty much the knock sensor of choice for the automobile industry. A drawing of a piezoceramic accelerometer knock sensor is shown in Fig. 8.2. In this particular design, the spring and top electrode have been combined into one part, but the mass is a separate metallic part between the piezoceramic disc and the spring. The whole assembly is stacked on a mandrel which extends up from the base-stud which forms most of the package.

8.3.3   Silicon Accelerometer

As previously noted, silicon itself cannot be made piezoelectric. However, it is possible to make a silicon micromachined accelerometer by anisotropically machining a cantilevered T-shaped structure into each cell of a silicon wafer, using a chemical etch. Strain gauges are diffused or implanted into the cantilever—the vertical bar of the T. The mass of the horizontal crossbar of the T and the spring constant of the cantilever provide the mechanical-to-strain transduction. Such accelerometers are in mass production for use in antiskid braking systems and as triggers for air bag safety devices. Whether or not they will replace piezoceramic knock sensors is primarily a matter of economics. Technically, the silicon accelerometer is satisfactory; its temperature limit is about 150 °C, which is adequate for on-block mounting.

8.3.4   Other Sensors

Instantaneous Cylinder Pressure Sensor. The direct measurement of instantaneous cylinder pressure permits the extraction of the pressure reverberation signal, which is the direct cause of knock. While this would be a very desirable signal to use for knock detection, it has not been implemented in on-board knock control systems for several reasons:

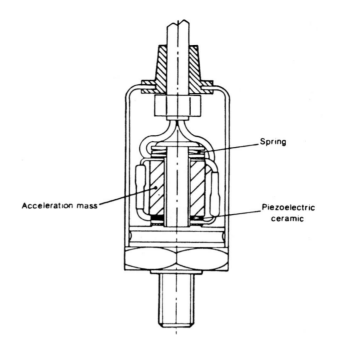

FIGURE 8.2   A piezoceramic accelerometer knock sensor.

- Either the same cylinder must always be the one to experience knock first and most severely, or one must have a sensor on every cylinder.
- The cylinder pressure wave is complex, and knock is only one of many signature elements present. Deriving a unique knock signal requires considerable signal processing in real time.
- While cylinder pressure sensors exist which are suitable for test purposes, a durable, low-cost, mass-producable on-board pressure sensor is not yet available.

In spite of these difficulties, work continues on cylinder pressure sensors for on-board control use, not so much to be used as knock-sensing devices as for use in deriving an instantaneous torque measurement (see Chap. 9). If this approach succeeds, then it is reasonable to suppose that the cylinder pressure sensor will be used to provide the inputs for obtaining both torque and knock measurements.

Since a spark-ignited engine already has a spark plug mounted in each cylinder head, it is possible to convert the spark plug into a kind of "poor man's pressure sensor" by mounting a piezoceramic washer held in compression between the spark plug and the cylinder head when the plug is torqued down. This arrangement has in fact appeared on a commercial passenger car engine. While the signal is not presently being used to extract a knock signal, suitable signal processing would make this possible.

Hydrophone in Coolant.   In Sec. 8.3.1, it was mentioned that the knock signal appears virtually everywhere on the block. In fact, it even appears in the coolant fluid faithfully reproduced. This fact led to experiments in which hydrophones were mounted in the coolant and used as knock sensors. This approach has never reached production because it has no advantage over a block-mounted sensor and is in fact more difficult to package and to mount on the engine.

8.4 SUMMARY

In a remarkably short span of time, the on-board sensing of knock and its control have become a rather standard feature of passenger car engine control electronics. At the same time, the on-board sensors have been developed and are now largely mature. Acceleration has become the parameter of choice for most of these control systems, and the required accelerometers are typically based upon piezoceramic technology; it seems likely that this will remain the case at least through the 1990s. The rapid proliferation of these systems was facilitated by three factors:

- A solid background of experimental knowledge about knock and how to control it was established in the laboratory during the several decades before lead-free gas was mandated.
- The three legislated pressures of emissions limits, CAFE fuel economy goals, and no-lead fuel, combined with a customer base used to engines without knock, made solving the knock problem a high priority.
- The already widespread use of digital microcomputer engine control made the addition of knock limit control a straightforward design change.

GLOSSARY

Curie temperature   The temperature above which a piezoelectric crystal or piezoceramic element no longer reliably retains its original piezoelectric characteristics.

Jerk sensor   A sensor which measures the third-time derivative of displacement.

Knock   Acoustic engine noise and vibration of characteristic frequency caused by uneven combustion in the engine cylinder(s).

Octane rating   A measure of the resistance of a gasoline fuel to knock, as compared to pure isooctane hydrocarbon.

Retarding   Causing engine combustion to occur at a larger angle past top dead center, by delaying the time at which the signal to start the spark event occurs.

Turbocharger   A device which compresses engine intake manifold air by using the engine exhaust to drive a turbine and compressor.

Wastegate valve   A valve in the exhaust system of a turbocharged diesel engine which causes part of the exhaust to bypass the turbine. The same name is also applied to a valve on a turbocharged gasoline engine which causes part of the boosted intake manifold air to dump to the atmosphere, dropping the manifold pressure.

REFERENCES

1. Paulius V. Puzinauskas, "Examination of methods used to characterize knock," SAE Paper 920808, Superflor Corp.
2. Karp P. Schmillen (FEV Motorentechnik, Aachen, Germany) and Manfred Rechs (Institute for Applied Thermodynamics, Technical University of Aachen, Germany), "Different methods of knock detection and knock control," SAE Paper 910858.
3. Masayoshi Kaneyasu (Hitachi America, Ltd.), Nobuo Kurihara, Kozo Katogi, and Hiroatsu Tokuda (Hitachi Ltd.), "Engine knock detection using multi-spectrum method," SAE Paper 920702.

ABOUT THE AUTHOR

William G. Wolber, executive engineer, Cummins Electronics Co., Inc., has 38 years' experience in the development of sensors, actuators, and instruments for application in automobiles and other products. Since 1981, he has been involved principally in the development of sensors and controls for heavy duty diesel engines for Cummins Electronics Co. He holds 15 U.S. patents and is the author of over 50 technical papers. He has lectured and conducted seminars internationally for the Society of Automotive Engineers and other organizations.

CHAPTER 9
ENGINE TORQUE SENSORS

William G. Wolber
Executive Engineer
Cummins Electronics Co. Inc.

9.1 INTRODUCTION

Torque is one of the primary state parameters of an engine; along with speed it is a fundamental measure related to the output power. Torque can be defined as the moment produced by the engine crankshaft tending to cause the output driveline to turn and thereby deliver power to the load. For rotary motion, the torque multiplied by the rotational speed equals the power delivered by the shaft. In derivative form, Newton's law states that torque T equals the rotational moment of inertia I times the angular acceleration α. Hence, at constant rotational speed, instantaneous power is proportional to instantaneous torque. This is an important relationship because torque and, thus, delivered power can change rapidly compared to rotational speed.

Portraying the engine as a torque-delivering device is a useful concept. When an engine is used in road service as prime mover power, the operator of the vehicle tends to ask the vehicle for positive or negative incremental acceleration, as the operator perceives it to be falling behind or closing upon the vehicle ahead. Hence, the operator asks the engine for more or less torque. If the engine is spark ignited, this happens naturally through the modulation of the engine air intake flow path. In a diesel engine, it happens indirectly. The operator controls fuel rate, which to first approximation is linearly related to power. For slowly varying engine speed and load, an incremental change in power results in a change in torque and therefore a change in acceleration.

9.1.1 Time-Scale Definitions

At this point, it is useful to define two time scales which will be used with regard to the engine. A reciprocating engine is never truly operating steady state. It is a cyclic succession of batch processes, a kind of system which chemical engineers have termed "continuous-by-jerks." Each cylinder absorbs shaft energy during the compression stroke and releases a larger amount of shaft energy through combustion during the power stroke. These actions are so interleaved that the drive shaft is continually accelerating and decelerating in step with cylinder events. Nevertheless, a quasi-steady-state model for the engine can be defined in which these rapid fluctuations are ignored and attention is focused on the more slowly varying state parameters which are nearly stationary during one engine revolution. This is the situation the operator senses and controls and it is also the primary focus of the control algorithms in a microcomputer-based engine control today. (As of 1994, all electronic engine controls operate on the "engine time scale.")

Quasi-Steady-State Torque.   Quasi-steady-state torque is defined as that running average value of torque that varies slowly with respect to the cylinder-to-cylinder period, but rapidly with respect to vehicle changes in motion and load. To quantize this state, it is noted that an unloaded engine coupled to flywheel inertia may accelerate from idle to maximum speed in one to five seconds when subjected to wide open throttle and that this performance is essentially reproduced whether the change in throttle position occurs in 20 ms or 1 ms. Quasi-steady-state torque is what the operator is interested in commanding, and so, if we visualize a torque command-feedback engine control, it is the parameter of interest.

Instantaneous Torque.   Today's electronic engine control can usefully respond much more rapidly than this for those state parameters having to do with each cylinder batch process itself. The preparation of the fuel and air charges and the timing of ignition take place on a time scale measured in fractions of a cylinder period, and thus the time scale of interest ranges from 30 μs to 20 ms. This time scale corresponds to the instantaneous engine state. It is the time scale of the torque impulses that are termed instantaneous torque.

In order to use instantaneous torque measurements, it must be recognized that the reciprocating engine is a cyclic machine in which major functions and the parameters that characterize them are tied together in sequence mechanically by the crankshaft and camshaft. Proper adjustment of those other parameters that are free to be changed independently of the train of instantaneous cylinder events allows optimization of the overall torque impulse generation in real time. For example, a theoretical examination of the internal combustion engine cycle has shown that the centroid of the cylinder pressure wave should occur about 15 crank-angle degrees after top dead center ("Powell's Magic Angle") to maximize the instantaneous incremental torque from that cylinder.[1,2] No spark or injection timing algorithm can do any better than to effect such timing of the torque impulse. Note, however, that we are stating where the centroid of the pressure wave should be for the best torque impulse, not where the fuel injection or ignition should be commanded.

State-of-the-art scheduled spark timing controls are based upon test data from one or more prototype engines run extensively in the laboratory on a dynamometer under quasi-steady-state conditions. From the data obtained, families of spark plug or injection timing (crank angle) surfaces versus engine speed, load, etc., are derived that correspond to optimum economy and performance while meeting emission requirements. These data then form the schedule embedded in the control microcomputer memory for all engines of that model produced. This type of scheduled computer control is standard throughout the industry today for all electronically controlled engines, both spark-ignited and compression ignition, with just two exceptions. These are the oxygen sensor feedback control loop, which keeps an engine equipped with a three-way catalyst in the stoichiometric "window" of the catalyst efficiency performance, and the speed governing feedback control algorithm used for power takeoff (PTO) operations, diesel all-speed governors, and generator-set frequency control.

By contrast, the addition of an on-board instantaneous torque measurement would permit the direct feedback control of several key engine control parameters. To take maximum advantage of such feedback control, an advanced instantaneous crankshaft position sensor is also required.

The controls which could be implemented through use of an instantaneous torque feedback control system are:

- Quasi-steady-state torque feedback control in response to torque command.

- Spark-ignition or compression-ignition timing control by feedback of instantaneous torque impulse timing compared to the norm of the "Magic Angle." Torque impulse amplitude can also be optimized against timing. These controls can be implemented on a cylinder-by-cylinder basis, for spark-ignited pulse sequential fuel injected engines, and for unit-injected diesel engines.

- Cylinder-by-cylinder torque-leveling feedback control can be implemented by adjusting the amount of fuel injected into each cylinder to obtain equal torque impulses from each one.

This results in a quiet, smoothly running engine with a somewhat improved maximum power, because the torque limit can be set for a more nearly constant cylinder event instead of for the worst case cylinder.

- The instantaneous torque signal is also rich in a variety of diagnostic information—for example, to measure engine power or for use as a miss detector.

9.2 AUTOMOTIVE APPLICATIONS OF TORQUE MEASUREMENT

9.2.1 Off-Board Measurement

The principal automotive use of torque measurement today is in the testing and evaluation of engines using the engine dynamometer. The torque sensor is inserted as a drive shaft between the engine and the dynamometer; the shaft of the sensor is a torsional Hooke's law member and its twist is measured. Typically the torque is actually measured using a strain gage bridge on the drive shaft. Full-scale twist is limited to no more than about a degree per foot of shaft for engines in the 50 to 500 hp range.

In a dc torque sensor, the strain gage bridge is powered from an external source through slip rings, and the offset voltage is taken off the bridge the same way (Fig. 9.1). The sensor is necessarily bulky, large, fragile, and costly. A more rugged ac strain gage sensor can be made using rotational transformers, as shown schematically in Fig. 9.2.

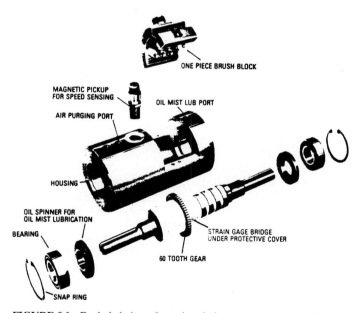

FIGURE 9.1 Exploded view of rotating shaft torque sensor with slip rings. *(Courtesy of the Lebow Div., the Eaton Corp.)*

Developmental Tests. In engine development, a good bit of the work involves fine-tuning the engine to get the maximum power and minimum fuel consumption at various engine conditions. Since power equals torque multiplied by engine speed, if tests are carried out at constant speed, maximum power occurs at maximum torque. Thus, the torque sensor can be used as a direct indicator of whether changes in the engine design or control will improve power.

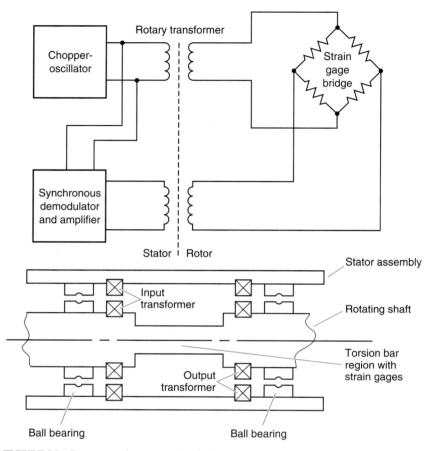

FIGURE 9.2   Rotary transformer rotating shaft torque sensor.

End-of-Line Manufacturing Tests.   Particularly in the case of heavy duty diesel engines, the price of the engine is directly related to engine rated horsepower. Such engines are in a real sense sold by the horsepower. The manufacturer certifies that a certain model will deliver no less than a certain horsepower when run at rated conditions. The engine is tested at the end of the assembly line for a number of attributes, chief among which is assurance that it exceeds stated horsepower at rated speed. The assurance is provided by accurate torque and speed measurements.

In-Service Tests.   Occasionally, torque sensors may be used with an engine that is being tested under field conditions. This is relatively straightforward when the engine is being used in a stationary application, but not if it is installed in a vehicle.

9.2.2   On-Board Measurements

To be most useful on board, a torque sensor should not only be accurate but also fast in response. Most of the sensors available today do not have this attribute, because they were developed for use in dynamometer tests.

To be a useful on-board engine control sensor, the torque sensor of the future also needs several other attributes:

- It must be extremely rugged, which for practical purposes means noncontacting with respect to the driveline.

- It must be able to withstand torque impulses of 10 to 20 times its full-scale measuring capability without degrading its accuracy. For strain gage type sensors, this means that the sensor would always have to measure in the lowest 5 to 10 percent of its range, where it is not very accurate.

- Installation of the sensor must not cause any significant change in the compliance of the driveline. This is a requirement imposed by engine application engineers to avoid spoiling the tradeoffs that have been made to avoid severe torsional vibrations.

- Ideally, the shaft of the sensor should be very short in length (in part to achieve the preceding characteristics). Unfortunately, for a torsional Hooke's law device, that means the full-scale shaft twist angle will be very small.

In spite of these formidable barriers to a satisfactory design, a wide variety of desirable applications could be made using an on-board instantaneous torque sensor. As a result, many researchers and developers both in academia and industry are working to achieve such a measurement directly or indirectly.

Power Measurement of Large Engines.   Means exist for field service personnel to measure engine power in the field for engines installed in a vehicle and rated at up to 400 to 500 hp. For larger vehicle-mounted engines, this measurement is a difficult problem for a number of reasons:

- A rugged on-board sensor is not available.

- These engines are often installed in very large machines such as mine-haul trucks and front-end loaders located off the road in remote areas.

- Dynamometers large enough to load down the engine to full power are not available except in a very few locations.

One of the most frequent customer complaints about heavy duty engines is perceived loss of power. Often such complaints must be resolved at the field location and on a subjective basis. The engine and vehicle can be fully loaded in actual work operation, and engine speed is known accurately. If an on-board torque sensor were available, such complaints could be quickly resolved, and it would be well worth installing on large engines.

Miss Detection.   The California Air Resources Board has mandated that all passenger vehicles shall be equipped with an engine diagnostic capability that includes a miss detector. While the regulation is not yet in force as of the time of this writing, the automotive industry knows that every segment will be affected by the requirement by the end of the decade. Many vehicle OEMs, first-tier automotive suppliers, entrepreneurial sensor firms, and academic researchers are working hard to meet the miss detector requirements, mainly basing their efforts on the same technologies useful for measuring or inferring torque.[3]

Torque Feedback Control.   The reciprocating engine could be configured in a feedback control mode if equipped with an on-board quasi-steady-state torque sensor capable of responding at least as fast as the engine/driveline. In a torque command drive-by-wire system, the operator input would be a command for a new torque, greater or less than the present torque. The engine control would do its best to provide the new torque as rapidly as possible. The feedback error signal would be the difference between the torque command and the sensor output. Of course, the new torque and the resulting acceleration or deceleration would have to be limited within bounds set by maxima for cylinder pressure, emissions production, exhaust gas temperature, fuel economy, and so on.

Feedback Control of Timing.   As was described in the introduction to this chapter, the measurement of instantaneous torque, on board, along with instantaneous crank angle position, would allow the engine control computer to use signature recognition to measure the crank angle at which the centroid of the torque impulse is located, for each cylinder. From this information, probably with some compensation for seriously off-normal engine conditions as stored in computer memory, the engine control can determine if that impulse was centered at Powell's Magic Angle, and, if not, how much earlier or later the chain of combustion events needs to be started. Most likely, the computer also needs to decide between updating that cylinder based upon that information alone and waiting a whole engine revolution to update, or also basing the correction upon abrupt changes in operator input, load, knock level, etc. In any case, under quasi-steady-state conditions, the best efficiency of that engine for converting chemical energy into shaft power by proper engine timing could be achieved this way whether the engine is spark-ignited or compression-ignition.

Cylinder Torque Leveling.   Individual trimming of the amount of fuel for each cylinder can be realized on pulse sequential fuel injected spark-ignited engines and on unit injector diesel engines by matching the torque impulse for each cylinder to the average of all cylinders. Then the average impulse can be raised to very nearly the maximum value the engine is designed for. In today's engines, the control must provide a guard band between the maximum torque for the worst case cylinder and the design limit for the engine (commonly called the maximum cylinder pressure limit or the peak torque limit). If the torque impulses delivered by each cylinder were known to be controlled to be equal, the guard band could be reduced and more power obtained from a given engine.

While cylinder-to-cylinder torque leveling is not the same as compression leveling, an engine controlled cylinder by cylinder for timing and torque leveling intuitively would appear to be as smoothly running and low in acoustic noise emission as can be visualized.

Engine Diagnostics.   The instantaneous torque signature is very rich in diagnostic information. A figure of merit for engine roughness can easily be obtained in real time, from which a lean-limit control signal can be derived. The miss detector responds to an extreme case of roughness. Ragged ignition and flame front formation, imperfect injection, poor distribution, and many other engine and control problems can be measured or inferred from such a signal, on board and in real time.

9.3   DIRECT TORQUE SENSORS

9.3.1   Reaction Force

The use of a strain-gaged torsional Hooke's law shaft to measure torque at the dynamometer has been described in Sec. 9.2.1. Torque can also be measured in the test cell by instrumenting the engine or dynamometer mounting with strain gage load cells to measure reaction torque. This is a useful way to measure quasi-steady-state torque, but is not a good measuring system for instantaneous torque, as both the engine and its load have considerable inertia and damping which attenuate the torque impulse and may introduce phase delay. It is also not a good on-board measurement because the engine mounts on a vehicle are designed to attenuate and damp out bouncing from road and load irregularities. Also, as a function of time, temperature, ozone concentration, and other variables, they tend to stiffen substantially and change the deflection of the engine at its mounts as a function of torque.

9.3.2   Torsional Strain (Twist) Sensors

Magnetic Vector Sensors.   The strain-gaged torsional Hooke's law sensor was described in Sec. 9.2.1. A more practical approach to an on-board torque sensor is a noncontacting design called a magnetic vector sensor.[4,5] This sensor operates on the principle that the magnetic domains in a ferromagnetic shaft delivering torque are randomly distributed when no torque is being delivered, but that each domain, on average, is slightly rotated in the tangential direction when torque is delivered by the shaft and twists it. If an ac-driven coil is placed near the shaft and surrounded by four sensing coils arranged mechanically and electrically as a bridge, the amplitude of the bridge offset is proportional to the magnetic vector tangential component, and therefore to twist and torque.

If the magnetic domains were truly statistically distributed over a small range of shaft angle, such a sensor would be able to measure instantaneous torque. Unfortunately, they are not. Over a small shaft angle increment, the average torque vector does not net to zero when torque is zero, and the output is characterized by a fixed pattern noise which repeats every 360°. The magnetic vector sensor is reasonably accurate measuring quasi-steady-state torque, but the signal-to-noise ratio becomes poor when an attempt is made to measure instantaneous torque.

Further work on this sensor simplified and miniaturized it.[6] The bridge was replaced by a single tangential coil, and the sensor was made small enough so that it could be mounted in the rear crankshaft bearing. However, it still was not able to measure instantaneous torque.

Investigation continues on techniques to reduce the fixed pattern noise, and some claims of progress have been made. However, at this writing, a production on-board torque sensor is not available.

Optical Twist Measurement.   Research work has been reported on a sensor that changes the duty factor of light pulses sensed after passing through sets of slits at both ends of a shaft.[7] The principle of its operation is shown in Fig. 9.3. Such a sensor is noncontacting and can be made robust, but it requires appreciable shaft length and therefore adds compliance to the driveline. The work has not been engineered to produce an economical on-board device.

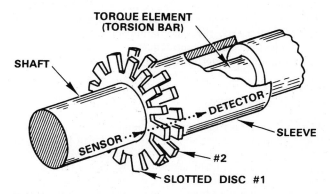

FIGURE 9.3   Optical torque meter. *(Courtesy of The Bendix Corp.)*

Capacitive Twist Sensor.   An electrode pattern can be made using interdigitated electrodes spaced one or two degrees apart on two facing flat discs.[8] One of the discs is stationary; the other rotates with the crankshaft. Two such pairs of electrodes can be operated with phase detection measurement to provide a virtually instantaneous signal proportional to the twist of the shaft; the rotating halves of the electrode pairs are attached to the ends of the Hooke's law torsional spring. Obviously, this arrangement has the same drawback as the optical sensor in that it has to have some shaft length to twist and, therefore, some compliance. However, it is robust, has good accuracy, and is a more practical on-board device than the optical twist sensor. This sensor can also yield an accurate crankshaft position measurement. Nevertheless, an on-board version is not available today.

9.4   INFERRED TORQUE MEASUREMENT

Indirect measurements of torque-related parameters can be made with a view to inferring torque from the measurements. Typically, such measurements require considerable real-time computation in the control microcomputer, along with precision measurement of the instantaneous crank angle position. Much work is in progress in a variety of locations to make these methods into practical instantaneous torque control signals.

9.4.1   Instantaneous Cylinder Pressure Sensors

Engine development engineers have long used piezoelectric crystal cylinder pressure sensors in the laboratory to make engine power and heat release measurements and as an aid to development. The best of these sensors use doped quartz single crystals. They are accurate and reasonably robust, but expensive and unforgiving if overranged or subjected to excessive temperatures. Much work continues on development of a mass-producable on-board cylinder pressure sensor.[9] One of the Japanese car manufacturers is reported to have a top-of-the-line passenger car model, available only in Japan, with engine control using piezoceramic cylinder pressure sensors.

The signals from cylinder pressure sensors need considerable real-time data processing to produce inferred "torque" signals. In one method, the noise always present is filtered, the pressure signal is multiplied by an instantaneous shaft angle term, and integrated over the angle range representative of the power stroke of the cylinder. From this a measure of torque contribution from that cylinder is obtained. The best digital signal processing (DSP) chips available in the early 1990s are barely able to keep up with cylinder events in such a process. Nevertheless, we can be confident that if the proper sensors are available in the late 90s, the microcomputer chip performance required will be available and cost effective too.

9.4.2   Digital Period Analysis (DPA)

When an engine is run at low speed and heavy load, the instantaneous angular velocity of its output shaft on the engine side of the flywheel varies at the fundamental frequency of the cylinders, since the compression stroke of each cylinder abstracts torque and the power stroke adds a larger amount. The signal-to-noise ratio of the measurement of instantaneous angular velocity (or rather of its reciprocal, instantaneous period) degrades with increasing engine speed and lighter load, but is a useful way to infer torque-like measures of engine performance.

Figure 9.4 shows an idealized plot of instantaneous crankshaft period against crank angle under constant speed, lean conditions. The instantaneous period wave is seen to be a variation about the mean period value. This waveform can actually be measured using a precision, multitoothed crankshaft position sensor. For reasons which will be explained later, the instantaneous angular velocity lags the torque inputs producing it. As a result, the period wave appears to lead the torque or cylinder pressure variations.

Timing Control by DPA.   The general case of the variation in crankshaft velocity in a four-cylinder engine can be described by:

$$T_N = AL\,P_N\,(\theta)\,\sin\theta = AL\,P_{(N+3)}\,(\theta)\,\sin\theta + T_F\,(\theta) + T_L + I\ddot{\theta} \tag{9.1}$$

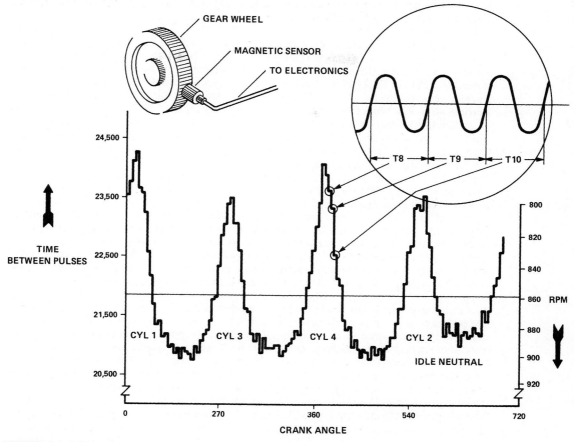

FIGURE 9.4   Digital period input.

where T_N = instantaneous torque due to burning gases in cylinder N at angle θ
                      A = area of piston
                      L = maximum effective crank lever arm
          $P_N(\theta)$ = pressure in cylinder N (a function of crank angle and many other variables)
      $P_{(N+3)}(\theta)$ = pressure in third cylinder to fire after N which is in its compression stroke when cylinder N is in its power stroke
          $T_F(\theta)$ = so-called "fixed load" torque due to friction, accessories, etc., and is generally a function of $d\theta/dt$
                T_L = torque delivered to the load
                   I = inertia of the engine, drivetrain, and vehicle reaction through the wheels
                   $\ddot{\theta}$ = instantaneous angular acceleration of the crankshaft

In order for Eq. (9.1) to remain valid, as T_N varies with angle θ due to the variations of $P_N(\theta)$ and the $\sin \theta$ term, some term in the right-hand side of the equation must vary correspondingly. In fact, the major effect is upon $\ddot{\theta}$, the angular acceleration, which varies both in magnitude and sign; being positive when P_N is large and θ is near $\pi/2$, and negative when P_N is small and θ is near 0 and π. If Eq. (9.1) is integrated as a function of θ from $\theta = 0$ to $\theta = \pi$ and then the summation is extended to angles larger than π by adding in the contributions of cylinders $N + 1$ and $N + 3$, the term in $I\ddot{\theta}$ becomes an average angular velocity over a complete engine cycle.

One important consequence of the preceding analysis is that, upon integration of the equation, the $\sin \theta$ term becomes $\cos \theta$—that is, the angular velocity wave lags the torque impulses causing it by $\pi/2$. Another consequence is that the amplitude of the period wave reflects the net contribution of the cylinders—if the load increases, and $P_N(\theta)$ increases to keep average angular velocity constant, the amplitude of the period wave must increase. The $I\ddot{\theta}$ term has become an $I\omega$, it is the reciprocal of this term which was plotted in Fig. 9.4.

When a spark plug fires or fuel is injected into a diesel cylinder, the pressure in the cylinder takes a finite length of time to build—first, because of a delay to get the fire started and then because of the finite and relatively constant flame propagation time, and second, because the temperature rise which causes pressure to rise, peaks only shortly before combustion is completed. Thereafter, pressure falls as the piston displaces under the pressure of the gases. Mean best torque (MBT) will be achieved from that cylinder when the pressure pulse, convolved with $\sin \theta$ yields a maximum upon integration. As described previously, researchers at Stanford University have found analytically and confirmed experimentally that this condition prevails for a fairly wide range of engine conditions when the centroid of the pressure pulse occurs at 15 degrees past top dead center (TDC). Because of the delays described previously, ignition must occur early enough to position the pressure peak near this value. It is this "anticipation" in spark plug firing that is termed *ignition advance*. The reason why advance angle has to be larger at higher speeds is now obvious: the flame propagation delay time covers more degrees of crank angle when the engine is running faster.

Further experiments by the Stanford researchers and others confirmed the suspicion that the period wave is a strong function of the crank angle, and that the angle associated with the centroid of the pressure wave is a unique function of the phase of the fundamental component of the period wave measured with respect to a crankshaft angle index point, say top dead center of cylinder no. 1. The period wave is measured with a sensor which is a precision version of a crankshaft position sensor.[10] It produces a fast, sharp pulse for every small and equal angle increment—say one degree—through which the shaft turns. Pulses from a high-frequency quartz crystal clock are counted to measure each period. The crankshaft angle index is available from the crankshaft position sensor. In principle, the period wave could be Fourier analyzed into the Fourier integral coefficients A_n and B_n by computing the Fourier integrals, and the phase of the fundamental (first harmonic) is then arctan B_1/A_1. To perform this computation in real time is a bit much to ask of today's microcomputer (but not tomorrow's!) and various shortcuts are utilized to achieve an approximate result. Remembering that the period wave appears to lead the torque impulses that cause it by $\pi/2$, the spark timing can now be varied so as to place the centroid of the pressure wave, on the average, at or very near the 15-degree-after-TDC point.

It is instructive to consider what performance is required of the DPA and crankshaft position sensors to achieve a given signal-to-noise ratio. The repeatability of the crankshaft angle marked by the sensor is a function of the diameter of the sensing disc. For the various magnetic sensors, a repeatability better than ± 0.5 degree can be achieved with a 10-cm-diameter disc. In the DPA sensor, the concern is for the period-to-period jitter. It is obviously worse for smaller angle increments both because the angle jitter is a larger part of the period, and also because the period-counting roundoff error is larger for any given clock frequency. At the same time, the more periods measured per revolution, the more fidelity the period wave will have for its high-frequency components. The period-to-period jitter of the magnetic sensor in this example is about ± 0.5 degree. This is satisfactory for 24 periods per revolution but marginal for 60 periods; a typical period wave amplitude is only ± 3 percent of the average period. On the other hand, even 60 periods per revolution is marginal for ignition or injection timing control.

The granularity due to counting roundoff also needs to be considered. Today's low-cost LSI circuits can count reliably at 20 MHz, so that is a practical clock frequency. If a four-cylinder engine is running at 1800 rev/min (30 Hz), the associated period wave will have a fundamental of 60 Hz. If the DPA sensor has one degree angle indices, referred to the crankshaft, each period will have about 2000 counts from the clock. Therefore, the period counting round-off noise will be ±1 part per 2000. Referred to a nominal ±3 percent amplitude period wave, this jitter amounts to ±2 percent of the peak value of the period wave (not of the period itself), not counting any smoothing.

For the fundamental of the period wave, the phase of which is used for DPA timing control, a good deal of smoothing can be realized, so that for a "clean" engine, estimation of the correct angle to ± one crankshaft degree is feasible.

Figure 9.5 shows an actual period wave measured using an electromagnetic DPA sensor with one-degree increments and a 10-MHz clock. Both the jitter described previously and a fixed pattern noise can be discerned in the signal. The latter effect is due to slight imperfections in the tooth spacing of the precision gear used as the sensing disc. Such systematic errors can be eliminated in the microcomputer, but they are troublesome and consume integration time. The better solution is to design a precision DPA sensor which minimizes fixed pattern noise.

DPA Used for Diagnostics.   During the 1980s, one of the heavy duty diesel engine manufacturers introduced an off-board diagnostic instrument capable of doing DPA on the engine with the clutch disengaged and using snap acceleration and deceleration to load the engine

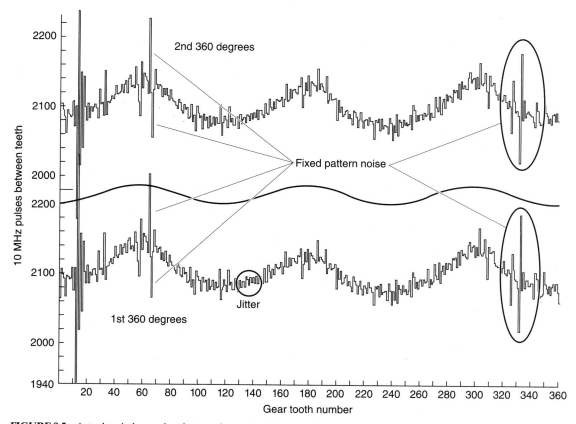

FIGURE 9.5   Actual period wave data from engine crankshaft; unsmoothed data. *(Courtesy of The Bendix Corp., Diesel Operation)*

inertially. This instrument used the very imperfect engine ring gear as the DPA target but solved the fixed pattern noise problem in a very elegant way.[11] The position sensor is actually a dual sensor, with the two magnetic circuits disposed tangential to the ring gear and closer together than one tooth pitch. A particular tooth is sensed by the first magnetic circuit and then by the second before the next tooth is sensed by the first circuit. Virtually all of the fixed pattern noise is eliminated.

What would be achieved in an on-board DPA system would be real-time, nearly ideal closed-loop control of spark timing. As with most controls for spark-ignited engines, there are some trims required to make the system work. Flame front propagation is in fact a complex process which has a substantial jitter in the time of propagation, so it is necessary to average the computation of the phase angle over a number of cylinder pulses in order to obtain a good phase estimator. Under transient conditions, the shape of the pressure pulse may change enough so that the angle for mean best torque (MBT) shifts slightly. These factors can also be incorporated in the control. A similar method could be used for compression-ignition engines; in fact, the period wave has a more reproducible signature than for a spark-ignited engine.

It is useful at this point to emphasize again that these principles hold under any conditions, but that the control works well only in the lean regime. As the air/fuel ratio nears stoichiometry, the amplitude of the period wave becomes quite small. Because the method of measuring the instantaneous period—counting clock pulses over a finite angle increment—is a differencing method, the signal-to-noise ratio (S/N) is always a problem, since a differencing process always yields a poorer S/N than that of the original function. Hence, the DPA technique yields poorer results the nearer the engine is to stoichiometry and the higher the engine speed.

Referring to Fig. 9.6, if a figure of merit is formed

$$R = \left| \frac{T_2 - T_1}{t_1 + t_2} \right| \tag{9.2}$$

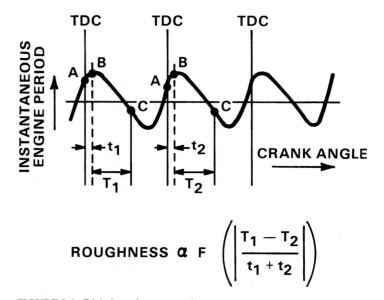

FIGURE 9.6   Digital roughness control.

we have a measure of the "roughness" of the engine useful for lean limit control or misfire detection. This is one example of many such optimizing algorithms which may be derived from DPA

9.5 SUMMARY

One can conclude from this chapter that torque measurement, whether direct or inferred, is a useful parameter for engine evaluation off-board, but that the proper sensors and computer analysis equipment for on-board control are not yet available. Yet the number of facilities working to advance this art, the resources being added, and the sporadic reports of progress are such that one can predict with some confidence that a breakthrough is imminent. Just what kind of control will first appear, and what kind or kinds will ultimately be successful, is not yet clear.

GLOSSARY

Algorithm A set of software instructions causing a digital computer to go through a prescribed routine. Because embedded computer engine controls have become so common, algorithm has become essentially synonymous with control law for automotive engineers.

Compression leveling A (theoretical) type of engine control which would cause each piston in each cylinder to compress its air charge to the same maximum pressure.

Dynamometer A machine to absorb power in a controlled manner, especially from an engine under test.

Hooke's law A relationship for an ideal elastic member which says that the displacement is proportional to the force.

Interdigitated An arrangement of two multiple-finger structures such that each pair of fingers from one structure has a finger from the other interposed.

Pulse sequential A type of fuel control for gasoline spark-ignited engines in which the fuel for each cylinder is injected into the air manifold near the intake valve for that cylinder just as it opens.

Robust Able to survive and operate properly in a severe environment.

Stoichiometric Pertaining to a combustion process in which the oxidizing agent (oxygen) and the reducing agent (fuel) are in balance such that, were the reaction to go to completion, there would be neither oxygen nor fuel left over, and all the reaction products such as carbon monoxide would be oxidized to their highest state—carbon dioxide.

Torsional Hooke's law A relationship for an ideal elastic shaft which says that the angle through which the shaft twists is proportional to the torque.

Torque The moment tending to make the output shaft of an engine turn. Torque can be expressed as a force acting perpendicular to a lever arm at a distance from the center of rotation. Its units are Newton-meters (pound force-feet).

Unit injector A type of fuel control for diesel engines which has fuel metered into a piston-barrel injector for injection into a specific cylinder at a specific time. Each engine cylinder has its own cam-driven injector, which operates something like a hypodermic syringe.

REFERENCES

1. J. A. Tennant, Rao, H. S., and Powell, J. David, "Engine characterization and optimal control," *Proceedings of the IEEE Conference on Decisions and Control* (including the 18th Symposium on Adaptive Processes), Ft. Lauderdale, Fla., Dec. 12–14, 1979. IEEE 79CH 7486-OCS, vol. 1, pp. 114–119.

2. Itshak Glaser and Powell, J. David, "Optimal closed-loop spark control of an automotive engine," SAE Paper No. 810058, Society of Automotive Engineers Inc., Warrendale, Pa.

3. Anders Unger and Smith, Kent, "Second-generation on-board diagnostics," *Automotive Engineering* vol. 102, no. 1, Jan. 1994, pp. 107–111.

4. William J. Fleming, "Automotive torque measurement: a summary of seven different methods," *IEEE Transactions on Vehicular Technology,* VT-31, No. 3, Aug. 1982, pp. 117–124.

5. William J. Fleming and Wood, P. W., "Non-contact miniature torque sensor for automotive applications," SAE Paper No. 820206.

6. Yutaka Nonomura; Sugiyama, Jun; Tsukado, Koja; Masahoru, Takeuchi; Itoh, Koji; and Konami, Toshiaki; "Measurements of engine torque with the intra-bearing torque sensor," SAE Paper No. 87042.

7. G. W. Pratt Jr., "An opto-electronic torquemeter for engine control," SAE Paper No. 760007.

8. Charles D. Hoyt, "DC excited capacitive shaft position transducer," U.S. Patent No. 4 862 752 Sept. 5, 1989.

9. Hiroki Kusakabe; Okauchi, Tohru; and Takigawa, Masuo; "A cylinder pressure sensor for internal combustion engine," SAE Paper No. 92071.

10. Stephen J. Citron and Orter, Kevin C., "On-line engine torque measurement utilizing crankshaft speed fluctuations," SAE Paper No. 850496.

11. Clarence E. Kincaid, "Computerized diagnostics for Cummins engines," *Proceedings of Convergence '84,* IEEE '84 CH 1988–5.

ABOUT THE AUTHOR

For biographical information on William G. Wolber, see Chap. 8.

CHAPTER 10
ACTUATORS

Klaus Müller

Manager, Development of Magnet Valves, Pressure Supply
Automotive Equipment Division 1
Robert Bosch GmbH, Stuttgart

10.1 PREFACE

10.1.1 Introductory Remarks

Numerous open- and closed-loop control systems find application in modern production vehicles, where they provide improved operating characteristics together with enhanced safety, comfort, and environmental compatibility.

The actuators respond to position commands from the electronic control unit to regulate energy, mass, and volume flows.

10.1.2 Actuators: Basic Design and Operating Principles

Conventional final-control elements (standard and spool valves, etc.) have been familiar for some time. A provision for electronic control is required for actuator applications in modern vehicles. The actuator consists of a transformer to convert the input signal from the control unit into (usually) mechanical output quantities, and the conventional final-control element which it governs. (See Fig. 10.1.)

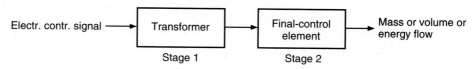

FIGURE 10.1 Basic actuator elements.

Either the control unit or the actuator itself will feature an integral electronic output amplifier. The energy conversion principles (stage 1) determine the classification of the actuators. Electromechanical actuators will also be discussed in the following pages.

10.2 TYPES OF ELECTROMECHANICAL ACTUATORS

10.2.1 Magnetic Actuators

dc Solenoids

Actuator Principles. In order to operate, actuators depend on the forces found at the interfaces in a coil-generated magnetic field when current passes through it. The solenoid actuation force F_m is calculated as

$$F_m = \frac{A\,B^2}{2\,\mu_o} \tag{10.1}$$

where A = pole face area
$\ B$ = magnetic induction
$\ \mu_o$ = permeability constant ($\mu_o = 4\,\pi\,10^{-7}\,\text{Vs/Am}$)

On the flat-armature solenoid illustrated in Fig. 10.2*a*, the total solenoid force is 2 F_m. Equation (10.1) can also be applied to versions equipped with a permanent magnet (Fig. 10.2*b*). A particular solenoid force is specified for each technical application. The pole face area, the magnetic circuit, and the coil are then determined for this force.

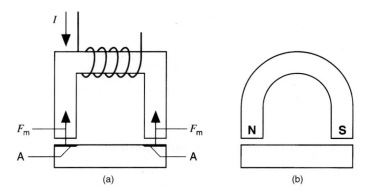

FIGURE 10.2 Flat-armature solenoid featuring field excitation (*a*) via coil; (*b*) via permanent magnet.

Determining Magnetic Circuit and Coil Specifications. The magnetic circuit consists of the working gap (between the armature and the base) and the ferrous regions. Permeability in iron is approximately three orders of magnitude greater than in air. For this reason, the iron regions conduct the field. If the effects of leakage flux are discounted, the absence of magnetic charge, $\oint B\,dA = 0$, means that the magnetic flux Φ_m remains constant for all cross sections A in the magnetic circuit:

$$\Phi_m = \iint_{A_1} B\,dA_1 = \iint_{A_2} B\,dA_2 = \iint_{A_i} B\,dA_i = \text{const.} \tag{10.2}$$

If the magnetic induction is assumed to be homogeneous for all cross sections A_i, then Eq. (10.2) can be simplified to:

$$\Phi_m = B_1\,A_1 = B_2\,A_2 = B_i\,A_i = \text{const.} \tag{10.3}$$

The induction lines run at a 90° angle to the surfaces A_i. Equation (10.3) defines the magnetic induction in each section of the magnetic circuit (Fig. 10.3). If, as an example, Index 1 is assigned to the gap section, then B_1 and A_1 are derived with the assistance of Eq. (10.1), and one can proceed to calculate B_i for the other sections.

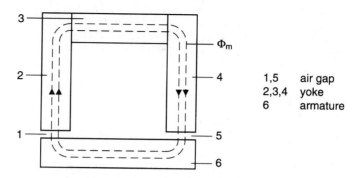

1,5	air gap
2,3,4	yoke
6	armature

FIGURE 10.3   Magnetic circuit divided into individual sections.

The magnitude of the magnetic field strength $\mathbf{H}_i$ is determined by the material properties (permeability μ_{ri}) of the section in question. Field strength $\mathbf{H}_i$:

$$\mathbf{B}_i = \mu_o \, \mu_{ri} \, \mathbf{H}_i \tag{10.4}$$

In air, $\mu_r = 1$. In ferromagnetic materials, μ_r does not remain constant. Rather, it varies as a function of the magnetic field strength $\mathbf{H}$ (see Fig. 10.4). The relationship between $\mathbf{B}$ and $\mathbf{H}$ is defined by the **B-H**-curve.

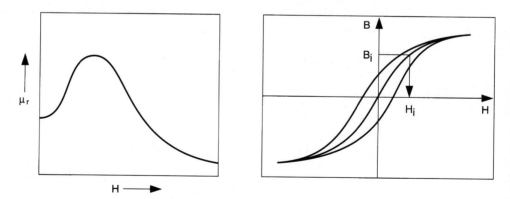

FIGURE 10.4   Progression of permeability and **B-H** curve.

Using the magnetic voltage $V_{mi} = \int \mathbf{H}_i \, d\mathbf{s}$ for the individual section, it is possible to calculate the peripheral magnetic voltage as the sum of the individual magnetic voltages V_{mi}. According to Ampere's law,

$$\Theta = \int \mathbf{H} \, d\mathbf{s} \tag{10.5}$$

this magnetic peripheral voltage is equal to the magnetomotive force Θ. It defines the *total current* of the coil, $\Theta = I \, w$. (I = current, w = number of windings.)

Because the preceding calculation fails to consider leakage flux, the results must frequently be treated as approximations only. It is possible to increase the precision of the calculations by portraying the magnetic circuit as a general network (with gaps and iron regions as reluctance elements) instead of as a series circuit. The results will then reflect the effects of a large proportion of the leakage flux. Maximum precision is achieved with numeric field calculations, which provide numerical solution of Maxwell's equations.

After magnetomotive force Θ has been determined, the field coil must be dimensioned to produce the required magnetic field. The formulas contained in Fig. 10.5 can be employed to determine the field coil's specifications. For a graphic interpretation, see Fig. 10.6.

$A_w = h \cdot l$

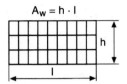

Winding cross section area:

$$A_w = \frac{R \pi \rho (d_a + d_i)(1 + \alpha \, \Delta\vartheta)^2 \, \Theta^2}{2 \, k_w \, U^2}$$

Winding number:

$$w = \left(\frac{2 A_w \, k_w \, R}{\Pi \rho (d_a + d_i)} \right)^{1/2}$$

Wire diameter:

$$d = \left(\frac{8 \rho (d_a + d_i) \, A_w \, k_w}{\pi R} \right)^{1/4}$$

A_w	Winding cross section area	$\Delta\vartheta$	Temperature differential between coil and room temperature
R	Coil resistance		
ρ	Specific resistance of coil wire	Θ	Magnetomotive force
		k_w	Coil space factor (ratio of total wire area (w/o insulation) to winding cross section area)
d_a	Outer diameter of windings		
d_i	Inside diameter of windings		
α	Thermal resistivity coefficient of coil wire	U	Voltage at coil

FIGURE 10.5   Determining coil data for specified coil resistance and voltage levels.

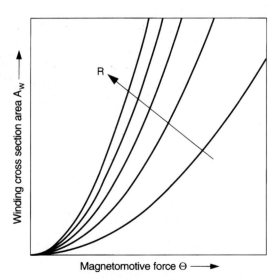

FIGURE 10.6   Area of winding A_w as function of magnetomotive force Θ (parameter coil resistance).

To minimize the size of the solenoid assembly, the magnetic circuit and the coil must be dimensioned to produce the smallest overall size. The formulas for coil dimensions (Fig. 10.7) can be used to minimize the volume of pot-shaped solenoids.

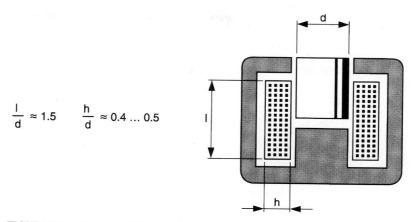

$$\frac{l}{d} \approx 1.5 \qquad \frac{h}{d} \approx 0.4 \ldots 0.5$$

FIGURE 10.7   Selecting coil dimensions for pot-shaped solenoids.

In general, the solenoid is iteratively optimized by changing geometry in those critical areas within the magnetic circuit requiring a high magnetic voltage V_{mi}. The magnetomotive force Θ is then recalculated for the modified magnetic circuit. Figure 10.8 shows the optimization of solenoid diameter D for a particular armature diameter d.

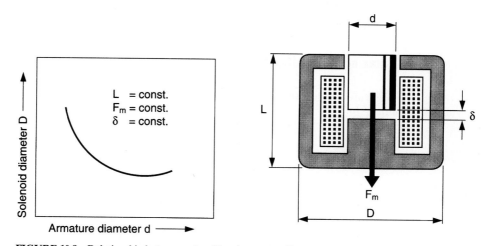

FIGURE 10.8   Relationship between solenoid and armature diameters.

Magnetic Force Curve.   When the unit is intended for use in an actuator, the relationship between magnetic force and stroke will be required. With a flat armature and base, and without including the iron regions, Ampere's law [Eq. (10.5)] and Eq. (10.4) provide the following:

$$\Theta = H_\delta\,\delta = \frac{B_\delta\delta}{\mu_o} \tag{10.6}$$

where δ = working gap

Together with the force relationship, Eq. (10.1), the following result is obtained:

$$F_m = \frac{\Theta^2\,\mu_o\,A_1}{2\,\delta^2}\,, \text{ i.e., } F_m \sim \frac{1}{\delta^2} \qquad (10.7)$$

The substantial drop in magnetic force will be undesirable in many applications. Modifications to the curve for magnetic force versus stroke represent an alternative to increases in solenoid dimensions. This expedient can be effected through control of the current in the coil or by means of design modifications to the armature and base (see Fig. 10.9).

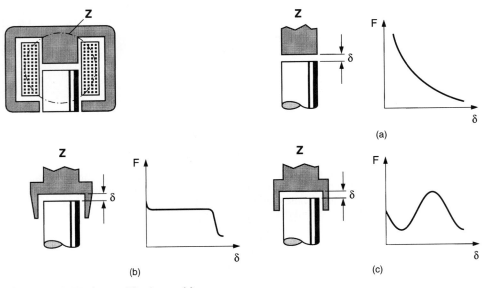

FIGURE 10.9 Design modifications and force curve.

The areas below the force-travel curves, a measure of the work performed, are always the same.

$$\int_0^\infty F_m\,(\delta)\,d\delta = \text{const.} \qquad (10.8)$$

with   I = const.

Configuration c can be employed together with a spring to produce a proportional solenoid in which armature travel can be regulated as a function of current. This type of system is sensitive to interference from extraneous factors such as mechanical friction, and hydraulic and pneumatic forces. Thus, final-control systems for high-precision applications must also incorporate a position sensor and a controller (Fig. 10.10).

Dynamic Response.   To show the dynamic response pattern more clearly, Fig. 10.11 provides a schematic illustration of the progression over time of three parameters: voltage u at the excitation coil, excitation current i, and armature position s.

The dynamic response pattern can be calculated using computer programs that apply Maxwell's equations (field propagation with eddy currents, self-induction) in conjunction with the motion equation.

Approximation formulas can be employed to derive rapid estimates (eddy currents and magnetic resistance in the iron regions are not taken into account):

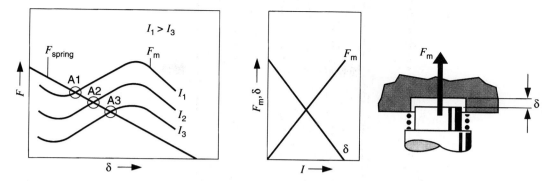

FIGURE 10.10   Operating points of a proportional solenoid.

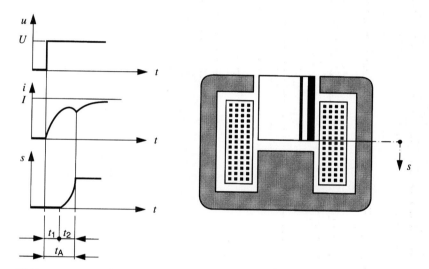

FIGURE 10.11   Progression of voltage, current, and armature travel.

$$t_1 \approx \frac{L_o}{R} \ln \frac{1}{1 - \dfrac{R}{U} \left(\dfrac{2\,F_{\text{mech}}\,\delta_o}{L_o} \right)^{1/2}} \tag{10.9a}$$

$$t_2 \approx \left(\frac{3\,\delta_o m}{U \left(\dfrac{F_{\text{mech}}}{2\,\delta_o\,L_o} \right)^{1/2} - R\,\dfrac{F_{\text{mech}}}{L_o}} \right)^{1/3} \tag{10.9b}$$

where L_o = initial inductance
R = coil resistance
U = voltage at solenoid
δ_o = gap with armature lowered
F_{mech} = armature counterforce (treated as constant)
and t_1, t_2, see Fig. 10.11

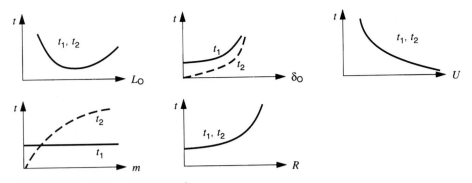

FIGURE 10.12   Relationships of t_1 and t_2.

Figure 10.12 provides an overview of the relationships between t_1 and t_2 and the parameters.

The eddy currents must also be considered in calculations dealing with electromagnets intended for operation at high speeds or switching frequencies. When the excitation current is applied suddenly, the progress over time for the magnetic force is

$$F_m(t) = F_{m0}(1 - e^{-t/\tau})^2 \qquad \text{for field generation}$$

and

$$F_m(t) = F_{m0}\, e^{-2t/\tau} \qquad \text{for field dissipation}$$

with

$$\tau = \frac{\mu_0 l_{Fe} ab}{\pi^2 \rho\, \delta\, (a/b + b/a)} \qquad \text{for rectangular cross sections}$$

with

$$\tau = \frac{\mu_0 l_{Fe} d^2}{4\,(2.405)^2 \rho\, \delta} \qquad \text{for circular cross sections}$$

where F_{m0} = static solenoid force according to Eq. (10.1)
    t = time
    l_{Fe} = length of iron core in which eddy currents occur
    a/b = height/width of iron core (rectangular cross section)
    d = diameter of iron core (circular cross section)
    ρ = specific resistance
    δ = working gap

Lamination to inhibit eddy currents in dc solenoids is not a standard procedure; its application is restricted to extreme cases.

Figures 10.6 and 10.12 illustrate the fact that at a given voltage, small coil resistances will furnish a small coil and short activation times. However, these benefits are accompanied by a simultaneous increase in the power loss $P_v = U^2/R$. The coil is thus designed to operate at the maximum permissible temperature.

Torque Motors.   The torque motor consists of a stator and an armature—both made of soft magnetic material—and a permanent magnet. The pivoting armature can be equipped with either one or two coils.

Figure 10.13*a* shows only the magnetic flux generated by the permanent magnet. The armature is resting at the center position. The magnitude of the magnetic induction is the same at all

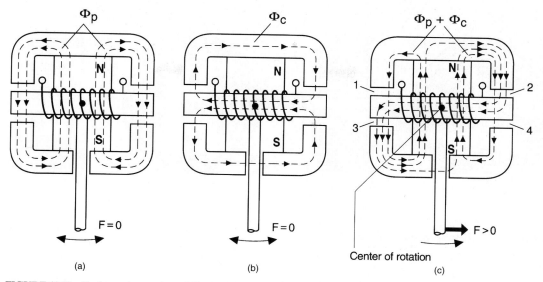

FIGURE 10.13 Design and operation of the torque motor.

gaps. Because equal amounts of force are generated at the armature ends, the forces acting on it exercise a mutual canceling effect.

Figure 10.13*b* illustrates only that magnetic flux which is generated at the coil. Figure 10.13*c* shows the cumulative pattern for the fluxes from *a* and *b*, with increased flow at gaps 2 and 3 ($\Phi_p/2 + \Phi_c/2$) accompanied by reductions at gaps 1 and 4 ($\Phi_p/2 - \Phi_c/2$). Using Eq. (10.1), the torque in the center position is

$$M = F_m\, r = \frac{r\, A B_p}{2\, s}\, w\, I, \text{i.e., } M \sim I \tag{10.10}$$

where r = armature radius
A = pole face area
B_p = magnetic induction in gap generated by permanent magnet
s = length of gap
w = number of coil windings
I = current.

Torque motors are used for applications in which substantial forces are required over small operating angles. They react more rapidly than electromagnets. In hydraulic and pneumatic applications, torque motors deliver good performance as drive units for flapper and nozzle systems.

Electromagnetic Step Motors.   Electromagnetic step motors are drive elements in which a special design operates in conjunction with pulse-shaped control signals to carry out rotary or linear stepped movements. Thus, one complete rotation of the motor shaft will be composed of a precisely defined number of increments, step angles ϕ_0. The magnitude of these angles is determined by the phase number q, the pole pair number p, and by the number of teeth z in the step motor. The step motor is thus capable of transforming digital control signals directly into discontinuous rotary motion. In principle, the step motor is essentially a combination of dc solenoids. The calculations employed for dc solenoids are thus also suitable for application with electromagnetic step motors. Depending upon the configuration of the magnetic circuit, a distinction is made between three types of step motors: the variable-reluctance step motor (neutral magnetic circuit), heteropolar units (polarized magnetic circuit), and hybrid devices.

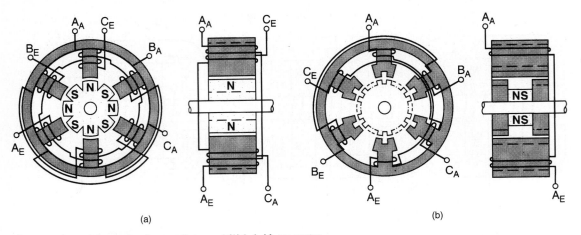

FIGURE 10.14 (*a*) Heteropolar step motor and (*b*) hybrid step motor.

Due to its positive operating characteristics (holding force available in power-off state, improved cushioning, lower control power requirement for a given volume), the polarized step motor has come to be the most widely applied (see Fig. 10.14).

Drive systems featuring electromagnetic step motors combine the following characteristics:

- Field forces induce controllable, incremental movements (minimal wear).
- Precisely graduated movements can be generated using an open-loop control circuit (without position monitors or feedback signals).
- High torque remains available at low angular velocities and in single-step operation.
- Brushless motor design makes it possible to create drive systems which combine reliability with long service life.

The operating characteristics of the rotational step motor can be described with the aid of a stationary torque-angle (M-ϕ) curve. A reasonable approximation can be obtained using sinus-shaped curves with a phase displacement reflecting the switching states of the phase windings (A, B, C) (Fig. 10.15a). Assuming that external torque inputs can be excluded, the

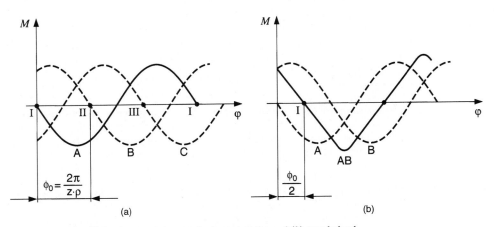

FIGURE 10.15 (*a*) Stationary torque-angle characteristics and (*b*) step-halved.

armature's stable position will be found where the backslope of the curve intersects the abscissa ($I, \Sigma\,M = 0, dM/d\phi < 0$). Phase B, C, etc., can then be activated to perpetuate rotation. The periodicity of the stable positions I, II, III is the step angle ϕ_0.

If phase A is followed by simultaneous excitation of A and B with current pulses of the same amplitude, the result is a summing pattern corresponding to Fig. 10.15b. The geometric step angle ϕ_0 can then be halved. Alternatively, simultaneous excitation with current pulses of different amplitudes (current control) can be used to subdivide ϕ_0 to almost any degree desired (microstep operation). However, the use of this strategy to enhance the step motor's positioning precision is not possible due to manufacturing tolerances. When step motors are used in drive systems which rely upon open-loop control methods, avoiding stepping errors becomes an important priority (synchronous response).

For critical applications, dynamic simulation of the step drive system's dynamic response pattern is recommended. Here, a good approximation is derived by portraying the step motor using a transfer function of a second-order system. Dynamic response can also be evaluated using the torque-step frequency pattern (M-f pattern) for potential step-error-free operation in a start-stop frequency range, Fig. 10.16a, and an operating frequency range, Fig. 10.16b.

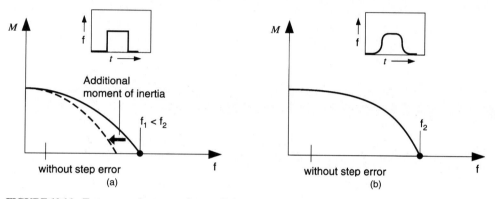

FIGURE 10.16   Torque-step frequency characteristic.

The range in which step error does not occur contracts in response to additional inertial torques or mobile masses. Impressed current induces an upward shift in the potential frequency range which is larger than that derived from impressed voltage. This demonstrates that the step motor's response pattern is strongly influenced by the electronic control strategy. The stepping frequency controls the angular velocity, the pulse distribution (A $\rightarrow$ B or A $\rightarrow$ C, see Fig. 10.15) determines the direction of rotation, and the number of pulses governs the pivot angle.

Step motors are only suitable for use as direct-drive elements (the motor's armature operates directly against the actuated unit, no gear drive) in those applications where the influence of load fluctuations and interference factors remains limited, as stepping errors can otherwise occur. For this reason, digital linear actuators featuring integrated rotary step motors and threaded spindles are becoming increasingly popular as linear-motion generators in high-demand applications. When operated within a closed-loop control system, step motors can provide improvements in dynamics, positioning precision, and sturdiness. However, the cost advantages associated with open-loop operation are forfeited.

Moving Coils.   The moving coil is an electrodynamic device (force applied to current-saturated conductor in a magnetic field). A spring-mounted coil is located in the ring gap of a magnetic circuit featuring a permanent magnet. When current flows through the coil, a force is exerted against it. The direction of this force is determined by the flow direction of the current itself.

The positioning force can be calculated using

$$F = B_A L_W I, \text{ i.e., } F \sim I \tag{10.11}$$

where B_A = magnetic induction in the gap
L_W = length of the coil wire
I = excitation current

As the force is not affected by the travel position, a spring can be included to produce a proportional relationship between travel and current.

The advantages of the moving coil include low hysteresis and good linear response. Low mass acts in combination with low coil inductance to provide excellent dynamic-response characteristics. The main liabilities of this design lie in the low force and limited work per stroke for any given unit dimensions.

dc Motors.   dc motors are used to discharge a multiplicity of functions in modern cars (today up to 70 motors per vehicle). These motors are generally permanently excited dc devices, as the magnetic field remains continually available without additional energy consumption. For economic reasons, these units are virtually always equipped with ferrite magnets.

Design and Operation.   The dc motor depends for its operation on the forces generated in a conductor within a magnetic field when current is applied.

The permanent-magnet-excited motor consists of

- The magnetic circuit consisting of a permanent magnet for generation and an iron core and a stator frame to conduct the magnetic flux
- Energized coils
- Carbon brushes and commutator, arranged to direct the current to the rotating coil while maintaining the force flow in a single direction

The stationary characteristic can be represented using the following equations (see Fig. 10.17).

$$U_1 = IR + U_i \tag{10.12a}$$

$$U_i = c\,z\,\Phi\,\omega \tag{10.12b}$$

$$M_i = M_v + M = c\,z\,\Phi\,I \tag{10.12c}$$

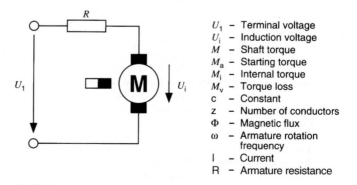

U_1 – Terminal voltage
U_i – Induction voltage
M – Shaft torque
M_a – Starting torque
M_i – Internal torque
M_v – Torque loss
c – Constant
z – Number of conductors
Φ – Magnetic flux
ω – Armature rotation frequency
I – Current
R – Armature resistance

FIGURE 10.17   dc motor, circuit diagram.

After inserting Eqs. (10.12*b*) and (10.12*c*) in (10.12*a*), with

$$\omega_{0i} = \frac{U_1}{c\,z\,\Phi} \qquad \text{(ideal idle speed)} \tag{10.13a}$$

$$M_a = c\,z\,\Phi\,\frac{U_1}{R} - M_v \qquad \text{(stall torque)} \tag{10.13b}$$

one obtains

$$\omega = \omega_{0i}\left(1 - \frac{M + M_v}{M_a + M_v}\right) \tag{10.14}$$

or, with idle speed $\omega_0 = \omega(M = 0)$

$$\omega = \omega_0\left(1 - \frac{M}{M_a}\right) \tag{10.15}$$

The motor draws power P_1 from the dc circuit.

$$P_1 = U_1\,I \tag{10.16}$$

or

$$P_1 = \frac{U_1}{c\,z\,\Phi}\,(M_v + M) = \omega_0\,\frac{M_v + M_a}{M_a}\,(M_v + M) \tag{10.17}$$

The output at the shaft is the mechanical power P_2

$$P_2 = M\,\omega = M\,\omega_0\left(1 - \frac{M}{M_a}\right) \tag{10.18}$$

Using Eqs. (10.17) and (10.18), the efficiency η can be calculated as a function of the shaft torque.

$$\eta = \frac{P_2}{P_1} = \frac{M(M - M_a)(M_v + M_a)}{M_a(M_v + M)} \tag{10.19}$$

Maximum efficiency as a function of load is obtained by setting the derivative $d\eta/dM = 0$ with

$$M_{\max} = M_v + [M_v(M_v + M_a)]^{1/2} \tag{10.20}$$

In comparison, the output power derived with Eq. (10.18) reaches a maximum at $M = M_a/2$, and thus at a higher value.

Figure 10.18 shows a performance diagram with speed *n*, current *I*, and efficiency η as function of the load torque *M*. It is not possible to determine speed and current separately.

Equations (10.12*a*) through (10.20) illustrate the interactions and the factors that affect the motor's performance curve. The influence of the design parameters is shown in Fig. 10.19.

The magnetic flux Φ is determined by the dimensions and intrinsic material characteristics of the magnet, and by the stack length of the armature and the rest of the magnetic circuit. The speed/torque curve responds to increasing magnetic flux Φ by tilting progressively to the horizontal axis; this response pattern is indicative of a more powerful motor (see Fig. 10.19*a*).

Variations in the number of turns *z* change the idle speed n_0 at the same starting torque (see Fig. 10.19*b*); changes in the armature's resistance (produced by selecting a different wire diameter *d*) affect the stall current, and thus the stall torque, obtained at any given idle speed n_0 (see Fig. 10.19*c*). The maximum achievable copper content is determined by the winding technique.

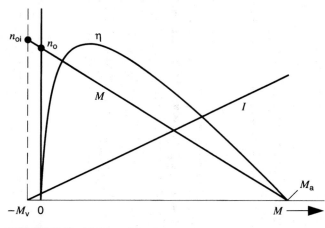

FIGURE 10.18   Motor performance curve.

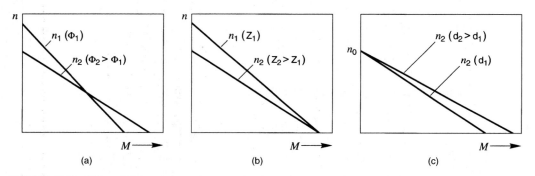

FIGURE 10.19   Effect of design parameters on rotational speed.

Units used in real-world applications display small deviations from the theoretical performance curve as a result of voltage drop at the carbon brushes, the current transfer to the commutator, the armature reaction field produced by the motor's current, and, finally, various rotational and flux losses.

The options for using the electrical parameters to affect the rotating speed are illustrated in Fig. 10.20. Variations in the voltage U (e.g., of the kind produced electronically with a pulse-width modulation) produce a parallel displacement in the speed curve (Fig. 10.20a). Other common options include the installation of a ballast resistor R_v and the inclusion of a third carbon brush. Less common (due to cost) is a design in which the winding is divided between two commutators; these can then be activated individually, in parallel, or in series. Servo motors generally operate for brief periods of time, but also over the entire range represented by the unit's characteristic curve.

Each motor must be built specifically for the operating conditions anticipated for the individual vehicle. Ferrite magnets must be selected for the lowest potential temperature, as it is here that the resistance to demagnetization is lowest. When circumstances demand, thermoswitches can also be included to provide protection against overheating.

Automotive actuators must be small and light. Motor volume is directly proportional to torque requirement. At the same time, the power output is proportional to torque multiplied

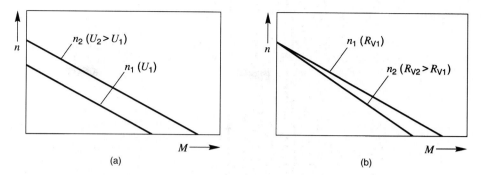

FIGURE 10.20   Speed variations in dc motors.

by rotating speed. Thus, the output can be increased by raising the operating speed; here the accompanying rise in noise levels is the limiting factor. Small motors are equipped with gear-drive units to obtain the required levels of actuating force.

Magnetostrictive Actuators.   Ferromagnetic materials respond to increased magnetic field strength by expanding or contracting (magnetostrictive effect). This is due to the Weiss' domains turning in the field direction. The maximum contraction obtained with iron is -8 μm/m. Highly magnetostrictive materials composed of rare-earth/iron alloys display a maximum elongation of 1500 to 2000 μm/m. Maximum potential elongation is obtained at the optimal mechanical pre-tension T_0 (Fig. 10.21).

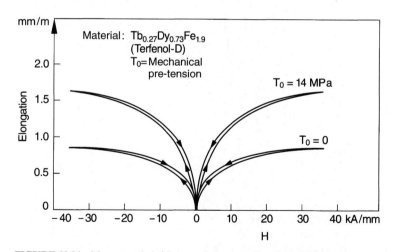

FIGURE 10.21   Magnetostrictive form variations as a function of field strength.

The specific advantages of the magnetostrictive transformer are high actuator forces, rapid response, good rigidity, and a high level of electromechanical efficiency.

The disadvantages include the small variations in length, the high power loss associated with generation of the large maximum field strengths which the unit requires (also in static operation), the length variation with hysteresis, the expense, and the limited availability of the requisite materials. The material is also brittle and difficult to machine.

The commercial availability of the transformers is limited to units designed for research purposes. We are not familiar with any applications in production motor vehicles.

10.2.2   Electrical Actuators

Piezoelectric Actuators.   When mechanical compression and tension are brought to bear on a piezoelectric body, they produce an asymmetrical displacement in the crystal structure and in the charge centers of the affected crystal ions. The result is charge separation. An electric voltage proportional to the mechanical pressure can be measured at the metallic electrodes (direct piezoelectric effect).

If electric voltage is applied to the electrodes on this same body, it will respond with a change in shape; the volume remains constant. This reciprocal piezoelectric effect can be exploited to produce actuators. Sintered ceramics, lead-zirconate-titanate (PZT), are the commonly used materials for these applications. The precise composition can be modified to obtain the desired material characteristics. The magnitude of the shape change depends on the electric field strength E. The relevant equation is $E = U / s$ (U = voltage, s = electrode gap). Single-element actuators require field strengths of up to 2 kV/mm and therefore very high voltage to achieve maximum travel (see Fig. 10.22).

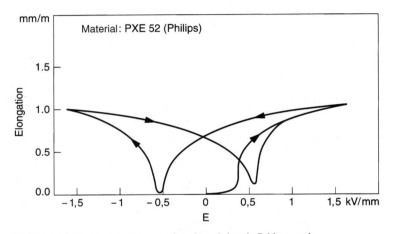

FIGURE 10.22   Form changes as a function of electric field strength.

Stacked-design translational devices consist of piezoelectric layers of between 0.3 and 1 mm in thickness, featuring a metallic electrode between each layer. This design is employed to lower the voltage (down to, for instance, 800 V) while simultaneously increasing the excursion rate. The layers are electrically parallel and form a series circuit (see Fig. 10.23a).

Flex elements are formed by joining two layers with varying intrinsic rates of elongation. The elongation occurs along the vertical axis of the direction in which the field strength is projected (transverse effect). Flex elements display larger excursion rates with lower actuating forces (see Fig. 10.23b).

New manufacturing techniques make it possible to produce multilayer piezoelectric devices with thinner layers; these can be used to obtain the required field strength at voltages as low as approximately 100 V and below.

However, due to the numerous parallel elements, the advantages associated with the low control voltage are obtained only at the price of increased capacitance and higher operating currents.

The positive attributes of the piezoelectric actuator include a high dynamic response level, substantial actuator force, voltage-proportional elongation, excursion with no power consumption in static operation, and (practically) no wear in the piezoelectric element.

The corresponding liabilities include minimal elongation changes, high operating voltage, hysteresis during elongation, a temperature-sensitive stroke, and a drift in operating response as the unit ages. The material itself is brittle and difficult to machine.

	a	**b**
Elongation Δl	Parallel to electrical field	Perpendicular to electrical field
Design types	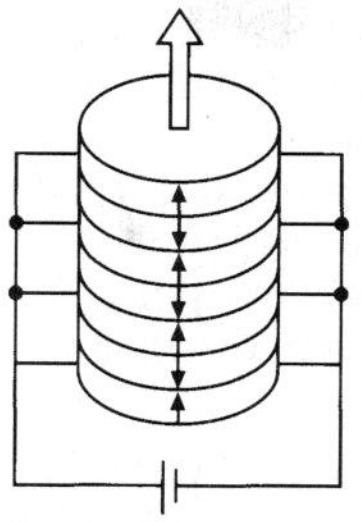	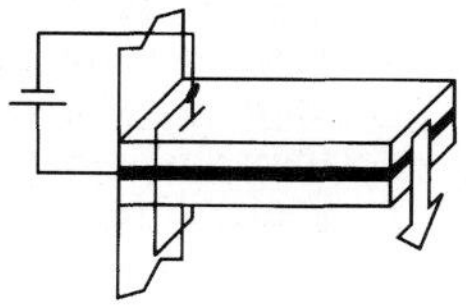
Typical regulation distance and elongation	$\dfrac{\Delta l}{l_0} = 0.17\ \%$	$\Delta l \leq 1000\ \mu m$ and more
max. statical load	$\leq 35\,000$ N	$\leq 0.01 \ldots 0.05$ N
Typical operation voltage	$150 \ldots 1000$ V $50 \ldots\ 150$ V (multilayer)	$10 \ldots 300$ V

FIGURE 10.23   Design and specifications of different transformer versions.

Piezoelectric actuators are applied in precision positioning devices and as active oscillation dampers. Potential automotive applications (with a voltage supply of 12 V) have yet to be thoroughly investigated. However, it is expected that the piezoelectric actuator—and the multilayer stacked-design device in particular—will gain popularity in closed-loop automotive control systems, where they will serve as a replacement for the conventional actuator in applications requiring a higher level of performance.

Electrostatic Actuators.   In the past, use of electrical field forces was restricted to some measurement devices and to the acceleration of charged particles. Microactuator technology makes it possible to apply these small forces in mechanical drive devices. These devices combine high switching speeds with much smaller energy loss than that found in electromagnetic actuators. The disadvantages are the force/travel limitations and the high operating voltages. At present, microactuators are rarely encountered outside the research laboratories; thus, the electrostatic actuator's current commercial significance is negligible.

Electrorheological Fluids.   The electrorheological effect is based on polarization processes in minute particles suspended in a fluid medium. These particles modify the fluid's viscosity according to the orientation in the electrical field. The effect can be employed to adjust the viscosity between "freely flowing" and "rigid." Reaction times are measured in ms. Among the disadvantages are interference factors, temperature sensitivity, high voltages, control powers of several hundred watts, and the price, which is still high. The electrorheological effect is exploited in controlled transfer and damping elements.

10.2.3 Thermal Actuators

Temperature-Sensitive Bimetallic Elements.   The temperature-sensitive bimetallic element is composed of at least two bonded components of varying thermal-expansion coefficients. When heat is applied, the components expand at different rates, causing the bimetallic element to bend. When electrically generated heat is applied, these devices become actuators.

The passive component is characterized by a lower thermal-expansion coefficient. Meanwhile, the active component should maintain a constant coefficient of thermal expansion over the largest possible range.

The passive element in the most common type of temperature-sensitive bimetallic device is invar ($FeNi_{36}$), while the active component is an alloy of iron, nickel, and manganese ($FeNi_{20}Mn_6$). Common element configurations include strips, coils, spirals, and wafers. Temperature-sensitive bimetallic devices are readily available and inexpensive. They can be applied at temperatures of up to roughly 650 °C, and display a high degree of consistency in their shape-change response (up to several million cycles). The drawbacks include the modest actuator forces, the low work potential for a given volume (energy density), and the fact that only a single type of shape modification (flexural) is possible.

Memory Alloys.   Memory alloys are metallic materials which exhibit a substantial degree of "shape memory." The explanation for this phenomenon can be found in the reversible, thermoelastic martensitic transformation, in which two different crystal structures are adopted. As long as the temperature remains below the transformation threshold, the structure remains martensitic. However, when the alloy is heated beyond the transformation temperature, it responds by becoming austenitic.

The element's shape is changed permanently by the one-way effect. If the element is heated to beyond the transformation temperature, it returns to its former shape. If the component is then reshaped after cooling, the entire process can be repeated. Thermomechanical pretreatment processes can be employed to achieve a two-way effect. The component then assumes one defined shape when heated, and another when cooled.

Yet another phenomenon is superelasticity. Application of loads produces an extension of up to 10 percent; the effect is reversed once the load is removed. However, because this effect is extremely sensitive to temperature, it has yet to be employed in the construction of actuators. The materials are commercially available, the base materials are nickel-titanium (NiTi–) and copper-zinc-aluminum alloys (CuZnAl–). The transformation temperatures of these alloys lie between –100 and +100 °C, with the one-way effect also being obtained outside this range.

The benefits of memory alloys include the high effective output for a given volume and the ability to complete work cycles within a minimal temperature interval of 10 to 30 °C. The memory components can be formed to suit the particular application. The wire's resistance can be employed for direct heating. The material itself can be formed with or without physical machining, and can also be welded. Among the disadvantages must be counted the limited thermal range of application and the high price.

Memory alloys are used as drive, final-control, and triggering elements in various technical applications (automotive, household appliances, heating and climate control, medical technology, etc.). The forms assumed by the actual components include triggering wires, coil springs, and flex and torsion elements.

The memory element can be used as sensor and actuator—for instance, in a liquid medium—in which temperature changes will induce shape changes in the component.

Expansion Elements.   The expansion element exploits the volume-versus-temperature response of specific solid and fluid media which exhibit large coefficients of thermal expansion. The volumetric response is converted to a stroke motion. The expansion medium is housed in a rigid container. The motion is converted to a stroke using diaphragms or elastomer inserts. Electrically controlled expansion elements find application as actuators. Expansion elements are inexpensive and robust, and combine large stroke travel with substantial positioning forces.

However, these devices are only suitable for application within a limited temperature range. Their dynamic response is also less than overwhelming. Expansion elements are widely applied in automotive technology (for instance, choke actuators on carbureted engines).

10.3 *AUTOMOTIVE ACTUATORS*

10.3.1   Antilock Braking

(See Chap. 15 and **traction control systems**, Chap. 16.)

Both antilock braking systems (ABS) and traction control systems (ASR) limit the rate of slip between tire and road surface. These systems enhance vehicle stability and steering response while maintaining optimal braking and acceleration characteristics. ABS and ASR employ a single set of actuators to modulate braking pressure. In addition, ASR devices supplement braking intervention by adjusting engine output.

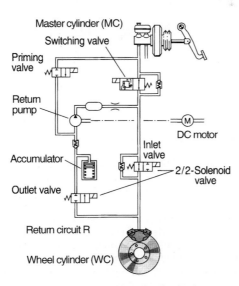

FIGURE 10.24   ABS/ASR hydraulic circuitry.

Actuators for Braking Intervention.   Braking pressure is regulated normally via 2/2 solenoid valves (valves with two ports and two switch positions, see Fig. 10.24). When no current is applied, the inlet valve remains open and the outlet valve is closed, allowing unrestricted wheel braking.

ABS/ASR systems modulate pressure by controlling two 2/2 solenoids for each wheel or for two wheels of one axle. With no current, the inlet valve remains open while the outlet valve stays closed. To maintain pressure, current is applied to the inlet valve. Pressure release is obtained by transmitting current to both valves.

Various pulse sequences applied to the inlet valve generate a step-by-step increase of the wheel braking pressure (wheel brake pressure modulation).

Using the same pulse sequence for the outlet valve while the inlet valve remains closed, a step-by-step brake pressure decrease in the wheel cylinders is achieved. Switching and priming valves of a 2/2 type can be incorporated in the circuit to provide the additional functions required for the ASR (Fig. 10.25).

Solenoid Valve Design.   One part of the magnetic circuit is located in the hydraulic chamber; here the armature and the pole piece simultaneously serve as valve elements in a design known as the wet solenoid. The solenoid coil and the other part of the magnetic iron circuit are located outside the hydraulic chamber. This design requires the presence of a pressure-resistant sealing element. This element must also be nonmagnetic, in order to ensure that the magnetic flux flows through the working gap and the armature in the desired fashion.

The solenoid circuit is designed to provide reliable switching and pressure maintenance at maximum temperature (maximum coil resistance), minimum voltage, and maximum pressure. At the same time, armature clearance and residual gap must both be adequate to ensure that the valve continues to function at low temperatures (brake-fluid viscosity changes exponentially (by three powers of ten) in the range between –40 and +120 °C). The maximum operating pressures can extend in extreme cases to more than 200 bar. Typical switching times are 4 to 10 ms. Dynamic response is evaluated according to the pressure variation at a specified control pulse. The duty-cycle requirements for ABS are minimal, but ASR switching and priming valves must be capable of 100 percent permanent duty. The maximum cycle numbers correspond to several million actuations.

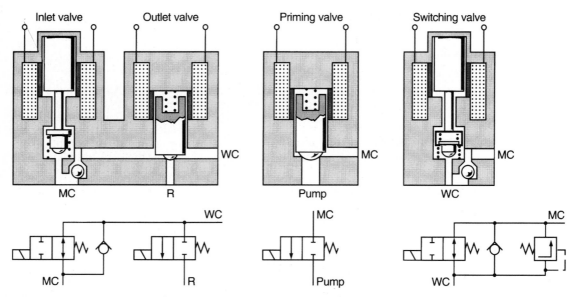

FIGURE 10.25   2/2 solenoid valves for ABS/ASR.

ETC with Throttle-Aperture Adjustment.   Either of two standard methods can be employed for throttle regulation. Electronic Throttle Control (ETC) systems feature an actuator (servo motor) mounted directly at the throttle valve. On systems incorporating a traction-control actuator, the actuator (servo motor) is installed in the throttle cable (Bowden cable).

The design configuration of the electronic throttle-control actuator is illustrated in Fig. 10.26. To enhance clarity and facilitate understanding, all rotating components (except the throttle plate) are portrayed as linear-motion devices. The throttle shaft travels between two

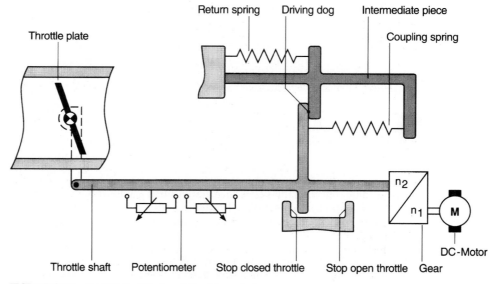

FIGURE 10.26   Operation of electronic throttle control.

motion limiters; these define the closed throttle and maximum aperture positions. The shaft is powered by a dc motor via a dual-gear drive. When the motor is off, a return spring pulls the intermediate piece back toward the idle-air stop. The driving dog pushes the throttle shaft toward the idle position. The coupling spring holds it in a defined idle position. This position corresponds to an idle speed ensuring adequate engine power to maintain power-steering and brake operation in the event of system failure.

Current can be applied to the dc motor in either direction. One direction opens the throttle plate and tensions the return spring. The other direction closes the throttle plate. When the throttle plate closes all the way, the coupling spring is tensioned. Two potentiometric throttle-position sensors are included in a design calculated to provide redundant system capacity. The electronic control unit uses the signals from these sensors to regulate motor current for the desired throttle position; the signals thus represent part of a closed-loop control system.

Traction-Control Actuator. The actuator can be installed in any of several locations within the engine compartment. No modifications to the throttle body are required.

Figure 10.27 illustrates the operating principles in a simplified linear flow pattern (the actuator components are actually rotary elements). The ends of the Bowden cable sections are connected to rotary cam/linkage spring assemblies.

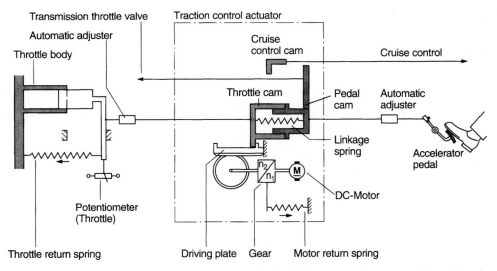

FIGURE 10.27 Operation of a traction-control actuator located between the accelerator pedal and throttle body.

Under normal operating conditions, the pressure applied at the accelerator pedal is relayed through the Bowden cable and linkage spring coupling to open the throttle valve. The servo motor comes to life when the ABS/ASR control unit transmits a command to reduce the throttle-valve aperture. The servo motor pulls the engagement mechanism to the left via gear drive and Bowden cable. Once the initial take-up range has been covered, the linkage is activated to reduce the throttle-valve opening. The servo motor is deactivated as soon as the ASR no longer requires throttle-valve regulation. A return spring then brings the motor back into its original position, allowing the traction control actuator to drive back to its original at rest position.

The traction-control actuator can also be used in conjunction with a cruise-control system. A separate cam connects the Bowden cable for the cruise control to the actuator assembly. This layout is employed to retain the option of traction-control intervention when the cruise-control system is activated.

Because the linkage spring must be considerably stronger than the throttle-return spring, it exerts a perceptible effect on the resistance at the accelerator pedal.

Another approach to engine intervention is embodied in a design in which the linkage spring is integrated within the throttle body. Yet a further option is to install a second throttle valve which remains open during normal operation; a separate Bowden cable is installed between this throttle body and the actuator to regulate the valve for active traction-control duties. Because the linkage spring is installed parallel to the throttle-return spring, the preload is substantially lower than that generated by the design described here; there is almost no perceptible feedback at the accelerator pedal. Actuator weight and dimensions are also reduced substantially.

10.3.2 Fuel-Injection for Spark-Ignition Engines

(See Chap. 12.)

Electronically controlled fuel injection systems meter fuel with the assistance of electromagnetic injectors. The injector's opening time determines the discharge of the correct amount of fuel.

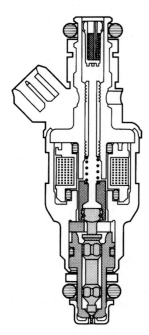

FIGURE 10.28 Injector unit for multipoint fuel injection system.

On single-point injection units, one injector unit is installed at a central location upstream from the throttle valve. Multipoint injection systems feature a separate injector at each cylinder (Fig. 10.28). This type of injector is located in the manifold tract just above the intake port into which it discharges its fuel.

Operating Requirements.   The injectors are 2/2 valves with coaxial fuel inlet and lateral plug. They operate with minimal strokes of less than $\frac{1}{10}$ mm.

Besides the precise opening and closing, the reliable sealing and the discharge pattern which an individual injector provides are all largely determined by the design of its metering apparatus, thus exercising a major effect on starting and response, fuel consumption, and emissions.

Electromagnetic injectors have to fulfill the demand for precise fuel metering, consistent linear response at minimal quantities, extended dynamic flow range (DFR), good spray formation and atomization, positive seal at injector seat, resistance to corrosion, operating consistency, and low noise.

Low-resistance injectors with current-controlled output stages achieve shorter switching times. See Table 10.1.

10.3.3 Fuel Injection for Diesel Engines

Distributor-Type Fuel Injection Pumps contain rotary solenoid actuators for injection quantity, and two position valves for engine operation and shutoff.

The fuel quantity injected by an in-line pump is a function of control-rack position and pump speed (Fig. 10.29).

TABLE 10.1 Typical Injector Specifications

	Units	Multipoint injection	Single-point injection
Line pressure . . . max.	kPa	200–380	100–300
Static flow at 250 kPa,	g/min	100–430	—
at 100 kPa,	g/min	—	200–520
Opening time	ms	1.5	0.75
Closing time	ms	0.8	0.65
Variation ratio (DFR)		1:10	1:16
Durability >mio.cycle		1000	1000
Needle/armature weight	g	4.3	2.7
Length	mm	77	53

The control rack of an EDC in-line pump is shifted by a linear-motion solenoid with a conic armature and base for long stroke application (see pages 10.5 and 10.6). The actuator is attached directly to the pump.

When no current is applied to the linear-motion solenoid, a spring pushes the control rack into the stop position and thus interrupts fuel delivery. As current increases, the control-rack travel and, with it the injection quantity, increase.

Typical operating data of the solenoid actuator are (full load, stationary condition): rack travel 13 mm, spring force 32 N, ECU current output 6 A, 200 Hz. By pulsation of the ECU-current, the actuator friction is minimized. Maximum rack travel is about 20 mm.

The electronically controlled unit injector (Fig. 10.30) has been developed to meet the future emissions regulations by realizing high injection pressures and precise control of start of injection and injection quantity.

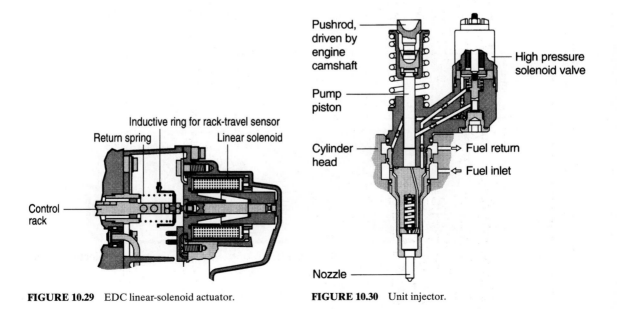

FIGURE 10.29 EDC linear-solenoid actuator.

FIGURE 10.30 Unit injector.

The unit injector combines injection pump and injection nozzle into a single unit, which is installed directly into the engine cylinder head and driven by the engine camshaft. High injection pressures of 1600 bar and more are readily attainable due to low dead volume of compressible fuel.

In order to control start and end of injection, each unit injector contains a time-controlled high-speed solenoid valve. When the valve is open, the unit injector plunger delivers fuel to the low-pressure fuel supply circuit without any injection into the engine cylinder. When the solenoid valve is closed, fuel is delivered to the nozzle for injection into the engine cylinder. Thus, the fuel injection quantity is determined by the time interval between closing and opening of the valve.

Typical switching times for a medium duty/heavy duty truck application are: closing period at rated power, 1000 µs; opening period at rated power, 600 µs. The whole injection process must be completed within a period of about 1 to 2 ms. Consequently, the solenoid-valve motion must occur with an accuracy of less than 10 µs in order to ensure compliance with the usual tolerances for fuel injection quantity and start of injection.

10.3.4 Actuators for Passenger Safety

(See Chap. 24.) Pyrotechnical actuators are used for passenger-restraint systems such as the air bag and the automatic seat belt tensioner. When an accident occurs, the actuators inflate the air bag (or tension the seat belt) at precisely the right instant. Specifications call for the belts to be fully tensioned ~ 10 ms after ignition, while ~ 30 ms are allowed between the ignition point and total inflation for the air bag.

Air bag actuators are available in various sizes, according to vehicle type and application (driver or passenger side), and they are dimensioned to generate gas volumes of between 30 and 200 dm^3. The gases and gas mixtures used for these devices are nontoxic. The section following describes the operating principles for various actuator types.

Pyrotechnical Air Bag Inflator (Gas Generator).   Figure 10.31 is an example of a driver-type inflator. When sufficient current is sent through the initiator, or squib, a thin metal filament covered by a sensitive pyrotechnic charge heats up and ignites this charge (Fig. 10.31*a*). The ignition of the squib provides enough energy to light a booster charge, whose combustion

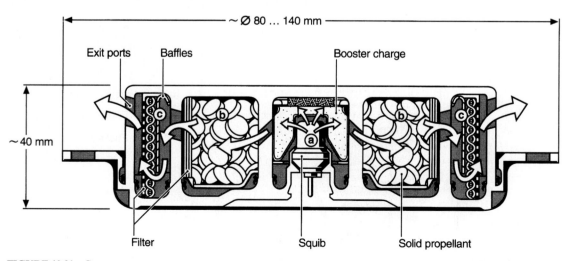

FIGURE 10.31   Gas generator.

builds up adequate pressure and heat to start the chemical reaction, converting the solid propellant, or gas generant, into gas (Fig. 10.31b). The resulting nontoxic hot gas flows over a series of screens, filters, and baffles, cooling down prior to leaving the inflator through exit ports located inside the air bag (Fig. 10.31c). The duration of this process is less than one-tenth of a second.

Hybrid (Compressed Gas and Pyrotechnic) Air Bag Inflator. Figure 10.32 is an example of a passenger-type tubular inflator. When sufficient current is sent through the initiator, or squib, a thin metal filament covered by a sensitive pyrotechnic charge heats up and ignites this charge (Fig. 10.32a). The ignition of the squib provides enough energy to propel a projectile through a rupture disk, allowing the escape of stored nontoxic compressed gas (Fig. 10.32b). The projectile also strikes two primers, lighting a solid pyrotechnic mass, which in turn heats the remaining stored gas (Fig. 10.32c). The expanding heated gas flows out of the inflator through exit ports located inside the air bag (Fig. 10.32d). The duration of this event is less than one-tenth of a second.

10.3.5 Actuators for Electronic Transmission Control

Continuous operation actuators are used to modulate pressure, while switching actuators function as supply and discharge valves for shift-point control.

In automatic transmissions, response times of 2 ms must be ensured in circuits with flow diameters of up to 2.4 mm, carrying up to 4 dm³ per minute at a differential pressure of 200 kPa, all within a temperature range extending from –40 to 150 °C; pressure can increase up to 2000 kPa.

On/Off Solenoids. Various versions of the on/off solenoid valve are in use (two-port, three-port, open base state, closed base state). These valves are normally employed for shifting gears, but can also serve in special applications such as control of converter lockup mechanisms or reverse lockouts. Substantial weight savings can be obtained from the use of plastics. On/off valves are controlled through basic switching output stages. Peak-and-hold control strategies can provide weight and size savings.

Variable-Pressure Solenoids (Pressure Regulators). Pressure regulation must remain precise during switching operations and when holding line pressure. Here, analog valves have

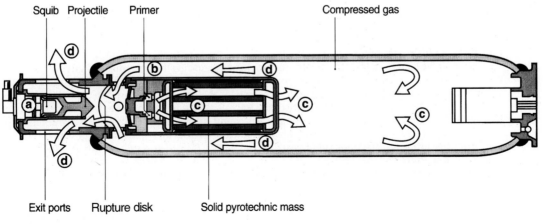

FIGURE 10.32 Hybrid air bag inflator.

proven extremely effective. Extremely stable output pressures are achieved by recirculating the controlled pressure to the valve element, making it possible to maintain stable output pressures in the face of interference factors like downstream leakage, supply-pressure fluctuations, and viscosity variations in the hydraulic fluid. Figure 10.33 shows a typical version of the three-way pressure-control valve, the spool valve. This design provides flow rates of 4 dm³/min at pressure differentials of 2 bar. In order to limit the effects of hysteresis on the pressure/flow response characteristic, mechanical friction must be minimized and materials with low coercive field force must be employed and heat-treating processes are also needed to minimize material-related hysteresis. Choppers in the current-controlled end stage reduce power loss and induce friction-reducing micromovement in the armature. Pressure regulators are also available as seat valves.

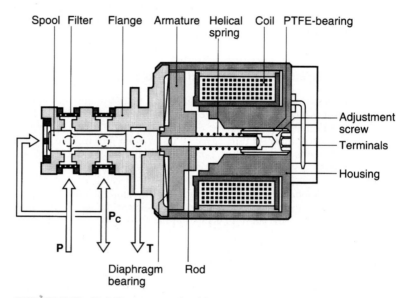

FIGURE 10.33 Variable-pressure solenoid.

PWM Solenoids (Pulse-Width Modulated Solenoid Valves).   On/off poppet valves are particularly well suited for direct actuation from microcomputers. The component layout is less complicated than that found in proportional valves, allowing reductions in manufacturing costs. Because microcomputers operate on the basis of discrete time, equidistant setpoint selection, direct valve actuation via constant-frequency pulse represents the optimum design configuration.

When the solenoid-actuated valve is switched on and off at a constant supply pressure, the resulting average outlet pressure is a function of the ratio between open and closed states. However, this design lacks the proportional valve's ability to compensate for interference due to such factors as system leakage, temperature, and fluctuations in supply pressure. This type of actuator thus represents a reasonably priced alternative for applications in which the control pressure is not the controlled variable, but rather is used as a manipulated variable.

These units can be used in automatic transmissions to select gear ratios, or to reduce torque-converter slip losses by modulating the contact pressure of the lockup clutch. Simple switching output stages or peak-and-hold circuits govern the electric control signal to the PWM valve. When used in conjunction with the appropriate valve design, this type of control can be used to obtain cycle frequencies in excess of 100 Hz. In some applications, such as continiously variable transmissions (CVT), a life expectancy of 2×10^9 cycles is demanded.

10.3.6   Actuators for Headlight Vertical Aim Control

Devices enabling adjustment of headlight range enhance safety by maintaining the correct aim under all vehicle-load conditions. Range adjustment can be manual, with a driver-operated switch, or it can be automatic. The same headlight-adjustment actuators are employed for both designs. The actuator is mounted directly on the headlamp bracket or housing, and adjusts the headlight insert or the reflector.

The actuators are dc or step motors producing a rotary motion which gear-drive units then convert to linear movement. Due to the fixed relationship between the motor's incremental response (steps) and the attendant linear motion, no travel sensor is required with step motors. The total adjustment range extends as far as 8 mm. A single step corresponds to a turning angle of 15 degrees, or an adjustment travel of 0.03 mm. The motor returns to the initial (zero) position (mechanical travel limiter) each time the system is activated in order to prevent step losses.

The step motor combines the following advantages:

- Extremely precise positioning through digital control.

- High adjustment speeds of up to 8 mm/s; different control frequencies can be selected to obtain variations. This system allows graduated adjustment at constant vehicle speeds (consistent lighting) and rapid response during acceleration and braking.

10.4   TECHNOLOGY FOR FUTURE APPLICATION

The motivation to develop new actuators is created by the potential advantages of new manufacturing and driving techniques in combination with new materials. The following examples illustrate representative fields of innovation.

10.4.1   Micromechanical Valves

Micromechanics technology stems from the adaptation of production methods employed in microelectronics. Lithographic miniaturization procedures and etching and assembly techniques make it possible to manufacture minute structures with a high degree of precision. Micromechanical production methods have already become established in the field of sensor manufacture. Electronic circuitry and sensors can be manufactured from the same material (primarily silicon) in simultaneous production processes to furnish integrated components; the benefits associated with this process represent numerous potential advantages.

In automotive applications, microactuators display potential as elements in open-loop control systems where low control power is to be converted, for instance, regulating the flow of fluids in hydraulic or pneumatic systems and metering fuel.

For micromechanical manufacturing, valve designs are required in which planar units with relatively low structure heights are stacked. The energy conversion principles employed to operate the valves correspond to the planar structure (e.g., electrostatic drive, electrothermal or piezoelectric flux converters).

The pressure-balanced seat valve is a basic example of this kind of microvalve (Fig. 10.34). This type of microvalve is produced in a manufacturing process entailing sequential structuring and bonding of four wafers. Depending on the required dimensions for the single valve and the resulting surface requirement, as many as several hundred elements can be produced simultaneously on each wafer stack. Further efforts must be directed to solving packaging problems before these microstructures can be used to control fluid supply and discharge processes.

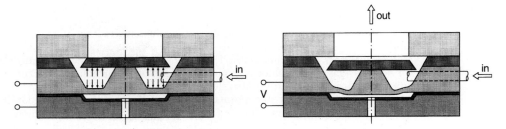

FIGURE 10.34   Pressure-compensated seat valve.

10.4.2   Positive-Engagement Friction Drives

Single piezoelectric actuators provide high dynamic positioning response over short actuating distances. The search for suitable mechanisms employing active piezoceramics to extend the effective travel range has given rise to a multiplicity of drive concepts sharing common attributes:

- Combination of single high-frequency motions (up to the ultrasonic range) to achieve a continuous drive movement
- Output element actuation using friction engagement

Ultrasonic Motor.   Of all the designs utilizing piezoelectric actuator technology, the ultrasonic traveling wave device has reached the most advanced stage of development (Fig. 10.35). A stator ring featuring teeth on the upper surface, and made of a material providing low material damping (bronze), is flex-mounted on an end shield via a central diaphragm. A flat piezoceramic ring is bonded to the underside of the stator ring. This piezoring is polarized along the vertical axis of the ring plane. The direction of the polarization changes segmentally (Fig. 10.36).

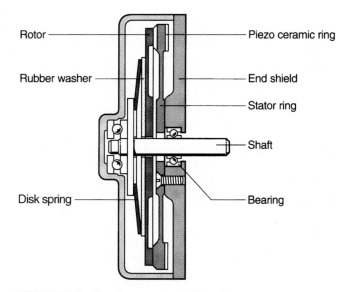

FIGURE 10.35   Traveling-wave motor, Shinsei type.

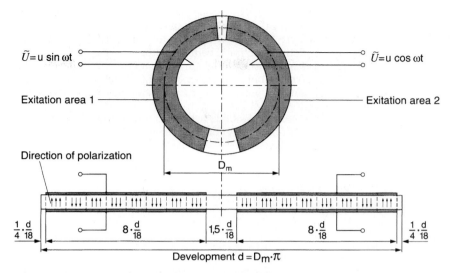

FIGURE 10.36   Segmentation and control of the piezoring.

The electrical contacts are arranged to provide two excitation regions, each featuring eight segments and two small zones. The zone length corresponds to either ½ or 1½ segments. Thus a segment of the excitation zone extends through ⅟₁₈ of the stator's circumference. When voltage is applied to an excitation region, the piezos of one polarization direction contract along the circumference direction (lateral piezo effect), while the piezos of the opposite polarization orientation expand. This effect produces a wave-shaped flux in the stator ring in the affected region.

If the region is then excited with ac voltage (for example, 100 V at approximately 40 kHz in existing motors), the result is an oscillation pattern which extends to encompass the entire stator ring. Excitation in the frequency of the ninth flex mode of the stator provokes a standing wave on the entire stator. Resonance step-up is employed to achieve amplitudes of 20 μm.

If an excitation current is now applied at the second excitation region with ac voltage at a 90° lateral displacement, the two waves overlap to form a traveling wave.

In addition to the up and down motion, one point on the upper surface of the stator produces—by means of tilting movement of those teeth which are situated above the neutral axis—a motion along the periphery (±2 μm). When the two motions combine, the surface points move in an elliptical pattern (Fig. 10.37).

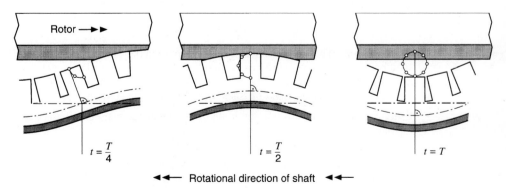

FIGURE 10.37   Drive mechanism.

A disc spring and a rubber washer are pressing the disk-shaped rotor in Fig. 10.35 against the stator. The elliptical motion of the stator teeth drives the rotor through friction contact with its contact layer. Speed is adjusted by, for example, varying the excitation frequency, with the stator's oscillation amplitude being monitored.

The salient characteristics of the ultrasonic motor are: high torque (up to 1.3 Nm), low rpm range (30 . . . 130 rpm), bidirectional operation, substantial characteristic retension force, free of clearance, no run-on, potentially precise positioning, noiseless operation, and flat unit configuration.

Ultrasonic motors are suitable for use as direct-drive devices. The disadvantages include the substantial, high-frequency control voltage, and the limitations on service life due to wear on the friction surface.

ACKNOWLEDGMENTS

The author wishes to acknowledge the contributions of D. Baumann, W. Brehm, O. Engfer, G. Genter, H. Gnuschke, U. Hafner, G. Hartz, Prof. E. Kallenbach, Technische Universität Ilmenau; T. Kamitsis, Morton International Inc., Odgen Utah; G. Keuper, H. M. Streib, U. Zillgitt. Unless otherwise stated, the collaborators are employees of Robert Bosch GmbH, Stuttgart.

The author acknowledges with gratitude the support of theoretical revision by Dietmar Baumann and the coordination done by Mr. Ortwin Engfer, as well as the typing of the manuscript by Dorothee Ludmann.

GLOSSARY

Actuator   The part of an open-loop or closed-loop control system which connects the electronic control unit with the process. The actuator consists of a transformer and a final-control element. Electric positioning signals are converted to mechanical output.

Closed-loop control   A process by which a variable is continuously measured, compared with a reference variable, and changes as a result of this comparison in such a manner that the deviation from the reference variable is reduced. The purpose of closed-loop control is to bring the value of the output variable as close as possible to the value specified by the reference variable in spite of disturbances. In contrast to open-loop control, a closed-loop control system acts to offset the effect of all disturbances.

Commutator   The commutator is a current switcher. For dc machines, the commutator switches the armature windings so that the resultant force always acts in the same rotary direction. This requires a reversal of the armature winding connection every 180°. The current supply to the armature is via brushes which contact the commutator.

Eddy current   In metals moving in an inhomogeneous magnetic field or located in a changing magnetic field, induced currents circulate throughout the volume. Because of their general circulatory nature, these currents are referred to as eddy currents.

Ferrite magnet   In small transformers where eddy current losses must be kept to a minimum, the cores are made of ferrites which are complex oxides of iron and other metals. These materials are ferromagnetic, but have relatively high resistivity.

Final-control element   The second or last stage of an actuator to control mechanical output.

Numeric field calculation   A method of numerically calculating fields with the help of computer programs, such as the methods of finite differences or finite elements.

Open-loop control   A process within a system in which one or more input variables act on output variables based on the inherent characteristics of the system. An open control loop is a series of elements that act on one another as links in a chain. In an open control loop, only disturbances that are measured by the control unit can be addressed. The open loop has no effect on other disturbances.

Peripheral magnetic voltage   The line integral of the magnetic field strength around a closed path.

$$V_m = \oint \mathbf{H} \cdot d\mathbf{s}$$

According to Ampere's law, the peripheral magnetic voltage is equal to the magnetomotive force Θ.

Piezoelectric effect   The direct piezoelectric effect is the ability of a piezoelectric crystal to produce an electric voltage when subjected to a force. The inverse piezoelectric effect is the ability of a piezoelectric crystal to deform when subjected to an electric voltage.

Pilot-controlled actuator   An actuator that uses one or more additional energy sources to transform the input signal to an output signal. The pilot-controlled actuator consists of a chain of energy positioners and energy transformers that produces an amplification due to their series configuration.

Self-induction   Every current is surrounded by a magnetic field with field lines that are interlinked with the current lines. This leads to an induced source voltage in the conductor or coil when the current strength is changed. This phenomenon is called self-induction.

Weiss' domains   Ferromagnetic materials have strong interaction among the atoms. Spontaneous local magnetization can occur, even though no external magnetic field is present. These so-called Weiss' domains, sized from 0.01 to 1 mm, are small elementary magnets, which are randomly distributed in the material and are first directed when an external field is applied.

BIBLIOGRAPHY

Actuators Basics

"DIN 19226 Regelungstechnik und Steuerungstechnik: Begriffe und Benennungen."

Janocha, H., *Aktoren: Grundlagen und Anwendungen,* Springer-Verlag, Berlin, Heidelberg, New York, 1992.

Kupfmüller, K., *Einführung in die theoretische Elektrotechnik,* Springer-Verlag, 1973.

Pregla, R., *Grundlagen der Elektrotechnik,* Teil I u. II, Hüthig-Verlag, Heidelberg, 1990.

Raab, U., "Modellgestützte digitale Regelung und Überwachung von Kraftfahrzeugaktuatoren," Reihe 8: Meβ-, Steuerungs- und Regelungstechnik Nr. 313, VDI-Verlag, Düsseldorf 1993.

Robert Bosch GmbH, *Automotive Handbook,* 3d ed., 1993.

Robert Bosch GmbH, "Elektronik und Mikrocomputer," 1987.

VDI/VDE-Technologiezentrum Informationstechnik GmbH, "Neue Aktoren," Fachbeilage Mikroperipherik, 1990.

dc Solenoids

Aldefeld, B., "Numerical Calculation of Electromagnetic Acutators," *Archiv für Electrotechnik,* Bd. 61, 1979, pp. 347–352.

Hickmann, W., "Ein Beitrag zur Rechnerunterstützten Auslegung und Optimierung von Gleichstrommagnetsystemen," Dissertation, TH Darmstadt, 1984.

Kallenbach, E., *Der Gleichstrommagnet,* Akademische Verlagsgesellschaft Geest & Portig KG, Leipzig, 1969.

Kallenbach, E., Bögelsack, G., *Gerätetechnische Antriebe,* Carl Hanser-Verlag, München, Wien, 1991.

Müller, W., "Numerical solution of 2- or 3-dimensional nonlinear field problems by means of the computer program PROFI," *Archiv für Elektrotechnik 6,* 1982, p. 299–307.

Roters, H. C., *Electromagnetic Devices,* John Wiley & Sons, New York, 1967.

Rüdenberg, *Elektrische Schaltvorgänge,* Springer, 1974.

Seely, S., *Electromechanical Energy Conversion,* McGraw-Hill New York, 1962. (Moskau: Energija, 1968).

Step Motors

Kuo, B. C., *Incremental Motion Control—Step Motors and Control Systems,* SRL Publishing Company, Champaign Ill., 1979.

Kuo, B. C., *Theory and Applications of Stepmotors,* West Publishing Co., New York, 1974.

Miller, T. J. E., *Brushless Permanent Magnet and Reluctance Motor Drives,* Clarendon Press, Oxford, 1989.

Takashi, Kenjo, *Stepping Motors and Their Microprocessor Controls,* Clarendon Press, Oxford, 1985.

dc Motors

Moeller, W. *Leitfaden der Electrotechnik,* Band II, Teil I, -Gleichstrommaschinen, Teubner, Stuttgart, 1979.

Ruschmeyer, K., *Motoren und Generatoren mit Dauermagneten,* Expert-Verlag, Grafenau, 1983, ISBN 3-88508-914-9.

Schüler, K., and K. Bringmann, *Dauermagnete,* Springer, Berlin, 1970.

Magnetostrictive Actuators

Clark, A. E., "Ferromagnetiv Materials," Chap. 7, Ed. E.P. Wohlfarth, North-Holland, 1980, pp. 531–589.

Dyberg, J., "Magnetostrictive Rods in Mechanical Applications," *Proc. 1st International Conference on Giant Magnetostrictive Alloys and Their Impact on Actuator and Sensor Technology,* Marbella, Spain, 1986.

Edge Technologies Inc., *TERFENOL-D Notes,* Vol. 3, No. 1, 1990.

Fahlander, M., and M. Richardson, "New Material for the Rapid Conversion of Electric Energy to Mechanical Motion," Feredyn AB, Uppsala, Sweden, 1988.

Janocha, H., and J. Schäfer, "Design Rules for Magnetostrictive Actuators," *Proc. Actuators 92,* VDI/VDE–Technologiezentrum Informationstechnik GmbH, Berlin, 1992.

Kvarnsjo, L., "Principles and Tools for Design of Magnetomechanical Devices Based on Giant Magnetostrictive Materials," Royal Institute of Technologie, Dept. of Plant Engineering, S-10044, Stockholm, Sweden, 1990.

Piezo Actuators

Galvagni, J., and B. Rawal, *Multilayer Electroactive Ceramic Actuators,* AVX Corporation, Myrtle Beach, 1991.

Janocha, H., and D. J. Jendritza, "Piezoaktuatoren—Möglichkeiten und Grenzen einer innovativen Stellgliedtechnologie," *VDI Berichte* Nr. 960, 1992.

Janocha, H., and D. J. Jendritza, "Piezoelektrische Aktoren praxisgerecht einsetzens," *Design & Elektronik 22;* Magna MediaVerlag, Haar bei München, 1992.

VDI/VDE-Technologiezentrum Informationstechnik GmbH, Piezokeramische Aktoren, Fachbeilage Mikroperipherik me Bd. 5, Heft 1, 1991.

Waanders, J. W., *Piezoelectric Ceramics: Properties and Applications,* Philips Components, 1991.

Electrostatic Actuators

Bart, S. E., T. A. Lober, R. T. Howe, J. H. Lang, and M. F. Schlecht, "Design considerations for microfabricated electric actuators," *Sensors and Actuators,* 14, 1988, pp. 269–292.

Price, R. H., J. E. Wood, and S. C. Jacobsen, "The modelling of electrostatic forces in small electrostatic actuators," *IEEE Solid-State Sensor and Actuator Workshop,* Hilton Head Island, S.C., 1988.

Trimmer, W. S., and K. J. Gabriel, "Design Considerations for a Practical Electrostatic Micromotor," *Sensors and Actuators,* 11, 1987, pp. 189–206.

Electrorheological Fluids

Block, H., and J. P. Kelly, "Electro-rheology—A Review Article," *J Phys. D. Appl. Phys,* 21, 1988, pp. 1661–1667.

Bonnecaze, R. T., and J. F. Brady, "Yield stress in electrorheological fluids," *J. Rheol.,* Vol. 36, No. 1, 1992, pp. 73–115.

Simmonds, A. J., "Electro-rheological valves in a hydraulic circuit," *IEE Proc-D,* Vol. 138, No. 4, 1991.

Stangroom, J. E., "Electrorheological Fluids," *J Physics Technology,* 14, 1983, pp. 290–296.

Memory Alloys

Brinson, L. C., "One Dimensional Constitutive Behavior of Shape Memory Alloys: Thermomechanical Derivation with Noncourtant Material Functions and Redefined Martensite Internal Variable," submitted for publication in *Journal of Intelligent Material Systems and Structures,* 1991.

Duerig, T. W., "Applications of shape memory," *Material Science Forum,* 56–58, 1990, pp. 679–692.

Duerig, T. W., K. N. Melton, D. Stoeckel, and C. M. Wayman, *Engineering Aspects of Shape Memory Alloys,* Butterworth-Heinemann, 1990.

Golestaneh, A., "Shape-memory phenomena," *Phys. Today,* Apr. 1984, pp. 62–70.

Tuominen, S. M., and R. J. Biermann, "Shape Memory Wires," *J. Metals,* 1988, p. 32.

Automotive Actuators for ABS/ASR-Systems

Huber, W., B. Lieberoth-Leden, W. Maisch, and A. Reppich, "New Approaches to Electronic Throttle Control," SAE 910085.

Maisch, W., W. D. Jonner, R. Mergenthaler, and A. Sigl, "ABS5 and ASR5: The New ABS/ASR Family to Optimize Directional Stability and Traction," SAE 930505.

Fuel Injection for Spark-Ignition Engines

Fuel Metering (Spark Ignition Engines), SAE 891832, Nov. 89.

Robert Bosch GmbH, *Automotive Electric/Electronic Systems,* SAE ISBN 0-89883-509-7, VDI ISBN 3-18-419110-9.

Fuel Injection for Diesel Engines

Fischer, W., W. Fuchs, H. Laufer, and U. Reuter, "Solenoid-Valve Controlled Diesel Distributor Injection Pump," SAE 930327.

Franke, G., B. G. Barker, and C. T. Timus, "Electronic Unit Injectors," SAE 885013.

Lauvin, P., A. Löffler, A. Schmitt, W. Zimmermann, and W. Fuchs, "Electronically Controlled High Pressure Unit Injector System for Diesel Engines," SAE 911819.

Mardell, J. E., and R. K. Cross, "An Integrated, Full Authority, Electrohydraulic Engine Valve and Diesel Fuel Injection System, SAE 880602.

Electronic Transmission Control

Brehm, W., and K. Neuffer, "Fast switching PWM-solenoid for automatic transmissions," *Proc. Seventh International Conference on Automotive Electronics,* London, Oct. 9–12, 1989, C 391/046 I Mech E, 1989.

Henry, James P., and David S. Dennis, "Predicting Solenoid Transient Performance," SAE Paper 870473.

Robinson, G., "A Practical Approach to Automatic Transmission Reliability," SAE Paper 910640.

U.S. Patent 4,535,816, "Pressure controller," 1985.

U.S. Patent 4,577,143, "Method and apparatus to convert an electrical value into a mechanical position by using an electromagnetic element subject to hysteresis," 1986.

Technology for Future Application

Fröschle, A., "Analyse eines Piezo-Wanderwellenmotors," Dissertation, Universität Stuttgart, 1992.

Huff, M. A., M. Mettner, A. A. Lober, and M. A. Schmidt, "A Pressure-Balanced Electrostatically-Actuated Microvalve," *Technical Digest, IEEE Solid-State Sensor and Actuator Workshop,* Hilton Head, S.C., June 4–9, 1990, p. 123.

Mettner, M., M. A. Huff, T. A. Lober, and M. A. Schmidt, "How to Design a Microvalve for High Pressure Application," *MME Micromechanics Europe '90,* Berlin, Nov. 26–27, 1990, p. 108.

ABOUT THE AUTHOR

Klaus Müller, after studying mechanical engineering, was employed at the University of Karlsruhe, Germany, investigating the field dynamic behavior of air conditioning system components. In 1976, he joined Robert Bosch GmbH, Stuttgart, where he began his work in advanced engineering of planar oxygen sensors, combustion sensors, and signal evaluation. This was followed by product development of hydraulic units for antilock braking systems and traction control.

P · A · R · T · 3

CONTROL SYSTEMS

CHAPTER 11
AUTOMOTIVE MICROCONTROLLERS

David S. Boehmer
Senior Applications Engineer
Intel Corporation

A microcontroller can be found at the heart of almost any automotive electronic control module or ECU in production today. Automotive systems such as antilock braking control (ABS), engine control, navigation, and vehicle dynamics all incorporate at least one microcontroller within their ECU to perform necessary control functions. Understanding the various features and offerings of microcontrollers that are available on the market today is important when making a selection for an application. This chapter is intended to provide a look at various microcontroller features and provide some insight into their characteristics from an automotive application point of view.

11.1 MICROCONTROLLER ARCHITECTURE AND PERFORMANCE CHARACTERISTICS

A microcontroller can essentially be thought of as a single-chip computer system and is often referred to as a single-chip microcomputer. It detects and processes input signals, and responds by asserting output signals to the rest of the ECU. Fabricated upon this highly integrated, single piece of silicon are all of the features necessary to perform embedded control functions. Microcontrollers are fabricated by many manufacturers and are offered in just about any imaginable mix of memory, I/O, and peripheral sets. The user customizes the operation of the microcontroller by programming it with his or her own unique program. The program configures the microcontroller to detect external events, manipulate the collected data, and respond with appropriate output. The user's program is commonly referred to as code and typically resides on-chip in either ROM or EPROM. In some cases where an excessive amount of code space is required, memory may exist off-chip on a separate piece of silicon. After power-up, a microcontroller executes the user's code and performs the desired embedded control function.

Microcontrollers differ from microprocessors in several ways. Microcontrollers can be thought of as a complete microcomputer on a chip that integrates a CPU with memory and various peripherals such as analog-to-digital converters (A/D), serial communication units (SIO, SSIO), high-speed input and output units (HSIO, EPA, PWM), timer/counter units, and standard low-speed input/output ports (LSIO). Microcontrollers are designed to be embedded within event-driven control applications and generally have all necessary peripherals integrated onto the same piece of silicon. Microcontrollers are utilized in applications ranging from automotive ABS to household appliances in which the microcontroller's function is predefined and limited user interface is required.

Microprocessors, on the other hand, typically require external peripheral devices to perform their intended function and are not suited to be utilized in single-chip designs. Microprocessors basically consist of a CPU with register arrays and interrupt handlers. Peripherals such as A/D and HSIO are rarely integrated onto microprocessor silicon. Microprocessors are designed to process large quantities of data and have the capability to handle large amounts of external memory. Although microprocessors are typically utilized in applications which are much more human-interface and I/O intensive such as personal computers and office workstations, they are beginning to find their way into embedded applications.

Choosing a microcontroller for an application is a process that takes careful investigation and thought. Items such as memory size, frequency, bus size, I/O requirements, and temperature range are all basic requirements that must be considered when choosing a microcontroller. The microcontroller family must possess the performance capability necessary to successfully accomplish the intended task. The family should also provide a memory, I/O, and frequency growth path that allows easy upgradability to meet market demands. Additionally, the microcontroller must meet the application's thermal requirements in order to guarantee functionality over the intended operating temperature range. Items such as these must all be considered when choosing a microcontroller for an automotive application.

11.1.1 Block Diagram

Usually the first item a designer will see when opening a microcontroller data book or data sheet is a block diagram. A block diagram provides a high-level pictorial representation of a microcontroller and depicts the various peripherals, I/O, and memory functions the microcontroller has to offer. The block diagram gives the designer a quick indication if the particular microcontroller will meet the basic memory, I/O, and peripheral needs of their application. Figure 11.1 shows a block diagram for a state-of-the-art microcontroller. It depicts 32 Kbytes

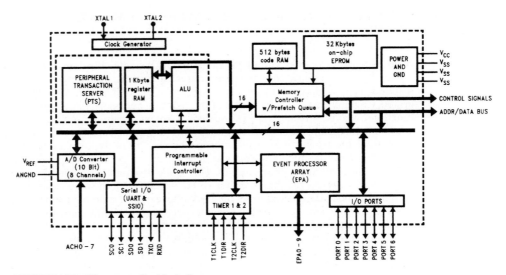

FIGURE 11.1 Microcontroller block diagram.

of EPROM, 1 Kbyte of register RAM, 6 I/O ports, an A-to-D converter, 2 timers, high-speed input/output (I/O) channels, as well as many other peripherals. These features may be "excessive" to a designer looking for a microcontroller to implement in an automotive trip-computer application but would be excellently suited for automotive ABS/traction control or engine control.

11.1.2 Pin-Out Diagram

A microcontroller's pin-out diagram is used to specify the functions assigned to pins relative to their position on a given package. An example pin-out diagram is shown in Fig. 11.2. Note that most pins have multiple functions assigned to them. Pins that can support more than one function are referred to as multifunction pins. The default function for multifunction pins is normally that of low-speed input and output (discussed later in this chapter). If the user should wish to select the secondary or special function associated with the pin, he or she can do so by writing to the appropriate special function register. There are some exceptions. A good example is pins used for interfacing to external memory. If the device is instructed to power-up executing from external memory as opposed to on-chip memory, the address data bus and associated control pins will revert to their special function as opposed to low-speed I/O.

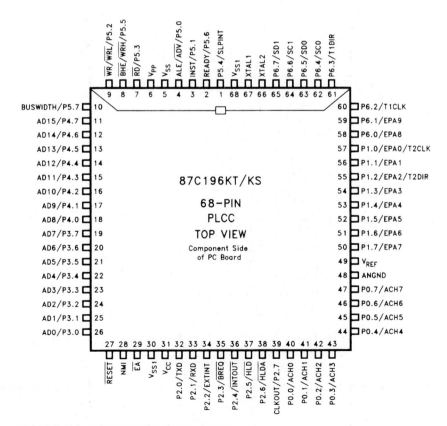

FIGURE 11.2 Microcontroller pin-out diagram.

11.1.3 Central Processing Unit

The central processing unit or CPU can be thought of as the brain of a microcontroller. The CPU is the circuitry within a microcontroller where instructions are executed and decisions are made. Mathematical calculations, data processing, and control signal generation all take place within the CPU. Major components of the CPU include the arithmetic logic unit (ALU), register file, instruction register, and a microcode engine. The CPU is connected to the bus controller and other peripherals via a bidirectional data bus.

Microcontrollers are, for the most part, digital devices. As digital devices, microcontrollers utilize a binary numbering system with a base of 2. Binary data digits or *bits* are expressed as either a logic "1" (boolean value of true) or a logic "0" (boolean value of false). In a 5-V system, a logic "1" may be simply defined as a +5-V state and a logic "0" may be defined as a 0-V state. A bit is a single memory or register location that can contain either a logic "1" or a logic "0" state. Bits of data can be arranged as a *nibble* (4 bits of data), a *byte* (8 bits of data), or as a *word* (16 bits of data). It should also be noted that, in some instances, a word may be defined as the data width that a given microcontroller can recognize at a time, be it 8 bits or 16 bits. For purposes of this chapter, we will refer to a word as being 16 bits. Data can also be expressed as a double word which is an unsigned 32-bit variable with a value between 0 and 4,294,967,295. Most architectures support this data only for shifts, dividends of a 32-by-16 divide, or for the product of a 16-by-16 multiply.

The most common way of referring to a microcontroller is by the width of its CPU. This indicates the width of data that the CPU can process at a time. A microcontroller with a CPU that can process 8 bits of data at a time is referred to as an 8-bit microcontroller. A microcontroller with a CPU that can process 16 bits of data at a time is referred to as a 16-bit microcontroller. With this in mind, it is easy to see why 16-bit microcontrollers offer higher performance than their 8-bit counterparts. Figure 11.3 illustrates a typical 16-bit CPU dia-

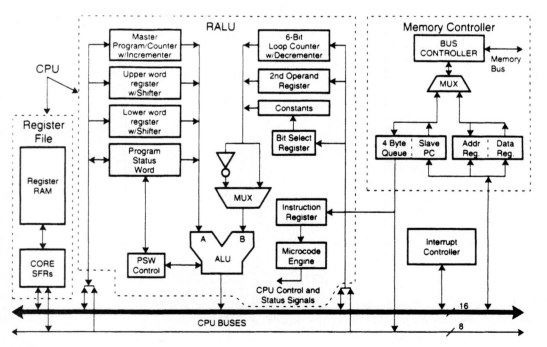

FIGURE 11.3 16-bit CPU.

gram. The microcode engine controls the CPU. Instructions to the CPU are taken from the instruction queue and temporarily stored in the instruction register. This queue is often referred to as a *prefetch queue* and it decreases execution time by staging instructions to be executed. The microcode engine then decodes the instructions and generates the correct sequence of events to have the ALU perform the desired function(s).

Arithmetic Logic Unit.   The ALU is the portion of the CPU that performs most mathematical and logic operations. After an instruction is decoded by the microcode engine, the data specified by the instruction is loaded into the ALU for processing. The ALU then processes the data as specified by the instruction.

Register File.   The register file consists of memory locations that are used as temporary storage locations while the user's code is executing. The register file is implemented as RAM and consists of both RAM memory locations and special function registers (SFRs). RAM memory locations are used as temporary data storage during execution of the user's code. After power-up, RAM memory locations default to a logic "0" and data in SFR locations contain default values as specified by the microcontroller manufacturer.

Special Function Registers.   SFRs allow the user to configure and monitor various peripherals and functions of the microcontroller. By writing specific data to an SFR, the users can configure the microcontroller to meet the exact needs of their application. Figure 11.4 shows an example of a serial port SFR used for configuration. Note that each bit location within the SFR determines a specific function and can be programmed to either a logic "1" or "0". If more than two configuration choices are possible, two or more bits will be combined to produce the multiple choices. An example of this would be the mode bits (M1 and M2) in the example SFR (Fig. 11.4). Bit locations marked "RSV" are reserved and should be written to with a value as indicated by the manufacturer.

SP_CON (1FBBH)

7	6	5	4	3	2	1	0
0	0	PAR	TB8	REN	PEN	M2	M1

M2, M1	Mode	Function
	00	Mode 0: Synchronous
	01	Mode 1: Standard asynchronous
	10	Mode 2: Asynchronous (receiver interrupt on 9th bit = 1)*
	11	Mode 3: Asynchronous (9th bit = parity or data)**
PEN		Parity Enable. Enables the Parity function for Mode 1 or Mode 3; cannot be enabled for Mode 2.
REN		Receiver Enable. Enables the receiver ;ɔ write to SBUF_RX.
TB8		Transmission Bit 8. Set the ninth data bit for transmission (Modes 2 and 3). Cleared after each transmission; not valid if parity is enabled.
PAR***		0 = even parity 1 = odd parity
Bits 6, 7		Reserved; write as zeros for future product compatibility.

* Mode 2: Asynchronous (receiver: interrupt on 9th bit = 1; transmitter: 9th bit = TB8)
** Mode 3: Asynchronous (receiver: always interrupt on 9th bit; transmitter: 9th bit = parity for PEN = 1
*** Par bit only available on 8XC196KT and KS devices.   9th bit = TB8 for PEN = 0
    For 8XC196KR, JR, KQ, JQ devices, this bit should be written as a zero
    to maintain compatibility with future devices.

FIGURE 11.4   Special function control register example.

SP_STAT (1FB9H)

7	6	5	4	3	2	1	0
RB8/RPE	RI	TI	FE	TXE	OE	X	X

Bits 0, 1   Reserved; ignore data.

OE   Set on buffer overrun error.

TXE   Set on transmitter empty. When set may write 2 bytes to transmit buffer.

FE   Framing error; set it no STOP bit is found at the end of a reception. When set may write
            1 byte to transmit buffer.

TI   Transmit interrupt; set at the beginning of the STOP bit transmission.

RI   Receive interrupt; set after the last data bit is received.

RPE   (Parity enabled) Receive parity error (Modes 1 and 3 only); set if parity is enabled and a
            parity error occurred.

RB8   (Parity disabled) Received Bit 8 (Modes 2 and 3 only); set if the 9th bit is high on reception.

FIGURE 11.5   Special function status register example.

Some SFRs can be read by the user to determine the current status of a given peripheral. Figure 11.5 shows an example of a serial port status register that, when read, indicates the current status of the microcontroller's serial port. Note that each bit location corresponds to a particular state of the serial port. Bit locations marked "RSV" are reserved and should be ignored when read.

Register Direct vs. Accumulator-Based Architectures.   Microcontroller architectures can be classified as either the register-direct or accumulator-based type. These terms refer to the means by which the CPU must handle data when performing mathematical, logical, or storage operations.

Register-direct architectures allow the programmer to essentially use most, if not all, of the microcontroller's entire RAM array as individual accumulators. That is, the programmer can perform mathematical or storage operations directly upon any of the RAM locations. This simplifies task switching because program variables may be left in their assigned registers while servicing interrupts. Figure 11.6 illustrates a register-to-register type architecture (such

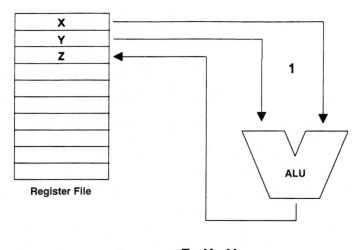

$$Z = X + Y$$

$$1. \ \text{MUL} \ Z,X,Y$$

FIGURE 11.6   Register-to-register architecture example.

as Intel's MCS®-96). This architecture essentially has 232 "accumulators" (more are available through a windowing mechanism) of which any can be operated on directly by the RALU. The true advantage of this type of architecture is that it reduces accumulator bottleneck and speeds throughput during program execution.

Accumulator-based architectures require the user to first store the data to be manipulated into a temporary storage location, referred to as an "accumulator," prior to performing any type of data operation. After the operation is completed, the user program must then store the result to the desired destination location. Figure 11.7 depicts an example of an accumulator-based architecture.

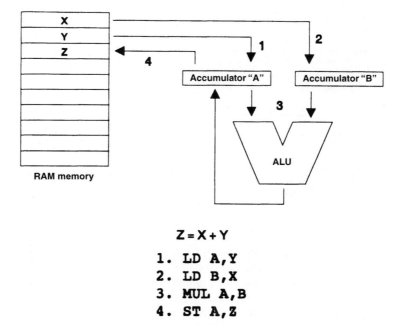

$$Z = X + Y$$

1. LD A,Y
2. LD B,X
3. MUL A,B
4. ST A,Z

FIGURE 11.7   Accumulator-based architecture.

Program Counter.   The Program Counter (PC) controls the sequencing of instructions to be executed. The PC is a 16-bit register located within the CPU which holds the address of the next instruction to be executed. After an instruction is fetched, the PC is automatically incremented to point to the next instruction.

SP starting address (SP+12):	
(SP+10):	80FFh
(SP+8):	A5A5h
(SP+6):	6E20h
(SP+4):	5555h
(SP+2):	0000h
SP ending address (SP):	8000h

FIGURE 11.8   Stack pointer example.

Stack and Stack Pointer.   The stack is an area of memory (typically user-assigned) that is used to store data temporarily in a FILO (first-in, last-out) fashion. The stack is primarily used for storing program information (such as the program counter or interrupt mask registers) when an interrupt service routine is invoked. It is also sometimes used to pass variables between subroutines. The stack is typically accessed through PUSH and POP instructions. Execution of the PUSH instruction "pushes" the contents of the specified operand onto the stack whereas the

POP instruction "pops" the contents of the specified operand off of the stack. The stack pointer (SP) is a register which points to the next available word location on the stack. Consider the example shown in Fig. 11.8 which shows the contents of the stack after the following code sequence is executed:

PUSH #80FFh	pushes immediate data 80FFh onto stack
PUSH #0A5A5h	pushes immediate data A5A5h onto stack
PUSH 82h	pushes data @ 82h (assume it's 6E20h) onto stack
PUSH #5555h	pushes immediate data 5555h onto stack
PUSH 4Eh	pushes data @ 4Eh (assume it's 0000h) onto stack
PUSH #8000h	pushes immediate data 8000h onto stack

Continuing with the preceding example, if a POP instruction were executed, the data at the current SP address (SP) would be "popped" off the stack and stored to the address specified by the instruction's operand. Executing the POP instruction results in the SP being incremented by 2.

Program Status Word and Flags. The program status word (PSW) is a collection of boolean flags which retain information concerning the state of the user's program. These flags are set or cleared depending upon the result obtained after executing certain instructions as specified by the microcontroller manufacturer. PSW flags are not directly accessible by the user's program; access is typically through instructions which test one or more of the flags to determine proper program flow. Following is a summary of common PSW flags as supported by Intel's MCS-96® architecture:

Z: The *Zero* flag is set when an operation generates a result equal to zero. The Z flag is never set by the add-with-carry (ADDC/ADDCB) or subtract-with-carry (SUBC/SUBCB) instructions, but is cleared if the result is nonzero. These two instructions are normally used in conjunction with ADD/ADDB and SUB/SUBB instructions to perform multiple-precision arithmetic. The operation of the Z flag for these instructions leaves it indicating the proper result for the entire multiple-precision calculation.

N: The *Negative* flag is set when an operation generates a negative result. Note that the N flag will be in the algebraically correct state even if overflow occurs. For shift operations, the N flag is set to the same value as the most significant bit of the result.

V: The *oVerflow* flag is set when an operation generates a result that is outside the range for the destination data type. For shift-left instructions, the V flag is set if the most significant bit of the operand changes at any time during the shift. For an unsigned word divide, the V flag is set if the quotient is greater than 65,535. For a signed word divide, the V flag is set if the quotient is less than −32,768 or greater than 32,767.

VT: The *oVerflow Trap* flag is set when the V flag is set, but it is only cleared by instructions which are specially designated to clear the VT flag (such as CLRVT, JVT, and JNVT). The VT flag allows for testing possible overflow conditions at the end of a sequence of related arithmetic operations. This is normally more efficient than testing the V flag after each instruction.

C: The *Carry* flag is set to indicate either (1) the state of the arithmetic carry from the most significant bit of the ALU for an arithmetic operation or (2) the state of the last bit shifted out of an operand for a shift. Arithmetic borrow after a subtract operation is the complement of the C flag (i.e., if the operation generated a borrow, then C = 0).

ST: The *STicky* bit flag is set to indicate that, during a right shift, a 1 has been shifted first into the C flag and then shifted out. The ST flag can be used along with the C flag to control rounding after a right shift. Imprecise rounding can be a major source of error in a numerical calculation; use of both the C and ST flags can increase accuracy as described in the following paragraphs.

Consider multiplying two 8-bit quantities and then scaling the result down to 12 bits:

MULUB   AX, CL, DL   (CL * DL = AX)

SHR   AX, #4   (AX is shifted right by 4 bits)

If the C flag is set after the shift, it indicates that the bits shifted off the end of the operand were greater than or equal to one-half the least significant bit of the 12-bit result. If the C flag is cleared after the shift, it indicates that the bits shifted off the end of the operand were less than half the LSB of the 12-bit result. Without the ST flag, the rounding decision must be made on the basis of the C flag alone. (Normally the result would be rounded up if the C flag is set.) The ST flag allows a finer resolution in the rounding decision as shown here:

C	ST	Bits shifted off
0	0	Value = 0
0	1	0 < Value < ½ LSB
1	0	Value = ½ LSB
1	1	Value > ½ LSB

Jump instructions are the most common instructions to utilize PSW flags for determining the operation to perform. Instructions that test PSW flags are very useful when program flow needs to be altered dependent upon the outcome of an arithmetic operation. The most common example of this would be for program loops that are to be executed a certain number of times. Following are examples of several MCS-96 instructions whose operation is dependent upon the state of one or more program status word flags:

JC   (Jump if C flag is set.) If the C (carry) bit is set, the program will jump to the address location specified by the operand. If the C flag is cleared, control will pass to the next sequential instruction.

JGT   (Jump if signed greater than.) If both the N (negative) and the Z (zero) flags are clear, the program will jump to the address location specified by the operand. If either of the flags is set, control will pass to the next sequential instruction.

JLE   (Jump if signed less than or equal.) If either the N or Z flags is set, the program will jump to the address location specified by the operand. If both the N and Z flags are cleared, control will pass to the next sequential instruction.

11.1.4   Bus Controller

The bus controller serves as the interface between the CPU and the internal program memory and the external memory spaces. The bus controller maintains a queue (commonly called the prefetch queue) of prefetched instruction bytes and responds to CPU requests for data memory references. The prefetch queue decreases execution time by staging instructions to be executed. The capacities of prefetch queues vary but for the MCS-96 architecture, it is 4 bytes deep.

When using a logic analyzer to debug code it is important to consider the effects of the prefetch queue. It is not possible to accurately determine when an instruction will execute by simply watching when it is fetched from external memory. This is because the prefetch queue is filled in advance of instruction execution. It is also important to consider the effects when a jump or branch occurs during program execution. When the program sequence changes because of a jump, interrupt, call, or return, the PC is loaded with the new address, the queue is flushed and processing continues. Consider the situation in which the external address/data bus is being monitored when a program branch occurs. Because of the prefetch queue, it will appear as if instructions past the branch point were executed, when in fact they were only loaded into the prefetch queue.

11.1.5 Frequency of Operation

Microcontrollers are being offered in an ever-increasing range of operating frequencies. Most high-end automotive applications currently use microcontrollers operating in the 12- to 20-MHz range, with 24 MHz becoming not so uncommon. Microcontrollers with frequencies as high as 30 and 32 MHz are available as prototypes and will soon be available for production. Operating frequency becomes especially important when a microcontroller must perform high-speed event control such as required in ABS braking and engine control. Applications such as these typically have to detect, calculate, and respond to external events within a given amount of time. In ABS applications, this time is commonly referred to as loop time and defines the amount of time that the microcontroller has to execute the main loop of the software algorithm to achieve optimal performance.

Operating frequency can be directly related to the speed at which a microcontroller will execute the user's code. For instance, let's look at how long it takes for a particular microcontroller to execute the following generic subroutine. For this example, consider the execution times rather than the operations each instruction is performing.

```
{6}    PUSHF
{3}    NOTB    PTS_COUNT_EPA1
{5}    ADDB    NUM_OF_PULSES_1, PTS_COUNT_EPA1, #00h
{5}    SUB     INV_SPEED_1, FTIME_1, ITIME_1
{27}   DIV     INV_SPEED_1, NUM_OF_PULSES_1
{5}    LD      Temp1+2, #Speed_high_constant
{5}    LD      Temp1, #Speed_low_constant
{27}   DIV     Temp1, INV_SPEED_1
{4}    ST      Temp1, EPA1_FREQ
{11}   RET
```

In this example, the numbers in brackets {} denote how many state times it will take the microcontroller to execute the given line of code. A state time is the basic time measurement for all microcontroller operations. For this MCS-96 family microcontroller, a state time is based on the crystal frequency divided by two. A state time for other microcontrollers may be based upon the crystal frequency divided by three. For this particular microcontroller, a state time can be calculated by the following formula (other microcontroller families use similar formulas):

$$1 \text{ state time} = 1[(\text{frequency of operation})/2]$$

Applying this formula, 1 state time = 125 ns when operating at 16 MHz, and 167 ns when operating at 12 MHz. The example code sequence takes the microcontroller 98 state times to execute. This equates to 16.37 μs to execute at an operating frequency of 12 MHz. At 16 MHz, it takes only 12.25 μs for the microcontroller to execute the subroutine. An operating frequency of 16 MHz results in the microcontroller executing approximately 34 percent more instructions in a given time than at a frequency of 12 MHz.

Another consideration when choosing an operating frequency is the clocking resolution of on-chip timer/counters. The maximum clocking rate of on-chip timer/counters is limited by the frequency the microcontroller is being clocked at. As an example, if an on-chip timer/counter is set up to increment/decrement at a rate determined by CLOCK/4, this would result in 333 ns resolution at 12 MHz. However, if the clock speed were increased to 16 MHz, a higher and more desirable resolution of 250 ns is achieved.

11.1.6 Instruction Set

An often overlooked feature that gives a microcontroller the capability to perform desired operations and manipulate data is its instruction set. A microcontroller's instruction set consists of a set of unique commands which the programmer uses to instruct the microcontroller on what operation to perform.

An *instruction* is a binary command which is recognized by the CPU as a request to perform a certain operation. Examples of typically supported operations are loads, moves, and stores which transfer data from one memory location to another. There are also jumps and branches which are used to alter program flow. Arithmetic instructions include various multiples, divides, subtracts, additions, increments, and decrements. Instructions such as ANDs, ORs, XORs, shifts, and so forth, allow the user to perform logical operations upon data. In addition to these basic instructions, microcontrollers often support specialized instructions unique to their architecture or intended application.

Instructions can be divided into two parts, the *opcode* and *operand*. The opcode (sometimes referred to as the machine instruction) specifies the operation to take place and the operand specifies the data to be operated upon. Instructions typically consist of either 0, 1, 2, or 3 operands to support various operations. As an example, consider the following MCS-96 architecture instructions:

PUSHF (0 operands) is an instruction that pushes the program status word (PSW) onto the stack. Since this instruction operates on a predefined location, no operand is necessary.

Format: PUSHF

PUSH (1 operand) is an instruction that pushes the specified word operand onto the stack.

Format: PUSH (SRC)

ADD (2 operands) adds two words together and places the result in the destination (leftmost) operand location.

Format: ADD (DST),(SRC)

ADD (3 operands) adds two words together as the 2-operand ADD instruction, but in this case, a third operand is specified as the destination.

Format: ADD (DEST),(SRC1),(SRC2)

Instructions support one or more of six basic addressing types to access operands within the address space of the microcontroller. If programmers wish to take full advantage of a microcontroller architecture, it is important that they fully understand the details of the supported addressing types. The six basic types of addressing modes are termed register-direct, indirect, indirect with autoincrement, immediate, short-indexed, and long-indexed. The following descriptions describe these modes as they are handled by hardware in register-to-register architectures.

The *register-direct* addressing mode is used to directly access registers within the lower 256 bytes of the on-chip register file. The register is selected by an 8-bit field within the instruction and the register address must conform to the operand type's alignment rules. Depending upon the instruction, typically up to three registers can take part in the calculation.

Examples:

ADD AX,BX,CX	AX = BX + CX
MUL AX,BX	AX = AX*BX
INCB CL	CL = CL + 1

The *indirect addressing* mode accesses a word in the lower register file containing the 16-bit operand address. The indirect address can refer to an operand anywhere within the address space of the microcontroller. The register containing the indirect address is selected by an 8-bit field within the instruction. An instruction may contain only one indirect reference; the remaining operands (if any) must be register-direct references.

Examples:

LD   BX,[AX]   BX = mem_word(AX)

In this example, assume that before execution:

   contents of AX = 2FC2h

   contents of 2FC2h = 3F26h

Then after execution,

   contents of BX = 3F26h

ADDB AL,BL,[CX]   AL = BL + mem_byte(CX)

The *indirect with autoincrement* addressing mode is the same as the indirect mode except that the variable that contains the indirect address is autoincremented after it is used to address the operand. If the instruction operates on bytes or short integers, the indirect address variable is incremented by one; if it operates on words or integers, the indirect address will be incremented by two.

Examples:

LD BX,[AX]+   BX = mem_word(AX)

                      AX = AX + 2

ADDB AL,BL,[CX]+   AL = BL + mem_byte(CX)

                      CX = CX + 1

For the *immediate addressing* mode, an operand itself is in a field in the instruction. An instruction may contain only one immediate reference; the remaining operand(s) must be register-direct references.

Example:

ADD AX,#340   AX = AX + 340 (decimal)

For the *short-indexed addressing* mode, an 8-bit field in the instruction selects a word variable (which is contained in square brackets) in the lower register file that contains an address. A second 8-bit field in the instruction stream is sign-extended and summed with the word variable to form an operand address.

Since the 8-bit field is sign-extended, the effective address can be up to 128 bytes before the address in the word variable and up to 127 bytes after it. An instruction may contain only one short-indexed reference; the remaining operand(s) must be register-direct references.

Example:

LD   AX,4[BX]   AX = mem_word(BX + 4)

In this example, assume that before execution:

   contents of BX = A152h

The operand address is then A152h + 04h = A156h

The *long-indexed addressing* mode is like the short-indexed mode except that a 16-bit field is taken from the instruction and added to the word variable to form the operand. No sign extension is necessary. An instruction may contain only one long-indexed reference and the remaining operand(s) must be register-direct references.

Examples:

ST AX,TABLE[BX]   mem_word(TABLE + BX) = AX

AND AX,BX,TABLE[CX]   AX = BX and mem_word(TABLE + CX)

11.1.7 Programming Languages

The two most common types of programming languages in use today for automotive micro-controllers are *assembly languages* and *high-level languages* (HLLs). Program development begins with the user writing code in either an assembly language or an HLL. This code is written as a text file and is referred to as a source file. The source file is then assembled or compiled using the appropriate assembler/compiler program. The assembler translates the source code into object code and creates what is referred to as an object file. The object file contains machine language instructions and data that can be loaded into an evaluation tool for debugging and validation. The object can also be converted into a hex file for EPROM programming or ROM mask generation as discussed later in this chapter. The program development process is illustrated in Fig. 11.9.

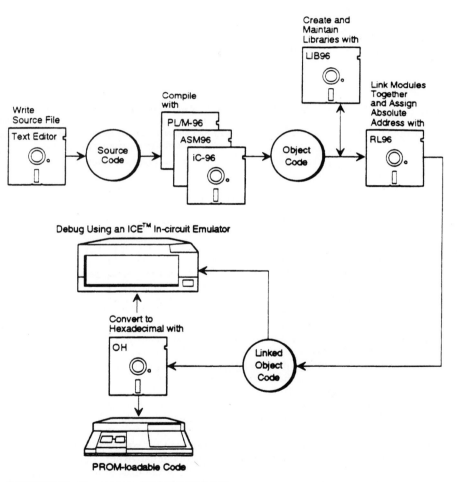

FIGURE 11.9 The program development process.

Assembly Language Programming.   An assembly language is a low-level programming language that is specific to a given microcontroller family. Assemblers translate language operation codes (mnemonics) directly into machine instructions that instruct the microcontroller on what operation to perform. Because the programmer is essentially using the microcontroller's machine code to write assembly language programs, more precise control of the device can be achieved through the direct manipulation of individual bits within registers. Because of their efficiency, assembly language programs require less code space than high-level languages. Assembly language programs consist of three parts: machine instructions, assembler directives, and assembler controls.

A *machine instruction* is a machine code that can be executed by the microcontroller's CPU. The collection of machine instructions that a particular microcontroller can execute is referred to as its instruction set. An example of a machine instruction is the opcode for the MULB instruction (Fig. 11.10) from Intel's MCS-96 assembly language. MULB is the mnemonic that represents the machine instruction which performs the specified multiplication operation. When executed by the microcontroller, the MULB opcode results in the multiplication of the two byte operands with the result being placed in a word destination location.

MULB (Three Operands)

Format	MULB wreg,breg,baop
Operation	The second and third byte operands are multiplied using signed arithmetic and the 16-bit result is stored into the destination (leftmost) operand. The sticky bit flag is undefined after the instruction is executed. (DEST) ← (SRC1) * (SRC2)
Opcode Pattern	11111110 | 010111aa | baop | breg | wreg
Flags Affected	ST

Examples	MULB DELTA, TIMER1, #2
	MULB ALPHA, BETA, GAMMA
	MULB ALPHA, DELTA, 10[GAMMA]

FIGURE 11.10   Machine instruction example: MULB.

Assembler directives allow the user to specify auxiliary information (such as storage reservation, location counter control, definition of nonexecutable code, object code relocation, and flow of assembler processing) that determines the manner in which the assembler generates object code from the user's source file input.

Assembler controls set the mode of operation for the assembler and direct the flow of the assembly process. Assembler controls can be classified into primary controls and general controls. Primary controls are set at the beginning of the assembly process and cannot be changed during the assembly. Primary controls allow the user to specify items such as print options, page lengths and widths, error messages, and cross-referencing. General controls can be specified in the invocation line or on control lines anywhere in the source file and can appear any number of times in the program. General controls either cause an immediate action or an immediate change of conditions in which the condition specified remains in effect until another general control causes it to change.

High-level Language Programming.   Unlike low-level languages (such as assembly languages), a high-level language is a general purpose language that can support numerous microcontroller architectures. The most common high-level language used for automotive applications is C. C programs are written with statements rather than specific instructions from a microcontroller's instruction set. High-level languages utilize a software program known as a *compiler* to translate the user's source code into the specific microcontroller's machine language. Each microcontroller family has its own unique compiler to support selected high-level languages. Although high-level languages tend to be less efficient than assembly languages, their advantage lies in ease of writing code and better debugging capability. The use of statements as opposed to specific instructions better suits high-level languages toward control of procedures (to implement complex software algorithms) as opposed to the microcontroller itself.

11.1.8 Interrupt Structure

The interrupt structure is one of the more important features of an automotive microcontroller. Applications such as automotive ABS and engine control can be referred to as event-driven control systems. Event-driven control systems require that normal code execution be halted to allow a higher-priority task or event to take place. These higher-priority tasks are known as interrupts and can initiate a change in the program flow to execute a specialized routine. When an interrupt occurs, instead of executing the next instruction, the CPU branches to an interrupt service routine (ISR). The branch can occur in response to a request from an on-chip peripheral, an external signal, or an instruction. In the simplest case, the microcontroller receives the request, performs the desired operation and returns to the task that was interrupted.

ISRs are typically serviced via software but it is becoming common for microcontroller manufacturers to implement special on-chip hardware ISR functions for commonly performed operations. These ISRs are typically microcoded or *hardwired* into the microcontroller as described later in this section.

Software, or Normal, Servicing of Interrupts.   The software servicing of interrupts is fairly straightforward as shown in Fig. 11.11. When an interrupt source is enabled by the user and a

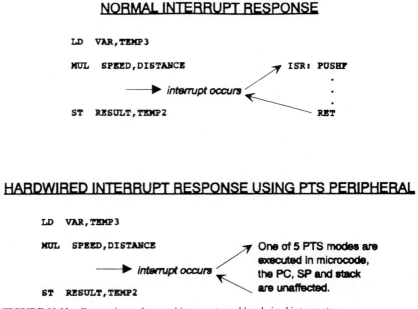

FIGURE 11.11 Comparison of normal interrupts and hardwired interrupts.

valid interrupt event occurs, the CPU will fetch the starting address of the ISR from the interrupt vector table. The interrupt vector table is a dedicated section of memory that contains the user-programmed start address of the various ISRs. After fetching the ISR address, the CPU automatically pushes the current program counter (PC) onto the stack and loads the PC with the ISR beginning address. This results in the program flow vectoring to the ISR address. The user-programmed ISR is then executed. The last instruction within the ISR is a return instruction that pops the old PC off the stack. This results in program flow continuing from where it was interrupted.

Interrupt mask registers allow the user to prevent or *mask* undesirable interrupts from occurring during various sections of the program. This is a very desirable feature and allows for custom tailoring of the interrupt structure to meet the needs of a particular application. Enabling or disabling of all interrupts (known as globally enabling/disabling) is typically supported with a software instruction such as DI (globally disable all interrupts) or EI (globally enable all interrupts).

Hardware, or Microcoded, Interrupt Structures.   Hardware interrupt structures differ from software interrupts in that the user doesn't have to provide the ISR to be executed when the interrupt occurs. With a hardware interrupt structure, the ISR is predefined by being hard-wired or *microcoded* into the microcontroller. This is advantageous because it requires less code space and requires less CPU overhead. Stack operations are not necessary since interrupt vectors do not have to be fetched. Most microcontroller manufacturers have their own proprietary solution for hardware ISR's, which are all somewhat similar to one another. For purposes of this section, we will briefly describe the peripheral transaction server as implemented on members of Intel's MCS-96 family of microcontrollers.

The PTS provides a microcoded hardware interrupt handler which can be used in place of a normal ISR. The PTS requires much less overhead than a normal ISR since it operates without modification of the stack. Any interrupt source can be selected by the user to trigger a PTS interrupt in place of a normal ISR. The PTS is similar to a direct memory access (DMA) controller in that when a PTS interrupt, or *cycle,* occurs, data is automatically moved from one location of memory to another as specified by the user. Figure 11.11 compares a regular ISR to a PTS interrupt cycle.

The PTS allows for five modes of operation; single-byte transfer, multiple-byte transfer, PWM, PWM toggle, and A/D scan mode. Each mode is configurable through an 8-byte, user-defined PTS control block (PTSCB) located in RAM. The user may enable virtually any normal interrupt source to be serviced by a PTS interrupt by simply writing to the appropriate bit in an SFR known as the PTS_SELECT register. When a PTS interrupt is enabled and the event occurs, a microcoded interrupt service routine executes in which the contents of the PTSCB are read to determine the specific operation to be performed. More details on the PTSCB can be found in the application example found in this section.

The major advantage of the PTS for automotive applications is its fast response time. The PTS is ideally suited for transferring single or multiple bytes/words of data in response to an interrupt. An example of this is the serial port example which will be described shortly. Another example of the usefulness of the PTS (using A/D scan mode) would be if the user wanted to automatically store A/D conversion results every time a conversion completed within a user-defined scan of A/D channels. The PTS could also be configured to automatically transfer a block of data between memory locations every time an interrupt occurs.

Application Example of PTS Single-Byte Transfer Mode.   This example shows how the PTS can be used to automatically transmit and receive 8-byte messages over the serial port. Data to be transmitted and received data are stored in separate tables. The use of the PTS for this purpose greatly reduces CPU overhead and code-space requirements. The layout of the user-defined PTSCB for single-byte transfer mode is shown in Fig. 11.12. PTS_DEST within the PTSCB contains the destination address for the data transfer and PTS_SOURCE contains the source address for the transfer.

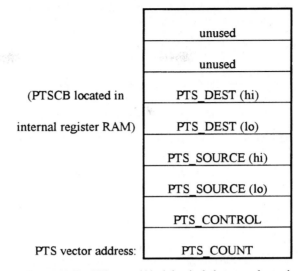

unused
unused
PTS_DEST (hi)
PTS_DEST (lo)
PTS_SOURCE (hi)
PTS_SOURCE (lo)
PTS_CONTROL
PTS_COUNT

(PTSCB located in internal register RAM)

PTS vector address:

FIGURE 11.12   PTS control block for single-byte transfer mode.

Two PTSCBs are set up for this example, one in response to receive (RX) interrupts and one in response to transmit (TX) interrupts. The RX PTSCB's PTS_DEST is initialized with the start address of the receive data table and the TX PTSCB's PTS_DEST is initialized with the address of the serial port's transmit buffer.

PTS_CONTROL is a byte that specifies the PTS operation to be performed. Its layout is shown in Fig. 11.13.

PTS_COUNT is a down counter that is used to keep track of how many PTS interrupts or cycles have occurred since the last initialization. PTS_COUNT is initialized by the user to any value below 256 and is decremented everytime the corresponding PTS cycle occurs. It is often used to keep track of how many pieces of data have been transferred. In this example, PTS_COUNT is used to determine when a complete 8-byte message has been transmitted or received. After PTS_COUNT expires, an "end-of-PTS" or "normal" ISR occurs, in which the user utilizes the data as required by the application. When an interrupt source is enabled by the user to be a PTS interrupt, the following sequence of events occurs every time the corresponding interrupt occurs:

1. Instead of a normal interrupt, the user has selected it to do a PTS cycle.
2. The microcoded PTS routine fetches the PTS_CONTROL byte from the PTSCB whose start address is specified by the user in the PTS interrupt vector table. The microcoded PTS routine then:

   reads data to be transferred from address specified by PTS_SOURCE

   writes the data to address specified by PTS_DEST

   optionally increments/updates PTS_SOURCE and PTS_DEST addresses

   decrements PTS_COUNT
3. When PTS_COUNT reaches "0", an end of PTS interrupt occurs and the normal ISR is executed in which the user utilizes the received data as necessary (for RX interrupts) or reloads the transmit table with new data (for TX interrupts).

Interrupt Latency.   Interrupt latency is defined as the time from when the interrupt event occurs (not when it is acknowledged) to when the microcontroller begins executing the first

PTS_CONTROL BYTE (for single and multiple-byte transfers)

7	6	5	4	3	2	1	0
M2	M1	M0	B/W	SU	DU	SI	DI

M2, M1, M0:	Mode	Function
	000	PTS Block Transfer
	100	PTS Single Transfer

B/W:	Byte/Word:	"0" = Word; "1" = Byte
SU:	Source Update:	"1" = update source address
DU:	Destination Update:	"1" = update destination address
SI:	Increment Source:	"1" = Increment Source address
DI:	Increment Destination:	"1" = Increment Destination address

FIGURE 11.13 PTS control byte for single- and multiple-byte transfer modes.

instruction of the interrupt service routine. Interrupt latency must be carefully considered in timing-critical code as is found in many automotive applications.

There is a delay between an interrupt's triggering and its acknowledgment. An interrupt is not acknowledged until the currently executing instruction is finished. Further, if the interrupt signal does not occur at least some specified (assume four for this discussion) state times before the end of the current instruction, the interrupt may not be acknowledged until after the next instruction has been executed. This is because an instruction is fetched and prepared for execution a few state times before it is actually executed. Thus, the maximum delay between interrupt generation and its acknowledgment is approximately four state times plus the execution time of the next instruction.

It should also be noted that most microcontrollers have protected instructions (such as RETURN, PUSH, POP) which inhibit interrupt acknowledgment until after the following instruction is executed. These instructions can increase interrupt-to-acknowledgment delay.

When an interrupt is acknowledged, the interrupt pending bit is cleared and a call is forced to the location indicated by the corresponding interrupt vector. This call occurs after the completion of the current instruction, except as noted previously. For the MCS-96 architecture, the procedure of fetching the interrupt vector and forcing the call requires 16 state times. The stack being located in external memory will add an additional two state times to this number.

Latency is the time from when an interrupt is generated (not acknowledged) until the microcontroller begins executing interrupt code. The maximum latency occurs when an interrupt occurs too late for acknowledgment following the current instruction. The worst case is calculated assuming that the current instruction is not a protected one. The worst-case latency is the sum of three terms:

1. The time for the current instruction to finish (assume four state times).
2. The state times required for the next instruction. This time is basically the time it takes to execute the longest instruction used in the user's code (assume it's a 16-state DIV instruction).
3. The response time (assume 16 states, 18 for an externally located stack).

Thus, for this scenario, the maximum delay would be 4 + 16 + 16 = 36 state times. This equates to approximately 4.5 μs for a MCS-96 microcontroller operating at 16 MHz. This latency can increase or decrease depending upon the longest execution-time instruction used. Figure 11.14 illustrates an example of this worst-case scenario.

Interrupt latency can be reduced by carefully selecting instructions in areas of code where interrupts are expected. Using a protected instruction followed immediately by a long instruction increases the maximum latency because an interrupt cannot occur after the protected instruction.

11.1.9 Fabrication Processes

The basic fabrication processes that are widely used for automotive microcontrollers today are NMOS (N-channel metal-oxide semiconductor) and CMOS (complementary MOS). The scope of this chapter does not allow for an in-depth discussion of these processes, although a brief description of the structures used to build on-chip circuitry will be discussed. These terms refer to the components used in the construction of MOSFET (MOS field effect transistor) inverters which are the basis of logic on digital devices. NMOS inverters are constructed of N-channel transistors only, whereas CMOS inverters are constructed of both N-channel and P-channel transistors. This section will describe the basic operation of each inverter along with its pros and cons.

Simply stated, a P-channel transistor conducts when a logic "0" is applied to its gate. Conversely, N-channel transistors conduct when a logic "1" is applied to their gate. Figures 11.15 and 11.16 show a simplified cross-sectional view and the electrical symbol for N- and P-channel devices, respectively.

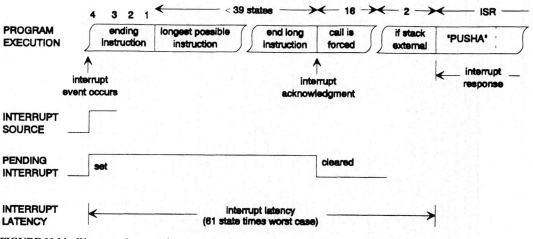

FIGURE 11.14   Worst case interrupt latency example.

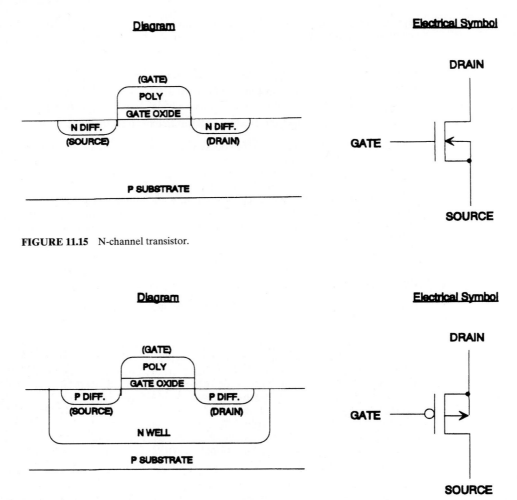

FIGURE 11.15 N-channel transistor.

FIGURE 11.16 P-channel transistor.

NMOS Inverters. NMOS inverters are constructed of two NMOS transistors in which one is utilized as a resistance (Q2) and the other is utilized as a switch (Q1). A depletion-mode NMOS transistor is commonly utilized for the resistance device. A basic NMOS inverter is shown in Fig. 11.17. Note that Q2 is always on and acts as a resistor.

When a logic "0" is applied to the inverter's input, Q1 is turned off, which results in Q2 driving a logic 1 at the output. When a logic "1" is applied to the inverter's input, Q1 is turned on and overcomes Q2. This results in a logic "0" at the output.

NMOS microcontrollers are still produced in large quantities today. An advantage of NMOS processes is the simplistic circuit configuration which results in higher chip densities. NMOS devices are also less sensitive to electrostatic discharge (ESD) than CMOS devices. An inherent disadvantage of NMOS design is the slower switching speeds and higher power dissipation due to the dc current path from power to ground through Q1 and Q2 when the inverter is driving a logic "0".

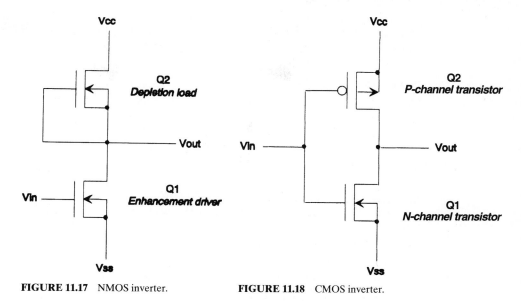

FIGURE 11.17   NMOS inverter.

FIGURE 11.18   CMOS inverter.

CMOS Inverters.   The CMOS is the most widely used process for automotive microcontrollers today. CMOS inverters are constructed of both P-channel and N-channel transistors that have their inputs tied together as shown in Fig. 11.18. When a logic "0" is applied to the inverter's input, Q1 is turned off and Q2 is turned on, which results in Q2 driving a logic "1" at the output. When a logic "1" is applied to the inverter's input, Q2 is turned off and Q1 is turned on, which results in Q1 driving a logic "0" at the output. Note that only one of these two devices will conduct at a time when the input is "1" or "0". While the input switches, both Q1 and Q2 may conduct for a short time resulting in a small amount of power dissipation.

The main advantages of CMOS logic are greatly improved switching times and lower power consumption, which is due to the complementary design of the inverter. A disadvantage of CMOS logic is that it is more expensive due to its increased complexity and more demanding fabrication process. CMOS logic is more susceptible to ESD damage, although microcontroller manufacturers have countered this by incorporating very effective ESD protection devices onto the silicon.

11.1.10   Temperature Range

Another important factor that must be considered when choosing a microcontroller is the temperature range in which it will be required to operate. The two most common temperature specifications specified by microcontroller manufacturers are *ambient temperature under bias* (TA) and *storage temperature*. These specifications are based upon package thermal characteristics as determined through device and package testing. Storage temperature refers to the temperature range that a microcontroller can be subjected to during periods of nonoperation. Storage temperature specifications are more extreme than ambient temperature under bias temperatures and are usually all the same regardless of the specified ambient temperature range. The common storage temperature range in industry is −60 to +150 °C. While powered-down, a given microcontroller must not be subjected to temperatures that exceed its specified storage temperature range.

Ambient temperature under bias (TA) refers to the temperature range that the microcontroller is guaranteed to operate at within a given application. While powered-up or operating, a microcontroller must not be subjected to temperatures that exceed its specified ambient temperature range. The most common ambient temperature ranges in industry are:

Commercial	0 to +70 °C
Extended	−40 to +85 °C
Automotive	−40 to +125 °C

11.2 MEMORY

Microcontrollers execute customized programs that are written by the user. These programs are stored in either on-chip or off-chip memory and are often referred to as the *user's code*. On-chip memory is actually integrated onto the same piece of silicon as the microcontroller and is accessed over the internal data bus. Off-chip memory exists on a separately packaged piece of silicon and is typically accessed by the microcontroller over an external address/data bus.

A memory map shows how memory addresses are arranged in a particular microcontroller. Figure 11.19 shows a typical microcontroller memory map.

Address	Memory Function		
0FFFFh 0A000h	External Memory		
9FFFh 2080h	Internal ROM/EPROM or External Memory		
207Fh 2000h	Internal ROM/EPROM or External Memory (Interrupt vectors, CCB's, Security Key, Reserved locations, etc.)		
1FFFh 1F00h	Internal Special Function Registers (SFR's)		
1EFFh 0600h	External Memory		
05FFh 0400h	INTERNAL RAM (Address with indirect or indexed modes.) (Also know as Code RAM)		
03FFh 0100h	Register RAM	Upper Register File (Address with indirect or indexed modes or through windows.)	Register File
00FFh 0018h	Register RAM	Lower Register File (Address with direct, indirect or indexed modes.)	
0017h 0000h	CPU SFRs		

FIGURE 11.19   Microcontroller memory map.

Memory is commonly referred to in terms of Kbytes of memory. One Kbyte is defined as 1024 bytes of data. Memory is most commonly arranged in bytes which consist of 8 bits of data. For instance, a common automotive EPROM is referred to as a "256k × 8 EPROM". This EPROM contains 256-Kbytes 8-bit memory locations or 2,097,152 bits of information.

11.2.1 On-Chip Memory

On-chip microcontroller memory consists of some mix of five basic types: random access memory (RAM), read-only memory (ROM), erasable ROM (EPROM), electrically erasable ROM (EPROM), and flash memory. RAM is typically utilized for run-time variable storage and SFRs. The various types of ROM are generally used for code storage and fixed data tables.

The advantages of on-chip memory are numerous, especially for automotive applications, which are very size and cost conscious. Utilizing on-chip memory eliminates the need for external memory and the "glue" logic necessary to implement an address/data bus system. External memory systems are also notorious generators of switching noise and RFI due to their high clock rates and fast switching times. Providing sufficient on-chip memory helps to greatly reduce these concerns.

RAM.   RAM may be defined as memory that has both read and write capabilities so that the stored information can be retrieved (read) and changed by applying new information to the cell (write). RAM found on microcontrollers is that of the static type that uses transistor cells connected as flip-flops. A typical six-transistor CMOS RAM cell is shown in Fig. 11.20. It consists of two cross-coupled CMOS inverters to store the data and two transmission gates, which provide the data path into or out of the cell. The most significant characteristic of static memory is that it loses its memory contents once power is removed. After power is removed, and once it is reapplied, static microcontroller RAM locations will revert to their default state of a logic "0". Because of the number of transistors used to construct a single cell, RAM memory is typically larger per bit than EPROM or ROM memory.

Although code typically cannot be executed from register RAM, a special type of RAM often referred to as *code RAM* is useful for downloading small segments of executable code. The difference between code and register RAM is that code RAM can be accessed via the

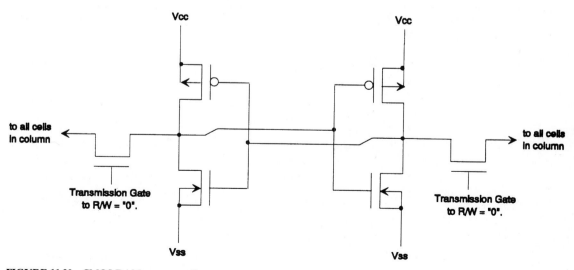

FIGURE 11.20   CMOS RAM memory cell.

memory controller, thus allowing code to be executed from it. Code RAM is especially useful for end-of-line testing during ECU manufacturing by allowing test code to be downloaded via the serial port peripheral.

ROM.   Read-only memory (ROM), as the name implies, is memory that can be read but not written to. ROM is used for storage of user code or data that does not change since it is a non-volatile memory that retains its contents after power is removed. Code or data is either entered during the manufacturing process (masked ROM, or MROM) or by later program-ming (programmable ROM, or PROM); either way, once entered it is unalterable.

A ROM cell by itself (Fig. 11.21) is nothing more than a transistor. ROM cells must be used in a matrix of word and bit lines (as shown in Fig. 11.22) in order to store information. The word lines are connected to the address decoder and the bit lines are connected to output buffers. The user's code is permanently stored by including or omitting individual cells at word and bit line junctions within the ROM array. For MROMs, this is done during wafer fabrica-tion. For PROMs, this is done by blowing a fuse in the source/drain connection of each cell. To read an address within the array, the address decoder applies the address to the memory matrix. For any given intersection of a word and bit line, the absence of a cell transistor allows no current to flow and causes the transistor to be off. This indicates an unprogrammed ROM cell. The presence of a complete cell conducts and is sensed as a logical "0", indicating a pro-grammed cell. The stored data on the bit lines is then driven to the output buffers.

MROMs are typically used for applications whose code is stable and in volume produc-tion. After the development process is complete and the user's program has been verified, the user submits the ROM code to the microcontroller manufacturer. The microcontroller manu-facturer then produces a mask that is used during manufacturing to permanently embed the program within the microcontroller. This mask layer either enables or disables individual ROM cells at the junctions of the word and bit lines. An advantage of MROM microcon-trollers is that they come with user code embedded, which saves time and money since post-production programming is not necessary. A disadvantage of MROM devices is that, since the mask with the user code has to be supplied early in the manufacturing process, throughput time (TPT) is longer.

Some versions of ROM (such as Intel's Quick-ROM) are actually not ROMs, but rather EPROMs, which are programmed at the factory. These devices are packaged in plastic devices, which prevents them from being erased since ultraviolet light cannot be applied to the actual EPROM array. Throughput time for QROMs is faster since the user code isn't required until after the actual manufacturing of the microcontroller is complete. As with

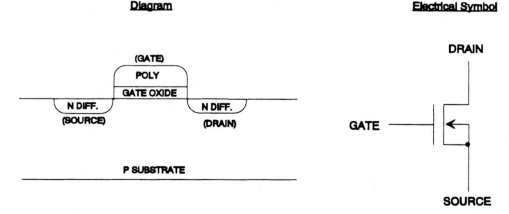

FIGURE 11.21   ROM memory cell.

WORD lines from address decoder

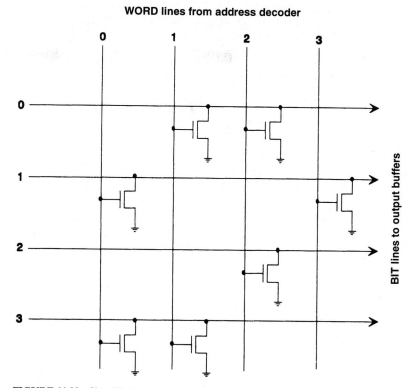

FIGURE 11.22 Simplified ROM memory matrix.

MROMs, the user supplies the ROM code to the microcontroller manufacturer. Instead of creating a mask with the ROM code, the manufacturer programs it into the device just prior to final test.

EPROM. EPROM devices are typically used during application development since this is when user code is changed often. EPROMs are delivered to the user unprogrammed. This allows the user to program the code into memory just prior to installation into an ECU module. Many EPROM microcontrollers actually provide a mechanism for in-module programming. This feature allows the user to program the device via the serial port while it is installed in the module. EPROM devices come assembled in packages either with or without a transparent window. Windowed devices are true EPROM devices that allow the user to erase the memory contents by exposing the EPROM array to ultraviolet light. These devices may be reprogrammed over and over again and thus are ideally suited for system development and debug during which code is changed often. EPROM devices assembled in a package without a window are commonly referred to as *one-time programmable devices* or OTPs. OTPs may only be programmed once, since the absence of a transparent window prevents UV erasure. OTPs are suited for limited production validation (PV) builds in which the code will not be erased.

A typical EPROM cell is shown in Fig. 11.23. It is basically an N-channel transistor that has an added poly1 floating gate to store charge. This floating gate is not connected and is surrounded by insulating oxide that prevents electron flow. The mechanism used to program an EPROM cell is known as *hot electron injection.* Hot electron injection occurs when very high drain (9-V) and select gate (12-V) voltages are applied. This gives the negatively charged electrons enough energy to surmount the oxide barrier and allows them to be stored on the gate.

This has the same effect as a negative applied gate voltage and turns the transistor off. When the cell is unprogrammed, it can be turned on like a normal transistor by applying 5 V to the poly2 select gate. When it is programmed, the 5 V will not turn on the cell. The state of the cell is determined by attempting to turn on the cell and detecting if it turns on. Erasure is performed through the application of ultraviolet (UV) light, which gives just the right amount of energy necessary for negatively charged electrons to surmount the oxide barrier and leave the floating gate.

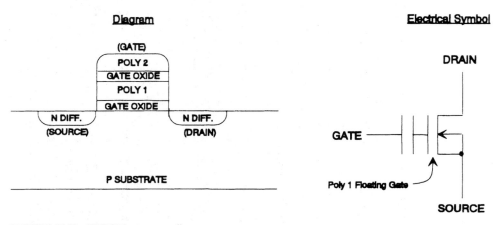

FIGURE 11.23 EPROM memory cell.

Flash. Flash memory is the newest nonvolatile memory technology and is very similar to EPROM. The key difference is that flash memory can be electrically erased. Once programmed, flash memory contents remain intact until an erase cycle is initiated via software. Like EEPROM, flash memory requires a programming and erase voltage of approximately 12.0 V. Since a clean, regulated 12-V reference is not readily available in automotive environments, this need is often provided for through the incorporation of an on-chip charge pump. The charge pump produces the voltage and current necessary for programming and erasure from the standard 5-V supply voltage. The advantage of flash is in its capability to be programmed *and* erased in-module without having to be removed. In-module reprogrammability is desirable since in-vehicle validation testing doesn't always allow for easy access to the microcontroller. Flash also allows for last-minute code changes, data table upgrades, and general code customization during ECU assembly. Since a flash cell is nearly identical in size to that of an EPROM cell, the high reliability and high device density capable with EPROM is retained. The main disadvantage of flash is the need for an on-chip charge pump and special program and erase circuitry, which adds cost.

A flash memory cell is essentially the same as an EPROM cell, with the exception of the floating gate. The difference is a thin oxide layer which allows the cell to be electrically erased. The mechanism used to erase data is known as *Fowler-Nordheim tunneling,* which allows the charge to be transferred from the floating gate when a large enough field is created. Hot electron injection is the mechanism used to program a cell, exactly as is done with EPROM cells. When the floating gate is positively charged, the cell will read a "1", when negatively charged, the cell will read a "0".

EEPROM. EEPROM (electrically erasable and programmable ROM, commonly referred to as E^2ROM) is a ROM that can be electrically erased and programmed. Once programmed, EEPROM contents remain intact until an erase cycle is initiated via software. Like flash, programming and erase voltages of approximately 12 V are required. Since a clean, regulated 12-V reference is not readily available in automotive environments, this requirement is satisfied using an on-chip charge pump as is done for flash memory arrays. Like flash, the advantage of EEPROM is its capability to be programmed and erased in-module. This allows the user to erase and program the device in the module without having to remove it. EEPROM's most significant disadvantage is the need for an on-chip charge pump. Special program and erase circuitry also adds cost.

An EEPROM cell is essentially the same as an EPROM cell with the exception of the floating gate being isolated by a thin oxide layer. The main difference from flash is that Fowler-Nordheim electron tunneling is used for *both* programming and erasure. This mechanism allows charge to be transferred to or from the floating gate (depending upon the polarity of the field) when a large enough field is created. When the floating gate is positively charged, the cell will read a "1"; when negatively charged, the cell will read a "0".

11.2.2 Off-Chip Memory

Off-chip memory offers the most flexibility to the system designer, but at a price; it takes up additional PCB real estate as well as additional I/O pins. In cost- and size-conscience applications, such as automotive ABS, system designers almost exclusively use on-chip memory. However, when memory requirements grow to sizes in excess of what is offered on-chip (such as is common in electronic engine control), the system designer must implement an off-chip memory system. Off-chip memory is flexible because the user can implement various memory devices in the configuration of his choice. Most microcontrollers on the market today offer a wide variety of control pins and timing modes to allow the system designer flexibility when interfacing to a wide range of external memory systems.

Accessing External Memory.   If circuit designers must use external memory in their applications, the type of external address/data bus incorporated onto the microcontroller should be considered. If external memory is not used, this will have, if any, impact upon the application. There are two basic types of interfaces used in external memory systems. Both of these are parallel interfaces in which bits of data are moved in a parallel fashion and are referred to as *multiplexed* and *demultiplexed* address/data buses.

Multiplexed Address/Data Buses.   As the name implies, multiplexed address/data buses allow the address as well as the data to be passed over the same microcontroller pins by multiplexing the two in time. Figure 11.24 illustrates a typical multiplexed 16-bit address/data bus system as is implemented with Intel's 8XC196Kx family of microcontrollers.

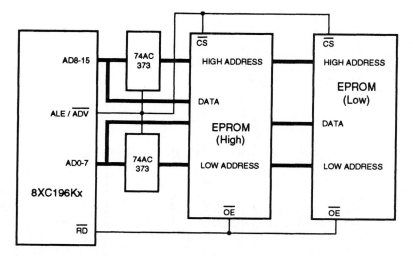

FIGURE 11.24 Multiplexed address/data bus system.

During a multiplexed bus cycle (refer to Fig. 11.25), the address is placed on the bus during the first half of the bus cycle and then latched by an external address data latch. The signal to latch the address comes from a signal generated by the microcontroller, called address latch enable (ALE). The address must be present on the bus for a specified amount of time prior to ALE being asserted. After the address is latched, the microcontroller asserts either a read (RD#) or a write (WR#) signal to the external memory device.

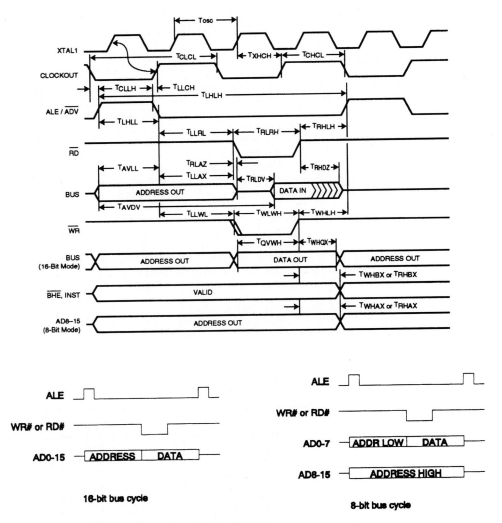

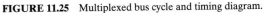

FIGURE 11.25 Multiplexed bus cycle and timing diagram.

For a read cycle, the microcontroller will pull its RD# output pin low and float the bus to allow the memory device to output the data located at the address latched on its address pins. The data returned from external memory must be on the bus and stable for a specified setup time before the rising edge or RD#, which is when the microcontroller latches the data.

For a write cycle, the microcontroller will pull its WR# pin low and then output data on the bus to be written to the external memory. After a specified setup time, the microcontroller will release its WR# signal, which signals to the memory device to latch the data on the bus into the address location present on its address pins.

Advantages of multiplexed address/data bus systems are that fewer microcontroller pins are required since address and data share the same pins. For a true 16-bit system, this translates into a multiplexed system requiring 16 fewer pins (for address and data) than would be required by a demultiplexed system. A disadvantage is that an external latch is required to hold the address during the second half of the bus cycle; this adds to the component count.

Demultiplexed Address/Data Buses.   Microcontrollers with demultiplexed address/data buses implement separate, dedicated address and data buses as shown in Fig. 11.26.

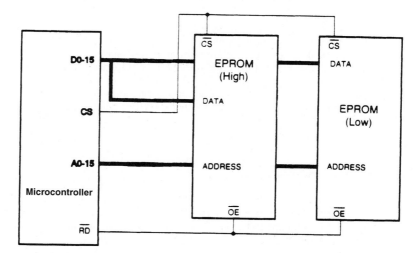

FIGURE 11.26   Typical demultiplexed address/data bus system.

The operation of a demultiplexed address/data bus is basically the same as the multiplexed type with the exception of not having an ALE signal to latch the address for the second half of the bus cycle. The operation of the RD#, WR#, address, and data lines is essentially the same as for that of a multiplexed system.

During a demultiplexed bus cycle, the microcontroller places the address on the address bus and holds it there for the entire bus cycle. For a read of external memory, the microcontroller asserts the RD# signal (or WR# for a write signal) just as would be done for a multiplexed bus cycle. The memory device will respond accordingly by either placing the data to be read on the data bus or by latching the data to be written off of the data bus. Figure 11.27 illustrates a simplified demultiplexed bus cycle.

An advantage of multiplexed address/data bus systems is that external data latches are not necessary, which saves on system component count. A disadvantage, as mentioned earlier, is that more microcontroller pins must be allocated for the interface, which leaves fewer pins for other I/O purposes.

11.3   LOW-SPEED INPUT/OUTPUT PORTS

Low-speed input/output (LSIO) ports allow the microcontroller to read input signals as well as provide output signals to and from other electronic components such as sensors, power drivers,

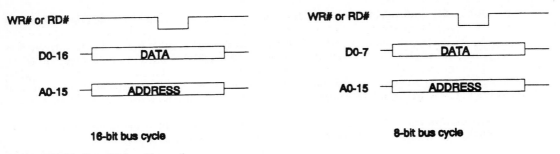

16-bit bus cycle   8-bit bus cycle

FIGURE 11.27 Demultiplexed bus cycle.

digital devices, actuators, and other microcontrollers. The term "low-speed" is used to describe these ports because unlike high-speed I/O (HSIO) ports which are interrupt driven, LSIO port data must be manually read and written by the user program. Interrupt-driven I/O is typically not possible on port pins configured for LSIO operation. It is common for modern high-performance microcontrollers to utilize multifunctional port pins which can be configured for a special function as well as LSIO. LSIO ports most commonly consist of eight port pins in parallel, which are supported by byte registers. For example, by writing to a single-byte special function register, an entire port can be configured, read, or written. Manipulating individual bits in the port register allows the user flexibility in accessing either single or multiple port pins.

11.3.1 Push-Pull Port Pin Configuration

The term *push-pull*, or *complementary*, output is commonly used to define a port pin that has the capability to output either a logic "1" or "0". Figure 11.28 shows a basic push-pull port pin configuration. Referring to Fig. 11.28, writing a "1" to the data output register enables the P-channel MOSFET and pulls the pin to +5 V, thus driving a logic "1" at the port pin. When a "0" is written

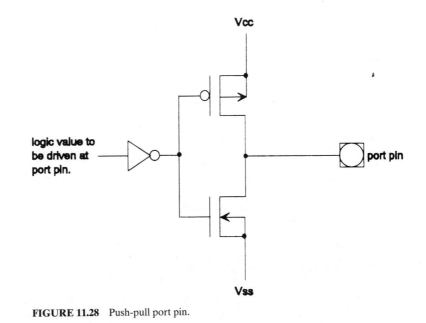

FIGURE 11.28 Push-pull port pin.

to the data register, the N-channel MOSFET is enabled and thus provides a current path to ground which results in a logic 0 at the port pin. Note that during this time the P-channel pull-up MOSFET is disabled to prevent contention at the port pin. Also note that the port logic design does not allow both the P-channel and the N-channel devices to be driving at the same time.

11.3.2 Open-Drain Port Pin Configuration

Open-drain port pins (Fig. 11.29) are useful for handshaking signals over which multiple devices will have control. The fact that the P-channel transistor is either omitted or disabled dictates the need for an external pull-up resistor. An example of an application for open-drain port pins would be for a bus contention line between two microcontrollers communicating on a common bus. During normal operation, the line is pulled high by the external pull-up resistor to signal to either microcontroller that no contention exists. If one of the microcontrollers should detect contention on the bus, it simply outputs a logic "0", which signals the contention to the other processor. To output the "0", the port only has to overcome the external pull-up which the user should appropriately size to match the port drive specifications.

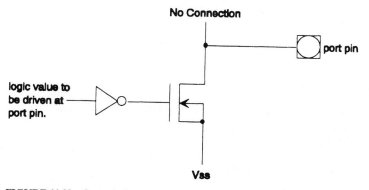

FIGURE 11.29 Open-drain port pin.

11.3.3 High-Impedance Input Port Pin Configuration

High impedance, or "Hi-z," port pins (Fig. 11.30) are used strictly as inputs since no drivers exist on these types of pins. Hi-z refers to the relatively high input impedance of the port pin. This high input impedance prevents the port pin circuitry from actively loading the input signal. Note that the pin is connected to the gates of a CMOS inverter, which drives internal circuitry. Usually a certain amount of hysteresis is built into these pins and is specified in the data sheet.

11.3.4 Quasi Bidirectional Port Pin Configuration

Quasi bidirectional (QBD) port pins are those that can be used as either input or output without the need for direction control logic. QBD port pins can output a strong low value or a weak high value. The weak high value can be externally overridden, providing an input function. Figure 11.31 shows a QBD port pin diagram and its transfer characteristic.

Writing a "1" to the port pin disables the strong low driver (Q2) and enables a very weak high driver (Q3). To get the pin to transition high quickly, a strong high driver (Q1) is enabled for one state time and then disabled (leaving only Q3 active).

It is important to keep in mind that since the port pin can be externally overridden with a logic "0", reading the port pin could falsely indicate that it was written as a logic "0".

The ability to overdrive the weak output driver is what gives the quasi bidirectional port pin its input capability. To reduce the amount of current that flows when the pin is externally pulled low, the weak output driver (Q4) is turned off when a valid logic "0" is detected. The input transfer characteristic of a quasi bidirectional port pin is shown in Fig. 11.31.

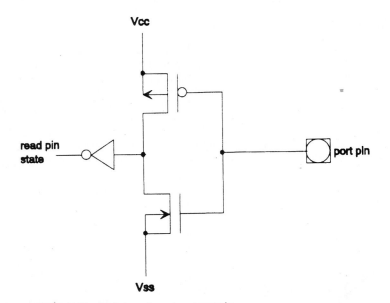

FIGURE 11.30   High-impedance input port pin.

11.3.5   Bidirectional Port Example

The following example describes the operation of a state-of-the-art bidirectional port structure. This particular structure is used upon newer members of Intel's MCS-96 automotive microcontroller family. A single port consists of eight multifunction, parallel port pins (see Fig. 11.32), which are controlled (on a by-pin basis) with four special function registers referred to as Px_PIN, Px_REG, Px_MODE, and Px_DIR. As is common with other high-performance microcontrollers, the pins of this port are shared with alternate special functions controlled by other on-chip peripherals. The Px_MODE register allows the programmer to choose either LSIO or the associated special function for any given port pin. Writing a "1" to the appropriate bit selects the corresponding pin as special function whereas a "0" selects LSIO. The function of the Px_PIN and Px_REG registers is fairly straightforward. In order to read the value on the pin, the user simply reads the Px_PIN register. To write a value to the Px_REG register, the user simply writes the desired output value to the Px_REG register. The Px_DIR register allows the user to configure the port pin as either input or output.

In order to prevent an undefined pin state during reset, port pins revert to a default state during reset. For the Intel Kx bidirectional port structure, this state is defined as a weak logic "1". The transistor that drives this state is labeled as WKPU in Fig. 11.32 and is asserted in reset until the user writes to the Px_MODE register to configure the port pin.

Ports such as this offer the user much flexibility in assigning their function within an application. Following are three examples that depict how these ports may be configured by the user by writing values to the appropriate bit within the port SFR. Also note that the eight pins of a port may be configured individually on a pin-by-pin basis.

To configure a given port pin as a high-impedance input pin, the user must write the following values to the corresponding bit within the port SFR.

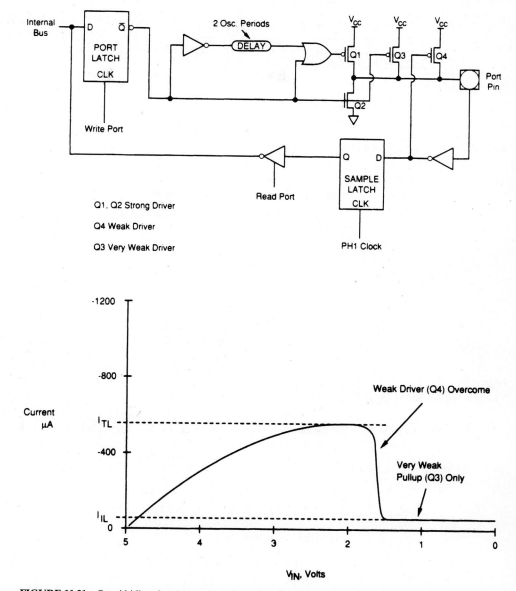

FIGURE 11.31 Quasi bidirectional port pin and transfer characteristic.

Px_MODE: "0" selects the pin as LSIO and disables weak pull-up.
Px_DIR: "1" disables operation of the N-channel transistor.
Px_REG: "1" disables the N-channel transistor.

To configure a given port pin for push-pull operation, the following values must be written to the corresponding bit within the port SFR.

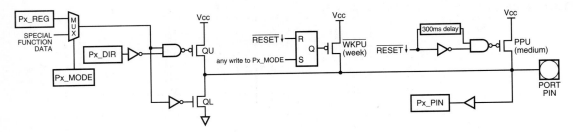

FIGURE 11.32 Bidirectional port structure example.

Px_MODE:	"0" selects the pin as LSIO and disables weak pull-up transistor.
Px_DIR:	"0" enables operation of both the N- and P-channel transistors.
Px_REG:	"0" or "1" drives that value at the port pin.

To configure a port pin for open-drain operation, the user must write the following values to the corresponding bits within the port SFR.

Px_MODE:	"0" selects the pin as LSIO and disables weak pull-up transistor.
Px_DIR:	"1" disables operation of the N-channel transistor.
Px_REG:	"1" disables the P-channel transistor / achieves Hi-Z state.
	"0" enables the N-channel transistor / drives "0" at pin.

11.4 HIGH-SPEED I/O PORTS

Perhaps the most demanding of automotive microcontroller applications is electronic engine control and antilock braking/traction control. These applications both require the microcontroller to detect, process, and respond to external signals or "events" within relatively short periods of time. Sometimes referred to as a capture/compare module, a microcontroller's HSIO (high-speed input/output) peripheral allows the microcontroller to capture an event as it occurs. The term *capture* refers to a series of events that begins with the microcontroller detecting a rising or falling edge upon a high-speed input pin. At the precise moment this edge is detected, the value of a software timer is loaded into a time register and an interrupt is triggered. This gives the microcontroller the relative time at which the event occurred. An HSIO peripheral also provides compare functions by detecting an internal event, such as a timer reaching a particular count value. When the particular count value is detected, the HSIO unit will generate a specified event (rising or falling edge) on a port pin. This feature is ideal for generating PWM waveforms or synchronizing external events with internal events.

For example, consider a typical ABS microcontroller which must detect, capture, and calculate wheel speeds; respond with signals to hydraulic solenoids; and perform many other background tasks all within a loop time of about 5 ms. The wheel speed signals are input to the microcontroller as square waves with frequencies up to 7000 Hz (approximately one edge every 71 μs). The microcontroller must have the performance necessary to capture and process these edges on as many as four wheel speed inputs. HSIO peripherals, along with the interrupt structure, play a major role in the microcontroller's ability to perform this function.

Nearly every microcontroller manufacturer has its own proprietary HSIO peripheral. For purposes of this section, the event processor array (EPA) HSIO peripheral, which is used by Intel's 87C196KT automotive microcontroller, will be discussed.

11.4.1   High-Speed Input and Output Peripheral

High-speed input/output peripherals typically consist of a given number of capture/compare modules, a timer/counter structure, control and status SFRs, and an interrupt structure of some type. Figure 11.33 shows a block diagram of the EPA peripheral. The main components of the EPA are ten capture/compare channels, two compare only channels, and two timer/counters. The capture/compare channels are configured independently of each other. The two timer/counters are shared between the various capture/compare channels. Each capture/compare channel has its own dedicated SFR's: EPAx_TIME and EPAx_CON (x designates the channel number).

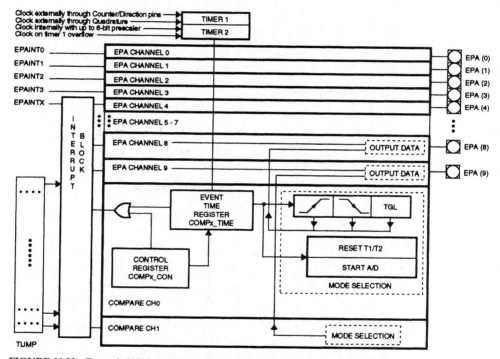

FIGURE 11.33   Example HSIO peripheral: Intel's EPA peripheral.

11.4.2   Timer/Counter Structures

High-performance microcontrollers typically integrate one or more timer/counters onto their silicon. A microcontroller's timer/counter structure provides a time base to which all HSIO events are referenced. Timers are clocked internally, whereas counters are clocked from an external clock source. Timers are often very flexible structures, in which programmers have the capability to configure the timer/counters to meet their application's particular needs. The 87C196KT has two 16-bit timer/counters referred to as TIMER1 and TIMER2. As 16-bit timer/counters, each timer has the capability of counting to 2^{16} or 65,536 before overflowing. The user has the option of triggering an interrupt upon overflow of a timer/counter. Each of these two timers can be independently configured using the TxCONTROL SFR as shown in Fig. 11.34, where x specifies either 1 or 2 for Timer1 or Timer2, respectively.

Bits number 3, 4, and 5 are the mode bits that allow the user to configure the clocking source and direction of each timer/counter. The clock rate can be based either upon the fre-

TxCONTROL SFR

7	6	5	4	3	2	1	0
CE	UD	M2	M1	M0	P2	P1	P0

CE: Count Enable: "0" = disable timer, "1" = enable timer

UD: Up/Down: "0" = count up, "1" = count down

MODE:

M2, M1, M0	Clock source	Direction determined by:
0 0 0	XTAL/4	state of UD bit
0 0 1	TxCLK pin	state of UD bit
0 1 0	XTAL/4	state of TxDIR pin
0 1 1	TxCLK pin	state of TxDIR pin
1 0 0	Timer1 overflow	state of UD bit
1 1 0	Timer1 overflow	same as Timer1
1 1 1	Quadrature clocking using TxCLK and TxDIR pins	

Prescale:

P2, P1, P0	Clock prescale values
0 0 0	÷ by 1 (250 ns @ 16 MHz xtal frequency)
0 0 1	÷ by 2 (500 ns @ 16 MHz xtal frequency)
0 1 0	÷ by 4 (1 μs @ 16 MHz xtal frequency)
0 1 1	÷ by 8 (2 μs @ 16 MHz xtal frequency)
1 0 0	÷ by 16 (4 μs @ 16 MHz xtal frequency)
1 0 1	÷ by 32 (8 μs @ 16 MHz xtal frequency)
1 1 0	÷ by 64 (16 μs @ 16 MHz xtal frequency)
1 1 1	reserved

FIGURE 11.34   Timer control SFR example.

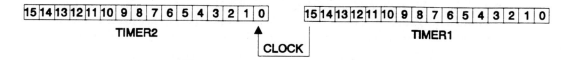

Overflow of TIMER1 clocks TIMER2 thus creating a 32-bit TIMER.

FIGURE 11.35   Cascading of timer/counters.

quency that the microcontroller is being clocked at the XTAL pins or upon the input frequency on another pin referred to as TxCLK. The user also has the option of either having the logic level of another pin (TxDIR) or the UD bits in TxCONTROL determine the direction (up/down) that the timer/counter is clocked.

For those applications that require a 32-bit timer/counter, the user has the option (using the mode bits) to direct the overflow of TIMER1 to clock TIMER2. This is known as cascading and essentially creates a 32-bit timer/counter as shown in Fig. 11.35.

11.4.3   Input Capture

Input capture refers to the process of capturing a current timer value when a specific type of event occurs. An excellent example of high-speed input capture can be illustrated with a basic automotive ABS input capture algorithm that calculates the frequency of a wheel speed input. The signals from the wheel speed sensors are input into the microcontroller's EPA pins as square waves. Consider the generic wheel speed input capture example shown in Fig. 11.36.

Two timers (1 and 2) are used in this example. Timer1 is used in conjunction with an EPA channel to provide a 5-ms software timer (this is a compare function that will be discussed in the next section). The 5 ms is the main loop time used in generic ABS algorithms. Timer2 is used in conjunction with one or more EPA channels to capture the relative times at which edges occur on wheel speed inputs. The EPA is configured to capture falling edges and initiate an interrupt, which stores the event time and increments an edge count. To simplify this example, we will consider only a single input channel.

The process starts by EPA interrupts being enabled after Timer1 starts a new 5-ms timer count. The first falling edge causes an interrupt that stores the event time (T2) into a variable *initial time* and increments an edge count. The next edge causes an interrupt in which the event time (T2+x) is stored into a variable called *final time* and increments the edge count.

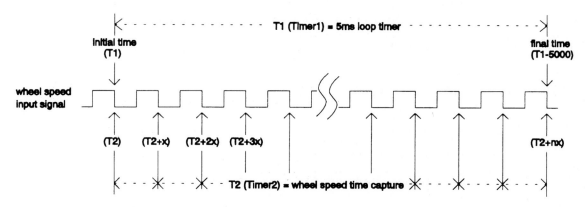

FIGURE 11.36   Input capture example using EPA peripheral.

Subsequent edges' event times are also stored into *final time* until Timer1's 5-ms count expires. At this point, final time contains the time at which the last edge to occur was captured. The average period of the input waveform can then be calculated with the following equation:

$$\text{input period} = (\textit{final time} - \textit{initial time}) \, / \, \text{edge count}$$

11.4.4   Output Compare

Output compare refers to the process of generating an event when a timer value matches a predetermined time value. The event may be to generate an interrupt, toggle an output pin, perform an A/D conversion, and so forth. Following is an example that shows the steps necessary to generate an event every 50 μs:

1. Enable the output compare channel's interrupt.
2. Initialize the timer to count up at 1 μs per timer tick.
3. Initialize the output compare channel to re-enable and reset the timer (to zero) when a timer match occurs.
4. Initialize the output compare channel to produce the desired event when a timer match occurs.
5. Write 32h (50 decimal) to the appropriate output compare channel's time register.
6. Enable the timer to start the process.
7. A compare channel interrupt will be generated every 50 μs.

Since the example re-enables and zeros the timer, the event will occur continuously until the user's program halts the process.

Software Timers.   Software timers such as the 5-ms timer used in the ABS wheel speed capture example can be set up easily using a compare channel and a timer. The following software timer procedure is very similar to that used in the previous output compare example:

1. Enable the compare channel's interrupt.
2. Initialize the timer to count up at 1 us per timer tick.
3. Initialize the output compare channel to re-enable and reset the timer (to zero) when a timer match occurs.
4. Initialize the output compare channel to produce an interrupt (5-ms ISR) when a timer match occurs.
5. Write 1388h (5000 decimal) to the appropriate output compare channel's time register.
6. Enable the timer to start the process.
7. An compare channel interrupt will be generated every 5 ms.

11.4.5   Pulse-Width Modulation (PWM)

Pulse-width modulation (PWM) peripherals provide the user with the ability to generate waveforms that have specified frequencies and duty cycles. PWM waveforms are typically used to generate pulsed waveforms used for motor control or they may be filtered to produce a smooth analog signal. HSIO peripherals typically provide for PWM waveform generation, although the methods are not usually as efficient as dedicated PWM peripherals. A basic example of creating a PWM waveform using an HSIO peripheral's output compare function is described in Sec. 11.4.4.

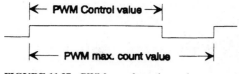

FIGURE 11.37   PWM waveform time values.

PWM Peripheral.   The components of a basic automotive microcontroller's PWM peripheral include a counter (typically 8-bit), a comparator, a holding register, and a control register. The counter typically has a prescaler that allows the user to select the clock rate of the counter, which allows for selectable PWM frequencies. Without prescaling capability, an 8-bit counter would only allow for a period of 256 state times. The PWM control register determines how long the PWM output is held high during the pulse, effectively controlling the duty cycle as shown in Fig. 11.37. For an 8-bit PWM counter, the value written to the PWM control register can be from 0 to 255 (equating to 255 state times with no prescaling). Note that PWM peripherals do not typically allow for a 100 percent duty cycle because the output must be reset when the counter reaches zero.

The operation of a PWM peripheral is rather simple. The PWM control register's value (assume 8-bit for this example) is loaded into a holding register when the 8-bit counter overflows. The comparator compares the contents of the holding register to the counter value. When the counter value is equal to zero, the PWM output is driven high. It remains high until the counter value matches the value in the holding register, at which time the output is pulled low. When the counter overflows, the output is again switched high. Figure 11.38 shows typical PWM output waveforms.

Duty Cycle	PWM Control Register Value	Output Waveform
0%	00	
10%	25	
50%	128	
90%	230	
99.6%	255	

FIGURE 11.38   PWM output waveforms.

11.5   SERIAL COMMUNICATIONS

It is often necessary for automotive microcontrollers to have the capability to communicate with other devices both internal and external to the ECU. Within an ECU a microcontroller may have to communicate with other devices such as backup processors, shift registers, watchdog timers, and so forth. It is not uncommon for automotive microcontrollers to communicate with devices external to the ECU, such as other modules within the vehicle and even diagnostic computers at a service station. All of these communication examples require a large quantity of data to be transmitted/received in a short period of time. Also consider that this communication must utilize as few pins of the microcontroller as possible in order to save valuable PCB board space. These requirements all support the need for serial communications.

Serial communications provides for efficient transfer of data while utilizing a minimum number of pins. Serial communications is performed by transferring a group of data bits, one at a time, sequentially over a single data line. Each transmission of a group of bits (typically a

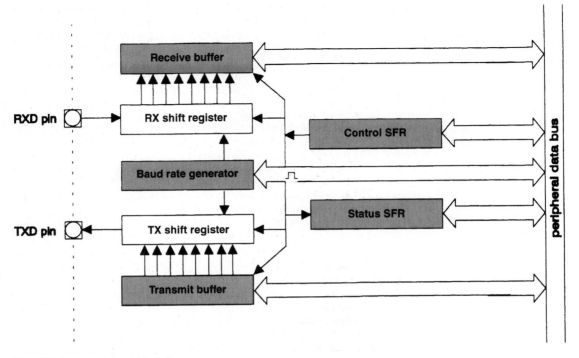

FIGURE 11.39 Serial port block diagram.

byte of data) is known as a data frame. This transfer of data takes place at a given speed, which is referred to as the baud rate and is typically specified in bits/second.

A typical microcontroller serial port consists of data buffers, data registers, and a baud rate generator. Interface to the outside world takes place via the transmit (TXD) and receive (RXD) pins. A block diagram for a typical serial port peripheral is shown in Fig. 11.39. By writing to the serial port control register, users are able to customize the operation of the serial port to their particular application's requirements.

The baud rate generator is used to provide the timing necessary for serial communications and determines the rate at which the bits are transmitted. In synchronous modes, the baud rate generator provides the timing reference used to create clock edges on the clock output pin. In asynchronous modes, the baud rate generator provides the timing reference used to latch data into the RX pin and clock it out of the TX pin.

11.5.1 Synchronous Serial Communications

Sometimes an application does not allow asynchronous serial communications to take place due to variations in clock frequency, which results in unacceptable baud rate error. Some applications simply require some sort of shift register I/O. Synchronous communication involves an additional clock pin, which is used to signal the other device that data being transferred are valid and ready to be read. Often when the user configures the serial port to work in a synchronous mode, the TXD pin automatically reverts to supplying the clock and the RXD pin automatically becomes the data pin. This configuration prevents an additional pin from having to be reserved for use as a serial clock pin. When a synchronous data transfer is initiated, a series of eight clock pulses is emitted from the clock pin at a predetermined baud rate as shown in Fig. 11.40.

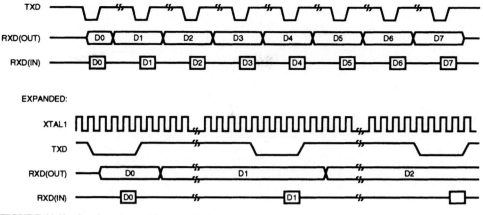

FIGURE 11.40   Synchronous serial mode data frame.

An example of synchronous serial communications is shown in Fig. 11.41. Assume that processor A is to transfer a byte of data to processor B. The program executing in processor A initiates a serial transmission by writing the data byte to be transmitted into the transmit buffer. Assuming microcontroller A's serial port is enabled for transmission, writing to the transmit buffer results in a series of eight clock pulses to be emitted from microcontroller A's clock pin. The first falling edge of the clock will signal to processor B that bit 0 (LSB) is ready to be read into its receive buffer. Microcontroller A will place the next data bit on the TXD pin with each rising clock edge. With B's serial port enabled for reception, each falling edge will result in another data bit being shifted into B's receive buffer. When B's receive buffer is full, the received data byte will be loaded into its receive register and will signal its CPU that the reception has been completed and the data is ready for use.

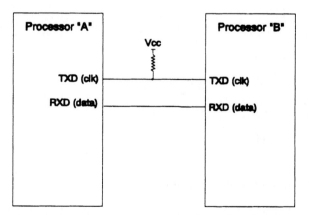

FIGURE 11.41   Synchronous serial communications example.

Shift Register Based I/O Expansion.   A common application for synchronous serial transmission is shift register based I/O expansion as shown in Fig. 11.42. In this circuit, a 74HC164 8-bit serial-in/parallel-out shift register is used to provide eight parallel outputs with a single serial input. The 74HC165 8-bit parallel-in/serial out shift register shown provides a single serial input resulting from eight parallel input signals. This allows the system designer to

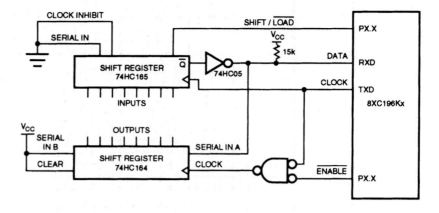

FIGURE 11.42   Shift register based I/O expansion example.

implement an additional 8-bit output port and additional 8-bit input port (16 signals total) using only four pins on the microcontroller. This expansion scheme allows a designer to achieve a greater number of I/O pins without having to upgrade to a microcontroller with a higher pin count.

To output data using this I/O expansion method, the user code simply writes a byte to the serial port transmit register to initiate data transfer. This causes the written byte to be shifted out of the microcontroller's RXD pin and into the 74HC164 one bit at a time. The data is reflected at the output pins of the 74HC164 as each bit is shifted in. For address/data bus emulation, another microcontroller pin may be utilized to indicate valid data to the intended receiving device.

To receive eight bits of data in parallel using this method, the user's code must latch the data on the 74HC165's input pins into its shift register by asserting the *shift/load* signal. After this is accomplished, the user's code simply needs to enable the serial port receive circuitry to receive the data one bit at a time into its receive buffer.

11.5.2   Asynchronous Serial Communications

The most common type of serial communications is asynchronous. As its name implies, asynchronous communication takes place between two devices without use of a clock line. Data is transmitted out the transmit buffer and received into the receive buffer independently at a speed determined by the baud rate generator. Most microcontrollers offer several modes of asynchronous serial communication.

Standard Asynchronous Mode.   The standard asynchronous mode consists of 10 bits: a start bit, eight data bits (LSB first), and a stop bit, as shown in Fig. 11.43. After the user initiates a transmission, data is automatically transmitted from the TX pin at the specified baud rate.

FIGURE 11.43   Standard asynchronous mode data frame.

A parity function is also implemented, which provides for a simple method of error-detection. Data transmitted will consist of either an odd or even number of logical "1"s. If even parity is enabled, the parity bit will either be set to a "1" or a "0" to make the number of "1"s in the data byte even. If odd parity is enabled, the parity bit will be set to the appropriate value to make the number of "1"s in the data byte odd. For instance, consider the data byte 11010010b. If even parity is enabled, the parity bit will be set to a "0" since there is already an even number of "1"s. If odd parity were enabled, the parity bit would be set to a "1" since another "1" would be needed to provide an odd number of "1"s. If the parity function is enabled (usually through a serial port control register), the parity bit is sent instead of the eighth data bit and parity is checked on reception. The occurrence of parity errors is typically flagged in a serial port status register to alert the microcontroller to corrupted data in the receive register.

Multiprocessor Asynchronous Serial Communications Modes.   Two other common serial communications modes which are used on automotive microcontrollers are the asynchronous 9th-bit recognition mode and the asynchronous 9th-bit mode. These two modes are commonly used together for multiprocessor communications where selective selection on a data link is required. Both modes are similar to the standard asynchronous mode with the exception of an additional ninth data bit in the data frame as shown in Fig. 11.44.

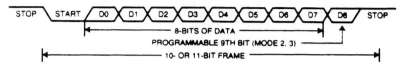

FIGURE 11.44   Asynchronous 9th-bit data frame.

The 9th-bit recognition mode consists of a start bit, nine data bits (LSB first), and a stop bit. For transmission, the ninth bit can be set to "1" by setting a corresponding bit in the serial port control register before writing to the transmit buffer. During reception, the receive interrupt bit is *not* set unless the ninth data bit being received is set to a logic "1".

The 9th-bit mode uses a data frame identical to that of the 9th-bit recognition mode. In this mode, a reception will always cause a receive interrupt, regardless of the state of the ninth data bit.

A multiprocessor data link is fairly simple to implement using these two modes. Microcontrollers within the system are connected as shown in Fig. 11.45. The master microcontroller is set to the 9th-bit recognition mode so that it is always interrupted by serial receptions. The slave microcontrollers are set to operate in the 9th-bit recognition mode so that they are interrupted on receptions only if the ninth data bit is set. Two types of data frames are used: address frames, which have the ninth bit set, and data frames, which have the ninth bit cleared. When the master processor wants to transmit a block of data to one of several slaves, it first sends out an address frame which identifies the target slave. Slaves in the 9th-bit recognition mode are not interrupted by a data frame, but an address frame interrupts all slaves. Each slave can examine the received byte and see if it is being addressed. The addressed slave then switches to the 9th-bit mode to receive data frames, while the slaves that were not addressed stay in the 9th-bit recognition mode and continue without interruption.

11.6   ANALOG-TO-DIGITAL CONVERTER

Analog-to-digital converter (A/D) peripherals allow automotive microcontrollers to sense and assign digital values to analog input voltages with considerable accuracy. An analog input

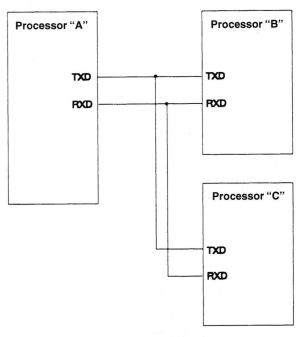

FIGURE 11.45 Asynchronous 9th-bit data frame.

may be defined as a voltage level that varies over a continuous range of values as opposed to the discrete values of digital signals.

11.6.1 Types of A/D Converters

The vast majority of A/D converters available on microcontrollers are of the successive approximation (S/A) type. Other types include flash A/D converters, in which conversions are completed in a parallel fashion and are performed at speeds measuring tens-of-nanoseconds. The drawback is that flash A/D converters require a great deal of die space when integrated on a microcontroller. It is because of their relatively large size that flash A/D converters are seldom offered on microcontrollers. Dual-slope A/D converters offer excellent A/D accuracy but typically take a relatively long period of time to complete a conversion. S/A A/D converters are very popular because they offer a compromise among accuracy, speed, and die-size requirements. The main drawback to successive approximation converters is that implementing the capacitor and resistor ladders takes a considerable amount of die space, although somewhat less than flash A/Ds. These converters are also somewhat susceptible to noise, although there are proven ways to reduce the effects of noise within a given application. The advantage of S/A converters is that they combine the best of other types of converters. They are relatively fast and do not take up excessive die space.

S/A converters typically consist of a resistor ladder, a sample capacitor, an input multiplexer, and a voltage comparator. A typical S/A converter is shown in Fig. 11.46. The resistor ladder is used to produce reference voltages for the input voltage comparison. A sample capacitor is utilized to capture the input voltage during a given period of time known as the sample time. Sample time can be defined as the amount of time that an A/D input voltage is applied to the sample capacitor.

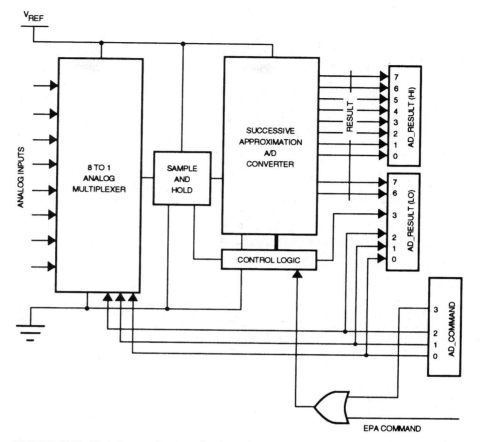

FIGURE 11.46 Typical successive approximation converter.

A successive approximation algorithm is used to perform the A/D conversion. A typical S/A converter consists of a 256-resistor ladder, a comparator, coupling capacitors, and a 10-bit successive approximation register (SAR), along with SFRs and logic to control the process. The resistor ladder provides 20-mV steps (with V_{ref} = 5.12 V), while capacitive coupling creates 5-mV steps within the 20-mV ladder voltages. Therefore, 1024 internal reference voltage levels are available for comparison against the analog input to generate a 10-bit conversion result. Eight-bit conversions use only the resistor ladder, providing 256 levels.

11.6.2 The A/D Conversion Process

The successive approximation conversion compares a reference voltage to the analog input voltage stored in the sampling capacitor. A binary search is performed for the reference voltage that most closely matches the input. The ½ full-scale reference voltage is the first tested. This corresponds to a 10-bit result in which the most significant bit is zero and all other bits are one (0111 1111 11b). If the analog input is less than the test voltage, bit 10 is left at zero and a new test voltage of ¼ full scale (0011 1111 11b) is tested. If this test voltage is less than the analog input voltage, bit 9 of the SAR is set and bit 8 is cleared for the next test (0101 1111

11b). This binary search continues until 8 or 10 tests have occurred, at which time the valid 8-bit or 10-bit result resides in the SAR where it can be read by software.

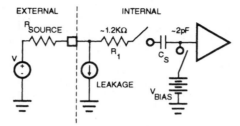

FIGURE 11.47 Idealized interface circuitry.

11.6.3 A/D Interfacing

The external interface circuitry to an analog input is highly dependent upon the application and can impact converter characteristics. Several important factors must be considered in the external interface design: input pin leakage, sample capacitor size, and multiplexer series resistance from the input pin to the sample capacitor. These factors are idealized in Fig. 11.47.

The following example is for a 1-μs sample time and a 10-bit conversion. The external input circuit must be able to charge a sample capacitor (C_S) through a series resistance (R_1) to an accurate voltage, given a dc leakage (I_L). For purposes of this example, assume C_S of 2 pf, R_1 of 1.2 kΩ, and I_L of 1 μA.

External circuits with source impedances of 1 kΩ or less can maintain an input voltage within a tolerance of about 0.2 LSB (1.0 kΩ × 1.0 μA = 1.0 mV) given the dc leakage. Source impedances above 5 kΩ can result in an external error of at least one LSB due to the voltage drop caused by the 1-μA leakage. In addition, source impedances above 25 kΩ may degrade converter accuracy because the internal sample capacitor will not charge completely during the sample time.

Typically, leakage is much lower than the maximum specification specified by the microcontroller manufacturer. Given typical leakage, source impedance may be increased substantially before a one-LSB error is apparent. However, a high source impedance may prevent the internal sample capacitor from fully charging during the sample window. This error can be calculated using the following formula:

$$\text{Error (LSBs)} = \left(e^{\frac{-T_{SAM}}{RC}} \right) \times 1024$$

where T_{SAM} = sample time, μs
$R = R_{SOURCE} + R_1$, Ω
$C = C_S$, μf

The effects of this error can be minimized by connecting an external capacitor C_{EXT} from the input pin to ANGND. The external signal will charge C_{EXT} to the source voltage. When the channel is sampled, a small portion of the charge stored in C_{EXT} will be transferred to the internal sample capacitor. The ratio of C_S to C_{EXT} causes the loss in accuracy. If C_{EXT} is .005 μf or greater, the maximum error will be −0.6 LSB.

Placing an external capacitor on each analog input also reduces the sensitivity to noise because the capacitor combines with series resistance in the external circuit to form a low-pass filter. In practice, one should include a small series resistance prior to the external capacitor on the analog input pin and choose the largest capacitor value practical, given the frequency of the signal being converted. This provides a low-pass filter on the input, while the resistor also limits input current during overvoltage conditions.

11.6.4 Analog References

To achieve maximum noise isolation, on-chip A/D converters typically separate the internal A/D power supply from the rest of the microcontroller's power supply lines. Separate supply pins, V_{ref} and An_{gnd}, usually supply both the reference and digital voltages for the A/D converter. Keep in mind that V_{ref} and An_{gnd} are the reference for a large resistor ladder on successive approximation converters. Any variation in these supplies will directly affect the reference voltage taps within the ladder, which in turn directly affect A/D conversion accuracy.

If the on-chip A/D converter is not being used, or if accuracy is not a concern, the Vref and Angnd pins can simply be connected to V_{cc} and V_{ss}, respectively. However, since the reference supply levels strongly influence the absolute accuracy of the A/D converter, a precision, well-regulated reference should be used to supply V_{ref} to achieve the highest performance levels. It is also important to use bypass capacitors between V_{ref} and An_{gnd} to minimize any noise that may be present on these supplies. In noise-sensitive applications running at higher frequencies, the use of separate ground planes within the PCB (circuit board) should be considered, possibly as shown in Fig. 11.48. This will help minimize ground loops and provide for a stable A/D reference.

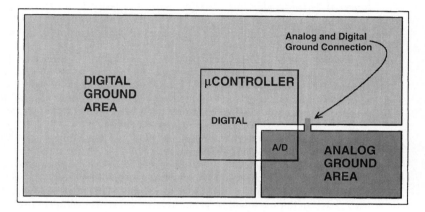

FIGURE 11.48   Example of separate analog and digital ground planes.

11.7   *FAILSAFE METHODOLOGIES*

The amount and complexity of automotive electronics incorporated into automobiles has increased at an incredible rate over the last decade. This trend has contributed significantly towards the impressive safety record of modern automobiles. Although microcontrollers are extremely reliable electronic devices, it is possible for failures to occur, either elsewhere in the module or within the microcontroller itself. It is critical that these failures be detected and responded to as quickly as possible in safety-related applications such as automotive antilock braking. If proper failsafe methodologies and good programming practices are followed, the chances of a failure going undetected are drastically reduced. The application of *failure mode and effect analysis* (FMEA) is an excellent tool for identifying potential failure modes, detection strategies, and containment methods. Used properly, FMEA will assist the designer in providing a high-quality, reliable automotive module. Although the scope of this chapter does not provide for a discussion on this topic, the author highly encourages the use of FMEA.

11.7.1   Hardware Failsafe Methods

Sometimes a hardware solution is required for detection of and response to certain failure modes. It is difficult for software alone to detect failures external to the device. As an example, consider a case in which electrical overstress (EOS) has damaged a port pin, causing it to read or drive an incorrect value. In this case, it can be difficult for software to detect because it would base its response on an incorrect value read from a pin.

Watchdog Timers (WDTs).   An on-chip hardware watchdog is an excellent method of detecting failures which otherwise may go undetected. An example of this would be a microcontroller fetching either erroneous address or data (due to noise, etc.) and becoming "lost." WDTs commonly utilize a dedicated 16-bit counter, which provides for a count of 2^{16}(65,536) clocked at a rate of one tick per state time. If users wish to take advantage of this feature, they simply write to a register to enable the count. Once enabled, the user program must periodically clear the watchdog by writing a specific bit pattern to the Watchdog SFR. Clearing the WDT at least every 4.1 ms (65,535 * 1 state time at 16 MHz) will prevent the device from being reset. The strategy is that if the WDT initiates a reset, the assumption can be made that a failure has occurred and the microcontroller has became lost.

External Failsafe Devices.   It is common for systems to incorporate an external failsafe device, such as another microcontroller or an *application-specific integrated circuit* (ASIC). The function of a failsafe device is to monitor the operation of the primary microcontroller and determine if it is operating properly.

The simplest failsafe devices output a signal such as a square wave for the microcontroller to detect and respond to. If the microcontroller doesn't respond correctly, a reset is typically asserted by the failsafe and the ECU reverts to a safe mode of operation. More complex failsafe devices will actually monitor several critical functions for failures such as low Vcc, stopped or decreased oscillator frequency, shorted/opened input signals, and so forth.

Oscillator Failure Detection.   It is possible for the clocking source (typically an oscillator) to fail for various reasons. Since most microcontrollers are static devices, a particularly difficult failure mode to detect is the clocking of the device at a reduced frequency. To detect this failure, an *oscillator failure detection* circuit is often integrated upon the microcontroller. This circuitry will detect if the oscillator clock input signal falls below a specified frequency, in which case an interrupt will be generated or the device will reset itself.

Redundancy/Cross-checking.   A common failsafe methodology is achieved by designing a redundant, or backup, processor into the module. In this case, the secondary microcontroller usually executes a subset of the main microcontroller's code. The secondary microcontroller typically processes critical input data and performs cross-checks periodically with the main microcontroller to insure proper operation. A failsafe routine is initiated if data exchanged between the two devices did not correlate.

11.7.2   Software Failsafe Techniques

Failsafe methodologies implemented in software are ideal for detecting failure modes that can interfere with proper program flow. Examples of these types of failures include noise glitches, which are notorious for causing external memory systems to fetch invalid addresses. ROM/EPROM memory corruption could cause an ISR start address to be fetched from an invalid interrupt vector location. Interrupts occurring at a rate faster than anticipated can cause problems such as an overflowing stack. Fortunately, failure modes such as these can be dealt with by implementing software failsafe methods. It is simply good programming practice to anticipate these types of failure modes and provide a failsafe strategy to deal with them. Following are several software strategies commonly used to deal with specific types of failure modes:

Checksum.   One possible error that must be accounted for is ROM/EPROM memory corruption. An effective method of detecting these types of failures is through the calculation of a checksum during the initialization phase of a user's program. A checksum is the final value obtained as the result of performing some arithmetic operation upon every ROM/EPROM memory location. The obtained checksum is then compared against a stored checksum. If the two match, the ROM/EPROM contents are intact. An error routine is called if the two checksums do not match. The most common arithmetic operation used to perform a checksum is addition. The checksum is calculated by adding the contents of all memory locations. When the addition is performed, the carry is ignored which provides for a byte or word checksum. The final result is then used as the checksum.

Unused Interrupt Vectors.   It is a rare occasion when all interrupt sources are enabled within an application. If, for some unforeseen reason, the program should vector to an unused interrupt source, some sort of failsafe routine should be implemented to respond to the failure. The failsafe routine could be as simple as vectoring to a reset instruction or it can be as complicated as the programmer wishes.

Unused Memory Locations.   A strategy should be in place to detect if, for some unforeseen reason, the program sequence should begin to execute in an unused area of ROM/EPROM. It is uncommon for the user's code to fill the entire ROM/EPROM array of a microcontroller. It is good programming practice to fill any unused locations with the opcode of an instruction such as *Reset*. On the MCS-96 family, executing the opcode FFh (which happens to be the blank state of EPROM) will initiate a reset sequence. Other microcontroller families have similar instructions.

Unimplemented Opcode Interrupt Vectors.   Microcontrollers often dedicate one or more interrupt vectors for failsafe purposes. An *unimplemented opcode* interrupt is designed to detect corrupted instruction fetches. The corresponding interrupt service routine is executed whenever an unsupported opcode is fetched for execution. The interrupt service routine contains the user's failsafe routine, which is tailored to address this failure for the specific application.

11.8 FUTURE TRENDS

There are several significant trends developing in automotive electronics as ECU manufacturers strive to meet the challenges of a demanding automotive electronics market. The challenges that are bringing about these trends are: decreasing cost targets, decreasing form-factor goals, increasing performance requirements, and increasing system-to-system communication requirements. As the most significant component of an ECU, microcontrollers are bearing the brunt of these demands. This section will discuss these challenges and provide some insight into some of the ways microcontroller manufacturers are addressing these trends.

11.8.1 Decreasing Cost Targets

Microcontroller manufacturers are aproaching cost reduction in two ways: indirectly and directly. *Indirect* cost reductions are achieved by integrating features onto the microcontroller which allow the system designer to reduce cost elsewhere in the system. The key to this approach being successful is in the microcontroller manufacturer's ability to integrate the feature cheaper than the cost of providing an external solution. Integration is not always the cheaper solution, therefore each feature must be evaluated individually to determine the feasability of integration. An example of an indirect cost reduction would be the integration of watchdog and failsafe functions onto the microcontroller. This would eliminate the need for external watchdog components and thus reduce cost.

Another example would be through the integration of communications protocols such as CAN (Controller Area Network) or J1850 onto the same piece of silicon as the microcontroller. This will reduce the system chip count (and thus cost) by at least one integrated circuit device (the CAN chip) and several interfacing components. In most cases, a reduced chip count will translate into a PCB size decrease and a cost savings.

By *directly* addressing decreasing cost targets, microcontroller manufacturers actually reduce the manufacturing cost of the microcontroller itself. An example of this would be utilizing smaller geometry processes for manufacturing. Process geometry refers to the transistor channel width that is implanted onto a piece of silicon for a given fabrication process. Smaller processes allow for a higher transistor density on an integrated circuit. Higher densities allow for smaller die sizes which relate to lower costs. Most automotive microcontrollers manufactured today are fabricated with a 1.0-micron, or larger, process. As technology advances, future automotive microcontrollers will be manufactured upon submicron processes, such as 0.6 micron.

11.8.2   Increasing Performance Requirements

Automotive applications, such as ABS and engine control, require the processing of a substantial amount of data within a limited period of time. Higher-performance microcontrollers are required as system complexity increases and new features, such as traction control and vehicle dynamics, are incorporated into the ECU.

Microcontroller performance can be directly related to speed. Therefore, a rather straightforward approach to increased performance is through increasing clock speed. Today, most automotive microcontrollers have the capability to operate at frequencies of 16 MHz with speeds up to 20 MHz becoming common. Future microcontrollers will have the ability to be operated at frequencies of 24 or even 32 MHz. This allows more code to be executed in the same amount of time, and thus improves performance.

The method of increasing performance is not limited to just increasing the clock frequency. Microcontrollers can also achieve higher performance by enhancing existing peripherals for more efficient operation. This may be in the form of improved data handling or new features which suit the needs of a specific automotive application.

11.8.3   Increasing System-to-System Communication Requirements

The increasing complexity of automotive electronics requires that an increasing amount of information (diagnostics, etc.) be shared between various ECUs within an automobile. To fulfill this need, high-speed data links are utilized to transfer messages between multiple ECUs utilizing protocols such as Bosch's Controller Area Network (CAN) and SAE's J1850. To provide further size and cost savings, it is becoming more and more common to see these protocols supported or integrated onto automotive microcontrollers as opposed to separate integrated circuits.

The theory of centralized body computing is also receiving a closer look due to increased government regulations concerning fuel economy and diagnostics. A centralized body computer would link all ECUs (ABS and traction control, engine, transmission, suspension, instrumentation, etc.) together over a high-speed, in-vehicle serial network. One common scenario would have the central computer (possibly a microprocessor as opposed to a microcontroller) performing the more intense data-crunching tasks, while peripheral microcontrollers located in each individual ECU would perform system I/O functions. These communication protocols provide for efficient two-wire, high-speed serial communications between multiple ECUs utilizing protocols such as CAN and J1850. Supporting these protocols places additional loading upon the microcontroller. Increased microcontroller performance is necessary to manage this loading.

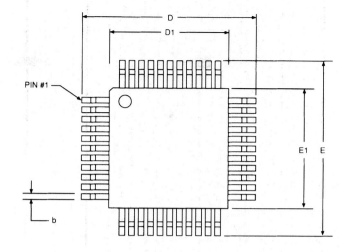

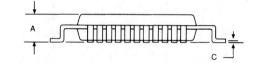

SHRINK QUAD FLATPACK				
SYMBOL	**DESCRIPTION**	**MIN.**	**NOM.**	**MAX.**
N	Lead Count		80	
A	Overall Height			1.66
A1	Stand Off	0.00		
b	Lead Width	0.14	0.20	0.26
c	Lead Thickness	0.117	0.127	0.177
D	Terminal Dimension	13.70	14.00	14.30
D1	Package Body		12.0	
E	Terminal Dimension	13.70	14.00	14.30
E1	Package Body		12.0	
e1	Lead Pitch	0.40	0.50	0.60
L1	Foot Length	0.35	0.50	0.70
T	Lead Angle	0.0°		10.0°
Y	Coplanarity			0.10

FIGURE 11.49   Shrink quad flat pack (SQFP) package.

11.8.4 Decreasing Form Factor Goals

Automobile manufacturers striving to build compact, more fuel efficient automobiles are putting pressure upon ECU suppliers to build smaller, lighter modules.

ECU size is directly affected by PCB size. The easiest way to achieve a smaller PCB is through integration and utilization of smaller integrated circuit packages. To support this demand, automotive microcontroller manufacturers are beginning to offer smaller, fine-pitch packages. A package commonly used today is the 68-lead plastic leaded chip carrier (PLCC) which has its pins placed on 1.27-mm centers and a body that is 24.3 mm^2. An example of a possible automotive package solution for the future would be the 80-lead shrink quad flat pack (SQFP, Fig. 11.49) which has pins on 0.50-mm centers and a body that is 12.0 mm^2. It is relatively easy to see that the SQFP package offers 12 additional pins in a package that is half the size of the PLCC. This high pin density, fine-pitch packaging allows for a smaller package to be utilized for the same size microcontroller die.

Another technology that is quickly becoming popular for automotive applications is referred to as *multichip modules* (MCMs). An MCM is a collection of unpackaged integrated circuit die (from various manufacturers) which are mounted upon a common substrate and packaged together. The advantage of MCMs is that they require much less PCB space than if the ICs were packaged separately.

GLOSSARY

Accumulator   A register within a microcontroller that holds data, particularly data on which arithmetic or logic operations are to be performed.

Arithmetic logic unit (ALU)   The part of a microcontroller that performs arithmetic and logic operations.

Analog-to-digital converter   An electronic device that produces a digital result that is proportional to the analog input voltage.

Assembly language   A low-level symbolic programming language closely resembling machine language.

Central processing unit (CPU)   The portion of a computer system or microcontroller that controls the interpretation and execution of instructions and includes arithmetic capability.

EPROM   Erasable and programmable read-only memory.

High-speed input/output unit (HSIO)   A microcontroller peripheral which has the capability to either capture the time at which a certain input event occurs or create an output event at a predetermined time, both relative to a common clock. HSIO events are configured by the programmer to occur automatically.

Interrupt service routine (ISR)   A predefined portion of a computer program which is executed in response to a specific event.

Low-speed input/output   The input/output of a digital signal by "manually" reading or writing a register location in software.

Machine language   A set of symbols, characters, or signs used to communicate with a computer in a form directly usable by the computer without translation.

Program counter (PC)   A microcontroller register which holds the address of the next instruction to be executed.

Program status word (PSW)   A microcontroller register that contains a set of boolean flags which are used to retain information regarding the state of the user's program.

Pulse-width modulation (PWM)   The precise and timely creation of negative and positive waveform edges to achieve a waveform with a specific frequency and duty cycle.

Random access memory (RAM)   A memory device which has both read and write capabilities so that the stored information (write) can be retrieved (reread) and be changed by applying new information to the inputs.

Read-only memory (ROM)   A memory that can only be read and not written to. Data is either entered during the manufacturing process or by later programming; once entered, it is unalterable.

Register/arithmetic logic unit (RALU)   A component of register-direct microcontroller architectures that allows the ALU to operate directly upon the entire register file.

Serial input/output (SIO)   A method of digital communication in which a group of data bits is transferred one at a time, sequentially over a single data line.

Special function register (SFR)   A microcontroller RAM register which has a specific, dedicated function assigned to it.

BIBLIOGRAPHY

ASM96 Assembler User's Manual, Intel Corp., 1992.

Automotive Electrics/Electronics, Robert Bosch GmbH, 1988.

Automotive Handbook, Intel Corporation, 1994.

Automotive Handbook, 2d ed., Robert Bosch GmbH, 1986.

Corell, Roger J., "How are semiconductor suppliers responding to the growing demand for automotive safety features?," *Intel Corp.,* 1993.

Davidson, Lee S., and Robert M. Kowalczyk, "Microcontroller technology enhancements to meet ever-increasing engine control requirements," Intel Corp., 1992.

Fink, Donald G., and Donald Christiansen, *Electronics Engineers' Handbook,* 3d ed. McGraw-Hill, 1989.

iC-96 Compiler User's Manual, Intel Corp., 1992.

Introduction to MOSFETS and EPROM Memories, Intel Corp., 1990.

MCS®-51 Microcontroller Family User's Manual, Intel Corp., 1993.

Millman, Jacob, and Arvin Grabel, *Microelectronics,* McGraw-Hill, 1987.

Packaging Handbook, Intel Corporation, 1994.

Ribbens, William B., *Understanding Automotive Electronics,* Howard Sams Company, Carmel, Ind. 1992.

8XC196Kx User's Manual, Intel Corporation, 1992.

8XC196KC/8XC196KD User's Manual, Intel Corp., 1992.

ABOUT THE AUTHOR

David S. Boehmer is currently a senior technical marketing engineer for the Automotive Operation of Intel's Embedded Microprocessor Division located in Chandler, Ariz. He is a member of SAE.

CHAPTER 12
ENGINE CONTROL

Gary C. Hirschlieb, Gottfried Schiller, and Shari Stottler
Robert Bosch GmbH

12.1 OBJECTIVES OF ELECTRONIC ENGINE CONTROL SYSTEMS

The electronic engine control system consists of sensing devices which continuously measure the operating conditions of the engine, an electronic control unit (ECU) which evaluates the sensor inputs using data tables and calculations and determines the output to the actuating devices, and actuating devices which are commanded by the ECU to perform an action in response to the sensor inputs.

The motive for using an electronic engine control system is to provide the needed accuracy and adaptability in order to minimize exhaust emissions and fuel consumption, provide optimal driveability for all operating conditions, minimize evaporative emissions, and provide system diagnosis when malfunctions occur.

In order for the control system to meet these objectives, considerable development time is required for each engine and vehicle application. A substantial amount of development must occur with an engine installed on an engine dynamometer under controlled conditions. Information gathered is used to develop the ECU data tables. A considerable amount of development effort is also required with the engine installed in the vehicle. Final determination of the data tables occurs during vehicle testing.

12.1.1 Exhaust Emissions

Exhaust Components. The engine exhaust consists of products from the combustion of the air and fuel mixture. Fuel is a mixture of chemical compounds, termed hydrocarbons (HC). The various fuel compounds are a combination of hydrogen and carbon. Under perfect combustion conditions, the hydrocarbons would combine in a thermal reaction with the oxygen in the air to form carbon dioxide (CO_2) and water (H_2O). Unfortunately, perfect combustion does not occur and in addition to CO_2 and H_2O, carbon monoxide (CO), oxides of nitrogen (NO_x), and hydrocarbons (HC) occur in the exhaust as a result of the combustion reaction. Additives and impurities in the fuel also contribute minute quantities of pollutants such as lead oxides, lead halogenides, and sulfur oxides. In compression ignition (diesel) engines, there is also an appreciable amount of soot (particulates) created. Federal statues regulate the allowable amount of HC, NO_x, and CO emitted in a vehicle's exhaust. On diesel engines, the amount of particulates emitted is also regulated.

Spark Ignition Engines

Air/fuel Ratio. The greatest effect on the combustion process, and therefore on the exhaust emissions, is the mass ratio of air to fuel. The air/fuel mixture ratio must lie within a certain range for optimal ignition and combustion. For a spark ignition engine, the mass ratio for complete fuel combustion is 14.7:1; i.e., 14.7 kg of air to 1 kg of fuel. This ratio is known as the stoichiometric ratio. In terms of volume, approximately 10,000 liters of air would be required for 1 liter of fuel. The air/fuel ratio is often described in terms of the excess-air factor known as lambda (λ). Lambda indicates the deviation of the actual air/fuel ratio from the theoretically required ratio:

$$\lambda = \frac{\text{quantity of air supplied}}{\text{theoretical requirement (14.7 for gasoline)}}$$

At stoichiometry: $\lambda = 1$
For a mixture with excess air (lean): $\lambda > 1$
For a mixture with deficient air (rich): $\lambda < 1$

Effect of Air/Fuel Ratio on Emissions

CO emissions. In the rich operating range ($\lambda < 1$), CO emissions increase almost linearly with an increasing amount of fuel. In the lean range ($\lambda > 1$), CO emissions are at their lowest. With an engine operating at ($\lambda = 1$), the CO emissions can be influenced by the cylinder distribution. If some cylinders are operating rich and others lean with the summation achieving $\lambda = 1$, the average CO emissions will be higher than if all cylinders were operating at $\lambda = 1$.

HC emissions. As with CO emissions, HC emissions increase with an increasing amount of fuel. The minimum HC emissions occur at $\lambda = 1.1 \ldots 1.2$. At very lean air/fuel ratios, the HC emissions again increase due to less than optimal combustion conditions resulting in unburned fuel.

NO$_x$ emissions. The effect of the air/fuel ratio on NO$_x$ emissions is the opposite of HC and CO on the rich side of stoichiometry. As the air content increases, the oxygen content increases and the result is more NO$_x$. On the lean side of stoichiometry, NO$_x$ emissions decrease with increasing air because the decreasing density lowers the combustion chamber temperature. The maximum NO$_x$ emissions occur at $\lambda = 1.05 \ldots 1.1$.

Catalytic Converters. To reduce the exhaust gas emission concentration, a catalytic converter is installed in the exhaust system. Chemical reactions occur in the converter that transform the exhaust emissions to less harmful chemical compounds. The most commonly used converter for a spark ignition engine is the three-way converter (TWC). As the name implies, it simultaneously reduces the concentration of all three regulated exhaust gases: HC, CO, and NO$_x$. The catalyst promotes reactions that oxidize HC and CO, converting them into CO$_2$ and H$_2$O, while reducing NO$_x$ emissions into N$_2$. The actual chemical reactions that occur are:

$$2CO + O_2 \rightarrow 2CO_2$$

$$2C_2H_6 + 7O_2 \rightarrow 4CO_2 + 6H_2O$$

$$2NO + 2CO \rightarrow N_2 + 2CO_2$$

In order for the catalytic converter to operate at the highest efficiency for conversion for all three gases (HC, CO, NO$_x$), the average air/fuel ratio must be maintained within less than 1 percent of stoichiometry. This small operating range is known as the *lambda window* or *catalytic converter window*. Figure 12.1 is a graph of lambda (λ) versus the exhaust emissions both before and after the catalytic converter. Up to 90 percent of the exhaust gases are converted to less harmful compounds by the catalytic converter.

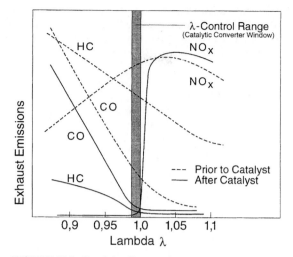

FIGURE 12.1 Lambda effect on exhaust emissions prior to and after catalyst treatment.

To remain within the catalytic converter window, the air/fuel ratio is controlled by the lambda closed-loop fuel control system, which is part of the electronic engine control system. The key component in this system is the lambda sensor. This sensor is installed in the exhaust system upstream of the catalytic converter and responds to the oxygen content in the exhaust gas. The oxygen content is a measure of the excess air (or deficiency of air) in the exhaust gases. A detailed discussion of the lambda closed-loop control system occurs in Sec. 12.2.1.

Ignition Timing.   The ignition timing is defined as the crankshaft angle before top dead center (TDC) at which the ignition spark occurs. The ignition timing of the air/fuel mixture has a decisive influence on the exhaust emissions.

Effect of ignition timing on exhaust emissions.

- CO emissions are almost completely independent of the ignition timing and are primarily a function of the air/fuel ratio.

- In general, the more the ignition is advanced, the higher the emissions of HCs. Reactions initiated in the combustion chamber continue to occur after the exhaust valve opens, which depletes the remaining HCs. With advanced timing due to lower exhaust temperatures, these postreactions do not readily occur.

- With increased timing advance, the combustion chamber temperatures increase. The temperature increase causes an increase in NO_x emissions regardless of air/fuel ratio.

To provide the optimal ignition timing for exhaust emissions, precise control of the ignition timing is required. It is imperative that the ignition timing be coordinated with the air/fuel ratio since they have a combined effect on exhaust emissions as well as fuel consumption and driveability. Ignition timing is generally controlled by the ECU. Ignition timing control is discussed in detail in Sec. 12.2.1.

Exhaust Gas Recirculation (EGR).   Exhaust gas recirculation (EGR) is a method of reducing emissions of oxides of nitrogen. A portion of the exhaust gas is recirculated back to the combustion chamber. Exhaust gas is an inert gas and, in the combustion chamber, it lowers the peak combustion temperature. Depending on the amount of EGR, NO_x emissions can be reduced by up to 60 percent, although an increase in HC emissions would occur at such high levels of EGR.

Some internal EGR occurs due to the overlap of the exhaust and intake valves. Additional quantities are supplied by a separate system linking the exhaust manifold to the intake manifold. The quantity of EGR flow to the intake system is metered by a pneumatic or electronic valve. The EGR valve is controlled by the ECU. The maximum flow of EGR is limited by an increase in HC emissions, fuel consumption, and engine roughness. EGR control is discussed in detail in Sec. 12.2.1.

Compression Ignition (Diesel) Engines.   There are some key distinctions between an SI engine and a CI engine. The CI engine uses high pressure and temperature instead of a spark to ignite the combustible air/fuel mixture. To achieve this, the CI engine compression ratio is in the range of 21:1, as opposed to roughly 10:1 for an SI engine. In a CI engine, the fuel is injected directly into the cylinder near the top of the compression stroke. Mixing of the fuel and air, therefore, occurs directly in the cylinder.

Air/fuel ratio.   Diesel engines always operate with excess air ($\lambda > 1$). Where:

$$\lambda = \frac{\text{quantity of air supplied}}{\text{theoretical requirement}}$$

The excess air ($\lambda = 1.1 \ldots 1.2$) reduces the amount of soot (particulates), HC, and CO emissions.

Catalytic Converters.   An oxidizing catalyst is used that converts CO and HC to CO_2 and H_2O. The NO_x reduction that occurs for an SI engine three-way catalyst (TWC) is not possible with a diesel because the diesel operates with excess air. The optimal conversion of NO_x requires a stoichiometric ratio ($\lambda = 1$) or a deficiency of air ($\lambda < 1$).

Injection Timing.   In a compression ignition engine, the start of combustion is determined by the start of fuel injection. In general, retarding the injection timing decreases NO_x emissions, while overretarding results in an increase in HC emissions. A $1°$ (crankshaft angle) deviation in injection timing can increase NO_x emissions by 5 percent and HC emissions by as much as 15 percent. Precise control of injection timing is critical. Injection timing on some systems is controlled by the ECU. Feedback on injection timing can be provided by a sensor installed on the injector nozzle. Further discussion on injection timing occurs in Sec. 12.3.1.

Exhaust Gas Recirculation (EGR).   As with an SI engine, exhaust gas can be recirculated to the combustion chamber to significantly reduce NO_x emissions. The quantity of EGR allowed to enter the intake is metered by the EGR valve. If the quantity is too high, HC emissions, CO emissions, and soot (particulates) increase as a result of an insufficient quantity of air. The EGR valve is controlled by the ECU, which determines how much EGR is tolerable under the current engine operating conditions.

12.1.2   Fuel Consumption

Federal statutes are currently in effect that require each automobile manufacturer to achieve a certain average fuel economy for all their models produced in one model year. The requirement is known as *corporate average fuel economy* or CAFE. The fuel economy for each vehicle type is determined during the federal test procedure, the same as for exhaust emissions determination, conducted on a chassis dynamometer. Because of the CAFE requirement, it is critical that fuel consumption be minimized for every vehicle type produced.

The electronic engine control system provides the fuel metering and ignition timing precision required to minimize fuel consumption. Optimum fuel economy occurs near $\lambda = 1.1$. However, as discussed previously, lean engine operation affects exhaust emissions and NO_x is at its maximum at $\lambda = 1.1$.

During coasting and braking, fuel consumption can be further reduced by shutting off the fuel until the engine speed decreases to slightly higher than the set idle speed. The ECU determines when fuel shutoff can occur by evaluating the throttle position, engine RPM, and vehicle speed.

The influence of ignition timing on fuel consumption is the opposite of its influence on exhaust emissions. As the air/fuel mixture becomes leaner, the ignition timing must be advanced to compensate for a slower combustion speed. However, as discussed previously, advancing the ignition timing increases the emissions of HC and NO_x. A sophisticated ignition control strategy permitting optimization of the ignition at each operating point is necessary to reach the compromise between fuel consumption and exhaust emissions. The electronic engine control system can provide this sophisticated strategy.

12.1.3   Driveability

Another requirement of the electronic engine control system is to provide acceptable driveability under all operating conditions. No stalls, hesitations, or other objectionable roughness should occur during vehicle operation. Driveability is influenced by almost every operation of the engine control system and, unlike exhaust emissions or fuel economy, is not easily measured. A significant contribution to driveability is determined by the fuel metering and ignition timing. When determining the best fuel and ignition compromises for fuel consumption and exhaust emissions, it is important to evaluate the driveability. Other factors that influence driveability are the idle speed control, EGR control, and evaporative emissions control.

12.1.4   Evaporative Emissions

Hydrocarbon (HC) emissions in the form of fuel vapors escaping from the vehicle are closely regulated by federal statutes. The prime source of these emissions is the fuel tank. Due to ambient heating of the fuel and the return of unused hot fuel from the engine, fuel vapor is generated in the tank. The evaporative emissions control system (EECS) is used to control the evaporative HC emissions. The fuel vapors are routed to the intake manifold via the EECS and they are burned in the combustion process. The quantity of fuel vapors delivered to the intake manifold must be metered such that exhaust emissions and driveability are not adversely affected. The metering is provided by a purge control valve whose function is controlled by the ECU. Further discussion on the operation of the evaporative emissions control system occurs in Sec. 12.2.1.

12.1.5   System Diagnostics

The purpose of system diagnostics is to provide a warning to the driver when the control system determines a malfunction of a component or system and to assist the service technician in identifying and correcting the failure (see Chap. 22). To the driver, the engine may appear to be operating correctly, but excessive amounts of pollutants may be emitted. The ECU determines a malfunction has occurred when a sensor signal received during normal engine operation or during a system test indicates there is a problem. For critical operations such as fuel metering and ignition control, if a required sensor input is faulty, a substitute value may be used by the ECU so that the engine will continue to operate.

When a failure occurs, the malfunction indicator light (MIL), visible to the driver, is illuminated. Information on the failure is stored in the ECU. A service technician can retrieve the information on the failure from the ECU and correct the problem. Detailed examples of system diagnostics are discussed in Sec. 12.2.3.

12.2   *SPARK IGNITION ENGINES*

12.2.1   Engine Control Functions

Fuel Control.   For the purpose of discussing fuel control strategies, a multipoint pulsed fuel injection system is assumed. Additional discussions of fuel control for different types of fuel systems such as carbureters, single-point injection, and multipoint continuous injection appear in Sec. 12.2.4 (Fuel Delivery Systems).

In order for the fuel metering system to provide the appropriate amount of fuel for the engine operating conditions, the mass flow rate of incoming air, known as the air charge, must be determined.

$$F_m = \frac{A_m}{\text{requested air-fuel ratio}}$$

where F_m = fuel mass flow rate
A_m = air mass flow rate

The air mass flow rate can be calculated from:

$$A_m = A_v A_d$$

where A_v = volume flow rate of intake air
A_d = air density

There are three methods commonly used for determining the air charge: speed density, air flow measurement, and air mass measurement. In the speed density method, the air charge is calculated by the engine electronic control unit based on the measurement of air inlet temperature, intake manifold pressure, and engine RPM. The temperature and pressure are used to determine the air density and the RPM is used to determine the volume flow rate. The engine acts as an air pump during the intake stroke. The calculated volume flow rate can be determined as follows:

$$A_{\text{RPM}} = \frac{\text{RPM}}{60} \times \frac{D}{2} \times V_E$$

where RPM = engine speed
D = engine displacement
V_E = volumetric efficiency

In an engine using exhaust gas recirculation (EGR), the volume flow rate of EGR must be subtracted from the calculated volume flow rate.

$$A_v = A_{\text{RPM}} - A_{\text{EGR}}$$

The volume flow rate of EGR can be determined empirically based on the EGR valve flow rate and the EGR control strategy being used.

In the air flow measurement method, the air flow is measured using a vane type meter and air density changes are compensated for by an air inlet temperature sensor. The vane meter uses the force of the incoming air to move a flap through a defined angle. This angular movement is converted by a potentiometer to a voltage ratio. Because only the fresh air charge is measured, no compensation is required for EGR.

In the air mass measurement method, the air charge is measured directly using a hot-wire or hot-film air mass flow sensor. The inlet air passes a heated element, either wire or film. The element is part of a bridge circuit that keeps the element at a constant temperature above the inlet air temperature. By measuring the heating current required by the bridge circuit and converting this to a voltage via a resistor, the air mass flow passing the element can be determined. Again, because only the fresh air charge is measured, no compensation for EGR is required. However, sensing errors may occur due to strong intake manifold reversion pulses, which occur under certain operating conditions. In such cases, a correction factor must be determined and applied.

Calculation of Injector Pulse Width.   The base pulse width is determined from the required fuel mass flow rate (F_m) and an empirical injector constant. The injector constant is determined by the design of the injector and is a function of the energized time versus the flow volume. This constant is normally determined with a constant differential pressure across the injector (from fuel rail to intake manifold). When the pressure across the injector does not remain constant (i.e., there is no pressure regulator intake manifold vacuum reference), an entire map of injector constants for different manifold pressures may be required.

The effective injector pulse width is a modification of the base pulse width. The base pulse width is adjusted by a number of correction factors depending on operating conditions. For example, a battery voltage correction is required to compensate for the electromechanical characteristics of the fuel injectors. Injector opening and closing rates differ depending on the voltage applied to the injector, which affects the amount of fuel injected for a given pulse width. Other common correction factors may include hot restart, cold operation, and transient operation corrections. Figure 12.2 is a flowchart of a typical injector effective pulse-width calculation method.

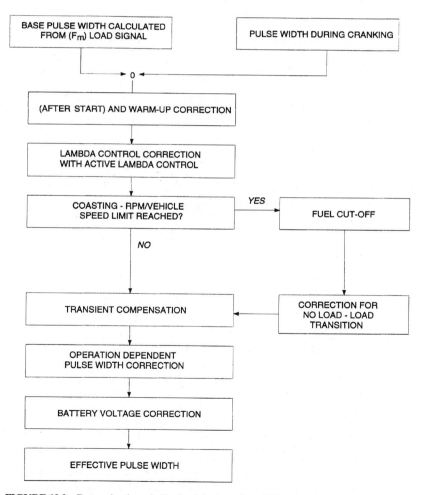

FIGURE 12.2   Determination of effective injector pulse width.

Injection Strategies. There are three commonly used fuel injection strategies for multipoint fuel metering systems: simultaneous injection, group injection, and sequential injection. Figure 12.3 is a diagram of the different strategies. Some engines use simultaneous injection during crank and switch over to sequential after the engine is running. This allows for shorter starting times since no synchronization with the camshaft is necessary before fuel injection begins. A description of each strategy follows.

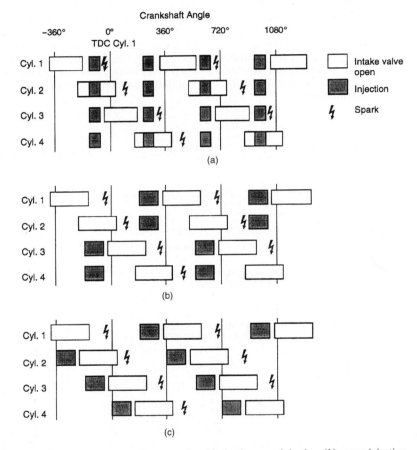

FIGURE 12.3 Fuel injection strategies: (*a*) simultaneous injection, (*b*) group injection, and (*c*) sequential injection.

Simultaneous injection. Injection of fuel occurs at the same time for all cylinders every revolution of the crankshaft. Therefore, fuel is injected twice within each four-stroke cycle. The injection timing is fixed with respect to crank/camshaft position.

Group injection. The injectors are divided into two groups that are controlled separately. Each group injects once per four-stroke cycle. The offset between the groups is one crankshaft revolution. This arrangement allows for injection timing selection that eliminates spraying fuel into an open intake valve.

Sequential injection. Each injector is controlled separately. Injection timing, both with reference to crank/camshaft position and pulse width, can be optimized for each individual cylinder.

Lambda Control.   A subsystem of the fuel control system is lambda closed-loop control. Lambda (λ) is defined as the excess-air factor that indicates the deviation of the actual air/fuel ratio from the theoretically required ratio:

$$\lambda = \frac{\text{quantity of air supplied}}{\text{theoretical requirement (14.7 for gasoline)}}$$

The lambda sensor, or exhaust gas oxygen sensor, is installed in the engine exhaust stream upstream of the catalytic converter. The sensor responds to the oxygen content of the exhaust gas. The signal from the lambda sensor serves as feedback to the fuel control system. This provides the fine-tuning needed to remain within the limited catalytic converter window for optimal catalyst performance. (See Sec. 12.1.1 for more discussion on the catalytic converter window.) For a lean mixture ($\lambda > 1$), sensor voltage is approximately 100 mV. For a rich mixture ($\lambda < 1$), the sensor voltage is approximately 800 mV. At roughly $\lambda = 1$ (a stoichiometric mixture), the sensor switches rapidly between the two voltages. The input from the lambda sensor is used to modify the base pulse width to achieve $\lambda = 1$.

Lambda closed-loop control requires an operationally ready lambda sensor, typically one which has reached an operating temperature threshold. Sensor output is monitored by the ECU to determine when the sensor is supplying usable information. An active sensor signal, along with other requirements, such as engine temperature, must be achieved before lambda closed-loop control will be activated.

Under steady state conditions, the lambda control system oscillates between rich and lean around the lambda window. As the lambda sensor switches, the injector pulse width is adjusted by the amount determined by a control factor until the lambda sensor switches again to the opposite condition. The control factor can be defined as the allowable increase or decrease in the commanded fuel injector pulse width. The frequency of oscillation is determined by the gas transport time and the magnitude of the control factor. The gas transport time is defined as the time from air/fuel mixture formation to lambda sensor measurement.

Under transient conditions, the gas transport time results in a delay before the lambda sensor can indicate that the operating conditions have changed. Using only the lambda sensor for closed-loop fuel control would result in poor driveability and exhaust emissions because of this delay. Therefore, the engine control unit uses an anticipatory control strategy that uses engine load and RPM to determine the approximate fuel requirement. The engine load information is provided by the manifold pressure sensor for speed density systems and by the air meter for air flow and air mass measurement systems and by the throttle valve position sensor. The engine control unit contains data tables for combinations of load and RPM. This allows for rapid response to changes in operating conditions. The lambda sensor still provides the feedback correction for each load/RPM point. The data used for these data tables are largely developed from system modeling and engine development testing.

Due to production variations in engines, variations in fuel and changes due to wear and aging, the control system must be able to adapt to function properly for every engine over the engine's life. Therefore, the electronic control unit has a feature for adapting changes in the fuel required for the load/RPM points. At each load/RPM point, the lambda sensor continuously provides information that allows the system to adjust the fuel to the commanded A/F ratio. The corrected information is stored in RAM (random access memory) so that the next time the engine reaches that operating point (load/RPM), the anticipatory value will require less correction. These values remain stored in the electronic control unit even after the engine is shut off. Only if power to the electronic control unit is disrupted (i.e., due to a dead battery), will the correction be lost. In that case, the electronic control unit will revert back to the original production values that are written in ROM (read-only memory).

Lambda sensors do not switch symmetrically from lean to rich and rich to lean. Because of this, the control strategy is modified to account for the asymmetry. This can be accomplished either by delaying the modification by the control factor after the sensor switches or by using control factors of different magnitudes for rich-to-lean and lean-to-rich switching.

Ignition Timing Control.   The goal of the engine control system for ignition timing is to provide spark advance which optimizes engine torque, exhaust emissions, fuel economy, and driveability, and which minimizes engine knock. Data tables with the base ignition timing, depending on engine load and RPM, are stored in ROM in the electronic control unit. The values in these tables are optimized for fuel economy, exhaust emissions, and engine torque. They are developed through engine experimentation, usually with an engine dynamometer. Corrections to the base timing values are needed for temperature effects, EGR, hot restart, barometric pressure, and engine knock. In addition, some systems use ignition timing to vary the engine torque for improvement in automatic transmission shift quality or for idle speed control. Figure 12.4 is a flowchart of a typical ignition timing calculation method.

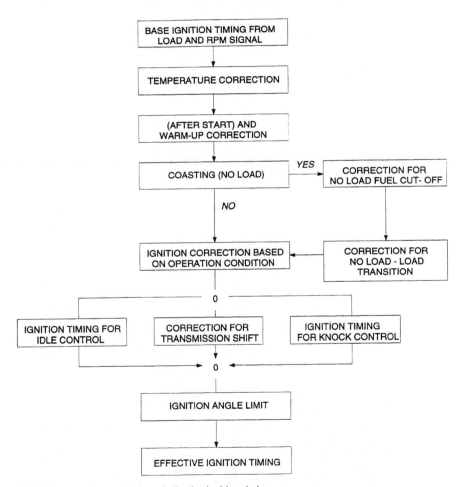

FIGURE 12.4   Determination of effective ignition timing.

Dwell Angle Control.   The dwell angle performance map stored in the electronic control unit controls the charging time of the ignition coil, depending on RPM and battery voltage. The dwell angle is controlled so that the desired primary current is reached at the end of the charging time just prior to the ignition point. This assures the necessary primary current, even with quick transients in RPM. A limit on the charge time in the upper RPM ranges allows for the necessary spark duration.

Knock Control. The ignition timing for optimization of torque, fuel economy, and exhaust emissions is in close proximity to the ignition timing that results in engine knock. Engine knock occurs when the ignition timing is advanced too far for the engine operating conditions and causes uncontrolled combustion that can lead to engine damage, depending on the severity and frequency. If a factor of safety was used when developing the base timing map for all conditions that contribute to knock, such as fuel quality and variations in compression ratio, the ignition timing would be significantly retarded from the optimum level, resulting in a significant loss in torque and fuel economy. To avoid this, a knock sensor (one or more) is installed on the engine to detect knocking (see Chap. 8). Knock sensors are usually acceleration sensors that provide an electric signal to the electronic control unit. From this signal, the engine control unit algorithm determines which cylinder or cylinders are knocking. Ignition timing is modified (retarded) for those cylinders until the knock is no longer detected. The ignition timing is then advanced again until knock is detected. (See Fig. 12.5.) Information on the amount of spark retard required to eliminate the knock for each cylinder under each load/RPM condition is saved in the electronic control unit RAM. This allows for quick access to the appropriate "learned" ignition timing for each condition. With this control system, the base timing can be more advanced for improved fuel economy and torque.

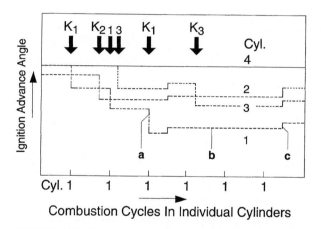

FIGURE 12.5 Knock control. Control algorithm for ignition adjustments for a four-cylinder engine. $K_{1...3}$ (knock in cylinders 1 . . . 3), cylinder number four (no knock), (*a*) (ignition retard), (*b*) (delay before return to original point, (*c*) (spark advance).

Evaporative Emissions Control. Hydrocarbon (HC) emissions in the form of fuel vapors escaping from the vehicle, primarily from the fuel tank, are closely regulated by federal statutes. There are two principal causes of fuel vapor in the fuel tank: increasing ambient temperature and return of unused hot fuel from the engine. In order to control the release of these emissions to the atmosphere, the evaporative emissions control system was developed.

Evaporative Emissions Control System. A vapor ventilation line exits the fuel tank and enters the fuel vapor canister. The canister consists of an active charcoal element which absorbs the vapor and allows only air to escape to the atmosphere. Only a certain volume of fuel vapor can be contained by the canister. The vapors in the canister must therefore be purged from and burned by the engine so that the canister can continue to store vapors as they are generated. To accomplish this, another line leads from the charcoal canister to the intake manifold. Included in this line is the canister purge solenoid valve. Figure 12.6 shows a layout of a typical evaporative emissions control system.

During engine operation, vacuum in the intake manifold causes flow through the charcoal canister because the canister vent opening, at the charcoal filter end, is at atmospheric pres-

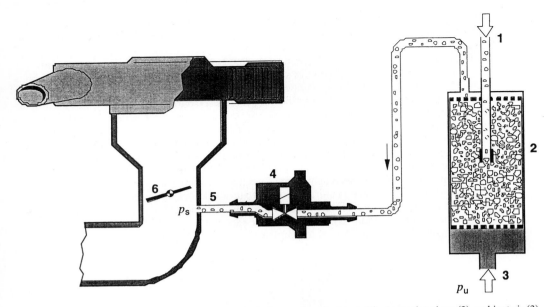

FIGURE 12.6 Evaporative emission control system: fuel vapor from fuel tank (1), charcoal canister (2), ambient air (3), canister purge control valve (4), purge line to intake manifold (5), throttle valve (6), p_s is intake manifold vacuum, and p_u is atmospheric pressure.

sure. The canister purge valve meters the amount of flow from the canister. The amount of fuel vapor in the canister and, therefore, contained in the flow stream, is not known. Therefore, it is critical that the lambda control system is operating and adjusting the fuel requirement as the vapors are being purged. Purge vapors could otherwise result in up to a 30 percent increase in air/fuel mixture richness in the engine.

Purge Valve Control.   Control of the purge valve must allow for two criteria:

- There must be enough vapor flow so that the charcoal canister does not become saturated and leak fuel vapors to the atmosphere
- Purge flow must generally occur under lambda closed-loop control so that the effect of the purge vapors on A/F ratio can be detected and the fuel metering corrected

When the electronic control unit commands the purge valve to meter vapor from the canister, it requests a duty cycle (ratio of ON time to total ON and OFF time). This allows the amount of vapor flow to be regulated depending on the engine operating conditions. When lambda control is not operating, only low duty cycles and, therefore, small amounts of purge vapors, are allowed. Under deceleration fuel cutoff, the purge valve is closed entirely to minimize the possibility of unburned HCs in the exhaust.

Turbocharger Boost Pressure Control.   The exhaust turbocharger consists of a compressor and an exhaust turbine arranged on a common shaft. Energy from the exhaust gas is converted to rotational energy by the exhaust turbine, which then drives the compressor. The compressed air leaves the compressor and passes through the air cooler (optional), throttle valve, intake manifold, and into the cylinders. In order to achieve near-constant air charge pressure over a wide RPM range, the turbocharger uses a circuit that allows for the bypass of the exhaust gases away from the exhaust turbine. The valve that regulates the bypass opens at a specified air charge pressure and is known as the wastegate.

   Engines that have turbochargers benefit significantly from electronic boost pressure control. If only a pneumatic-mechanical wastegate is used, only one boost pressure point for the entire operating range is used to divert the exhaust gas. This creates a compromise for part-load conditions, which results in increased exhaust backpressure, more turbocharger work, more residual exhaust gas in the cylinders, and higher-charge air temperatures.

   By controlling the wastegate with a pulse-width modulated solenoid valve, different wastegate opening pressures can be specified, depending on the engine operating conditions (Fig. 12.7). Therefore, only the level of air charge pressure required is developed. The electronic control unit uses information on engine load from either manifold pressure or the air meter and RPM and throttle position. From this information, a data table is referenced and the proper boost pressure (actually a duty cycle of the control valve) is determined. On systems using manifold pressure sensors, a closed-loop control system can be developed to compare the specified value with the measured value.

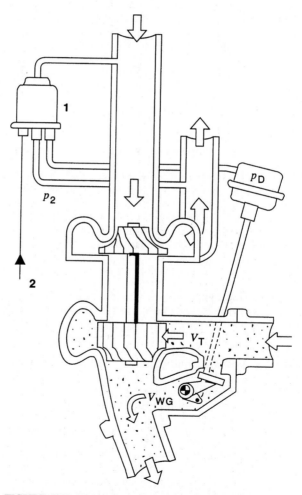

FIGURE 12.7 Electronic turbocharger boost control: solenoid valve (1), control signal from ECU (2), boost pressure (p_D), volume flow through turbine (V_T), volume flow through wastegate (V_{WG}).

The boost pressure control system is usually used in combination with knock control for turbocharged engines. When the ignition timing is retarded due to knock, an increase in already high exhaust temperatures for turbocharged engines occurs. To counteract the temperature increase, the boost pressure is reduced when the ignition timing is retarded past a predetermined threshold.

Engine/Vehicle Speed Control.   Using the inputs of engine RPM and vehicle speed to the electronic control unit, thresholds can be established for limiting these variables with fuel cutoff. When the maximum speed is achieved, the fuel injectors are shut off. When the speed decreases below the threshold, fuel injection resumes.

EGR Control.   By mixing a portion of the exhaust gas with the fresh intake air/fuel mixture, oxides of nitrogen (NO_x) can be reduced by lowering the peak combustion temperatures. However, the addition of exhaust gas can degrade driveability by causing combustion instability, especially at idle and low speeds and with a cold engine. The ECU references an engine RPM/load table of optimal EGR valve openings. The data table is developed on the engine dynamometer by analyzing the exhaust emissions. With increasing EGR, a point is reached where hydrocarbon (HC) emissions begin to increase. The optimal percent of EGR is just prior to that point.

The electronic control unit regulates a pneumatic- or solenoid-type valve to meter a certain quantity of exhaust gas back to the intake manifold. Typically, an engine coolant temperature threshold is also required before EGR is activated to avoid poor driveability. Under acceleration and at idle, EGR is deactivated.

Camshaft Control.   There are two types of camshaft controls: phasing (i.e., overlap or intake/exhaust valve opening point) and valve lift and opening duration.

Camshaft Phasing Control.   Valve overlap is a function of the rotation of the intake camshaft with respect to the exhaust camshaft. Overlap can be controlled by an electrohydraulic actuator. At idle and at high RPM, it is desirable to have the intake valves open and close later, which reduces the overlap. For idle, this reduces the residual exhaust gases that return with the fresh charge air and improves idle stability. At high RPM, late closing of the intake valve provides the best condition for maximum cylinder filling and, therefore, maximum output. For partial loads, a large valve overlap, where the intake opens early, is desirable. This allows for an increase in residual exhaust gas for improved exhaust emissions (Fig. 12.8).

Valve Lift and Opening Duration Control.   Control of the valve lift and opening duration is accomplished by switching between two camshaft profiles. An initial cam specifies the optimal lift and duration for the low to middle RPM range. A second cam profile controls a higher valve lift and duration for high-RPM operation. By monitoring engine load and RPM, the ECU actuates the electrohydraulic device that switches from one cam profile to the other (Fig. 12.9).

Variable Intake Manifold Control.   The goal of the engine design is to achieve the highest possible torque at low engine RPM as well as high output at high engine RPM. The torque curve of an engine is proportional to the air charge at any given engine speed. Therefore, a primary influence on the torque is the intake manifold geometric design. The simplest type of air charging uses the dynamics of the drawn-in air. The standard intake manifolds for multipoint engines consist of several intake runners and collectors converging at the throttle valve.

In general, short intake runners result in a high output at high RPM with a simultaneous loss of torque at low RPM. Long intake runners have the opposite effect. Due to intake valve and piston dynamics, pressure waves occur that oscillate within the intake manifold. Proper selection of runner lengths and collector sizes can result in the pressure waves arriving at the intake valves just before they are closing. This has a supercharging effect. The limitation of this method is that, for a given intake manifold configuration, the tuning peak can only occur at one operating point.

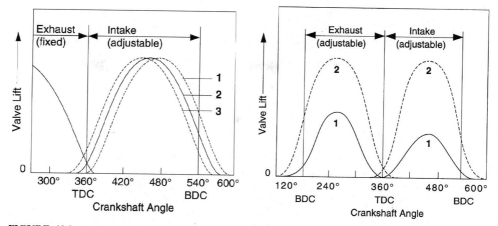

FIGURE 12.8 Adjustment angle for intake cam-shaft: retard (1), standard (2), advance (3).

FIGURE 12.9 Selective camshaft lobe actuation: base cam lobe (1), auxiliary cam lobe (2).

Variable Intake Systems.   To optimize the benefits of intake manifold charging, several systems have been developed that allow for changes in runner length and collector volume, depending on engine operating conditions. This allows for tuning peaks at more than one operating point. One method developed uses electronically controlled valves to close off areas of the intake manifold (Fig. 12.10). Inputs of engine load, RPM, and throttle angle determine the position of the valves.

12.2.2 Engine Control Modes

Engine Crank and Start.   During engine cranking, the goal is to get the engine started with the minimal amount of delay. To accomplish this, fuel must be delivered that meets the requirements for starting for any combination of engine coolant and ambient temperatures. For a cold engine, an increase in the commanded air/fuel ratio is required due to poor fuel vaporization and "wall wetting," which decreases the amount of usable fuel. Wall wetting is the condensation of some of the vaporized fuel on the cold metal surfaces in the intake port and combustion chamber. It is critical that the fuel does not wet the spark plugs, which can reduce the effectiveness of the spark plug and prevent the plug from firing. Should plug wetting occur, it may be impossible to start the engine.

Fuel Requirement.   Within the ECU ROM there are specific data tables to establish cold-start fuel based on engine coolant temperature. For two reasons, the lambda sensor output cannot be used during crank: the lambda sensor is below its minimum operating temperature and the air/fuel ratio required is outside the lambda sensor control window.

Many starting sequences use a front-loading strategy for fueling whereby the quantity of fuel is reduced after a speed threshold (RPM) is achieved, after a certain number of revolutions or at a defined time after the initial crank. Some systems also switch over from simultaneous injection to sequential injection after a speed threshold is achieved. For cold temperature starting, the fuel mixture may remain richer than $\lambda = 1$ after starting, due the continuing poor mixture formation in the cold induction system.

Ignition Timing Requirement.   Ignition timing is controlled by the ECU during crank and is determined by engine coolant temperature and cranking speed. For a cold engine with low cranking speeds, ideal timing is near TDC. For higher cranking speeds, a slightly more advanced timing is optimal. Timing advance must be limited during cranking to avoid igniting

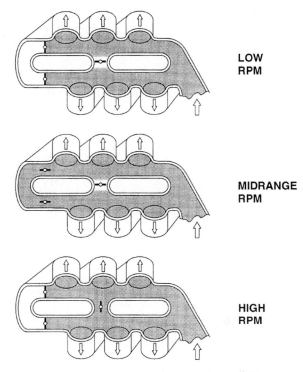

LOW
RPM

MIDRANGE
RPM

HIGH
RPM

FIGURE 12.10 Variable configuration intake manifold.

the air/fuel mixture before the crankshaft reaches top dead center (TDC). A damaging torque reversal could occur that would damage the starter. After the engine starts, ignition timing is advanced to improve cold engine running as well as to reduce the need for fuel enrichment.

Engine Warm-Up. During the warm-up phase, there are three conflicting objectives: keep the engine operating smoothly (i.e., no stalls or driveability problems), increase exhaust temperature to quickly achieve operational temperature for catalyst (light-off) and lambda sensor so that closed-loop fuel control can begin operating, and keep exhaust emissions and fuel consumption to a minimum. The best method for achieving these objectives is very dependent on the specific engine application.

If the engine is still cold, fuel enrichment will be required to keep the engine running smoothly due, again, to poor fuel vaporization and wall wetting effects. The amount of enrichment is dependent on engine temperature and is a correction factor to the injector pulse width. This enrichment, combined with secondary air injection, also helps achieve the desired increase in catalyst temperature. To provide secondary air injection, an external air pump delivers fresh air downstream of the exhaust valves for a short time after start. The excess air causes oxidation (burning) of the excess HC and CO from the rich mixture in the exhaust manifold, which rapidly increases the temperature of the catalytic converter. The oxidation also removes harmful pollutants from the exhaust stream.

It is possible to increase the exhaust temperature by increasing the idle speed during warm-up. The increased idle speed may also be combined with a slightly retarded ignition timing, which increases temperatures in the exhaust, thereby promoting rapid warm-up of the catalyst.

Transient Compensation.   During transitions such as acceleration or deceleration, the objective of the engine control system is to provide a smooth transition from one engine operating condition to another (i.e., no hesitations, stalls, bumps, or other objectionable driveability concerns), and keep exhaust emissions and fuel consumption to a minimum.

Acceleration Enrichment.   When an increase in engine load and throttle angle occurs, a corresponding increase in fuel mixture richness is required to compensate for the increased wall wetting. The sudden increase in air results in a lean mixture that must be corrected swiftly to obtain good transitional response. The rate of change of engine load and throttle angle are used to determine the quantity of fuel during acceleration enrichment. The amount of fuel must be enough to provide the desired performance, but not so much as to degrade exhaust emissions and fuel economy.

During acceleration enrichment, the ignition timing is set for maximum torque without knocking. Additionally, when a large change in engine load occurs, some systems delay the ignition timing advance briefly to prevent engine knock, which may arise from a momentary lean mixture or from transient ignition timing errors.

Deceleration Enleanment.   During deceleration modes, such as coasting or braking, there is no torque requirement. Therefore, the fuel may be shut off until either an increase in throttle angle is detected or the engine speed falls to a speed slightly above the idle RPM. Fuel shutoff or cutoff can decrease exhaust emissions by eliminating unburned HC and CO and may also improve fuel consumption. Fuel cutoff is also used to protect the catalytic converter from extreme high temperatures during extended overrun conditions. During transition to fuel cutoff, the ignition timing is retarded from its current setting to reduce engine torque and to assist in engine braking. The fuel is then shut off. During the transition, the throttle bypass valve or the main throttle valve may remain open for a short period to allow fresh air to oxidize the remaining unburned HC and CO to further reduce exhaust emissions. During development of the fuel cutoff strategy, the advantage of reduced emission effects and catalyst temperature control must be balanced against driveability requirements. The use of fuel cutoff may change the perceived amount of engine braking felt by the driver. In addition, care must be taken to avoid a "bump" feel when entering the fuel cutoff mode, due to the change in torque.

Full Load.   Under steady state full-load conditions, such as for climbing a grade, it is desirable to control the air/fuel mixture and ignition timing to obtain maximum power and to also limit engine and exhaust temperatures. The best engine torque is typically delivered at about $\lambda = 0.9$ to 0.95. When the ECU determines the engine is operating at full load via the throttle valve sensor (at WOT), the commanded air/fuel mixture, if required, can be enriched. The lambda sensor signal cannot be used to provide correction to the air/fuel mixture because the rich operating point lies outside the lambda control window.

The ignition timing at full load is set to achieve the maximum torque without knocking. This initial value is determined through engine dynamometer testing. With a knock control system (see Sec. 12.2.1), the ignition timing is modified (retarded) when engine knock occurs. The modification required to eliminate the knock may be saved in the ECU so that the next time that engine RPM/load point occurs, less knocking will occur and less correction will be required.

Idle Speed Control.   The objectives of the engine control system during idle are:

- Provide a balance between the engine torque produced and the changing engine loads, thus achieving a consistent idle speed even with various load changes due to accessories (i.e., air conditioning, power steering, and electrical loads) being turned on and off and during engagement of the automatic transmission. In addition, the idle speed control must be able to compensate for long-term changes in engine load, such as the reduction in engine friction that occurs with engine break-in.

- Provide the lowest idle speed that allows smooth running to achieve the lowest exhaust emissions and fuel consumption (up to 30 percent of a vehicle's fuel consumption in city driving occurs during idling).

To control the idle speed, the ECU uses inputs from the throttle position sensor, air conditioning, automatic transmission, power steering, charging system, engine RPM, and vehicle speed. There are currently two strategies used to control idle speed: air control and ignition control.

Air Control.   The amount of air entering the intake manifold is controlled either by a bypass valve or by an actuator acting directly on the throttle valve. The bypass valve uses, for example, an electronically controlled motor controlled by the ECU that opens or closes a fixed amount. For large throttle valves, it may be desirable to use a bypass valve because a small change in throttle angle may result in a large change in air flow and, therefore, idle speed may be difficult to control. Using engine RPM feedback input, the ECU adjusts the air flow to increase or decrease the idle speed. A disadvantage to air control is that the response to load changes is relatively slow. To overcome this, air control is often combined with ignition timing control to provide acceptable idle speed control. The fuel quantity required at idle is determined by engine load and RPM. During closed-loop operation, this value is optimized by the lambda sensor closed-loop control.

Ignition Timing Control.   Engine torque may be increased or decreased by advancing or retarding the ignition timing within an established window. This principle can be employed to help control idle speed. Ignition timing control is particularly desirable for responding to idle load changes because engine torque output changes more rapidly in response to a change in ignition timing than to a change in air valve position. Using the same inputs as for air control, the ECU adjusts the spark advance to either raise or lower the idle speed.

Anticipating Accessory Loads.   Specific electric inputs to the ECU, such as a pressure switch located in the power steering system, are used to anticipate accessory loads so that the idle control system can compensate more quickly. This "feed forward" strategy allows better idle control than a strictly feedback system which does not respond until the idle speed begins to fall. When an accessory can be controlled by the ECU, further improvement in idle speed control is obtained. By delaying the load briefly after it is requested, the compensation sequence can begin before the load is actually applied. Such a load delay strategy is effective for controlling air conditioning compressor loads, for example. In this case, when the air conditioner is requested, the ECU begins to increase the idle speed first and then activates the A/C compressor.

12.2.3   Engine Control Diagnostics

The purpose of system diagnostics is to provide a warning to the driver when the control system determines that a malfunction of a component or system has occurred and to assist the service technician in identifying and correcting the failure (see Chap. 22). In many cases, to the driver, the engine may appear to be operating correctly, but excessive amounts of pollutants may be emitted. The ECU determines that a malfunction has occurred when a sensor signal received during normal engine operation or during a system test indicates there is a problem. For critical operations such as fuel metering and ignition control, if a required sensor input is faulty, a substitute value may be used by the ECU so that the engine will continue to operate, but likely not at optimal performance. It is also possible to apply an emergency measure if the failure of a component may result in engine or emission system damage. For example, if repeated misfires are detected in one cylinder, perhaps due to an ignition failure, the fuel injector feeding that cylinder can be shut off to avoid damage to the catalytic converter. When a failure occurs, the malfunction indicator light (MIL), visible to the driver, is illuminated. Information on the failure is stored in the ECU. A service technician can retrieve the information on the failure from the ECU and correct the problem.

Air Mass Sensor.   For air mass measurement systems, the pulse width of the fuel injectors is calculated in the ECU from the air mass sensor input. As a comparison, the pulse width is also calculated from the throttle valve sensor and the engine RPM. If the pulse width values deviate by a predetermined amount, the discrepancy is stored in the ECU. Then, while the vehicle is being driven, plausibility tests determine which input is incorrect. When this has been determined, the appropriate failure code is saved in the ECU.

Misfire Detection.   Misfiring is the lack of combustion in the cylinder. Misfiring can be caused by several factors including fouled or worn spark plugs, poor fuel metering, or faulty electrical connections. Even a small number of misfires may result in excessive exhaust emissions due to the unburned mixture. Increased misfire rates can damage the catalytic converter.

To determine if the engine is experiencing a misfire, the crankshaft speed fluctuation is monitored. If a misfire occurs, no torque is created during the power stroke of the cylinder(s) that is misfiring. A small decrease in the rotational speed of the crankshaft occurs. Because the change in speed is very small, highly accurate sensing of the crankshaft speed is required. In addition, a fairly complicated calculation process is required in order to distinguish misfiring from other influences on crankshaft speed. As was mentioned previously, if a cylinder repeatedly misfires, it is possible to shut off the fuel to that cylinder to prevent damage to the catalytic converter.

Catalytic Converter Monitoring.   During the useful life of a catalytic converter, its efficiency decreases. If subjected to engine misfire, the decrease in efficiency occurs more rapidly. A loss in efficiency results in an increase in exhaust pollutants. For this reason, the catalytic converter is monitored. A properly operating catalytic converter transforms O_2, HC, CO, and NO_x into H_2O, CO_2, and N_2. The incoming air/fuel ratio oscillates from rich to lean due to the lambda closed-loop control strategy discussed in Sec. 12.2.1. Only a properly functioning catalytic converter is able to dampen these oscillations by storing and converting the incoming components. As the catalyst ages, this storage effect is diminished. To monitor the catalytic converter, an additional lambda sensor is installed downstream of the catalyst. The ECU compares the signal of the lambda sensor upstream with the lambda sensor downstream and determines if the catalytic converter is operating properly. If not, the ECU illuminates the malfunction indicator light (MIL) and stores a failure code.

Lambda Sensor Monitoring.   To minimize exhaust emissions, the engine must operate within the catalytic converter window for air/fuel ratio (see Sec. 12.1.1 for a detailed description of the catalytic converter window). Output from the lambda sensor serves as feedback to the ECU to control the fuel within that window. When a lambda sensor is exposed to high heat for a long period of time, it may respond more slowly to changes in the air/fuel mixture. This can cause a deviation in the air/fuel mixture from the window, which would affect the exhaust emissions.

If the upstream lambda sensor operation is determined to be too slow, which can be detected by the system operation frequency, the ECU illuminates the malfunction indicator light (MIL) and a failure code is stored. Additionally, the ECU compares the output signal of the additional lambda sensor downstream of the catalytic converter with the lambda sensor signal upstream. With this, the ECU is able to detect deviations of the average value in air/fuel ratio.

For heated lambda sensors, the electric current and voltage of the heater circuit is monitored. To accomplish this, the heater is directly controlled by the ECU, not through a relay.

Fuel System Monitoring.   To provide the correct air/fuel ratio, the ECU uses a preset data map with the optimal fuel required for each load and RPM point. The lambda closed-loop control system (see Sec. 12.2.1) provides feedback to the ECU on the necessary correction to the preset data points. The corrected information is stored in the ECU's RAM so that the next time that operating point is reached, less correction of the air/fuel ratio will be required. If the ECU correction passes a predetermined threshold, it is an indication that some component in the fuel supply system is outside of its operating range. Some examples are defective pressure regulator, defective manifold pressure sensor, intake system leakage, or exhaust system leakage. When the ECU determines a problem exists, the MIL is illuminated and a code is stored in the ECU.

Exhaust Gas Recirculation (EGR) Monitoring.   There are currently two methods used to monitor EGR operation. One method confirms that hot exhaust gases are returning to the intake manifold during EGR operation by use of a temperature sensor in the intake manifold. The second method requires the EGR valve to be fully opened during coast operation, where high intake manifold vacuum occurs. The exhaust gas flowing into the manifold causes a measurable increase in pressure. Thus, if a measured increase in pressure does not occur, the EGR system is not operating.

Evaporative Emissions Control System (EECS) Monitoring.   In general, a valve will be installed at the atmospheric side of the purge canister. During idle, this valve would close and the purge valve would open. Intake manifold vacuum would occur in the entire EECS. A pressure sensor in the fuel tank would provide a pressure profile during this test to the ECU, which would then determine if a leak existed in the system.

12.2.4   Fuel Delivery Systems

Overview.   Fuel management in the spark ignition engine consists of metering the fuel, formation of the air/fuel mixture, transportation of the air/fuel mixture, and distribution of the air/fuel mixture. The driver operates the throttle valve, which determines the quantity of air inducted by the engine. The fuel delivery system must provide the proper quantity of fuel to create a combustible mixture in the engine cylinder. In general, two fuel delivery system configurations exist: *single-point* and *multipoint* (Fig. 12.11).

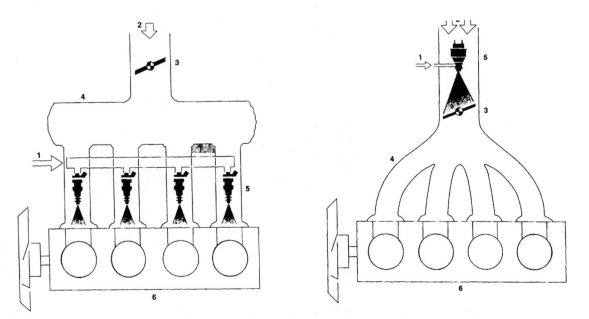

FIGURE 12.11   Air-fuel mixture preparation: right, single-point fuel injection; left, multipoint fuel injection with fuel (1), air (2), throttle valve (3), intake manifold (4), injector(s) (5), and engine (6).

For single-point systems such as carburetors or single-point fuel injection, the fuel is metered in the vicinity of the throttle valve. Mixture formation occurs in the intake manifold. Some of the fuel droplets evaporate to form fuel vapor (desirable) while others condense to form a film on the intake manifold walls (undesirable). Mixture transport and distribution is a function of intake manifold design. Uniform distribution under all operating conditions is difficult to achieve in a single-point system.

For multipoint systems, the fuel is injected near the intake valve. Mixture formation is supplemented by the evaporation of the fuel on the back of the hot intake valve. Mixture transport and distribution occurs only in the vicinity of the intake valve. The influence of the intake manifold design on uniform mixture distribution is minimized. Since mixture transport and distribution is not an issue, the intake manifold design can be optimized for air flow.

Single-Point Injection Systems   A single-point injection system uses one or, in some cases, two electronic fuel injectors to inject fuel into the intake air stream. The main component is the fuel injection unit which is located upstream of the intake manifold.

Component Description.   An electric fuel pump provides fuel at a medium pressure (typically 0.7 to 1.0 bar) to the electronic fuel injection unit (Fig. 12.12). The fuel injection unit houses the solenoid-operated fuel injector, which is located in the intake air flow above the throttle valve. This allows for homogeneous mixture formation and distribution. The injector spray pattern is designed to allow fuel to pass between the throttle valve and the throttle bore. To prevent vapor lock of the injector, fuel flows through the injector at all times. Fuel not used by the engine is returned to the fuel tank. The injector is activated in relation to the speed of the engine, typically once per ignition event. The length of the pulse width determines the quantity of fuel provided.

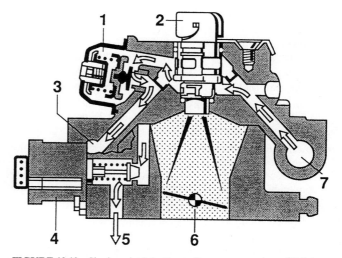

FIGURE 12.12   Single-point injection unit: pressure regulator (1), injector (2), fuel return (3), stepper motor for idle speed control (4), to intake manifold (5), throttle valve (6), and fuel inlet (7).

The electronic injection unit also houses the throttle position sensor and, in some cases, an inlet air temperature sensor which provides operating condition information to the ECU. The throttle valve actuator and fuel pressure regulator are also mounted on the injection unit. In addition, some units contain an air bypass valve for idle speed control. Engine temperature, battery voltage, and engine speed via the ignition system are all inputs to the ECU. The single-point injection system also uses lambda closed-loop fuel control to optimize fuel metering within the lambda control window (see Sec. 12.2.1).

Adaptation to Operating Conditions.   For cold-start and engine warm-up, the ECU uses engine temperature information to determine the correct amount of fuel and commands the fuel injector via a pulse width. Due to wall wetting and poor fuel vaporization when the engine is cold, an increase in mixture richness is required. As the engine warms up to operating temperature, the commanded pulse width is reduced.

During an acceleration transition, the ECU adds a correction factor (an increase) to the commanded injector pulse width. The sudden increase in air results in a lean mixture which must be corrected swiftly to obtain good transitional response. During a deceleration transition, the fuel can be shut off by simply not providing a pulse width signal to the injector to minimize exhaust emissions and fuel consumption.

During full-load operation, the air/fuel mixture can be enriched ($\lambda < 1$) to deliver maximum torque. The ECU determines full-load operation by the throttle position sensor (at or near wide-open throttle) and adds a correction to the injector pulse width to achieve the desired air/fuel mixture richness.

The single-point system can control the idle speed by ECU control of either a throttle valve actuator or a bypass valve. Idle speed is a function of engine operating temperature, whether the transmission is in drive, and what accessories are in use. Fuel metering at idle is determined by engine RPM and load as well as lambda closed-loop control.

Multipoint Fuel Injection Systems.   A multipoint fuel injection system supplies fuel to each cylinder individually via a mechanical or solenoid-operated fuel injector located just upstream of the intake valve. Advantages of this system type compared to SPI systems are numerous:

- *Increased fuel economy.*   On an SPI engine, due to the intake manifold configuration, mixture formation will differ at each cylinder. To provide adequate fuel for the leanest cylinder, too much fuel must be metered overall. In addition, during engine load changes, a film of fuel is deposited on the intake manifold walls. This leads to further variations in mixture from cylinder to cylinder. Multipoint injection provides the same quantity of fuel to each cylinder.

- *Higher power output.*   With the fuel being injected near the intake valve, the rest of the intake manifold can be optimized for maximum air flow. The result is increased torque.

- *Improved throttle response.*   Because the fuel is injected onto the intake valves, responses to increases in throttle position are swift. With an SPI system, the increased fuel required must travel the length of the intake manifold before entering the cylinder.

- *Lower exhaust emissions.*   As was discussed for fuel economy, mixture variation in an SPI system creates increased exhaust emissions. Metering of the fuel at the intake valve decreases this variation. In addition, the system transport time is reduced, increasing the frequency at which the lambda closed-loop control system can switch air/fuel ratio. Catalytic converter efficiency is increased.

Although there are numerous advantages of the MPI systems over the SPI systems, there is still one important advantage the SPI systems have over the MPI systems. In general, SPI systems have better fuel preparation, similar to a carburetor.

Mechanically Controlled Continuous Injection System.   This type of system meters the fuel as a function of the intake air quantity and injects it continuously onto the intake valves. This is accomplished by measuring the air flow as it passes through the air flow meter by means of deflection of a meter plate. The fuel is supplied through a fuel accumulator to the fuel distributor by an electric fuel pump. A primary-pressure regulator in the fuel distributor maintains constant fuel pressure. The fuel distributor, through its interface with the air flow meter and warm-up regulator, meters fuel to the continuously flowing fuel injectors.

Component Description

Mixture control unit.   The mixture control unit houses the air flow meter and the fuel distributor. In the air flow meter, the measurement of the intake air serves as the basis for determining the amount of fuel to be metered to the injectors. The air flow meter is located upstream of the throttle valve so that it measures all the air entering the engine. It consists of an air funnel, in which a sensor plate is free to pivot. Intake air flowing through the funnel causes a deflection of the sensor plate. The sensor plate is mechanically linked to a control plunger and movement of the plate results in movement of the control plunger. The control plunger movement determines the amount of fuel to be injected.

In the fuel distributor, the control plunger moves up and down in a cylindrically shaped device (barrel) with rectangular openings (metering slit), one for each engine cylinder. Increased air flow causes the control plunger to move upward, uncovering a larger area of the metering slit and increasing the fuel metered. Downstream of each metering slit is a differential-pressure valve that maintains a constant pressure drop across the metering slits at different flow rates. Due to the constant pressure, the fuel flow through the slits is directly proportional to the position of the control plunger (Fig. 12.13).

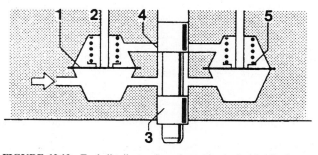

FIGURE 12.13 Fuel distributor for mixture control unit: diaphragm (1), to injector (2), control plunger (3), metering slot (4), differential pressure regulator (5).

Warm-up regulator.   The warm-up regulator is used to richen the fuel mixture under cold engine conditions. It consists of a diaphragm valve and an electrically heated bimetallic spring. Under cold conditions, the warm-up regulator lowers the control pressure on the control plunger. The control pressure acts on the opposite end of the plunger from the air flow meter plate. A lower control pressure results in a lower force required to move the meter plate. Therefore, the same air flow causes the meter plate and control plunger to move a greater distance and additional fuel is metered to the injectors.

Fuel injectors.   The injectors open at a pressure of approximately 3.6 bar. Atomization of the fuel occurs through oscillation (audible chatter) of the valve needle caused by the fuel flowing through it. The injectors remain open as long as fuel is provided above the opening pressure. Fuel is injected continuously into the intake port. When the intake valve opens, the mixture is drawn into the cylinder.

Auxiliary air valve.   The auxiliary air valve provides additional air to the engine by bypassing the throttle valve during cold engine operation. This creates an increase in the idle speed needed during cold operation.

Thermo-time switch.   The thermo-time switch controls the cold start valve as a function of time and engine temperature. Fuel enters the intake manifold from the cold start valve and further enriches the mixture to improve cold-starting at low ambient temperatures. When the engine is warm, the contacts in the thermo-time switch open and the cold-start valve is not used in starting the engine.

Lambda sensor.   With the addition of a lambda sensor in the exhaust stream, a frequency valve, a modified fuel distributor, and an electronic control unit, the mechanically controlled fuel system can operate under lambda closed-loop control. The lambda sensor signal is read by the ECU. The ECU outputs electric pulses to an electromagnetic (frequency) valve. The frequency valve modulates the pressure to the lower chambers of the differential-pressure valves in the fuel distributor. This results in a modification of the pressure drop across the metering slits, effectively increasing or decreasing the amount of fuel injected. Figure 12.14 is a schematic of a typical mechanically controlled continuous injection system.

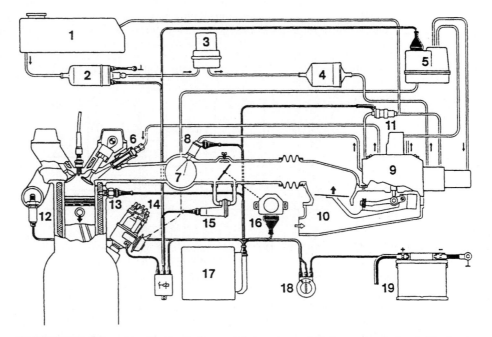

FIGURE 12.14 Schematic of mechanically controlled continuous injection system: fuel tank (1), electric fuel pump (2), fuel accumulator (3), fuel filter (4), warm-up regulator (5), injector (6), intake plenum (7), cold-start valve (8), fuel distributor (9), air flow sensor (10), electrohydraulic pressure actuator (11), lambda sensor (12), thermo-time switch (13), ignition distributor (14), auxiliary air valve (15), throttle switch (16), ECU (17), ignition switch (18), and battery (19).

Depending on the engine temperature, the cold-start valve injects extra fuel into the intake manifold for a limited period during cold start. The injection period is determined by a combination of time and temperature and is controlled by the thermo-time switch. As the engine temperature increases, this additional enrichment is no longer required and the thermo-time switch turns off the cold-start valve. For repeated start attempts or long cranking, the thermo-time switch turns off the cold-start injector after a given time. This minimizes engine flooding when engine start has not occurred.

As the engine continues to warm up, wall wetting and poor fuel vaporization still occur and mixture enrichment is still required until the engine reaches operating temperature. This enrichment is controlled as a function of temperature by the warm-up regulator. As the temperature increases, the warm-up regulator commands less and less additional fuel by increasing the control pressure.

For acceleration response, the air flow sensor "overswings" during quick throttle increases. This causes an additional quantity of fuel to be injected for acceleration enrichment. For full-load enrichment to achieve maximum power, a special warm-up regulator that uses intake manifold pressure is required. At increased manifold pressures, i.e., during wide-open throttle, the warm-up regulator lowers the control pressure, which results in an increase in fuel delivery. Deceleration fuel shutoff is accomplished by diverting all intake air through an air bypass around the air flow sensor plate. With no air flow past the air flow sensor plate, the fuel pressure to the injectors is decreased below the opening pressure.

Idle speed for the cold-running engine is increased by the auxiliary air valve. The amount of additional air varies with engine temperature until the auxiliary air valve is closed and the idle speed is then controlled only be the air passing the throttle valve.

Electronically Controlled Continuous Injection.   The basis of the electronically controlled continuous injection is still the mechanical hydraulic injection system discussed previously. This is supplemented by an electronic control unit (ECU) that allows for an increase in flexibility and the use of additional functions. This system incorporates additional sensors for detecting the engine temperature, the throttle valve position (load signal), and the air flow sensor plate deflection. This information is processed by the ECU, which then commands an electrohydraulic pressure actuator to adapt the injected fuel quantity for the present operating conditions.

In contrast to the mechanical system mentioned previously, the control pressure or counterpressure on the control plunger is not varied by a warm-up regulator. The control pressure remains constant and is the same as the primary pressure. The function of the warm-up regulator is now handled by the ECU and the electrohydraulic pressure actuator. Figure 12.15 is a schematic of a typical electronically controlled continuous injection system.

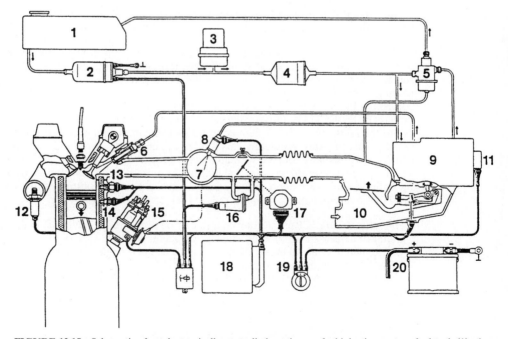

FIGURE 12.15   Schematic of an electronically controlled continuous fuel injection system: fuel tank (1), electric fuel pump (2), fuel accumulator (3), fuel filter (4), fuel pressure regulator (5), injector (6), intake plenum (7), cold-start valve (8), fuel distributor (9), air flow sensor (10), electrohydraulic pressure actuator (11), lambda sensor (12), thermo-time switch (13), coolant temperature sensor (14), ignition distributor (15), auxiliary air valve (16), throttle valve switch (17), ECU (18), ignition switch (19), and battery (20).

Component description—electrohydraulic pressure actuator.   The main difference in the componentry between the purely mechanical system and the electronically controlled system is the addition of the electrohydraulic actuator and the elimination of the warm-up regulator. With the addition of the ECU control of fuel metering, the purely mechanical warm-up regulator is no longer required. Depending on the signal received from the ECU, the electrohydraulic pressure actuator varies the pressure in the lower chambers of the differential pressure valves. This changes the amount of fuel delivered to the injectors.

Lambda closed-loop control.   As with the mechanical system, the lambda sensor signal is processed by the ECU to determine mixture composition. The difference is that the ECU now commands the electrohydraulic actuator to modify the fuel metered, as opposed to the separate frequency valve, which is no longer necessary.

Adaptation to operating conditions. Depending on the engine temperature, the cold-start valve injects extra fuel into the intake manifold for a limited period during cold-start. The quantity to be injected is controlled by the ECU and is a function of engine temperature (from the engine temperature sensor). The thermo-time switch controls how long the cold-start valve remains active, depending on engine temperature and time.

Acceleration enrichment is controlled by the ECU. Input from the air flow sensor plate position sensor provides the ECU with information on how quickly the engine load has increased. The ECU commands additional enrichment via the electrohydraulic pressure actuator. For full-load enrichment for maximum power, the ECU receives input from the throttle position sensor that the throttle is wide open. The ECU then commands additional enrichment via the electrohydraulic pressure actuator. Deceleration fuel shutoff is also controlled by the ECU when the throttle valve switch indicates the throttle is closed and the engine speed is above idle RPM. The ECU signals the electrohydraulic pressure actuator to interrupt fuel delivery to the injectors.

Idle speed control can be a closed-loop function with the addition of the idle actuator valve. This valve is ECU-controlled and the RPM signal from the ignition, combined with the engine temperature signal, is used to determine its position for the correct idle speed.

Pulsed Fuel Injection Systems.   Pulsed fuel injection systems are a further enhancement of the continuous injection systems. Today, most continuous injection systems have been replaced with pulsed fuel injection systems. Instead of injecting fuel continuously and controlling the quantity of fuel by modifying the delivery volume flow rate, the fuel quantity is controlled by the open time of the solenoid-operated injectors. The injectors are controlled directly by the ECU. For most systems, the fuel pressure drop across the injector, from the fuel rail to the intake manifold, is kept constant by using intake manifold air pressure to compensate the fuel pressure regulator. This type of system allows for still greater precision of fuel control and is usually coupled with an equally precise ignition timing control system.

Component description.   Several multipoint pulsed injection systems exist in various configurations. The components discussed here serve as a general outline of this system type. Figure 12.16 is a schematic of a typical pulsed fuel injection system.

- *Inlet air sensing.*   The inlet air charge can be measured directly using either an air flow meter or a mass air flow meter. The air flow meter is a vane-type meter, which uses the force of the incoming air to move a flap through a defined angle. The angular movement is converted by a potentiometer to a voltage ratio. The air flow meter requires an air inlet temperature sensor to correct for air density changes. The air mass flow meter measures the air mass directly by hot-wire or hot-film element. As the inlet air flow passes the heated element, a bridge circuit keeps the element at a constant temperature above the inlet temperature. The heating current required by the bridge circuit to maintain the element at a constant temperature is measured and converted to an air density value.

   The air charge can also be measured indirectly by measuring the inlet air temperature, intake manifold pressure, and engine RPM and then calculating the air charge (see Sec. 12.2.1 for further discussion on the calculation method which is called speed density air measurement).

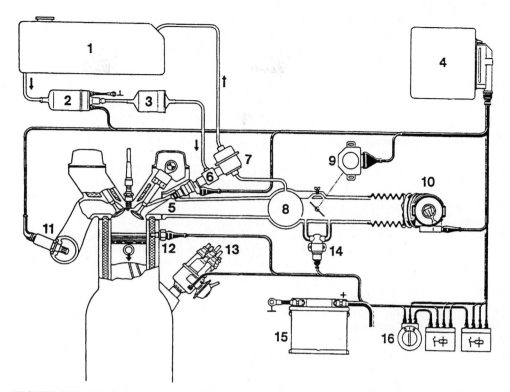

FIGURE 12.16   Schematic of a pulsed fuel injection system: fuel tank (1), electric fuel pump (2), fuel filter (3), ECU (4), injector (5), fuel distributor (6), fuel pressure regulator (7), intake plenum (8), throttle valve switch (9), hot-wire mass air flow sensor (10), lambda sensor (11), coolant temperature sensor (12), ignition distributor (13), idle speed actuator (14), battery (15), and ignition switch (16).

• *Fuel metering.*   The fuel supply system includes an electric fuel pump, fuel filter, fuel rail, pressure regulator, and solenoid-operated injectors. The fuel pump provides more fuel than the maximum required by the engine. Fuel not used by the engine is returned to the fuel tank. The fuel rail supplies all injectors with an equal quantity of fuel and ensures the same fuel pressure at all injectors.

The pressure regulator keeps the pressure differential across the injectors constant. It contains a diaphragm that has intake manifold pressure on one side and fuel rail pressure on the other. Normally, it is mounted at the outlet end of the fuel rail. The diaphragm operates a valve which opens at a differential pressure between 2.0 and 3.5 bar and allows excess fuel to return to the fuel tank.

The fuel injectors are solenoid-operated valves that are opened and closed by means of electric pulses from the ECU. The injectors are mounted in the intake manifold and spray onto the back of the intake valves. In general, one injector is used for each cylinder.

In addition, some systems also use a separate cold-start injector mounted in the intake manifold just downstream of the throttle valve. This injector ensures good fuel vaporization during cold-start and supplies the additional enrichment needed to start the cold engine. Control of the cold-start valve is either by the ECU directly or in conjunction with a thermo-time switch.

- *Lambda closed-loop control.*   The lambda sensor signal is processed by the ECU. The ECU determines the required injector pulse width to maintain the air/fuel ratio within the lambda control window (see Sec. 12.2.1 for further discussion on lambda closed-loop control).

Adaptation to operating conditions.   For cranking, the fuel required is determined by a data table in the ECU with reference to engine temperature. The ECU then commands a pulse width for the fuel injectors. The air/fuel mixture is greatly enriched due to poor fuel vaporization and wall wetting, which reduces the amount of usable fuel. After start, the fuel mixture remains rich due to continuing poor air/fuel mixture formation. The amount of enrichment should be minimized to obtain good emission results. The target is to stay close to lambda (λ) = 1.

For acceleration enrichment, the throttle valve position sensor indicates that the throttle has moved rapidly. The ECU adds a correction factor to increase the pulse width so that a smooth transition occurs. For deceleration, the ECU uses input from the throttle position sensor and engine RPM to indicate that the throttle has closed and the engine speed is above the idle speed. Since no torque is required under this condition, the ECU provides no pulse width to the injectors and they are therefore closed. For full-load enrichment, when necessary, the ECU can provide an injector pulse width that would result in the engine achieving its maximum torque (roughly $\lambda = 0.9$). Fuel metering during idle is primarily controlled by lambda closed-loop control when the engine has reached operating temperature.

12.2.5   Ignition Systems

Overview.   The purpose of the ignition system in the spark ignition engine is to initiate combustion of the air/fuel mixture by delivering a spark at precisely the right moment. The spark consists of an electrical arc generated across the electrodes of the spark plug. Two important factors for proper ignition are the energy of the spark and the point in the four-stroke cycle when the spark occurs (ignition timing).

Electrical Energy.   The energy required for a spark to ignite an air/fuel mixture at stoichiometry depends on specific engine conditions. If there is insufficient energy available to ignite the air/fuel mixture, misfiring will occur. Misfiring will result in poor engine operation, high exhaust emissions, and possible catalytic converter damage. Therefore, the amount of ignition energy available must always exceed the amount necessary to ensure ignition even under adverse conditions.

Some of the conditions that affect ignitability of the air/fuel mixture are fuel atomization, access of the mixture to the spark, spark duration, and spark physical length. Fuel atomization is controlled by the fuel system and the engine design. Access to the spark depends on combustion chamber and spark plug design. Spark duration is a function of the ignition system. Spark physical length is determined by the spark plug dimensions (gap).

Ignition Timing.   The ignition timing must be selected to meet the following objectives: maximize engine performance, limit fuel consumption, minimize engine knock, and minimize exhaust emissions. Unfortunately, all of these objectives cannot be achieved simultaneously under all operating conditions and compromises must be made.

It is desirable in the SI engine to have ignition of the combustible mixture occur prior to the piston reaching TDC on the compression stroke to achieve the best engine performance. The ignition spark must occur early enough to ensure that the peak cylinder combustion pressure occurs at the correct point after top dead center (ADC) under all operating conditions. Figure 12.17 is a graph of ignition angle vs. combustion pressure. The length of the combustion process from initial ignition to final combustion is approximately 2 ms. This combustion time remains relatively constant with respect to engine speed. Therefore, as the engine speed increases, the ignition spark must occur earlier in terms of crankshaft angle to ensure complete combustion.

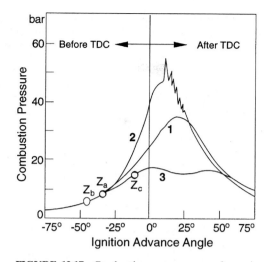

FIGURE 12.17 Combustion pressure curve for various ignition timing points: correct ignition advance Z_a (1), excessive ignition advance Z_b (2), and excessive ignition retard Z_c (3).

At low engine loads, the lower air charge and the residual gas content, due to valve overlap, serve to lengthen the time required for complete combustion. To compensate for this effect, the ignition timing is advanced at low loads to ensure that complete combustion occurs.

Ignition timing influences exhaust emissions and fuel consumption. With more advanced timing, the emission of unburned hydrocarbons (HC) and of oxides of nitrogen (NO_x) increases. Carbon monoxide (CO) emissions are not influenced greatly by ignition timing. To achieve improvements in fuel consumption, the air/fuel mixture must be lean. To ensure complete combustion for a lean mixture, the ignition timing must be advanced. However, as previously stated, advanced timing increases emissions of HC and NO_x.

Spark Ignition Systems.   The general configuration of an ignition system consists of the following components: energy storage device, ignition timing mechanism, ignition triggering mechanism, spark distribution system, and spark plugs and high tension wires.

Inductive ignition systems use an ignition coil as the energy storage device. The coil also functions as a transformer, boosting the secondary ignition voltage. A typical turns-ratio of the primary to secondary winding is 1:100. Electrical energy is supplied to the coil's primary winding from the vehicle electrical system. Before the ignition point, the coil is charged during the dwell period to its interruption current. Open- or closed-loop dwell angle control ensures a sufficient interruption current even at high speeds. Sufficient ignition energy at the interruption current is ensured by an adequate coil design. At the ignition point, the primary current will be interrupted. The rapid change of the magnetic field induces the secondary voltage in the secondary winding. A distribution system assigns the high voltage to the corresponding spark plug. After exceeding the arcing over voltage at the spark plug, the coil will be discharged during the spark duration.

The ignition timing mechanism, ignition triggering mechanism, and the spark distribution system differ between ignition systems. Further discussion of these will occur within the discussion of each ignition system type.

The spark plugs provide the ignition energy via the high-tension wires to the air/fuel mixture in the cylinder to initiate combustion. The voltage required at the spark plug can be more than 30 kV. Because the spark plug extends into the combustion chamber, it is exposed to extreme temperature and pressure conditions. Spark plug design and materials are chosen to ensure long-term operation under tough operating conditions.

A typical spark plug consists of a pair of electrodes, called a center and ground electrode, separated by a gap. The size of the gap is important and is specified for each plug type and engine. The center electrode is electrically connected to the top terminal of the plug which is attached to the high-tension wire. The electrical energy travels through the high-tension wire to the top terminal and down to the center electrode. The ground electrode is part of the threaded portion of the spark plug that is installed in the cylinder head. The ground electrode is at electrical ground potential because the negative terminal of the battery is also connected to the engine. The spark is produced when the high-voltage pulse travels to the center electrode and jumps the gap to the ground electrode.

Ignition System Types.   Table 12.1 summarizes the various ignition systems used on SI engines.

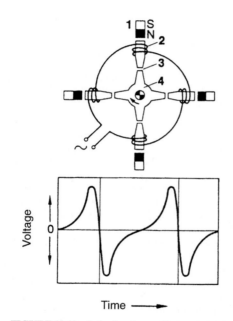

FIGURE 12.18   Induction-type pulse generator: permanent magnet (1), induction winding with core (2), variable air gap (3), trigger wheel (4).

Coil ignition.   Breaker-triggered coil ignition systems have been replaced by breakerless transistorized ignition systems and are no longer installed as original equipment.

On breakerless transistorized ignition systems, the contact breaker's function is replaced by a magnetic pulse generator. The pulse generator is installed in the distributor and turns with the distributor shaft. There are commonly two types of pulse generators: induction-type and Hall-type. Induction-type pulse generators consist of a stator and a trigger wheel (Fig. 12.18). The stator consists of a permanent magnet, inductive winding, and core, and remains fixed. The trigger wheel teeth correspond to the number of cylinders, and the trigger wheel turns with the distributor shaft. The operating principle is that as the air gap changes between the stator and the rotor, the magnetic flux changes. The change in magnetic flux induces an ac voltage in the inductive winding. The frequency and magnitude of the alternating current increases with increasing engine speed. The electronic control unit or trigger box uses this information to trigger the ignition timing.

TABLE 12.1   Overview of Various Ignition Systems

	Ignition designation				
Ignition function	Coil system	Transistorized coil system	Capacitor discharge system	Electronic system with distributor	Electronic distributorless system
Ignition triggering	Mechanical	Electronic	Electronic	Electronic	Electronic
Ignition timing	Mechanical	Mechanical	Electronic	Electronic	Electronic
High-voltage generation	Inductive	Inductive	Capacitive	Inductive	Inductive
Spark distribution to appropriate cylinder	Mechanical	Mechanical	Mechanical	Mechanical	Electronic

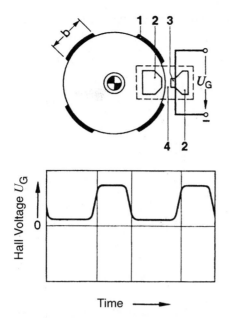

FIGURE 12.19 Hall-type pulse generator: vane (1), soft magnetic conductive elements (2), Hall IC (3), and air gap, UG-Hall sensor voltage (4).

Hall-type pulse generators utilize the Hall effect (Fig. 12.19). As the distributor shaft turns, the vanes of the rotor move through the air gap of the magnetic barrier. When the vane is not in front of the Hall IC, the sensor is subjected to a magnetic field. The magnetic flux density is high and thus the voltage U_G is at a maximum. As soon as the rotor vane enters the air gap, the magnetic flux runs through the vane area and is largely prevented from reaching the Hall layer. The voltage U_G is at a minimum. The resulting pulses switch the primary current off and on.

The distributor disburses the ignition pulses to the spark plugs via the high-tension wires in a specific sequence. It also adjusts the ignition timing by means of spark advance mechanisms. The distributor rotor is turned by the engine at one-half the crankshaft speed. The electrical energy is fed to the center of the rotor. While the rotor turns, the rotor electrode aligns with the outer electrodes that are connected to the high-tension wires. One outer electrode and high-tension wire connection exists for each cylinder. When alignment occurs between the center and outer electrode, the spark is distributed to that particular cylinder.

The spark advance mechanisms advance the ignition timing by rotating the distributor plate relative to the distributor shaft. The centrifugal advance increases the spark advance with increasing engine speed. The vacuum advance, using intake manifold vacuum, increases the spark advance at low engine speeds.

Capacitor discharge ignition system. The capacitive discharge system differs from the coil-type ignition systems previously discussed. Ignition energy is stored in the electrical field of a capacitor. Capacitance and charge voltage of the capacitor determine the amount of energy that is stored. The ignition transformer converts the primary voltage discharged from the capacitor to the required high voltage.

Electronic ignition—with distributor. Electronic ignition calculates the ignition timing electronically (Fig. 12.20). This replaces the function of the centrifugal advance and vacuum advance in the distributor discussed on the previous coil ignition systems. Because the ignition timing is not limited by mechanical devices, the optimal timing can be chosen for each engine operating point. Figure 12.21 is a comparison of an ignition map from a mechanical advance system and a map of an electronically optimized system. Also, additional influences such as engine knock detection can be used to modify the ignition timing. The engine speed input and crankshaft position input can be obtained from a sensor mounted near the crankshaft. Precision is improved over using the distributor-mounted trigger. This input is provided to the electronic control unit (ECU) along with the engine temperature and engine load. The ECU references data tables to determine the optimal spark advance for each engine operating condition. Additional corrections to the spark timing, such as for EGR usage or knock sensor detection, are made in the ECU.

Electronic ignition—distributorless. On distributorless ignition systems, the high voltage distribution is accomplished by using either single or double spark ignition coils. Ignition timing is determined by the ECU, as discussed for electronic ignition with distributor. For the double spark ignition coils, one coil exists for two corresponding cylinders. Two high-tension

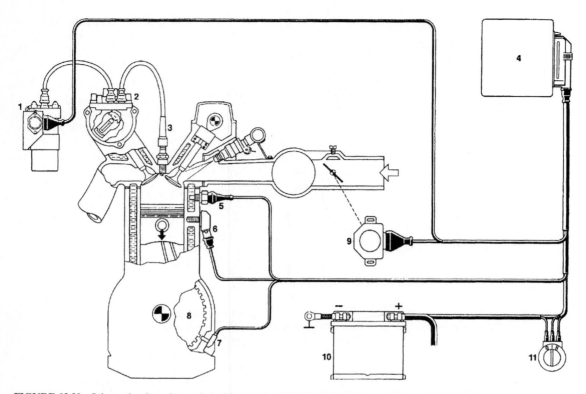

FIGURE 12.20 Schematic of an electronic ignition system with distributor: ignition coil (1), high-voltage distributor (2), spark plug (3), ECU (4), coolant temperature sensor (5), knock sensor (6), engine speed and crankshaft reference sensor (7), sensor wheel (8), throttle valve (9), battery (10), and ignition switch (11).

wires are routed from each coil to two cylinders, which are 360° out of phase. When the coil output stage is triggered via the ECU, a spark is delivered to both cylinders. One cylinder will be on the compression stroke, the other on the exhaust stroke. Because both cylinders are fired together, for a given crankshaft rotation, one will always be on the compression stroke and the other on the exhaust stroke. Therefore, there is no need to know which cylinder is compressing the ignitable mixture.

On single spark ignition coils, one coil exists for each cylinder. Each coil triggers only once during the four-stroke cycle. Because of this, it must be known which cylinder is on the compression stroke. Synchronization with the camshaft must occur. The information needed on camshaft position is supplied by a phase sensor mounted on the camshaft.

12.3 COMPRESSION IGNITION ENGINES

12.3.1 Engine Control Functions

Electronic engine controls are now being used on compression ignition (diesel) engines. These controls offer greater precision and control of fuel injection quantity and timing, engine speed, EGR, turbocharger boost pressure, and auxiliary starting devices. The following inputs

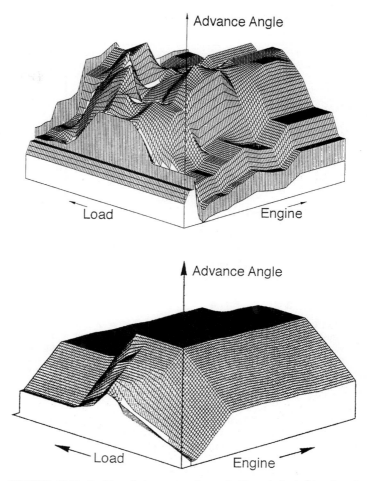

FIGURE 12.21 Ignition timing maps: electronically optimized (*above*) and mechanical advance system (*below*).

are used to provide the ECU with information on current engine operating conditions: engine speed; accelerator position; engine coolant, fuel, and inlet air temperatures; turbocharger boost pressure, vehicle speed, control rack, or control collar position (for control of fuel quantity); and amospheric pressure. Figure 12.22 is a schematic of an electronic engine control system on an in-line diesel fuel injection pump application.

Fuel Quantity and Timing. The fuel quantity alone controls a compression ignition engine's speed and load. The intake air is not throttled as in a spark ignition engine. The quantity of fuel to be delivered is changed by increasing or decreasing the length of fuel delivery time per injection. On the injection pump, the delivery time is controlled by the position of the control rack on in-line pumps and the position of the control collar on distributor-type pumps. An ECU-controlled actuator is used to move the control rack or the collar to increase or decrease the fuel delivery time. The ECU determines the correct length of delivery time (expressed as a function of control rack or collar position) using performance maps based on engine speed and calculated fuel quantity. Corrections and/or limitations as functions of

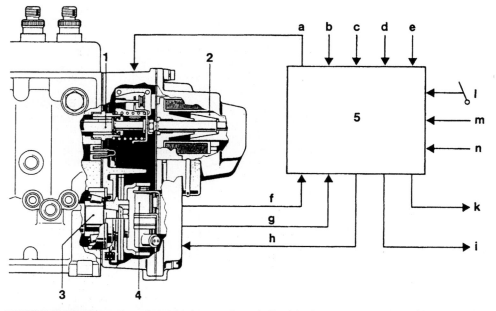

FIGURE 12.22   Electronic engine control system for an in-line injection pump: control rack (1), actuator (2), camshaft (3), engine speed sensor (4), ECU (5). Input/output: redundant fuel shutoff (a), boost pressure (b), vehicle speed (c), temperature—water, air, fuel (d), intervention in injection fuel quantity (e), speed (f), control rack position (g), solenoid position (h), fuel consumption and engine speed display (i), system diagnosis information (k), accelerator position (l), preset speed (m), and clutch, brakes, engine brake (n).

engine speed, temperature, and turbocharger boost pressure are used to modify the delivery time. In addition, the control rack or collar actuator contains a position sensor that provides feedback to the ECU on controller position. If the requested position differs from the commanded position, the ECU continues to move the controller via the actuator until the commanded and actual position are the same.

The start of injection time of the fuel at the cylinder is a function of the wave propagation speed (i.e., the speed of sound) of the fuel from the fuel injection pump to the injector. Because this time remains a constant, at increasing engine speed the delivery of fuel at the cylinder would be delayed with reference to crankshaft angle. Therefore, the timing at the injection pump must be advanced with increasing engine speed so that the start of injection occurs at the same crankshaft angle at higher engine speeds. Selection of injection timing has a large impact on exhaust emissions and engine noise. Delaying the start of injection reduces NO_x emissions, but excessive delay increases HCs in the exhaust. A 1° deviation in injection timing can increase NO_x emissions by 5 percent and HC emissions by as much as 15 percent. Therefore, precise control of the start of injection is essential.

Although many systems use mechanical devices to control injection timing, electronic control of injection timing is being used on some pump types. The advantage of electronic control is that a sophisticated timing data map can be used that provides the best injection timing for exhaust emissions under various operating conditions. On electronic control systems, the start of injection is monitored at the injector nozzle by a needle-motion sensor. The ECU uses this information to determine and control the injection timing. The timing is then modified by control of a pulse-width modulated solenoid valve. The valve varies the pressure exerted on the spring-loaded timing device plunger. The plunger rotates the pump's collar ring (for distributor type pumps) in the opposite direction of the pump's rotation which advances the timing.

Speed Control.   As was mentioned previously, for a CI engine, fuel quantity alone controls the engine's speed and load. Therefore, presuming adequate injected fuel quantity, an unloaded CI engine can speed up out of control and destroy itself. Because of this, a governor is required to limit the engine's maximum speed. In addition, governors are also used for low idle and cruise control to maintain a constant engine or vehicle speed and meter the correct fuel for cold-starting. Fuel is also controlled as a function of speed and boost pressure to limit smoke levels, engine torque, and exhaust gas temperatures. On an electronically controlled CI engine, the governor's functions are controlled by the fuel delivery system described previously. Engine speed is provided by an RPM sensor that monitors the periods of angular segments between the reference marks on the engine's flywheel or in the in-line injection pump.

EGR Control.   Rerouting of exhaust gases into the intake air stream is known as exhaust gas recirculation (EGR). EGR reduces the amount of oxygen in the fresh intake charge while increasing its specific heat. This lowers combustion temperatures and results in lower NO_x emissions. However, excessive amounts of EGR result in higher emissions of soot (particulates), CO, and HCs all due to insufficient air. Also, the introduction of EGR can have an adverse affect on driveability during cold-engine operation, full-load operation, and at idle. It is best, therefore, to control the EGR valve with the ECU. Both pneumatically controlled and solenoid-controlled EGR valves are in use. The ECU determines when and how much EGR will occur based on engine temperature and accelerator position.

Turbocharger Boost Pressure Control.   Engines that have turbochargers benefit significantly from electronic boost pressure control. If only a pneumatic-mechanical wastegate is used, only one boost pressure point for the entire operating range is used to divert the exhaust gas away from the turbine side of the turbocharger. This creates a compromise for part-load conditions because all the exhaust gases must pass the turbine. The result is increased exhaust backpressure, more turbocharger work, more residual exhaust gas in the cylinders, and higher charge air temperatures.

By controlling the wastegate with a pulse-width-modulated solenoid valve, the wastegate can be opened at different pressures depending on the engine operating conditions. Therefore, only the level of air charge pressure required is developed. The electronic control unit uses information on engine speed and accelerator position to reference a data table and the proper boost pressure (actually, duty cycle of the control valve) is determined. On systems using intake manifold pressure sensors, a closed-loop control system can be developed to compare the specified value with the measured value.

Glow Plug Control.   Electronic control of the glow plug duration can be handled by the ECU or a separate control unit. Input for determining glow time is from an engine coolant temperature sensor. At the end of the specified glow period, the controller turns out the start indicator light to signal the driver that the engine can be started. The glow plugs remain energized while the starter is engaged. An engine load monitor is used to switch off the glow process after start. To limit the loads on the battery and the glow plugs, a safety override is also used.

12.3.2 Fuel Delivery Systems

The diesel fuel delivery system comprises a low- and high-pressure side. On the low-pressure side is the fuel tank, fuel filter, fuel supply pump, overflow valve, and fuel supply lines. The high-pressure side is initiated in the plunger and barrel assembly and continues through the delivery valve, high-pressure injection lines, and injection nozzle.

The fuel injection pump must deliver fuel at a pressure between 350 and 1200 bar, depending on the engine's combustion configuration. The quantity and timing of injection must be precisely controlled to achieve good mixture quality and to minimize exhaust emissions.

Fuel Injection Process.   An engine-driven camshaft (in-line pump) or cam plate (distributor pump) drives the injection pump's plunger in the supply direction, creating pressure in the high-pressure gallery. The delivery valve responds to the increase in pressure by opening. This sends a pressure wave to the injection nozzle at the speed of sound. The needle valve in the nozzle overcomes the spring force of the injection nozzle spring and lifts from its seat when the opening pressure is reached. Fuel is then injected from the spray orifices into the engine's combustion chamber. The injection process ends with the opening of the spill port in the plunger and barrel assembly. This causes the pressure in the pump chamber to collapse, which then causes the delivery valve to close. Due to the action of the delivery valve relief collar, the pressure in the injection line is reduced to the "stand-by pressure." The stand-by pressure is determined to ensure that the injector nozzle closes quickly to eliminate fuel dribble, and the residual pressure waves in the lines prevent the nozzles from reopening.

ABOUT THE AUTHORS

GARY C. HIRSCHLIEB is chief engineer, engine management systems, for the Robert Bosch Corp. He previously held various engineering and sales responsibilities with Bosch. In his earlier career, he worked as a senior engineer in powertrain development for Ford tractor operations, and as a sales engineer with GTE, and as an engineer in plant engineering for GM Truck and Coach.

GOTTFRIED SCHILLER is engineering manager, engine management systems, for Robert Bosch Corp. His previous positions with Bosch included applications engineering, engine management systems; application engineer, diesel systems; and development engineer, diesel products.

SHARI STOTTLER is now a self-employed technical writer, but, until 1993, she was a senior application engineer with Robert Bosch Corp. Prior to that she had been an engineering project coordinator for Honda of North America, Manufacturing, and a product engineer with General Motors Corp.

CHAPTER 13
TRANSMISSION CONTROL

Kurt Neuffer, Wolfgang Bullmer, and Werner Brehm
Robert Bosch GmbH

13.1 INTRODUCTION

In North America and Japan, 80 to 90 percent of all passenger cars sold have automatic transmissions (ATs), but in Europe only 10 to 15 percent of passenger cars sold have ATs. There are two main reasons for the difference. In Europe, drivers tend to view ATs, compared to manual transmissions, as detrimental to driveability and responsible for a somewhat higher fuel consumption. But implementation of electronic control concepts has invalidated both of those arguments.

Since the introduction of electronic transmission controls units (TCUs) in the early 1980s by Renault and BMW (together with a four-speed transmission from Zahnradfabrik Friedrichshafen, or ZF), the acceptance of the AT rose steeply, even in Europe. For this reason, all new ATs are designed with electronic control. The market for ATs is divided into stepped and continuously variable transmissions (CVTs). For both types the driver gets many advantages. In stepped transmissions, the smooth shifts can be optimized by the reduction of engine torque during gear shift, combined with the correctly matched oil pressure for the friction elements (clutches, brake bands). The reduction of shift shocks to a very low or even to an unnoticeable level has allowed the design of five-speed ATs where a slightly higher number of gear shifts occur. In today's standard systems, the driver can choose between sport and economic drive programs by operating a selector switch. In highly sophisticated newer systems, the selection can be replaced by the self-adaptation of shift strategies. This leads not only to better driveability but also to a significant reduction in fuel consumption. Additionally, a well-matched electronic control of the torque converter lockup helps to improve the yield of the overall system. Both automotive and transmission manufacturers benefit from the reduced expense resulting from the application of different car/engine combinations. Different shift characteristics are easy to implement in software, and much adaptation can be achieved by data change, leaving the transmission hardware and TCU unchanged. The reduction of power losses in friction elements increases the life expectancy and enables the optimization of transmission hardware design.

With the CVT, one of the biggest obstacles to the potential reduction in fuel consumption by operating the engine at its optimal working point is the power loss from the transmission's oil pump. Only with electronic control is it possible to achieve the required yield by matching the oil mass-stream and oil pressure for the pulleys to the actual working conditions.

To guarantee the overall economic solution for an electronically controlled transmission, either stepped or CVT, the availability of precision electrohydraulic actuators is imperative.

13.2 *SYSTEM COMPONENTS*

The components of an electronic transmission control system are a transmission which is adapted to the electronic control requirements and an electronic control unit with corresponding inputs and outputs and attached sensor elements.

13.2.1 Transmission

The greatest share of electronically controlled transmissions currently on the market consists of four- or five-speed units with a torque converter lockup clutch, commanded by the control unit. Market share for five-speed transmissions is continuously increasing. With electronically controlled transmissions there are numerous possibilities to substitute mechanical and hydraulic components with electromechanical or electrohydraulic components. One basic method is to substitute only the shift point control. In a conventional pure hydraulic AT, the gear shifts are carried out by mechanical and hydraulic components. These are controlled by a centrifugal governor that detects the vehicle speed, and a wire cable connected to the throttle plate lever. With an electronic shift point control, on the other hand, an electronic control unit detects and controls the relevant components. In the transmission's hydraulic control unit, mechanical and hydraulic components are replaced by electrohydraulic controlling elements, usually in the form of electrohydraulic on/off solenoids. This way the number of solenoids, as well as the control logic, can be varied over a wide range. For example, for each gear, one specific solenoid can operate the relevant clutch for this gear shift. Alternatively, there can be one solenoid for each gear change, which is switched corresponding to the shift command. In this way, only three solenoids are required in a four-speed transmission. In some current designs, the gears are controlled by a logical combination of solenoid states. This design needs only two gear-controlling solenoids for a four-speed transmission. For five-speed applications, accordingly, three solenoids are required (Table 13.1)

TABLE 13.1 Example of a Gear-Solenoid Combination for a Five-Speed Transmission Application

	Solenoid 1	Solenoid 2	Solenoid 3
1st gear	on	on	on
2nd gear	on	on	off
3rd gear	on	off	off
4th gear	off	off	off
5th gear	off	on	off

The hydraulic pressure is controlled in this basic application by a hydraulic proportional valve which is, in turn, controlled by a wire cable connected to the throttle plate lever. With this design, the shift points can be determined by the electronic TCU, resulting in a wide range of freely selectable driving behaviors regarding the shift points. It is also possible to use different shift maps according to switch or sensor signals. The influence on driving comfort during gear shifting in this electronic transmission control application has important restrictions. The only possible way to control shift smoothness is with an interface to the electronic engine management. This way, the engine output torque is influenced during gear shifting. A systematic wide-range control of the hydraulic pressure during and after the gear shift necessitates the replacement of the hydraulic pressure governor with an electronically controlled hydraulic solenoid. This design allows the use of either a pulse-width-modulated (PWM) solenoid or a pressure regulator. The choice of which type of pressure control solenoid to use results from the requirements concerning shift comfort under all driving conditions. For present-day designs with high requirements for shift comfort during the entire life of the transmission, at all temperatures, and with varying oil quality, the analog pressure control solenoid is superior to the usual PWM solenoid, providing there is no pressure sensor in operation as a guideline for pressure regulation. This application usually uses one central controlling element in the transmission for the pressure regulation to control the shift quality.

In other transmission developments, the shift quality is further increased using electronically controllable brake elements (brake bands) for some specific gear changes. In this case, the flywheel effect of the revolving elements is limited by an electronic control of a brake band according to an algorithm or special timing conditions.

The most sophisticated transmission application to date is so designed that overrunning clutches are eliminated and gear changes are exclusively controlled by the electronic control unit with pressure regulator solenoids.[1] This application is characterized by extremely high demands on the electronic TCU concerning real-time behavior and data handling. The relationship between weight, transmission outline, and transferrable torque has reached a high level. Compared to transmissions with overrun clutches, the necessary fitting dimensions are reduced.

Present electronically controlled ATs usually have an electronically commanded torque converter clutch, which can lock up the torque converter between the engine output and the transmission input. The torque converter clutch is activated under certain driving conditions by a solenoid controlled by the electronic TCU. The solenoid design, depending on the requirements of TCC functions and shift comfort, can either be an on/off solenoid, a PWM solenoid, or a pressure regulator. Locking up the torque converter eliminates the slip of the converter, and the efficiency of the transmission system is increased. This results in an even lower fuel consumption for cars equipped with AT.

13.2.2   Electronic Control Unit

Another important component in electronic transmission control is the electronic control unit, which is designed according to the requirements of the transmission and the car environments. The electronic control unit can be divided into two main parts: the hardware and the corresponding software.

Hardware.   The hardware of the electronic control unit consists of the housing, the plug, the carrier for the electronic devices, and the devices themselves. The housing, according to the requirements, is available as an unsealed design for applications inside the passenger compartment or within the luggage compartment. It is also possible to have sealed variants for mounting conditions inside the engine compartment or at the bulkhead. The materials for the housing can be either various plastics or metals. There are many different nonstandardized housings on the market. The various outlines and plug configurations differ, depending upon the manufacturer of the electronic unit. The plug configuration, i.e., the number of pins and the shape, depends on the functions and the requirements of the automotive manufacturer. The number of pins is usually less than 100. Some control unit manufacturers try to standardize their plugs and housings throughout all their electronic control units, such as engine management, ABS, traction control, and others. This is important to simplify and to standardize the unit production and the tests during manufacturing.

The carrier for the electronic devices is usually a conventional printed circuit board (PCB). The number of layers on the PCB depends on the application. For units with a complex device structure and high demands for electromagnetic compatibility, multilayer applications are in use. In special cases, it is possible to use ceramics as a carrier. There are usually some parts of the electronic circuit, resistors for example, designed as a thick-film circuit on the hybrid. In this case the electronic unit is manufactured as a solder hybrid or as a bond hybrid with direct-bonded integrated circuit devices. Some single applications exist with a flex-foil as a carrier for the electronic devices. These applications are limited to very special requirements.

The transmission control area requires some specially designed electronic devices, in particular, the output stages for the actuators of pressure regulation and torque converter clutch control. These actuators for pressure control have extremely high demands regarding accuracy of the actuator current over the whole temperature range and under all conditions independent of battery voltage and over the entire lifetime. There are some known applications of customer-specific integrated circuits or devices. Here, special attention paid to quality and reliability over the entire lifetime is necessary to meet the continuously increasing quality requirements of the automotive market. Currently, there is an increasing spread of surface-mounted devices in transmission control applications. This is why the unit size is continuously decreasing despite an increasing number of functions.

On the functional side, the hardware configuration can be divided into power supply, input signal transfer circuits, output stages, and microcontroller, including peripheral components and monitoring and safety circuits (Fig. 13.1). The power supply converts the vehicle battery voltage into a constant voltage required by the electronic devices inside the control unit. Accordingly, special attention must be paid to the protection of the internal devices against destruction by transients from the vehicle electrical system such as load dump, reverse battery polarity, and voltage peaks. Particular attention is also necessary in the design of the elec-

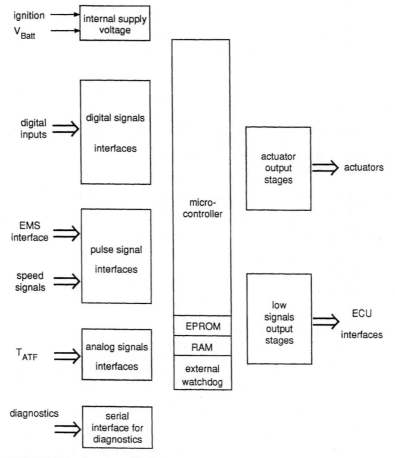

FIGURE 13.1 Overview of hardware parts.

tronic ground concept for the control unit, especially where the electromagnetic compatibility and RF interference is concerned. This is very important to prevent undesired gear shifting that may be troublesome for drivers. One part of the input circuit is the preparation of the digital signals, such as position switch, program selector, and kickdown switch. A second part is the transfer of the analog signals like ATF temperature and voltages according to potentiometer states. The third part is the interface to other electronic control units, especially to the engine management system. Here the single signal lines between the control units will be increasingly substituted by bus systems like CAN. The fourth part is the preparation of the transmission-specific signals from the speed sensors inside the transmission.

The calculators inside the control units are usually microcontrollers. The real-time requirements and the directly addressable program storage size of the selected microcontrollers are determined by the functions of the transmission control and the car environment. In present applications, either 8-bit or 16-bit microcontrollers are in use. There are systems with 32-bit microcontrollers in development for new, highly sophisticated control systems with increasing functional and extreme real-time requirements originating from the transmission concept. The memory devices for program and data are usually EPROMS. Their storage capacity is, in present applications, up to 64 Kbytes. Future applications will necessitate storage sizes up to 128 Kbytes. The failure storages for diagnostics and the storage for adaptive data are in conventional applications, battery voltage-supplied RAMs. These are increasingly being replaced by EEPROMs.

There are usually watchdog circuits in various configurations in use regarding safety and monitoring. These can be either a second, low-performance microcontroller, a customer-specific circuit, or a circuit with common available devices. The output stages can be divided into high-power stages for the transmission actuator control and low-power stages like lamp drivers or interfaces to other electronic control units. The low-power output stages are mostly conventional output drivers either in single or in multiple applications, which are mainly protected against short circuits and voltage overloads.

For the transmission solenoid control, special output stages are necessary, and they are specialized for operation with inductive actuators. The pressure regulation during shifting in some applications requires high accuracy and current-regulated output stages are needed. These are mainly designed as customer-specific devices. The type and number of solenoid output stages depend on the control philosophy of the transmission: they are generally of a special design for specific transmission applications. During the preparation of the speed sensor signals, attention must be paid to the electromagnetic compatibility and radio frequency interference conditions.

Software.   The software within the electronic transmission control system is gaining increasing importance due to the increasing number of functions which, in turn, requires increasing software volume. The software for the control unit can be divided into two parts: the program and the data. The program structure is defined by the functions. The data are specific for the relevant program parts and have to be fixed during the calibration stage. The most difficult software requirements result from the real-time conditions coming from the transmission design. This is also the main criterion for the selection of the microcontroller (Fig. 13.2).

The program is generally made up in several parts:

- Software according to the special microcontroller hardware; e.g., I/O preparation and filter, driver functions, initialization of the microcontroller and the control unit, internal services for the controller peripheral devices, and internal software services like operating systems.

- Software coming from the defined functions, originating from specific transmission and car functions.

- Parts concerning safety functions like output switch-off, substitute values for the input signals, and safety states of the microcontroller environment in case of failures. Depending on the requirements, there can be a software watchdog or a hardware-configured watchdog circuit in use. The watchdog instruction is also part of the security software.

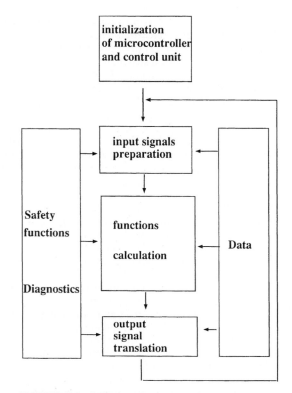

FIGURE 13.2   Software structure overview.

- Diagnostic and communication software for the self-test of the control unit and also the test of the control unit environment.

These functions are related to the defined functions of the electronic control system. Parts of the software component are usually the output stages monitoring, the input monitoring, and the diagnosis of the microcontroller environment. Failure handling and storage is gaining importance as system complexity increases. These diagnostic functions are also very useful for the service station to determine the reason for eventual problems. Part of these functions is reserved for the communication software needed for the test equipment to read the failures stored during car service. Current protocols are standardized communication protocols like ISO 9141. There is an increasing share of bus systems for communication with other electronic control units, using standardized protocols like CAN, VAN, or J1850. These bus systems allow an increasing unit function by changing software when other control units are added to the bus.

Most software models are written directly in an assembler to meet the real-time requirements and because there is a limited memory size in common mass production units. The number of powerful, cost-effective microcontrollers is continuously increasing. The availability of memory components with larger storage sizes suitable for automotive use is also rising, making it possible to use a higher programming language in future developments. This allows an ingenious structure of software models and an application of operating systems. This can be followed by an effective distribution of functions during and outside gear shifting with related time requirements and event management. This type of program structure improves the function of the electronic TCU because of the accelerated handling of time-critical functions during gear shifting.

The second software part, data, can be divided into fixed data, which is related to fixed attributes of the system; e.g., the number of actuators, and calibration data for system tuning. The calibration data can be adapted to changing parameters of the system such as the engine, vehicle, and transmission characteristics. The fixing of calibration data takes place during the tuning stage of the vehicle and has to be redetermined for each type of vehicle and transmission. With some applications, the calibration data are added to a basic program during the vehicle production according to different types of cars by the so-called end-of-line programming. This means that the units can be programmed with the calibration data with closed housings by a special interface. The share of software development in relation to the total development time is increasing continuously. The requirements for real-time behavior and memory size are rising in accordance with the considerably increasing demands for shift comfort and self-learning functions. This requires an ingenious structure of the software and an event-related distribution of software models, especially during gear shifting. The rising software complexity with simultaneously increasing quality requirements causes higher demands for software quality control.

13.2.3 Actuators

Electrohydraulic actuators are important components of the electronic transmission control systems.[2] Continuously operating actuators are used to modulate pressure, while switching actuators function as supply and discharge valves for shift-point control. Figure 13.3 provides a basic overview of these types of solenoids.

Important qualities for the use of actuators in ATs are low hydraulic resistance to achieve high flow rates, operation temperature range from −40 to +150 °C, small power loss, minimized heat dissipation in the ECU's output stages, small size and low weight, highest reliability in heavily contaminated oils, maximum accuracy and repeatability over lifetime, short reaction times, pressure range up to 2000 kPa, maximum vibration acceleration of 300 m/s^2, and high number of switch operations.

A very important aspect is that the hardware and software of the ECU be developed, taking into account the electrical specifications of the solenoid to obtain an optimized complete system concerning performance and cost.[6,7] For further details in design and application, refer to Sec. 10.3.5.

It should be noted that these characteristics can be varied over a wide range and that many other types of solenoids exist or are in development for the special requirements of new applications.

13.3 SYSTEM FUNCTIONS

Functions can be designated at systems functions if the individual components of the total electronic transmission control system cooperate efficiently to provide a desired behavior of the transmission and the vehicle. There are different stages of functionality which have different effects on driving behavior and shift characteristics (Fig. 13.4). In general, there is an increasing complexity of the system relating to all components to improve the translation of driver behavior into transmission action. That means that the expense of actuators, sensors, and links to other control units is increasing, as is the expense of the TCU software and hardware in the case of high-level requirements regarding driveability and shift comfort. Figure 13.4 shows three main areas. These will be discussed in detail in the following material.

13.3.1 Basic Functions

The basic functions of the transmission control are the shift point control, the lockup control, engine torque control during shifting, related safety functions, and diagnostic functions for

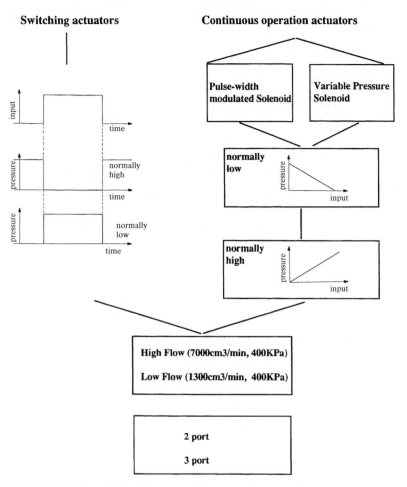

FIGURE 13.3 Electrohydraulic actuators for automatic transmissions.

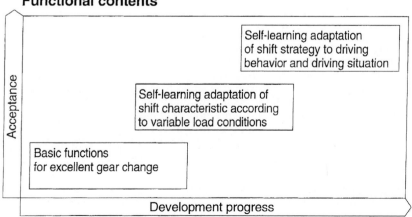

FIGURE 13.4 Relationship between driving characteristic and function complexity.

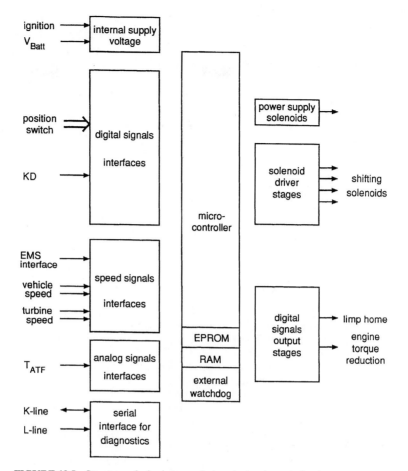

FIGURE 13.5 Structure of a basic transmission electronic control unit.

vehicle service. The pressure control in transmission systems with electrical operating possibilities for the pressure during and outside shifting can also be considered as a basic function. Figure 13.5 shows the necessary inputs and outputs as well as the block diagram of an electronic TCU suitable for the basic functions.

Shift Point Control. The basic shift point control uses shift maps, which are defined in data in the unit memory. These shift maps are selectable over a wide range. The shift point limitations are made, on the one hand, by the highest admissible engine speed for each application and, on the other hand, by the lowest engine speed that is practical for driving comfort and noise emission. The inputs of the shift point determination are the throttle position, the accelerator pedal position, and the vehicle speed (determined by the transmission output speed). Figure 13.6 shows a typical shift map application of a four-speed transmission.

To prevent overly frequent shifting between two gears, a hysteresis between the upshift and the downshift characteristic is incorporated. The hysteresis is determined by the desired shifting habit of the transmission and, alternatively, the car behavior. In the event that the particular shift characteristic is crossed by one of either of the two input valves, the electronic ECU releases the shift by activating the related actuators. This can be a direct shift into the

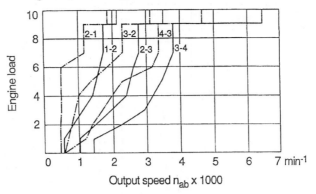

FIGURE 13.6 Shift characteristics of a four-speed application.

target gear or by a serial activation of specific actuators in a fixed sequence to the target gear, depending on the transmission hardware design.

Lockup Control/Torque Converter Clutch.[8] The torque converter clutch connects both functional components of the hydraulic converter, the pump and the turbine. The lockup of the clutch reduces the power losses coming from the torque converter slip. This is a permanent slip because it is necessary in principle to have a slip between the pumpwheel and the turbine to translate torque from the engine output to the transmission input. To increase the efficiency of the lockup, it is necessary to close the clutch as often as possible. On the other hand, the torque converter is an important component to prevent vibrations of the powertrain. The activation of the lockup is, therefore, a compromise between low fuel consumption and high driving comfort. The shift points of the lockup are determined in the same way as the determination of the shift point in the gear shift point control. Usually there is one separate characteristic curve for the lockup for each gear. To prevent powertrain vibrations, it is advisable to open the lockup during coasting to use the damping effect of the torque converter. In the case of a high positive gradient of the accelerator pedal with low engine speed, the converter clutch has to open to use the torque gain of the converter for better acceleration of the car. In some applications, the lockup is opened during shifting for improved shift comfort. After shifting, the lockup can be closed again. When driving in first gear, the lockup is usually open, because the time spent in first gear is usually very low and, therefore, the frequency of lockup shifting versus gear shifting becomes very high. This may result in decreased driving comfort. A second reason is the improved acceleration of the car in first gear when using the converter gain for wheel torque.

Engine Torque Control During Shifting.[8] The engine torque control requires an interface to an electronic engine management system. The target of the engine torque control, torque reduction during shifting, is to support the synchronization of the transmission and to prevent shift shocks.

In conventional applications, the engine torque reduction originates from an ignition angle control. The timing and absolute value of the ignition control depends on the operating conditions concerning actual engine torque and shifting type.

Upshift. The upshift occurs without an interruption of the tractive power. The engine torque reduction may be activated if the clutch of the target gear stays with the translation of torque. The beginning of the engine torque reduction is determined by the course of engine or transmission input speed. There it is important to detect a decreasing speed. The start of the torque reduction is characterized by a specific speed difference. The end of the torque reduction is activated at an applicable speed lead before reaching the synchronous speed of the new gear.

The power losses, which have to be picked up by the clutches, are dependent on the engine torque and the slipping time

$$Q = f \times (M_{eng} \times t_s + Q_{kin})$$ (13.1)

where Q = power losses
M_{eng} = engine torque
t_s = slipping time
Q_{kin} = kinetic energy of revolving elements

It is possible to reduce the temperature stress to the clutches by reducing the engine torque and, consequently, by increasing the slipping time at a fixed possible maximum power loss Q [Eq. (13.1)]. Figure 13.7 shows a typical upshift characteristic.

Shift Quality Comparison

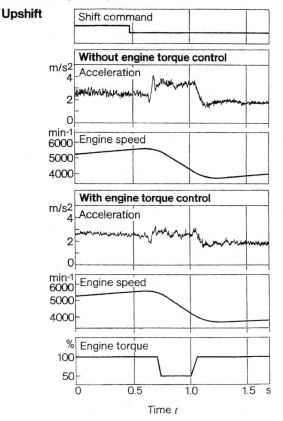

FIGURE 13.7   Timing of engine torque reduction during upshift.

Downshift.   Downshift under driving conditions results in a short interruption of the tractive power. At the synchronous point, the tractive power is in operation. The higher revolving energy, on the other hand, results in undesired vibrations of the powertrain. To prevent such vibrations, it is necessary to reduce the engine output torque before reaching the synchronous point of the new gear. When the transmission input speed reaches the synchronous speed of the new gear, the engine torque has to increase to the nominal value. The increase is usually applied as a torque ramp. Figure 13.8 shows a typical characteristic of a downshift. The values and timing of the engine torque reduction are generally part of the special calibration data for each combination of vehicle, engine, and transmission.

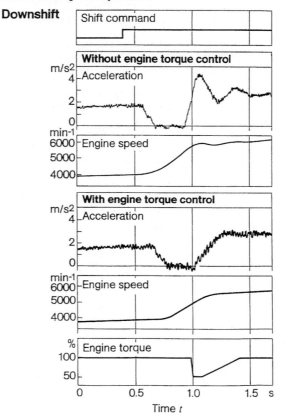

FIGURE 13.8   Timing of engine torque reduction during downshift.

Pressure Control.[8]   The timing and absolute values of the pressure, which is responsible for the torque translation of the friction elements, is, aside from the engine torque reduction, the most important influence to shift comfort. The electronic TCU offers additional possibilities for better function than a conventional hydraulic system.

The pressure values during and outside shifting can be calculated by different algorithms or can be determined by characteristic maps. The inputs for a pressure calculation are engine torque, transmission input speed, turbine torque, throttle position, and so on. The inputs depend on the special signal availability in different systems as well as the requirement concerning shift comfort. The variable pressure components are usually added to a constant pressure value according to the different transmission designs. Equation (13.2) gives a typical algorithm for a pressure calculation.

$$P_{\text{mod}} = P_{\text{const}} + k_n \times P_n + k_{\text{tor}} \times P_{\text{tor}} + k_s \times P_s \qquad (13.2)$$

where P_{mod} = pressure
  P_{const} = constant pressure value
  k_n = adaptation factor for input speed
  P_n = pressure component dependent on the revolution signal
  k_{tor} = adaptation factor for engine torque
  P_{tor} = pressure component dependent on torque
  k_s = adaptation factor for vehicle speed
  P_s = pressure component dependent on vehicle speed

During applications, the factors must be defined in the calibration phase. In general, the determination of these factors requires many vehicle tests, because the dynamic characteristic of the total system has an important influence on shift comfort. Another possibility for the pressure determination is to use characteristic maps which have to be defined during the calibration phase. This kind of pressure determination allows an improved selection of the optimum pressure at various extreme points independent of an algorithm.

Safety and Diagnostic Functions.   The functions, which are usually known as diagnostic functions of the electronic TCU, can be divided into real safety functions to prevent critical driving conditions and diagnostic functions which affect an increasing availability of the car and a better failure detection for servicing. The boundary between safety and diagnostic functions depends on the philosophy of the automotive manufacturer. In the category of real safety functions belong all security functions that prevent uncontrollable shifting, especially unintended downshifting. One section is the monitoring of the microcontroller and its related peripheral devices. The monitoring of the transmission, like gear ratio detection, is also a part of this functional block, as are the actuator and speed sensor monitoring. The microcontroller monitor is usually a watchdog circuit. One possibility is to use the controller internal watchdog. In common applications, it is necessary to use an external watchdog circuit for safety reasons. This can be done with a second, low-performance microcontroller or by a separate hardware watchdog designed as an ASIC or as a conventional circuit device. Usually there is a safety logic circuit connected to the watchdog, which, in the case of a microcontroller breakdown, activates the failure signal and switches the outputs for the transmission actuators to a safety condition.

For the detection of the watchdog, it is necessary to test the watchdog function after each power-on during the electronic initialization. The monitoring of the controller peripheral components, in general EPROM, RAM, and chip-select circuits, works continuously with specific algorithms; e.g., by writing fixed data values to the storage cells and following comparison with the read value or by checksum comparison with fixed sum values. The actuator monitoring includes detection of short circuit to supply voltage and ground, as well as open-load conditions.

In case of actuator malfunction, the limp home mode is selected. This means that the transmission runs in a fixed, safe gear, depending on the driving conditions. The safe state of the actuators is the noncurrent condition, which is secured by the electronic control unit. The control unit can put the output stages into the noncurrent stage separate for each output or by a common supply switch, usually a relay or a transistor. There are some applications that use a combination of both the watchdog and safety circuits.

The monitoring of the transmission-specific sensors, such as input speed, output speed, and oil temperature, works as a plausability check. For example the transmission input speed can be calculated as a combination of the transmission output speed and the gear ratio. In case of a detected speed sensor malfunction, the limp home mode is generally required. With a temperature sensor failure, the TCU usually works with a substitute value.

The diagnostic functions, which facilitate the finding of failures in the service station, contain the failure storage and the communication to the service tester, which allow the stored failures of the electronic TCU to be read. The communication between the control unit and the service tester is mainly car manufacturer-specific and must be defined by the car manufacturer before going into series production. The communication runs on a bidirectional, separate communication link.

The failure storage takes place in a nonvolatile memory device; e.g., in a permanent supplied RAM or in an EEPROM. It is also possible to store sporadic failures to detect such problems during the next service. The failure codes, number of stored failures, the handling of the failure storage, as well as the reaction of the TCU in case of a particular failure, is manufacturer-specific and is part of the unit specification. The real safety functions are part of the basic functions of an electronic TCU. The diagnostic functions concerning service tester and communication protocols are, over a wide range, manufacturer-specific. These range from a simple blink code up to a real self-test of the electronic unit, including all peripheral components.

13.3.2 Improvement of Shift Control

In a second development stage, the basic functions can be revised by a modification of the software functions and by adding new parts to the basic functions. This action results in a significant enhancement of the driving and shifting comfort. By a revision of the basic safety and diagnostic functions with so-called substitute functions, it is possible to increase the availability of the vehicle with AT as well as the driveability in case of a malfunction.

Shift Point Control. The basic function can be improved significantly by adding a software function, the so-called adaptive shift point control.[8] This function requires only signals which are available in an electronic TCU with basic functions. The adaptive shift point control is able to prevent an often-criticized attribute, the tendency for shift hunting especially when hill climbing and under heavy load conditions.

The adaptive function calculates the vehicle acceleration from the transmission output speed over time. The value of the actual acceleration in relation to a set value of the acceleration is the input for the shift point correction. The set value is given by the traction resistance characteristic. For a certain difference between set and actual value, the adaptation of the shift point occurs. The dimension of the shift point correction can be determined by calibration data and depends in general also on the actual vehicle speed and the engine load.

The shift point correction leads to higher hysteresis between upshift and downshift characteristics. With a high difference between set and actual values, it is also possible to forbid certain gears. The return to the basic shift point control is organized by software and can be fixed by calibration data. Usually, in the case of power-on, the adaptive shift point control is reset (Figs. 13.9 and 13.10).

In addition to these functions, different shift maps can be implemented into the data field of the TCU. For example, it is possible to have one shift map for low fuel consumption, which has shift points in the range of the best efficiency of the engine, and additionally to have another map for power operation, where the shift points are placed at points of highest engine output power. The character and number of different shift maps can be selected over a wide range. The choice of the different shift maps can be done by a selector push button or switch commanded by the driver. In further applications, the changing of the different shift programs is possible by self-learning strategies. It is also possible to implement a manual program in which fixed gears are specific to predetermined positions of the selector lever.

Lockup Control. There are some additional functions which can improve considerably the shift comfort of the lockup. In a first step, it is possible to replace the on/off control of the lockup actuator by a pulse control during opening and closing. This can be achieved using conventional hardware only by a software modification. In a further step, the on/off solenoid is replaced by a pressure regulator or a PWM solenoid.

By coordinating intelligent control strategies and corresponding output stages within the electronic TCU, a considerable improvement of the shift behavior of the lockup results. Here

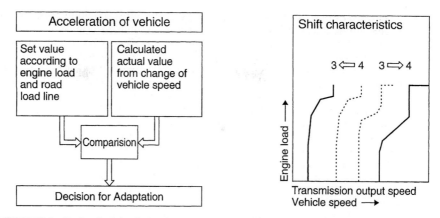

FIGURE 13.9   Basic principle of adaptive shift point control.

FIGURE 13.10   Shift characteristics before (- - -) and after (—) adaptation.

it is possible to close the lockup at low engine speed and low engine load with good shift comfort, resulting in decreased fuel consumption.

Engine Torque Reduction During Gear Shifting.   By an improved interface design to the engine management system, it is possible to extend the engine torque reduction function. It is necessary to use a PWM signal with related fixed values or a bus interface. The engine torque reduction is controlled directly by the TCU. The advantage of such an interface is an independent calibration of the TCU data over a wide range without changing the engine management data. A further advantage is the improved possibility for the coordination of the engine torque reduction and the pressure control within the TCU. The improvement of this interface can be extended up to a real torque interface, especially when using a bus communication link.

Pressure Control.[8]   The pressure control can be improved in a similar way as the shift point control with an adaptive software strategy. The required inputs for the adaptive pressure control are calculated from available signals in the transmission control. The main reasons for the implementation of the adaptive pressure control are the variations of the attributes of the transmission components like clutch surfaces and oil quality as well as the changing engine output torque over the lifetime of the car.

The principle of adaptive pressure control is a comparison of a set value for the shift time with an actual value, measured by the transmission input speed course. At a specific difference of the set value to the actual value, the pressure value is corrected by a certain increment in the positive or negative direction. The original adaptation time and the pressure value increment were fixed during the calibration phase. For safety reasons, the total deviation of the pressure value from a given value is limited, depending on the particular application. Usually the correction values are stored in the nonvolatile memory to have the correct values available after power-on of the electronic TCU.

Safety and Diagnostic Functions.   The safety functions extend over better monitoring of the selector lever and functions concerning misuse by the driver. With a corresponding transmission hardware design, the implementation of a reverse gear inhibit function is possible; i.e, above a certain vehicle speed, the position R is blocked hydraulically by a single solenoid or by a particular solenoid combination commanded by the electronic TCU. This function prevents the destruction of the transmission in the event of an unintentional shift to the reverse gear. Downshift prevention is part of the safety function, especially during manual shifting by the driver. Here the synchronous speed of the new gear is calculated and compared with the admissable maximum engine speed. In the case of a calculated synchronous speed above the maximum engine speed, the downshift is prohibited by the TCU. This function can be supported by an overrun safeguard which releases the limp home mode in case of exceeding the admissable maximum engine speed.

All of those functions can be extended and have to be defined during the development stage by the automobile transmission and electronic TCU manufacturers. To increase availability of the AT system, even with the failure of certain signals, it is possible to provide a substitute operation with better drivability than in the limp home mode. This can be done by substitute functions. The electronic TCU falls back on substitute values or signals in the case of a breakdown of certain interfaces. There is, for example, the possibility to run with a programmable fixed throttle value with a breakdown of the throttle position signal. This results in a reduction of the shift characteristics to shift points. Shifting into all gears is possible, however, with reduced shift comfort. A further method is to use secondary signals in case the original signals break down. For example, the calculation of vehicle speed can be from wheel speed during breakdown of the transmission output speed signal. This technique usually requires a connection between ABS and transmission control. The third variant is the canceling of certain functions if the necessary input signals are missed. For example, in the case of a kickdown switch failure, the kickdown function is canceled. This results in no downshift after operation of the kickdown. Downshifts are nevertheless still possible via the full-throttle opening point according to the full-load shift characteristic.

The availability and driveability of automobiles equipped with electronic TCU in case of system failures can be improved significantly with the implementation of substitute functions. This results in a considerable increase in acceptance by the drivers of automobiles with electronic transmission control.

13.3.3   Adaptation to Driver's Behavior and Traffic Situations

In certain driving conditions, some disadvantages of the conventional AT can be prevented by using self-learning strategies.[9] This is especially valid when improving the compromise in the shift characteristics regarding gear selection under particular driving conditions and under difficult environmental conditions. The intention of the self-learning functions is to provide the appropriate shift characteristic suitable to the driver under all driving conditions. Additionally, the behavior of the car under special conditions can be improved by suitable functions. Available input signals of the car, provided by the related electronic TCUs from interfaces and communication links, are processed by the TCU with specific algorithms. The self-learning functions can be divided into a long respectively medium term adaptation for driver's style detection and into a short-term adaptation which reacts to the present driving situation, such as hills or curves.

The core of the adaptive strategies is the driver's style detection. The driver's style can be detected by monitoring of the accelerator pedal movements. The inputs are operation speed, operation frequency, and the rating position of the accelerator pedal. These inputs are processed depending on priorities with special algorithms related to the desired driving behavior of the car. The calculated driver style is related to certain shift maps. There is a large choice of shift maps available. With the currently known applications, there are mostly four different shift maps ranging from fuel economic to extremely sporty vehicle behavior. The calculated driver's style can also depend on the actual vehicle speed and the share of constant driving conditions during a certain driving cycle. These self-learning functions can be calibrated by the car manufacturer, depending on his philosophy and target market. In this way, the number of shift maps and the speed of the adaptation have the main influence. A further possibility to match the driver's style is by rating the accelerator pedal operation during vehicle start, for example, after a red light stop. In this way the operation speed and frequency of the accelerator pedal below a certain vehicle speed can be interpreted and calculated as part of the driver's style rating. In the event of kickdown, the shift maps of the driver's style rating are shut down by a priority command. The driver has the usual behavior of the car during kickdown, generally a downshift, providing no other safety function is in operation.

To prevent shift hunting, the self-learning functions are carried out over a long respectively medium term adaptation with the adaptation timer ranging from several seconds up to one minute. The second part of the self-learning functions is the driving condition detection. There is a correlation between the input signals of the transmission control and the driving condition.

One of the main disadvantages of a conventional electronic transmission control is the upshifting at constant vehicle speed by crossing the upshift characteristic with a reduction of the accelerator pedal angle. This results in an unintended gear shift, especially when cornering and when approaching a crossing or an obstacle. To prevent these gear shifts it is possible to use so-called upshift prevention. Cornering can be detected by the acceleration of the car along the driving direction related to the vehicle speed. The vehicle speed is calculated from the transmission output speed. The acceleration can be detected by an acceleration sensor or by the difference between the nondriven wheel speeds. In this way it is possible to prevent the upshift when cornering, resulting in a considerable improvement in vehicle stability.

The detection of a crossing or obstacle approach is possible by the detection of a fast off condition of the accelerator pedal. At a certain gradient of the pedal position, the upshift is prevented. This is a considerable advantage especially when overtaking low-speed vehicles. With this strategy the correct gear is available without a shift delay.

Another part of the driving situation detection is the recognition of uphill driving and full-load conditions. This is possible by adding special functions to the adaptive gear shift control. When driving downhill, it makes sense to support the engine braking effect for a better deceleration of the car. Downhill driving can be detected by a comparison of throttle position and vehicle speed gradient. An upshift is prevented and, in some special cases, a downshift is activated by the electronic TCU.

A further section of the self-learning functions is the environmental monitoring with related shift strategies. A special application can be a self-learning winter program. The wheel slip of the driven wheels is compared with a set value of a combination of given wheel torque and vehicle speed. When exceeding a set limit of wheel slip, a special shift strategy is chosen. For example, the vehicle starts off in second gear or an upshift takes place at lower engine speeds.

The development of adaptive shift strategies started a few years ago and is currently one of the main areas in electronic transmission development. The efficiency of the self-learning functions has led to a wide acceptance of AT-equipped vehicles. The future development concerning new adaptive functions and an improvement of the already known functions is an important area in control development. This can be supported by an increasing share of electronic units and interfaces for the communication between units. With multiple use of sensors providing the necessary input signals, the total system gains increased functionality, especially with bus systems.

At present, an increasing share of manual programs with an AT can be registrated. The driver instructs the AT to shift via a switch or a push button. In this manner, the driver can operate the AT like a manual gearbox independently of other shift maps, with only the safety functions in operation. This has led to a broad acceptance, especially in the sports car market. These functions can all be calibrated and applied by the car manufacturer with data relating to his philosophy and to the target market. The result is the prevention of the known disadvantages of the conventional AT control without canceling the advantages in driving comfort and safety.

13.4 COMMUNICATIONS WITH OTHER ELECTRONIC CONTROL UNITS

With the existence of electronic control units for various applications in vehicles, many opportunities exist to link these ECUs and to establish communications between them. The main partner of the TCU is the engine management system. Due to the coupling of engine and transmission within the vehicle powertrain, it is necessary to have an interface between these ECUs for a functional coupling and an interchange of signals. It is essential for the pressure control inside the transmission control to sensor the engine load, the engine speed, and the throttle position. The engine torque reduction during shifting is also important to establish a good shift comfort and a satisfactory lifetime for the clutches. By handing over certain signals like position lever state, lockup condition, or shift commands to the engine management, the driving comfort of the vehicle can be improved significantly. An interface to ABS and traction control is useful for some self-learning functions in the transmission control when using the wheel speeds.

It is possible to implement certain shift strategies in the transmission control as an active support for ABS and traction control. A link to the electronic throttle control or cruise control makes it possible to optimize certain functions for the total vehicle. By interfaces between the ECUs, a reduction of the sensor expense results by a multiple use via communications. Suitable links include, especially, PWM or bus configurations for trouble-free communication. Bus systems in particular have the advantage of the link-up of additional ECUs without changing their existing hardware. Additional coupling requires only a software change. The interchange of required supplementary signals for new functions is possible without any problems. An example of powertrain management by coupling the powertrain ECUs to achieve lower fuel consumption, simultaneously improving the driveability, is described as follows.

13.5   OPTIMIZATION OF THE DRIVETRAIN

The newest generation of transmission controllers has overcome the former disadvantage regarding fuel efficiency. Adaptive functions in cooperation with carefully designed torque converter clutch control,[8] which allows the clutch to be closed even at low gears, have improved fuel consumption significantly. Based on the driver's behavior, together with an adaptive shift strategy as previously described, part of the TCU's adaptive program software may select an economy or even super-economy shift strategy whenever possible. There is, however, still more potential for fuel economy by optimization of the drivetrain.

The concept called Mastershift[10] is shown in Fig. 13.11. The basic idea is to interpret the accelerator pedal position as an acceleration request. That acceleration request, or a request for wheel torque, has to be converted by operating the engine at high torque, i.e., open throttle and low rpm values. In order to realize this, it is necessary to use an electronic throttle control system. The communication between the electronic throttle, the engine, and transmission is shown in Fig. 13.12.

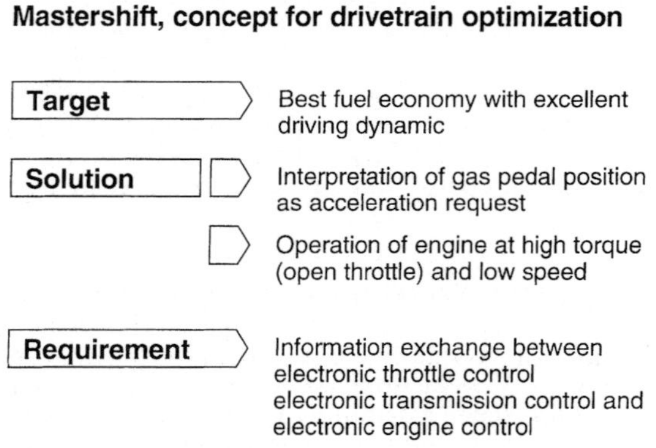

Mastershift, concept for drivetrain optimization

Target	Best fuel economy with excellent driving dynamic
Solution	Interpretation of gas pedal position as acceleration request
	Operation of engine at high torque (open throttle) and low speed
Requirement	Information exchange between electronic throttle control electronic transmission control and electronic engine control

FIGURE 13.11   Drivetrain operation.

Mastershift – logical structure

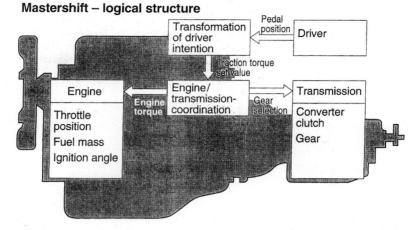
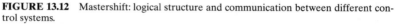

FIGURE 13.12 Mastershift: logical structure and communication between different control systems.

In such a system, a well-defined coordination between the engine torque, mainly given by throttle position (air mass), fuel mass, and ignition angle on one side and selection of the appropriate gear including torque converter clutch on the other side, is imperative. Depending on the type of engine, fuel consumption can be reduced further by 5 to 10 percent with this optimized Mastershift concept. Because the average engine operation is at higher torque levels compared to standard systems, a greater number of gear shifts may occur. This is important to guarantee optimal shift comfort. Figure 13.13 shows how that can be accomplished by using the additional degree of freedom given by the electronic throttle control. It is possible to operate the throttle angle during the gear shift in such a way as to achieve constant wheel torque before and after downshifts.

13.6 FUTURE DEVELOPMENTS

In future years, development work will be concentrated on redesign of hardware components for cost reduction, improvement of yield to reduce fuel consumption, and improvement of driveability. A good approach to meet cost targets on the electronic hardware side would be to integrate two or more individual control modules into a common housing. Regarding the electronic components, one could continue using two separate microcontrollers. This would have the advantage that the software development and application could be done individually for two different systems, for example engine and transmission controllers. Another approach could be to mount the TCU on the transmission housing itself. This could lead to a significant reduction in the expense for the wiring harness. Here, however, the problem of hostile ambient temperatures on electronic components has to be solved. Today's stand-alone actuators could be integrated into a common housing similar to the solution shown by Chrysler Corp. in its A 604 transmission.

The improvement of the yield is a main topic for designers of ATs. Oil pumps and torque converters are a major source of energy losses. A significant improvement of yield will be possible as soon as torque converter clutches are available with the capability for continuous slip operation. The torque converter clutch can then be operated in low gears and at low engine speeds without facing problems from drivetrain oscillations and/or noise emission.

The driveability is the most important feature for the drivers' acceptance of ATs. In addition to the self-adaptive functions described, the implementation of shift strategies benefiting from control algorithms using fuzzy theory may further improve driveability.

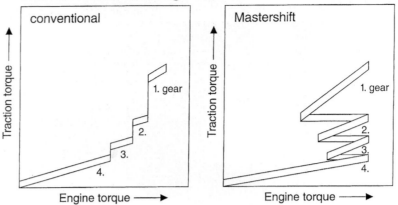

FIGURE 13.13 Constant traction torque by operation of throttle opening during gear shift.

GLOSSARY

ASIC Application-specific integrated circuit.

AT Automatic transmission.

ATF Automatic transmission fluid.

CAN Controller area network.

CVT Continuously variable transmission.

EEPROM Electrically erasable and programmable read-only memory.

EMC Electromagnetic compatibility.

EPROM Erasable programmable read-only memory.

PWM Pulse-width modulation.

RAM Random access memory.

RFI Radio frequency interference.

TCC Torque converter clutch.

TCU Transmission control unit.

REFERENCES

1. F. Kucukay and Lorenz, K., "Das neue Fünfgang-Automatikgetriebe für V8-Motoren in der 7er Bau-reihe von BMW," *ATZ Automobiltechnische Zeitschrift 94,* Heft 7/8, 1992.

2. K. Neuffer, "Recent development of AT-control: adaptive functions and actuators," Symposium No. 9313, *Advanced Technologies in Automotive Propulsion Systems,* Society of Automotive Engineers of Japan Inc., 1993, pp. 42–49.

3. J. G. Eleftherakis and Khalil, A., "Development of a laboratory test contaminant for transmissions," SAE Paper 90 0561, Society of Automotive Engineers, Warrendale, Pa.

4. B. Aldefeld, "Numerical calculation of electromagnetic actuators," *Archiv für Elektrotechnik,* Bd. 61, 1979, pp. 347–352

5. K. Hasuuaka, Takagi, K., and Sinji, W., "A study on electro-hydraulic control for automatic transmissions," SAE Paper 89 2000, Society of Automotive Engineers, Warrendale, Pa.

6. P. C. Sen, "Principles of electric machines and power electronics," J. Wiley, New York, 1989.

7. "Method and Apparatus to Convert an Electrical Value into a Mechanical Position by Using an Electromagnetic Element Subject to Hysteresis," U. S. Patent 4,577,143 March 18, 1986.

8. K. Neuffer, "Electronische Getriebesteuerung von Bosch," *ATZ Automobiltechnische Zeitschrift 94,* Heft 9, 1992, pp. 442–449.

9. A. Welter, et al., "Die Adaptive Getriegesteuerung für Automatikgetriebe der BMW-Fahrzeuge mit Zwolfzylindermotor," *ATZ Automobiltechnische Zeitschrift 94,* 1992, pp. 428–436.

10. H. M. Streib and R. Leonhard, "Hierarchical control strategy for powertrain function," *XXIV Fisita Congress,* London, 1992.

ABOUT THE AUTHORS

KURT NEUFFER is responsible at Robert Bosch GmbH for the development of electronic control units for automatic transmissions and also for the development of actuators. He was educated in electronics engineering at the University of Stuttgart and holds a Dr. Ing. in the field of basic semiconductor research. He has been in the field of automotive component development for 10 years.

WOLFGANG BULLMER is responsible at Bosch for systems and software development of electronic control units for automatic transmissions. He was educated in electronics engineering at the University of Stuttgart. He has been working in the area of transmission control unit development for eight years.

WERNER BREHM is a Bosch section manager for the design of electrohydraulic actuators used in electronically controlled automatic transmissions. He was educated in mechanical engineering at the University of Stuttgart and has worked on components engineering for antilock braking systems in passenger cars.

CHAPTER 14
CRUISE CONTROL

Richard Valentine
Motorola Inc.

14.1 CRUISE CONTROL SYSTEM

A vehicle speed control system can range from a simple throttle latching device to a sophisticated digital controller that constantly maintains a set speed under varying driving conditions. The next generation of electronic speed control systems will probably still use a separate module (black box), the same as present-day systems, but will share data from the engine, ABS, and transmission control systems. Futuristic cruise control systems that include radar sensors to measure the rate of closure to other vehicles and adjust the speed to maintain a constant distance are possible but need significant cost reductions for widespread private vehicle usage.

The objective of an automatic vehicle cruise control is to sustain a steady speed under varying road conditions, thus allowing the vehicle operator to relax from constant foot throttle manipulation. In some cases, the cruise control system may actually improve the vehicle's fuel efficiency value by limiting throttle excursions to small steps. By using the power and speed of a microcontroller device and fuzzy logic software design, an excellent cruise control system can be designed.

14.1.1 Functional Elements

The cruise control system is a closed-loop speed control as shown in Fig. 14.1. The key input signals are the driver's speed setpoint and the vehicle's actual speed. Other important inputs are the faster-accel/slower-coast driver adjustments, resume, on/off, brake switch, and engine control messages. The key output signals are the throttle control servo actuator values. Additional output signals include cruise ON and service indicators, plus messages to the engine and/or transmission control system and possibly data for diagnostics.

14.1.2 Performance Expectations

The ideal cruise system features would include the following specifications:

- *Speed performance:* ±0.5 m/h control at less than 5 percent grade, and ±1 m/h control or vehicle limit over 5 percent grade.
- *Reliability:* Circuit designed to withstand overvoltage transients, reverse voltages, and power dissipation of components kept to minimum.

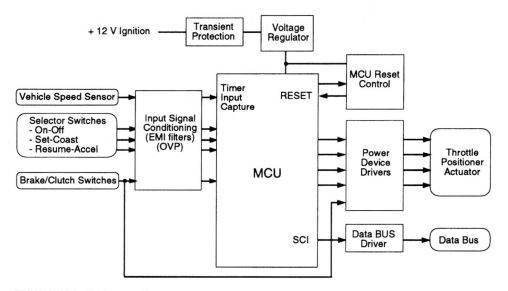

FIGURE 14.1 Cruise control system.

- *Application options:* By changing EEPROM via a simple serial data interface or over the MUX network, the cruise software can be upgraded and optimized for specific vehicle types. These provisions allow for various sensors, servos, and speed ranges.

- *Driver adaptability:* The response time of the cruise control can be adjusted to match the driver's preferences within the constraints of the vehicle's performance.

- *Favorable price-to-performance ratio:* The use of integrated actuator drivers and a high-functionality MCU reduce component counts, increase reliability, and decrease the cruise control module's footprint.

14.1.3 Safety Considerations (Failsafe)

Several safety factors need to be considered for a vehicle speed control design. The most basic is a method designed into the throttle control circuit to insure a failsafe mode of operation in the event that the microcontroller or actuator drivers should fail. This electronic fail-safe circuit shuts off the control servos so that the throttle linkage will be released when the brake switch or cruise off switch is activated, no matter the condition of the MCU or servo actuator control transistors. (This assumes the actuators are mechanically in good shape and will release.)

Other safety-related items include program code to detect abnormal operating conditions and preserving into memory the data points associated with the abnormal condition for later diagnostics. Abnormal conditions, for example, could be an intermittent vehicle speed sensor, or erratic driver switch signals. A test could also be made during the initial ignition "key on time" plus any time the cruise is activated to verify the integrity of the cruise system, with any faults resulting in a warning indicator to the driver. Obviously, the most serious fault to avoid is runaway acceleration. Continuous monitoring of the MCU and key control elements will help minimize the potential for this type of fault.

14.2 MICROCONTROLLER REQUIREMENTS FOR CRUISE CONTROL

The MCU for cruise control applications requires high functionality. The MCU would include the following:

- a precise internal timebase for the speed measurement calculations
- A/D inputs
- PWM outputs
- timer input capture
- timer output compares
- serial data port (MUX port)
- internal watchdog
- EEPROM
- low-power CMOS technology

14.2.1 Input Signals

The speed sensor is one of the most critical parts in the system, because the microcontroller calculates the vehicle speed from the speed sensor's signal to within ½ m/h. Any speedometer cable whip or oscillation can cause errors to be introduced into the speed calculation. An averaging routine in the speed calculations can minimize this effect. The speedometer sensor drives the microcontroller's timer input capture line or the external interrupt line. The MCU then calculates the vehicle's speed from the frequency of the sensor signals and the MCU internal timebase. The vehicle's speed value is continually updated and stored into RAM for use by the basic speed control program. Speed sensors traditionally have been a simple ac generator located in the transmission or speedometer cable. The ac generator produces an ac voltage waveform with its frequency proportional to the sensor's rpm and vehicle speed. Optical sensors in the speedometer head can also be incorporated. Usually the speed sensor produces a number of pulses or cycles per km or mile. With the increasing ABS system usage, a backup speed sensor value could be obtained from the ABS wheel speed sensors. The ABS speed data could be obtained by way of a MUX network.

The user command switch signals could either be single MCU input lines to each switch contact or a more complex analog resistor divider type to an A/D input line. Other input signals of interest to the cruise system program would be throttle position, transmission or clutch status, A/C status, actuator diagnostics, engine status, etc., which could be obtained over the MUX data network.

14.2.2 Program Flow

The microcontroller is programmed to measure the rate of vehicle speed and note how much, and in which direction, the vehicle speed is drifting. The standard PI (proportional-integral) method produces one output signal p that is proportional to the difference between the set-speed and actual vehicle speed (the error value) by a proportional gain block Kp. Another signal i is generated that ramps up or down at a rate set by the error signal magnitude. The gains of both Ki and Kp are chosen to provide a quick response, but with little instability. In effect, the PI system adds up the error rate over time, and, therefore, if an underspeed condition occurs as in a long uphill grade, the error signal will begin to greatly increase to try to compensate. Under level driving conditions, the integral control block Ki will tend toward zero

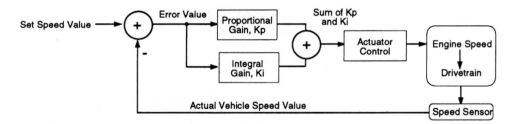

FIGURE 14.2   PI speed error control.

because there is less error over time. The vehicle's weight, engine performance, and rolling resistance all factor in to determine the PI gain constants. In summary, the PI method allows fast response to abrupt grades or mountains and stable operation under light grades or hills. Figure 14.2 shows the traditional PI cruise control diagram.

14.2.3   Output Controls

When the error signal has been computed, an output signal to the servo actuators is generated to increase, hold, or decrease the throttle position. The servo is updated at a rate that is within the servo's mechanical operating specifications, which could be several milliseconds. The error signal can be computed at a much faster rate and, therefore, gives extra time for some averaging of the vehicle speed sensor signal.

Throttle positioning is traditionally either a vacuum type servo or motor. The vacuum supply to the vacuum servo/actuator is discharged as a failsafe measure whenever the brake system is engaged in addition to the normal turn-off of the actuator driver coils. Electric servo type motors require more complex drive electronics and some type of mechanical failsafe linked backed to the brake system.

14.3   CRUISE CONTROL SOFTWARE

The cruise error calculation algorithm can be designed around traditional math models such as PI or fuzzy logic.

14.3.1   Fuzzy Logic Examples

Fuzzy logic allows somewhat easier implementation of the speed error calculation because its design syntax uses simple linguistics. For example: IF speed difference negative and small, THEN increase throttle slightly.

The output is then adjusted to slightly increase the throttle. The throttle position update rate is determined by another fuzzy program which looks for the driver's cruise performance request (slow, medium, or fast reaction), the application type (small, medium, or large engine size), and other cruise system factory preset parameters. Figure 14.3 shows one part of a fuzzy logic design for computing normal throttle position. Other parts would compute the effects of other inputs, such as resume, driver habits, engine type, and the like.

Other program design requirements include verification that the input signals fall within expected boundaries. For example, a broken or intermittent speed sensor could be detected.

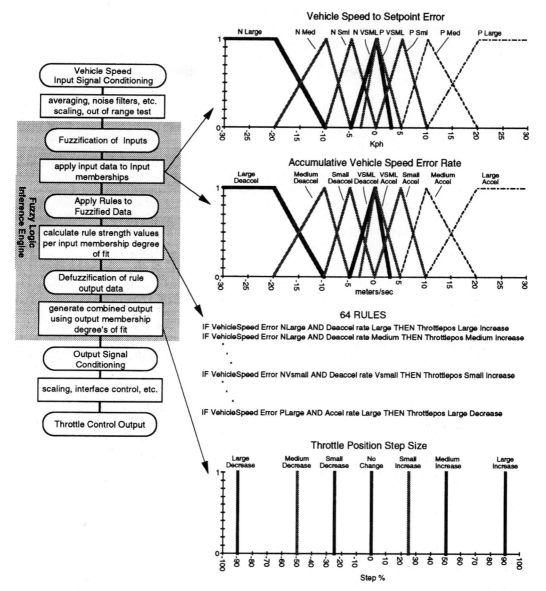

FIGURE 14.3   Fuzzy speed error program flow.

A heavily loaded vehicle with a small engine may not be able to maintain a high setpoint speed up a steep grade, and the cruise control needs to be disengaged to protect the engine from sustained full-throttle operation under a heavy load. This could be preset to occur 20 percent below the setpoint speed. Another program can test the vehicle speed to resume setpoint speed and prevent unsafe acceleration under certain conditions. For example, if a high-performance vehicle (>200-kW or 268-hp engine) has a setpoint speed of 125 km/h (78 mi/h), and drives from the freeway into heavy city traffic doing 48 km/h (30 mi/h) and the vehicle's driver fortuitously hits the cruise resume switch at this low speed, the cruise control invokes a near full-throttle action, and an accident is likely. A fuzzy design can limit the acceleration upon resume using simple rules such as IF resume and big speed error, THEN increase throttle slightly.

14.3.2 Adaptive Programming

The response time and gain of the cruise system can be adjusted to match individual drivers. For example, some drivers may prefer to allow the vehicle to slow down somewhat when climbing a grade and then respond quickly to maintain a setspeed; other drivers may prefer a constant speed at all times, while still other drivers may prefer a very slow responding cruise system to maximize fuel efficiency. The cruise system can be adapted either by a user selection switch (slow, medium, fast) or by analyzing the driver's acceleration/deacceleration habits during noncruise operation. Once these habits are analyzed, they can be grouped into the three previously mentioned categories. One drawback of a totally automatic adaptive cruise system is when various drivers with vastly different driving preferences operate the vehicle on the same trip. The cruise system would have to be "retrained" for each driver.

14.4 CRUISE CONTROL DESIGN

Many of the required elements of a cruise control can be integrated into one single-chip MCU device. For example, the actuator drivers can be designed in the MCU if their power requirements are on the low side.

14.4.1 Automatic Cruise System

Figure 14.4 shows an experimental system design for a cruise control based upon a semicustom 8 or 16-bit single-chip MCU that incorporates special high-power output driver elements and a built-in voltage regulator.

14.4.2 Safety Backup Examples

The design of a cruise control system should include many safeguards:

- A test to determine vehicle speed conditions or command inputs that do not fall within the normal conditions for operation of the cruise control function.
- A test to determine if the vehicle speed has decreased below what the cruise routine can compensate for.
- Speed setpoint minimums and maximums (30 km/h min to 125 km/h max, for example) are checked and, if exceeded, will cause the cruise function to turn off.
- Speedometer cable failure is detected by checking for speed sensor electrical output pulses over a 100-ms time period and, if these pulses are absent, the system is disengaged.
- Software program traps should also be scattered throughout the program and, if memory permits, at the end of each program loop. These will catch an out-of-control program and initiate a vector restart.

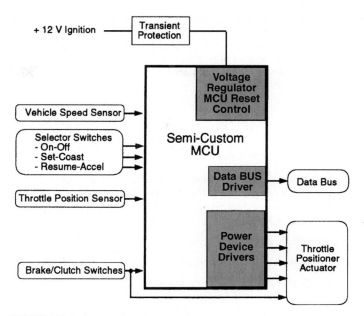

FIGURE 14.4 Automatic cruise control.

14.4.3 EMI and RFI Noise Problems

As with any electronic design, consideration must be given to suppressing RFI (radio frequency interference) from the circuit, besides minimizing effects of external EMI (electromagnetic interference) and RFI to the circuit's normal operation. It is not uncommon that the circuit must operate in RF fields up to 200 V/m intensity. This requires careful layout of the module's PCB (printed circuit board) and RF filters on all lines going in or out of the module. The module case may even have to contain some type of RF shielding. Minimizing generated RFI from the cruise circuit can be accomplished by operating the MCU's crystal oscillator at a minimal power level (this is controlled mostly by the MCU internal design), careful PCB trace layout of the MCU oscillator area, metal shielding over the MCU, ground planes on the PCB under the MCU, and setting the actuator switching edge transition times to over 10 ms. (See Chaps. 27 and 28.)

14.5 FUTURE CRUISE CONCEPTS

Several research projects are underway to develop a crash avoidance system that could be interconnected with a cruise system. The development of a low-cost distance sensor that can measure up to a few hundred meters away with a tight focal point in all weather conditions is proving to be a challenge. When a practical vehicular distance sensor is available, the cruise control can be programmed to maintain either constant speed or constant distance to another vehicle. Other methods of cruise control could include receiving a roadside signal that gives an optimum speed value for the vehicle when travelling within certain traffic control areas.

14.5.1   Road Conditions Integration with IVHS

The IVHS (Intelligent Vehicle-Highway System) network may be a more practical approach to setting optimum cruise speed values for groups of vehicles. The IVHS can monitor road conditions, local weather, etc., and broadcast optimal speed data values for vehicles in its zone. (See Chap. 29.)

GLOSSARY

Analog input   Sensors usually generate electrical signals that are directly proportional to the mechanism being sensed. The signal is, therefore, analog or can vary from a minimum limit to a maximum limit. Normally, an 8-bit MCU A/D input using a 5-V reference, the analog input resolution is 1 bit, which is 1/256 of 5 V or 0.0193 V.

Defuzzification   The process of translating output grades to analog output values.

Fuzzification   The process of translating analog input values to input memberships or labels.

Fuzzy logic   Software design based upon a reasoning model rather than fixed mathematical algorithms. A fuzzy logic design allows the system engineer to participate in the software design because the fuzzy language is linguistic and built upon easy-to-comprehend fundamentals.

Inference engine   The internal software program that produces output values through fuzzy rules for given input values. The inference process involves three steps: fuzzification, rule evaluation, and defuzzification.

Input memberships   The input signal or sensor range is divided into degrees of membership, i.e., low, medium, high or cold, cool, comfortable, warm, hot. Each of these membership labels is assigned numerical values or grades.

Output memberships   The output signal is divided into grades such as off, slow, medium, fast, and full-on. Numerical values are assigned to each grade. Grades can be either singleton (one value) or Mandani (a range of values per grade).

Rule evaluation   Output values are computed per the input memberships and their relationship to the output memberships. The number of rules is usually set by the total number of input memberships and the total number of output memberships. The rules consist of IF inputvarA is x, AND inputvarB is y, THEN outvar is z.

Semicustom MCU   An MCU (microcontroller unit) that incorporates normal MCU elements plus user-specified peripheral devices such as higher-power port outputs, special timer units, etc. Mixed semiconductor technologies, such as high-density CMOS (HCMOS) and bipolar analog, are available in a semicustom MCU. Generally, HCMOS is limited to 10 V, whereas bipolar-analog is usable to 60 V.

BIBLIOGRAPHY

Bannatyne, R., "Fuzzy logic—A new approach to embedded control solutions," Motorola Semiconductor Design Concept, DC410, 1992.

Catherwood, M., "Designing for electromagnetic compatibility (EMC) with HCMOS microcontrollers," Motorola Semiconductor Application Note, AN1050, 1989.

Chaudhuri, et al., "Speed control integrated into the powertrain computer," *New Trends in Electronic Management and Driveline Controls,* SAE SP-653, 1986, pp. 65–72.

Hosaka, T., et al., "Vehicle control system and method therefore," U.S. Patent 4809175, May 29, 1990.

Hosaka, T., et al., "Vehicle control system," U.S. Patent 4930084, Feb. 28, 1989.

Mamdani, E. H., "Application of fuzzy logic to approximate reasoning using linguistic synthesis," *IEEE Transactions on Computers,* C-26-12, 1977, pp. 1182–1191.

Ribbens, W., "Vehicle Motion Control," *Understanding Automotive Electronics,* 4th ed., 1992, pp. 247–257.

Takahashi, Hioshi, "Automatic speed control device using self-tuning fuzzy logic," *IEEE Workshop on Automotive Applications of Electronics,* 88THO321, 1988, pp. 65–71.

Self, Kevin, "Designing with fuzzy logic," *IEEE Spectrum,* Nov. 1990, pp. 42–44, 105.

Sibigtroth, J., "Implementing fuzzy expert rules in hardware," *AI Expert,* April 1992.

Stefanides, E. J., "Cruise control components packaged as one unit," *Design News,* Oct. 1, 1990, pp. 162–163.

Zadeh, L. A., "Fuzzy sets, information and control," vol. 8, 1965, pp. 338–353.

ABOUT THE AUTHOR

Richard J. Valentine is a principal staff engineer at Motorola SPS in Phoenix, Ariz. His present assignments include engineering evaluation of advanced semiconductor products for emerging automotive systems. He holds two patents and has published 29 technical articles during his 24 years at Motorola.

CHAPTER 15
BRAKING CONTROL

Jerry L. Cage
AlliedSignal Inc.

15.1 INTRODUCTION

This chapter describes braking by first examining vehicle braking fundamentals, including the tire-to-road interface, vehicle dynamics, and conventional brake system components, and progressing to antilock systems objectives, components, safety considerations, control logic, and testing. The chapter concludes with a discussion of future vehicle braking systems.

For simplicity and because of applicability to the majority of automotive vehicles on the road, hydraulic brake systems as used on two-axle, nonarticulated vehicles will be discussed exclusively; this type of brake system is used on passenger cars, light trucks, and, in North America, on medium trucks.

15.2 VEHICLE BRAKING FUNDAMENTALS

Essential to the understanding of the technology associated with modern automotive vehicle braking is knowledge of the tire-to-road interface, vehicle dynamics during braking, and the components of a brake system. This section discusses these subjects to a system level of understanding.

15.2.1 Tire-to-Road Interface

The braking force generated at each wheel of a vehicle during a braking maneuver is a function of the normal force on the wheel and the coefficient of friction between the tire and the road. The simplified relationship between the weight on a wheel and the resulting frictional (braking) force is shown in Eq. (15.1).

$$F_x = \mu W_{wh} \tag{15.1}$$

where F_x = friction force $\times$ direction
μ = coefficient of friction, tire-to-road
W_{wh} = static and dynamic weight on the wheel

The tire-to-road coefficient of friction is not a constant but is a function of factors, most prominent being type of road surface and the relative longitudinal slip between the tire and the road. General curves relating coefficient of friction to wheel slip on various surfaces are shown in Fig. 15.1. From this figure and Eq. (15.1), the following observations are evident:

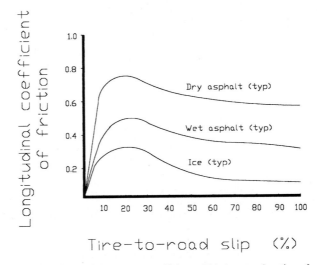

FIGURE 15.1   Longitudinal coefficient of friction as a function of wheel slip.

- The generation of frictional forces depends on wheel slip. If the tire is rolling at the same tangential velocity as the road surface, there is no longitudinal (braking) force. This relationship is fundamental in understanding braking and is not easily observed: wheel slip other than near 100 percent (no rotational wheel speed) is difficult to discern without instrumentation.
- The peak frictional (braking) force occurs under conditions of relatively little slip. This indicates that a hard apply of the brakes which causes a 100 percent slip typically does not produce the most braking force and an evenly modulated, controlled brake pressure applied by a skilled driver or through antilock control tends to produce shorter stops on most surfaces.
- The frictional (braking) force generated varies widely with road surface. The result of this relationship is obvious to both drivers and passengers in terms of stopping distance and deceleration if dry asphalt braking is compared with braking on ice.
- Typically, beyond the peak coefficient of friction attainable on a given road surface, the slope of the curve becomes negative. This phenomenon (essentially indicating that, beyond the slip resulting in peak frictional force, more pedal force results in less braking) explains why a skilled driver can attain significantly shorter stopping distances than can a less experienced driver and why electronic vehicle braking control is as complicated as it is. Also, the amount of "peak" in the coefficient of friction curves varies widely with road surface. More braking force benefit can be gained through slip control on surfaces such as ice than on dry asphalt, for example.

Another characteristic of automotive tires important in braking is lateral force versus slip. Lateral force is the force keeping a tire from sliding in a direction normal to the direction of the vehicle. The equation for lateral force is as follows:

$$F_y = \mu_{\text{lateral}} W_{wh}$$

where F_y = friction force, by direction
        μ_{lateral} = lateral coefficient of friction, tire-to-road

The lateral coefficient of friction drops off quickly once a wheel begins to slip longitudinally, as can happen during braking. Excessive wheel slip at the rear wheels of a vehicle and the resulting loss of lateral frictional force will contribute to instability as the rear of the vehicle tends to slide sideways with relatively small lateral forces on the vehicle. Excessive wheel slip and the resulting loss of lateral friction force on the front wheels of a vehicle will contribute to loss of steerability; this loss of steering phenomenon is common during panic stops on low coefficient surfaces such as ice, as a hard apply of the brakes puts the tires in a 100 percent slip situation.

15.2.2   Vehicle Dynamics During Braking

An equation for braking performance can be obtained from Newton's second law: the sum of the external forces acting on a body in a given direction is equal to the product of its mass and the acceleration in that direction. Relating this law to straight-line vehicle braking, the significant factors are shown in Eq. (15.2) and the sum of the forces acting on the vehicle is shown in Fig. 15.2.[1]

$$\Sigma F = Ma_x = \frac{+W}{g} D_x = + F_{xf} + F_{xr} + D_A + W \sin \Theta + f_r W \cos \Theta \tag{15.2}$$

where M = mass of the vehicle
       a_x = linear acceleration in the x direction
       W = weight of the vehicle
       g = acceleration due to gravity
       $D_x = - a_x$ = linear deceleration
       F_{xf} = front axle braking force
       F_{xr} = rear axle braking force
       D_A = aerodynamic drag (considered to be acting at a point)
       Θ = angle of roadway
       f_r = rolling resistance coefficient = $(R_{xf} + R_{xr}) / W\cos\Theta$

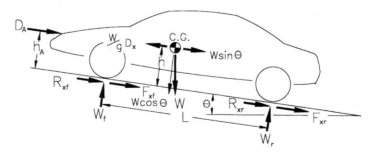

FIGURE 15.2 Significant forces' action on a vehicle during braking.

If braking forces are held constant and the vehicle velocity effects on aerodynamic drag and rolling resistance are neglected, the time for a vehicle velocity change, Eq. (15.3), and the distance traveled during a velocity change, Eq. (15.4), can also be derived from Newton's second law.[2]

$$t = \frac{M}{F_{xt}}(V_o - V_f) \tag{15.3}$$

where F_{xt} = total of all longitudinal deceleration forces on the vehicle
$\quad\quad t$ = time
$\quad\quad V_o$ = initial velocity
and $\quad V_f$ = final velocity

$$x = \frac{M}{F_{xt}}\left(\frac{V_o^2}{2} - \frac{V_f^2}{2}\right) \tag{15.4}$$

where x = distance in forward direction

These approximations indicate that the time to stop is proportional to vehicle velocity and the stopping distance is proportional to the square of the vehicle velocity.

During braking, the dynamic load transfer that occurs is a function of the height of the center of gravity, the weight of the vehicle, the wheelbase, and the deceleration rate. Equation 15.5 describes this dynamic load shift.

$$W_d = \left(\frac{h}{L}\right)\left(\frac{W}{g}\right)D_x - \frac{h_A}{L}D_A \tag{15.5}$$

where W_d = dynamic weight
$\quad\quad h$ = center of gravity height
$\quad\quad L$ = wheelbase
$\quad\quad W$ = static vehicle weight
$\quad\quad g$ = acceleration due to gravity
$\quad\quad D_x$ = deceleration in the forward direction
$\quad\quad h_A$ = height of the aerodynamic drag

Considering two-axle vehicles, this load transfer is additive to the front wheels and subtractive to the rear wheels during braking, as shown in Eq. (15.6) and (15.7), respectively.

$$F_{xmf} = \mu_p\left(W_{fs} + \frac{hWD_x}{Lg} - \frac{h_A}{L}D_A\right) \tag{15.6}$$

where F_{xmf} = maximum friction force in the longitudinal direction on the front wheels
$\quad\quad \mu_p$ = peak coefficient of friction
$\quad\quad W_{fs}$ = static weight on the front wheels

$$F_{xmr} = \mu\left(W_{rs} - \frac{hWD_x}{Lg} + \frac{h_A}{L}D_A\right) \tag{15.7}$$

where F_{xmr} = maximum friction force in the longitudinal direction on the rear wheels
$\quad\quad W_{rs}$ = static weight on the rear wheels

Simplifying Eq. (15.2) for the case of $\Theta = 0°$ and negligible aerodynamic drag and rolling resistance yields the following:

$$\sum F = \frac{W}{g}D_x = +F_{xf} + F_{xr}$$

Solving for D_x and substituting in simplified Eqs. (15.6) and (15.7) yields Eq. (15.8) and (15.9), respectively:

$$F_{xmf} = \mu \frac{\left(W_{fs} + \dfrac{hF_{xmr}}{L} \right)}{1 - \mu_p \dfrac{h}{L}} \qquad (15.8)$$

$$F_{xmr} = \mu \frac{\left(W_{rs} + \dfrac{hF_{xmf}}{L} \right)}{1 - \mu_p \dfrac{h}{L}} \qquad (15.9)$$

These relationships indicate that the maximum braking force on the front wheels is dependent on the braking force on the rear wheels through the deceleration and the associated forward load transfer and, in a similar fashion, the braking force on the rear wheels is dependent on the braking force on the front wheels.

Through application of the preceding equations, brake systems designers can determine the total braking force required to achieve the desired deceleration, and the brake system components can be sized appropriately. Safety and legal requirements dictate that system designers consider deceleration under vehicle loaded and unloaded conditions as well as under partially failed brake system conditions (either half-system failures or loss of brake boost to the entire system). Because of these considerations and numerous others, such as desired customer pedal stroke and pedal force/deceleration expectations, vehicle brake system sizing is a complicated engineering effort usually accomplished with the aid of a vehicle simulator computer program.

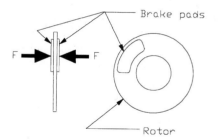

FIGURE 15.3   Disk brake schematic.

15.2.3   Brake System Components

Disk Brakes. Figure 15.3 shows a schematic diagram of a disc brake. In this type of brake, force is applied equally to both sides of a rotor and braking action is achieved through the frictional action of inboard and outboard brake pads against the rotor. The pads are contained within a caliper (not shown), as is the wheel cylinder. Although not a high-gain type of brake, disk brakes have the advantage of providing relatively linear braking with lower susceptibility to fading than drum brakes.

Force applied to the rotor by the pads is a function of hydraulic pressure in the brake system and the area of the wheel cylinder (or cylinders, as the design dictates). Static brake torque can be calculated using the following equation:

$$T = PAER \qquad (15.10)$$

where T = brake torque
 P = application pressure
 A = wheel cylinder area
 E = effectiveness factor: ratio of the disk rubbing surface to the input force on the shoes
 R = brake radius

The static brake force can be calculated with the following relationship:

$$F_b = \frac{T}{r}$$

where F_b = brake force
r = tire rolling radius

Drum Brakes. Figure 15.4 depicts a schematic diagram of a drum brake. In drum brakes, force is applied to a pair of brake shoes in a variety of configurations, including leading/trailing shoe (simplex), duo-duplex, and duo-servo. Drum brakes feature high gains relative to disk brakes, but some configurations tend to be more nonlinear and sensitive to fading and other brake lining coefficient-of-friction changes.

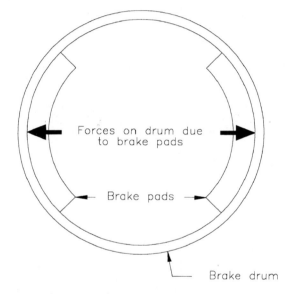

Forces on drum due
to brake pads

Brake pads

Brake drum

FIGURE 15.4 Drum brake schematic.

The static brake torque equation previously presented for disk brakes, Eq. (15.10), is equally applicable to drum brakes with design-specific changes for drum brake radius and effectiveness factor. By design, the brake radius for a drum brake is one-half the drum diameter. The effectiveness factor represents the major functional difference between drum and disk brakes; the geometry of drum brakes may allow a moment to be produced by the friction force on the shoe in such a manner as to rotate it against the drum and increase the friction force developed. This action can yield a mechanical advantage that significantly increases the gain of the brake and the effectiveness factor as compared with disk brakes. The dynamic brake force calculation for drum and disk brakes is more complex since the brake lining coefficient of friction is a function of temperature; as the lining heats during a braking maneuver, the effective coefficient of friction increases and less pressure is needed to maintain a constant brake torque.

Booster and Master Cylinder. Figure 15.5 is a schematic of a brake pedal, a vacuum booster, and a master cylinder. In actual practice, in passenger cars and light trucks the mechanical force gain due to the brake pedal geometry is usually 3 to 4 and the gain through a vacuum

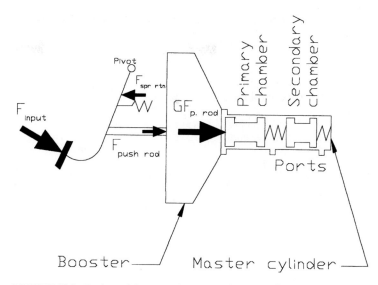

FIGURE 15.5 Brake pedal, vacuum booster, and master cylinder schematics.

booster is typically 5 to 9 after the booster reaches its crack point and before runout occurs. Therefore, force applied by the operator typically will be multiplied by a factor of 12 to 36 at the master cylinder in order to achieve the pressure necessary for braking. The resulting pressure in the master cylinder is as follows:

$$P_{MC} = \eta \frac{(F_{op}G_{mech}G_{boost} - F_s)}{A_{piston}}$$

where η = mechanical efficiency
P_{MC} = master cylinder pressure
F_{op} = operator force on the brake pedal
G_{mech} = mechanical gain primarily related to the brake pedal assembly geometry and the instantaneous return spring force
G_{boost} = brake booster gain, a function with the nonlinearities of a minimum crack force being necessary to initiate boost and a runout phenomenon resulting in a decreased force gain after a given input force is applied
F_s = return spring force
A_{piston} = area in the master cylinder on which the force is acting (chamber piston area)

Master cylinders are separated into primary and secondary chambers to improve safety by avoiding total brake system loss in case of a failure in one portion of the system. The most common configuration is shown in Fig. 15.5 with two chambers in a single bore.

Proportioning Valve. Due to the dynamic weight shift, as shown in Eq. (15.5), brake pressures that are appropriate for high-deceleration braking on front wheels usually are too high for the rear wheels; the result is that the rear wheels will tend to lock during braking. This problem can be decreased significantly through the use of proportioning valves. Standard proportioning valves allow equal front and rear brake pressures during low input pressures (corresponding to low deceleration rates and little dynamic load shift) but decrease the gain through the valve to less than one when a fixed input pressure (crack pressure) is reached. More sophisticated load-sensing valves are used in some applications when necessary, such as when dynamic load shifts and vehicle loading changes are wide enough to make a fixed proportioning valve insufficient for proper braking in all conditions. Load-sensing valves feature a means to measure the weight on the rear wheels and adjust the gain through the valve accordingly.

Figure 15.6 shows the two most common passenger car and light truck system schematics including proportioning valves. The vertically split brake system typically is used on rear-wheel-drive vehicles and the diagonally split system is typically used on front-wheel-drive vehicles.

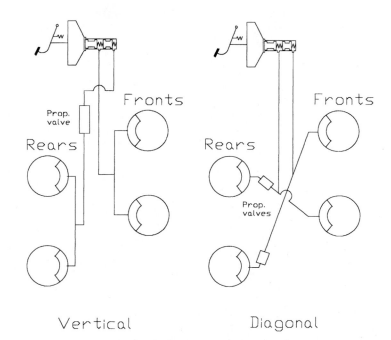

FIGURE 15.6   Vertical and diagonal split brake systems schematics.

Widespread use of diagonally split systems has been a direct result of the popularity of front-wheel-drive vehicles. Current law requires a half-system (hydraulic) failure stopping rate that is difficult to meet if the half system is the rear brakes (on a vertically split system) and the vehicle weight is significantly shifted towards the front as it is in front-wheel-drive vehicles. Diagonally split systems afford the use of one front brake regardless of the half-system failure, and front-wheel-drive vehicles can be made to pass the legal requirements despite the typically large difference between the weight on the front and on the rear wheels. However, diagonally split systems require two proportioning valves and tend to require more complex hydraulic plumbing than do vertically split systems.

15.3   ANTILOCK SYSTEMS

Although antilock concepts have been known for decades, widespread use of antilock (also called antiskid and ABS) began in the 1980s with systems developed with digital microprocessors/microcontrollers replacing the earlier analog units. An antilock system consists of a hydraulic modulator and hydraulic power source that may or may not be integrated with the system master cylinder and booster, wheel speed sensors, and an electronic control unit. The fundamental function of an antilock system is to prohibit wheel lock by sensing impending wheel lock and taking action through the hydraulic modulator to reduce the brake pressure in the wheel sufficiently to bring the wheel speed back to the slip level range necessary for near-optimum braking performance.

15.3.1   Objectives

The objectives of antilock systems are threefold: to reduce stopping distances, to improve stability, and to improve steerability during braking.

Stopping Distance.   As shown in Eq. (15.4), the distance to stop ($V_f = 0$) is a function of the initial velocity, the mass of the vehicle, and the braking force. From this equation it can be seen that by maximizing the braking force the stopping distance will be minimized, all other factors remaining constant. From Fig. 15.1 it is evident that on all types of surfaces, to a greater or lesser extent, there exists a peak frictional force. It follows that by keeping all of the wheels of a vehicle near the peak, an antilock system can attain maximum frictional force and, therefore, minimum stopping distance. This is an objective of antilock systems; however, it is tempered by the need for vehicle stability and steerability.

Stability.   Although decelerating and stopping vehicles constitutes a fundamental purpose of braking systems, maximum friction force may not be desirable in all cases. For example, if a vehicle is on a split-coefficient surface, (asphalt and ice, for example), such that significantly more braking force is obtainable on one side of the vehicle than on the other side, applying maximum braking force on both sides will result in a yaw moment that will tend to pull the vehicle to the high-coefficient side and contribute to vehicle instability. Typically, on short-wheelbase vehicles a control strategy is employed to control the pressure in the rear wheels together to improve stability; similarly, it is common for a front-wheel strategy to be employed to limit the initial side-to-side pressure difference so as to not induce excessive moment changes in the steering wheel and force the operator to make excessive steering corrections to counteract the yaw moment.

If an antilock system can keep the vehicle wheels near the peak frictional force range, then lateral force is reasonably high, though not maximized. This contributes to stability and is an objective of antilock systems.

Steerability.   Steerability depends on high lateral force. Good peak frictional force control is necessary in order to achieve satisfactory lateral force and, therefore, satisfactory steerability. Steerability while braking is important not only for minor course corrections but also for the possibility of steering around an obstacle. Antilock systems provide this feature through control to the peak frictional force range.

15.3.2   Antilock Components

The components of an antilock system are the wheel speed sensors, the hydraulic modulator, the hydraulic power source (usually an electric motor/pump), and the electronic control unit.

Wheel Speed Sensors.   Due to simplicity and proven reliability, variable reluctance wheel speed sensors typically are used in antilock systems. Used in conjunction with exciter rings, this type of sensor produces a sinusoidal output that is directly proportional in frequency and amplitude to the angular velocity of the sensed wheel.

Depending on the design of the sensor and exciter ring and the gap between them, the sensor output amplitude may be as low as 100 mV at very low vehicle speeds and over 100 V at high vehicle speeds.

Both single-pole and dual-pole variable reluctance sensors are used, depending on the application: single-pole sensors tend to have higher outputs and dual-pole sensors tend to have better immunity to some types of noise. A limitation of this technology is that the very low speed output tends to be too low to be sensed reliably by the electronic control unit, given the electrically noisy environment typical of vehicles. This can result in errors below 1 to 3 m/h and cumulative inaccuracies if this sensor is used in conjunction with an odometer function; normally, antilock function is inhibited at very low speeds. Both single-ended and balanced inputs are used in electronic control units to receive wheel speed signals. A variety of active sensor technologies, including Hall effect and magnetoresistive, can be used in applications requiring very low speed sensing and in applications in which an appropriate signal level cannot be achieved with conventional variable reluctance sensors.

Hydraulic Modulators. Hydraulic modulators typically take two forms in production antilock systems: solenoid valves and electric motors. A simplified solenoid valve system schematic is shown in Fig. 15.7. In this system, if the solenoid valves are de-energized, hydraulic fluid is free to flow between the master cylinder and the brakes. If too much pressure is presented to the brakes and wheel lock is imminent, the antilock system will actuate a solenoid valve and energize the hydraulic pump. Actuation of the solenoid valve allows pressure to decrease from the brake through the valve to a low-pressure accumulator/sump. The fluid is temporarily stored in the sump prior to being pumped back into the system by the hydraulic pump. Through repetitive energization/de-energization cycles, average pressure to a given wheel can be regulated to the level necessary to achieve the desired braking force. Typical brake pressure and resulting wheel speed cycling is shown in Fig. 15.8.

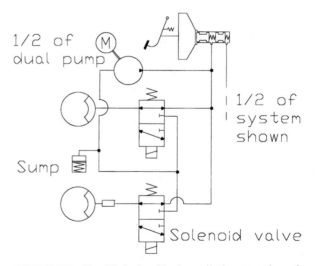

FIGURE 15.7 Simplified solenoid valve antilock system schematic.

Electric Motor/Pump. Although some antilock systems use multiple electric motors driving pistons to provide multiple-channel pressure reduction and rebuild, usually an electric motor-driven pump is used in conjunction with solenoid valves to achieve individual brake or brake channel pressure reduction and rebuild. A dual pump is often used to maintain a complete hydraulic separation of the two channels of the brake system. This is done to ensure that failure in one channel of the brake system will not affect operation of the other channel.

Electronic Control Unit. Control of the hydraulic modulator and electric motor/pump is performed by the electronic control unit. Modern customer expectations coupled with

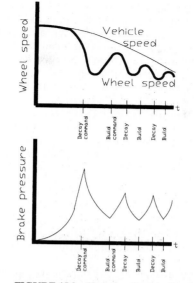

FIGURE 15.8   Typical antilock brake cycling.

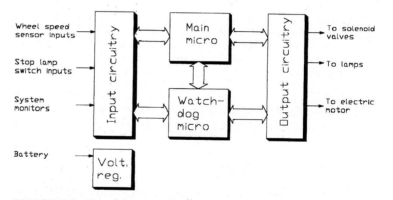

FIGURE 15.9   Electronic control unit block diagram.

decreasing microcontroller costs have made microcontroller-based electronic control units the norm rather than the exception. Although the control units can be either engine compartment-mounted or passenger compartment-mounted, reduced wiring costs favors the former. Also, for enhanced reliability, electronic control units may be either attached to or integrated with the hydraulic modulator.

15.3.3 Safety Considerations

Standard automotive brake systems have been developed and refined over the years to be highly reliable and safe. Because of its ability to decrease pressure in brakes, an antilock system must be designed using a disciplined methodology and must be rigorously tested prior to release for production.

Failure Mode and Effects Analyses/Fault Tree Analyses.   Failure mode and effects analyses (or fault tree analyses) are essential to the proper design of antilock systems. Both system-level and subsystem-level analyses need to be performed and fault effects and detection assumptions must be tested. No single failure can result in an unsafe condition and, if a fault is undetectable in the field, that fault in conjunction with any other fault must not result in an unsafe condition. Because of the complexity of the electronic control units, simulation techniques are used to test those fault effects in which bench or field testing is impractical.

Common Design Techniques to Improve Safety.   One of the most common techniques used to improve safety in antilock systems is to include extensive built-in-test within the electronic control unit. Typically, all inputs to the electronic control unit and outputs to the other components of the antilock system are tested for proper signals and loads, respectively, and all functions internal to the electronic control unit are extensively tested.

In addition, redundant processing is commonly used to insure the proper internal working of a microcontroller. This may take the form either of identical microcontrollers or of a main and a watchdog microcontroller that can inhibit operation.

In order to ensure inhibition of faulty antilock operation, antilock systems employ a relay function to remove actuation power from the output actuators; this function may take the form of a discrete relay or it may be a transistorized circuit. This relay function is a key element of the design since it affords a secondary method in which to inhibit energization of valves or the motor/pump and, therefore, a second level of safety relative to improper antilock operation.

Figure 15.9 is a typical electronic control unit block diagram.[3] Inputs are filtered and buffered prior to being presented to the microcontrollers for processing. Likewise, the microcontroller outputs are buffered/amplified and filtered prior to exiting the electronic control unit. In the diagram shown, the main microcontroller is responsible for the majority of processing and control of the outputs; the watchdog microcontroller, as its name implies, is responsible for monitoring for proper operation and inhibiting antilock if faults are indicated. A characteristic of modern antilock electronic control units is bidirectional communication between functional blocks; this is a result of the high level of built-in-test designed into the control units. For example, the output circuitry may be commanded to test the solenoid valves for proper current draw and convey the test results to the microcontrollers; similarly, the input circuitry may be commanded to perform tests on the sensors and other antilock components external to the electronic control unit, and convey the test results to the microcontrollers.

15.3.4   Antilock Control Logic Fundamentals

Due to the complexity of antilock braking and the requirements of stability and steerability as well as good stopping distance, the brake control algorithm is more easily represented as a state-space diagram than as a classical proportional-integrative-derivative control scheme.

A simplified state diagram for a single-channel antilock system is shown in Fig. 15.10. In this diagram, a vehicle not braking or decelerating would be in the NORMAL BRAKING state. If antilock action is warranted, it is because the brake pressure on a given channel has caused the wheel to begin to lock; the first action would be to decrease the brake pressure (DECAY state) in an effort to permit the locking wheel to reaccelerate. Fine control of the brake pressure is indicated by the states labeled HOLD OR BUILD/DECAY and SLOW BUILD and course control is indicated by the FAST BUILD state. (The course control is typically used during rapidly changing road surface conditions such as ice-to-asphalt transitions.) During the antilock cycle the state will change, as needed, to attain the type of brake pressure and resulting wheel speed activity as shown in Fig. 15.8. Once the need for antilock action has ended, the END ANTILOCK state is entered, the pump motor is de-energized, the valves are de-energized, and the system can return to the original NORMAL BRAKING state.[4]

How this state-space approach is integrated into a typical microcontroller flowchart is shown in Fig. 15.11. After RESET and INITIALIZATION, a microcontroller enters into a

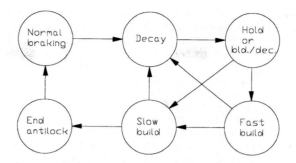

FIGURE 15.10   Simplified single-channel state diagram.

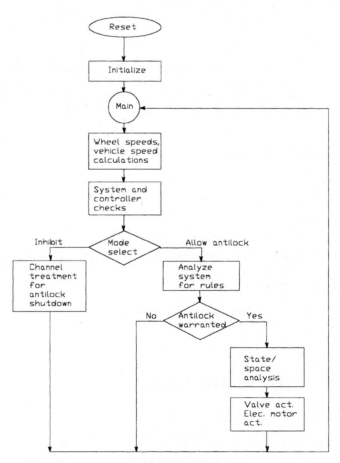

FIGURE 15.11   Simplified antilock flowchart.

MAIN loop that includes extensive system and electronic control unit checks as well as calculations of wheel speeds, prediction of vehicle speed, analysis of conditions warranting antilock action/state-space control law, and valve and motor/pump actuations.

Calculation of wheel speeds consists of scaling the wheel speed sensor inputs to a more usable form and possibly filtering noise due to axle deflection, brake squeal, other electrical systems, etc. A consideration is that the bandwidth of wheel acceleration and deceleration is large—50 g's may be attainable.

The vehicle velocity prediction is critical to many control schemes because wheel velocity relative to vehicle velocity, as well as wheel slip, may be used as a factor in determining appropriate valve action. Vehicle velocity prediction becomes difficult once the wheels begin to lock because the sensors will no longer be reliable indicators of vehicle speed. The methods used to predict vehicle velocity once the wheels have begun to lock consist of a set of rules that have been developed by antilock manufacturers through years of experience to ensure a prediction that has a high degree of accuracy to true vehicle speed.

The antilock system checks typically consist of sensor and valve/motor continuity tests and system voltage range tests. In addition, the checks normally include tests internal to the electronic control unit, such as inter-microcontroller communication.

Once it is determined that conditions are such that antilock action can be safely invoked if warranted, the wheel speed conditions are analyzed to establish the appropriate state for that channel. Primary indicators for most antilock control schemes are wheel slip and wheel deceleration. Another factor considered is the effect on vehicle stability if a particular state is commanded.

Actuation of the valves or electric motor actuators is a direct result of the decisions made in the analysis/state-space logic. Other than actuators requiring pulse-width modulation drives, the actuators normally will remain in the commanded state until the microcontroller loops back through the code (usually a few milliseconds).

15.3.5 Antilock System Testing

Antilock vehicle testing has evolved over the years to include the following most common tests:

- Straight-line stopping
- Braking in a turn
- Split coefficient stopping with associated stability criteria
- Transitional road surface testing including checkerboard and low/high and high/low coefficient surfaces
- Lane change maneuver

All of these tests may be performed on a variety of surfaces, at a variety of speeds, and with lightly loaded and heavily loaded vehicles.

15.4 FUTURE VEHICLE BRAKING SYSTEMS

A trend that will impact braking systems is the industry's desire to reduce vehicle wiring through the use of multiplexing techniques. As increasing numbers of vehicles are outfitted with antilock, this trend is expected to result in an increased number of antilock systems communicating with other vehicle systems through a multiplex link. In addition to the wheel speed/vehicle velocity information available from the antilock system, the antilock electronic control unit could benefit from this technology by being able to receive engine, transmission, steering angle, and other subsystem information.

Another trend in advanced electronically controlled braking systems is vehicle dynamics control during nonbraking maneuvers, as well as during braking. This is accomplished through use of the traction control actuators normally integrated in antilock hydraulic modulators, the addition of sensors to more accurately determine the dynamic state of the vehicle, and communication links with the drivetrain electronic controllers. Vehicle dynamic control holds the promise of safer vehicle operation through improved stability in all maneuvers.

The vehicle brake systems engineering community also is investigating the addition of radar to individual vehicles. This addition could lead to semiautomatic or automatic braking in emergency situations as the brake system anticipates the potential problem and aids the operator in safely applying the vehicle brakes in time to avoid a collision. This concept also lends itself to automatic braking in nonemergency situations to maintain safe distances between vehicles at high speeds.

Continuing interest in electric vehicles and the need for regenerative braking in these vehicles likely will significantly impact future braking systems. It is expected that the regenerative braking function will not be sufficient to provide adequate braking deceleration under all conditions and to provide operators the comfort and safety obtainable with conventional friction brake systems augmented by antilock systems. It is expected that a more complex electronic control system will be used in conjunction with electric vehicles to afford optimum power regeneration without sacrificing braking stopping distance, stability, or steerability.

These trends point to a continued use of friction brake systems through the end of the century and a significant expansion of the role of electronics in these systems.

GLOSSARY

Antilock (or ABS or Antiskid)   A system designed to prevent wheel lock during overbraking.

Antilock hydraulic modulator   A hydraulic brake pressure modulation actuator used in antilock systems.

Booster   A brake pedal force amplifier, typically vacuum or hydraulically powered.

Booster crack point   The brake pedal/push rod travel point initiating booster force amplification.

Booster runout   A condition in which the brake booster can no longer provide the gain required due to high input forces and the input force/output force slope becomes less positive.

Brake caliper   A part of a disc brake that contains the brake pads and the brake cylinder.

Braking force   A force tending to stop a moving vehicle. Usually applied to the force resulting from brake torque being applied to a wheel of a moving vehicle.

Braking maneuver   Any vehicle braking action intended to decelerate a moving vehicle, including partial as well as full stops.

Diagonal split brake system   A brake system configuration in which a front brake and its opposing rear brake are included in the same brake channel. This technique is used to allow braking on one front wheel in the case of catastrophic failure of the other brake channel.

Disk brake   A type of brake characterized by force being applied to both sides of a rotor, thereby creating braking torque.

Drum brake   A type of brake characterized by brake force being applied to the inner surface of a drum, thereby creating braking torque.

Dynamic load transfer   The characteristic of weight shift during deceleration that places more weight on the front wheels and reduces weight on the rear wheels.

Electric motor/pump   The typical hydraulic power source used in antilock systems; an electric motor driving a hydraulic pump.

Lateral force   Force perpendicular to the direction of travel.

Longitudinal slip   Relative slip between the wheels and the road surface in the direction of travel.

Master cylinder   A two-chambered hydraulic cylinder operated by the driver through actuation of the brake pedal.

Proportioning valve   A hydraulic valve designed to reduce pressure to the rear brakes relative to the front brakes once a crack point is reached. The valve may be fixed or load-sensing.

Regenerative braking   A type of braking used in electric vehicles in which the drive motor is used as a generator during braking, and it serves as the load to brake the vehicle. This technique is used to reclaim a portion of the energy expended during vehicle motion.

Vertical split brake system   A brake system configuration in which both front brakes are on one channel and both rear brakes are on the other channel.

Wheel slip   The difference between tangential wheel speed and road speed. A rolling tire with no braking torque on it exhibits 0 percent slip; a nonrotating tire on a moving vehicle exhibits 100 percent slip.

REFERENCES

1. J. Y. Wong, *Theory of Ground Vehicles,* John Wiley & Sons, New York, 1978.
2. T. D. Gillespie, *Fundamentals of Vehicle Dynamics,* Society of Automotive Engineers, Inc., Warrendale, Pa., 1992.
3. J. L. Cage, "The Bendix ABS underhood electronic control unit," *Automotive Technology International '90,* Sterling Publications International Limited, London, 1990.
4. J. L. Cage, and J. T. Hargenrader, "Safe electronic modules for antilock applications," *Automotive Technology International '91,* Sterling Publications International Limited, London, 1991.

ABOUT THE AUTHOR

Jerry L. Cage is the manager of electrical/electronics engineering, AlliedSignal Braking Systems. He has over 20 years experience in the design and development of automotive and aerospace control systems and harsh environment electronics. He has been awarded five U.S. patents in electronics and electrohydraulics.

CHAPTER 16
TRACTION CONTROL

Armin Czinczel
Development Engineer
Robert Bosch GmbH

16.1 INTRODUCTION

Traction control systems designed to prevent the drive wheels from spinning in response to application of excess throttle have been on the market since 1987. Vehicles with powerful engines are particularly susceptible to drive-wheel slip under acceleration from standstill and/or on low-traction road surfaces. The results include attenuated steering response on front-wheel-drive (FWD) vehicles, diminished vehicle stability on rear-wheel-drive (RWD) cars, and loss of effective accelerative force.

Large mutual discrepancies in left- and right-side traction levels engender early drive-wheel slip on slick surfaces. Under these conditions, the effective accelerative forces at both drive wheels are limited to a level corresponding to the adhesion available at the low-traction side. The traction control system inhibits wheelspin, allowing the wheel on the high-traction surface to apply maximum accelerative force to the road.

16.1.1 Optimizing Stability (Steering Control)

The essential requirement for systems designed to optimize vehicle stability (with RWD) and steering control (with FWD) is to maintain adequate lateral traction. The most basic arrangements achieve this end by controlling engine torque alone. Both drive wheels transmit the same level of motive force, dosed in accordance with the adhesion available at the low-traction wheel and thereby providing particularly large lateral-traction reserves at the wheel with the greater adhesion. When the traction levels are roughly equal at both drive wheels, the system enhances vehicle stability (steering control) while providing a certain increase in available effective accelerative force beyond that available on an uncontrolled vehicle with slipping wheels.

16.1.2 Optimizing Traction

The optimization of traction becomes a top priority when the motive force must be transmitted to surfaces on which the adhesion varies substantially between sides.

The typical passenger car features a differential unit at the drive axle; this unit allows virtually loss-free differences in wheel speed (for instance, in corners) in combination with uniform torque distribution to the drive wheels. This layout generally provides favorable dynamic vehicle response, as the equal distribution of drive torque inhibits vehicle yaw. However, a difference in the force-transmission potentials at the drive wheels can combine with demands for maximum traction to expose basic liabilities in the design principle.

Figure 16.1 illustrates the system dynamics of drive shaft, differential, and drive wheels on road surfaces affording differing levels of traction with adhesion coefficients μ_H, μ_L (high wheel, low wheel). The torque emanating from the driveshaft is distributed equally between the drive wheels. The low wheel responds to inadequate adhesion potential by spinning during brief wheel acceleration. The accelerative force transmitted through the high wheel then corresponds to the sum of the accelerative force at the low wheel plus its inertia $\Theta_R [\dot{\Omega}]/R$. Once the low wheel reaches its terminal speed, the accelerative force available at both wheels is limited to the maximum at the low wheel.

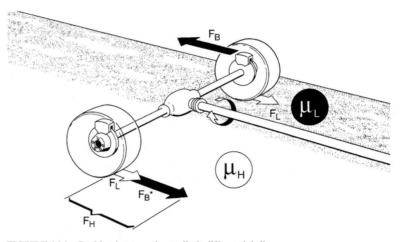

FIGURE 16.1 Braking intervention to limit differential slip.

The only way to increase the accelerative force at the high wheel is to prevent the low wheel from spinning. The first option, application of the wheel brake, is illustrated in Fig. 16.1. The application of braking force F_B at the low wheel prevents it from spinning. This makes the additional accelerative force F_B^* (the product of F_B multiplied by the ratio of effective braking radius to wheel radius) available at the high wheel.

A second option for maximum exploitation of traction potential is represented by the application of fixed, variable, or controlled differential-slip limitation mechanisms. These provide fixed coupling to ensure equal slippage rates at the drive wheels, thereby allowing them to develop maximum accelerative force.

During cornering at high rates of lateral acceleration, lateral variations in drive-wheel load occur, again producing a difference in acceleration potential. Brakes and limited-slip differential arrangements can also be applied to assist in ensuring maximum traction under these conditions.

16.1.3 Optimizing Stability and Traction

Traction-control systems incorporating engine-torque control and supplementary braking intervention (or controlled differentials) can be applied simultaneously to ensure consistent vehicle stability (steering control) and optimal acceleration within the limits imposed by physical constraints. Engine-torque control is the preferred method on road surfaces affording uniform adhesion, while application of braking force (or differential control) provides optimal acceleration at both drive wheels for dealing with surfaces displaying lateral variations in traction.

16.2   FORCES AFFECTING WHEEL TRACTION: FUNDAMENTAL CONCEPTS

The dynamic forces that define the tires' braking response on straights and during cornering are already familiar from the technical literature. The transmission of accelerative force in straight-line operation and in curves is subject to the same qualitative principles that apply during braking. The slip ratio which applies for braking.

$$\lambda_B = \frac{V_F - \Theta_R R}{V_F}$$

is replaced by the ratio

$$\lambda_A = \frac{\Theta_R r - V_F}{V_F} \quad \text{with} \quad \Theta_R r \geq V_F$$

Acceleration slip rates can range all the way from 0 to the very high numbers used to describe the conditions that can occur when the drive wheels spin freely during attempts to accelerate from rest.

Figures 16.2 to 16.4 show acceleration and side-force coefficients as a function of the acceleration slip. Figure 16.2 applies for acceleration during straight-line operation. The demand for reserves in lateral adhesion is fairly diminutive under these conditions (including, for instance, compensation for side winds); thus, traction remains the salient factor.

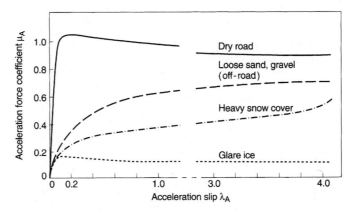

FIGURE 16.2   Adhesion coefficient for acceleration μ_A as a function of acceleration slip λ_A.

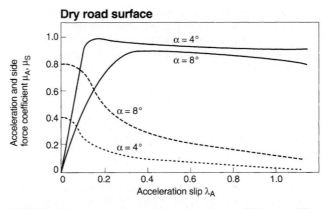

FIGURE 16.3 Acceleration and lateral traction coefficients at different slip angles α.

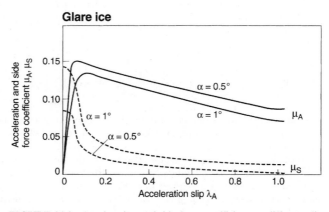

FIGURE 16.4 Acceleration and side-force coefficients at different slip angles α.

On dry road surfaces, maximum accelerative force is available at slip rates of 10 to 30 percent, with traction enhancements of 5 to 10 percent possible relative to spinning drive wheels.

On glare ice, maximum traction is achieved at extremely diminutive acceleration slip levels (2 to 5 percent). On loose sand and gravel and in deep snow (especially in combination with snow chains), the coefficient of acceleration force increases continually along with the slip rate, with the respective maxima only being reached somewhere beyond 60 percent. Thus, the slip rates of 2 to 20 percent found within the ASR's operating range will not provide adequate traction under all operating conditions.

For this reason, all known ASR systems incorporate slip-threshold switches or ASR deactivation switches, which allow the vehicle operator to either reset the ASR slip-control threshold to substantially higher levels, or to switch the system off entirely should the need arise.

Figures 16.3 and 16.4 apply to acceleration during cornering; under these conditions the drive wheels are subject to various degrees of lateral force as a function of the vehicle's rate of lateral acceleration. Increasing acceleration slip (and increasing accelerative forces) cause a drop in the lateral forces, which then respond to still higher slip rates by collapsing to small residual levels.

Figure 16.3 represents the response pattern on a dry road surface. The curve starts at a rate of acceleration slip of zero. Initially, the side-force coefficient displays a moderate downward trend. However, continuing increases in the coefficient of acceleration force induce a substantial fall in the side-force coefficient. The figure shows that the accelerative force must be limited to a fraction of its ultimate potential if sufficient lateral forces are to be maintained.

On glare ice (Fig. 16.4), the extremely limited friction potential means that vehicle stability under acceleration remains available only at relatively small slip angles (ca. ≤2°). Relatively diminutive slip angles (≤0.05°) will be sufficient to induce a radical drop in the side-force coefficient. This makes it clear that an extremely precise and sensitive slip control is required on glare ice (and other low-friction road surfaces). The traction-control system must thus exhibit a high degree of monitoring accuracy, while signal processing and actuation of the final-control elements must be rapid and precise.

16.3 CONTROLLED VARIABLES

The four wheel speeds used for the ABS supply the following closed-loop control parameters for the ASR traction control system: the acceleration slip from the lateral variation in the rotation speeds of the driven and nondriven wheels, and the angular acceleration of the driven wheels.

The following secondary control parameters are also calculated: vehicle velocity and acceleration based on the speeds of the nondriven wheels, and curve recognition, derived from comparisons of the speeds of the nondriven wheels.

The target value for acceleration slip is defined as the mean rotational velocity of the nondriven wheels plus a specified speed difference known as the slip threshold setpoint. The main goal of regulating acceleration slip can thus be divided into two subsidiary objectives: closed-loop control of acceleration slip to maintain slip rates at the specified levels with maximum precision, and calculation of optimal slip setpoints for different operating conditions and their implementation as control objectives.

Depending on the final-control strategy being used, various control concepts can be employed to meet the first objective. With throttle-valve control, a setpoint calculated from a number of signals is adopted for regulation as soon as the closed-loop control enters operation. The subsequent control process basically corresponds to that of a PI controller. When the brakes are used, arrangements are necessary to compensate for the nonlinear pressure-volume curve which governs the response in the brake calipers. The first stage of the closed-loop control program thus employs a sensing pulse corresponding to a relatively large volume; this compensates for compliance in the brake caliper. In the next stage, the system responds to positive deviations from the setpoint with graduated pressure increases; the rate of increase corresponds to the degree of divergence. A subsequent drop below the control setpoint initiates a pressure-relief stage (sequence of defined pressure-relief and holding phases). This impulse series, in which the length of the pressure-relief phases increases continually, is followed by termination of braking intervention.

Ignition and fuel-injection intervention essentially conform to the D controller closed-loop control concept. The difficulty associated with determining satisfactory setpoint values results from the fact that optimal acceleration and lateral forces cannot be achieved simultaneously. The ASR control algorithm must therefore meet varying operator demands for linear traction and lateral adhesion by using priority-control strategies and adaptive response patterns.

High vehicle speeds are accompanied by lower operator requirements for traction, especially with low coefficients of adhesion. At the same time, reductions in vehicle stability and steering response are not acceptable. The control strategy is thus designed to provide progressively lower slip threshold setpoints as the vehicle speed increases, with priority being shifted from linear traction to lateral adhesion.

The vehicle's acceleration rate and the regulated level of engine output provide the basis for reliable conclusions regarding the coefficient of friction. Thus, another important strategy takes into account the coefficient of friction at the road surface. The slip threshold setpoint is raised in response to higher friction coefficients. This ensures that an ASR system designed for optimum performance on low-friction surfaces will not intervene prematurely on high-traction surfaces.

Yet another important control strategy is based on the cornering detection mentioned previously. This system employs the difference in the wheel speeds of the nondriven wheels as a basis for reductions in the slip setpoint to enhance stability in curves. This speed differential can be used to calculate the vehicle's rate of lateral acceleration. A large discrepancy indicates a high rate of lateral acceleration, meaning that a high coefficient of friction may also be assumed. In this case, the slip setpoint should not be reduced, but rather increased.

16.4   CONTROL MODES

16.4.1   Modulation of Engine Torque

Various control intervention procedures can be employed, either singularly or in combination, to regulate engine torque:

- Throttle-valve control with the assistance of the electronic performance control or an automatic throttle-valve actuator (ADS)
- Adjustment of the ignition-advance angle
- Selective ignition cutout, combined with suppression of fuel injection
- Fuel injection suppression alone

Slippage at the drive wheels generally occurs in response to an excess of torque relative to the coefficient of friction available at the road surface. Controlled reduction of engine torque is thus a logical step. It is always the most suitable method in cases where virtually identical adhesion is present at both drive wheels. At the same time, the response times for the individual engine controls must be considered if adequate vehicle stability is to be ensured (see Fig. 16.5).

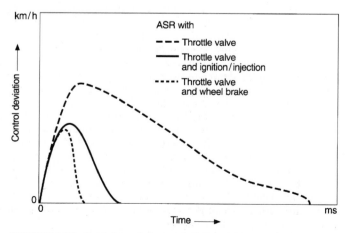

FIGURE 16.5 Deviation of the controlled variable during first control cycle with different actuators.

If control is restricted to the throttle-valve position alone, the throttle valve's response time, response delays within the intake tract, inertial forces in the engine, and drivetrain compliance will all result in palpable wheel slippage continuing for a relatively long period of time. Throttle regulation alone cannot ensure adequate vehicle stability on rear-wheel-drive vehicles. This qualification is particularly applicable to vehicles with a high power-to-weight ratio. On FWD and 4WD vehicles, throttle-valve control alone can be sufficiently effective if response delays are minimized.

Arrangements combining throttle-valve regulation with interruptions in the fuel injection produce substantial reductions in the amplitude and duration of wheel slip. Thus, this concept can be used to guarantee good vehicle stability regardless of which axles are driven.

In principle, it is also possible to design an ASR system based solely on regulation of the ignition and injection systems. This concept employs a system with sequential fuel injection. It alternately cuts out individual cylinders, while the ignition is also adjusted for the duration of the control process. Although this concept can be employed to ensure adequate vehicle stability regardless of drive configuration, certain sacrifices in comfort are unavoidable, especially during operation on ice and during the warm-up phase.

16.4.2 Brake Torque Control

The brakes at the drive wheels are capable of converting large amounts of kinetic energy into heat, at least for limited periods of time. In addition, the response times can be held extremely short, making it possible to limit slippage increases to very low levels.

ASR systems relying exclusively on braking intervention appear suitable for regulating spin at the drive wheels.

Traction enhancements during starts and under acceleration on road surfaces affording varying levels of adhesion at the left and right sides are especially significant with this system.

The ASR hydraulic unit used to generate the braking forces employs components which are already present for the ABS. Cost considerations make it important that ASR hydraulic systems require an absolute minimum in additional components beyond those already available for the ABS.

The hydraulic concepts can be classified in two categories, according to whether stored hydraulic energy is employed or not. A dual-strategy system including rapid braking intervention with stored hydraulic energy is always to be recommended where the engine torque control is based entirely on throttle valve adjustments with their relatively long response times.

Figures 16.6 and 16.7 illustrate two examples of ASR braking intervention using stored energy.

Brake Torque Control with Stored Energy. In this ASR system, designed for RWD vehicles in the upper price range, engine torque is regulated exclusively by the engine performance control (EPS) unit. Rapid braking intervention is required for enhanced regulation of vehicle stability; this also ensures optimal traction at both drive wheels, especially with lateral variations in adhesion potential. This system offers optimal vehicle stability and traction combined with a high level of comfort. Figure 16.6 illustrates the design of the integrated ABS/ASR hydraulic unit.

The primer pump draws brake fluid from the master-cylinder reservoir and supplies it to the ABS return pump under small positive pressure. To meet the requirements of the ABS system, the dual-circuit ABS return pump is expanded to include a third plunger, which assumes responsibility for the ASR storage charge. For "rapid" braking intervention, the pressure in the wheel cylinder must escalate from 0 to 50 bar in less than 200 ms. A hydropump, with its limited supply capacity, is not capable of providing this order of pressure build-up in the required time, necessitating the use of a high-pressure accumulator to supply the required brake fluid with adequate alacrity.

When the traction control system is activated, the switchover valve moves to the third position and brake fluid from the reservoir is supplied to the two ABS/ASR control valves. While

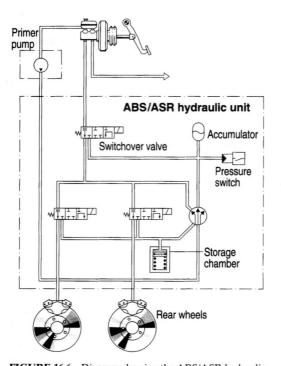

FIGURE 16.6   Diagram showing the ABS/ASR hydarulic circuit using braking force with stored energy (integrated system).

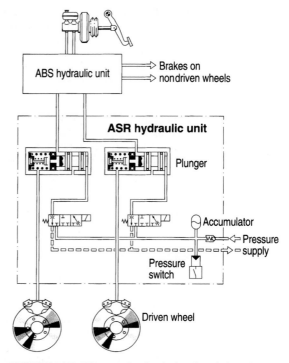

FIGURE 16.7   Diagram showing hydraulic unit for ASR system with braking intervention using stored energy via plunger.

an ABS solenoid valve can satisfy the requirements of the ABS hydraulic circuit, two solenoid valves are needed for the ABS/ASR hydraulic unit in order to allow individual braking control at the drive wheels.

These two solenoid valves regulate brake pressures at the driven wheels in accordance with the ASR control commands. Accumulator charging is controlled by the pressure switch and continues during normal vehicle operation. A special low-noise pump design is employed to meet stringent customer specifications.

ABS/ASR System with Brake Intervention Using Stored Energy (separate design).   One version employs a high-pressure accumulator to provide hydraulic energy for ASR braking. An engine-driven pump (level control) supplies hydraulic fluid to the accumulator. The system includes a plunger for each driven-wheel brake. An additional 3/3 ABS valve is also installed to govern the supply of hydraulic fluid from the reservoir to the primary side of the plunger and to separate this medium from the brake fluid present on the secondary side. The solenoid valves respond to the position commands from the ABS/ASR control unit to control pressure accumulation, maintenance, and release operations to maintain the required pressure level on the plungers' primary sides. The plungers move to the left. Initially, a central valve closes to block the connection with the master cylinder. The plunger's displacement pressurizes the brake fluid on the secondary side to produce the desired pressure level in the wheel cylinder.

ASR designs relying on stored energy to activate plungers are always worthy of consideration in those cases where the vehicle is already equipped with a hydraulic energy supply for other purposes (e.g., power steering, level control).

Brake Torque Control without Stored Energy.   Each of the ASR hydraulic units described requires a high-pressure accumulator to ensure that the braking energy can be provided quickly enough. This means additional design complication with attendant expenditure.

Another system differs from those already described by using the supply circuit of the ABS return pump exclusively to regulate the braking force at the drive wheels. The return pump forms part of a self-priming circuit, thus employing the (already installed) ABS return pump as an inexpensive source of energy for braking. The ASR braking function can thus be achieved with a minimum of additional design complication.

Figure 16.8 shows the hydraulic circuit for a passenger car with a K-pattern brake circuit and front-wheel-drive. When the intake valve opens, the self-priming pump extracts brake fluid from the reservoir and draws it into its circuit before supplying it directly to the ABS/ASR control valve at the drive wheel. The control valve regulates braking force by building up, maintaining, and releasing pressure in accordance with the respective position commands from the control unit. The fluid bled by the control valve in the pressure-release mode is returned to the pump's intake side. A switchover valve connects the high-pressure side of the self-priming return pump with the second brake circuit (governing the other front-wheel brake) and the pressure-relief valve responsible for regulating the ASR system pressure. With the exception of the suction line, the second brake circuit features a symmetrical layout. The passage to the master cylinder is also closed.

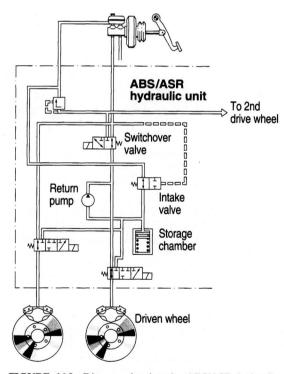

FIGURE 16.8 Diagram showing the ABS/ASR hydraulic unit employed for braking intervention without stored energy.

This ASR system can be installed in rear-wheel-drive vehicles with TT brake circuit configurations with even less expenditure: because both drive-wheel brakes are then in the same circuit, only a single switchover valve is required.

New Design for Brake Torque Control without Stored Energy.   The principle of braking intervention without stored energy has been developed further for a new generation of ASR systems entering production in 1993. (See Fig. 16.9.)

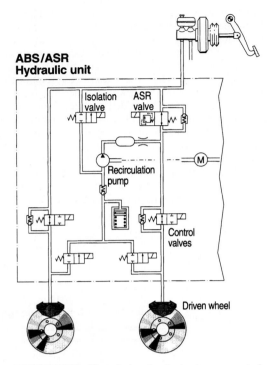

FIGURE 16.9 New design for brake torque control without stored energy.

The self-priming recirculation pump draws fluid from the master cylinder through an electrically controlled isolation valve, obviating the requirement for an additional intake line. Meanwhile, the pressure-relief valve can be integrated within the ASR valve. This configuration allows creation of a self-contained system combining simplified installation with enhanced safety. In addition, the reduction in the number of components improves reliability.

The 3/3 valves employed on earlier versions have been replaced by extremely small 2/2 solenoid valves.

16.4.3 Differential Slip Modulation

ABS/ASR System Regulating Differential Slip on Rear-Wheel-Drive Vehicles.   This system controls the differential's lateral slip to improve traction for starting off and for simultaneous acceleration and cornering on road surfaces affording different levels of traction from left to right. The slip-limitation mode remains active until a specific vehicle speed is attained, and is deactivated completely at higher speeds.

When the vehicle starts off, the rotation speeds of the wheels on the outside of the curve are subjected to a mutual comparison. The lock is activated once a specific difference in the two speeds is exceeded. There then follows a comparison of the rotation speeds of the driven

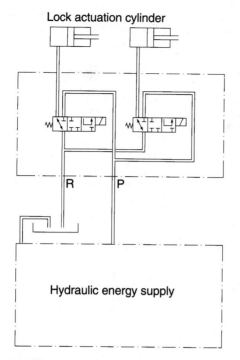

Lock actuation cylinder

R P

Hydraulic energy supply

FIGURE 16.10 Hydraulic unit for control of rear-axle and interaxle differential locks.

wheels. The lock is deactivated as soon as the difference in rotation speeds drops below a specified level.

ABS/ASR System for Controlling Rear-Axle and Interaxle Differential Slip Rates on 4WD Passenger Cars. This version incorporates an additional interaxle control feature.

Four-wheel drive passenger cars employ a specific fixed front-to-rear distribution of engine output to provide optimum vehicle characteristics within the stable range (that is, with limited amounts of acceleration slip). One or both wheels at either axle can respond to throttle application on low-traction surfaces with immoderate wheelspin. This is where the interaxle slip limiter is activated to adapt the distribution of engine torque to the traction available at the respective axles, thereby improving traction while also enhancing vehicle stability and steering response.

Figure 16.10 illustrates the design of the hydraulic unit used to control the lateral and interaxle slip-limitation mechanisms. An electric pump supplies a high-pressure accumulator. The accumulator, in turn, provides pressure to a 3/3 solenoid valve for control of the lateral and interaxle locking mechanisms. The return volume from the pressure-relief phase is conducted to a separate reservoir.

16.5   TRACTION CONTROL COMPONENTS

The following is a selection of the components used in Bosch traction control systems.

16.5.1   Wheel-Speed Sensors

The system employs the same wheel-speed sensors that provide the information for the antilock braking system.

16.5.2   Electronic Control Unit

Figure 16.11 shows an ASR circuit diagram. An input amplifier IC receives the signals from the wheel-speed sensor; the signal frequency indicates the wheel speed. Two microcontrollers then process the signals to determine the wheel speed and acceleration rate. These data, in turn, provide the basis for calculations to determine the actual and desired values for slip control. Overall signal processing, the control algorithm, and the monitoring software are present in each of these microcontrollers to provide the system with backup capabilities.

Three output amplifiers control the solenoid valves, the ABS and ASR indicator lamps, the driver-information lamp, and the motor and valve relay. An additional IC is required to monitor the braking requirement and pump-motor voltage and for diagnosis.

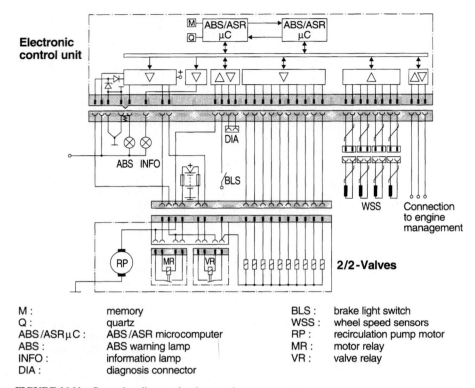

M :	memory	BLS :	brake light switch
Q :	quartz	WSS :	wheel speed sensors
ABS/ASRμC :	ABS/ASR microcomputer	RP :	recirculation pump motor
ABS :	ABS warning lamp	MR :	motor relay
INFO :	information lamp	VR :	valve relay
DIA :	diagnosis connector		

FIGURE 16.11 Operation diagram for the complete system.

16.5.3 Hydraulic Unit

Four examples of ASR hydraulic units were given in Sec. 16.4.2.

16.5.4 Electronic Throttle Control Actuator

See Sec. 10.3.1.

16.5.5 Simplified Throttle Control Actuator

See Sec. 10.3.1.

16.5.6 Fuel Injection and Ignition Control

This system reduces engine output by suppressing the fuel injection process.

Complete fuel injection suppression would lead to a total loss of engine output—a smooth, graduated response would be impossible with this kind of arrangement. In contrast, selective suppression of the injection process at individual cylinders can be employed to achieve a good compromise between quick response and a graduated reduction of engine power. This is the design principle behind the new concept.

With suppression according to individual cylinders, the number of control increments is the same as the number of cylinders. Because this limited number of control stages is still inadequate for a (as an example) four-cylinder engine, a supplementary strategy is employed: this is referred to as alternating injection suppression. It consists of varying the number of active cylinders by one after every two crankshaft rotations to produce a mean torque lying between the torques produced at the two cylinder stages. This method doubles the number of control stages to achieve an acceptable level of driving comfort, while complementary reductions in ignition advance can be employed to provide additional incremental adjustments.

In cases where the excess torque is substantial, injection suppression can be supplemented by short-term ignition cutout to provide extremely rapid output reductions. Figure 16.12 shows the design of the system. In addition to the modest expense, this system also offers vehicle manufacturers an additional advantage in the form of space savings (no additional space required) and simplicity (limited amount of extra wiring).

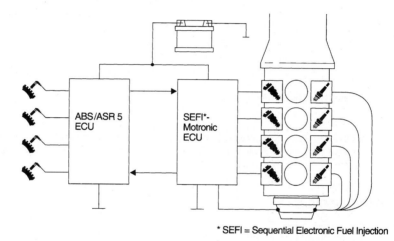

* SEFI = Sequential Electronic Fuel Injection

FIGURE 16.12   ASR EZ system.

16.6 APPLICATIONS ON HEAVY COMMERCIAL VEHICLES

Heavy commercial vehicles are used in a highly variegated range of applications. In principle, the ASR installed on these vehicles employs the same control strategies used for passenger cars: engine-output control and braking intervention.

Differences in vehicle application can make it necessary to employ ASR systems in various levels of complexity (for instance, relying on braking control or engine output control exclusively). The control unit recognizes the design stage and carries out its control functions accordingly. This makes it possible to employ the most economical ASR system for each vehicle type and particular application.

Figure 16.13 features a schematic diagram showing a typical 4×2 vehicle equipped with a top-of-the-line ABS/ASR system. During acceleration on μ-split surfaces, the brake-force regulator limits slip between the drive wheels. The ASR valve (4) is activated on the side with the spinning wheel, while the ABS pressure-control valve (3) allows graduated increases in pressure at the wheel cylinder.

If both drive wheels start to spin on a road surface affording equal traction on both sides, the engine-output controller responds by reducing the drive slip to optimum values. In this example, the electric performance control (EPC) (10) assumes the role of final-control ele-

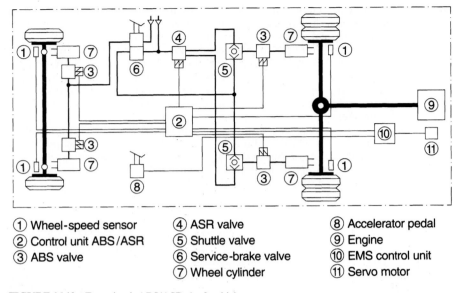

FIGURE 16.13   Four-circuit ABS/ASR, 4 × 2 vehicle.

1. Wheel-speed sensor
2. Control unit ABS/ASR
3. ABS valve
4. ASR valve
5. Shuttle valve
6. Service-brake valve
7. Wheel cylinder
8. Accelerator pedal
9. Engine
10. EMS control unit
11. Servo motor

ment. The ABS/ASR control unit (2) transmits the desired increment of reduction to the EPC control unit via interface, and also controls the electric motor at the injection pump.

16.7   FUTURE TRENDS

Ensuring driving stability is the most important task of ASR with rear-wheel-drive cars. This task can be achieved by a fast engine torque control or a combination of throttle control and a fast brake control.

ASR systems with a fast engine torque control (ignition and injection intervention) and brake control without stored energy will be widely used.

Although the application of controllable differential locks also offers efficient ASR control, the higher costs of this system will prevent wide usage.

The predominant demand on ASR systems for front-wheel-drive cars is that of traction optimization. Therefore, an ASR system with brake torque control is needed. The combination of brake torque control and engine torque control results in a complex, efficient system.

In the future, only ASR systems with brake torque control will be widely used with front-wheel-drive cars. Especially the combination of brake torque control and engine torque control with ignition and injection intervention will be widely used.

GLOSSARY

ABS return pump   A piston pump that draws back brake fluid to the master cylinder.

Alternating injection suppression   A variation of the number of active cylinders by one after every two crankshaft rotations in order to modulate the engine torque.

ASR deactivation switch   A device to switch off ASR on sand and loose gravel in order to achieve maximum traction on these surfaces.

Automatic throttle valve actuator   A simple actuator for automatic throttle angle reduction in case of excessive acceleration slip.

Braking intervention   Automatic brake application at drive wheels in case of excessive acceleration slip.

D controller   A controller with differentiating characteristics.

Electronic performance control   Electronic accelerator control.

Engine torque control   An actuator to modulate engine torque in case of excessive acceleration slip.

PI controller   Controller with proportional and integral characteristics.

Slip threshold switch   Switch to increase desired slip threshold on sand and loose gravel.

Switchover valve   A valve to switch hydraulic performance from normal braking to ASR performance.

Throttle valve control   ASR actuator to modulate the throttle angle.

3/3 ABS valve   A valve with three connections and three positions for ABS wheel pressure modulation.

BIBLIOGRAPHY

Maisch, Wolfgang, Jonner Wolf-Dieter, and Alfred Sigl, "Traction control—a logical addition to ABS," *SAE International Congress and Exposition,* Detroit, Feb. 23–27, 1987.

Kolberg, Gerhard, "Elektronische Motorsteuerung für Kraftfahrzeuge," *Motortechnische Zeitschrift,* Germany, 1985.

Demel, H., and A. Czinczel, "ABS-task, design, and function," *I Mech E Conference,* London, 1988-6, pp. 89–94.

Buschmann, G., N. Ocvirk, and P. Volz, "Integrated traction control function—the consequent extension of highly sophisticated anti-lock systems," *I Mech E Conference,* 1988-6, pp. 103–112.

Klein, Hans-Christof, "PkW-ABV-Bremssysteme mit weiteren integrierten Funktionen," *Automobilindustrie,* May 1989, pp. 659–673.

Kupper, R., and N. Hover "Anti-slip-control system with high safety and comfort," *I Mech E,* C382/113, 1989, pp. 523–531.

Sigl, A., and H. Demel, "ASR-traction control, state of the art and some prospects," SAE 900.24.

Sigl, A., and A. Czinczel, "ABS/ASR5—the new ABS/ASR system for passenger cars," *I Mech E Conference,* London, 1993, pp. 81–87.

ABOUT THE AUTHOR

Dipl. Ing. Armin Czinczel received a degree in mechanical engineering at the Technical University in Hanover, Germany. He started his professional career with development work on navigation systems. He joined Bosch in 1968, working on ABS development until his retirement in 1994.

CHAPTER 17
SUSPENSION CONTROL

Akatsu Yohsuke
Manager, Vehicle Research Laboratory
Nissan Motor Co., Ltd.

The function of a suspension system in an automobile is to improve ride comfort and stability. An important consideration in suspension design is how to obtain both improved ride comfort and stability, since they are normally in conflict. Advances in electronic control technology, applied to the automobile, can resolve this conflict.

17.1 SHOCK ABSORBER CONTROL SYSTEM

During the past 20 years, many different damping control systems have been studied. The main purpose of all these systems is to select the optimum damping force for various driving conditions. The first function of a shock absorber is to control vehicle movement against inertial forces, such as roll when the vehicle turns and pitch when the vehicle is braked. The second function is to prevent vehicle vibration caused by road surface inputs. To satisfy both functions it is necessary to control damping forces.

There are three basic parts of a damping control system: a damping control device (actuator), sensors, and software (control strategy). Optimum damping forces should be set for various running conditions in order to improve ride comfort and handling stability.

17.1.1 System Configuration

One of the damping control system configurations is shown in Fig. 17.1. This system uses five sensors, including a supersonic road sensor, to detect running conditions. Control signals are sent to adjust the damping force of the variable shock absorbers to optimum values. A main advantage to this type of system is that, through the use of a road sensor, it can provide optimum control in accordance with the actual road conditions. This system incorporates three discrete damper characteristics. Sensors used are: a vehicle speed sensor, a steering angle sensor, an acceleration and deceleration sensor, a brake sensor, and a supersonic sensor to detect road conditions.

One system uses four piezo sensors and four piezo actuators on each wheel in order to change the damping forces as quickly as possible. This system incorporates two discrete damper characteristics. Sensors used are: four piezo sensors on each wheel, a stop lamp switch, a steering sensor, and a vehicle speed sensor.

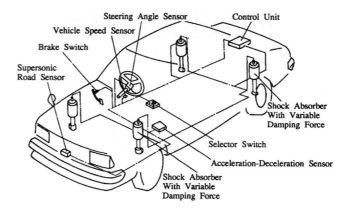

FIGURE 17.1   Principal components of a damping control system.

17.1.2   Actuator and Sensor

Actuator.   Discrete damping control actuators often use a built-in motor to change the damping force. This motor turns a rotary valve to select the orifice diameter for three different damping levels: soft, medium, and hard. The stopping position of the rotary valve is controlled by encoder signals.

Another actuator is a piezo actuator consisting of 88 piezo elements, and it is installed in the piston rod of a shock absorber. When a high voltage (500 V) is applied to the piezo actuator, it expands about 50 μm with reverse piezoelectric effect. Elongation in the piezo actuator causes the plunger pin to be pushed out through the displacement hydraulic coupling unit. As a result, the plunger pin moves down to open the bypass of the damping force switching valve. The result is a soft damping force. Figure 17.2 shows this valve.

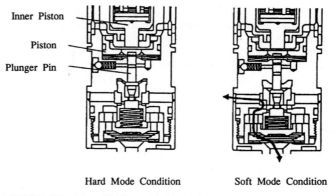

FIGURE 17.2   Damping force switching valve.

Sensor.   A sensor using a supersonic wave to detect the road surface is shown in Fig. 17.3. The vehicle height from road to body is calculated on the basis of reflection time T. Judgment of the road condition is made by analyzing the pattern of change in vehicle height.

A sensor using the piezoelectric effect is shown in Fig. 17.4. Installed in the piston rod of a shock absorber, the sensor generates an electric charge in accordance with axial force from the road surface.

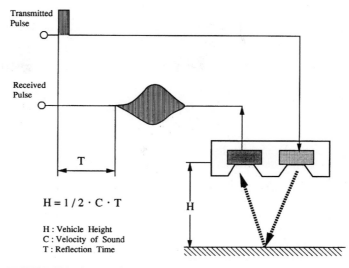

FIGURE 17.3   Supersonic sensor.

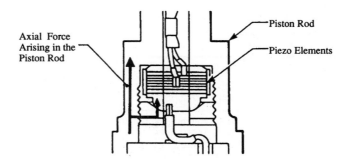

FIGURE 17.4   Piezoelectric sensor.

17.1.3 Control System

The control system of Fig. 17.1 is shown in Table 17.1. The occurrence of roll and pitch can be predicted from various sensors. Single bumps or dips are detected from changes in vehicle height. The outline of the road surface judgment logic is shown in Table 17.2.

The block diagram of the system using four piezo sensors and four piezo actuators is shown in Fig. 17.5. The damping force arising in an absorber increases instantaneously as the tire or wheel goes up or down in accordance with unevenness of the road surface. Each piezo sensor outputs to the electronic control unit continuous signals indicating damping force differential. If the value of damping force differential exceeds a predetermined level, the system switches from firm mode to soft mode. The system is designed so that the firm mode re-engages immediately after the vibrations due to poor road surface cease.

Many of the limitations and disadvantages of the conventional shock absorber can be eliminated by the damping control systems. They include semiactive suspension systems which are capable of providing both ride comfort and good handling.

TABLE 17.1   Damping Force Control System

| | | Sensors used | | | | | Damping force |
	Control objectives	Vehicle speed	Steering angle	Accel/ decel	Brake	Road condition	Front / Rear
Roll	Roll reduction for quick steering operation	O	O				Hard / Hard
Pitch	Reduction of nose diving by braking				O	O	Hard / Hard
	Reduction of pitching when accelerating and decelerating	O		O			Medium / Medium
Bouncing	Reduction of light, bouncy vibrations in bottoming	O				O	Medium / Medium
	Reduction of light, bouncy vibrations in bouncing on a heaving road	O				O	Medium / Medium
Road holding performance	Road holding performance improvement when running on rough roads	O				O	Medium / Medium
Others	Stability improvement at high speed	O					Medium / Soft
	Prevention of shaking when stopping and rocking when passengers exit or enter	O					Hard / Hard

TABLE 17.2   Road Condition Judgment Logic

| High-frequency components | Low-frequency components | |
	Small	Large
Small	Smooth road damping force control unnecessary	Heaving road
Large		Rough road

17.2   HYDROPNEUMATIC SUSPENSION CONTROL SYSTEM

A hermetically sealed quantity of gas is used in the hydropneumatic suspension control system. The gas and hydraulic oil are separated by a rubber diaphragm, as shown in Fig. 17.6a. The mechanical springs are replaced by gas. The shock absorber damping mechanism is achieved by the orifice fitted with valves.

17.2.1   System Configuration

As shown in Fig. 17.6b, by adding an additional sphere to the hydropneumatic system, a controllable hydropneumatic system can be realized. If the regulator is closed, the system is in a firm mode. If the regulator is open, the spring constant of the suspension system becomes lower by increasing the total volume of the sphere, and the total damping force is reduced.

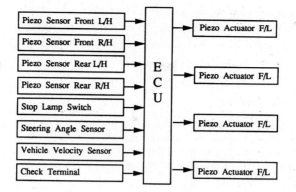

FIGURE 17.5   Block diagram of damping control system.

Depending on the sensors used, which detect vehicle driving and road surface conditions, this system can change the regulator characteristics in order to achieve both good ride comfort and handling stability.

17.3   ELECTRONIC LEVELING CONTROL SYSTEM

In a pneumatic and hydropneumatic suspension, the vehicle body can be maintained at a constant height from the road surface, keeping a low spring constant. The advantages of an electronic control system are:

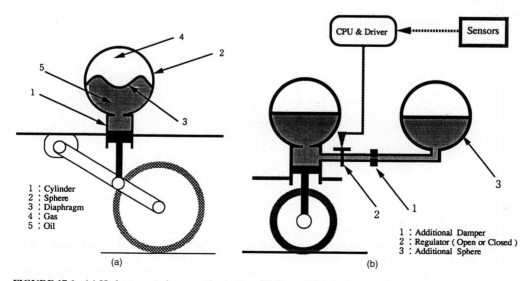

FIGURE 17.6   (*a*) Hydropneumatic suspension system; (*b*) Controllable hydropneumatic suspension system.

- Keeping a low spring rate to achieve good ride comfort independent of load conditions
- Increase in vehicle body height on rough road surfaces
- Changing spring rate and damping force in accordance with driving conditions and road surfaces

17.3.1   System Configuration

The system is shown in Fig. 17.7. It consists of eight sensors, a mode select switch, air spring/shock absorber units on four wheels, actuators to operate the changing valves in the unit, a compressor unit and five height control valves for air springs, and an electronic control unit (ECU). The system configuration is shown in Fig. 17.8.

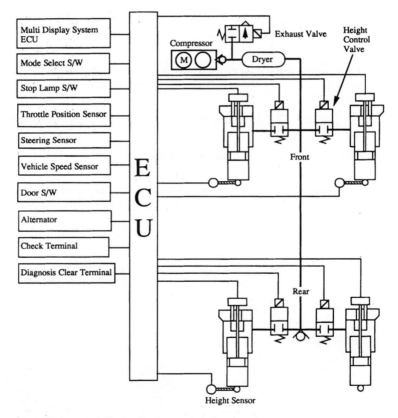

FIGURE 17.7   Principal components of an air suspension system.

17.3.2   Components

The structure of the air suspension unit consists of a shock absorber, a pneumatic piston surrounding the shock absorber, main and sub-air chambers, a rolling diaphragm, and valves which change the suspension stroke.

The actuator uses a dc motor, which has two shafts to operate the valves for the air spring and the shock absorber. The rotation of the motor is reduced by the sector gear and operates

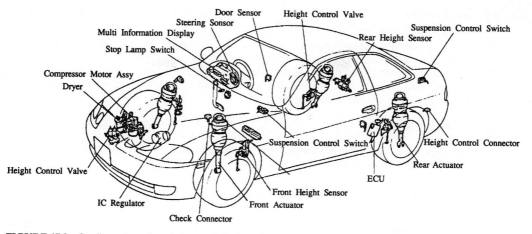

FIGURE 17.8 Configuration of an air suspension system.

the rotary valve to change the damping force. At the same time, another gear engaged with the sector gear operates the air valve to change the spring rate.

17.3.3 Control System

This system can change the spring rate and the damping force into three levels and vehicle height levels of low, normal, or high can be selected. One of the control logics is shown in Table 17.3. This is a control which changes the suspension characteristics in response to vehicle speed and road conditions. The spring rate/damping force and the vehicle height are controlled independently according to each control logic.

Electronic leveling control systems do not need much energy to control vehicle height. They control both spring rate and damping force. As a result of keeping the low spring rate, electronic leveling control systems can provide both good ride comfort and handling stability.

TABLE 17.3 Basic Control Logic of Air Suspension System

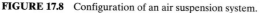

		Spring rate, damping force					
		Soft mode			Medium mode		
Function	Operating condition	Soft	Medium	Firm	Soft	Medium	Firm
Antiroll	Rapid steering	○──────→	○	●	○──→		●
Antidive	Braking at V* > 60 km/h	○──────→	○	●	○──→	●	
Antisquat	Rapid starting at V < 20 km/h	○────────→		●	○──────→		●

* V: Vehicle speed.

17.4 ACTIVE SUSPENSION

Suspension control systems for passenger cars have evolved through several stages over the years. Work in the field began with the air suspension for controlling vehicle height and then progressed to the hydropneumatic suspension and suspensions with variable damping force and spring rate control. Now efforts are underway to develop an active suspension. It is defined as one that has the following features:

- Energy is constantly supplied to the suspension and the force generated by that energy is continuously controlled
- The suspension incorporates various types of sensors and a unit for processing their signals that generates forces that are a function of the signal outputs

17.4.1 System Configurations

Basic Configuration.   Hydraulic active suspension can be divided into two large systems: the hydraulic system and the control system, as shown in Fig. 17.9. The hydraulic pressure of each of the actuators located on each wheel is controlled in accordance with the output values from the G sensors to suppress changes in vehicle body position (bounce, pitch, roll) and reduce vibration from the road surface.

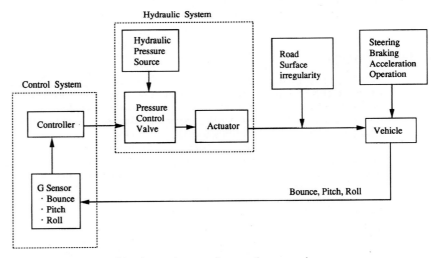

FIGURE 17.9   Hydraulic and control systems for an active suspension.

Hydraulic and Control System Configuration.   A basic overview of the system is shown in Fig. 17.10. The functions of the main units of the hydraulic system are shown in Table 17.4.

As shown in Fig. 17.11, the control system contains the controller and all of the sensors including the vertical G sensors, lateral G sensors, fore and aft G sensors, and vehicle height sensors.

17.4.2 Components

Oil Pump.   The oil pump has seven cylinders arranged around the circumference and can output a maximum oil flow of 12 liters per minute. The pump is connected in tandem with the power steering vane pump.

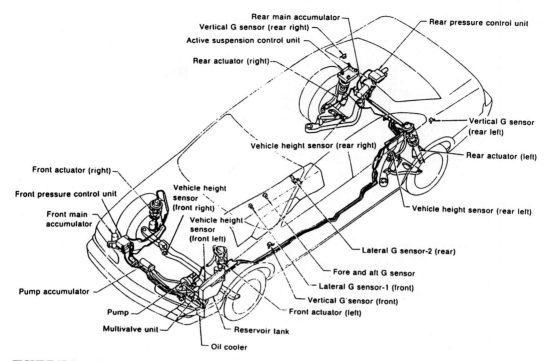

FIGURE 17.10   Principal components of an active suspension system.

Pump Accumulator.   To dampen pulsating hydraulic pressure generated by the oil pump, pump accumulators are installed in the hydraulic supply unit, including one on the side of the oil pump. To dampen the high-frequency pulsations, a metal-bellows-type accumulator is used.

Multivalve Unit.   As shown in Fig. 17.12, the multivalve unit contains valves for many different functions. The main purpose of the multivalve unit is the basic control of hydraulic pressure for the whole system. The function of the multivalve unit is shown in Table 17.5.

Main Accumulator.   The main accumulator is positioned at both the front and rear axles. The main accumulator has two principal functions: it stores oil from the multivalve unit and provides extra flow to the actuators when necessary, and it preserves vehicle height when the engine is turned off.

TABLE 17.4   The Functions of Main Units of the Hydraulic Systems

	Main basic function
Oil pump	Supplies the necessary oil for system operation (power supply)
Pump accumulator	Removes the pulsating action from pressurized oil supplied by the oil pump
Multivalve unit	Controls the supply of pressurized oil, failsafe function, etc.
Main accumulator	Maintains oil pressure, compensates when large amount of flow is required and preserves vehicle body height
Pressure control unit	Controls the hydraulics for the actuators on each wheel according to signals received from the control unit
Actuator	Controls vehicle attitude and absorbs external forces from the road surface

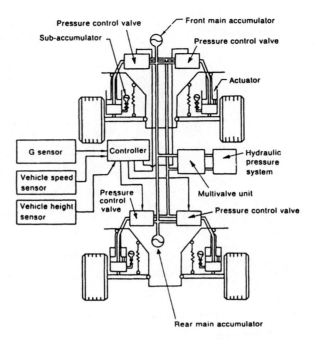

FIGURE 17.11 Controls for an active suspension system.

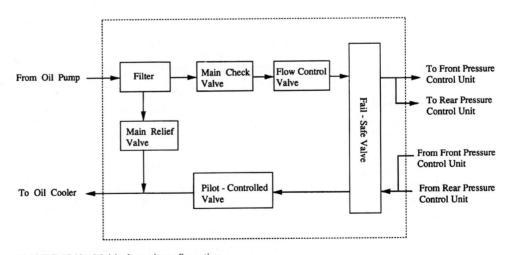

FIGURE 17.12 Multivalve unit configuration.

Pressure Control Unit. As shown in Fig. 17.13, the pressure control unit controls the hydraulic movement of the actuator of each wheel in accordance with instructions received from the control unit. Table 17.6 shows the valve's construction and operating principle.

The electrohydraulic pressure control system consists of a pressure actuator and a pressure control valve. The actuator is of the single acting type and is provided with a damping valve and an accumulator below the cylinder. The pressure control valve is built with three ports

TABLE 17.5 Multivalve Unit Functions

Function	Valve	Outline
Pressure supply management function	Main relief valve	When the oil pressure exceeds a constant value, the main relief valve will return some of the oil flow. This keeps the oil supply pressure at a constant pressure.
Vehicle height maintenance function	Main check valve Pilot-controlled check valve	The main check valve is a nonreturn valve that controls the flow from the line filter and directs it to the flow control valve. The pilot controlled check valve is a supply-pressure-reaction-type open/closed valve. When the hydraulic pressure exceeds a constant value, the valve opens and when the hydraulic pressure falls below that level, it closes. In addition, it maintains the hydraulic pressure at a constant level when the engine is turned off.
Vehicle height control function	Flow control valve	When the engine is turned off, the flow control valve closes the main passage and directs the flow through the bypass passage orifice, slowly increasing the hydraulic pressure, after which the main passage is opened. This prevents any sudden changes in vehicle height when starting the engine.
Failsafe function	Failsafe valve	When any irregularities occur in the electronic system, it changes the hydraulic passage, preventing any sudden changes in vehicle height.

and employs a pilot type proportional electromagnetic control valve. This pressure control valve has two main functions:

- It controls the pressure of the actuator according to the control input. This is accomplished by driving the solenoid so that it adjusts the pilot valve, causing the spool to move.
- Feedback control is applied to move the spool in response to fluctuations in actuator pressure caused by road surface inputs; the action of the spool works to keep the actuator pressure at a certain fixed level.

Actuator. As shown in Fig. 17.14, the actuator consists of the hydraulic power cylinder, subaccumulator, damping valve, etc. Auxiliary coil springs are also employed to reduce the pressure necessary for the overall system and to reduce the amount of horsepower expended. The subaccumulator and damping valve at the bottom of the hydraulic power cylinder absorb and damp the high-frequency vibration from the road surface.

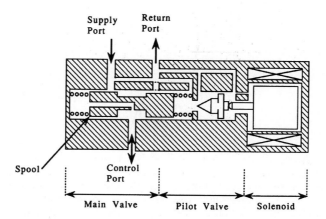

FIGURE 17.13 Pressure control valve construction.

TABLE 17.6   Pressure Control Valve Functions

Active control function	The pressure in the control port (actuator) is controlled in response to the electric current applied to the solenoid, thus controlling the vehicle attitude.
Passive damping function	When various pressure levels are caused in the interior of the actuator by road surface forces, this pressure passes through the control port, causing feedback on the spool and the generation of appropriate damping forces.

Controller.   As shown in Fig. 17.15, the controller is constructed using two 16-bit microcomputers, MCU1 and MCU2.

MCU1 processes signals from the G sensors and then sends attitude control signals to the pressure control valve solenoid drive circuit. MCU2 processes signals from the vehicle height sensors and then sends attitude control signals to the solenoid drive circuit.

MCU1 and MCU2 normally perform mutual transmission, but should an irregularity occur, the signal will be sent to the failsafe circuit, causing the failsafe valve to operate and thus guarantee a high degree of safety.

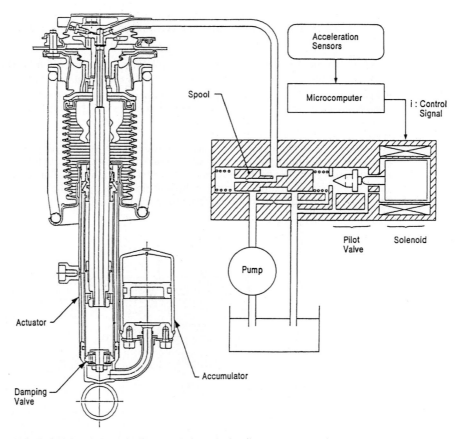

FIGURE 17.14   Schematic diagram of electrohydraulic pressure control system.

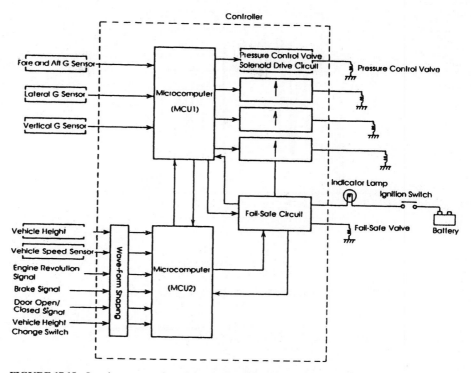

FIGURE 17.15 Interior construction of the electrohydraulic pressure controller.

G Sensors. The G sensors are ball position detection type sensors. They detect changes in the magnetic field caused by the position change of a steel ball as the result of acceleration.

17.4.3 Control System

Roll Control. The inertia force, which causes the car to roll, is detected by the lateral G sensor. Roll control is initiated by increasing the control pressure on the wheels on the outside of the turn and by decreasing the control pressure for the wheels on the inside of the turn. Figure 17.16 shows this operating principle.

The relation between the lateral G and the force generated by the actuator is:

$$F = m\alpha \qquad (17.1)$$

$$Fh = \Delta Fd$$

$$\Delta F = \frac{Fh}{d} = \frac{m\alpha h}{d}$$

Pitch Control. During braking, inertia is generated at the vehicle's center of gravity and causes pitching. The longitudinal G sensor detects this inertia and cancels it to suppress nose dive by increasing the control pressure to the front and decreasing control pressure to the rear, as shown in Fig. 17.17. The relationship between longitudinal G and the actuator generated force is:

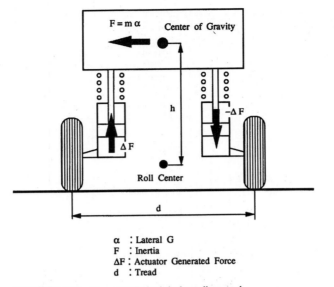

α : Lateral G
F : Inertia
ΔF : Actuator Generated Force
d : Tread

FIGURE 17.16   Operating principle for roll control.

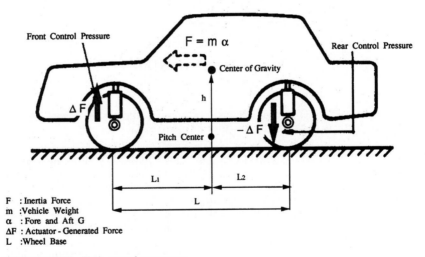

F : Inertia Force
m : Vehicle Weight
α : Fore and Aft G
ΔF : Actuator - Generated Force
L : Wheel Base

FIGURE 17.17   Pitch control parameters.

$$Fh = \Delta F \, (L_1 + L_2)$$

$$\Delta F = \frac{Fh}{(L_1 + L_2)} = \frac{m\alpha h}{L} \qquad (17.2)$$

Bounce Control.   The vertical G sensor attached to the vehicle body detects the value for vehicle body acceleration. By integration of the acceleration, the absolute velocity of the body is calculated. A force proportional to the absolute velocity is generated by the pressure control valve.

This control method, called skyhook damper control, is adapted. It dampens the motion of the car body regardless of any input from the road surface.

In the case of a passive damper, the vertical motion of the body relative to the road surface inputs can be given as:

$$\frac{X_2}{X_1} = \frac{2j\omega_2 \xi_2 \omega + \omega_2^2}{-\omega^2 + 2j\omega_2 \xi_2 \omega + \omega_2^2} \tag{17.3}$$

The vibration transmission rate at the resonant point is:

$$\left| \frac{X_2}{X_1} \right|_{\omega = \omega_2} = \sqrt{1 + \frac{1}{4\xi_2^2}} \tag{17.4}$$

and always has a value greater than one.

By contrast, the vibration characteristics of the skyhook damper are given as:

$$\frac{X_2}{X_1} = \frac{2j\omega_2 \xi_2 \omega + \omega_2^2}{-\omega^2 + 2j\omega_2 (\xi_2 + \xi_s)\omega + \omega_2^2} \tag{17.5}$$

The vibration transmission ratio at the resonant point is:

$$\left| \frac{X_2}{X_1} \right|_{\omega = \omega_2} = \frac{\sqrt{4\xi_2^2 + 1}}{2(\xi_2 + \xi_s)} \tag{17.6}$$

hence,

$$\xi_s \geq \sqrt{\xi_2^2 + \frac{1}{4}} - \xi_2 \tag{17.7}$$

and it is possible to reduce the ratio to less than one.

The effects of the hydraulic active suspension are organized in Table 17.7 according to those related to the vehicle.

17.4.4 Effectiveness

Figure 17.18 shows the lateral G and angle of roll during cornering. Figure 17.19 shows the fore and aft G force, angle of nose dive, and squat angle during starts and stops. In either case, the car with the hydraulic active suspension outperformed the other cars with conventional suspensions.

TABLE 17.7 Effect of Active Suspension Control

Control	Vehicle-related effects
Roll control	During transient control of wheel loading, as when changing lanes, the steering characteristics of the vehicle can be optimally controlled. The tires are used to their utmost performance ability because there is minimal roll, minimal change in the camber of the tires to the ground, and because the tires are continually kept in square contact with the road.
Pitch control	Nose dive and tail lift are minimized during braking. Squats are minimized during starts and rapid acceleration.
Bounce control	Vertical vibration of the vehicle is reduced and continuity is improved. Vertical load fluctuation is minimal, and the contact of the tires with the road is greatly improved.

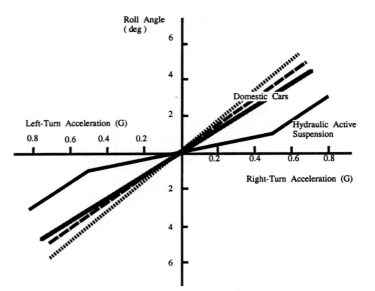

FIGURE 17.18 Comparison of roll angles during cornering.

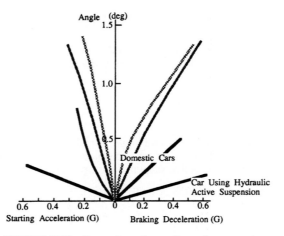

FIGURE 17.19 Comparison of nose dive and squat angles.

Figure 17.20 shows the effects of bounce control for the skyhook damper. Compared with cars using conventional suspension systems, the car with the hydraulic active suspension system exhibited superior performance and low vibration levels.

Figure 17.21 shows the ride characteristics and roll rate for various cars with some suspension systems. As the results clearly demonstrated, the hydraulic active suspension system, through advanced roll control and bounce control, provides a ride and a level of control far superior to that of other suspension systems.

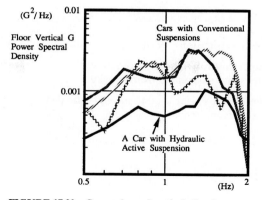

FIGURE 17.20 Comparison of vertical vibrations.

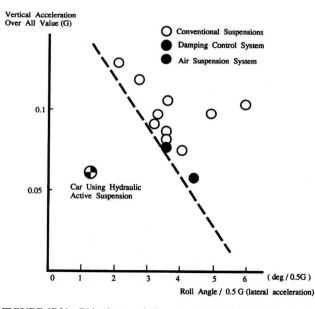

FIGURE 17.21 Ride characteristics and roll rate for various cars with different suspension systems.

17.5 CONCLUSION

The active suspension system provides outstanding levels of performance which are unobtainable with other suspension control systems and conventional passive suspensions. Evaluations made with actual vehicles confirmed the effectiveness of the active suspension system in improving ride comfort and handling properties.

GLOSSARY

Hydropneumatic suspension   A suspension system using oil or air to support the car body.

Skyhook damper control   The control law applied to control the vehicle as if it were fixed within absolute space suspended from the sky.

Supersonic sensor   A sensor used to measure the distance between a car body and the road surface using supersonic waves.

NOMENCLATURE

C_2:   passive damping coefficient

C_s: active damping coefficient

K_1:   tire stiffness

K_2:   spring stiffness

M_1:   unsprung mass

M_2:   sprung mass

$\omega_1 = (K_1/M_1)^{1/2}$ natural frequency of unsprung mass

$\omega_2 = (K_2/M_2)^{1/2}$ natural frequency of sprung mass

$\xi_2 = (C_2/2)\,(M_2K_2)^{1/2}$ active damping ratio

$\xi_s = (C_s/2)\,(M_2/K_2)^{1/2}$ passive damping ratio

BIBLIOGRAPHY

Decker, H., and W. Scramm, "An optimized approach to suspension control," SAE Paper 900661, 1990.

Decker, H., W. Scramm, and R. Kallenbach, "A modular concept for suspension control," *XXIII Fisita Congress,* Torino, Italy, 1990, 905124.

Decker, H., W. Scramm, and R. Kallenbach, "A practical approach toward advanced suspension systems," *Proc. IMechE International Conference on Advanced Suspensions,* London, 1988, S. 93–99.

Doi, S., E. Yasuda, and Y. Hayashi, "An experimental study of optimal vibration adjustment using adaptive control methods," *Proceedings of the Institution of Mechanical Engineers,* London, Oct. 24–25, 1988.

Guy, Y., M. B. Lizell, and M. W. Kerastas, "A solenoid-actuated pilot valve in a semi-active damping system," SAE Paper 881139, Aug. 1988.

Haget, K. H., et al., "Continuous adjustable shock absorbers for rapid-acting ride control systems (RCS)," *XXIII Fisita Congress,* Torino, Italy, 1990, 905125.

Hennecke, D., P. Baier, B. Jordan, and E. Walek, "EDCIII—the new variable damper system for BMW's top models—a further development of our adaptive, frequency-dependent damper control," SAE Paper 900662.

Hennecke, D., P. Baier, B. Jordan, and E. Walek, "Further market-oriented development of adaptive damper force control," *XXIII Fisita Congress,* Torino, Italy, 1990, 905143.

Hennecke, D., B. Jordan, and U. Ochner, "Electronic damper control—a fully automatic adaptive system for damping force adjustment on the BMW 635 CSi," *ATZ 89,* 9, 1987, pp. 471–479.

Hrovat, D., D. L. Margolis, and M. Hubbard, "An approach toward the optimal semi-active suspension," *Transactions of the ASME,* 288, vol. 110, Sept. 1988.

Karnop, D., and D. L. Margolis, "Adaptive suspension concepts for road vehicles," *Vehicle System Dynamics,* 13, 1984, pp. 145–160.

Karnop, D., M. J. Crosby, and R. A. Harwood, "Vibration control using semi-active force generators," *ASME Journal of Engineering for Industry Transactions of the ASME,* No. 96, 1974, S. 613–626.

Margolis, D. L., "Semi-active control of wheel hop in ground vehicles," *Vehicle System Dynamics,* 12, 1983, pp. 317–330.

Sharp, R. S., and S. A. Hassan, "Performance and design considerations for dissipative semi-active suspension systems for automobiles," *Proceedings Institution of Mechanical Engineers,* vol. 201, no. D2, pp. 149–153.

Sugasawa, F., et al., "Electronically controlled shock absorber system used as a road sensor which utilizes super sonic waves," SAE Paper 851652, 1985.

Tsutsumi, Y., H. Sato, H. Kawaguchi, and M. Hirose, "Development of Piezo TEMS (Toyota Electronic Modulated Suspension)," SAE Paper 901745, 1990.

Yokota, Y., K. Asami, and T. Hajima, "Toyota electronic modulated suspension system for the 1983 Soarer," SAE Paper 840341, 1984.

Hydropneumatic Suspension

Akatsu, Y., N. Fukushima, K. Takahashi, M. Satoh, and Y. Kawarazaki, "An active suspension employing an electrohydraulic pressure control system," *XXIII Fisita Congress,* Torino, Italy, 1990, 905123.

Carbonaro, O., "Hydractive suspension electronic control system," *XXIII Fisita Congress,* Torino, Italy, 1990, 905101.

Dominy, J., and D. N. Bulman, "An active suspension for a Formula One Grand Prix racing car," *Transactions ASME, Journal Dynamic Systems Measurement Control,* vol. 107, 1, 1985, pp. 73–78.

Hedrick, J. K., "Railway vehicle active suspensions," *Vehicle System Dynamics* **10**, 1981, pp. 267–283.

Henning, H., "Citroen SM V6," *ATZ 92,* 1990, pp. 23–27.

Hrovat, D., "Optimal active suspension structures for quarter-car vehicle models," *Automatica,* vol. 26, 5, 1990, pp. 845–860.

Karnop, D., "Active damping in road vehicle suspension systems," *Vehicle System Dynamics* **12**, 1983, pp. 291–316.

Sharp, R. S., and S. A. Hassan, "An evaluation of passive automotive suspension systems with variable stiffness and damping parameters," *Vehicle System Dynamics,* **15**(6):1986, pp. 335–350.

Tanahashi, H., K. Shindo, T. Nogami, and T. Oonuma, "Toyota electronic modulated air suspension for the 1986 Soarer," SAE Paper 870541, 1987.

Thompson, A. G., "An active suspension with optimal linear state feedback," *Vehicle System Dynamics* **5**, 1976, pp. 187–203.

Tobata, H., N. Fukushima, K. Fukuyama, and T. Kimura, "Advanced control method of active suspension," *Avec92,* Yokohama, Japan, 1992, 923023.

Wright, P., "The application of active suspension to high performance road vehicle," *I MechE,* C239/84, 1984.

ABOUT THE AUTHOR

Akatsu Yohsuke has been Vehicle Research Manager for Nissan Motor Co., Ltd., since 1980. He was awarded the B.E. degree from the Tokyo Institute of Technology in 1978 and the M.E. degree from there in 1980.

CHAPTER 18
STEERING CONTROL

Makoto Sato
Honda R&D Co., Ltd.

The application of electronic control technology to vehicle steering systems is still in the development stage. The structure and functioning of such systems are not yet clearly defined. Accordingly, the material that follows is intended primarily to introduce systems which have already been published, and it is devoted entirely to the electronic aspects of those systems and does not include descriptions of the basic operation of hydraulic power steering systems.

18.1 VARIABLE-ASSIST STEERING

18.1.1 Fundamentals of Electronically Controlled Power Steering

Electronically controlled power steering improves steering feel and power-saving effectiveness, and increases steering performance. It does so with control mechanisms that reduce the steering effort. An electronic control system, for example, may be added to the hydraulic booster or the whole system may be composed of electronic and electric components.

The intent of electronic controls, initially, was to reduce the steering effort when driving at low speeds and to supply feedback for the appropriate steering reaction force when driving at high speeds. In order to achieve those goals, devices such as vehicle speed sensors were used to detect vehicle speed in order to make smooth and continuous changes in the steering assist rate under conditions ranging from steering maneuvers at zero speed to those at high speeds. However, as vehicles became equipped with electrohydraulic systems and fully electronic and electric systems, the emphasis for these systems started to include reduction in power requirements and higher performance.

The main functions required for electronically controlled power steering are listed in Table 18.1.

18.1.2 Types of Electronically Controlled Power Steering

Electronically controlled power steering systems presently available commercially can be classified according to their basic structure and basic principles into three types: hydraulic, hybrid, and full electric systems, as shown in Table 18.2. Detailed explanations of these systems are given as follows.

TABLE 18.1   Functions Required for Electronically Controlled Power Steering

Reduction of driver's burden when turning the steering wheel and improvement in the steering feel	• Reduction in steering effort • Smoothness of steering operation • Feedback of appropriate steering reaction forces • Reduction of kickback[1] • Improvement in convergence[2] • Creation of other new functions
Power saving	
Failsafe	• Maintaining of manual steering function in the event of any malfunctions

TABLE 18.2   Classification of Electronically Controlled Power Steering System

Basic structure	Control method	Control objects	Sensors				Actuator	Major effects	
			Vehicle speed	Steering torque	Angular velocity	Current		Steering force responsive to vehicle speed	Power saving
Electronically controlled hydraulic system	Flow	Flow supply to power cylinder	○			○	Solenoid	○	○
	Cylinder bypass	Effective actuation pressure given to cylinder	○			○	Solenoid	○	
	Valve characteristics	Pressure generated at control value	○			○	Solenoid	○	
	Hydraulic reaction force control	Pressure acting on the hydraulic reaction force mechanism	○			○	Solenoid	○	
Hybrid system	Flow	Flow supply to power cylinder	○		○	○	Motor	○	○
Full electric system	Current	Motor torque	○	○		○	Motor	○	○
	Voltage	Motor power	○	○	○	○	Motor	○	○

18.1.3   Explanations of Each System

Electronically Controlled Hydraulic System.   This system consists of a linear solenoid valve, a vehicle speed sensor, and other electronic devices located in part of the hydraulic circuit of the hydraulic system. The opening of the solenoid valve is controlled based on signals from the vehicle speed sensor. The flow and pressure of the hydraulic fluid is controlled by means of the opening of the solenoid valve.

The assist rate is smoothly and continuously varied in response to the vehicle speed, so that when the vehicle is stationary, the opening of the solenoid valve is small to ensure that the steering effort is appropriately light. When the vehicle is moving at high speed, the opening of the solenoid valve is large to ensure that the steering effort is appropriately heavy.

Flow Control Method.   In this method, a solenoid valve is located at the pump discharge port as shown in Fig. 18.1. The electronic control device regulates the solenoid valve opening at high vehicle speeds to reduce the pump discharge volume, thus increasing the required steering effort. By reducing the resistance of the circuit between the pump and the power cylinder, power requirements are reduced. Figure 18.2 shows the position of the solenoid

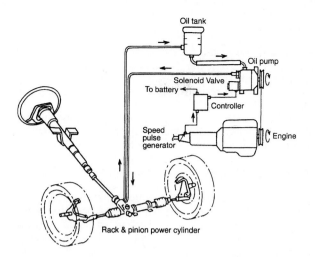

FIGURE 18.1 Vehicle speed-responsive pump discharge flow volume control type.[1]

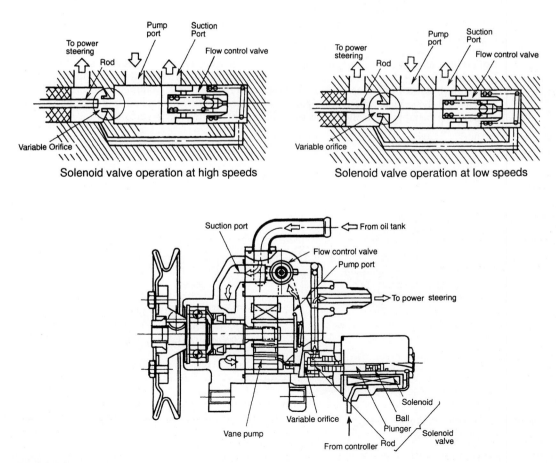

FIGURE 18.2 Structure and operation of pump with solenoid valve.[1]

valve at the pump, with separate diagrams showing the operation at high and low vehicle speeds.

The flow of hydraulic fluid to the power cylinder is reduced when driving at high speeds, so that, for this method, the magnitude of the steering response rate and the steering reaction force are balanced at a point of equilibrium.

Cylinder Bypass Control Method.   In this method, a solenoid valve and a bypass line are located between both chambers of the power cylinder.[2] The opening of the valve is extended by the electronic control equipment in accordance with increases in vehicle speed, thus reducing the hydraulic pressure in the power cylinder and increasing the steering effort. Like the flow control method, this system may also seek the equilibrium point for the steering response rate and the steering reaction force.

Valve Characteristics Control Method.   In this method, the pressure control restrictions of the rotary valve (control valve) mechanism, which control the volume and pressure of the hydraulic fluid supplied to the power cylinder, are divided into second and third parts. A fourth part, controlled by means of the vehicle speed signal, is provided in the hydraulic line between the second and third parts as shown in Fig. 18.3. The structure of this system is shown in Fig. 18.4. The steering effort is controlled by carrying out variable control of the fourth part to vary the assist ratio. Because the structure is simple and the flow from the pump to the cylinder is supplied efficiently without waste, this system exhibits a good response rate. Figure 18.5 shows the hydraulic pressure characteristics in the valve characteristics control method with the driving current of the solenoid valve in accordance to the vehicle speed control signal as a parameter. When the current is 0.3 A, the valve is fully open, and this represents the high-speed driving condition.

Hydraulic Reaction Force Control Method.   In this method, the steering effort is controlled by means of a hydraulic reaction force mechanism, which is located at the rotary valve (control valve). A hydraulic reaction force control valve increases the hydraulic pressure (reaction pressure) introduced into the hydraulic reaction force chamber in accordance with increases in the vehicle speed. The rigidity of the reaction force mechanism (equivalent spring constant) is variably controlled so as to directly control the steering effort.

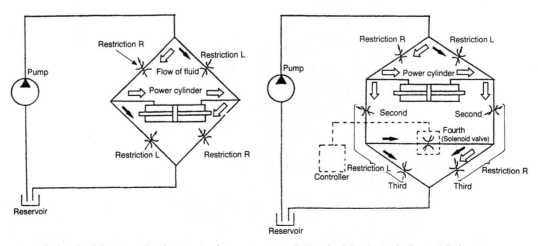

Bridge circuit for conventional power steering

Bridge circuit for electronically-controlled power steering

FIGURE 18.3   Closing bridge circuit for control valve.[2]

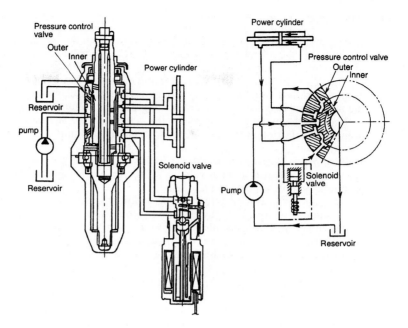

Cross-section of rotary valve structure   Hydraulic pressure circuit of rotary valve

FIGURE 18.4   Valve characteristics control method.[1]

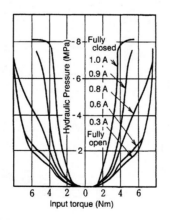

FIGURE 18.5   Valve characteristics in response to vehicle speed.[1]

This method requires the inclusion of a reaction force mechanism, which makes the structure of the control valve more complex, which in turn increases the cost. However, because the rigidity of the reaction force mechanism increases in accordance with increases in the vehicle speed, there is no vagueness in the steering feel in the area around the straightforward steering position. Because this method assigns the steering reaction force irrespective of the volume of hydraulic fluid supplied to the power cylinder, the magnitude of the steering reaction force can be set freely without the need to sacrifice any of the steering response rate.

18.1.4 Hybrid Systems

Hybrid systems utilize a flow control method in which the hydraulic power steering pump is driven by an electric motor. The steering effort is controlled by controlling the rotating speed of the pump (discharge flow).

The drive efficiency of the generator and motor are low compared to that of the hydraulic pump, which is driven by the vehicle engine. But because any residual flow is not discharged, the power loss is lower than that of the engine pump when driving at high speeds.

Because the pump is not driven by the vehicle engine, there is also a large degree of freedom in the selection of the mounting location for the pump.

Driving Mode Responsive Method.   In this method, the control system consists of a vehicle speed sensor, steering angular velocity sensor, an electronic control unit, and a motor driven hydraulic pump, as shown in Fig. 18.6.

As is shown in Fig. 18.7, the driving conditions (such as driving in urban areas, country areas, winding regions, or highways) are automatically judged, and the pump flow rate is controlled in accordance with this condition in order to provide the appropriate steering effort for the driving conditions. Fine control adjustments are achieved by means of this method as compared with vehicle speed-responsive types mentioned previously.

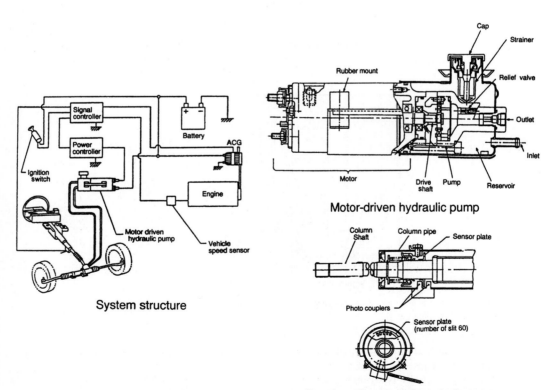

FIGURE 18.6   Driving mode responsive-type hybrid power steering.[3]

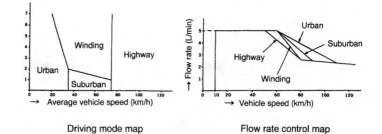

Driving mode map   Flow rate control map

FIGURE 18.7   Driving mode and pump flow rate.[3]

Steering Wheel Speed Responsive Method.   For this method, the system consists of components such as a vehicle speed sensor, steering wheel angular velocity sensor, an electronic control unit, and a motor-driven hydraulic pump, as shown in Fig. 18.8. The pump flow volume is controlled in accordance with the angular velocity of the steering wheel and the vehicle speed as shown in Fig. 18.9. As mentioned previously, the discharge flow volume of the pump is reduced and the steering response drops when the vehicle is driven at high speeds. Therefore, in this system, the speed of the motor is increased in accordance with the detected angular velocity of the steering wheel in order to increase the discharge flow volume to solve the problem. Accordingly, losses in power resulting from the circulation of residual flow within the system are kept to the minimum possible level, and the magnitude of the reaction force can be controlled freely without sacrificing any of the steering response rate.

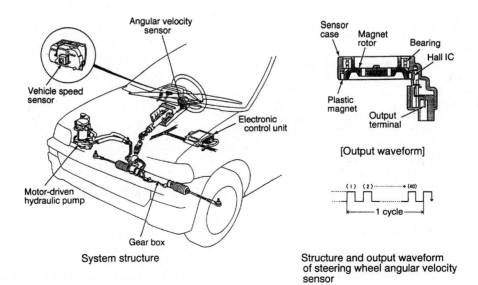

System structure

Structure and output waveform
of steering wheel angular velocity
sensor

FIGURE 18.8   Steering speed-responsive-type hybrid power steering.[4]

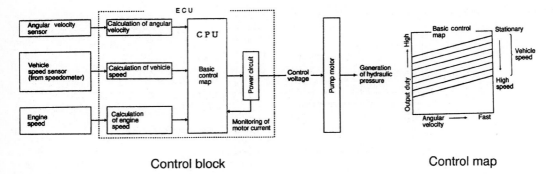

Control block   Control map

FIGURE 18.9   Basic control.[4]

18.1.5 Electric Power Steering

Electric power steering (EPS) is a fully electric system, which reduces the amount of steering effort by directly applying the output from an electric motor to the steering system. This system consists of vehicle speed sensors, a steering sensor (torque, angular velocity), an electronic control unit, a drive unit, and a motor, as shown in Fig. 18.10. Signal outputs from each sensor are input to the electronic control unit, where the necessary steering assistance is calculated and applied by the drive unit to control the operation of the motor.

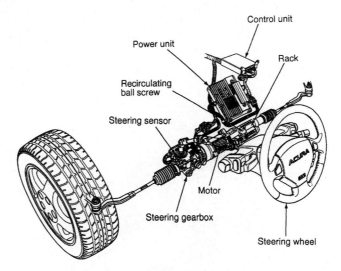

FIGURE 18.10   Structure of EPS System[5] (rack assist-type ball screw drive).

Because the motor output is controlled directly in this system, the setting range for the steering effort is large, and also because it is possible to supply only the amount of power that is necessary when the steering wheel is turned, a large reduction in power requirements can be effectively achieved with no power losses. This means, in contrast to hydraulic systems, that it is not necessary for the pump to keep operating continuously when the steering wheel is not being turned.

TABLE 18.3   Classification of Motor Drive Mechanism in EPS

Method	Motor drive method	Power transmission mechanism	Figure
Pinion assist	Column shaft drive	Motor→worm gear→column shaft→pinion shaft	18.11
	Pinion shaft drive	Motor→gear train→pinion shaft	18.12
Rack assist	Another shaft pinion drive	Motor→planetary gear train→another shaft pinion→rack shaft	
	Ball screw drive	Motor→ball screw→rack shaft	18.10

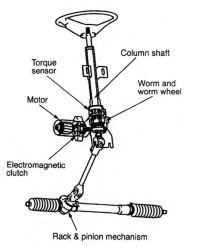

FIGURE 18.11   Column shaft drive method.[1]

In rack-and-pinion steering mechanisms, the EPS system applies the motor power to the pinion gear shaft or to the rack shaft. Several reduction gears are incorporated to amplify the torque of the motor. This system can be classified according to the drive method as given in Table 18.3 and Figs. 18.10 to 18.12. The maximum amount of assist, the smoothness of the steering feel, and the degree of noise occurring during steering are, by and large, determined by the power transmission systems in this table. In general, it is possible to obtain a greater amount of assist from the rack assist method than from the pinion assist method, and the rack assist method is optimal for vehicles in which the front axle load is high.

Details of the respective sensors, controls, and the results achieved thereby are given as follows under common headings.

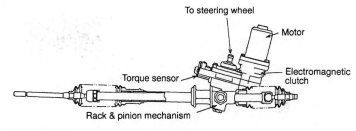

FIGURE 18.12   Pinion shaft drive method.[1]

Sensors.   The EPS system utilizes a variety of sensors to control the motor. These sensors include a torque sensor, which detects the steering effort of the steering wheel; a steering wheel angular velocity sensor, which detects the angular velocity of the steering wheel; a battery sensor, which detects the battery voltage; a current sensor, which detects the motor current and the battery current; and a vehicle speed sensor. Of these sensors, the torque sensor and the steering wheel angular velocity sensor, which form the core of the EPS system, are described as follows. (Also see Chap. 3.)

Torque Sensor.   The pinion shaft in the rack-and-pinion steering mechanism is divided into two sections of input shaft and pinion gear. The torque sensor comprises a torsion bar

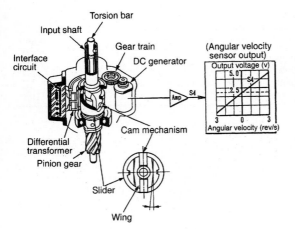

FIGURE 18.13   Torque sensor and angular velocity sensor.[5]

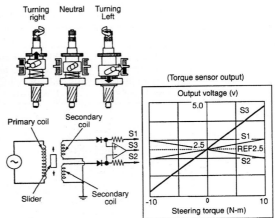

FIGURE 18.14   Diagram of torque sensor operation.[5]

that connects the two sections, a slider with a movable iron core, a cam mechanism that converts the twist torque of both sections of the shaft into an axial direction displacement, and a differential transformer that converts the axial direction displacement of the slider into an electric signal.

The structure is shown in Fig. 18.13. Figure 18.14 shows examples of the detection of the magnitude and direction of the slider displacement. Signal S3 is the output signal of torque and S1 and S2 are outputs for diagnosis use. The differential transformer-type torque sensor has a dual electric structure to provide differential outputs, so that a high sensing accuracy and good temperature characteristics can be obtained, and detection of failure can also be made accurately.

In addition to this type of torque sensor, there are other torque sensors that use a potentiometer instead of a differential transformer, and also types in which the relative displacement in the turning direction is measured in a noncontact manner using a coil, without there being a mechanically movable part such as the slider.

Angular Velocity Sensor.   The angular velocity sensor consists of a gear train, which is located around the input shaft, and a dc generator, which is driven at an increase of speed by this gear train. The structure is shown in Fig. 18.13. The turning direction and angular velocity of the steering wheel are detected by the turning direction and angular velocity of this dc generator. Signal S4 indicates the output from the steering wheel angular velocity sensor.

Electronic Control Unit (ECU).   The ECU consists of an interface circuit that coordinates the signals from the various sensors, an A/D converter and a PWM unit that are all built into an 8-bit one-chip microprocessor, a watchdog timer (WDT) circuit that monitors the operation of this microprocessor, and a PWM drive circuit that drives the power unit mentioned previously. The ECU conducts a search for data according to a table lookup method based on the signals input from each sensor and carries out a prescribed calculation using this data to obtain the assist force.

In addition, trouble diagnosis for the sensors and the microprocessor is also carried out. When a problem is detected, power to the motor is interrupted, an indicator lamp illuminates, and the problem condition is memorized. Then this problem mode flashes on a display as necessary.

Power Unit.   The power unit comprises a power MOSFET (metal oxide semiconductor field effect transistor) bridge circuit which drives the motor in a forward or reverse direction, a drive circuit which controls the respective power MOSFET of this power MOSFET bridge circuit, a current sensor, and a relay which turns the motor current ON and OFF.

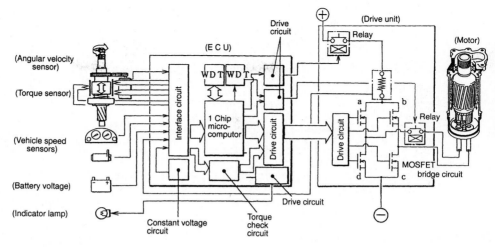

FIGURE 18.15   ECU and drive unit.[6]

The structure is shown in Fig. 18.15. The motor is driven based on instructions from the ECU. The current at this time is monitored by the ECU, and the power supplied to the motor is interrupted in the event of an abnormality.

Depending on the magnitude of the current, some systems are provided with an integrated ECU and power unit, while other systems have each section separate.

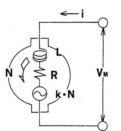

FIGURE 18.16   Motor equivalent circuit.[6]

Motor Control Methods.   In the equivalent circuit of the motor, which is shown in Fig. 18.16, the relationship between the terminal voltage V_M, the impedance L, the resistance R, the induced voltage constant k, the revolution speed N, the current i, and the time t, is expressed by the following equation:

$$V_M = L(di/dt) + R \cdot i + k \cdot N \quad (18.1)$$

$$\doteqdot R \cdot i + k \cdot N \quad (18.2)$$

And it is known that the current **i** is proportional to the motor torque T_M.

As can be understood from Eq. (18.2), there are two control methods. In the motor current control method (refer to Fig. 18.17), the target motor current I_T, which is proportional to the motor assist torque T_M, is determined from the signal output T from the torque sensor, and control is performed so that there is no difference between this target current value I_T and the value detected through feedback from the current sensor I_M.

In the motor voltage control method (refer to Fig. 18.18), the motor voltage component ($V_{M1} = R \cdot i = k_T \cdot T_M$; k_T is a proportional constant) which corresponds to the motor assist torque as calculated from the output signal T from the torque sensor, and the motor voltage component ($V_{M2} = k \cdot N$) which corresponds to the motor speed as calculated from the output signal $\dot\theta_1$ from the steering wheel angular velocity sensor. These two voltage components are then added and output.

Current Control Method.   In this method, the target value for the motor current, which corresponds to the motor assist torque, is set so that it is equal to the vehicle speed response type derived from the signal of the vehicle speed sensor.

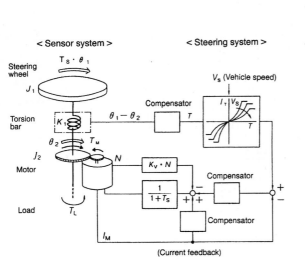

FIGURE 18.17 Diagram of principle of motor current control method.[7]

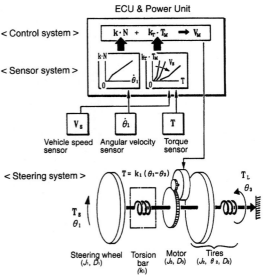

FIGURE 18.18 Diagram of principle of motor voltage control method.[8]

Voltage Control Method. In this method, both the motor torque and the motor speed can be controlled by the output from the torque sensor and the steering wheel angular velocity sensor. When the vehicle is traveling at low speeds, *normal control* is carried out. With this control, the value for $(R \cdot i + k \cdot N)$ in Eq. (18.2) is output to the motor to obtain a good motor response rate (steering response rate) and thus provide a comfortable steering performance. When the vehicle is traveling at high speeds, it is possible to carry out two types of control. In the first method, *return control,* the value for $(k \cdot N)$ is made smaller so that a damping torque which is proportional to the motor speed is generated. In the second method, *damper control,* motor torque is generated in the opposite direction of motor rotation with $V = 0$ when the steering wheel is released in turning.

Normal Control. This is a method of drive control for steering with a reduced steering effort and a good steering response rate. As is shown in Table 18.4, when the steering wheel is turned to the right, FET (a) is ON at the same time that FET (c) is carrying out PWM drive, and current flows to the FET bridge circuit as shown in Fig. 18.19 based on the value of V_M in Eq. (18.2). If the angular velocity of the steering wheel increases, the PWM duty also increases.

An example of the steering characteristics in an actual vehicle can be seen in Fig. 18.20. Figure 18.20*a* represents the assist characteristics during stationary swing, with the dotted line representing the steering characteristics when no assist force is provided. Figure 18.20*b* is the steering response rate; Fig. 18.20*c* is the steering characteristics corresponding to the vehicle speed; and Fig. 18.20*d* is the steering characteristics relative to the lateral acceleration of the vehicle.

TABLE 18.4 FET Drive During Normal Control[5]

Steering condition	FET (a)	FET (b)	FET (c)	FET (d)	Motor operation
Steering to right	ON	OFF	PWM	OFF	Operates in direction steering to the right
Straight ahead	OFF	OFF	OFF	OFF	Stops
Steering to left	OFF	ON	OFF	PWM	Operates in direction steering to the left

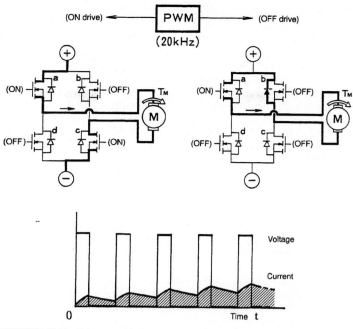

FIGURE 18.19 Diagram of bridge circuit operation.[6]

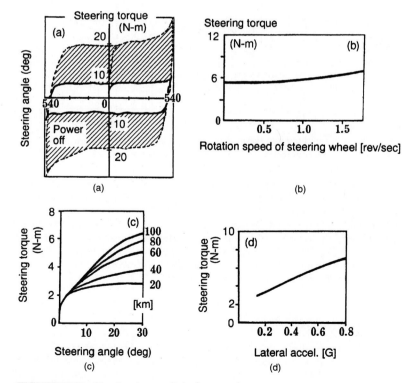

FIGURE 18.20 Steering characteristics.[8]

Return Control. This method of drive control is for varying the steering wheel return characteristics. When the driver is returning the steering wheel to the neutral position at low-speed driving, the motor current is immediately reduced in order to make the motor operate in the reverse direction to the torque generating directions. As a result, a good returnability of the steering wheel should be obtained. At high-speed driving, motor current is gradually reduced in order to suppress returnability and obtain more stable steering characteristics.

As shown in Table 18.5, when the steering wheel returns to the straightforward position after being turned to the right, FET (a) carries out PWM-r drive based on the signals from the steering wheel angular velocity sensor, and, at the same time, FET (c) also carries out PWM drive based on the signals from the torque sensor.

TABLE 18.5 FET Drive During Return Control[5]

Steering condition	FET (a)	FET (b)	FET (c)	FET (d)
Return from right steering to straight ahead	PWM-r	OFF	PWM	OFF
Return from left steering to straight ahead	OFF	PWM-r	OFF	PWM

The results obtained by means of this return control are shown in Fig. 18.21. Figure 18.21*a* represents the steering characteristics when return control is not applied, and Fig. 18.21*b* represents the steering characteristics when return control is operating. The hysteresis is greater and the returnability is weaker than in Fig. 18.21*a*.

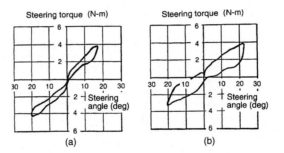

FIGURE 18.21 Comparison of steering wheel return characteristics.[6]

Damper Control. This method of drive control is for improving the convergence of the steering wheel when the vehicle is traveling at high speeds and for eliminating wandering of the steering wheel caused by the tire inputs.

As shown in Fig. 18.22, when the motor terminals are shorted, it is possible to generate motor torque in the reverse direction in proportion to the speed of the motor as is shown by the equation in Fig. 18.22, and this characteristic is utilized for control. Figure 18.23 shows the results of the application of damper control during a convergence test carried out at a vehicle speed of 120 km/h.

18.1.6 Power-Saving Effectiveness

Because the EPS system is a "power-on-demand" system, which supplies only the necessary amount of power at the necessary time, almost no power losses occur when the steering wheel is not being turned. Because of this, the system has extremely high fuel efficiency. Table 18.6 shows the results of measurements of fuel consumption during different driving modes to compare EPS with the hydraulic system. The LA-4 mode corresponds to urban road driving.

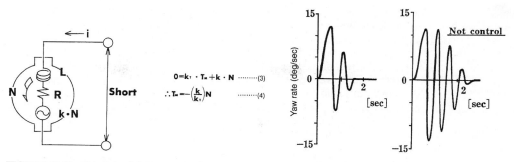

FIGURE 18.22   Principle of damper control.

FIGURE 18.23   Effect of damper control.

18.1.7   Trends in Research and Development

The demands for faster speed, higher quality, and reduced power requirements in vehicles is continually increasing. In order to respond to these demands, research and development is under way on the application of electronic control systems with the aim of further improving functions and performance. Features that are being proposed include the introduction of fuzzy logic and the application of power steering, which responds to the driving environment by varying the assist amount in accordance with the traffic conditions or the road surface conditions in order to provide steering feel to fit the sensitivities of human operators. The most important of these is probably active reaction power steering, which provides feedback to the driver regarding the behavior of the vehicle in the form of steering reaction force. Such a system provides the driver with information regarding the operating conditions of the vehicle, for instance, the yaw velocity and/or lateral acceleration, as steering reaction forces. Not only would it improve the relationship between the driver and the vehicle to make it possible to achieve a steering feel that better suits the sensitivities of the driver, but a function that automatically compensates for irregularities in vehicle behavior caused by disturbances could also be expected.

Figure 18.24 is a system control block diagram in which the yaw rate is fed back as a steering reaction force.

Figure 18.25 shows an example of the effect of suppressing irregularities in vehicle behavior caused by side disturbances by comparing the amount of lateral removal when braking on a rut of road surface with the case for conventional power steering.

18.2   FOUR-WHEEL STEERING SYSTEMS (4WS)

For vehicles with extremely long wheel bases and vehicles which need to be operated in narrow places, the concept of a four-wheel steering system is attractive. In such systems, the rear wheels are turned in the opposite direction to the steering direction of the front wheels in

TABLE 18.6   Measurement Results on Mode Fuel Consumption[6]

Mode	EPS (mpg)	Hydraulic power steering (mpg)	Improvement in fuel consumption	
			Fuel consumption difference (mpg)	Improved rate (%)
LA-4	20.51	20.01	0.80	2.50
Highway	28.88	28.18	1.14	2.52

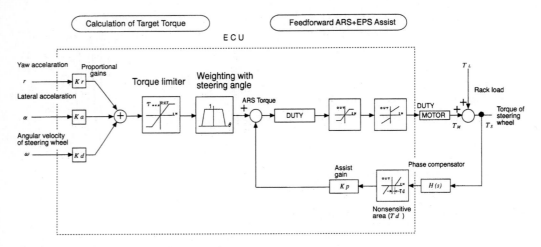

FIGURE 18.24   Block diagram of active reaction control.

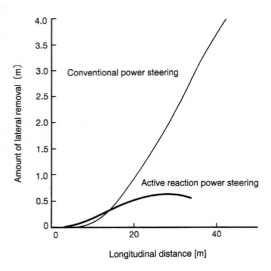

FIGURE 18.25   Effect of active reaction power steering.

order to make the turning radius as small as possible and to improve the handling ability. Such 4WS systems have been under development for some time. However, the concept of the system being used in passenger vehicles for the purpose of improving vehicle stability and steering response at medium to high speeds is relatively new.

A 4WS system for passenger cars has the following two aims:

- Reducing the turning motion (yawing) of the vehicle by steering the rear wheels in the same direction as the front wheels, thus improving the vehicle stability at high speeds
- Improving the steering response at medium speeds, while at the same time reducing the turning circle radius at low speed, by steering the rear wheels in the opposite direction to the front wheels

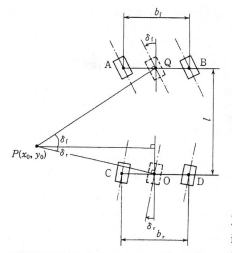

FIGURE 18.26   Half vehicle model of 4WS.[1]

18.2.1   Basic Principles of 4WS

Shortening the Minimum Turning Radius. As shown in Fig. 18.26, provided the origin point of the coordinate is set at the center of the rear tread, the coordinates of the turning center of the vehicle $P(X_0, Y_0)^v$ when the rear wheels are turned in the opposite direction from the front wheels are given in the following equations:

$$x_0 = \iota \,/\, (\tan \delta_f + \tan \delta_r) \qquad (18.3)$$

$$y_0 = \iota \,(\iota \cdot \tan \delta_1) \,/\, (\tan \delta_f + \tan \delta_r) \quad (18.4)$$

And, if the turning radius for the front outer wheel is R and the difference between the turning radius of the front and rear outer wheels is ΔR, then:

$$R = \overline{BP} = \sqrt{\left(\frac{b_f}{2} + X_0\right)^2 + (\iota - y_0)^2} \cdot \sqrt{\left(\frac{b_f}{2} + \frac{\iota}{\tan \delta_f + \tan \delta_r}\right)^2 + \left(\frac{\iota \cdot \tan \delta_f}{\tan \delta_f + \tan \delta_r}\right)^2} \quad (18.5)$$

$$\Delta R = \overline{AP} - \overline{CP}$$

$$= \sqrt{\left(-\frac{b_f}{2} + X_0\right)^2 + (\iota - y_0)^2} - \sqrt{\left(-\frac{b_r}{2} + X_0\right)^2 + y_0^2}$$

$$= \sqrt{\left(-\frac{b_f}{2} + \frac{\iota}{\tan \delta_f + \tan \delta_r}\right)^2 + \left(\frac{\iota \cdot \tan \delta_f}{\tan \delta_f + \tan \delta_r}\right)^2}$$

$$- \sqrt{\left(-\frac{b_r}{2} + \frac{\iota}{\tan \delta_f + \tan \delta_r}\right)^2 + \left(\frac{\iota \cdot \tan \delta_f}{\tan \delta_f + \tan \delta_r}\right)^2} \qquad (18.6)$$

In these equations, δ_f is the front wheel steering angle (average of left and right wheels), δ_r is the rear wheel steering angle (average of left and right wheels), b_f is the tread of the front wheels, b_r is the tread of the rear wheels, and ι is the wheelbase.

$$R = \overline{PQ} = \frac{\iota}{\sin\delta_f + \cos\delta_f + \tan\delta_f} \qquad (18.7)$$

$$\Delta R = \overline{PQ} - \overline{PO} \qquad (18.8)$$

$$= \frac{\iota}{\sin\delta_f + \cos\delta_f + \tan\delta_f}$$

$$- \frac{\iota}{\sin\delta_f + \cos\delta_f + \tan\delta_f}$$

It can be seen from Eq. (18.7) that when the rear wheels steer in the opposite direction as the front wheels, the turning radius becomes smaller than when the rear wheels are not steered ($\delta_r = 0$). In addition, it can be seen from Eq. (18.8) that when the steering amount for the front and rear wheels is the same ($\delta_f = \delta_r$), then it becomes possible to obtain a difference of 0 between the turning radius of the front and rear wheels

Improvement in Stability and Maneuverability When Driving at Medium to High Speeds.
The steering characteristics in yaw velocity and lateral acceleration of the vehicle with 4WS in which the rear wheels are steered in proportion to the front wheels steering angle in the same direction, are shown in Table 18.7, along with that for a vehicle yaw 2WS system. However, the half-car vehicle model shown in Fig. 18.26 is used as the vehicle model.

From Table 18.7, in a system in which the rear wheels are turned in the same direction as the front wheels, the stability factor K, the damping ratio ζ, and the natural oscillation of yawing ωn are not different from the values for conventional vehicles with 2WS, so that the intrinsic stability of the vehicle will not vary. On the other hand, because the lateral acceleration response delay will become smaller as the coefficients of numerators s and s^2 increase and the steady state gain in the yaw velocity will drop by the proportion to $(1 - k)$, the yawing movement which accompanies the lateral movement of the vehicle will become less and the stability within the range of practical use will be improved. If, however, the rear wheels are steered in the opposite direction to the front wheels, $k < 0$ and so $1 - k > 1$. This means that the steady state gain of the yaw velocity will increase, with the result that the steering response will be improved. The symbols used in Table 18.7 and Fig. 18.27 are explained in Table 18.8.

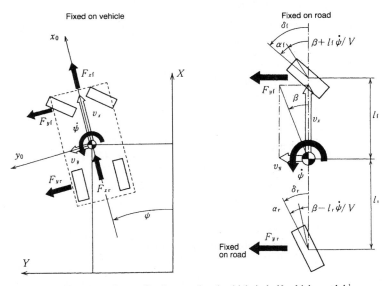

FIGURE 18.27   Coordinates fixed on road and vehicle in half vehicle model.[1]

18.2.2   Classification of 4WS

Four-wheel steering systems that are currently being implemented in vehicles are classified according to their functions and mechanisms. The aims and characteristics of each system are briefly explained in Tables 18.9 and 18.10. Because the fully mechanically controlled system shown in Table 18.10 has a low degree of control freedom, there is less tendency for it to be used. Regardless of its low cost, however, this system provides every basic function of 4WS, so that there is a possibility that it may be used in the future, primarily in smaller vehicles.

TABLE 18.7[1]

Symbol	Name	
K	Stability factor (s^2/m^2)	
A	Steady state gain in yaw velocity	(1/s)
B_f, B_r	Steady state gain vehicle side slip angle for front and rear	(s)
T_f, T_r	Time constant for front/rear yaw velocity	(s)
τ_f, τ_r	Time constant for front/rear side slip angle	(s)
ω_n	ω_n : Response frequency	(rad/s)
	$f_n(\omega_n/2\pi)$: Natural frequency	(Hz)
$\zeta \cdot \omega_n$	$\zeta \cdot \omega_n$:	(1/s)
	$\zeta \cdot \omega_n \times V$: Steering capacity	(m/s^2)
	ζ : Damping rate	

	Vehicle with 2WS	Vehicle with 4WS in which the rear steering angle is proportional to front
Stability factor	$\dfrac{m(l_r K_r - l_f K_f)}{2l^2 K_f K_r} = K$	K
Steady state gain in yaw velocity	$\dfrac{1}{1+KV^2} \cdot \dfrac{V}{l}$	$\dfrac{1}{1+KV^2} \cdot \dfrac{V}{l}$
Damping rate	$\dfrac{1}{2} \cdot \dfrac{(k_f + K_r I_t + (K_f l_f + K_r l_r^2)m}{\sqrt{mI_z K_f K_r l^2(1+KV^2)}} = \zeta$	ζ
Response frequency	$\dfrac{2l}{V} \cdot \sqrt{\dfrac{K_f K_r(1+KV^2)}{I_z m}} = \omega_n$	ω_n
Steering capacity	$\dfrac{1}{V}\left(\dfrac{K_f + K_r}{m} + \dfrac{K_f l_f^2 + K_r l_r^2}{l_z}\right) = \zeta \cdot \omega_x$	$\zeta \cdot \omega_n$
$\dfrac{\dot{\varphi}}{\delta_H}$	$\dfrac{1}{i_s} G_\varphi(0)\dfrac{1+T_f s}{1+\dfrac{2\zeta}{\omega_n}s+\dfrac{1}{\omega_n^2}s^2}$ $G\varphi(0) = \dfrac{1}{1+KV^2} \cdot \dfrac{V}{l}$	$\dfrac{1-k}{i_s} G\varphi(0)\dfrac{1+(1+\lambda\phi)T_f s}{1+\dfrac{2\zeta}{\omega_n}s+\dfrac{1}{\omega_n^2}s^2}$ $G\phi(0) = \dfrac{1}{1+KV^2} \cdot \dfrac{V}{l}$ $\lambda\varphi = \dfrac{k}{1-k} \cdot \dfrac{T_f - T_r}{T_f}$
$\dfrac{\alpha_y}{\delta_H}$	$\dfrac{1}{i_s} G_{ay}(0) = \dfrac{1+T_{ay1}s+T_{ay2}s^2}{1+\dfrac{2\zeta}{\omega_n}s+\dfrac{1}{\omega_n^2}s^2}$ $G_{ay}(0) = \dfrac{1}{1+KV^2} \cdot \dfrac{V^2}{l}$ $T_{ay1} = \dfrac{l_r}{V}, \qquad T_{ay2} = \dfrac{l_z}{2K_r l}$	$\dfrac{1-k}{i_s} G_{ay}(0) \cdot \dfrac{1+(1+\lambda_{ay1})T_{ay1}s+(1+\lambda_{ay2})T_{ay2}s^2}{1+\dfrac{2\zeta}{\omega_n}s+\dfrac{1}{\omega_n^2}s^2}$ $G_{ay}(0) = \dfrac{1}{1+KV^2} \cdot \dfrac{V^2}{l}$ $\lambda_{ay1} = \dfrac{k}{1-k} \cdot \dfrac{T_{ay1}+T'_{ay1}}{T_{ay1}}$ $\lambda_{ay2} = \dfrac{k}{1-k} \cdot \dfrac{T_{ay2}+T'_{ay2}}{T_{ay2}}$ $T_{ay1} = \dfrac{l_r}{V}, \qquad T_{ay2} = \dfrac{l_f}{V}$ $T_{ay2} = \dfrac{l_z}{2K_r l}, \qquad T'_{ay2} = \dfrac{l_z}{2K_f l}$

TABLE 18.8[1]

Symbol	Dimension	Name
m	kg	Mass of the vehicle
I_z	kg · m^2	Moment of the inertia of vehicle
l	m	Wheel base
l_f, l_r	m	Distance between center of gravity and front/rear wheel shaft
V	m/s	Vehicle speed $V = \sqrt{v_x^2 + v_y^2}$
v_x, v_y	m/s	Longitudinal and lateral velocity of the center of gravity
a_x, a_y	m/s^2	Longitudinal and lateral acceleration of the center of gravity
ψ, ϕ	rad	Yaw angle, roll angle
$\dot{\psi}, \dot{\phi}$	rad/s	Yaw velocity roll rate
β	rad	Side slip angle of the center of gravity
δ_f, δ_r	rad	Front/rear wheel steering angle
α_f, α_r	rad	Front/rear side slip angle
K_f, K_r	N/rad	Equivalent cornering power of front/rear
δ_H	rad	Steering wheel angle
i_s	I	Steering ratio in over all

TABLE 18.9[1]

Classification by functions	Aims
Small range of rear steer angle only controlled electronically	Improvement of steering response and vehicle stability in medium to high speed
Not only small range in medium to high speed but large range in low speed of rear steering angle are controlled electronically	In addition to the above, making the minimum turning radius small

TABLE 18.10[1]

Classification by mechanism	Feature
Full mechanical system	Simple mechanism
Electronic-hydraulic system	High degree for control freedom (compact actuator)
Electronic-mechanical-hydraulic system	High degree of freedom (mechanism is not simple)
Full electric system (electronic-electric system)	High degree of control freedom simple mechanism

18.2.3 Introduction to Each System

Fully Mechanical System.   This was the first 4WS system used in passenger vehicles. It was adopted in the Honda Prelude in 1987 and in the Honda Accord in 1989. This system is a front-wheel steering angle responsive-type system in which the rear-wheel steering angle is determined wholly by the steering angle of the front wheels. The structure and fabrication of this system are shown in Figs. 18.28 and 18.29.

In rack-and-pinion type steering gearboxes for the front wheels, a rear-wheel steering pinion is provided in order to transmit the steering angle of the front wheels to the rear wheels. The displacement in the steering angle is transmitted to the rear steering gearbox via the center steering shaft. As shown in the figure, the rear steering gearbox consists of a combination of an eccentric shaft and a planetary gear. The input and output characteristics that can be obtained are shown in Fig. 18.30. The result of this is that when the steering angle for the front

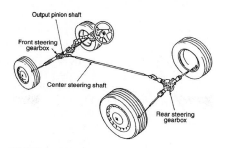

FIGURE 18.28 Fully mechanical 4WS.

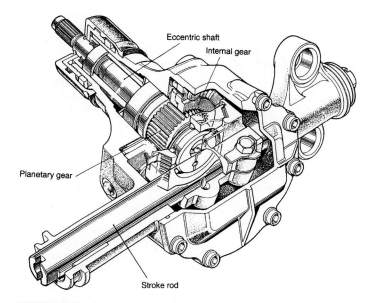

FIGURE 18.29 Rear steering actuator of full mechanical 4WS.

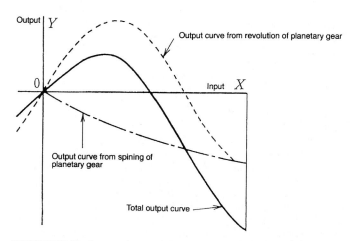

FIGURE 18.30 Input-output characteristics of rear steering gearbox.

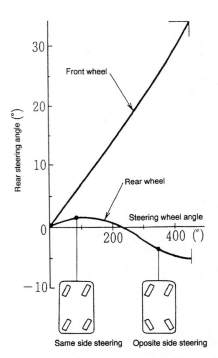

wheels is small, the rear wheels turn in the same direction, but when the steering angle for the front wheels is large, the rear wheels turn in the opposite direction, as shown in Fig. 18.31. During high-speed driving, since the front wheels are only turned by very small amounts, the rear wheels thus turn in the same direction, and driving stability is improved. At extremely low speeds where the front wheels are steered through much larger angles, the rear wheels turn in the opposite direction and the turning radius becomes small, thus, the working ability should be improved.

Electronic-Hydraulic Control System

Vehicle Speed/Lateral Acceleration Responsive Type. This system was installed in vehicles like the 1986 Nissan Skyline. The structure of the system and the construction of the rear gearbox are shown in Figs. 18.32 and 18.33, respectively. In this system, a special hydraulic valve, which generates hydraulic pressure balanced with the reaction force from the front wheels in proportion to the lateral acceleration, is provided in the front-wheel power steering system, and this hydraulic pressure is transmitted to the actuator for the rear wheels. The rear-wheel actuator

FIGURE 18.31 Characteristics of front steering speed-responsive 4WS.

contains a high spring rate spring which allows displacement of the output rod to the position that balances the hydraulic pressure received. The rear wheels are steered in the same direction as the front wheels by means of the displacement of this rod. Accordingly, the relationship between the vehicle speed and the steering angle of the rear wheels varies in accordance with

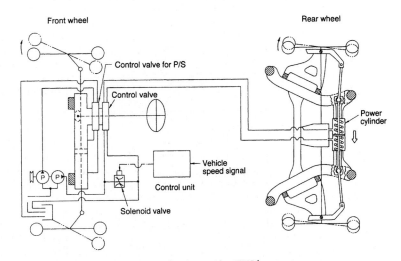

FIGURE 18.32 Lateral acceleration-responsive 4WS.[1]

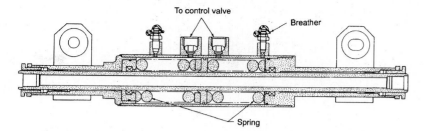

FIGURE 18.33 Rear steering actuator of lateral acceleration-responsive 4WS.[1]

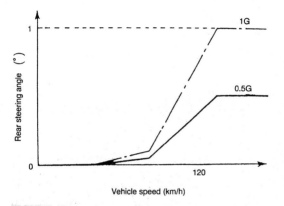

FIGURE 18.34 Characteristics of rear steering angle.[1]

the lateral acceleration as shown in Fig. 18.34. In this system, the maximum steering angle of the rear wheels is confined to a fairly low value, so that it is not intended to be a system for improving the minimum turning radius of the vehicle at very low speeds.

Vehicle Speed/Front-Wheel Steering Angle/Steering Wheel Velocity Responsive Type. This system was installed in vehicles such as the 1988 Nissan Sylvia, and was developed for the purpose of further improvement of vehicle stability and maneuverability during medium- to high-speed driving. The structure of the system and the construction of the rear-wheel actuator (solenoid servo valve) are shown in Figs. 18.35 and 18.36, respectively. In this system, the working fluid discharged from the hydraulic pump is directly introduced to the solenoid servo valve and controlled by instructions from an ECU (electronic control unit), after which it is sent to the power cylinder.

The ECU detects the front-wheel turning angle and the steering speed of the steering wheel by means of signals from the steering wheel angle sensor located in the steering wheel. The values thus calculated and the vehicle speed are used to determine the steering angle for the rear wheels. The maximum steering angle of the rear wheels is confined to a fairly low value in this system also, so that it was intended only to be a system for improving the vehicle stability and maneuverability at medium to high speeds. However, it does not improve only the stability by turning the rear wheels in the same direction, but also improves the maneuverability by momentarily turning the rear wheels in the opposite direction to the front wheels when the steering wheel is turned quickly at medium vehicle speeds. That is, the initial yawing movement (yaw velocity) of the vehicle is improved and steering response is thus improved. Figure 18.37 shows the steering angle pattern of the rear wheels with time expressed along the horizontal axis.

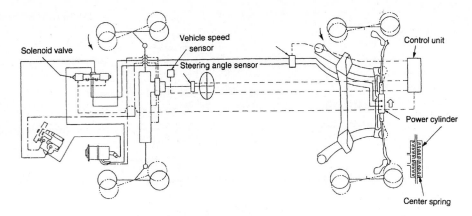

FIGURE 18.35 System construction of front-wheel-responsive 4WS.[1]

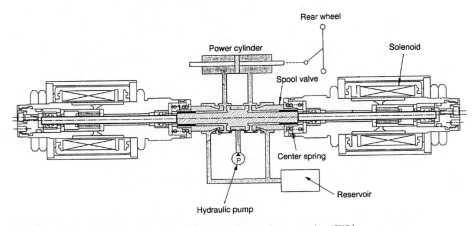

FIGURE 18.36 Solenoid servo valve of front steering angle-responsive 4WS.[1]

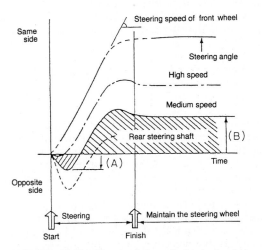

FIGURE 18.37 Characteristics of front steering angle-responsive 4WS.[1]

Electronic-Hydraulic-Mechanical Systems

Vehicle Speed/Front-Wheel Steering Angle Responsive Type.   This system was introduced in the 1987 Mazda Capella, and was designed with the aim of being a system for improving both stability when driving at high speeds, like the fully mechanical system, and vehicle minimum turning radius at low speeds. The structure of the system and the construction of the rear actuator are shown in Figs. 18.38 and 18.39, respectively. This system can be broadly divided into the power assist section and the phase control section. The power assist section consists of a linear spool valve and a power piston, and utilizes hydraulic pressure as the dynamic force. The phase control section comprises a bevel gear which engages with the input shaft, a control yoke, and a control rod which is connected to a valve. The angle of the control yoke is driven by a stepping motor via a worm gear, thus controlling the turning direction of the rear wheels so that the rear wheels can be turned, not only in the same direction, but also in the opposite direction as the front wheels.

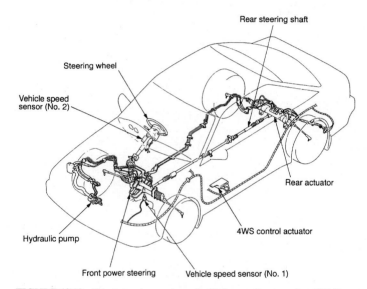

FIGURE 18.38   Front steering angle and vehicle speed-responsive 4WS.[11]

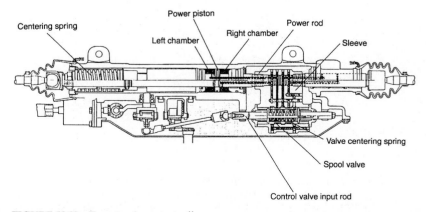

FIGURE 18.39   Rear steering actuator.[11]

In Fig. 18.40, *a* represents the situation in which the rear wheels are turned in the same direction, and *b* represents the situation in which the rear wheels are in the opposite direction. The direction of movement of the valve spool in relation to the turning direction of the input shaft is opposite for *a* and *b* as shown. Figure 18.41 shows the situation in which the ratio of the steering angle of the rear wheels with respect to the steering angle of the front wheels is continuously changing with respect to the vehicle speed.

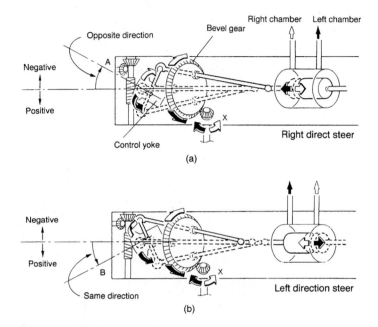

FIGURE 18.40   Explanation diagram of rear actuator.[11]

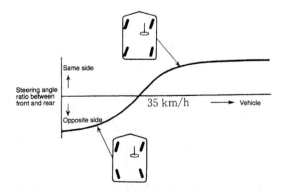

FIGURE 18.41   Characteristics of front steering angle and vehicle speed-responsive 4WS.[1]

Vehicle Speed/Front-Wheel Steering Angle/Yaw Velocity Responsive Type.   This system was introduced in the 1992 Toyota Soarer. Figures 18.42 and 18.43 show the system structure and the construction of the rear-wheel steering actuator, respectively. The system consists of two sections: a *mechanical-hydraulic type* steering mechanism to steer the rear wheels by a

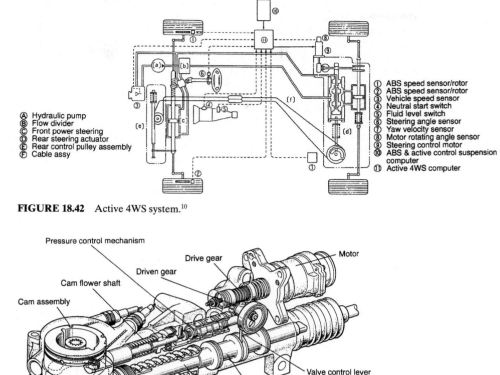

(A) Hydraulic pump
(B) Flow divider
(C) Front power steering
(D) Rear steering actuator
(E) Rear control pulley assembly
(F) Cable assy

(1) ABS speed sensor/rotor
(2) ABS speed sensor/rotor
(3) Vehicle speed sensor
(4) Neutral start switch
(5) Fluid level switch
(6) Steering angle sensor
(7) Yaw velocity sensor
(8) Motor rotating angle sensor
(9) Steering control motor
(10) ABS & active control suspension computer
(11) Active 4WS computer

FIGURE 18.42 Active 4WS system.[10]

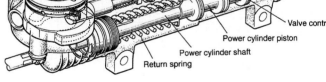

FIGURE 18.43 Rear steering actuator unit.[10]

considerably large steering angle in the opposite direction to the front wheels in order to make the turning radius small at low speeds, and an *electronic-hydraulic type* steering mechanism to steer the rear wheels by a considerably smaller value in order to not only improve the steering response and the stability during middle- to high-speed driving, but also to suppress the unexpected movements due to the outside disturbances.

Mechanical-Hydraulic Type Steering Mechanism.   This mechanism consists of steering angle transmission cables, which transmit information concerning the steering angle of the front wheels to the rear-wheel steering actuator; a joint to connect the front and rear cables; a pulley assembly, which converts the displacement of the front-wheel steering rack into cable movement; a cam, which converts the movement of the cable into displacement of the sleeve valve inside the rear-wheel steering actuator; and a copy valve, which steers the rear wheels as far as the instruction given by the sleeve valve and maintains them in position. Furthermore, a dead zone is provided in the pulley assembly so that the rear wheels are not steered in the opposite direction to the front wheels when the vehicle is traveling at high speed.

Electronic-Hydraulic Type Steering Mechanism.   This mechanism is designed to improve the steering response and the stability of the vehicle and to suppress the unexpected movements from outside disturbances when the vehicle is traveling at medium to high speeds. For this purpose, the system consists of five types of sensors for detecting the driving conditions and the steering situations, an ECU which determines the steering angle for the rear wheels based on the signals from these sensors, a pulse motor which drives the gear mechanism based on instructions from the ECU, a gear mechanism which converts the rotation of the pulse motor into a spool valve displacement, and a hydraulic copy valve which steers the rear wheels as far as the instruction given by the sleeve valve and maintains them in that position.

Control Method. The basic algorithm to determine the steering angle for the rear wheels is given in Fig. 18.44. When driving in the medium- to high-speed range, the front-wheel steering angle proportional gain for the rear wheels is set to 0; instead of that, the yaw velocity proportional gain in the direction which suppresses the yaw rate is set. Accordingly, in the medium- to high-speed range, the rear wheels are turned in the same direction as front wheels, with the same effect as that of the other system mentioned before. The feature of this system is that a yaw rate sensor is provided to detect the vehicle dynamics and utilizes its signal as a control parameter. The effect of this is the addition of a function which automatically compensates the confusion in vehicle behavior caused by outside disturbance.

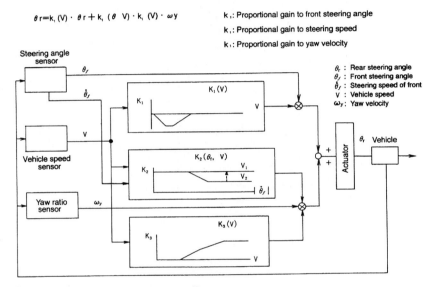

FIGURE 18.44 Control block diagram.[10]

18.2.4 Electronic-Electric Control Systems

Vehicle Speed/Front-Wheel Steering Angle/Steering Speed Responsive Type. This system was introduced in the 1991 Honda Prelude. The system structure is shown in Fig. 18.45, and the construction of the rear-wheel actuator is shown in Fig. 18.46. This system has a structure whereby the rotation of an electric motor that is controlled by the ECU is converted into linear motion by means of a ball screw to directly drive the rear wheels. The system is easy to install. Cross sections of the structures of the front-wheel steering angle sensor and the rear-wheel steering angle sensor are shown in Figs. 18.47 and Fig. 18.48, respectively.

Also in this system, the turning of the rear wheels is determined by the vehicle speed, the front steering angle, and the steering wheel velocity. The determining algorithm is similar to the system mentioned previously. In this system, improvements in the stability at high speeds, improvement in the steering response when the steering wheel is turned quickly, and improvement in the turning radius of the vehicle at low speeds have been realized simultaneously.

The most recent example of an electronic-electric system is the system[12] that has been installed in the 1993 Nissan Laurel. The approach to control in this system is the same as in the

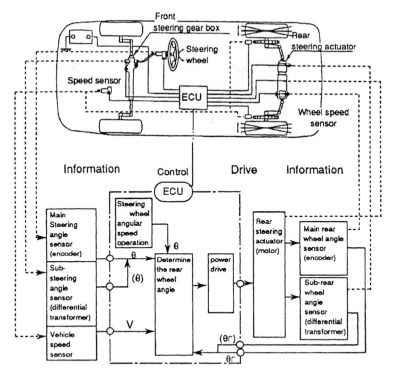

FIGURE 18.45   Block diagram of the full-electric 4WS.

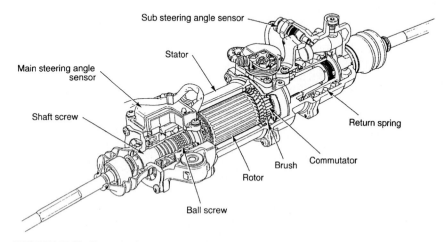

FIGURE 18.46   Rear steering actuator.

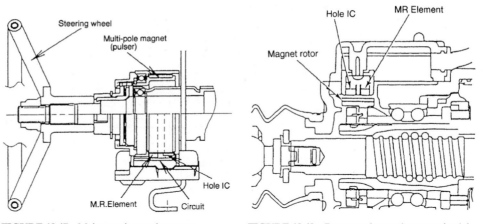

FIGURE 18.47   Main steering angle sensor.   **FIGURE 18.48**   Rear steering angle sensor (main).

vehicle speed/front-wheel steering angle/steering wheel velocity responsive type system mentioned before, but by using an electric actuator, the space taken up by the system has been reduced and ease of installation improved.

Figure 18.49 shows the system structure, and Fig. 18.50 shows the steering angle generation modes for the rear wheels.

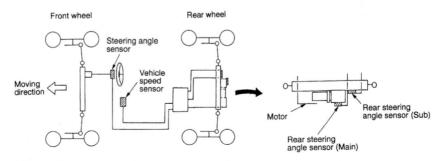

FIGURE 18.49   System construction of HICAS.[12]

18.2.5   Trends in Research and Development

Four-wheel steering systems that have been installed in current vehicles mainly adopt the program control technique in which the rear-wheel steering angle is programmably determined based on the beforehand scheduling relationship with the vehicle speed, the front steering angle, and steering wheel velocity. The aim of the system is the improvement of the insufficient performances in handling characteristics of the vehicle under special steering situations.

Recently, however, the system based on the new concept is being earnestly researched in order to drastically improve the handling characteristics in any region for practical use. Such technology is similar to that of CCV (control configured vehicle), which is used in airplanes, and named as *active control technology* in general. In this section, a basic introduction to the following two representative concepts concerning the active four-wheel steering system (A-4WS), which adopts the active control technology in the 4WS systems, will be given.

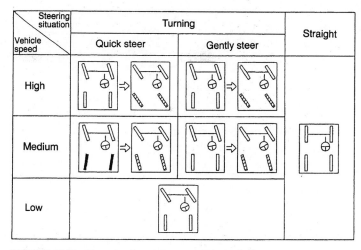

Steering situation / Vehicle speed	Turning				Straight
	Quick steer		Gently steer		
High					
Medium					
Low					

FIGURE 18.50   Rear steering angle generation mode.[12]

Vehicle's Slip Angle Control System.   Generally, the moving direction of the center of gravity of the vehicle is not the same as the heading direction of the vehicle while the vehicle is turning, and the angle between these two directions is called the *side slip angle of the vehicle*. When the side slip angle of the vehicle is large, the driver is forced to drive with an oblique line of vision. This can be considered one cause of increased driving difficulties. From this point of view, the control concept has been proposed whereby the side slip angle of the vehicle while driving is always kept close to 0. In addition, the cause of the increasing of phase delay in lateral acceleration according to the vehicle speed is that the steady state gain in the sideslip angle is reduced together with the vehicle speed and becomes negative at high speed. In order to eliminate such phenomena, the concept which keeps the sideslip angle close to 0 may also be desirable.

The sideslip angle B can be expressed in general by the following equation:

$$\beta = \frac{1}{POL(s)}\{B_f(1 + \tau_f \cdot s)\delta_f + B_r(1 + \tau \cdot s)\delta_r\} \tag{18.9}$$

$$B_f: \frac{2l_r lk_r - l_f m v^2}{2lk_r V} \cdot A, B_r: \frac{2l_f lk_f - l_r m v^2}{2lk_f V} \cdot A$$

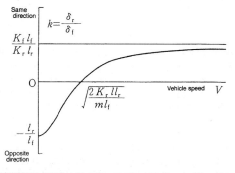

FIGURE 18.51   Steering angle ratio for making the vehicle sideslip angle equal to 0.[1]

Provided the numerator s in Eq. (18.9) = 0, the steering angle ratio between the front and rear wheels that is required for realizing a sideslip angle of 0 can be obtained from Eq. (18.10) as a function of the vehicle speed. This is shown graphically in Fig. 18.51.

$$\frac{\delta_r}{\delta_f} = -\frac{B_f - B_f \tau_{fs}}{_Br + B_r \tau_r s} \tag{18.10}$$

$$= \frac{-l_{f+} + (l_r m/2k_f A)V^2 - (I_z/2K_r l)V \cdot s}{l_{f+} + (l_r m/2k_f A)V^2 - (I_z/2K_f A)V \cdot s}$$

If the front- and rear-wheel control principle that includes the phase proceeding func-

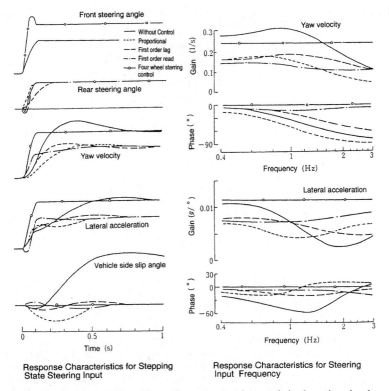

FIGURE 18.52 Affections in steering response characteristics by using the delay/advanced control means.[1]

tion for the front-wheel steering angle is employed, the vehicle characteristics can be set more freely. An example of the simulation analysis when the front and rear wheels are steered with a control principle such as the above is shown in Fig. 18.52.

Model Following Control System. In this system, the desirable vehicle behavior in accordance with the driver's steering operations is predetermined as a reference model, and the control is carried out so that the actual vehicle behavior fits this model. Generally, the lateral acceleration and the yaw velocity are used as the parameters for expressing the lateral movement of the vehicle. If the independent models are set for both of these characteristics, and make the actual vehicle behavior follow them, it is necessary to actively control both of the front and rear wheels. Research into systems such as this is currently being carried out, but in this section, a system for controlling the steering angle of the rear wheels that uses a range model for $D*$ which is defined by the linear combined Eq. (18.11) for the yaw velocity and the lateral acceleration will be introduced.

$$D* = da_y + (1 - d)V\phi \qquad (18.11)$$

If the weighted constant d in Eq. (18.11) equals 0, this control system becomes a yaw velocity model following control system, and if $d = 1$, then it is a lateral acceleration following control system.

GLOSSARY

Convergence   Yaw stability of the vehicle when driver inputs a rapid steering wheel movement and releases the steering wheel.

Kickback   Steering torque and angle arising from inverse input through the tires from uneven concrete road or other surface.

REFERENCES

1. "Steering," chap. 8, *Handbook of Society of Automotive Engineers of Japan* vol. 2 (Design), Society of Automotive Engineers of Japan, Inc., 1991.
2. Nissan Ciema, guidebook in Japan, 1991.
3. Shigeru Iga, et al., "Motor driven power steering for the maximum steering sensation in every driving situation," SAE paper 880705, 1988.
4. *Honda Today* service manual in Japan, 1991.
5. Acura NSX service manual, 1991.
6. Yasuo Shimizu, et al., "Development of electric power steering," SAE paper 910014.
7. Syunichi Wada, et al., "Electric power steering system," Mitsubishi Denk Giho, vol. 66, no. 9, 1992.
8. Yasuo Shimizu, et al., "Control of electric power steering (EPS)," *The 68th JSME Spring Annual Meeting,* vol. C 1605, 1991.
9. Naohiro Yuhara, et al., "Improvement of vehicle handling quality through active control of steering reaction torque," *International Symposium on Advanced Vehicle Control 1992,* no. 923073.
10. *Toyota Technical Review,* vol. 41, no. 1, 1989.
11. Mazda Motor Company Introduction to Capella (new car), 89-5-NM005, 1989.
12. Nissan Motor Company Introduction to Laurel (new car), F005705, 1989.

ABOUT THE AUTHOR

Makoto Sato, executive chief engineer of Honda R&D Co., Ltd., was graduated from Nagoya Institute of Technology in 1960 and began his career with Kokusan Electric Co. He moved to Honda R&D Co., Ltd. in 1968 and began working on vehicle dynamics control systems with electronic technologies. He is now researching new safety technologies with intelligent electronics, especially in the area of crash avoidance.

CHAPTER 19
LIGHTING, WIPERS, AIR CONDITIONING/HEATING

Richard Valentine
Motorola Inc.

19.1 LIGHTING CONTROLS

Controlling lamps with power electronics offers many advantages and a few disadvantages over conventional switches or relays. An important advantage includes easier diagnostics compared to the classical mechanical switch or relay approach, while a significant disadvantage includes the higher cost of the electronics. Because some lights, such as headlamps, turn signals, and brake lamps are safety related, a method to test the integrity of these lamps is an advantageous feature. The power electronic design can not only turn lights on or off, but it can vary the light's intensity and detect abnormal conditions such as open or shorted lamps. The cost tradeoff issue becomes more interesting when the power electronics load control is connected onto a data bus or multiplexed network (see Chap. 26).

The typical automotive lamp can range from small-wattage panel lamps to large 60-W or higher headlamps (refer to SAE ref HS-34/93 for auto lamp standards). Tungsten and halogen types prevail for many vehicular lamp designs. The prime difference between standard tungsten nonhalogen and halogen lamps is in light efficiency. Halogen types produce about 20 percent more light for each watt of energy consumed. Other types of lamps, such as light-emitting diodes (LEDs), fluorescents, or gas discharge, are somewhat adaptable for vehicular applications. The power electronics operating requirements vary for each lamp technology category.

19.1.1 Incandescent/Halogen

The single most important rule when switching normal incandescent lamps is to select a power transistor that can sustain a 10 to 15 times inrush current level. For example, a 2-A-rated stop lamp requires a 20- to 30-A-rated power transistor for an electronic switch design. When designing a lamp-driven circuit, other considerations besides inrush currents must be taken into account: maximum power transistor operating temperatures, shorted load protection, voltage supply transients, reverse voltage supply condition, open load detection, high or low side design topology, MCU interface, switching edge speed limits, and variable brightness control. In addition, the electronic lamp switch should not drop more than 0.3 V to ensure that the lamp's intensity is not degraded. Incandescent lamp light output is very sensitive to the lamp's operating voltage. A 20 percent drop in an incandescent lamp's nominal operating voltage can reduce its light output by 50 percent.

Inrush Current Effects. Lamp loads behave like high positive temperature coefficient resistors. When the lamp is cold, the resistance value of its filament is about 1/10 of its normal operating resistance. Lab tests show a definite relationship between the lamp's peak inrush current level and light output intensity with respect to time. If the lamp current is limited to its nominal value, it takes longer—one-half second or more—for the filament to reach its nominal temperature, but if the current supply is unlimited, the lamp heats up very quickly. The lamp response time and the available supply current must be considered for applications when an instantaneous light output is desired, such as with turn signals or brake lights in a vehicle. A 1-s delay at 89 km/h (55m/h) equals 24.6 m (81 ft). Four seconds of time is about how long some vehicles take to stop at a vehicle speed of 89 km/h. If the driver has exerted maximum braking, and his stop lamp waits for 1 s to convey this action to trailing vehicles, the driver will almost be halfway stopped before the trailing vehicle has a stop light indication. This is not acceptable, and the delay time in stop or possibly in turn signal indicators must be minimized to benefit the reaction time for other drivers.

Limiting the lamp's inrush current will probably increase the lamp's longevity in high duty cycle applications, such as a flasher, because the mechanical stress on the filament is reduced. A limited inrush current design should decrease the chances of the lamp failing during the initial turn on. In vehicular applications when external induced filament vibration is high, the lamp reliability may not be improved enough to justify a current limiting design. A current limiting design does increase the power transistor's peak heat dissipation, and when operating with an energy source that is capable of supplying high peak currents, such as an automotive battery, the rationale to include current limiting would be to use a smaller, less expensive transistor or to minimize voltage sags in the wire bus when several lamps are switched on at the same time. A current limiting design may include a network to control the switching transition times from OFF to ON to OFF.

Setting the switching times to over 0.001 s would help minimize EMI effects. Most power transistors can switch in less than 1 μs, with some power FETs able to switch in 50 ns. These RF switching speeds are undesirable and will be detectable by other electronic systems in the vehicle, such as the AM radio.

Lamp Driver Design. The power electronics can drive the lamp in one of two simple ways. One is *low side switching* (Fig. 19.1) with the lamp connected between the power supply and the transistor, or *high side switching* (Fig. 19.2) with the lamp connected between the transistor and common. The main drawback to low side switching is that one side of the lamp is always connected directly to the battery supply, and if this lead is shorted to common, very high currents will occur. A high side switch disconnects the power supply from the load, so if the switch is off, the chances of an accidental power supply short when replacing or troubleshooting the lamp are minimal. On the other hand, in the high side switch design, a switch ON condition will cause very high current levels to flow through the power transistor in the event of a short. The selection between high or low side switching is affected by the lamp's environment.

In a low side design, leakage currents that may flow from the lamp's socket or connectors can be a concern. This is especially true if the lamp is operated in a salt-laden, high-moisture atmosphere. This problem occurs because of the constant voltage potential at the socket and is one reason why most exterior vehicular lighting systems use high side switching. Other applications, such as instrument backlighting or signal indicators that are usually located inside the vehicle, can be a low side design to take advantage of lower-cost NPN transistors or N-channel power FETs. N-channel power FETs can be used for high side switching by adding a charge pump as shown in Fig. 19.2a. Special power linear devices are also available that incorporate a charge pump for high side switching of small lamps. These power linear IC devices (MC3399, MC33091, or equivalent) will find more usage as their pricing and reliability become more attractive for automotive application.

Power Control Device Selection. When the drive topology has been decided upon, a power device can be chosen. There are numerous tradeoffs between bipolar and power FET transistors. The N-channel power FET device requires minimal drive power for a low side switch and

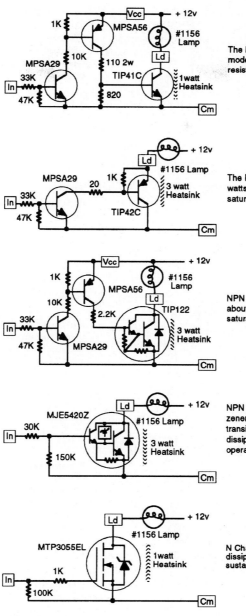

The NPN transistor runs in full saturation mode, but requires 1.5 watt base drive resistor.

The PNP transistor dissipates about 3 watts since it does not operate in saturation mode.

NPN Darlington transistor dissipates about 3 watts since it does not operate in saturation mode.

NPN Darlington transistor has internal active zener element to clamp over voltage transients in forward SOA mode. Device dissipates about 3 watts since it does not operate in saturation mode.

N Channel MOSFET transistor dissipates about .8 watts, and can sustain low energy voltage spikes.

FIGURE 19.1   Low side switching.

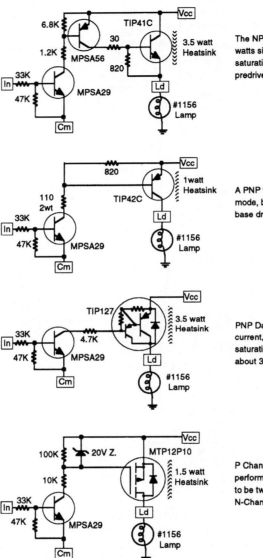

The NPN transistor dissipates about 3 watts since it does not operate in saturation mode. Circuit requires two predrivers.

A PNP transistor can run in saturation mode, but dissipates about 1.5 watts in base drive resistor.

PNP Darlington requires small base current, but can't operate in saturation mode, and dissipates about 3 watts.

P Channel MOSFET offers best electrical performance, but the internal silicon die has to be twice as large as similar rated N-Channel MOSFET.

FIGURE 19.2   High side switching.

is cost-competitive with similar rated bipolars. Low side switching can easily use N-power FETs, whereas a high side switch would need more expensive P power FETs. Power FET transistors will usually be able to conduct the high peak inrush currents much more readily than bipolar transistors. This is because power FETs have higher transconductance than bipolars. Bipolars are usually biased for operation at the lamp's average load current and will therefore operate in a linear mode during the lamp's initial turn on, thereby offering some current-limiting at the expense of increased peak junction temperature. The power FET will usually con-

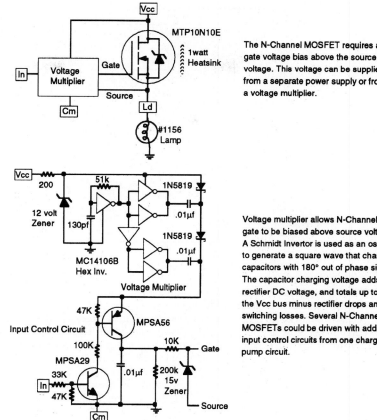

The N-Channel MOSFET requires a gate voltage bias above the source voltage. This voltage can be supplied from a separate power supply or from a voltage multiplier.

Voltage multiplier allows N-Channel gate to be biased above source voltage. A Schmidt Invertor is used as an oscillator to generate a square wave that charges capacitors with 180° out of phase signals. The capacitor charging voltage adds to the rectifier DC voltage, and totals up to 3x the Vcc bus minus rectifier drops and switching losses. Several N-Channel MOSFETs could be driven with additional input control circuits from one charge pump circuit.

FIGURE 19.2a   N FET high side design.

duct many times its average current without going into a linear mode, provided the overcurrent condition time period is fairly short, less than 100 ms.

Lamp driver long-term reliability is determined mainly by the power transistor's heat dissipation and somewhat by the solder joint totals. Selecting P-power FET devices for the high side configuration because of the low number of parts, ease of drive interface, and low power dissipation appears best, but P-channel FET devices are usually 50 percent more costly. The N-channel devices win both for cost and reliability in a low side switch design. Table 19.1 summarizes the various lamp driver designs.

Short-Circuit Protection.   Another consideration is shorted circuits. The bipolar transistor is typically biased for minimum base drive power loss. During a shorted load condition, the bipolar will pull out of saturation, enter into a linear operation mode, and may fail due to excessive junction temperatures, ordinarily before a fuse will blow. A properly sized power FET may be able to safely conduct enough shorted load current to blow the fusing element. Power FET devices of 50 V are available that exhibit less than 0.01 ohm forward ON resistance in a fingernail-sized surface-mount package such as a MTB75N05HD or the equivalent.

TABLE 19.1   Lamp Switch Design Comparison

Device type	Driver stage loss, W	Output device loss, W	Pwr. eff. in/out, %	Relative system cost	Parts count total, pcs	Solder joints total, pts	Relative reliability
High side switch configurations for 2.1-A lamp load							
NPN	0.2	2.7	89	high	9	25	low
PNP	1.31	0.8	92	medium	6	18	medium
Darlington PNP	0.03	2.7	89	high	5	13	low
P-channel MOSFET	0.01	0.9	96	high	7	19	medium
N-channel MOSFET	0.05	0.7	97	highest	19	54	low
Low side switch configurations for 2.1-A lamp load							
NPN	1.32	0.8	91	medium	9	23	medium
PNP	0.13	3.2	88	high	5	15	low
NPN Darlington	0.08	2.7	90	high	8	23	low
NPN Darlington w/Zener	0.0004	2.7	90	low	3	10	medium
N-channel MOSFET	0.0002	0.7	97	low	3	10	high

Power supply voltage = 12 V

This type of device could safely conduct 14 A continuously (assuming a 50 °C ambient temperature and 2 W constant power dissipation, $[I = (P/R)^{1/2}]$.

Another way of protecting a transistor against excessive current levels is to monitor the current value by the insertion of a low-value power resistor in series with the load. A comparator is used to detect the current sense resistor's voltage drop and will toggle if this voltage drop exceeds the comparator's reference voltage. The comparator output is tied to an R-S flip-flop logic network that latches off the input signal. Some power FET devices are now manufactured with an internal current mirror element and eliminate the need for an external large power resistor. A basic circuit is shown in Fig. 19.3 for an internal current-sensing power

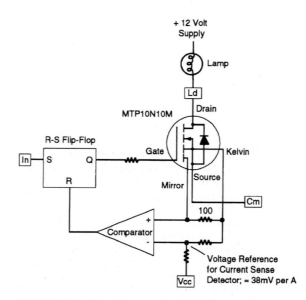

FIGURE 19.3   Internal current-sensing FET lamp drive.

FET lamp driver. This circuit uses an RS flip-flop that will shut off the gate voltage. When the RS flip-flop has been toggled by the comparator, the RS input (set line) has to be retoggled to turn on the current-sensing power FET again. When an overcurrent condition occurs, the current-sensing power FET is latched off until the input is retoggled.

The transistor's voltage rating will be determined by the maximum voltage transients on the power supply line. In vehicular battery-charging systems, the normal 12-V supply can reach over 85 V due to intermittent battery connections when the alternator is operating. If the transistor is not avalanche-rated and enters a second breakdown due to excessive power supply voltages, it will fail shorted. Higher-voltage systems require much higher-voltage-rated devices.

MCU-based Lamp Driver. The current-sensing power FET can be directly interfaced to a single-chip microcomputer. The use of a single-chip microcomputer can allow the switch control circuit to perform many tasks: open load detection, shorted load protection, variable intensity, and diagnostics. The MCU concept is especially attractive when several lamps are clustered together and driven from the same module. Figure 19.4 shows the use of a single-

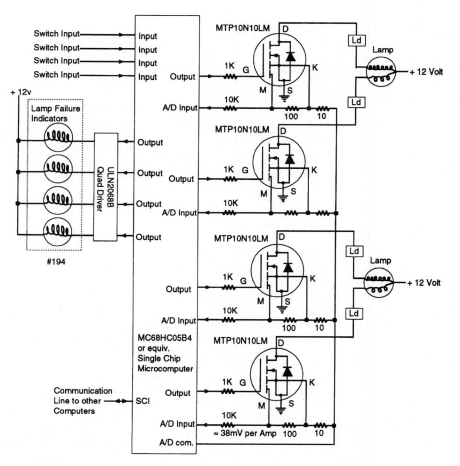

FIGURE 19.4 MCU lamp control.

chip MCU for controlling four lamp filaments. Many more lamps could easily be added to this design. Low side switching is used to accommodate the use of logic level N-channel current-sensing power FETs. The MCU's program is set to sustain a shorted load condition for less than 50 ms; this allows a cold lamp turn-on condition to be tolerated. If a shorted load occurs after the initial turn on, the program can shut off the load in less than 1 ms, wait for 1 s, and then try to renenergize the lamp. A diagnostic fault lamp is energized to alert the user that a fault has occurred. An open load can be detected when the lamp is energized by having the program monitor the A/D inputs for a zero value. An 8-bit A/D converter will resolve to about 0.02 V when referenced from a 5-V supply. Therefore, a normal load current of 2 A will generate about a 0.084-V level, which will be read as a 04-hex number by the program. A value of 00 to 01 H would be considered an open, and a value of greater than 06 H would constitute a shorted load. A distinction could be made in the lamp failure indicator between an open and shorted load by turning the failure indicator full on for an open, and then flashing it at a 1-Hz rate for a shorted condition. The failure indicators are 3-W lamps for bright visibility, such as is required in vehicular dashboards. High-efficiency LEDs could be used when the 3-W lamp's brilliance is not required, and the LEDs may be directly driven from the MCU's output ports when connected in a low side switch configuration.

Variable light intensity can be obtained by programming a 100-Hz frequency with 0 to 100 percent pulse-width modulation. The 8-bit MCU can vary the pulse width by 256 steps, which would appear as an infinite intensity control to the human observer. One difficulty with PWM is when its duty cycle is producing very narrow pulses, such as at 1 percent or 99 percent. These narrow pulses may not allow the power stage to completely switch on or off. One method to minimize narrow PWM pulses is to force the PWM to jump from 0 percent to about 5 percent, and from 95 to 100 percent. This can easily be accomplished in the software design.

An external communication link can be established via the MCU's serial data port. This would allow the light control functions to be remotely accessible by another computer.

In summary, standard discrete power FET or bipolar transistors can effectively control incandescent lamp loads. Power FETs are preferred because of their low drive power requirement and high transconductance. The addition of an MCU enables the lamp control design to include many desirable features, such as shorted load protection, and minimizes the need for more advanced lamp driver semiconductors such as smartpower or power IC devices. MCUs are available with a built-in MUX port to communicate with other load control modules for remote operation of several lamps or other loads.

19.1.2 Fluorescent Lamps

A fluorescent lamp is commonly defined as a light source that produces light by the interaction of an arc with the gas mixture inside a glass vacuum tube. When this gas mixture is ionized by means of a high-voltage pulse from the tube's end terminals, its internal resistance decreases from megohms to several hundreds of ohms. Fluorescent lamps are typically 2 to 3 times more power efficient than standard incandescent lamps. The automotive lamp applications for fluorescents may include inside lighting, instrument back panel lighting, and other areas where an unfocused and discontinuous light spectrum, but highly efficient light source, can be utilized. The main drawback to fluorescent lamps is that they require a fairly high voltage to initiate the arc and a means to limit the lamp current once the arc is established. In other words, the fluorescent design will cost much more than a similar incandescent-sized light. This is an important consideration when operating the fluorescent lamp from a 12-V supply.

A 12-V powered fluorescent driver design requires an 8- to 16-V input to about 300-V output convertor with current limiting. These types of circuits usually operate at high frequencies (20 to 100 kHz) to minimize the size of passive components, such as transformers and capacitors, and to minimize audible noise. This type of circuit can generate significant EMI and RFI if not properly shielded and filtered. Figure 19.5 shows a block diagram of a 12-V fluorescent driver.

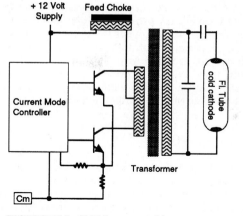

FIGURE 19.5   12-V fluorescent driver.

19.1.3   High-Intensity Gas Discharge Lamps

This class of lights includes mercury vapor, metal halide, and low- or high-pressure sodium. Some progress has been made to incorporate HID (high-intensity discharge) lamps in automotive applications. The HID metal halide type lamp offers high efficiency, up to four times more lumens per watt than incandescent, and high light output in a small package that can be utilized for headlamps. Again, the main drawback is the cost of the necessary power driver electronics. HID lamps require a circuit design similar to fluorescent drivers but at much higher power levels. The cost of the HID driver electronics limits their widespread use for automotive usage.

19.1.4   Electroluminescent (EL)

These low-intensity blue-green color light sources are used for decorative night lighting purposes and as backlighting for liquid crystal displays (LCD). EL lighting generally requires a low-current 100-V ac source. A 12-V dc to 100-V ac invertor is required for vehicular systems.

19.1.5   Light Emitting Diodes (LEDs)

Red LEDs may be adapted for stop light indicators. The LED produces a true red and does not require colored lenses. By combining several series LED strings together in one assembly, a stop light indicator is possible. A constant current source can be utilized to maintain a constant LED illumination level as shown in Fig. 19.6.

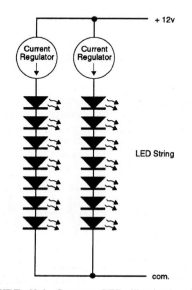

FIGURE 19.6   Constant LED illumination level design.

19.2   WINDSHIELD WIPER CONTROL

Windshield wiper (WW) systems are required by government regulations and therefore should be designed for high reliability. The motor control usually allows for low- and high-speed operation, or variable speed. The mechanical wiping motion is accomplished by a worm-gear design which gives torque multiplication and connects to the windshield wiper mechanical arm assembly. The key design specification is that the motor must sustain a "stalled" wiper condition without damage. The motor must also provide sufficient torque to run the wiper mechanism under worst-case conditions, such as blades frozen to the windshield. Electronic controls are used with WW systems, usually for intermittent operation plus variable speed. The driver adjusts a time interval control potentiometer for a one- to several-seconds wiper rate. The electronic circuit activates the motor with the appropriate time interval. A travel limit switch is normally used to insure that the wipe cycle is completed, and that the blades are returned to their nominal position.

Automatic windshield wiper designs are possible with today's technology that utilize a moisture detector to determine the degree of WW action required.

19.2.1   PM Motor Speed Control

The auto industry uses dc PM motors because they are economical to produce and ensure good performance. The motor's speed can be varied by either a simple voltage dropping passive resistor or an active linear voltage regulator. This simplistic method is widely used for vehicular motors requiring variable speed control. It does have a serious drawback in terms of power efficiency. For example, to control the speed of a motor that draws 20 A at full speed requires about 10 A at half speed. At full speed, the overall motor control system's efficiency will be around 80 percent. If the speed is reduced to half, the system's efficiency drops to 40 percent. This is because there is a heat loss of 70 W in the series voltage dropping element, in addition to the 14 W lost in the motor. A more efficient speed control system is therefore a desirable goal and can be accomplished by interrupting the motor's voltage at a variable duty cycle or by using a switching power supply. A switching power supply to control up to 300 W would cost more than the motor because of its high-frequency transformers and other components.

PWM Speed Control Design.   Electronic permanent magnet motor speed designs can range from a single power transistor to turn the motor on or off to an "H" bridge microcontroller-based system with closed-loop speed control. The design of a unidirectional 280-W 20-A motor speed control will be examined that uses power FET semiconductor technologies.

Since the PM motor is a dynamic machine with the armature acting as a flywheel, the voltage interruption or chopping rate could be 1000 Hz or slower, before the motor's speed actually pulsates. A problem at 1000 Hz or other audible rates is noise generated from within the motor. This audible motor sound may not be tolerable for drivers or passengers. At higher frequencies—16 kHz or greater—the audible noise is minimized. Another noise issue is the significant electronic radio frequency interference (RFI) that radiates into the electrical system, including the vehicle's radio equipment. This RFI is generated by the fast switching edges of the PWM signal. The drawing in Fig. 19.7 illustrates slow and fast switching speeds and the resultant power transistor dissipation relationships. Slowing down the switching edges minimizes the radio frequency interference (RFI), but the switching speed parameters also play a crucial role in the overall controller system. High transitional speeds are desirable to minimize switching losses and to improve reliability, but very fast switching speeds become impractical beyond a certain point due to the inherent inductance in the wire and component leads. A compromise has to be made between the edge speeds and power device heat loss.

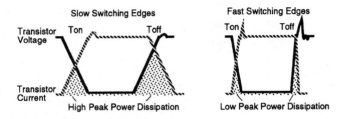

FIGURE 19.7   Slow vs. fast power loss.

Switching Speed Effects.   Figure 19.8 graphs the switching edge speed effects upon the power transistor's power dissipation when switching a 20-A motor load from a 14.4-V power supply. Three different operating frequencies are plotted, one at 20 kHz, one at 16 kHz, and the last at 2 kHz. Note how the 2-kHz switching times are less critical than the higher 16-kHz and 20-kHz frequencies. In order to minimize audible noise, the 16- or 20-kHz frequency can be used, but, unfortunately, the 200- to 500-ns switching speeds required to minimize switching losses cause the intrinsic inductance in the hookup wiring, components, and motor to become critical. These faster edge speeds will generate significant voltage spikes across the hookup wiring and may lead to reliability problems unless precautions are made to minimize stray inductance in this wiring.

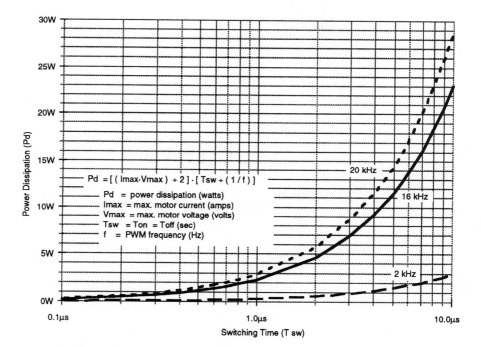

FIGURE 19.8   Power loss vs. switching speeds.

If the motor controller design has lead lengths that exceed 25 mm (1 in), their inductance values must be considered. An inductance value of 0.12 μH can be obtained in about 127 mm (5 in) of wire length with a #12 wire size, as shown in Fig. 19.9. This 0.12-μH value may not sound like much, but a plot (Fig. 19.10) of power line inductance versus switching transition times shows that just 0.1 μH of lead inductance can generate a 10-V voltage spike (at 20-A motor current) when switching edges are about 0.2 μs. Therefore, if fast switching edges are to be used, as with a 20-kHz operating frequency, a capacitor filter network is mandatory near the motor's power lead and controller. This filter network actually has to smooth out both the 20-kHz, and the much higher frequencies associated with the 200- to 1000-ns switching edges. To summarize, when fast switching edges are generated, filter networks are mandatory, or the hookup wiring will act as an antenna.

Motor Inductance Clamping.   The kickback voltage from the motor's inductance also has to be contained, as the motor's inductance value will be dominant over the hookup wiring. This high-energy-laden voltage spike must be dealt with or the power transistor will enter an

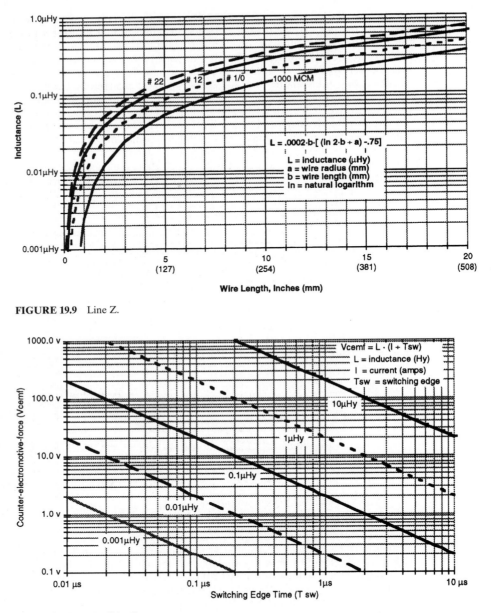

FIGURE 19.9 Line Z.

FIGURE 19.10 L di/dt effects.

avalanche or second breakdown mode, which is something to be avoided. The energy content of the motor's inductive kickback voltage is mainly determined by the motor's current, the motor's internal and external wire inductance value, and the rate at which the current is switched off. A high-current-rated freewheeling rectifier network can be connected across the controller's battery and motor terminals to clamp the motor's inductive kickback voltage spike. The reverse recovery times of these freewheeling rectifiers do affect the power transistor's switching performance.

When operating at a frequency of 20 kHz or a 50-μs repetition rate, the motor's inductance value is large enough to keep the freewheeling rectifier in a forward conduction mode until the next 50-μs cycle occurs. For example, if the PWM is set to a 25 percent duty cycle, the power transistor is on for the first 12.5 μs, and the freewheeling rectifier is in conduction for the remaining 37.5 μs. This means that when the next cycle occurs, the power transistor is switching on while the freewheeling rectifier is still in conduction. The result is that the power transistor and freewheeling rectifier conduct a high level "shoot-through" current spike. The magnitude and duration of this current spike are directly related to the rectifier's reverse recovery time rating, lead inductances, and the battery supply source impedance at the rectifier and power transistor location. Selecting freewheeling rectifiers with a "soft" reverse recovery characteristic will help minimize the shoot-through current problem.

The motor's back-emf, is produced from the rotating armature in a magnetic flux from the permanent magnets (PM). The PM motor's back-emf with a fixed mechanical load is normally lower than its power supply voltage and should therefore not exceed the voltage ratings of the power transistor.

Motor Current. When the motor's inductive generated transients are safely contained, one needs to deal with stalled and shorted motor conditions. Note that the motor's copper windings exhibit a positive temperature coefficient of 0.00393 per °C. Therefore, a 0.25-ohm motor resistance value at 25 °C room temperature would be about 0.18 ohm at −40 °C. Using the 20-A motor as the load, the maximum stalled or locked rotor current can be calculated as shown below.

$$I_{max} = E_{max} \div R_{mtr} = 14.4 \div 0.18 = 77 \text{ A}$$

where E_{max} = maximum power supply voltage
R_{mtr} = minimum motor resistance*

Power Transistor Specifications. When the maximum motor current has been established, the power transistor device specifications can be determined. In this case, the device needs an average current rating of at least 77 A, but the prime consideration for reliable power transistor operation is its worst-case heat dissipation.

The worst case scenario would include maximum values for the supply voltage, ambient temperature, and motor current. A maximum junction temperature of 150 °C for the power transistors is used as a maximum point. It should be noted that the reliability will increase by about one order of magnitude for each 10 °C drop in the power transistor's junction temperature. The following equations calculate the power transistor's maximum allowable heat dissipation for use in an 85 °C environment using a 2.7 °C/W heatsink unit and a 1 °C/W junction to case power FET thermal resistance.

$$PD_{max} = (TJ_{max} - TA_{max}) \div (R\text{ø}JC + R\text{ø}CS + R\text{ø}SA)$$

$$= (150 - 85) \div (1 + .1 + 2.7)$$

$$= 17.1 \text{ W}$$

where TJ_{max} = maximum allowable junction temperature
TA_{max} = maximum ambient temperature
$R\text{ø}JC$ = junction to case thermal resistance
$R\text{ø}CS$ = case to heatsink interface thermal resistance
$R\text{ø}SA$ = heatsink to ambient thermal resistance

---

* Formula for calculating the motor's cold resistance value is $R_{mtrcold} = [(\text{delta temp.} \times R_{coef}) \, R_{mtr}] + R_{mtr} = [(-65 \times 0.00393) \times 0.25] + 0.25 = 0.18$.

After the maximum transistor power dissipation is known, the maximum forward voltage drop, VDS_{on}, and ON resistance can be calculated as shown:

$$VDS_{on} = PD_{max} \div I_{max}$$
$$= 17.1 \div 77$$
$$= 0.22 \text{ V at } 150\ ^\circ\text{C Tj}$$
$$RDS_{on} = VdS_{on} \div I_{max}$$
$$= 0.22 \div 77$$
$$= 0.003 \text{ ohm at } 150\ ^\circ\text{C Tj}$$

In order to obtain a 0.003-ohm power FET ON resistance value at 150 °C Tj, several power FET devices will need to be paralleled. Bipolar devices were not even considered because of their high-current base drive requirements. Power FETs exhibit about a 75 percent ON resistance increase from a 25 to 150 °C rise in junction temperature. Therefore, six MTB75N05HD or equivalent devices in parallel would be required to achieve 0.003-ohm total ON resistance value when operating in an 85 °C ambient with a 2.7 °C/W heatsink. Six devices may not be economically attractive, so a larger heatsink may be more desirable. If the heatsink's thermal resistance is lowered to 1 °C/W, an ON resistance of 0.005 ohm would be required, which is three MTB75N05HD or equivalent paralleled devices. This is an example of the cost tradeoff between heatsink size and power FET ON resistance. It also points out that the power FETs ON resistance must be considered at the actual worst-case operating temperatures.

Short Current Protection.   Some form of overcurrent protection would minimize power transistor failures in the event of a shorted motor, as might happen if the motor leads touched each other. Assuming motor's internal resistance will always present at least 90 percent of its nominal value, the shorted motor leads is the worst possible overcurrent condition. If three 75-A-rated power FETs are used in parallel, they would be capable of conducting well over 200 A. This current level may clear a 30-A fuse or activate a circuit breaker before the power FETs start to seriously overheat. In some wiring systems a *fuse link* is used to protect against a catastrophic wiring harness fire. The fuse link is usually just a short piece of copper wire that is encased in flame resistant insulation and is one wire-size smaller than the motor harness wire. The fuse link would probably not clear before the failed power transistors had shorted and blown open. If a fuse is selected that is slightly larger than the motor's normal run current, the power transistors may be capable of sustaining the shorted load current levels long enough to blow out the fuse before the transistors fail. A more reliable shorted load protective concept may still be necessary.

It may be desirable to latch off the power transistor during shorted load conditions. Load current sensing can be accomplished in three ways, as shown in Fig. 19.11. The voltage drop across the power transistor can be monitored, and, when a certain threshold is reached, the gate drive is latched off until the next operating cycle. Another method is to insert a series resistor in the source's path and monitor the voltage drop across the resistor. An internal current-sensing power FET device can also be substituted for one of the power FETs, with its current mirror voltage representing a portion of the total load current.

The method of measuring the transistor's forward ON voltage does have some inher-

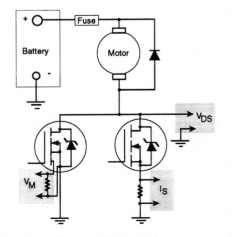

FIGURE 19.11   Load current sensing.

ent drawbacks. The drain-to-source measurement circuit has to be synchronized with the gate drive voltage, and the forward voltage will change by at least 2 to 1 at a nominal current level over a −40 to +175 °C junction temperature range. The temperature drift of 2 to 1 means that, at 175 °C, a 60-A overcurrent would read the same as 120 A at −40 °C. Therefore, at high temperatures, the overcurrent detector may falsely shut down with a stalled motor, and, at cold temperatures, the overcurrent may not shut down at all. The most accurate current measurement method is to use a series resistor added in the high current path.

A single-chip microcontroller could greatly enhance the operation of this design by allowing more functionality. For example, a stalled motor condition could be detected and a preset shutdown mode invoked to protect the motor against burnout. The MCU would include internal A/D for current detection directly from the current-sensing resistor or from the internal current-sensing power FET. The PWM signal would also be generated from the MCU. Figure 19.12 shows an MCU-based speed control conceptual design that uses an 8-bit single-chip microcomputer.

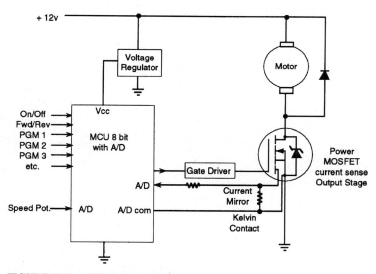

FIGURE 19.12   MCU motor control.

19.3   AIR CONDITIONER/HEATER CONTROL

Electronic controls allow an automatic climate control system to be designed for the comfort of the driver and passengers. An upscale automatic HVAC (heater and air conditioning) system, Fig. 19.13, may utilize an MCU to compute the most effective heat and ac flow rates. The heater and ac evaporator fan motor speed control designs can be similar to the WW variable speed design previously discussed if PM motors are selected. Brushless motors (BLMs) offer several features for this application. The BLM offers no brush-to-commutator noise. This feature alone is desirable in luxury vehicles, and, when one considers the increased mechanical reliability gained by the elimination of the brush-commutator assembly, the BLM cost-to-performance ratio seems more reasonable.

19.3.1   BLM System

If a motor-driven load requires closed-loop speed and direction control, the cost disadvantage of a BLM system becomes less significant. Figure 19.14 shows a typical permanent magnet brush motor compared with a BLM with both motors utilizing speed and directional control

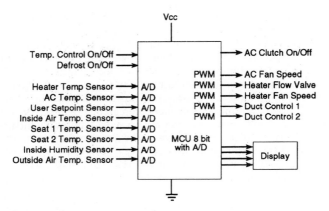

FIGURE 19.13   Climate control system.

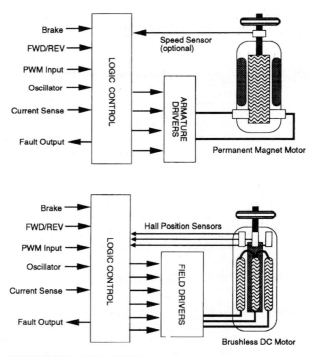

FIGURE 19.14   PM vs. BLM.

networks. Note that the BLM system uses only about one-third more drive electronics than the PM motor.

The BLM drive electronics may consist of a BLM linear bipolar integrated circuit, such as an MC33035 or similar device, that not only contains logic gates for commutation timing, but also includes internal driver stages capable of driving either power bipolar or power FET output transistors, or the MCU itself can be used to generate the necessary BLM control signals. One possible system may include the MC33035 linear bipolar IC and six power FETs. Three of the power FETs are internal current-sensing types. These current-sensing FET signals are conditioned and fed back to the MCU and to the linear IC as signals representing a motor normal condition or a motor overload condition. When the MCU detects a motor overload condition, a predetermined course of action takes place. First, the overload is counted as an event. The MCU timer allows the overload to continue for a length of time depending on how much time has elapsed from the previous overload. This is done to allow for the thermal heat buildup that will occur when the motor is overloaded or stalled on a repetitive basis, enabling the motor to have a high starting torque when cold, but to protect the windings, bearings, and drive electronics when the motor's temperature has become dangerously high due to repeated starts with a faulty load. The MCU's EEROM is used to remember user settings such as temperature preferences, as well as for interfacing into a multiplex data network.

19.3.2 Clutch Coil Control

The HVAC system also controls the ac clutch coil, plus other small duct motors or solenoids. Care must be taken when switching these highly inductive loads with power transistors. Figure 19.15 shows several possible voltage clamping networks to prevent damage to the power module when the inductive loads are switched off. The following formula should always be on hand and used when designing power-switching circuits that drive coils or solenoids.

$$V_{pk} = L \ (Di/Dt)$$

where V_{pk} = maximum inductive generated voltage
Di = coil's peak current level when switched off
Dt = switching time of the coil's current level

A typical air-conditioner clutch coil may exhibit 15 mH of inductance and 3 ohms resistance (or 4.8 A of current), and, when operating from a 14.4-V battery, would generate about 720 V when switched off in 100 μs ($V_{pk} = 0.015 \times (4.8/.0001)$). Needless to say, this would severely stress or destroy a typical 50-V-rated power transistor. Some form of voltage clamping is required.

A fully automatic HVAC system can monitor the inside and outside air temperatures. The MCU program can monitor these inputs plus the user's temperature setpoint and then compute the heater and/or ac fan motor's speed plus heater core flow rate and/or ac clutch to achieve the desired inside temperature. The HVAC MCU software design can be implemented using fuzzy logic rules rather than standard control algorithms or massive lookup tables.

19.3.3 Fuzzy HVAC Control

Fuzzy logic design can be used to develop an HVAC control program. In general terms, a fuzzy logic design allows the software programming of an MCU-based controller to be simplified and is especially useful for complex nonlinear control dynamics. At this time, standard MCU devices can be used for fuzzy programming. Future MCU devices will probably be available that will enhance a fuzzy program. Programmers who can easily understand how to compose assembly language programs for converting various input signal conditions into the required output signals may not contemplate a fuzzy logic design, but, for many system designers, the fuzzy program method will shorten the software design and can allow the program design to be evaluated with the use of fuzzy development tools even before the hardware has been constructed.

A fuzzy logic implementation using an 8-, 16-, or 32-bit single-chip microcontroller (MC68HC11, MC68HC16, MC68332, etc.) requires the control system's behavior to be well defined from an intuitive sense. The designer defines the input conditions and desired output in a subjective manner. For example, if the auto's inside temperature is 25 °C, most people would probably find that value comfortable. In fuzzy terms, 25 would be 100 percent true for an input

ELECTRONIC MODULE PROTECTION

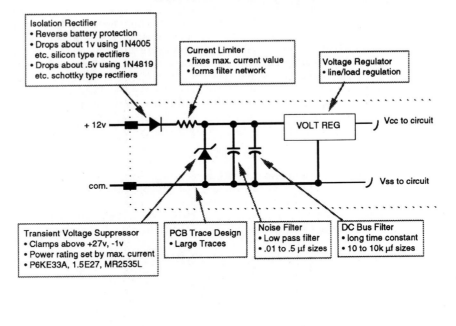

Isolation Rectifier
• Reverse battery protection
• Drops about 1v using 1N4005
  etc. silicon type rectifiers
• Drops about .5v using 1N4819
  etc. schottky type rectifiers

Current Limiter
• fixes max. current value
• forms filter network

Voltage Regulator
• line/load regulation

Transient Voltage Suppressor
• Clamps above +27v, -1v
• Power rating set by max. current
• P6KE33A, 1.5E27, MR2535L

PCB Trace Design
• Large Traces

Noise Filter
• Low pass filter
• .01 to .5 µf sizes

DC Bus Filter
• long time constant
• 10 to 10k µf sizes

SIGNAL INPUT LINE PROTECTION

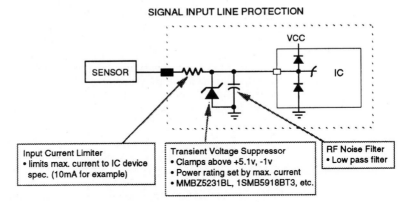

Input Current Limiter
• limits max. current to IC device
  spec. (10mA for example)

Transient Voltage Suppressor
• Clamps above +5.1v, -1v
• Power rating set by max. current
• MMBZ5231BL, 1SMB5918BT3, etc.

RF Noise Filter
• Low pass filter

FIGURE 19.15   Voltage clamping networks.

membership called "comfortable," whereas 20 °C might be 0 percent and 30 °C might be 0 percent. Memberships could include "icycold," "cold," "cool," "comf.," "warm," and "hot." This thinking process fuzzifies the input temperature analog signal into numerical values that are attached to each membership. The user setpoint temperature is also divided into membership functions. The user setpoint temperature input is also fuzzified. Figure 19.16 shows the ambient and user setpoint memberships graphically. Other inputs, such as outside temperature, humidity, solar radiation, etc., could also be incorporated to produce a high-performance HVAC system. Once the input signals have been fuzzified, the first of three parts of a fuzzy design has been completed.

A second part of the fuzzy design is to assign membership functions as shown in Fig. 19.17 to the output control signals. In this example, only the heater side is shown. The output mem-

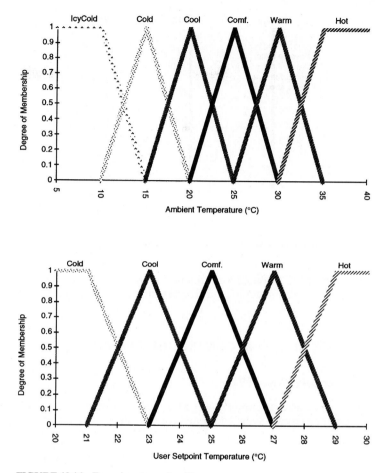

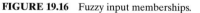

FIGURE 19.16 Fuzzy input memberships.

bership functions are classified as singletons, which only gives one value per membership. This approach trades precision for memory size.

The third part of a fuzzy design uses the min-max inference method to establish rules. A matrix representation of the input and output memberships and rules is helpful as shown in Fig. 19.18. The matrix size is determined by the input membership quantity, which is 5 for the user setpoint and 6 for the ambient temperature. This means a total of 30 rules are possible (5 × 6 = 30). The designer selects which output membership function occurs for each input membership function.

Fuzzy logic development tools are available that can simulate the fuzzy design. These programming design tools simplify testing the program's performance before production. A 3-D interactive graphic display allows the designer to visually examine the input to output relationships. Irregularities can be traced back and corrected before the first prototype is built. The availability of integrated fuzzy design software for personal computers allows the system engineer to evaluate the fuzzy design approach.

In summary, the fuzzy design method requires: the input data to be applied to the input membership functions or fuzzified, invoking the rule set to the fuzzified data, and, finally, generating an output or defuzzification based upon the rules and output function type. The fuzzy

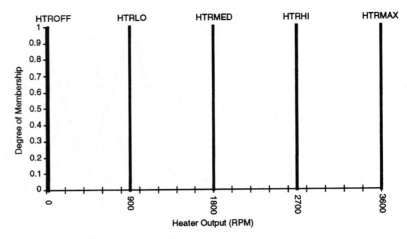

FIGURE 19.17   Fuzzy output memberships.

design can be modified with common-sense rules and rule strengths, whereas the conventional algorithm design method may require modifications at the most basic assembly code levels.

19.4   *MISCELLANEOUS LOAD CONTROL REFERENCE*

19.4.1   Current-Sensing Power FETs

Internal current-sensing power FETs can be used for current sensing, but their implementation may require some additional considerations. The current-sensing power FET device is a

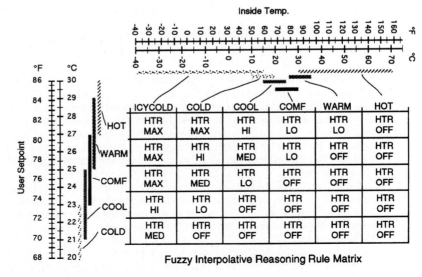

FIGURE 19.18   Fuzzy rules.

normal power FET transistor with a very small portion of its active die area set aside for a current mirror. To use its current-sensing ability, an external resistor is connected between the current mirror output and the Kelvin output. The voltage drop across this resistor will be directly proportional to the device's current level when the device is operated in the active region. Choosing the correct value of the sense resistor is important to maintain an accurate drain current-to-sense voltage ratio over wide temperature ranges and when the unit is operated in the full ON or ohmic region.

When operating in the full ON region, the current mirror network changes from a constant current mode to a voltage source mode. This mode change occurs because the forward transconductance of the current mirror FET cells is decreasing due to the lower drain-to-source voltage. The result lowers the mirror current level to the sense resistor during full ON conditions when the load is connected between the drain and Vcc.

By selecting a sense resistance value that is less than 10 percent of the ohmic or rM(ON) value, the current mirror accuracy can be maintained. For example, if the current-sensing power FET device's rDS(ON) is 0.16 ohm and the current mirror ratio is 1800, the rM(ON) will be about 288 ohms ($0.16 \times 1800 = 288$). Therefore, a sense resistor value of less than 28 ohms is required. If a lower rDS(ON) current-sensing power FET device is used, for example, 0.026 ohm, and the current mirror ratio is 950, a sense resistor of less than 2.5 ohms should be used.

The use of an amplifier stage is still required to boost the current mirror's output signal level, which is similar to a traditional current-sensing network that uses very low resistance values (0.005 to 0.1 ohm). A low-cost operational amplifier (op-amp), LM324A, for example, will give fair performance over wide temperature ranges. The input offset voltage range of the op-amp will be a determining factor in the overall accuracy of the current-sensing power FET circuit design because of the low-millivolt current mirror signals. Instrument-grade op-amps can be used when higher accuracy is required. The op-amp circuit layout should be connected in close proximity to the current-sensing power FET's Kelvin and mirror output pins to minimize external noise pickup.

19.4.2 Overvoltage, "Load Dump," Reverse Battery

A hazard to any automotive electronics is reversed power supply connections. The power FET's internal rectifier will become forward-biased and will turn on the motor or lamp load. The FET's power dissipation will increase about 5 times normal since its voltage drop is now about 1 volt instead of the nominal 0.2 V. A standard bipolar transistor does not have the internal collector-to-emitter rectifier, but it still will suffer from a reversed power supply condition. The emitter-base junction avalanches at around 6 to 8 V, and the base-collector forms a rectifier. Therefore, the typical bipolar transistor is cooking itself into oblivion with about an 8-V drop while conducting about 1 A of lamp current. Most auto manufacturers specify that any electronic or electrical device must be able to withstand a reverse battery connection. The exact magnitude of the reverse voltage requirement varies per manufacturer, but the worst case seems to be −24 V for 10 min. This requirement is especially troublesome when the load requires an inductive kickback clamp rectifier, and either a power FET or bipolar transistor is used as the load driver. The power transistor's intrinsic rectifier and the load rectifier become forward-biased as shown in Fig. 19.19. The result? The clamp rectifier fails by shorting, the transistor shorts, and then the fuse may blow unless the rectifier or power transistor blows open first. A simple reverse battery isolator relay can be used to guard against incorrect battery polarity connections. This simple relay has been incorporated in the power supply line, which will open the line in the event of a power supply voltage reversal or if the power supply should exceed 32 V.

There are several other hazards for 12-V vehicular electronics that have to be considered. These can be divided into two groups: minimum/maximum operational voltages and voltage transients.

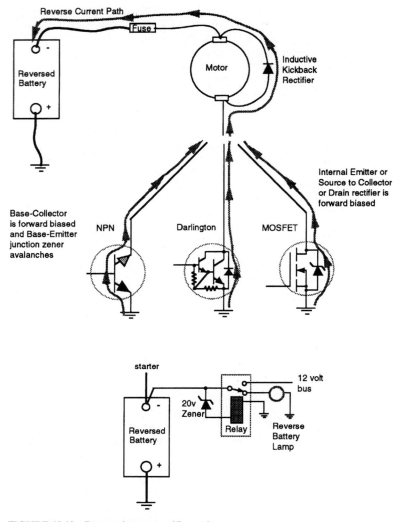

FIGURE 19.19 Reverse battery rectifier path.

The typical power supply voltage operating range for nonengine functions is 8 to 16 V. Most nonengine vehicular loads are either lamps or motors, and these types of loads will function in some proportion all the way down to near zero voltage when controlled by simple switches. When electronic control circuits are used with these loads, a power supply voltage threshold level occurs, and the load abruptly stops functioning. This threshold level normally takes place between 3 to 8 V and is dependent upon the control circuit's biasing networks and internal transistor technologies. The important criterion is that the electronic control should behave in a stable fashion when the power supply voltage varies between nominal levels and zero. A smooth transition during power supply on/off conditions in the electronic designs can be implemented with some form of hysteresis element for the analog portions and a low-voltage interrupt/reset for MCU/digital circuits.

Voltage transients tend to be either high-energy, up to 125-V levels, or low-energy, high-voltage spikes. The alternator "load dump" voltage spike ranges from about 85 to 125 V for a duration of approximately ½ second. This voltage spike is of a high-energy nature because of the alternator's low source impedance. By using Zener-type rectifiers in the alternator in place of the alternator's normal rectifiers, the load dump voltage can be clamped to under 40 V.

High-voltage transients are generated by the fast turnoff of high-current inductive loads, such as air-conditioning compressor clutches. The polarity of high-voltage inductive kickback spikes depends upon the control switch configuration. Adding a rectifier across the inductive load to clamp the turnoff voltage spike will affect the mechanical performance of some solenoids, actuators, or relays. The mechanical turnoff will slow down. As the solenoid's magnetic field collapses, a countervoltage is generated that, in turn, causes the magnetic field to reverse, which speeds up the solenoid's turnoff action. The insertion of a back-emf rectifier clamps or shunts the counter voltage, and therefore minimizes any significant reversal of the magnetic field. Using back-to-back Zener rectifiers across the inductive load that are selected will allow satisfactory mechanical turnoff action, and yet will protect the power electronics.

Another form of electrical stress that the motor control system has to sustain is ESD or electrostatic discharge. The ESD is normally encountered in the manufacturing cycle, but can occur in the application. To minimize ESD, the control shafts, switch handles, user faceplate, etc., should be designed to dissipate ESD through a ground path away from the electronic module.

19.4.3 Microcomputer I/O Line Protection

Voltage transients on MCU input or output (I/O) lines can cause the MCU to fail. Figure 19.20 shows three different methods to contain excessive MCU input or output line voltage spikes.

Single input line protection is accomplished by a 5.1-V Zener clamp to contain positive-going transients and a Schottky rectifier for the negative-going transients. The Schottky rectifier does have temperature problems at both ends. At 125 °C, its leakage current may reach 50 μA when the input line is at a 5-V level. Therefore, the input signal may lose 50 μA of current to the Schottky which may reduce its voltage level too much for the MCU input port to respond properly. Another problem occurs at cold temperatures. At −40 °C, the forward voltage rises to about 0.47 V, which is getting close to the −0.50-V maximum level specification for most HCMOS-type microcomputer chips. A simple RF low pass filter network is also a good idea to incorporate on each input line. The RC network will minimize problems from high-energy RF fields and will limit excessive current levels from flowing through the MCU's internal substrate.

Multiple input line protection uses two Schottky rectifiers per line for clamping positive- and negative-going voltage transients. A single 4.7-V Zener is used as a common clamp to all input lines.

MCU output line protection uses a resistor, capacitor, Zener, and Schottky rectifiers. The resistor is connected in series to the load, and will therefore have to be sized to drop about 5 to 10 percent of the nominal load voltage. The resistor's main function is to limit reverse current into the MCU in case the output line is raised above Vdd or below Vss, and no other protective devices are used. Adding a small value capacitor at the load output will help minimize RFI, at the expense of reducing switching time from the MCU. Adding a Schottky and Zener rectifier to the MCU output line will protect against both negative- and positive-going transients.

Adding program traps in the MCU software will help to restart the MCU in the advent of a software crash. Experiments have shown MCU-based electronic modules that fail (program crashes, and MCU locks up until hardware restarts it) due to high bursts EMI or RFI, will still perform, but at reduced throughput, when software traps are used. One method uses a trap consisting of three NOP instructions followed by a JMP to RESET instruction. These traps

Input Line Protection

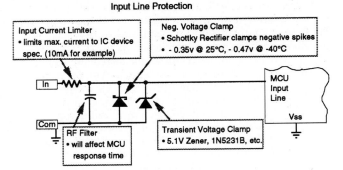

Multiple Input Line Protection with one Zener

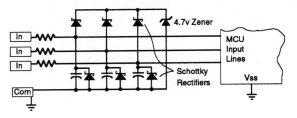

Output Line Protection

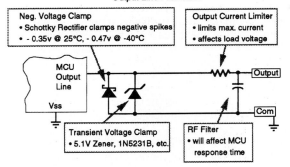

FIGURE 19.20 MCU I/O voltage spike clamping.

are used after loops or subroutines. These software traps, in addition to a watchdog timer if the MCU has this feature, will help in catching an out-of-control program.

The location of the watchdog timer reset instruction code is also important. If the watchdog timer is reset from within an interrupt routine, there is a possibility that the program could still be out of control, but that the interrupt vectors could still be working, and will therefore not reset. A good place to locate the watchdog update code is in a main program path rather than in an interrupt routine.

The PCB or thick-film design layout affects the MPU's reliability in terms of overvoltage transients. The clamping networks should be located physically close to the input socket pins and common. The MPU common traces should not be in the path of any voltage-clamping networks. It may also be a good idea to place an inexpensive metal shield around the MPU PCB area to protect against RFI and ESD problems.

19.4.4 Wire Size Reference

Most wire tables only give basic weight, dimensions, and dc resistance. A more complete version would include straight-line inductance as shown in Table 19.2. Unlike resistance which adds in a linear proportion to its length, inductance adds up on a logarithmic scale.

19.5 FUTURE LOAD CONTROL CONCEPTS

Higher integrated or more complex semiconductor power devices are available for specific load controls that can justify the extra cost of these smarter power types. The tradeoff is that the extra internal circuitry in the device usually limits its application to specific loads.

TABLE 19.2 Wire Gage Resistance and Inductance

Wire #	Dia., mm	Dia., in	Ohms per 305 mm (ft)	L of 25 mm (1 in), μH	L of 305 mm (1 ft), μH	L of 914 mm (1 yd), μH
1000 MCM	29.261	1.1520	0.000008	.003	.182	.746
500 MCM	20.650	0.8130	0.000016	.004	.203	.810
250 MCM	14.605	0.5750	0.000031	.006	.224	.873
0000	11.684	0.4600	0.000049	.007	.238	.914
000	10.404	0.4096	0.000062	.008	.245	.935
00	09.266	0.3648	0.000078	.008	.252	.956
0	08.252	0.3249	0.000098	.009	.259	.977
1	07.348	0.2893	0.000124	.010	.266	.999
2	06.553	0.2580	0.000156	.010	.273	1.019
4	05.189	0.2043	0.000248	.011	.287	1.062
6	04.115	0.1620	0.000395	.012	.301	1.105
8	03.264	0.1285	0.000628	.014	.315	1.147
10	02.588	0.1019	0.000999	.015	.329	1.189
12	02.052	0.0808	0.001589	.016	.344	1.232
14	01.628	0.0641	0.002526	.017	.358	1.274
16	01.291	0.0508	0.004016	.018	.372	1.317
18	01.024	0.0403	0.006386	.020	.386	1.359
20	00.812	0.0320	0.010154	.021	.400	1.401
22	00.644	0.0254	0.016139	.022	.414	1.444
24	00.511	0.0201	0.025671	.023	.428	1.486
26	00.405	0.0159	0.040818	.024	.443	1.529
28	00.321	0.0126	0.064914	.025	.457	1.571
30	00.255	0.0100	0.103093	.027	.471	1.613
32	00.202	0.0080	0.164095	.028	.485	1.656
34	00.160	0.0063	0.260891	.029	.499	1.698
36	00.127	0.0050	0.414849	.030	.513	1.741
38	00.101	0.0040	0.659695	.031	.527	1.783
40	00.080	0.0031	1.048548	.033	.542	1.825

$R_{ohm} = 4 Lp/\pi D^2$. L = length in meters, D = length in mm, p = resistivity .017241Ω per μΩm (= Ω mm²/m). (Ref: *Automotive Handbook,* 2d ed, Bosch, 1986, pp. 176–177.)

$L\mu H = (0.0002 L)*[(IN(2*L/(D/2)) - 0.75)]$. L = length in mm, IN = nat. log., D = dia. in mm. (Ref: *ARRL Handbook,* 1988, pp. 2–18.)

Some form of more intelligent brake indicator system may help minimize the classic chain vehicle crashes that occur in poor driving conditions. One possible method using electronic switched stop lamps would involve a rate of closure detector system to determine if the vehicle's speed is safe for objects ahead of it. If the closure rate is unsafe, the stop lights could be activated to alert trailing (or tailgating) drivers to a pending accident.

19.5.1 Fully Integrated Power Devices

The concept of putting the MCU and power drivers on one piece of silicon is viable at limited power levels and breakdown voltages. The MC68HC05V8 MCU is but one of several semiconductor industry examples of this technology.

GLOSSARY

Charge pump A circuit that usually consists of an oscillator driving logic gates that yield out-of-phase signals that are applied to a rectifier voltage doubler network. The charge pump circuit can be integrated into MCUs and other power analog integrated circuits.

Current mirror A design that generates a signal whose level is directly proportional to another current level. The current mirror concept is used in current-sensing power MOSFETs.

Electromagnetic interference (EMI) Unwanted magnetically coupled voltages that affect the normal operation of electronic systems. EMI is a problem when high-energy circuits are in close proximity to high-impedance sensors, or any low-energy electronic control circuit. EMI also occurs in a wiring harness. One wire conducting a high-energy pulse in this harness will couple the pulse into the other harness wires. Twisted wire pairs are often used to minimize EMI susceptibility.

Freewheeling rectifier A rectifier that is connected across an inductive load or transistor switching device to suppress the voltage spike generated when the load is turned off.

H-bridge A design utilizing four power devices that are connected to reverse the voltage across both terminals of a load. H-bridges are used for bidirectional motor controls.

Half H-bridge A design using two power devices that are connected in series from the positive power supply bus to common, and a load terminal connected to the transistor's middle-connection. Two half H-bridges can make a full H-bridge. Three half H-bridges are commonly used in three-phase motor controls.

Intrinsic rectifier A rectifier that is inherently part of a semiconductor design. Most power MOSFET transistors have a drain-to-source rectifier that is formed by the nature of the MOSFET design structure. In battery-powered designs, the intrinsic rectifier is a concern during reversed battery hookups.

Load dump The effect of disconnecting the load from an alternator running at full power. In automotive equipment this condition can be caused by intermittent battery connections when the alternator is applying maximum current to the battery. When the load is abruptly disconnected, the alternator control circuitry shuts off the field current, but this current takes up to ¼ s to decay, and allows the alternator to produce a voltage much higher than its nominal value, up to 125 V in some cases. This abnormal voltage tracks the field current decay.

Pulse-width modulation A common control signal modulation method used in dc speed controls. The signal's frequency is fixed at a rate of 100 Hz to 20 kHz, but its pulse width is varied from 0 to 100 percent. The variable pulse width, in effect, acts like a variable voltage source when driving most automotive type loads.

P-channel MOSFET   Usually a power transistor that requires a negative gate-to-source control voltage of 3 to 10 V. P-channel MOSFETs are normally connected between power supply positive bus and the load, and can operate from a positive voltage bus.

N-channel MOSFET   Usually a power transistor that requires a positive gate-to-source control voltage of 3 to 10 V. N-channel MOSFETs are normally connected between common and the load, and operate from a positive voltage bus. The gate input characteristics are capacitive with gate power loss occurring during the switching edge transition period.

Radio frequency interference (RFI)   High-frequency signals of sufficient magnitude to influence the normal operation of electronic systems. RFI sources from automotive equipment include spark plug arcing, dc motor brush arcing, electrical contact switching, and fast transitional voltage pulses from power electronic circuits.

Saturation   A power transistor's forward ON region normally defined as when an increase in drive input voltage or current has little effect upon further reducing the transistors forward ON voltage. Saturation regions vary from less than 0.1 to over 3 V depending on the transistor technology and design.

Zener rectifier   A semiconductor rectifier device that is designed to operate in a reverse bias mode. When the reverse voltage reaches the Zener voltage, the device abruptly starts conducting current. Zener rectifiers are used for shunt voltage regulators, overvoltage protection, and voltage level detectors. Zener rectifiers are also designed specifically for high-power voltage transient suppression. These devices are constructed to handle very high momentary current levels.

Note

Based in part on the article by Richard Valentine, "Don't underestimate transistor-based lamp driver design," *EDN,* June 7, 1990, pp. 119–124.

BIBLIOGRAPHY

Aptronix Inc., *FIDE Users Manual,* 1992.

Bairanzade, M., "The electronic control of fluorescent lamps," Motorola Semiconductor Application Note, AN1049, 1990.

Bannatyne, R., "Using fuzzy logic in practical applications," *Motorola Semiconductor Engineering Bulletin,* EB412, 1993.

Bacelis, O. W., et al., "The automotive primary power supply system," SAE Technical Paper 741208, 1974.

Berringer, Ken, "High-current DC motor drive uses low on-resistance surface mount MOSFETs," Motorola Semiconductor Application Note, AN1317, 1992.

Catherwood, M., "Designing for EMC compatibility with HCMOS MCUs," Motorola Semiconductor Application Note, AN1050, 1989.

Davis, B., et al., "The impact of higher system voltage on automotive semiconductors," SAE technical paper 911658, 1991.

Gauen, K., and J. Alberkrack, "Three piece solution for brushless motor controller design," Motorola Semiconductor Application Note, AN1046, 1989.

Graham, D., and J. Savage, "Brushless DC motor technology," *Second IAVD Congress on Vehicle Design & Components,* Mar. 1985, pp. c1–23.

Hollander, D., "The hidden dangers of electrostatic discharge," Motorola Semiconductor Application Note, AR300, 1987.

Huettl, T., and R. Valentine, "Simplified control for brushless motors," *Machine Design,* Feb. 21, 1985, pp. 236–241.

Mihin, M., and R. Valentine, "New rectifiers clamp alternator voltage levels," SAE technical paper 872002, 1987.

Motorola Inc., "Reducing A/D errors in microcontroller applications," Motorola Semiconductor Application Note, AN1058, 1990.

Motorola Inc., TMOS power MOSFET transistor data, Chap. 2, DL135 Rev. 4, 1992.

Schultz, W., "New components simplify brush DC motor drives," Motorola Semiconductor Application Note, AN1078, 1989.

Society of Automotive Engineers, *SAE Ground Vehicle Lighting Standards Manual,* SAE HS-34, 1993.

Tal, J., "Design and analysis of pulsewidth-modulated amplifiers for DC servo systems," *IEEE Transactions on IECI,* vol. 23, no. 1, Feb. 1976, pp. 47–55.

Valentine, Richard, "Brushless DC motor control," *Control Engineering,* July 1985, pp. 134–140.

Valentine, Richard, "Don't underestimate transistor-based lamp-driver design," *EDN,* June 7, 1990, pp. 119–124.

Zhang, W., "Temperature control 2," FIDE Application Note 005-920903, Aptronix Inc., 1992.

ABOUT THE AUTHOR

Richard J. Valentine is a principal staff engineer at Motorola SPS in Phoenix, Ariz. His present assignments include engineering evaluation of advanced semiconductor products for emerging automotive systems. He holds two patents and has published 29 technical articles during his 24 years at Motorola.

DISPLAYS AND INFORMATION SYSTEMS

CHAPTER 20
INSTRUMENT PANEL DISPLAYS

Ronald K. Jurgen, Editor

20.1 THE EVOLUTION TO ELECTRONIC DISPLAYS

In the early automobile years, cars had analog displays that contained minimal information, usually just car speed and oil pressure. As the use of electronics increased in cars dramatically from the late 1970s on, however, the traditional mechanical or electromechanical analog displays with a circular dial face and a pointer began to be challenged by newer technologies. The major ones included gas discharge or plasma displays, vacuum fluorescent displays (VFDs), liquid crystal displays (LCDs), cathode-ray tubes (CRTs), and more recently, head-up displays (HUDs). These newer technologies made it possible for car makers to give drivers a broad spectrum of information, including sophisticated graphics.

In 1978, the first production electronic digital display, a gas plasma device, was used in the Cadillac Seville; in 1984, the first standard equipment production LCD cluster was used in the Chevrolet Corvette; and in 1985, the first full-color CRT was used in a production vehicle, the Toyota Soarer.[1]

The initial rush by car makers to use electronic displays has now abated somewhat. Drivers, in many instances, did not take kindly to overkill with electronic displays—any more than they did to electronically generated voice messages—and today's use of displays tends to be more conservative. In fact, one approach fast gaining popularity is electronic analog displays rather than strictly digital ones.

This chapter will describe typical electronic displays used in cars. It is not intended to be all-inclusive. That would be beyond the scope of this handbook. But the display examples given are representative of what can be found in cars today.

20.2 VACUUM FLUORESCENT DISPLAYS

One of the most widely used electronic displays is the vacuum fluorescent display. It was first used in automotive clocks and has since been applied in other ways including audio systems, air conditioning/heating, message centers, and head-up displays. Its popularity stems from features that include availability of a variety of colors, high luminance, low voltage operation, reliability, and long life.

The basic structure of a modern VFD, Fig. 20.1, consists of a cathode, grid, and anode.[2] The tungsten-wire cathode emits thermal electrons that are accelerated when a positive voltage is applied to the anode and grid. The phosphor-coated anode emits a blue-green light when struck by the emitted electrons. Other colors such as yellow-green, green-yellow, yellow-orange, orange, and red-orange colors, obtained through the use of optical filters, can be used independently within the same display. Thick- or thin-film screens are used to shape the phosphor pattern in any desired manner. VFDs produce maximum perceived brightness at low input power.

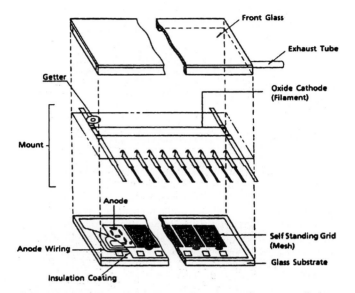

FIGURE 20.1 The basic structure of a vacuum fluorescent display. *(Reprinted with permission from SAE SP-858 ©1991 Society of Automotive Engineers, Inc.)*

Initial VFDs were single-digit displays. Multiple-digit displays followed and now single large-scale VFDs contain multiple functions such as speedometer, fuel and temperature gages, trip odometer, turn indicators, and warning signals.

A typical application of VFDs was in the electronic instrument panel on the 1985 Chrysler LeBaron.[3] The VFDs are controlled (Fig. 20.2) by a Motorola MC6805R3 8-bit, HMOS, single-chip microprocessor with internal analog-to-digital converters. Another microprocessor, a 4-bit device, is used to generate a high switching rate for the center display in the instrument panel.

20.3   LIQUID CRYSTAL DISPLAYS

LCDs are fluids consisting of organic compounds whose molecular orientation rotates polarized light by 90 degrees as light passes through the material.[4] When an electric field is applied to the fluid, its molecular orientation is altered as is its polarizing ability. The change is visible in reflected or transmitted light and can be used to form predetermined patterns or characters.

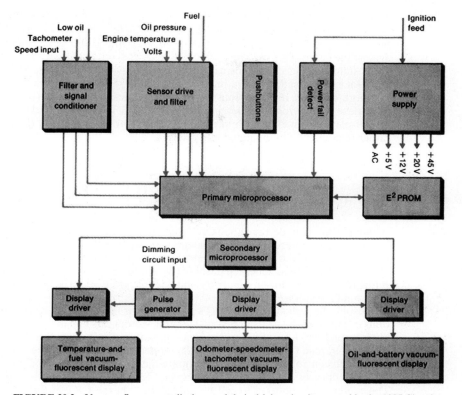

FIGURE 20.2 Vacuum fluorescent displays and their driving circuits as used in the 1985 Chrysler LeBaron. (*©1984 IEEE*)

There are three general classes of liquid crystals called *nematic, smectic,* and *cholesteric.*[5] In nematic liquid crystals, the molecules are lined up in one dimension but have random order in the other two directions. In smectic liquid crystals the ordering of the molecules is similar except that it is much higher. In cholesteric liquid crystals, the molecules stack in layers that have a twist and tilt that gives the molecules a spiral configuration.

Certain chemical substances applied on top of the two electrodes of a liquid crystal display orient the long axes of the molecules so that they line up parallel to the surface of the glass plate. The display cell is assembled so that the long axes of the molecules on the top plate are oriented at 90 degrees to the direction of the molecules on the bottom plate. The molecules between the plates assume a spiral configuration.

A polarizer is placed on top of the display cell. When light enters the liquid crystal region of the display, the direction of polarization is rotated as the light travels along the spiral configuration. A second polarizer behind the bottom plate is oriented to allow the light with its altered polarization to pass through. The display then appears bright to the observer. An electric field applied across the display cell, the molecules realign with their long axes parallel to the direction of the field. The polarized light entering the cell is no longer twisted and the second polarizer cuts off the light passing through the liquid crystal. The observer sees a dark screen.

In what is called a dichroic LCD, no polarizers are used, but a dichroic dye is combined with the liquid crystal material.[4] The dye molecules combine with the liquid crystal molecules to produce unique spectral absorption characteristics. With no voltage applied, the dye absorbs certain wavelengths of the incident ambient light and the observer sees a colored background. When the display is activated, the observer sees colorless display elements against the colored background.

In simple liquid crystal displays containing only a few seven-segment characters, each numeral is addressed by activating the appropriate segments to form a specific numeral. But for more complex displays, consisting of many picture elements (pixels) that are twisted nematic cells, this type of addressing is too cumbersome and matrix addressing is used instead. The pixels are turned on by applying voltage to both their row and their column electrodes rather than directly to the individual pixels.

20.4   CATHODE-RAY TUBE DISPLAYS

Although the cathode-ray tube (CRT) has found wide success in a variety of applications including television receivers, instruments, and radar and medical equipment, it has been far less successful in the automotive field. Some of the reasons for its lack of impact are the amount of space needed behind dashboards to house the CRT, possible washed-out images in sunlight, lack of instant-on capability, and possible safety hazards from x-ray exposure, implosion, and high voltages.[6]

Despite the difficulties that CRTs present to car makers, there have been limited applications in cars over the years in several General Motors cars and in some Ford Motor Company models. In 1986, for example, the General Motors Corp. introduced a CRT-based display called a Graphic Control Center in 1986-model Buick Rivieras.[7] The center combined diagnostic with control functions in an integrated information system and handled inputs from 7 to 10 microprocessors with the actual number dependent on the number of options on the car. The center could be used to call up information on the CRT in the basic areas of climate, radio, trip monitor, and gages, in addition to diagnostics information. The display for each area would appear as a "page" of information. In some cases, there would be more than one page, starting with the general and proceeding to the more specific.

When the ignition key was turned on, a summary page would appear displaying key information from all the basic areas. To access more detailed information, the driver simply touched an appropriate spot on the screen. A Mylar switch panel positioned over the screen used ultrathin wires encoded by rows and columns to send signals to the control circuits.

Although General Motors had CRT systems in the Riviera and subsequently the Buick Reatta and a somewhat similar system in the Oldsmobile Toronado and Trofeo, they were eventually dropped. One of the main drawbacks was that the driver had to take his or her eyes off the road in order, for example, to tune the radio. The Oldsmobile system improved on the Buick version in this regard by careful placement of some of the more commonly used controls so that the driver could activate them while still looking at the road. But car buyers, by and large, never became convinced that the CRT system was necessary or desirable.

A possible comeback for the CRT may be in the offing when automobile navigation systems take hold (see Chap. 29). Many of those systems use CRTs to provide the driver with useful trip information.

20.5   HEAD-UP DISPLAYS

A head-up display (HUD) is aptly named since it allows viewing of data superimposed on the driver's visual field with his or her head up. HUDs have been used in the military aircraft industry for over 20 years and more recently have had limited application in automobiles. A main advantage of a HUD in a car is that the driver need not constantly refocus his or her eyes as when switching them from the road to conventional dashboards and back again. The first applications in production automobiles were in the 1988 Nissan Silvia model and in special editions of the 1988 Oldsmobile Cutlass Supreme.

One of the first HUDs to appear in cars was in 1988 when the Oldsmobile Cutlass Supreme Indianapolis 500 Pace Car and its 54 replicas were equipped with the systems.[7] This was followed by offering the HUD as an option on the 1989 Oldsmobile Cutlass Supreme and on the Pontiac Grand Prix. Those systems were developed jointly by General Motors engineers from the Hughes Aircraft Corp., Delco Electronics Corp., and C-P-C Engineering. HUDs continue to be offered today by General Motors on some models.

The heart of the original GM system was an image source—a custom-designed, high-intensity, blue-green vacuum fluorescent tube made by Futaba Corp. of America. High brightness was made possible by keeping the cathode energized at all times and the electrodes at higher voltages than would be used in vacuum fluorescent tubes for conventional purposes.

The system works as follows. Speed and other sensor inputs are processed by an electronic module which then sends signals to the vacuum-fluorescent tube to activate segments of seven-segment numbers or graphic symbols in the tube. Optical elements then project the light from those energized segments onto the windshield of the car. The driver sees virtual images that seemingly float in space near the front end of the car (Fig. 20.3).

FIGURE 20.3   This head-up display, showing a virtual image of car speed, was standard on General Motors' Pontiac Division's 1993 Bonneville SSEi and is available as an option on the Bonneville SSE and on all Grand Prix models. Information that is projected onto the windshield includes vehicle speed, turn signal indicator, high-beam lights, check gages warning, and low-fuel alert.

The images can display car speed in either mi/h or km/h, left and right arrows for turn signal indications, a headlight symbol for high-beam indicator, and a gas pump for low-fuel warning.

As shown in Fig. 20.4, the image is projected from the image source onto the car's windshield by mirrors. A proprietary optical design keeps the image in the correct aspect ratio. The driver can adjust both the brightness and the vertical location of the image but the horizontal

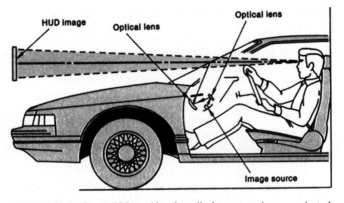

FIGURE 20.4   General Motors' head-up display uses an image projected onto the windshield of the car but the driver sees a virtual image of the projected information positioned at the front of the car. *(©1988 IEEE)*

location is fixed. Making it variable would require expensive variable-magnification changes in the system optics.

20.6   ELECTRONIC ANALOG DISPLAYS

Despite the proliferation of electronic digital displays in cars, many drivers still prefer analog displays. To satisfy this need while at the same time taking advantage of advances in electronics, many car makers have introduced electronic analog displays. These displays, despite their dependence on electronic circuits, present the driver with essentially the same type of display as in the electromechanical speedometer, for example.

Some car makers have seized the opportunity to offer their customers unique analog displays. One notable example is the high-precision electronic analog display in the Toyota Lexus LS 400.[8] Called a combination meter, Fig. 20.5, it uses a smoked-filter glass to cover the

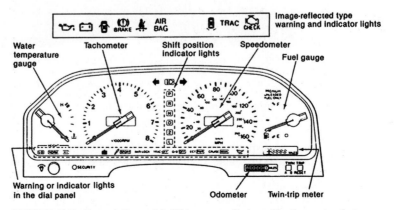

FIGURE 20.5   Toyota's Lexus LS 400 has a so-called combination meter that presents analog displays that are electronically activated. *(©1989 IEEE)*

entire display area that is blacked out when the ignition switch is turned off. Cold-cathode tubes containing mercury gas light the light-transmitting dial panel. When powered, the tubes emit a white light to illuminate the dials when the ignition switch is turned on.

The speedometer, tachometer, fuel gage, and water temperature gage all have self-light-emitting needles consisting of cold-cathode tubes with a sealed-in mixture of neon and xenon gases that emit white light when energized. A cableless speedometer driven by a moving coil indicates speed based on pulse signals from the transmission speed sensor.

20.7 RECONFIGURABLE DISPLAYS

What may be a future trend in displays was presented at the Society of Automotive Engineers annual meeting in Detroit, Mich., in 1993. A reconfigurable automotive display system was described that displays multifunctional information on a dot matrix fluorescent indicator panel.[9] An advanced 8-bit microcontroller with real-time processing capabilities is used in the system to perform display refreshing, keypad scanning, and serial communications.

The dot matrix display in the system is a vacuum fluorescent type composed of an 80 by 16 matrix of pixels in a 9.85-mm-high by 50.5-mm-long graphics area. Two lines of 13 characters each can be displayed using a 5 by 7 font. The system can display text messages of different sizes, locations, and font types as well as graphics symbols. The advantage is that several fixed segment display systems can be replaced with a single dot matrix display system to cut costs and packaging space.

REFERENCES

1. Eric M. Ethington, Gary A. Streelman, and David R. Clark, "What information does an operator expect in an automobile display?," *Automotive Information Systems and Electronic Displays: Recent Developments,* SP-770, Society of Automotive Engineers, Inc., Feb. 1989, pp. 51–54.

2. Nobuo Akiba; Robert J. Davis; Kato, Satoro; Tatiyoshi, Sadao; Torkai, Masahiro; and Tsunesumi, Satoshi, "Technological improvements of vacuum fluorescent displays for automotive applications," *Vehicle Information Systems & Electronic Display Technology,* SP-858, Society of Automotive Engineers, Inc., Feb. 1991, pp. 59–68.

3. Ronald K. Jurgen, "More electronics in Detroit's 1985 models," *IEEE Spectrum,* Oct. 1984, pp. 54–60.

4. Lawrence A. Lopez, "Display Technology," *Proceedings International Congress on Transportation Electronics,* P-111, Society of Automotive Engineers, Inc., Oct. 1982, pp. 191–197.

5. Charles M. Apt, "Perfecting the picture," *IEEE Spectrum,* July 1985, pp. 60–66.

6. Ronald K. Jurgen, "All electronic dashboards coming," *IEEE Spectrum,* June 1981, pp. 34–37.

7. Ronald K. Jurgen, "New frontiers for Detroit's Big Three," *IEEE Spectrum,* Oct. 1988, pp. 32–34.

8. Ronald K. Jurgen, "Global '90 cars: electronics-aided," *IEEE Spectrum,* Dec. 1989, pp. 45–49.

9. Gregory T. Gumkowski and Adnan Shaout, "Reconfigurable automotive display system," *Automotive Display Systems and IVHS,* Society of Automotive Engineers Inc., pp. 13–19.

CHAPTER 21
TRIP COMPUTERS

Ronald K. Jurgen, Editor

21.1 *TRIP COMPUTER BASICS*

Trip computers have evolved over the years from simple systems that estimate only the distance that can be traveled with the remaining fuel to sophisticated systems that also offer such features as instantaneous and average fuel economies, amount of fuel used, average speed, amount of fuel remaining, estimated time of arrival, oil life indicator, and diagnostic capabilities.

21.1.1 Basic System Configurations

A simple distance-to-empty system such as that shown in Fig. 21.1[1] has transducers that convert distance and fuel quantity into time-varying voltages or currents. Electronic signal pro-

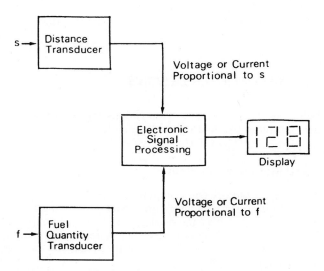

FIGURE 21.1 Elements of a basic distance-to-empty system. *(Reprinted with permission from SAE Technical Paper 800240 ©1980 Society of Automotive Engineers, Inc.)*

cessing operates on those voltages or currents to produce a distance-to-empty estimate that is formatted for transmission to a display device.

A basic trip computer, shown in Fig. 21.2,[2] in addition to distance-to-empty, computes instantaneous fuel consumption, average fuel consumption, and average cruising speed. Through use of a sequential selector button, the driver causes the readouts to appear in order on the display.

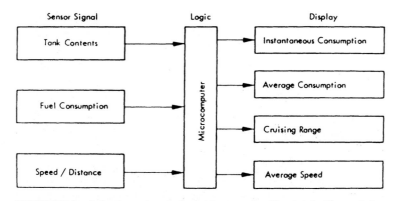

FIGURE 21.2   A simple version of a basic trip computer. *(Reprinted with permission from SAE Technical Paper 810302 ©1981 Society of Automotive Engineers, Inc.)*

21.1.2   A Full-Function Trip Computer

A full-function trip computer, shown in Fig. 21.3,[2] incorporates many more functions. The driver can feed information into the computer at the beginning of a trip—distance to destination, for example. During the trip, the driver can request specific information.

21.2   *SPECIFIC TRIP COMPUTER DESIGNS*

Different car makers have taken various approaches to trip computers for their car models over the years. Two selected examples follow.

21.2.1   The General Motors Trip Computer

The General Motors Trip Computer was first available as a high-cost option on the Cadillac Seville in 1978. The computer's principal four parts are a function-select keyboard, the central processing unit (CPU), the displays, and the interconnecting special wiring. The CPU translates the various engine and vehicle sensor inputs into the appropriate information needed by the driver and also provides constant speed and fuel displays, generator system information, and diagnostic features.

A block diagram of the bus-oriented CPU designed around the Motorola M6800 microcomputer family with N-channel, 8-bit parallel processing is shown in Fig. 21.4.[3] A 16-bit

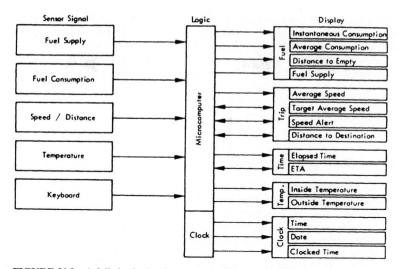

FIGURE 21.3   A full-size basic trip computer. *(Reprinted with permission from SAE Technical Paper 810302 ©1981 Society of Automotive Engineers, Inc.)*

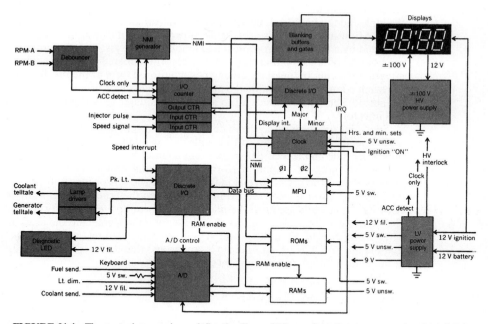

FIGURE 21.4   The central processing unit for the General Motors Trip Computer contains the following software routines in ROM: major loop (fuel-flow content and correction, distance and speed information, trip time and average speed time, fuel sense and display, time-of-day clock, clock colon control, keyboard requests, dimmer information, coolant sensor, system voltage, engine r/min, self-diagnostics); minor loop (keyboard call-up, diagnostic LED control); display-interrupt service (multiplexing, nonvolatile RAM information update, keyboard select saved for minor loop, engine r/min), speed-interrupt service (distance information maintenance for RAM, vehicle-speed information maintenance for RAM); initialization (displays and telltales, setup computer control registers, update trip parameters for "ignition off" time); nonmaskable interrupt service (display blanking, RAM disabling during power down). *(©1978 IEEE)*

address bus provides addressing capability of up to 65,536 word locations. The ROMs hold the instruction op code and the control program data. The RAMs provide software registers, software accumulators, and a stack area for the control program.

The trip computer contains self-diagnostics. When a light-emitting diode on the outside of the computer case is lit, it indicates certain failures. For example, if after sampling the critical +9 V of the A/D chip multiplexer channel, a failure is noted, it is flagged and saved in the RAM for servicing by the minor loop, Fig. 21.4, and then activates the LED on the computer case by way of the discrete I/O.

21.2.2 Ford's Second Generation Tripminder

Ford Motor Company's 1982 Tripminder was a second-generation vehicle trip computer. It performs computations on five input variables to generate the functions available to the driver. It was available in three versions—high, mid, and low series—for use in the Continental, Ford of Europe Granada, and Ford/Mercury Thunderbird/XR-7, respectively.

A block diagram of the Tripminder hardware is shown in Fig. 21.5a and software architecture in Fig. 21.5b.[4] The 8050 microprocessor could support 4K of internal ROM and 256 bytes of keep-alive RAM used for trip-log functions.

Computations are performed on five input variables. One of them, time, is produced by a precision crystal oscillator internal to the Tripminder. The others are sensed from the vehicle environment. The European and high-series versions have a distance-to-empty feature requiring a fuel-tank-level input. Driving range available is based on the amount of fuel left in the tank and the historical fuel economy of the car.

Fuel flow information is acceptable in two forms. In carbureted engines, fuel flow data is provided by a fuel flow sensor installed in the fuel line just ahead of the carburetor. The sensor's output of 48,000 pulses per gallon is recorded in an 8-bit event counter in the interface integrated circuit. In fuel injected engines, a buffered form of the fuel injector signal is sent to the event counter to determine the number of fuel injector firings that occurred during a sample period. The signal is also sent to an interval counter to determine the total on time of the fuel injector.

Speed information comes from either an electronic speedometer or from a variable reluctance speed sensor installed in line with the speedometer cable. The data consists of 8000 pulses per mile and is recorded in an event counter.

The TIC integrated circuit performs fundamental system control and timekeeping operations as well as the data conversion functions for the sensor inputs. It is a CMOS device that must be continuously powered. At midnight, when the time clock registers roll over, the TIC circuit automatically starts up the microprocessor to update the software calendars. The TIC circuit also continuously monitors the accessory input signal and the clock keyboard button. Sequencing on and off of the power supplies is controlled by the TIC circuit to make certain that the microprocessor is initialized correctly and that the keep-alive memory in RAM is not accidentally written into during power supply transients.

21.3 CONCLUSION

Trip computers vary from relatively simple versions to complex designs that give the driver a wealth of information. Some trip computers also provide a means for on-board diagnostics (see Chap. 22). What a trip computer can do depends on how many sensor inputs are fed to it. But the bottom line, as with any automotive component, is cost tied in with perceived value to the customer.

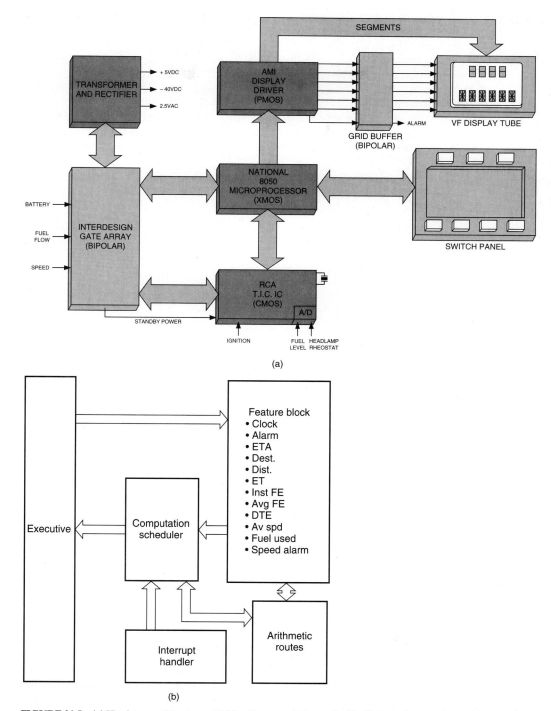

FIGURE 21.5 (*a*) Hardware architecture and (*b*) software architecture for Ford Motor Company's second generation Trip-minder. (*Reprinted with permission from SAE Technical Paper 820107 ©1982 Society of Automotive Engineers, Inc.*)

REFERENCES

1. D. R. Sendelback and T. J. Wood, "Response and accuracy limitations for a fuel level based distance-to-empty calculation," *Automotive Electronic Instrumentation—Displays and Sensors,* SP-457, Society of Automotive Engineers, Feb. 1980, pp. 21–24.

2. W. H. Hucho, "The evolution towards a new driver information system," *Electronic Displays and Information Systems,* P-92, Society of Automotive Engineers, Feb. 1981, pp. 67–75.

3. Ronald K. Jurgen, "For Detroit: smaller and smarter chips," *IEEE Spectrum,* Nov. 1978, pp. 33–35.

4. G. Cilibraise, "The second generation family of Ford Tripcomputers—the Tripminder," *Electronic Displays and Information Systems and On-Board Electronics,* P-103, Society of Automotive Engineers, Inc., Feb. 1982, pp. 127–135.

CHAPTER 22
ON- AND OFF-BOARD DIAGNOSTICS

Wolfgang Bremer, Frieder Heintz, and Robert Hugel
Robert Bosch GmbH

22.1   WHY DIAGNOSTICS?

The desire for greater safety, driving comfort, and environmental compatibility is leading to a rapid increase in electronic control units and sensors in upper class, medium-sized, and compact vehicles. Additional functions and their corresponding equipment in today's cars create a bewildering tangle of cables and confusing functional connections. As a result, it has become more and more difficult to diagnose faults in such systems and to resolve them within a reasonable period.

22.1.1   Diagnostics in the Past and Today

On-board diagnosis has been limited thus far to a few error displays and fault storage achieved by relatively simple means. It has been left more or less to each manufacturer to decide to what extent diagnosis would be carried out. Diagnosis always means the working together of man and machine and consists essentially of three major components: registration of the actual condition, knowledge of the vehicle and its nominal condition, and strategy—how to find the smallest exchangeable deficient component by means of combining and comparing both the nominal and actual conditions.

All three points are inseparably connected. Only the means to the end have changed over time. The oldest and simplest method of diagnosis is that done with the help of our sense organs, but the limits of this kind of diagnosis are obvious. In fact, the objective in the development of diagnostic techniques is the extension of human abilities with the aid of diagnostic tools in order to be able to measure more precisely and more directly, to compare more objectively, and to draw definite conclusions.

The development of control techniques was essentially determined by the following items: the development of automotive engineering; the structure of workshops—that is, essentially the relation between the costs of labor and materials; and the development of electronics and data processing.

For a long time, motor diagnosis was limited to ignition control and timing. In the 1960s, new exhaust-gas measuring instruments for fuel injection adjustment were developed, but the mechanic still had to make the diagnosis. In the 1980s, the introduction of electronics in the vehicle was followed by a new generation of measuring instruments in the workshops. Not

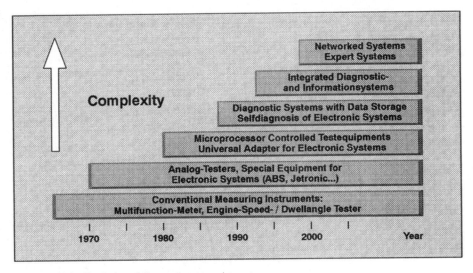

FIGURE 22.1 Evolution of diagnostic test equipment.

only were separate measurements combined with comprehensive test procedures, but also the information about the nominal condition of the vehicle was stored in a data memory.[1] A view of the development is shown in Fig. 22.1.

As more and more electronic systems were added to cars, the more difficult it became to determine the actual condition in case of a defect. Soon a multitude of connecting cables and adapters were required to reach the necessary measuring points. Moreover there was an increasing amount of information needed to make an effective diagnosis. In the majority of workshops, diagnosis is carried out as shown in Fig. 22.2. The most important test points of

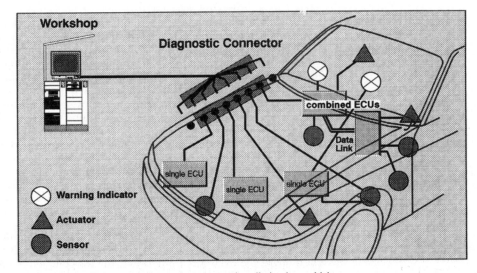

FIGURE 22.2 Present-day diagnostic connector installation in a vehicle.

control units and sensors are tied to a diagnostic connector which is plugged into the measuring instrument with a corresponding adapter for the respective vehicle. Because of the permanently increasing amount of electronic functions, it is necessary to develop connectors with more and more contacts. It is evident that this method soon will become too unwieldy.

Modern electronics in vehicles support diagnosis by comparing the registered actual values with the internally stored nominal values with the help of control units and their self-diagnosis, thus detecting faults. By interconnecting the measuring instruments, a detailed survey of the entire condition of the vehicle is available and an intelligent on-board diagnostic system is able to carry out a more precise and more definite localization of the defect.[2] With the help of an interconnection and standardization of the interface leading to the external tester, the many different complex and expensive adapters have become superfluous. Modern diagnosis will look like what is shown in Fig. 22.3.

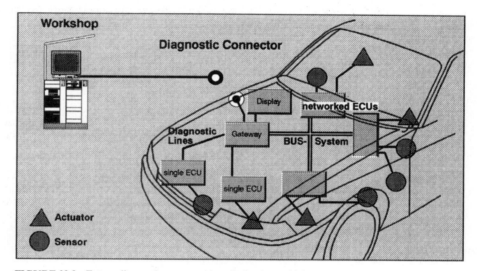

FIGURE 22.3   Future diagnostic connector installation in a vehicle.

Instead of a multiplicity of adapters there is only a single standardized interface, provided by the diagnostic processor. By means of interconnection, the diagnostic processor is provided with all available data and the condition of the vehicle is known. With the help of the diagnostic processor, the external measuring instrument has access to the measuring and diagnostic values of the sensors and is able to directly reach the actuator for measuring purposes.[3]

Such a diagnosis also demands a certain change in the functional structure of a vehicle. Corresponding hierarchical models have already been presented.[4]

22.1.2 Reasons for Diagnostics in Vehicles

Which are the most important reasons for diagnostics as demanded and desired in today's vehicles?

Existing Diagnostic Problems.   A number of diagnostic problems must be resolved:

- Early diagnostic information was related only to single components and control units. In case of a defective comprehensive system, every unit, component, sensor, and connecting cable of the system had to be tested and controlled. This was a very time consuming and expensive process.

- Because of the single component and control unit checks, it was impossible to analyze all the additional data correlated with a particular defect.

- In the case of a defect in single sensors or units, the car was often inoperable. Taking into consideration all available information about the vehicle, it is possible to use alternative parameters and procedures in order to achieve at least a so-called limp-home function and sometimes continue the use of the vehicle under only slightly limited operating conditions.

- Usually there was only a global error display with an often ambiguous warning light available for the driver. Drivers desire more detailed information and especially guidelines for what procedures should be followed.

- The multitude of adapter cables, plugs, diagnostic equipment, and communication interfaces in a workshop has become so complex that the effectiveness decreased dramatically, with the repair costs increasing disproportionally.

New Legal Proposals. Worldwide new legal proposals and governmental regulations [e.g., California Air Resources Board (CARB), On Board Diagnostics II (OBDII), Environmental Protection Agency (EPA)] are forcing manufacturers and subcontractors to seek more profitable, effective, and convincing diagnosis of vehicles.

Serial Data Networks. New serial data networks for the connection of control units and vehicle body components, installed in the vehicle, offer the possibility of absolutely new optimum approaches and even anticipate maintenance and diagnosis up to the introduction of autodidactic data processing systems and external data bases.[5,6,7,8]

International Initiatives for Standardization. Initiated by legislative and governmental demands for better diagnostics in the area of emission control, initiatives for standardization in the entire diagnostic field in vehicles were launched during recent years to achieve worldwide standardization of tools, interfaces, connectors, and protocols.

22.1.3 Diagnostic Tasks in Vehicles

In order to minimize the number of defects or even to completely avoid them, a vehicle requires regular checks. In case of an inevitable defect, a clear and directed diagnosis is required and has to be followed by a prompt, reliable, and inexpensive repair. Therefore appropriate diagnostic systems are being developed considering the following targets: simplification of maintenance, fault indication in time, guidelines for the driver in case of a defect, and safer and faster repairs with the help of a specific fault indication.

In addition to technical considerations, environmental aspects are now being taken into consideration as reflected in the diagnostic concepts. In the future, only perfect systems will be accepted, in order to keep environmental pollution to a minimum. It is understandable, therefore, that legislators insist on increased monitoring standards, particularly for exhaust-related components.

As an example of the new monitoring standards, consider the requirements of CARB and EPA in the United States and the resulting consequences for diagnosis. At the moment, the extent of such a detailed monitoring has to be a compromise between the different requirements and the possible technical and economical solutions, but the environmental aspects will gain more and more importance. The increased amount of available data will certainly permit a considerably higher rate of in-depth fault localization and will also allow clear fault identification without interactive outside intervention. Having knowledge of the functional interrelationships and access to all essential data, a picture of the defect can be created with the help of individual pieces of information. The driver and the workshop can then be provided with appropriate instructions. In this context, on-board expert systems are being considered.

For an effective and successful diagnosis today and in the future the following tasks and targets can be defined.

Fault Storage with Boundary Conditions.   A very important aspect of modern diagnosis is the clear and reliable analysis of the respective fault. During the self-diagnosis, it is absolutely necessary to store not only the respective fault information but also all relevant marginal parameters in the control unit, e.g., ambient temperature, velocity, engine speed, engine knock, and so on. The additional data can be stored when a defect occurs as well as during specified intervals around the moment of a defect. Such additional data is called "freeze frame" data.[9]

Fault Localization.   Mechanics must be able to locate a defective control unit quickly and then determine which component of that control unit is at fault so that it can be replaced.

Data Correlation, Recognition of Imminent Faults.   A large amount of data useful for the analysis of a vehicle is now available and even more will be available in the future. These data will have to be evaluated and compared with the help of modern data processing techniques, including fuzzy logic, neural networks, autodidactic systems, and expert systems. These techniques will not only enable the diagnosis of the actual condition of the vehicle but will also determine future maintenance needs. As a result, the reliability and availability of a vehicle will be increased and the possible consequences of a defect kept to a minimum. The driver can also be forewarned about imminent problems and can then take appropriate steps before starting on a trip.

Parameter Substitution.   The breakdown of a sensor in modern diagnostic procedures is not necessarily followed by a lack of the respective information. After having diagnosed a fault, the diagnostic computer—with the aid of the available information—is often able to compute an auxiliary parameter to replace the original one. As a result, either a limp-home condition is possible or else the nominal function can be assured but under slightly limited conditions. Simple examples for such a calculated parameter are vehicle speed (considering the gear and the synchronous speed, or the antilock braking information, or the data of the navigation system), motor temperature (considering the outside temperature and the operating time), and the amount of remaining fuel (considering the last actual fuel content and the calculated consumption).

Providing Guidelines.   As mentioned earlier, a diagnostic system has to provide clear information to the driver in case of a defect. A global warning indication is not sufficient. The driver needs to learn the extent of the defect and its consequences by appropriate text, graphics, or synthetic voice. In addition, the driver needs to be told the steps that have to be taken (e.g., "refill cooling water," "minimum speed to the next service station, risk of engine breakdown," "stop, brake system out of order").[10]

The diagnostic monitoring system can also be used, if there is no service station nearby, as a substitutional off-board system. The defect is then localized by an interactive working together of the indicating system and an appropriate input medium.

External Diagnostic Access.   For off-board diagnosis, the diagnostic system of the vehicle has to provide a standardized access to all relevant components, control units, and stored information. This standardized access might also be used by the vehicle manufacturer, legislator, application engineer, and the end-of-the-line programmer. The access itself has to be controlled with the help of an appropriate mechanism to prevent possible abuse.[11]

Logbook Function.   The control unit or the diagnostic computer of the vehicle is supposed to store every repair that has been carried out in the format of a logbook. It should contain the time and name of the workshop, every exchanged and newly installed element, every inspection carried out, and so forth.

22.2   ON-BOARD DIAGNOSTICS

The more complex automobiles became, the greater the number of electronic systems and the more difficult became the registration of the actual condition in case of a defect. To reach the necessary measuring points, many connecting cables and adapters were required. In addition, much data about the different systems and their working together was needed to allow a system-specific diagnosis. Modern electronics with self-diagnosis supports the service mechanic by registrating the actual values, comparing them with the nominal values, and diagnosing faults that are stored for repair purposes. Actually, the internal functions are checked whenever an ECU is turned on.

First, the checksum of the program memory is checked together with its function and the correct version. Then a read and write test of the RAM cells is performed. Special peripheral elements (e.g., AD converters) are also checked within this test cycle. During the entire operating time of the vehicle, the ECUs are constantly supervising the sensors they are connected to. With the help of an adequate interpretation of the hardware, controllers are able to determine whether a sensor has a short circuit to ground or battery voltage, or if a cable to the sensor is interrupted. By comparing the measured values and the stored technical data, a controller is able to determine whether the measured values exceed the limits, drift away, or are still within the tolerable limits. The combination of information provided by other sensors allows the monitoring for plausibleness of the measured values.

Sensors are tested similarly to the way actuators are monitored for short circuits or interruptions of cables. The check is carried out by measuring the electric current or reading the diagnostic output of intelligent driver circuits. The function of an actuator under certain conditions can be tested by powering the actuator and observing the corresponding reaction of the system. If discrepancies to the nominal values are diagnosed, the information is stored in an internal fault memory together with relevant outside parameters, e.g., the motor temperature or the engine speed. Thus, defects that appear once or under certain conditions can be diagnosed. If a fault occurs only once during several journeys, it is deleted. The fault memory can be read later in the workshop and provides valuable information for the mechanic.

In case of a detected defective sensor, the measured values are replaced by nominal values or an alternative value is formed using the information of other sensors to provide at least a limp-home function.

With the help of an appropriate interface, a tester can communicate with the ECUs, read the fault memory and the measured values, and send signals to the actuators. In order to be able to use self-diagnosis as universally as possible, manufacturers aim at the standardization of the interface and the determination of appropriate protocols for data exchange.

Another task of self-diagnosis is the indication of a defect to the driver. Faults are mostly indicated by one or more warning lights on the dashboard. Modern developments aim at more comprehensive information using displays for text and graphics, which provide priority-controlled information for the driver. Legal regulations concerning exhaust-gas gave rise to an essential extension of self diagnosis. The control units have to be able to control all exhaust-relevant functions and components and to clearly indicate a defective function or the exceeding of the permissible exhaust limits. Some of the demanded functions require an enormous amount of additional instructions; therefore, the extent of self-diagnosis already reaches up to 40 percent of the entire software of the control unit.

22.3   OFF-BOARD DIAGNOSTICS

The continual increase in the use of electronics within the broad range of different vehicles represents one of the major challenges for customer service and workshop operations. Modern diagnosis and information systems must cope with this challenge and manufacturers of test equipments must provide instruments that are flexible and easy to handle. Quick and reliable fault diagnosis in modern vehicles requires extensive technical knowledge, detailed vehicle information, and up-to-date testing systems.

Due to the different demands of the service providers, there are many different test equipments on the market. They can be subdivided into two main categories: handheld or portable instruments and stationary equipments. Handheld instruments are commonly used for the control of engine functions like ignition or fuel injection and the request of error codes of the electronic control units (ECUs). Stationary test equipment, on the other hand, covers the whole range of function and performance checks of the engine, gear, brakes, chassis, and exhaust monitoring.

Most of the common testers are used for the diagnosis of the engine. The Bosch MOT 250, for example, offers the following functions:

- Engine speed by means of the top dead center (TDC) transmitter, cylinder 1 or terminal 1 signal
- Ignition timing with TDC sensor or stroboscope
- Dwell angle in percent, degrees, or dwell time
- On/off-ratio in percent
- Injection timing or other times measured at the valve or other suitable measuring points
- Electric cylinder balance in absolute or relative terms
- Voltage to ground or floating potential including lambda-sensor voltages or dynamic voltage at terminal 1
- Current with two test adapters for maximum 20 A and 600 A
- Resistances from milliohms to megohms
- Temperature with oil-temperature sensor

For most variables, a maximum of four blocks of measured variables can be stored and recalled one after the other. Twelve blocks can be stored for the cylinder balance function. A digital storage oscilloscope records and stores up to 32 oscillograms of ignition voltages, alternator ripple, and current or voltage transients in the electric or electronic systems. Two RS232 interfaces are provided for documentation purposes and data exchange.

For repair, service, and maintenance, many different manuals and microfiches are stored in the workshops. It is a time-consuming task to collect all the necessary information, especially when vehicles of different makes have to be repaired. To avoid unnecessary paper, information and communication systems among workshop, dealer, and manufacturer are built up. The corresponding manuals have to be standardized and distributed on electronic data processing media, preferably on CD-ROMs.

Every garage or workshop, equipped with the appropriate data system (basically a tester connected to a PC), will receive servicing aids and updates via telephone line or by periodic receipt of updated CDs. A committee of the SAE is preparing rules for the standardization of manuals. There are already published draft international standards (DIS) for terms and definitions (J1930) used in the manuals, for diagnostic codes/messages (J2012), or electronic access/service information (J2008) (see the following). Most of the available test equipment is capable of storing operator manuals within its memory and offers menu-guided assistance to the service personnel. Automatic vehicle and component identification by the tester and the availability of corresponding data at the workbench eases troubleshooting and repairs.

22.4 LEGISLATION AND STANDARDIZATION

22.4.1 CARB, EPA, OBD II

The following is an abstract of the California Air Resource Board (CARB) Regulations for On-Board-Diagnosis two(OBDII):

> All 1994 and subsequent model-year passenger cars, light-duty trucks, and medium-duty vehicles shall be equipped with a malfunction indicator light (MIL) located on the instrument panel that will automatically inform the vehicle operator in the event of a malfunction of any power train component which can affect emission and which provide input to, or receive output from, the on-board computer(s) or of the malfunction of the on-board computer(s) itself. The MIL shall not be used for any other purpose.
>
> . . . .
>
> All 1994 and subsequent model-year passenger cars, light-duty trucks, and medium-duty vehicles required to have MIL pursuant to paragraph above shall also be equipped with an on-board diagnostic system capable of identifying the likely area of the malfunction by means of fault codes stored in the computer memory. These vehicles shall be equipped with a standardized electrical connector to provide access to the stored fault codes . . . Starting with model-year 1995, manufacturers of non-complying systems shall be subject to fines pursuant to section 43016 of the California Health and Safety Code for each deficiency identified, after the second, in a vehicle model. For the third deficiency and every deficiency thereafter identified in a vehicle model, the fines shall be in the amount of $50 per deficiency per vehicle for non-compliance with any of the monitoring requirements . . .

Systems to Be Monitored

OBD II Functions.   These include catalyst monitoring, misfire monitoring, evaporative system monitoring, secondary air system monitoring, fuel systems monitoring, oxygen sensor monitoring, exhaust-gas-recirculation (EGR) system monitoring, and comprehensive component monitoring.

Catalyst.   Legal requirements (CARB excerpt): "The diagnostic system shall individually monitor the front catalyst or catalysts which receive untreated engine out exhaust-gas for malfunction. A catalyst is regarded as malfunctioning when the average hydrocarbon conversion efficiency falls between 50 and 60 percent."

Technical solution: In addition to the oxygen sensor upstream the catalyst, another sensor is mounted downstream.

A properly working catalyst shows a storage effect so that the oscillation of the lambda-controller appears damped at the downstream lambda probe. A worn-out catalyst has a reduced damping effect and the signals of up- and downstream sensors are equivalent.

The ratio of the signal amplitudes is a measure of the conversion efficiency. The electronic system that controls the fuel injection monitors these signals together with other relevant engine conditions to derive the catalyst efficiency.

Misfire Detection.   Legal requirements (CARB excerpt): "To avoid catalyst damage, the diagnostic system shall monitor engine misfire and identify the specific cylinder experiencing misfire."

Technical solution: Misfire can be caused by worn-out spark plugs or defective electrical wiring. Unburned fuel reaches the catalyst and may destroy it by overheating. Even the least amount of misfire rates influences the emission and therefore single misfire events must be detected.

The speed of the engine is measured very precisely. In case of misfire, the momentum, which is normally produced by the combustion, is lacking. Thus abnormal variations of speed-changes at steady state conditions may be considered as misfire. To distinguish clearly between misfire and other malfunctions, complicated calculations have to be carried out.

If a certain percentage of misfires within 200 or 1000 revolutions is detected, a fault code is stored in the control unit and the fault is indicated to the driver.

Oxygen Sensor.   Legal requirements (CARB excerpt): "The diagnostic system shall monitor the output voltage, the response rate, and any other parameter which can affect emission and all fuel control oxygen sensors for malfunction."

Technical solution: The control unit has a special input circuit for detecting shorts or breaks and monitors the switching frequency of the control loop.

By means of a second lambda probe behind the catalyst, it is possible to monitor the lambda probe in front of the catalyst for its correct position. A lambda probe which is subject to an increased temperature for extensive periods may react slower on variations of the air/fuel mixture, thus increasing the period of the lambda-probe regulation. The diagnostic system of the control unit controls the regular frequency and indicates slow sensors to the driver by means of a warning light.

Heated sensors are monitored for correct heater current and voltage by hardware means within the control unit.

Evaporative System.   Legal requirements (CARB excerpt): "The diagnostic system shall control the air flow of the complete evaporative system. In addition, the diagnostic system shall also monitor the complete evaporative system for the emission of HC vapor into the atmosphere by performing a pressure or vacuum check of the complete evaporative system. From time to time, manufacturers may occasionally turn off the evaporative purge system in order to carry out a check."

Technical solution: At idle position, the canister purge valve is activated and the lambda controller is monitored for its reaction. For leak detection of the evaporative system, the output to the active carbon filter is shut off and the canister pressure is decreased to about -1.5 kPa. Then the complete system is turned off and the pressure within the canister is monitored for variation with time. The pressure gradient, together with other parameters like the amount of fuel, may indicate possible leaks.

Secondary Air System.   Legal requirements: "Any vehicle equipped with any form of a secondary air delivery system shall have the diagnostic system monitor the proper functioning of the secondary air delivery system and any air switching valve."

Technical solution: The lambda controller is monitored for correlated deviations when the secondary air flow is changed.

Fuel System.   Legal requirements: "The diagnostic system shall monitor the fuel delivery system for its ability to provide compliance with emission standards."

Deviations of the stochiometric ratio which last for a longer time are stored within the adaptive mixture controller. If these values exceed defined limits, components of the fuel system obviously do not correspond to the specification.

Exhaust-Gas Recirculation (EGR) System.   Legal requirement: "The diagnostic system shall monitor the EGR system on vehicles for low and high flow rate malfunctions."

Technical solution: (1) At overrun, the fuel is cut off and the EGR valve is completely opened. The flow of exhaust gas to the manifold raises the manifold pressure, which is recorded and allows statements about the function of the EGR valve. (2) Another possibility is to control the increase of the manifold intake temperature when the EGR valve is opened.

In a conclusion to the previously described OBD II requirements and technical solutions, we can define the following four quality demands for electronic control units:

- Guarantee for exhaust-gas-relevant components with repair costs >$300 for seven years or 70,000 miles for all 1990 and subsequent model-year vehicles (CARB).
- Guarantee for exhaust-gas-relevant components with repair costs >$200 for eight years or 80,000 miles for all 1994 and subsequent model-year vehicles (EPA/Clean Air Act).
- Guarantee protocols in case of a reclamation rate of exhaust-gas-relevant components higher than 1 percent (CARB).
- Recall of vehicles in case of a calculated reclamation rate of more than 20,000 ppm within a period of five years/50,000 miles (CARB).

22.4.2 International Standardizations

Because of the manifold requirements on modern diagnostics, the national and international standardization committees soon came to the conclusion that with the help of appropriate and, if possible, international agreements about protocols, connectors, tools and auxiliaries, the process of diagnosis can be standardized, thus reducing time and costs.

Figure 22.4 shows how, in a standardized graphic, control units and diagnostic tools are connected and diagnostic data exchanged.

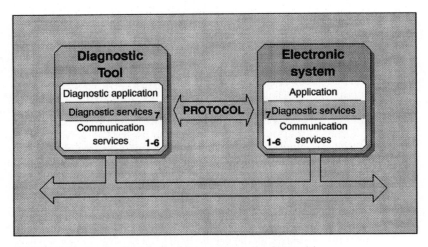

FIGURE 22.4 Standardized testing link according to the OSI model.

For data exchange, electronic systems are structured and described according to a seven-layer model (OSI model, open system interconnection) developed by the ISO (International Standardization Organization). Every unit connected to a data network can be structured with the help of this model—control units as well as diagnostic tools.

The diagnostic services that the controller may use during the diagnostic process are regulated in the seventh layer. Diagnostic service means definite instructions, which actuate determined and standardized diagnostic procedures, e.g. "start diagnostic session," "read diagnostic trouble codes," "read freeze frame data," and so on. There are different sequences of bits and bytes code for such instructions. On the hardware level (plugs, cables, potentials), the sequences are finally transmitted from unit to unit. The ISO and the SAE (Society of Automotive Engineers) developed corresponding standards in the area of service definition

TABLE 22.1   ISO Diagnostic Services

Diagnostic management
StartDiagnosticSession
StopDiagnosticSession
SecurityAccess
TesterPresent
EcuReset
ReadEcuIdentification
DisableNormalMessageTransmission
EnableNormalMessageTransmission
Data transmission
ReadDataByLocalIdentifier
ReadDataByGlobalIdentifier
ReadMemoryByAddress
WriteDataByLocalIdentifier
WriteDataByGlobalIdentifier
WriteMemoryByAddress
SetDataRates
StopRepeatedDataTransmission
Input/output control
InputOutputControlByGlobalIdentifier
InputOutputControlByLocalIdentifier
Stored data transmission
ReadNumberOfDiagnosticTroubleCodes
ReadDiagnosticTroubleCode
ReadDiagnosticTroubleCodesByStatus
ReadStatusOfDiagnosticTroubleCodes
ReadFreezeFrameData
ClearDiagnosticInformation
Remote activation of routine
StartRoutineByLocalIdentifier
StartRoutineByAddress
StopRoutineByLocalIdentifier
StopRoutineByAddress
RequestRoutineResultsByLocalIdentifier
RequestRoutineResultsByAddress
Upload download
RequestDownload
RequestUpload
TransferData
RequestTransferExit

as well as in the area of communication. Table 22.1 shows the diagnostic services as proposed by the ISO.

Figure 22.5 presents the determined standards with some essential technical details as developed for the field of communication.

Unfortunately the whole spectrum of available standards has become very complex and difficult to use. The following explanations try to provide a unified system for the existing standards in the area of diagnosis.

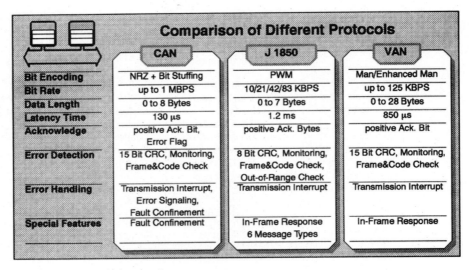

FIGURE 22.5 In-vehicle networks.

Figure 22.6 shows a general model for diagnostic concepts. The three main levels comprehensively describe the whole area of diagnostics. The three levels are hierarchically structured, closely linked together with flowing transition from one level to the other. Although there are certain similarities between this model and the seven-layer model of the OSI, both models do not correlate.

The upper level comprises the elements, which are essential for the user or generator of diagnostic applications. The term "user" includes the driver, the legislator, the mechanic, and the manufacturer. This upper level can be subdivided into three main fields of activities: user

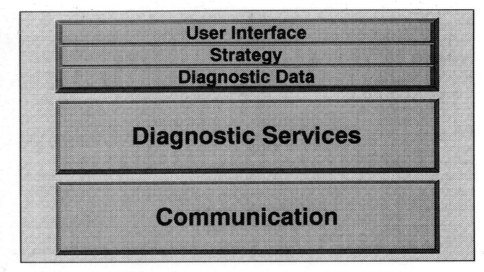

FIGURE 22.6 Model for diagnostic concept.

interface, strategy, and diagnostic data. Although presented as layers, these activities do not correlate hierarchically, but each is associated with a service or group of services.

The "user interface" describes how information flows between the user and the diagnostic service. This includes a functional description of scan tools, handheld testers, monitoring systems, and so on.

The term "strategies" stands for strategic details, which are essential for the diagnosis or repair of a vehicle, including communication access, diagnostic data and information.

The term "diagnostic data" includes the data that are necessary for the diagnosis itself. The details concerning parameters, trouble codes, and so on are described here.

The intermediate level describes the diagnostic services, defining a set of services and a set of commands for general purpose, which allow the diagnosis of a vehicle. The set of commands is supposed to cover the needs of users concerning repair and maintenance as described by the strategies and diagnostic data.

The lowest level deals with the communication area. It describes every technical detail that is necessary for communication and provides the information about how to start communication (initialization). It also specifies the appropriate Baud rate, the suitable protocol, and the necessary hardware (connector, cable, and so on).

This model offers a general description of the essential fields of diagnostic interest and allows the categorization of all ISO and SAE standardization activities in the three main levels of the diagnostic concept model.

Figures 22.7 and 22.8 are presented in the same graphic form (three-level structure). They provide a summary of the concrete standardization activities of the SAE and ISO. Figure 22.7 shows the existing standards or drafts of automotive diagnosis for general purpose.

The user interface for general purposes is undefined. The SAE J2186 (Data Link Security) and the SAE J2008 (Electronic Access/Service Information) are strategic documents, though most strategies are not standardized and diagnostic data is described in documents SAE J2012 (Diagnostic Codes and Messages) and SAE J2190-2 (Parameters—in preparation).

On the level of diagnostic services, the standardization activities can be divided in two fields called service definition and service implementation. The term "service definition" describes a set of useful diagnostic services, which enable the user to run a diagnostic session

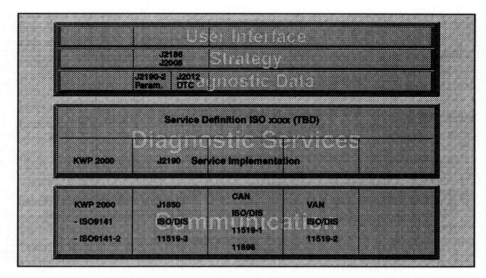

FIGURE 22.7   Realization for general automotive diagnosis.

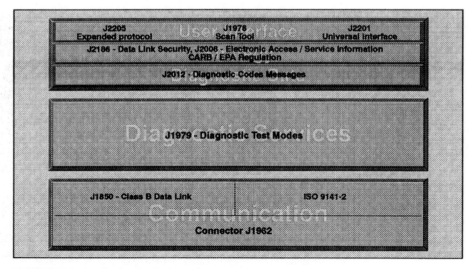

FIGURE 22.8   Realization for CARB and EPA requirements.

independently of the knowledge of any technical detail in the communication area as described in the level below.

This set of diagnostic services for general purpose can now be mapped on different protocols. Any bit representation of the different services can be built up. This is called service implementation. At the moment, there are two implementations available, the SAE J2190 (Diagnostic Test Modes) and the KWP 2000 (ISO Draft: Keyword Protocol 2000). The lowest level (the Communication level) shows the standardized details of communication such as the data formats and the physical layers; e.g., the KWP 2000 uses the physical layer of ISO 9141 or ISO 9141-2, the SAE J2190 uses the SAE J1850 Class B network (ISO/DIS 11519-3). It is shown that communication can also be built up with a CAN or a VAN network.

Figure 22.8 shows the standardization activities for the special requirements of the CARB and the EPA using the same three-level-concept.

The user interface, a generic scan tool, is standardized within the SAE J1978, including the SAE J2205 (Expanded Diagnostic Protocol) and the SAE J2201 (Universal Interface). Some aspects of the diagnostic strategy are described in the SAE J2186 (Data Link Security), the SAE J2008 (Electronic Access/Service Information), and some in the regulations. The diagnostic data is described in the document SAE J2012—Diagnostic Codes and Messages.

The level of diagnostic services defines one SAE J1979 standard—Diagnostic Test Modes. This standard is a closely linked combination of a service definition and a service implementation (referring to the SAE as "modes").

In the field of communication, the possible networks are described in the SAE J1850 (Class B Data Network) and the ISO 9141-2 (CARB Requirements for Interchange of Digital Information).

A standard for the physical connector (SAE J1962) has also been developed. Figure 22.9 shows the status of diagnostic standards for trucks and buses and for passenger cars in Europe and in the United States. It shows also a time schedule for the development of standards. A comparison of the communication and diagnostic services levels has already been realized. The titles of the different SAE and ISO numbers are shown in Tables 22.2 and 22.3, where all ISO and SAE papers, relevant for diagnostics, are listed. Table 22.3 offers a detailed list of trucks and bus activities (J1939).

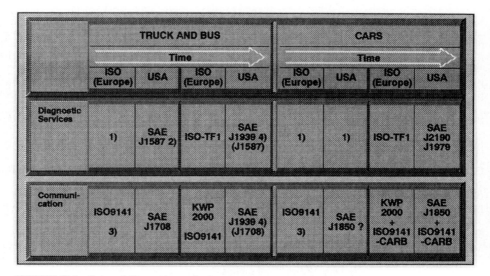

	TRUCK AND BUS				CARS			
	Time →				Time →			
	ISO (Europe)	USA	ISO (Europe)	USA	ISO (Europe)	USA	ISO (Europe)	USA
Diagnostic Services	1)	SAE J1587 2)	ISO-TF1	SAE J1939 4) (J1587)	1)	1)	ISO-TF1	SAE J2190 J1979
Communication	ISO9141 3)	SAE J1708	KWP 2000 ISO9141	SAE J1939 4) (J1708)	ISO9141 3)	SAE J1850 ?	KWP 2000 + ISO9141 -CARB	SAE J1850 + ISO9141 -CARB

FIGURE 22.9   Status of diagnostic standards.

22.5   *FUTURE DIAGNOSTIC CONCEPTS*

As yet, most vehicle manufacturers have installed a diagnostic connector in the engine compartment in order to offer essential electric signals for diagnostic purposes. Due to the multitude of different equipments and philosophies of car makers, the connectors have different shapes and contact arrangements. Therefore, a workshop has to keep a lot of different expensive cables and adaptors in store.

For future diagnostic systems, the connection between control unit and vehicle is supposed to be realized with the help of a standardized connector. A connector for the legally demanded exhaust-gas diagnosis was defined by an SAE draft (J1962), concerning form, contact arrangement, and installation position. (Fig. 22.10)

With this connector and a so-called generic scan tool, anyone is able to read the fault-memory in regard to exhaust-gas-relevant defects. The interconnection of the control units allows the access to the entire electronics of the vehicle.

The necessary protocols are partly defined and developed further in standardization committees of the ISO. At the moment, there are two actual standards available:

1. *ISO 9141-2:*   Determination of the requirements on hardware and communication protocols. The requirements on hardware are essentially determined by the maximum Baud rate of data transfer and the maximum number of control units simultaneously connected with the diagnostic cable.

Communication is started by means of a trigger address, and is followed by a synchronization byte of the control unit(s), which is necessary for the automatic setting of the Baud rate. The trigger address calls either a particular control unit or a function, that may also address several control units.

After transmission of the synchronization byte, the control unit waits for the tester to set the Baud rate, then sends two key-bytes that inform the tester about the suitable data transfer protocol. The tester responds with the last inverted key-byte, in order to confirm the correct receipt. The connection between tester and control unit is now established.

TABLE 22.2   ISO and SAE Documents

ISO 9141		Road Vehicles—Diagnostic System—Requirements for Interchange of Digital Information
ISO/DIS 9141-2		Road Vehicles—Diagnostic System—Part 2: CARB Requirements for Interchange of Digital Information
ISO/DIS 11519-1		Road Vehicles—Low-Speed Serial Data Communication—Part 1: General Definitions
ISO/DIS 11519-2		Road Vehicles—Low-Speed Serial Data Communication—Part 2: Low Speed Controller Area Network (CAN)
ISO/DIS 11519-3		Road Vehicles—Low-Speed Serial Data Communication—Part 3: Vehicle Area Network (VAN)
ISO/DIS 11519-4		Road Vehicles—Low-Speed Serial Data Communication—Part 4: Class B Data Communication Network Interface (J1850)
ISO/DIS 11898		Road Vehicles—Interchange of Digital Information—Controller Area Network (CAN) for High-Speed Communication
ISO/WD 14229		Diagnostic Systems—Diagnostic Services Specification
ISO/WD 14230		Diagnostic Systems—Keyword Protocol 2000 (3 parts: 1: Physical Layer, 2: Data Link Layer, 3: Implementation)
SAE J 1213/1	IR	Glossary of Vehicle Networks for Multiplexing and Data Communications
SAE J 1583	IR	Controller Area Network (CAN), An In-Vehicle Serial Communication Protocol
SAE J 1587	RP	Joint SAE/TMC Electronic Data Interchange Between Microcomputer Systems in Heavy-Duty Vehicle Applications
SAE J 1699	RP	J 1850 Verification Test Procedures
SAE J 1708	RP	Serial Data Communications Between Microcomputer Systems in Heavy-Duty Vehicle Application
SAE J 1724		Vehicle Electronic Identification (New Task Force)
SAE J 1850	RP	Class B Data Communication Network Interface
SAE J 1930	RP	Electrical/Electronic Systems Diagnostic Terms, Definitions, Abreviations and Acronyms
SAE J1939/xx		Truck + Bus, Details next page
SAE J 1962	RP	Diagnostic Connector
SAE J 1978	RP	OBD II Scan Tool
SAE J 1979	RP	E/E Diagnostic Test Modes
SAE J 2008	RP	Electronic Access/Service Information
SAE J 2012	RP	Diagnostic Trouble Code Definitions
SAE J 2037	IR	Off-Board Diagnostic Message Formats
SAE J 2054	IR	E/E Diagnostic Data Communications
SAE J 2056/1	RP	Class C Application Requirement Considerations (Part 2: IR: Survey of Known Protocols, Part 3: IR: Selection of Transmission Media)
SAE J 2057/1	IR	Class A Application/Definition (Part 3: IR: Class A Multiplexing Sensors, Part 4: IR: Class A Multiplexing Architecture Strategies)
SAE J 2106	IR	Token Slot Network for Automotive Control
SAE J 2112	IR	Diagnostic Technician Questionnaire Summary
SAE J 2178	RP	Class B Data Communication Network Messages (Part 1: Detailed Header Formats and Physical Address Assignments, Part 2: Data Parameter Definitions, Part 3: Frame Ids for Single Byte Forms of Headers, Part 4: Message Definition for Three Byte Headers)
SAE J 2186	RP	E/E Data Link Security
SAE J 2190	RP	Enhanced E/E Diagnostic Test Modes
SAE J 2201	RP	Universal Interface for OBD II Scan Tool
SAE J 2205	RP	Diagnostic Specific Functionality Protocol
SAE J 2216	RP	Application of the Clean Air Act Amendment of 1990 (Section 207, Paragraph M5)

RP = Recommended Practice, IR = Information Report

TABLE 22.3   SAE Truck and Bus Documents

SAE J 1939	RP	Serial Control and Communication Vehicle Network (Class C)
SAE J 1939/01		Truck and Bus Control and Communication Vehicle Network (Class C)
SAE J 1939/02		Agricultural Equipment Control and Communication Network
SAE J 1939/1x		Physical Layer, x refers to a specific version
SAE J 1939/11		Physical Layer, 250 kBaud, Twisted Shielded Pair
SAE J 1939/12		Physical Layer, 125 kBaud, Twisted Pair
SAE J 1939/13		Physical Layer, 250 kBaud, Twisted Pair with Ground
SAE J 1939/14		Physical Layer, 1 MBaud, Fiber Optic
SAE J 1939/15		Physical Layer, 50 kBaud, German Agricultural
SAE J 1939/21		CAN 29 Bit Identifier Data Link Layer
SAE J 1939/3x		Network Layer, x refers to a specific version
SAE J 1939/31		Truck + Bus Network Layer
SAE J 1939/4x		Transport Layer, x refers to a specific version
SAE J 1939/5x		Session Layer, x refers to a specific version
SAE J 1939/6x		Presentation Layer, x refers to a specific version
SAE J 1939/7x		Application Layer, x refers to a specific version
SAE J 1939/71		Truck, Bus, Agricultural and Construction Equipment Application Layer
SAE J 1939/72		Virtual Terminal
SAE J 1939/73		Application Layer—Diagnostics
SAE J 1939/81		Network Management
SAE J 1939/??		Tractor-Trailer-Interface

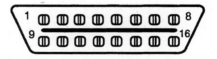

PIN #	Assignment
1	discretionary
2	BUS + Line of SAE J1850
3	discretionary
4	Chassis Ground
5	Signal Ground
6	discretionary
7	K Line of ISO 9141-2
8	discretionary
9	discretionary
10	BUS - Line of SAE J1850
11	discretionary
12	discretionary
13	discretionary
14	discretionary
15	L Line of ISO 9141-2
16	Unswitched Vehicle Battery Positive

Note: Assignment of pins 1, 3, 6, 8, 9, 11, 12, 13, and 14 is left to the discretion of the vehicle manufacturer

FIGURE 22.10   SAE J1962 diagnostic connector.

2. *Interface according to the SAE J1850 (Class B Data Communication Network Interface):*
The SAE J1850 defines means and methods for serial data exchange for automotive application at the physical and data link layer of the OSI model. It is used for networked systems and for diagnostic purposes.

Two implementations are characterized: pulse-width modulation (PWM) at 41.6 kbps transmitted on twisted pair wires, and variable pulse-width modulation (VPM) at 10.4 kbps, transmitted on a single wire.[12]

A generic scan tool, as mentioned, therefore, has to handle the three different interfaces.

A new protocol, *Keyword 2000,* is prepared by the ISO committees. It is supposed to combine the protocols that have been used up to now.

With the introduction of more and more diagnostic functions and networked systems in the vehicle, the functional structure will be modified (Fig. 22.11).

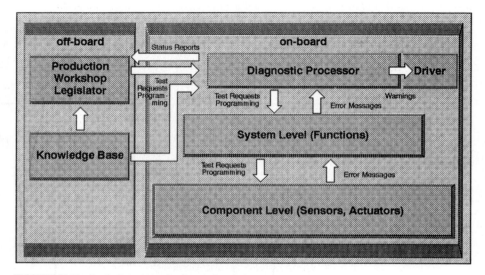

FIGURE 22.11   Logical structure for future diagnosis.

A diagnostic processor on top of a hierarchical structure of functions has access to every system via the network. It can request status information of the functions of the levels below, or of the sensors and actuators, and receives warning messages if problems are detected by the self-diagnosis of the different subsystems. The diagnostic processor serves as a man-machine interface to the driver and as a gate to the outside. It is the only secure access to the entire system of the vehicle.

GLOSSARY

CAN   Controller Area Network (standardized protocol developed by Bosch for networked systems).

CARB   California Air Resources Board.

CD-ROM   Compact disk read only memory, a data storage medium.

DIS   Draft International Standard.

ECU   Electronic control unit.

EGR   Exhaust-gas recirculation.

EPA   Environmental Protection Agency.

Freeze frame   Faults stored together with various related parameters.

HC   Hydrocarbon.

ISO   International Standardization Organization.

ISO 9141-2   Standardized protocol for data exchange between ECUs and testers.

Lambda controller   Electronic system for controlling the air/fuel ratio.

Lambda sensor   A sensor for air/fuel ratio (oxygen sensor).

MIL   Malfunction indicator lamp (indicates emission-related faults to the driver).

OBDII   On Board Diagnostics II.

Off-board diagnosis   Diagnosis performed by means outside a vehicle.

On-board diagnosis   Diagnosis performed by means within a vehicle.

OSI   Open System Interconnection.

PC   Personal computer.

PWM   Pulse-width modulation.

RS 232   Standardized data link (hardware).

Scan tool   Small tester that can be connected to the diagnostic connector to interrogate emission-related fault codes.

SAE   Society of Automotive Engineers.

TDC   Top dead center.

Terminal 1   Connection to a signal related to ignition timing.

VAN   Vehicle Area Network (French proposal for network protocol).

VPM   Variable pulse-width modulation.

REFERENCES

1. W. Bremer and Heintz, F., "Was bieten die Karosserie-Zentral-Elektronik mit Kabelbaum-Multiplex und die On-Board-Diagnose?," (Advantages of a central body-electronic with multiplex and on-board diagnosis), Bosch Customer Information, 1977.

2. W. Bremer, Heintz, F., and Hugel, R., "Diagnosis in Networked Systems," *International Conference Automotive Diagnostics,* London, 1990.

3. K. Dieterich and Unruh, J., "CAN—A Bus System for Serial Data Transfer," *23. FISITA Congress "The promise of new technology in the automotive industry,"* 1990.

4. T. Goelzer and Leonhard, R., "A new Architecture for Car Electronics", *International Symposium Vehicle Electronics Integration ATA-EL 91,* 1991.

5. W. Kremer and Kaminski, D., "Integrated Vehicle Electronics with CAN," *23. FISITA Congress "The promise of new technology in the automotive industry,"* 1990.

6. T. Kühner and Kaminski, D., "Structuring of vehicle electronics in cars for an effective on-board-diagnosis system," *VDI Reports "Electronic in Vehicles,"* Nr. 819, 1990.

7. E. Hipp, Jung, C., and Morizur, P., "On Board Diagnosis as the Central Interface for Modern Vehicle Electronics," *International Symposium Vehicle Electronics Integration ATA-EL 91,* 1991.

8. W. Botzenhardt, Litschel, M., and Unruh, J., "Bussysteme für Kfz-Sterugeräte" (Bus systems for vehicle electronic control units), *VDI Reports "Electronic in Vehicles,"* Nr. 612, 1986.

9. B. Przbylla, "Eigendiagnose von elektronischen Steuergeräten im Kraftfahrzeug" (Self-diagnosis of electronic control units in the vehicle), *VDI Reports "Electronic in Vehicles,"* Nr. 612, 1986.

10. W. Bremer, "Möglichkeiten der fahrzeugfesten Überwachung mit Kabelbaum-Multiplex," (Possibilities of On-Board Diagnostics with Multiplex), *Status-seminar of the German Ministry of Research and Technology,* 1978.

11. D. Nemec, "Möglichkeiten komfortabler Testgeräte zur Auswertung der Eigendiagnose von Steuergeräten" (Possibilities of comfortable test equipment for the evaluation of selfdiagnostic data of control systems), *VDI Reports "Electronic in Vehicles,"* Nr. 687, 1988.

12. A. W. Millsap, Lowden, M. T., Folkerts, M. A., Unruh, J., and Dais, S., "Mapping J1850 Messages into CAN Version 2.0," *SAE International Congress,* Paper 930437, 1993.

ABOUT THE AUTHORS

WOLFGANG BREMER studied electrical communication techniques from 1962 to 1968 at the University of Karlsruhe (Germany). Afterwards he was engaged with Siemens AG in Karlsruhe in the development of high-precision electronic balances. Since 1970, he has been working in the advanced engineering department of measurement and information techniques of Robert Bosch GmbH and is responsible for the development of serial communication and diagnostic systems in the chassis area of vehicles. He is working in several ISO and SAE committees and working groups in the field of diagnosis.

FRIEDER HEINTZ studied electrical communication techniques from 1954 to 1959 at the University of Karlsruhe. Afterwards he was engaged in research and development of process-control computers with Siemens AG in Karlsruhe, Munich, and New York. Since 1969, he has been the head of the advanced engineering department for measurement and information techniques at Robert Bosch GmbH. For 20 years, he has managed national and international working groups for diagnosis and serial data transfer in vehicles within the ISO (International Organization for Standardization).

ROBERT HUGEL studied physics at the University of Karlsruhe from 1967 to 1972. Then he was engaged for six years in the development, production, and sales of infrared spectrometers, two years in the development of laser-based measuring systems, and the last 13 years in developing various automotive electronics at Robert Bosch in the advanced engineering department for measurement and information techniques.

P · A · R · T · 5

SAFETY, CONVENIENCE, ENTERTAINMENT, AND OTHER SYSTEMS

CHAPTER 23
PASSENGER SAFETY AND CONVENIENCE

Bernhard K. Mattes
Electrical Engineer
Robert Bosch GmbH

23.1 PASSENGER SAFETY SYSTEMS

Electronically controlled passenger safety systems, such as air bags, seat belt tensioner, and rollover sensor systems, help to avoid injuries or to reduce injury severity in an accident. If the passenger compartment cell is not too heavily deformed, then these systems are effective in minimizing the acceleration or load forces acting on the vehicle occupants. During a rollover accident, the rollover protection system helps provide the necessary survival space. In an open vehicle, a rollover bar, as well as protection elements such as extending headrests behind the rear seats, considerably increase occupant safety.

Such occupant protection systems are also classified as passive restraint systems, since the protective function is independent of any active contribution by the passengers.

23.1.1 Air Bag and Seat Belt Tensioner Sensor Systems: Principle Sensor Function and Timing Sequences

The functional components of electronically controlled air bag and seat belt tensioner initiation consist of crash detection sensors, signal processing, squib triggering, and system monitoring. Whereas a vehicle in a crash situation is rapidly decelerated by contact with an external obstacle, the occupants continue to move forward until restrained or contact within the vehicle occurs (steering wheel, windshield, dashboard, or other rigid structural parts). Air bags and seat belt tensioners are designed to reduce impacts of passengers within the vehicle.

The igniter (squib) activates the pyrotechnical inflator used for both air bag deployment and seat belt tightening. The sensor range comprises an angular sensitivity of $\pm30°$ to the longitudinal axis. Normally, electronic sensor units contain one or more accelerometers with main sensitivity along the longitudinal axis.

Crash conditions demand a timely activation of restraining devices. It is equally important, however, that they are also released only when required.

Depending on the kind of collision (frontal, oblique, offset, pole, underride, etc.) the triggering time must be calculated correctly, so that the allowed forward displacement will not be exceeded by the time the air bag is inflated or the seat belts are tensioned.

In most cases, the allowable forward passenger travel with an air bag system is 12.5 cm (5-inches rule). For seat belt tensioning systems, the acceptable displacement drops to about 1 cm. Approximately 30 ms are required to inflate air bags, and the time required to tension a seat belt with a pyrotechnically activated seat belt retractor is approximately 10 ms. Thus, trigger commands must be given by the time the maximally allowable forward displacement will be reached minus the activation time of the respective restraining device. Effective injury prevention requires timely firing based on detection of acceleration or deceleration crash signals and their processing by the crash discrimination algorithm or electromechanical sensor.

Different crash-sensing schemes are shown in Fig. 23.1.

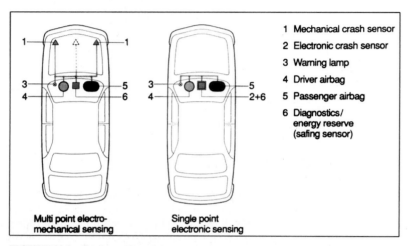

FIGURE 23.1 Crash-sensing schemes.

23.1.2 Multipoint Electromechanical Sensing Systems or Distributed Air Bag Systems

A distributed air bag sensing system or multipoint electromechanical sensing system consists of two to four electromechanical crash discrimination sensors, strategically mounted in the vehicle's crush zone, plus an additional arming sensor mounted in the passenger compartment inside an electronic control unit including diagnostics, energy reserve, and voltage converter.

Sensors. Two typical types of electromechanical sensors are based on the *ball-in-tube* respectively or the *rolamite* principle. The function of the ball-in-tube sensor is shown in Fig. 23.2. A ball held in position by a permanent magnet begins to move if the inertial force acting on it due to the vehicle's deceleration exceeds the magnetic restraining force. A narrow air gap between ball and tube results in viscous air damping and integration behavior of the relative motion. Upon reaching the other end of the tube, the gold-plated ball closes a mechanical switch.

Closure of at least one of the sensors located in the vehicle's crush zone and simultaneous closure of the arming switch inside the passenger compartment directly connect the igniters to battery plus and minus and initiate air bag deployment. The two-stage passenger inflator is ignited in series. A transistor turns on the ignition current for the second stage approximately 10 to 15 ms after the first stage. This delay time provides a softer passenger bag inflation and slower pressure increase inside the passenger compartment.

Such electromechanical spring mass sensors obey second-order differential equations of motion. Parameters like restraining magnetic force, damping factor, mass of the ball and

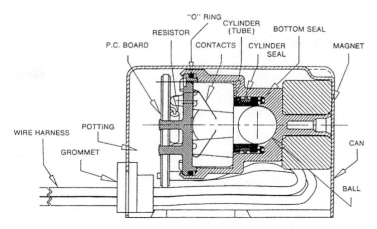

FIGURE 23.2 Ball-in-tube sensor. (*Courtesy Breed Technologies Inc.*)

travel distance determine the sensor's dynamic characteristics and have to be designed according to the vehicle's crash behavior.

The function of the rolamite sensor is as follows. A sheet metal spring band wound around a metal cylinder keeps the roller in its rest position as long as the retaining spring force is bigger than the inertial force acting on the roller cylinder. The rolling of the cylinder over the convex guide is thus kinematically constrained by the guide and the spring to translation along the guide's surface. After having reached or exceeded a specified travel distance, the firing contact is closed.

Normally, the arming sensor inside the diagnostics and energy reserve module is of the same type as the discriminating sensors used in the crush zone.

The advantage of such systems is that the discriminating sensors can be installed in front end positions where high acceleration amplitudes can be sensed in early stages of impact. Disadvantages range from no crash prediction capabilities, no sensor "stuck open" indication in the field, high cost and installation expense, as well as no seat belt tensioner function.

Diagnostics and Energy Reserve Module.   A system readiness indicator is legally required for air bag-equipped vehicles (with the exception of all-mechanical systems). This means that air bag system-readiness has to be constantly monitored. Electronic diagnostics and energy reserve modules *periodically* perform the following diagnostic functions:

Monitor.   This diagnostic function includes the following checks:

- All ignition loops for too high or too low resistances
- All ignition loops for leakages to battery plus or minus
- External crash discrimination sensors for continuity (there is a diagnostic resistor in parallel to the contact), for cable harness short circuits to battery plus or ground, and for too long contact closure (longer than 1 s)
- Internal arming sensor for continuity and for too long contact closure
- Warning lamp output for short circuits to battery plus or minus and for interruption
- Energy reserve capacitor(s) for correct voltage(s) and capacitance(s)

Control.   This diagnostic function includes the following checks:

- Battery supply for too low and too high voltage
- Internal regulated voltage (normally = 5 V) for too low or too high level
- Diagnostics interface for short circuits

After the initialization phase at power turn-on, the following checks are done once:

- RAM, ROM, EEPROM-read check
- Watchdog check
- Output transistor check for 2d passenger stage (if it exists)

Each fault type is characterized by a special fault code and stored into EEPROM after being judged as faulty. There are different modes of fault assessment and different degrees of fault tolerance.

Fault Clock.   State-of-the-art diagnostics and energy reserve modules have one fault clock counting the elapsed time of the faults in total. But there are also modules with individual fault clocks for each fault type.

Storage capacity of the fault time counter normally includes 50 to 100 h with a time resolution of 1 to 5 min.

Crash Recorder.   The sequence of crash-relevant events like closure of discriminating sensors, arming sensor, battery voltage level, energy reserve voltage, turn-on of power stages (if existing), can be stored in the EEPROM. This can be done in the form of time-discrete "snapshots" of system conditions for approximately 10 to 20 ms before and approximately 30 to 50 ms after deployment. Advanced crash recorders also store acceleration and deceleration values of some time period before and after the firing moment. This is done to get information about impact energy of real-world crashes.

Serial Diagnostic Interface.   EEPROM content (type of unit, fault codes, fault time, crash recorder) can be retrieved via a bidirectional diagnostics interface. Initiation of communication, diagnostics concept, and software depend on the car manufacturer's requirements.

Energy Reserve and Voltage Converter.   If battery supply is lost in a crash, ignition function and crash recorder storage is maintained by the energy reserve. This backup supply is performed by one or more capacitors (acting as energy reservoir(s). For the ignition loops, the energy reserve is wired or with vehicle battery voltage. For the monitoring circuits part, the energy reserve is switched on to the voltage regulator input in case of too low battery. Survival time of such components ranges between 0.1 and 1 s.

There are systems with an individual energy reserve for each ignition loop as well as one for the monitoring circuit. In such systems, there is no loss of function for the rest of the ignition loops and the crash recorder if one loop gets short circuited in a crash and its energy reserve capacitor is discharged.

A step-up converter keeps the energy reserve(s) charged up to voltages nominally higher than battery voltage (e.g., $V_{ER} = 22$ V to $V_{ER} = 35$ V).

23.1.3 Single-Point Electronic Sensing Systems or Central Air Bag Systems

With single-point electronic sensing systems (or central air bag systems), the electronic control module is located in the passenger compartment. There are no external sensors in the crush zone. The electronic circuits include acceleration sensors, signal-processing algorithms, diagnostics, output stages, energy reserve, and voltage converter.

Historical Evolution.   Production of single-point sensing electronic air bag units started in 1980. This first concept used a strain gage acceleration sensor and a mercury switch as "arming" or "safing" sensor. The signal processing was performed by analog integration of the acceleration signal and resulted in a value related to velocity change during the impact, a so-called Δv-value.

If Δv exceeded a vehicle-specifically set threshold and the mercury switch was closed, then the restraining devices were triggered. The first systems comprised three electronic components: sensor, analog circuitry, and diagnostic unit; voltage converter unit; and energy reserve unit.

In the beginning of 1987, another analog integrating system went into production and consisted of two electronic components: sensor and diagnostic unit, and voltage converter and energy reserve unit. This was the first air bag sensor system based on using a piezoelectric accelerometer, and contained a microcontroller only for monitoring functions. Storage of fault codes, fault clock, and crash recorder in an EEPROM were included as well. The unit was designed for triggering the driver air bag, as well as the driver and passenger belt tensioners.

Mid-1987 marked the production start of the first air bag sensor unit with a digital single-point sensing algorithm. With this system, all the functions could be integrated into one box. Figure 23.3 shows a block diagram of this unit.

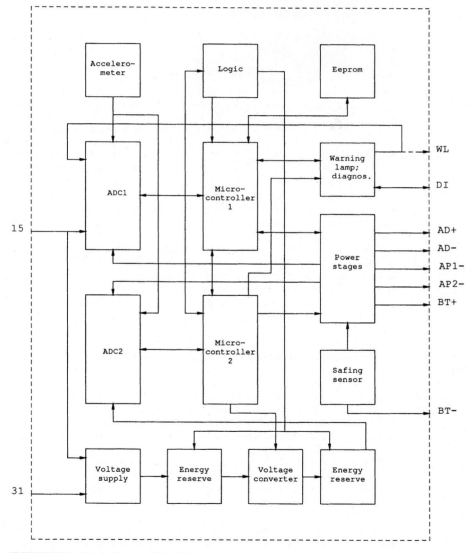

FIGURE 23.3 Block diagram AB 3-ECU.

20 mm

FIGURE 23.4   Piezoelectric accelerometer BSA 6.

For redundancy against inadvertent deployment, this unit was a two-microcontroller design (parallel processing) and contained a mercury switch as arming sensor. In 1989, this mercury switch was replaced by a reed switch.

Current Systems.   The key features of a single-point air bag electronic control unit (ECU) are the accelerometer, the digital single-point sensing algorithm, the degree of function availability, the safety against inadvertent release, and the degree of fault tolerance of the system.

Electronic Accelerometers.

Piezoelectric accelerometers.   Current accelerometers have been upgraded and are robust against electromagnetic interferences. Dual-channel accelerometers exist that deliver differential mode output signals and offer the possibility to design all-electronic air bag ECUs and remove the need for the untestable mechanical arming sensor. Inverse polarity of the sensor signals allows the unit to distinguish from common mode signals which can result from electrical disturbances. Figure 23.4 shows a dual-channel accelerometer.

Diagnosis of the electrical function of these sensors can be performed after initialization, and, thus, function reliability and system readiness are monitorable. Other piezoelectric accelerometers contain mechanically deflectable sensing elements, (e.g. by piezoelectric actuators), for verification of system integrity.

Micromachined accelerometers.   Micromachined accelerometers can be mounted directly on the printed circuit board. The required interface circuitry is included on the same chip with the monolithic capacitive accelerometer. High linearity is guaranteed by closed-loop operation. This means that the movable beam is always electrostatically centered by a feedback voltage proportional to deflection (= acceleration/deceleration). The measurement range is ± 50 g. For self-test, the functional beam is electrostatically deflected.

Single-point sensing algorithm.   Different types of digital crash-sensing algorithms are currently in use. The sampling rate of the acceleration signal varies between 0.5 and 1 ms.

Mathematical manipulation of the crash signal (differentiation, multiplication, integration) and release threshold variation by software allows an early discrimination of different impact types (frontal, oblique, offset, pole, underride). Furthermore, application of the appropriate prediction model for forward displacement and determination of the correct trigger point is possible.

Digital sensing algorithms increase the possibility both to detect problem crashes such as underrides with perceived damage, and to distinguish between deployment and nondeployment impacts. This shows a distinct improvement over hardwired analog integration systems. The digital approach allows the end of line programming of sensitivity parameters for different car models. Thus sensitivity parameters are programmed into the EEPROM of the microcontroller which allow the use of the same ROM-mask for different car types.

Electronic control modules.   Today, state-of-the-art ECUs use a one-channel acceleration sensor and an arming sensor in series to the output stages. Such units are a mix of electronic and mechanical control. The first *all-electronic* single-point sensing ECU went into production in mid-1992. This module incorporated a dual-channel electronic accelerometer and no mechanical safing switch. Figure 23.5 shows the block diagram of a state-of-the-art electronic control module.

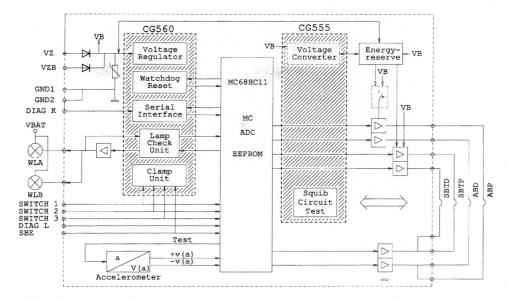

FIGURE 23.5   Block diagram AB6.3-ECU.

AC-firing.   Normally squibs are fired with a dc pulse (dc-firing). The first unit with ac-firing went into production in mid-1993. With ac-firing, there is a capacitor inside the squib connector in series to the squib. This capacitor is periodically charged up and discharged so that a firing is only possible with alternating current (ac-firing).

AC-firing was introduced because of faults occurring in the vehicle periphery (outside the ECU). Typical faults consist of short circuits in the air bag module (= squib + inflator + bag + cover) by metal (splinters), defects in the contact unit for the driver air bag (= clock spring), and short circuits in the harness. Igniters are very sensitive to short current pulses (3 A for 60 μs can be sufficient to fire the air bag).

The main benefit of ac-firing is an immunity to all short circuits to dc-vehicle voltages with and without the ECU, as well as immunity from inadvertent deployments with all types of static ECU defects. The danger of false triggering is reduced because the push-pull output stages can only fire if activated with the correct asynchronous sequence of pulses by the microcontroller. A microcontroller disturbance inadvertently producing such a pulse sequence is highly unlikely.

A disadvantage of the current ac-firing system is the more complex ignition loop diagnostics required in the ECU. These diagnostics have to monitor the resistance and capacitance in the loop.

23.1.4 Rollover Sensors

Convertibles can overturn in almost any direction (although a backward turnover around the lateral axis is not very likely). Thus a rollover sensor unit has to sense in practically every direction in the horizontal plane. The kind of sensing and the signal evaluation times are the differences between rollover and air bag sensor units. A rollover accident has to be detected within approximately 200 ms; the activation time of the mechanical protection device takes approximately 300 ms.

The following rollover sensing concepts are used. The first concept (URS = *Überrollsensor*) went into production in 1989: omnidirectional tilt switch in conjunction with rear-axle switches, and longitudinal and lateral accelerometers. These are the same ones as used for air bag ECUs.

The tilt switch consists of a rocker cylinder with a permanent magnet mounted on top. A Hall-IC placed in the lid of the switch senses the rocker cylinders position. The discrimination threshold can be adjusted to the desired angle (e.g., 22°).

Rear-axle switches open if one or both half-axles of the vehicle are completely unloaded. This means that a potential vehicle rollover is indicated by an airborne wheel.

The system cannot release the rollover protection device (e.g., the rollover bar) if the respective rear wheel cannot move any more because of a fender deformed during impact. To avoid this, and for redundancy purposes, the sensor unit also senses the acceleration in every horizontal direction. It contains a longitudinal and a lateral piezoelectric accelerometer whose signals are squared and added. Exceeding the release threshold of approximately 5 g causes activation of the rollover protection element(s) located behind the rear seats. This sensor also unlocks the central locking system after a vehicle rollover.

Rear-axle switches are one way to provide a redundant signal for the rollover indication. Another system (ÜRSS = *Überroll-Schutz-System*) is based on a combination of three "spirit level" sensors, optically evaluated by LEDs and photo transistor-light barriers, and a vertical gravitation switch consisting of a magnet, a spring, and a reed contact.

Two of the level sensors are mounted ±52° to the horizontal plane and sense overturning around the vehicle's longitudinal axis. They also close if an acceleration greater than 1.3 g is exceeded for more than 80 ms. The third-level sensor is inclined by 80° to the horizontal plane and senses overturning around the lateral axis in the forward direction. This sensor closes for an acceleration exceeding 5.7 g for more than 80 ms.

The reed contact in the vertical acceleration switch is closed after the vehicle loses ground contact, since it is no longer possible to sense gravity in the vehicle if it is airborne. Thus, a spring with a restoring force of approximately 10 percent of the magnet's normal weight is enough to move the magnet over the reed contact and cause its closure. The rollover protection is then activated after a delay of approximately 300 ms. This activation can be initiated either by one of the level sensors or by the vertical acceleration switch.

A release of the rollover protection equipment in the case of a backward turnover around the vehicle's lateral axis would require an additional fourth-level sensor in the sensor unit.

23.1.5 Tire Pressure Control Systems

Tires must have the correct pressure in order to provide expected driving performance like the transfer of high breaking or lateral adhesion forces to the road surface. They must have good aquaplaning properties, which also depend on the tire pressure. In addition to safety considerations, improved economy can be expected since low tire pressure generally increases rubber abrasion and fuel consumption.

Electronic tire pressure control systems alert the driver in case of pressure loss. Low pressure indication is performed using a reference pressure switch mounted in the rim which compares the tire pressure with the reference pressure in a box hermetically sealed by a high-grade steel diaphragm. A contact opens if tire pressure falls below the reference pressure. Temperature dependancy of the pressure switch is negligible since the temperature of tire air is practically identical to temperature of reference gas.

A high-frequency sensor mounted on the axle detects if the pressure switch is closed. At each pass, the closed pressure switch contact activates a serial resonance circuit by energy absorption out of the axle-mounted high-frequency transmitter. So, rotation can only be sensed if the tire pressure is high enough.

An ECU for each wheel compares transmitter signal with wheel rotation signal of a rotation sensor. As there is a defined relation between these signals, any discrepancy within a specified driving distance can be detected, and the driver warned.

23.2 PASSENGER CONVENIENCE SYSTEMS

23.2.1 Electromechanical Window Drives

There are three different systems currently in use.

Lift Mechanism System.   An electric gear motor drives a spur gear meshing in a gear segment. This segment acts on the window lift mechanism.

Flexible Cable System.   An electric gear motor drives a system of flexible cables to lift the window.

Stiff Cable System.   An electric gear motor is connected with the window via a tension and compression stiff cable. This cable is driven by a toothed wheel.

Window Lift Motors.   The limited space inside the door requires window lift motors with a flat design. The lift mechanism consists of a self-locking worm gear system, which keeps its position if not intentionally activated and which must resist trials to open the window by force. An elastic claw clutch provides good damping behavior.

Window Lift Controls.   Activation is performed using rocker switches.

Best driver comfort results from a combination of window drives and the central door-locking system. Here the windows are either automatically closed after leaving and locking the vehicle, or they are driven to a designated ventilating position. Such an automatic system requires the use of a driving force limiting or jamming protection. This protection must be effective during upward motion of the window within a range of 200 to 4 mm before the upper window stop.

Jamming force must not exceed 100 N, and the rise of force must remain less than 10 N/mm. Hall sensors monitor the rotation speed of the lift motors. If a speed decrease is detected, the rotation direction is immediately reversed. A complete window closure is enabled by turning off the jamming protection just before the window is driven into the door gasket. Thus, the motor can be driven just to blocking (if necessary). On this occasion, initialization of the window position is done.

An ECU for all window lifts can either be mounted centrally, or the electronic controls can be integrated into the window lift motors in order to save harness expense. Such drives would be preferable when used in conjunction with bus systems.

23.2.2 Electromechanical Sunroof Drives

State-of-the-art sunroof drives incorporate the functions of a lifting and sliding roof. Lifting or sliding motions are initiated by electronic or electromechanical controls. Electromechanical controls include mechanical interlocks of limit switches which allow the closed sunroof to be opened or lifted. Reversing the polarity of the drive motor lowers or closes an opened or lifted sunroof. In case the sunroof control is connected to a central locking system, then an electronic unit with jamming protection would be advantageous.

Additional functions such as preselectable position control, closing if demanded by a rain detector, and data bus connection can be realized with low extra expense.

The permanent magnet drive motor has a rated output of approximately 40 W and is coupled to a worm gear unit. Sunroof motors have a thermal overload protection implemented by thermal circuit breakers. The sunroof is moved either by flexible cable drives or by contraction/tension-stiff cables. It must be possible to close the sunroof using simple on-board tools in case there is a failure of the electrical system.

23.2.3 Electromechanical Seat and Steering Wheel Adjustment

Electrically adjustable seats are especially well suited for vehicles frequently driven by different persons of various size. After each driver change, the seat can be adjusted to best fit the new driver's requirements.

Up to five motors per front seat allow the following position changes: height adjustment of front edge of seat plane, height adjustment of rear edge of seat plane, longitudinal adjustment of seat, tilt adjustment of back rest, and height adjustment of headrest. Electric motors drive gear units via flexible shafts for longitudinal and vertical adjustments of the seat.

There are seat adjustment controls currently on the market with programmable non-volatile memories, allowing a readjustment of the seat to positions stored in the EEPROM. Adjustments of the external mirror and the height of the seat belt guide can be programmed as well, according to individual demands. Furthermore, seating comfort in passenger cars is improved using electromechanically adjustable steering columns and tiltable steering wheels. The adjustment is performed via a self-locking gear unit with an electric motor and is integrated directly into the steering column. Adjustment can be achieved by manual activation of a position switch, or by connection to the programmable seat memory unit.

23.2.4 Central Locking Systems

Central locking of the doors, trunk lid, and tank cap is done either by pneumatic or electromotor driven actuators.

With the pneumatic system a bipressure pump provides the over- and underpressure to the system. To achieve this, the pump is driven by an electromotor in both rotation directions. The system can be operated from different locations: central position switch, driver door lock, passenger door lock, and trunk lid lock.

All-electric motor-driven central locking systems are based on the same concept. A small electric motor with reduction gear drives to position a bar for closing or opening the lock.

In case of power loss, it must be possible to open the doors with the mechanical key or with the internal door handle. On central locking systems with integrated theft alarm, opening is only possible with the mechanical vehicle key.

There are central locking systems which can be operated by ultrasonic remote control. These systems offer keyless closure or entry and thus high operational comfort.

23.2.5 Reverse Parking Warner

The system consists of an ECU, LCD, and sensors. It is equipped with ultrasonic transmitter/receiver sensors using the echo depth sounder method. Bursts of ultrasonic waves at approximately 30 kHz are transmitted for 30 ms. The travel time of the first echo signal gives information about the distance to the obstacle.

Upon shifting into the rear gear, the system is activated and completes a self-check by turning on all display characters for a specified short time period and checking the ultrasonic sensors. A space up to 0 to 160 cm behind the vehicle is observed and divided into different warning sectors. The most critical distance is an obstacle within 30 cm. In this case, the optical display flashes and the acoustical warner gives a permanent signal.

23.2.6 Emergency Light Flasher

An ECU turns on the blinking lights. Synchronous flashing of all blinkers of a vehicle must be possible with the ignition turned on or off. A specific control lamp to indicate the status of the emergency light flashers must be included inside the vehicle. Usually this lamp is integrated into the on/off switch.

GLOSSARY

Accelerometer   Inertial deflection of this sensing element results in an electric signal proportional to acceleration or deceleration of the vehicle.

Airbag   Gas-filled cushion for impact energy absorption of vehicle occupants during a crash.

Allowable forward displacement   Forward displacement of the occupant which is allowed before the restraining device has reached its full protection capability.

Arming sensor   An electromechanical acceleration switch integrated in the electronic control unit located inside the passenger compartment. Activation of the restraining device is only possible if the arming sensor completes the triggering circuit.

EEPROM   Electrically erasable and programmable read only memory.

Energy reserve   Backup power supply for the restraining system in case of battery loss.

Forward displacement   Forward travel of the occupant during a crash which occurs until there is contact with the restraining device or vehicle interior.

Hall IC   Integrated circuit containing a Hall sensor plus appropriate evaluation circuitry. The Hall sensor delivers an electric voltage proportional to the magnetic field strength by which it is affected.

Igniter   Electrically activated initiation element for firing of an inflator.

Inflator   Gas-producing unit for air bag inflation or activation of seat belt tensioner.

Piezoelectric   Materials, e.g., special ceramics, which have the capability to convert mechanical deformation into electric signals (voltage and/or charge) and vice versa, are known as piezoelectric materials.

RAM   Random access memory.

Reed contact   Mechanical, magnetic-field-sensitive switch, hermetically sealed inside a glass tube.

Restraining device   Air bag, seat belt, and seat belt tensioner.

ROM   Read only memory.

Safing sensor   Another expression for arming sensor.

Seat belt tensioner   Pyrotechnically or spring-activated device to tighten the seat belt during a crash.

Squib   Electrically activated initiation element for firing an inflator (another expression for igniter).

Voltage converter   Electronic device to keep the energy reserve charged up to a voltage normally higher than battery voltage.

Watchdog   Electronic circuit for checking the correct flow of the microcontroller program.

BIBLIOGRAPHY

Analog Devices Specifications for "Monolithic accelerometer with signal conditioning ADXL50,*" edition C1808-20-6/93. (*Patent pending.)
Bosch Automotive Handbook, 2d ed., 1986.

"Bosch Kraftfahrtechnisches Taschenbuch," 21. Auflage, July 31, 1991. Bosch internal design documentation of electronic control units for restraint systems.

Handout of lecture "Der BMW-Überrollsensor (ÜRSS)," given by M. Jost on 13. Conference "Elektronik im Kraftfahrzeug," Haus der Technik, Essen, Germany, June 15–16, 1993.

ABOUT THE AUTHOR

Bernhard Mattes has been employed with Robert Bosch GmbH since he was graduated from the Technical University of Stuttgart, Germany, as a Diplom-Ingenieur in 1968. He began work at Bosch as an electrical engineer in an automotive electronics design department and has been a section manager since 1984. His working fields at Bosch have included electronic gear box controls, cruise controls, crash-sensing systems for front and side impacts, sensing systems for rollovers, accelerometer and safing sensor development, and tilt and rotation sensor development.

CHAPTER 24
ANTITHEFT SYSTEMS

Shinichi Kato
Manager, Electronics Design Section No. 2
Nissan Motor Co., Ltd.

24.1   VEHICLE THEFT CIRCUMSTANCES

24.1.1   Vehicle Theft in the United States

In the United States, the number of thefts from vehicles exceeds the number of actual vehicles stolen. A much larger profile is given to stolen cars, however, because of the economic losses suffered by car owners and the tie-in with stolen cars and drug abuse and other crimes.

The number of vehicle thefts in the United States has increased continuously to a 1991 level of approximately 1.7 million. The ease with which thefts can be carried out, the light punishments given to car thieves, and the ready availability of car theft tools and information on how to use them, has led to a systematic network of organized car crimes and the establishment of black markets for both stolen cars and parts.

24.1.2   Vehicle Theft in Europe

By 1992, the number of vehicle thefts in France, Germany, and the United Kingdom totaled 1.08 million, a radical 64 percent increase since 1988. The breakdown of communism in eastern Europe, adding to the existing black market for vehicles and spare parts, the trend toward joyriding in stolen vehicles, and other social problems similar to those in the United States, have all been contributing factors in the increase.

24.1.3   Vehicle Theft Worldwide

The United Kingdom has the largest incidence of vehicle theft followed in order by Australia, Sweden, the United States, and France.

24.1.4   Reasons for Vehicle Theft

The reasons for vehicle theft vary from country to country and between different areas of the same country. In the United Kingdom and Australia, for example, joyriding is the cause of most auto thefts. In the United States, on the other hand, the theft of vehicle contents ranks highest.

24.1.5   Methods of Entry

In the United States, "slim-jims" or similar devices to unlock car doors and gain entry are the most popular among car thieves. Vehicle contents can then be removed or the steering lock broken and the vehicle hot-wired and driven away. The use of roughly ground ceramic has recently gained popularity over traditional methods of breaking windows such as hammers or spring-punches because of ceramic's ease of use and lack of noise when used.

With the advent of keyless entry systems, devices to "steal" the code while the driver operates the keyfob and transmit it back when the thief chooses, have been developed and readily available to the aspiring thief.

24.2   OVERVIEW OF ANTITHEFT REGULATIONS

The total cost to the public of vehicle thefts in the United States alone is estimated at $8.3 billion per year, taking into account the vehicle and insurance losses and the expense of police time. Due to these economic pressures and spiraling vehicle-theft-related crime, regulations are now being introduced to help protect the vehicle-buying public and insurance companies.

24.2.1   Vehicle Security Regulations in the United States

Three types of vehicle security regulations exist in the United States:

- The vehicle must be fitted with an audible warning that operates when the ignition key remains in the ignition and the driver's door is opened.
- As vehicle theft is not consistent among vehicle types and different areas of the country, 11 states (Florida, Illinois, Kentucky, Massachusetts, Michigan, New York, New Jersey, Pennsylvania, Rhode Island, Texas, and Washington) have introduced regulations to deduct 5 to 15 percent from insurance premiums if vehicles are equipped with certain antitheft systems.
- The Vehicle Theft Act (1986) makes it mandatory for vehicles with a particular theft rating or above to have specified parts of the vehicle clearly marked.

Although this places a cost burden on car makers, they do not need to mark parts on vehicles they equip with antitheft systems approved by the National Highway Traffic and Safety Administration.

24.2.2   Vehicle Safety Regulations in Europe

The United Kingdom.   In an attempt to improve vehicle security, insurance companies in Europe define the effectiveness of individual antitheft systems. For example, in the United Kingdom, Thatcham (a survey division of the Association of British Insurers) classifies all vehicles with regard to their antitheft worthiness. This is done on a points basis, with points awarded as shown in Fig. 24.1.

Effective in 1994, Thatcham criteria indicate that the two most important attributes of a vehicle security system are a two-way mobilizer to prevent theft of the vehicle and interior sensors to deter unauthorized entry and theft from the vehicle. Any vehicle judged to have adequate antitheft devices gets significant savings on insurance premiums, thereby offering a powerful incentive to car buyers.

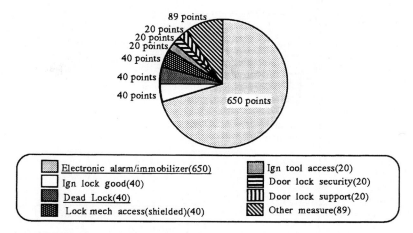

89 points
20 points
20 points
20 points
40 points
40 points
40 points
650 points

Electronic alarm/immobilizer(650)
Ign lock good(40)
Dead Lock(40)
Lock mech access(shielded)(40)
Ign tool access(20)
Door lock security(20)
Door lock support(20)
Other measure(89)

FIGURE 24.1   United Kingdom's Thatcham point system, which assigns points to various antitheft devices.

Germany.   In Germany, the country's largest vehicle insurer is Allianz. It announced the policy detailed in Table 24.1 whereby heavy financial penalties are introduced to encourage car owners to ensure that their vehicles meet security standards. These penalties exist in the form of 10 percent premium increases and only 90 percent repayments from insurers in the case of a stolen vehicle that has no antitheft systems. As in the United Kingdom, the application of antitheft systems is likely to spread as more customers demand more secure vehicles from car makers.

TABLE 24.1   Allianz Insurance Company Antitheft Policy

Timing	Scope	Antitheft system	Impact noncompliance
07/01/93	Vehicle to be fitted with aftermarket system	Immobilizer step 1: interrupt at least 3 systems • Starter circuit • Fuel supply • Ignition system • Other system	In case of theft claim, customer only gets back 90 percent of car value
01/01/95	Standard fitment for all new registrations	Immobilizer step 2: engine management operation (electronic code)	↑

24.3   A BASIC ANTITHEFT SYSTEM

A basic antitheft system, Fig. 24.2, must do three things: sense unauthorized entry into the vehicle or unauthorized movement of the vehicle, detect unauthorized attempts to start the vehicle or to disarm the alarm system, and upon detecting any unauthorized act actuate an

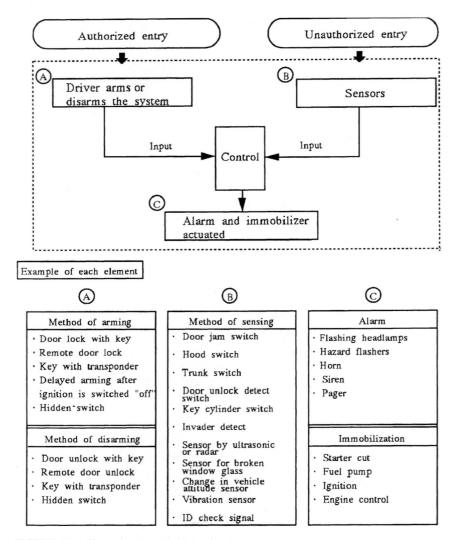

FIGURE 24.2   The basic structure of an antitheft system.

alarm and inhibit the vehicle from starting. Many vehicles now include visual indication in the form of stickers or flashing lights to indicate that they are equipped with an antitheft system.

Antitheft systems use active and passive arming systems. In an active system, the driver can arm the system with an ultrasonic or infrared keyfob or by throwing a hidden switch. In a passive arming system, operating the door key switch automatically arms the system when the driver leaves the vehicle. Insurers in the United States feel that the passive system is more effective and, consequently, give a larger insurance premium deduction for vehicles equipped with such systems. Two thirds of all vehicle security systems are passive, while almost all factory fit systems fall into this category.

24.3.1 Unauthorized Entry Detection

A tamper switch detects any abnormal forces applied to the door and trunk lock key cylinders, while make-break switches sense opening of all apertures. Ultrasonic beams inside the vehicle can detect the vibration from broken glass or movement within the car. The trigger level of these units is particularly sensitive, because too low a level can lead to false alarms.

24.3.2 Alarm and Immobilization

Alarm activation is indicated by the sounding of the car horn or siren combined with the flashing of the vehicle's headlights and taillights. A recent innovation has been the application of radio paging systems to indicate stolen vehicles. The vehicle is also immobilized by causing an interrupt in circuits vital to vehicle operation such as the starter motor, fuel pump, and ignition systems.

24.3.3 A Typical System Example

The following explanation relates to one of the more popular vehicle alarm configurations shown in Figs. 24.3 and Fig. 24.4. Abnormal conditions or unauthorized entries are detected as inputs from door, hood, and trunk switches, ignition switch, and ultrasonic sensors. When any of these conditions occurs, the horn sounds and the vehicle's lights flash for a predetermined period (usually one to three minutes).

A circuit example using a custom integrated circuit is shown in Fig. 24.4. A flow chart of the system operation is shown in Fig. 24.5.

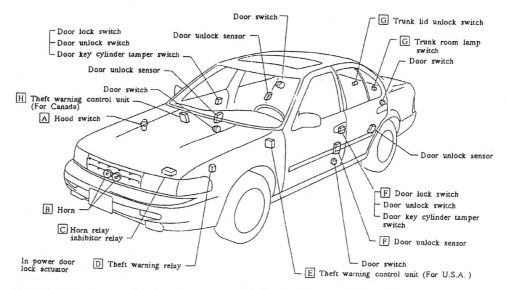

FIGURE 24.3 Component parts and harness connector location for an antitheft warning system.

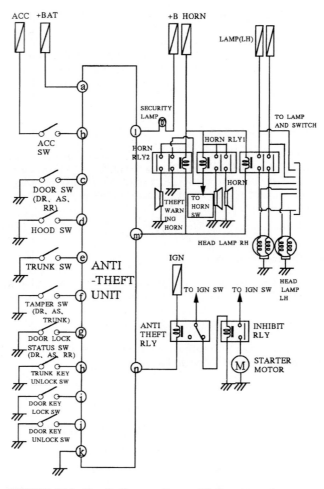

FIGURE 24.4 Circuit diagram of an antitheft system using a custom IC.

24.3.4 Immobilizer

Because of the frequency of false alarms activated by oversensitive invasion sensors, vehicles with alarms sounding are increasingly being ignored by people in the vicinity. Therefore, as a deterrent to vehicle theft, unauthorized entry detection systems alone are no longer considered effective by insurance companies. They prefer—and reduce premium reductions accordingly—to have, in addition, an immobilizer to electrically or mechanically disable the vehicle unless it is correctly disarmed.

Now that most vehicles are equipped with electronic engine control units, car makers feel that they provide the best means for immobilization. This is accomplished with three basic driver interfaces for arming and disarming (Fig. 24.6):

- An ID code input to the ECU by means of a keyboard, which may be separate or combined with another electronic dashboard device such as the radio

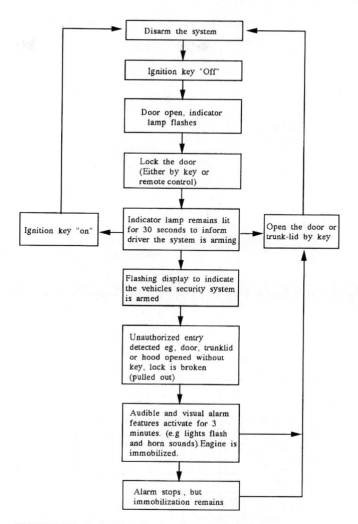

FIGURE 24.5   A flowchart for the system shown in Fig. 24.4.

- An ID signal transmitted by a keyfob to a receiver and decoding unit in the vehicle
- An ID signal received from a transponder built into the ignition key

The transponder built into the ignition key is the most recent innovation (Fig. 24.7). The ignition key contains a transponder device. A reader unit is installed in the vehicle close to the ignition key cylinder. A "power pulse" is transmitted by the reader's antenna shortly after the ignition key is inserted into the lock. This power pulse is received as energy by the transponder and stored in a capacitor. The power is then used to transmit an ID code signal back to the reader. The reader identifies the received signal as authorized or not and, if authorized, enables the ECU to start the vehicle.

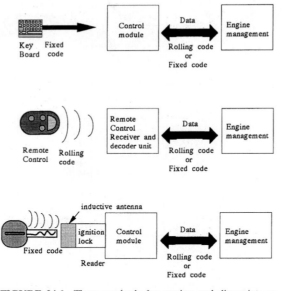

FIGURE 24.6 Three methods for arming and disarming an antitheft system.

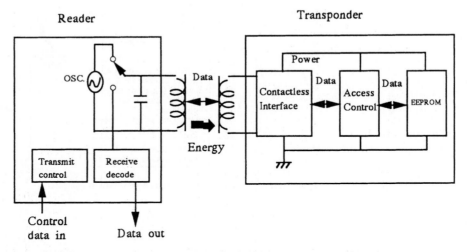

FIGURE 24.7 A block diagram of a typical antitheft system incorporating a transponder built into the ignition key and a reader unit installed near the ignition key cylinder.

ABOUT THE AUTHOR

Shinichi Kato was graduated from Tokyo Institute of Technology in 1973 and joined Nissan Motors Co. Ltd. that same year in charge of electric parts design. He was sent to Nissan Research and Development in Michigan in 1988, where he was in charge of the Ford and Nissan joint project as an electrical design engineer. He returned to Japan in 1992 as the manager of Nissan's electrical design department.

CHAPTER 25
ENTERTAINMENT PRODUCTS

Tom Chrapkiewicz
Philips Semiconductors

25.1 FUNDAMENTALS OF AUDIO SYSTEMS

The purpose of an automotive audio system is to present a realistic illusion of a musical event. While this chapter is concerned primarily with automotive audio systems, it is appropriate to cover some of the basics of audio systems and the human auditory system.

25.1.1 Characteristics of Sound

Sound has a dual nature: it may be considered a physical disturbance in a medium such as air, or it may be considered a psychophysical perception resulting from nerve impulses stimulating the acoustic cortex of the brain. In audio, we are vitally concerned with both. The ear itself determines the quality of sound signals, but the sound is carried to the ear through physical stimuli. Acoustics is the branch of physics that deals with this transmission of sound in a medium to the ear. The complex relationship process that relates stimulus and sensation is the field of psychoacoustics.

Basic Acoustics[1]. For sound to be transmitted from one place to another, a medium is required that has elasticity and inertia. Air has these characteristics, as do other materials such as water, steel, wood, etc. When an air particle is moved by something vibrating, it moves, passing on momentum to adjoining particles as it strikes them. The original air particle is then pulled back toward its equilibrium position by elastic forces residing in the air. Any particular air particle vibrates about its equilibrium position, receives momentum from collisions, and passes momentum on to other particles, which pass it on to others, and so on. Consider a wave traveling through a pond of water. The wave progresses through the water, but each individual water molecule remains at (relatively) the same location. The actual transmission of sound through a medium is a type of longitudinal wave propagation.

The velocity at which an acoustic wave moves through a medium is dependent on that medium. The velocity of sound in air at standard temperature and pressure is approximately 344 m/s. This is considerably slower than the speed of light (3×10^8 m/s). Table 25.1 gives the velocity of sound in different media.

Any audible sound is of an alternating character with a characteristic frequency and amplitude. As this sound moves through the air, it has a particular wavelength, determined by its frequency and propagation velocity. The wavelength is calculated as:

TABLE 25.1   The Speed of Sound in Various Media

Media	Speed of sound, m/s	Speed of sound, ft/s
Air, 21 °C	344	1,129
Fresh water	1,480	4,856
Salt water, 21 °C, 3.5% salinity	1,520	4,987
Plexiglass	1,800	5,906
Wood, soft	3,350	10,991
Fir timber	3,800	12,467
Concrete	3,400	11,155
Mild steel	5,050	16,568
Aluminum	5,150	16,896
Glass	5,200	17,060
Gypsum board	6,800	22,310

$$\lambda = \frac{c}{f}$$

Thus, a sound with a frequency of 1000 Hz has a wavelength of about 0.344 m.

25.1.2   Characteristics of Audible Sound

Amplitude Range of Sound.   Obviously, sounds can be very loud or very quiet. Since the range of levels of sound is so large, a logarithmic scale is used. The unit of this measurement level is the Bel (named after Alexander Graham Bell). The threshold of hearing is about 20×10^{-6} Pa (1 Pascal = 1 Newton per square meter). The threshold of pain is over 100 Pa. This represents a ratio of over 5 million. In logarithmic terms, this ratio of 5 million is log (p1/p2) or about 6.7. Since one Bel represents a rather large difference, the decibel (or one-tenth of a Bel) is usually used. So, a ratio in decibels (or dB) is $10 \times$ log (p1/p2). Also, since the square of sound pressure is proportional to acoustic power, we use $20 \times$ log (p1/p2). Thus, the *dynamic range,* as it's called, of the human auditory system is: $20 \times$ log ($100/20 \times 10^{-6}$) or about 134 dB.

Frequency Range of Sound.   As mentioned, any sound has a characteristic frequency. The average range of the human auditory system is from 20 Hz to 20 kHz. This represents a wavelength range of 1.72 cm at 20 kHz to 17.2 m at 20 Hz. A particular sound does not consist of all frequencies within this range, but only one or (usually) several frequencies (recall Fourier). Also, the human auditory system does not respond equally to all frequencies. The human auditory system is most sensitive at about 3 kHz. Some well-known frequency ranges are detailed in Fig. 25.1.

25.1.3   Basic Psychoacoustics[2]

The Human Hearing System.   The human ear is commonly considered to have three parts: the outer, middle, and inner ear.[2,3] The sound is gathered and modified by the pinna, directed down the auditory canal, and terminates in the tympanic membrane (eardrum). The ear canal is about 0.7 cm in diameter and about 3 cm long. Notice that a quarter-wavelength of a wave 3 cm long is 2870 Hz, which is near the frequency at which the human auditory system is most sensitive. The other side of the tympanic membrane faces the middle ear. The middle ear is filled with air, and air pressure equalization takes place through the Eustachian tube opening into the pharynx (throat) so that static pressure is the same on both sides of the eardrum.

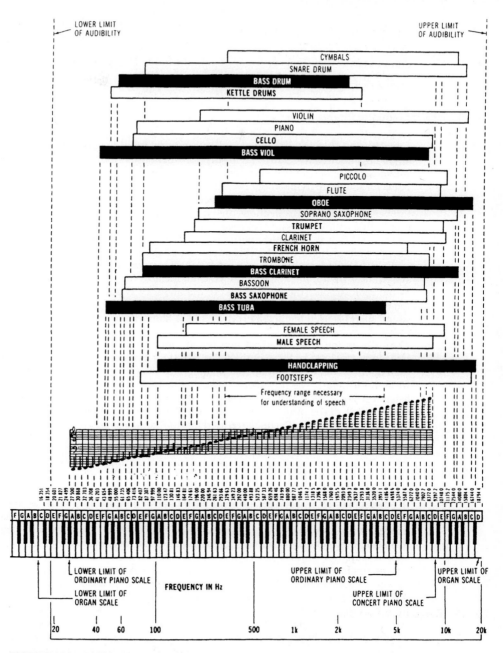

FIGURE 25.1   Audible frequency detail.

Fastened to the tympanic membrane is one of the ossicles. The three bones of the ossicles form a lever, the end of which excites the oval window of the cochlea. The cochlea is filled with an incompressible liquid which carries the sound waves. The cochlea is lined with hair cells (about 25,000) that send nerve impulses to the brain. The cochlea is basically a mechanical-to-electric transducer.

25.1.4 Psychoacoustic Phenomena

Localization.   In localizing a sound, our ear and brain mechanism utilizes several types of angle-dependent data. Due to air absorption, there are the amplitude differences between the sounds arriving at the two ears. Since our ears are 8 or 9 inches apart, there is a time delay between sounds arriving at the two ears.

There are also differences in the spectrum of the sound entering the two ears. These differences are caused by reflections on the pinna and head diffraction. It has long been believed that both ears are necessary for localization, but more recent studies have shown that listeners can be trained to localize with only one ear.[4] Ear canal measurements have shown frequency nulls around 8.2 kHz. This implies a reflected wave with a delay of about 61 μs. In an audio system with multiple loudspeakers, the ear senses multiple sound sources. The auditory system uses the timing and spectral clues to localize the apparent sound sources. In addition to the real sources (the loudspeakers), the auditory system creates virtual sources between the real sources. This effect is known as imaging. The image (sometimes also referred to as the sound stage) is used by media producers to enhance the aural experience of the listener.

Echo Perception.   As noted previously, time delays of less than hundreds of microseconds are utilized as localization clues in the hearing system. For delays much greater than this, but less than about 50 ms, the auditory system integrates the energy, and perceives a fuller sound than without the delays. The precedence effect refers to the fact that if a delayed signal reaches the listener from a different direction within 50 ms of the first, the apparent sound source is still in the direction of the original signal. For delays greater than 50 ms, the listener perceives a discrete echo. Additions of echoes are used in room or hall simulation (see Sec. 25.4.2).

25.2   A BRIEF HISTORY OF AUTOMOTIVE ENTERTAINMENT

It is most curious that the gestation of both radio broadcasting and the automobile occurred almost simultaneously. In 1885, Karl Benz produced the first automobile at Mannheim, Germany. It was powered by a spark-ignited gasoline engine. In 1886, Professor Heinrich Hertz of Karlsrule Polytechnic in Germany demonstrated the transmission of electromagnetic energy from a spark.

The first automotive entertainment system was installed in 1926. William M. Heina filed a patent Sept. 16, 1926, for a "Portable Radio Apparatus." It was issued as patent #1,626,464 on April 26, 1947. The patent made no revolutionary claims, but it served as a model for many future installations. Unsubstantiated reports indicate that Radio Auto Distributors and All American Mohawk had offered automotive radios in 1926.[5] Many milestones in radio broadcasting had already occurred. In 1910, spark-gap transmission tests of the Chalmers-Detroit Motor Car Company and the 1915 experiments of DeForest and Sarnoff led to the first broadcasts of the Detroit Station 8MK (later to become WWJ) on Aug. 20, 1920, and the broadcasts of KDKA on Nov. 2, 1920 (earlier known as 8XK).

The radio circuits of the day were based on vacuum-tube designs and consequently required high voltages and power consumption. By 1931, the dynamic loudspeaker (which was pioneered by Magnavox in 1928) was installed in automobiles. (This is the fundamentally the same type of loudspeaker used today) This offered quite an advantage, since earlier electrodynamic loudspeakers had quiescent current consumption of about 1 A. Tremendous growth had occurred leading to 1930. By that time many manufacturers of automotive radios were in existence: Automatic Radio Manufacturing Company, United American Bosch Corporation, Carteret Radio Laboratories, Inc., Crosley Radio Corporation, Charles Hoodwin Co., Galvin Mfg. Corporation (later to become Motorola), National Company, Philco-Transitone, Pilot Radio & Tube Corporation, Sparks-Withington Company, and The United States Radio & Television Corporation.

The predominant medium of transmission to the automobile was via the AM band. While FM had been in existence since 1940, it was not until 1957 that the first FM radios were installed in automobiles. The year 1966 gave us the first OEM installation of 8-track tape players after a joint effort among Ford Motor, Lear Manufacturing, Motorola, and RCA. This was the medium of choice through the early 1970s, only to be replaced by the more rugged compact cassette (see Sec. 25.3.1 on Media). There were other short-lived intermediate media such as vinyl records and other obscure tape cartridges. Their life and breadth of application were very limited, although they paved the way for the media of today. Modern media such as the compact disk have limited installation rates. The medium provides superior performance, yet is not nearly as popular as cassette installations. The near-future of media may rest with the digital compact cassette (DCC) or the MiniDisc (MD).

25.3 CONTEMPORARY AUDIO SYSTEMS

An audio system could more correctly be called a high-fidelity sound reproduction system. The goal of any audio system, be it in an automobile, home, or movie theater, is to reproduce an actual or intended acoustic event. Most commercially available recordings (cassette, compact disc, or LP record) are recordings of actual acoustic events—that is, all performers performing together interacting with each other. Modern multitrack recording technology, however, has removed this restriction from the artists. The intended or virtual event that is captured may have never really occurred; it may be an imaginary event in the mind of the producer. A duet may be performed with the singers separated by many miles and even years.[6] Modern digital signal-processing (DSP) technology has allowed the artist to create not only virtual events such as this, but also virtual performers that have not ever performed a piece.[7]

The first audio system was invented by Thomas Edison between August and December 1877.[8, 9] This hand-cranked system consisted of a grooved metal cylinder, a mouthpiece, and tin foil as the recording medium. The indentations in the foil cylinder were an analog reproduction of the sound waves impressed on the foil. These analog indentations were of a vertical or "hill-and-dale" nature. By 1896, Emile Berliner developed the disc recording system, in which the sound was stored on a flat disc as lateral grooves in the surface of the disc. This basic method has remained in use to this day (1994) on records otherwise known as LPs (although LPs are increasingly difficult to find). By 1926, the recording and playback of these discs had been transformed from a strictly acoustical system to an electrical system. In 1931, Alan Blumlein of Columbia Laboratories conducted experiments in stereo reproduction of sound (from the Greek *stereos,* meaning solid). These systems required two information channels and early attempts to do this on a disc failed. By 1957, commercially available stereo records became available. These had the two channels of information stored in the two walls of a single groove. It was not until the 1970s that stereo records became universal and the older, monaural records were no longer produced. During this same time period, the system of magnetic tape for audio storage was being developed, first in Germany in the 1940s and imported to the United States by the Ampex Corporation. This system stores one or more channels of information in analog form on an oxide- or metal-coated plastic tape. This system is still in use today in the form of the analog cassette (originally called the compact cassette). The compact cassette was developed in the late 1960s by Philips Corporation for use in dictation equipment and was shortly thereafter adapted to audio system usage. In the late 1970s, Philips and Sony Corporation began development of the compact disc system. This was the first consumer system to use a digital storage medium. The information is stored in digital form using an optical medium. By the late 1980s, the compact disc was the dominant format in dollar sales. In the early 1990s, there were several competing digital audio recording formats [digital audio tape (DAT), digital compact cassette (DCC), and recordable minicompact disc) for the home, although it is not yet clear which one will dominate the market.

A typical audio system controls a stereo signal which is obtained from any medium such as a radio broadcast tuner (AM, FM, etc.), turntable (record player), cassette tape, or compact disc. These media contain two discrete channels (left and right) of sound. Ideally, there is an infinite amount of separation between these two channels, but the human auditory system cannot distinguish separation beyond about 25 dB. In actual recordings, the information contained in these two channels is usually very similar, but different depending on the tastes of the musician and producer. The differences in the two channels is what gives recordings vastly different spatial characteristics.

Typically, these two channels are first processed by the volume, tone, and balance controls and are ultimately transformed to an acoustic signal at the loudspeakers. The analog signal levels in a modern audio system are about −10 dBu (where 0 dBu is 0.775 V), or about 0.3 V RMS with very little current capability (on the order of milliamperes). This is what is commonly referred to as a *line-level* signal. After the power amplifier stage, the signal is at a level of about 1 to 50 V with a current capability of up to 10 A. Recall that these analog signals have a 20-Hz to 20-kHz bandwidth and a 90-dB dynamic range. Digital signals in a consumer audio system (while currently rare but gaining popularity), are about 0.5 V peak-to-peak, requiring a bandwidth of about 4 megabits per second.

25.3.1   Media

AM and AM Stereo.   Amplitude modulation is defined as the process of changing the amplitude of a high-frequency carrier in accordance with the amplitude of the signal to be transmitted. Commercial AM broadcasting in the United States is within the carrier band of 530 to 1600 kHz. When there is no signal to be transmitted, the carrier is of a constant frequency and amplitude. When an audio signal is to be transmitted, the amplitude of the carrier is modulated in accordance with the amplitude of the audio signal. Within the 530- to 1600-kHz band, each AM station is spaced 10 kHz apart. This allows for a maximum audio frequency of about 10 kHz to be transmitted. Thus, the AM media is limited to a maximum transmitted signal frequency of 10 kHz and a dynamic range of about 40 dB. Primary markets for AM are news, talk radio, sports, and limited music broadcasts. The nature of the AM system allows for easy corruption of the amplitude envelope from atmospheric noise, electromagnetic interference, and lightning.[10]

Experimentation as early as the 1950s and 1960s by Philco and CBS proposed AM stereo broadcasting.[11] These systems were not compatible with existing monaural systems and were consequently rejected by the Federal Communications Commission (FCC). By the late 1970s, several competing and compatible AM stereo systems were proposed. The most notable competitors were Harris, Motorola, and Kahn. The system that is in widespread use today is the Motorola C-Quam® System.[11]

FM and FM Multiplex Stereo.   Frequency modulation is defined as the process of changing the frequency of a high-frequency carrier in accordance with the amplitude of the signal to be transmitted. Commercial FM broadcasting in the United States is within the carrier band of 88 to 108 MHz. When there is no signal to be transmitted, the carrier is of a constant frequency and amplitude. When an audio signal is transmitted, the frequency of the carrier is modulated in accordance with the amplitude of the audio signal. Notice that the amplitude of the transmitted modulated carrier is of a constant amplitude at all times. See Fig. 25.2 for an example of a typical signal and the resultant carrier in an FM system. Within the 88- to 108-MHz band, each FM station is spaced 200 kHz apart. This allows for a maximum audio frequency of about 15 kHz to be transmitted. Thus, the FM medium is limited to a maximum transmitted signal frequency of 15 kHz. Primary markets for FM have been music. The nature of the FM system provides for a very robust noise-free transmission, since any amplitude irregularities of the received signal can be ignored. Any interference which may cause amplitude irregularities can therefore be eliminated.

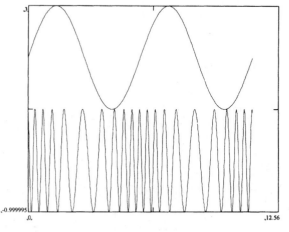

FIGURE 25.2   Signal and FM modulated carrier.

The Frequency Modulation Multiplex (FM MPX) system was developed in the early 1960s as an extension of the existing FM system. Channel-spacing is maintained at 200-kHz increments. A sum signal, the sum of the left and right channels (L + R), is frequency modulated on the carrier frequency exactly as in the monaural system. A 19-kHz pilot at 10 percent modulation level indicates the presence of a stereo signal. A difference signal (L-R) is modulated about a suppressed subcarrier of 38 kHz. The FM stereo tuner circuit demodulates and decodes these signals and outputs the left and right audio signals for further audio processing. The audio signals are limited to a 15-kHz bandwidth and a dynamic range of greater than 60 dB.[12]

FM Reception Difficulties.   Due to the relatively high carrier frequency, FM broadcast reception is less susceptible to the interference and poor reception of AM systems. However, FM reception can be limited by signal cancellation which is commonly called multipath distortion.[13–15] Multipath distortion is the loss of FM signal encountered when a direct and reflected signal simultaneously arrive at the receiver out of phase and cancel, resulting in a loss of signal. Since in an automotive receiver, the receiver is constantly moving through these null zones, the familiar spitting sound results. A method for compensating for these signal losses is what is called a diversity antenna system. This is a system of two or more antennas in extreme locations on the vehicle. Since the antennas will be more than one half-wavelength apart, at least one of them will not be in a null zone. The tuner then monitors the signal content at all antennas and switches to the antenna with the best signal. Antenna switching can be accomplished in less than 30 μs of detecting multipath interference. To eliminate antenna switching noise, the switching can be synchronized with the zero crossings of the audio signal.[14–18]

The second most common FM reception problem is ignition noise.[13, 14] This problem continues to increase as automotive ignition systems become increasingly complex. This problem is exacerbated by the fact that conventional methods of eliminating high-frequency radiation, such as resistance wires and grounding straps, do not eliminate the problems in the FM frequency band.

The circuit that detects and eliminates ignition noise is known by several different names: electronic ignition suppression (EIS), interference absorption circuit (IAC), and noise blanker (NB). Strategies for detecting ignition noise pulses vary greatly among manufacturers. The noise-blanking system may momentarily mute the audio signal or perform some type of piecewise linear approximation to the signal being repaired.

Analog Cassette.   The analog compact cassette (commonly known today as the cassette) is based on conventional multiple-track stereo analog magnetic recording technology.[14, 19] The cassette as we know it today was developed in 1963 by Philips Corporation primarily as a dictation medium. Advances in magnetic tape formulations and the advent of the Dolby™ B Type Noise Reduction System transformed the cassette into a high-fidelity music storage medium. Modern cassette players can achieve a dynamic range of over 70 dB and a frequency response approaching 20 kHz. Through the early 1990s, the cassette continued to be the largest revenue-producing medium for prerecorded music. More recent advances such as improved noise reduction systems and improved tape formulations are continuing to extend the life of this robust magnetic medium. As a result of its maturity and ruggedness, the cassette continues to be the most popular music carrier for automotive applications.

Compact Disc.   The fundamental technology that led to the development of the compact disc[14] began in the 1970s at Philips Laboratories. The compact disc format as it exists today was code-veloped in 1980 by Philips Corporation and Sony Corporation. The basic system is an optical, noncontact system, which is also used for video (laser disc), information storage (CD-ROM), interactive media (CD-I), photo storage (Photo-CD), and other applications (CD-V, CD-G).

The playback system for a compact disc is composed of two basic subsystems: the servo and control system and the audio data processing system (Fig. 25.3). The data is read from the disc via a laser diode pickup. The focus and tracking of the pickup is controlled via the closed loop servo control system. The audio information is stored in digital form at a sampling rate of 44.1 kHz (early proposals called for a rate of 44.056 kHz for compatibility with existing video storage formats) with a resolution of 16 bits. This provides a dynamic range of over 90 dB and frequency response to 20 kHz. This digital bitstream is stored as a continuous spiral

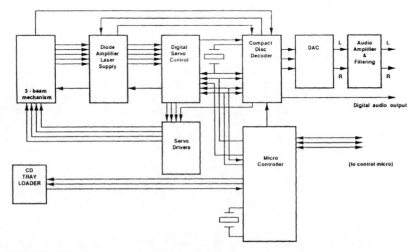

FIGURE 25.3   Typical compact disc playback system.

track beginning at the center of the disc. The data is interleaved throughout the disc to provide robustness to errors due to scratches or dust. To further minimize errors, a Cross Interleaved Reed-Solomon Code (CIRC) is used. Due to the overhead required for interleaving and error correction, the raw bit rate from a compact disc is about 4 megabits per second. The ultimate output of a CD system can be a stereo analog output and/or a digital bitstream output. This digital output has been error-corrected and can be in one of several forms. The most common are the IEC[20] serial format which is also known as SPDIF (Sony-Philips Digital Interface Format) or I²S. The IEC format is transmitted via a single wire or possibly via a fiber optic cable. The I²S format contains separate data, bit clock, and word (L/R) clock signals.[18]

25.3.2 Signal Processing

Frequency Response Modification: Tone Controls and Graphic Equalizers and Loudness Compensation. Personal taste is certainly an important aspect in the enjoyment of any audio system. Given that the listener is presented with a music source that is somewhat flat in the frequency domain, that listener may still prefer to accentuate (boost) or attenuate (cut) certain frequency bands. The bass and treble controls provided on most of even the simplest automotive radios provide the user with the flexibility to do this. The bass control can either boost or cut the low-frequency extreme of the audio spectrum; the treble control can boost or cut the high-frequency extreme of the audio spectrum. Figure 25.4 shows the response of a typical set of bass and treble controls. For further frequency content modification, a graphic equalizer provides greater flexibility and control over the audio spectrum. This device divides the audio spectrum into several bands and allows boost or cut within these bands. Figure 25.5 shows a composite response of a typical graphic equalizer. The type of frequency response alterations described here are user-adjustable. Many automotive audio systems, particularly the higher-end systems, employ fixed equaliza-

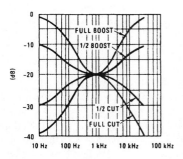

FIGURE 25.4 Bass/treble characteristic.

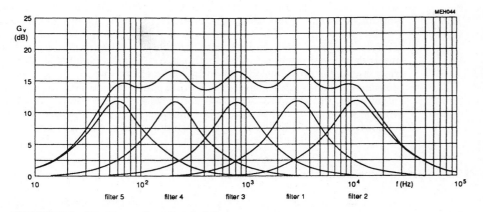

FIGURE 25.5 Graphic equalizer characteristic.

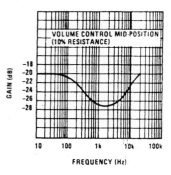

FIGURE 25.6 Loudness characteristic.

tion, which compensates for the acoustics of the vehicle interior. This type of vehicle-specific equalization is not adjustable by the user, but certainly provides an improved sound quality in the vehicle (see Vehicle Acoustics in Sec. 25.3.3).

Given the nonlinear response of the human ear to changes in level (recall the amplitude response curves), many users find it desirable to have the audio system automatically compensate for the decreasing sensitivity of the ear at low frequencies. The loudness feature is a type of automatic low-frequency boost. At lower settings of the volume control, the low-frequency output of the system is automatically boosted. This has the added benefit in an automotive environment in that a significant portion of the noise floor in an automobile cabin is low frequency (see Fig. 25.6 for a typical loudness characteristic). Some loudness characteristics also boost the high frequencies at lower volume settings. The loudness function is often hardwired into the audio system and cannot be defeated by the user.

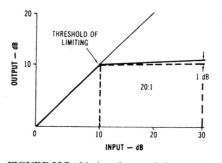

FIGURE 25.7 Limiter characteristic.

Dynamic Range Modification: Compressors and Limiters. Given the extreme capabilities of digital media such as the compact disk, compressors and/or limiters may be installed in the audio system. In order to limit these excursions, a limiting circuit may be applied (see Fig. 25.7 for the transfer function of a typical limiter). Note that in this example transfer function, for a signal above the threshold, a 20-dB change in input level will result in a 1-dB change in output level.

Wide dynamic range results in music with both extremely loud and extremely quiet passages. Given that the noise floor in an automobile environment is about 50 dB, quiet passages below that level will not be heard. A compressor will not only make the louder sounds quieter, but will also make the quieter sounds louder, thus bringing the low signal levels above the noise floor. Limiter and compressor functions may be user-switchable or hardwired on by the system manufacturer.

Power Amplifiers. For the listener to perceive sound, the air must be compressed. The transducer that accomplishes this is the loudspeaker. The power amplifiers in the audio system are responsible for providing the relatively high current drive to these loudspeakers. Modern automotive audio systems have six or more separate channel amplifiers, each of which may be required to provide up to 24 W. In order to achieve these power levels with an automobile voltage source of about 14 V, circuit techniques such as bridge-tied-load (BTL) are used.[14] Other techniques on the horizon promise more efficient delivery of power.

25.3.3 System Considerations

Signal Distribution. In the earliest days of automotive audio systems, the output of the radio was a simple loudspeaker signal which drove the loudspeaker directly. Modern systems, with multiple tuners and speakers, require new signal distribution for signal distribution. Further, the automotive audio system may have other essential portions of the system located outside of the traditional location in the instrument panel. For instance, recent systems locate the tuner directly at the antenna to reduce losses in the antenna wiring. Also, to reduce the I^2R losses in the speaker wiring and connectors, audio amplifiers will be located at or near the loudspeakers. This siting also minimizes the weight of lengthy high-gage wiring to the loudspeakers.

With these requirements, it is now required that system suppliers distribute audio and possibly RF signals throughout the vehicle. Depending on the noise environment of the vehicle, this may require something more elaborate than the old standard 14-gage lengths of stranded wire. Audio signals with a bandwidth of 20 kHz and nominal peak-to-peak amplitudes of 3 V must be distributed with great care. Alternatives are balanced signal drivers driving a twisted pair of wires which may have an integral shield. The twisted wire and shield minimize noise coupling into the wire. Then a receiving amplifier with good common mode rejection ratio is used to cancel out any noise pickup that may have occurred.

With increased digitization of the automotive audio system, it is worth considering distributing the signal in digital form[20] (see Sec. 25.4.1 on Media and sec. 25.4 on Future Trends). This provides a most robust method of distributing the signal without concern for noise pickup. The distribution media can be wire or fiber optic cable. If a wire is used, a shielded cable should be used to prevent radiation from the signal cable.

Standards are being proposed which may lead to control information being simultaneously transmitted along with the digital audio bitstream.[21] Thus, signal and control information share the same signal distribution media, further lessening the weight and cost impacts of multiple interconnects. This is an extension to the SPDIF standard which would provide for the automotive audio system components to be tied together via a "ring" not unlike a business computer network.

Vehicle Acoustics (Vehicle Cabin Characteristics). The interior cabin of a vehicle presents a most challenging acoustic environment. The small cabin dimensions produce standing waves which cause peaks and valleys in the low-frequency acoustic response of the vehicle interior. The highly absorptive materials (carpeting, seat material) combined with highly reflective glass, generate frequency response abberations across the audio frequency band. It should be noted that when making acoustic measurements on a vehicle, one must not rely on spot measurements. The response at any one point in the interior volume is quite irregular, and the response at various points throughout the interior volume can vary greatly. It is recommended that some type of averaged response be used to give an accurate view of what the response at various points in the interior truly is.[22]

Several techniques can be used to combat problems in vehicle acoustic problems. Acoustically transparent materials for speaker grilles are essential. Some common sense is easy to apply here: Carpeting is not acoustically transparent. Loudspeakers aimed at the listener's ears rather than pointed at a reflective surface (or within a map pocket) provide a more acoustically transparent response. Many premium or high-level audio systems provide fixed equalization, which is usually applied in the head unit or power amplifier signal processing sections. This equalization is ideally the mirror image of the vehicle cabin response, resulting in a combined response that is near flat.[22]

There is an easy way to demonstrate the frequency response irregularities caused by reflective surfaces: listen to someone talking with their hands cupped around both sides of their mouth, as they would do while shouting, or have that person hold two hardcover textbooks on either side of their mouth while talking.[23] The nasal type of sound experienced is due to the reflections within the hands or books.

A more subtle experience while listening to an automotive audio system is that of the virtual acoustic image. A note on imaging is appropriate here. Presumably, one has experienced the virtual image formed while listening to a home audio system. Any musical material that is produced equally from the left and right speakers of a properly set up audio system will appear to come from a virtual loudspeaker midway between the two real speakers. The ideal acoustic image within a vehicle would be front and center with the musical instruments spread across the vehicle interior. Due to the nonideal placement of the loudspeakers, the image in the vehicle may appear somewhere in the floor, the back seat, or some other nonideal location. A simple approach—although often difficult to execute—to combat this problem is to locate the loudspeakers at or close to ear level and direct them at the listener's ears. Furthermore, in a vehicle, the listener(s) are never located centrally between the loudspeakers. An interesting approach to fixing the noncentral location of the listener is to apply delays appropriate to center the image.[24]

25.4   FUTURE TRENDS

The future of automotive audio systems proves to be most exciting. Driven by the rapid increase of more powerful microcomputers, new communication techniques, improved media, and data storage techniques, the systems will change drastically through the end of this millennium.

25.4.1   Media

Radio Broadcast Data System (RBDS).   The Radio Broadcast Data System is an extension of the Radio Data System (RDS) which has been in use in the European community since 1984. The system allows the broadcaster to transmit text information at the rate of about 1200 bits per second. The information is transmitted on a 57-kHz suppressed subcarrier as part of the FM MPX signal.[25,26]

RBDS was developed for the North American market by the National Radio Systems Committee (NRSC), a joint committee composed of the Electronic Industries Association (EIA) and the National Association of Broadcasters (NAB). The possibilities for applications of text transmission to the vehicle are numerous. For instance, song title and artist, traffic, accident and road hazard information, stock information, or weather. In emergency situations, the audio system can be enabled to interrupt the cassette, CD, or normal radio broadcast to alert the user, then return. Currently there are at least 50 FM stations in the United States transmitting and testing the RBDS system.[27] The system is not quite mature as of this writing, but it is anticipated to mature rapidly over the next five years.

Digital Audio Broadcast (DAB).   Digital Audio Broadcasting is designed to provide high-quality, multiservice digital radio broadcasting for reception by stationary and automotive receivers. It is being designed to operate at any frequency up to 3 GHz. The system as being investigated has been developed by the Eureka 147 Consortium. This system is being demonstrated and extensively tested in Europe, Canada, and the United States. The system is a rugged, yet highly spectrum- and power-efficient sound and data broadcasting system. It uses advanced digital techniques to remove redundancy and perceptually irrelevant information from the audio source signal, then applies closely controlled redundancy to the transmitted signal for error correction (see section on recordable media that follows). The transmitted information is then spread in both the frequency and the time domains so a high-quality signal is obtained in the receiver, even under severe multipath propagation conditions. The feature of frequency reuse will permit broadcasters to be extended, virtually without limit, using additional transmitters, all operating on the same radiated frequency. A common worldwide frequency in the L band (around 1.5 GHz) is being considered, although some disagreement still exists.[28,29] The implementation of DAB is inevitable. The only question is when.

Recordable Media. Recent advances in recording technologies and digital signal processing have driven the development of two competing recordable media formats: digital compact cassette (DCC) and MiniDisc. The digital audio tape (DAT) has not been forgotten, but its position as an automotive medium is dubious.

Digital Compact Cassette. The DCC was invented by Philips as the marriage of the compact cassette and compact disk quality digital audio. Market forces of existing libraries of analog cassettes were deciding factors in developing a physically compatible format. A DCC player can also play analog compact cassettes. Although very similar physically, construction and recording technique used in the DCC is vastly different from the analog compact cassette. The DCC is a stationary head magnetic recording system using nine parallel tracks, each 185 mm wide. To achieve these miniature dimensions, the DCC record/playback head assembly calls on the high-tech thin-film head technology already well proven in multichannel professional recording. In order to accommodate playback of analog compact cassettes, the head unit also provides analog heads (Fig. 25.8).

In order to achieve high-quality digital audio in a limited bandwidth, the DCC relies on the psychoacoustic properties of the human hearing system. The DCC system compresses the digital audio data according to the masking properties of the human hearing system. The threshold of hearing referred to earlier in this chapter is a static characteristic and is actually a dynamic threshold. The characteristics vary with the type of sound presented to the ear (Fig. 25.9). When the ear is presented with a relatively loud sound, it cannot detect a quieter one. This phenomenon depends on the relative frequency and amplitude of the signals involved. Philips has developed the precision adaptive sub-coding (PASC) technique which implements in high-speed digital signal processing (DSP) circuits the masking properties of the human hearing system. The system determines what portion of the audible spectrum the listener is able to hear and dedicates signal processing and compression algorithms to store that portion of the signal most efficiently.[30] Testing has shown that the DCC system is actually capable of storing digital audio data to a better resolution than the compact disc.[31]

Eight of the nine tracks contain all the PASC and error correction data. The ninth track holds mainly track and time information, similar to the compact disc. The PASC data is spread across the tape in a checkerboard pattern that increases the system's robustness against dropouts. This technique is similar to the interleaving of data used in the compact disc. Cross Interleaved Reed-Solomon Code (CIRC) protects the data against further errors. Like with the compact disc, a significant portion of data can be lost without affecting the data output

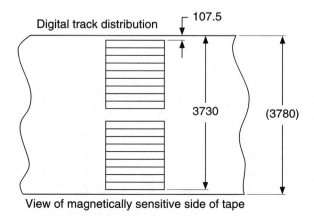

FIGURE 25.8 DCC head assembly.

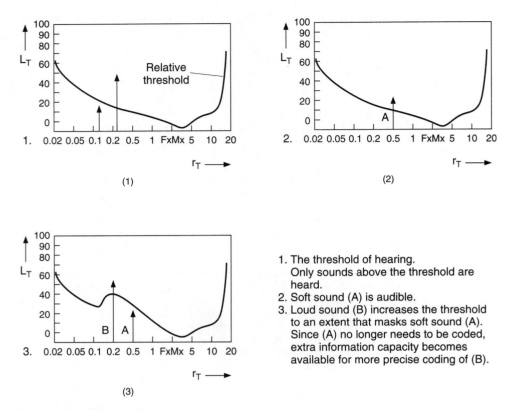

1. The threshold of hearing.
   Only sounds above the threshold are
   heard.
2. Soft sound (A) is audible.
3. Loud sound (B) increases the threshold
   to an extent that masks soft sound (A).
   Since (A) no longer needs to be coded,
   extra information capacity becomes
   available for more precise coding of (B).

FIGURE 25.9   Hearing threshold.

(Fig. 25.10). The data storage requirements of the DCC require a digital bitstream of a maximum of 353 kilobits per second. This is as compared to the uncompressed bitstream which has a data rate of 1.4 megabits per second. This is a data reduction of four times. Notice that this requires a significant amount of computational power. Special-purpose, hardwired digital signal processors are used to accomplish the decoding task in real time (see Fig. 25.11 for a block diagram of and Table 25.2 for specifications of a complete DCC system).

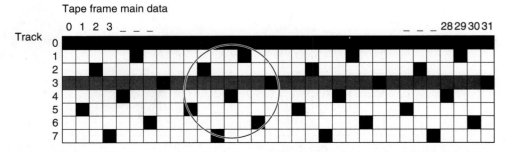

FIGURE 25.10   DCC data storage. A block as large as the circle, or an entire track can be lost without affecting data recovery.

TABLE 25.2 Digital Compact Cassette Technical Specifications

Achievable audio performance	
Number of channels	Stereo
Frequency range at fs = 48 kHz	5–20,000 Hz
at fs = 44.1 kHz	5–20,000 Hz
at fs = 32 kHz	5–14,500 Hz
Dynamic range	>105 dB
THD (including noise)	>95 dB
Wow and flutter	Quartz crystal precision
Signal format	
Sampling frequencies	48 kHz, 44.1 kHz, 32 kHz
Coding	PASC
Audio bit rate	384 bits/s (at 48 kHz)
Error correction systems	C1, C2 Reed-Solomon block code
Modulation system	8–10 (ETM)
Pre-emphasis	Optional
Cassette	
Recording time	Up to 2 × 45 min (D90)
	Provision for 2 × 60 min (D120)
Tape type	(Video) chrome or equivalent
Tape width	3.78 mm
Tape speed	4.76 cm/s
Number of tracks	8 digital audio, 1 subcode
Track width	>185 μm
Track pitch	195 μm

MiniDisc (MD).   The MiniDisc[32] was developed by Sony as a combination of the compact disc and a recordable medium. The recording technology used is a magneto-optical (MO) system. The form factor of the medium is very similar to a common 3.5-in floppy disk. The encoding technique in principle is similar to the PASC system. The encoding technique employed here is known as ATRAC. The MD is certainly a rugged portable medium, although subjective testing indicates that the response of the MD ATRAC system is not quite capable of encoding compact disc quality sound.

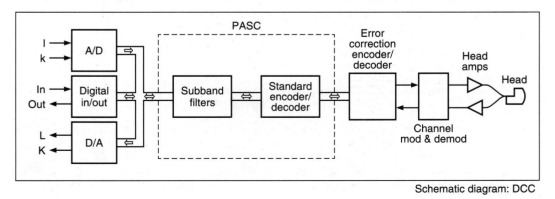

FIGURE 25.11 Complete DCC playback system.

25.4.2 Signal Processing

Digital Signal Processing Technology.   Currently, we are within a radical change in signal processing in all fields of consumer and industrial electronics. The proliferation of sound capabilities in the commonplace personal computer is a testament to this change, with further improvements and functionality coming yearly. Driven by the requirement of increased feature content and the rapidly reducing price of high-speed digital semiconductors, we will truly see a radical change in signal-processing architectures through the end of the century. Consider that the price of a state-of-the-art programmable digital signal processor (DSP) integrated circuit in 1980 was hundreds of dollars. This part could perform on the order of 1 to 5 million instructions per second (MIPS).[33] Today, a state-of-the-art programmable DSP is certainly less than one hundred dollars, with numerous units available for five dollars. Furthermore, today's DSPs will support advanced features such as shared memory, parallel processing, and high-level language support. We are beginning to see further levels of functional integration whereby formerly external functions such as analog-to-digital converters, digital-to-analog converters, and memory management units are integrated directly on the DSP. Simultaneously, these parts are exceeding 50 MIPS.[34] Additional advances are being made in integrating fixed function digital logic on the DSP. The result is that future DSPs will be tailored to specific tasks with further reduced cost. Current state-of-the-art integrated circuit manufacturing technologies are at the 1-micron feature width. Trends indicate that this will be approaching (and likely surpassing) the 0.5-micron level within the next decade. Thus, we can expect a quadrupling of functionality in the same silicon die area.

Automotive Audio Applications.   Certainly the impact of the rapid advances in DSP technology on automotive entertainment systems will be far reaching. The initial impact has already happened in the area of simple audio signal processing. Numerous aftermarket and OEM offerings contain room emulation or Hall effect features. Similar to the effect available in home entertainment systems, this effect simply emulates the reflective and absorptive properties of various listening environments in the automobile. The user can then experience the ambience of a jazz room, stadium, or concert hall. Here, DSP is an enabling technology. While room emulation can be done in analog technology, it is most expensive and performs poorly. Given the sampling frequency of 44.1 kHz of most digital audio media, the DSP must be capable of processing the signal data within one sample period (about 27 µs). This is relatively easy with available DSP chips. The proliferation of digital media furthers this enabling. Analog media must first be converted to digital before the signal can be processed in the digital domain. Given that a medium (DCC, MD, or DAB) exists in a digital form, processing the signal immediately is straightforward; no conversion is necessary. A discussion of the relative merits of analog versus digital signal processing is beyond the scope of this discussion. The significant features of digital signal processing are accurate design results, ease of feature addition and extension, predictable quality, and ease of manufacturability. Consider the requirement for the addition of adding particular equalizer characteristics to an analog radio that does not have the equalizer feature installed. Considerable redesign is required to add the analog components required to achieve the equalizer function. In a DSP system, adding the equalizer function is simply a matter of adding the proper algorithms in the coding of the processor to achieve the desired signal response.

With the rapid increase in speed of DSP circuits, the amount of signal processing that can be done with the DSP is rapidly increasing. Speeds of commercially available DSP chips are such that they are capable of processing the multiplex signals of an FM receiver. Now the methods of combating multiplex distortion and other reception problems are transferred from the realm of analog circuits to the implementation of DSP algorithms. This movement of the processing towards the front end of the receiver will continue. Processing the radio frequency signal directly seems to be just over the horizon.

The signal-processing capabilities of automotive entertainment systems have seen a many-orders-of-magnitude increase and have been driven by the fact that, today, transistors are less costly than staples.[35] Consider that in 1930 we had radios with six vacuum tubes. Before the year 2000 we will have audio systems with multiple control microprocessors and multiple DSPs totaling the equivalent of hundreds of thousands of transistors performing calculations on the order of GIPS (10^9 instructions per second).

GLOSSARY

Acoustics   The study of the generation, transmission, and reception of sound.

Analog signal   A signal in which the information of interest is communicated in the form of a continuous signal. The magnitude of this signal is proportional (or *analog*ous) to the actual quantity of interest.

CIRC (Cross Interleaved Reed-Solomon Code)   The encoding process used for playback error correction in the compact disc playback system.

Digital signal   A signal in which the information of interest is communication in the form of a number. The magnitude of this number is proportional to (within the limitations of the resolution of the number) the actual quantity of interest.

Digital signal processing   (often abbreviated DSP—as a verb). The processing of analog signals which have been converted to digital form. The processing usually involves repeated additions and multiplications.

Digital signal processor   (often abbreviated DSP—as a noun). A monolithic integrated circuit optimized for digital signal-processing applications. Portions of the device are similar to a conventional microprocessor. The architecture is highly optimized for the rapid, repeated additions and multiplications required for digital signal processing. Digital signal processors may be implemented as programmable devices or may be realized as dedicated high-speed logic.

Dynamic loudness compensation   A type of loudness compensation which is dependent on the actual signal level rather than the position of the volume control. This is greatly enabled through the use of digital signal processor integrated circuits.

Equalization   The modification of the frequency response of a system. This may be done to compensate for deficiencies in the transmission/reception system or based on the subjective requirements of the user.

Loudness compensation   The characteristic of an audio system to boost the low- and (sometimes) high-frequency components of an audio signal. This is to compensate for the human ear's decreasing sensitivities at these ends of the spectrum. The amount of boost is usually dependent on the position of the volume or level control. See also **Dynamic loudness compensation**.

Monaural   Traditionally refers to an audio signal that has only one channel of information. Also may refer to the signal component in a stereo transmission which is common between the two (left and right) channels. Also commonly referred to as "mono."

Multiplex stereo   The system standardized in the early 1960s to transmit and receive a stereo signal. This system was designed to be compatible with existing FM systems which were monaural. See text for details.

Psychoacoustics   The study of the interaction of acoustics and the human hearing and brain systems.

Signal   A fluctuating quantity that is proportional to some physical quantity. In the context here, the signal is usually in the form of a voltage or current. See also **Analog signal** and **Digital signal**.

Signal processing   Modification of the time or frequency characteristics of a signal.

Stereo   Classically, from the Greek *stereos,* meaning "solid." Traditionally refers to an audio system which has two or more independent channels of audio information. A typical stereo system consists of primarily a left and a right channel. Modern surround sound systems contain from four to as many as seven channels of information.

Sound   A vibratory disturbance in the pressure and density of a fluid or in the elastic strain in a solid, with frequency in the range of about 20 to 20,000 cycles per second, capable of being detected by the organs of the human hearing system.

REFERENCES

1. F. Alton Everest, "Fundamentals of Sound," Chap. 1 in Ballou (ed.), *Handbook for Sound Engineers,* 2d ed., Howard Sams, Indianapolis, Ind. 1987.
2. F. Alton Everest, "Psychoacoustics," Chap. 2 in Ballou (ed.), *Handbook for Sound Engineers,* 2d ed., Howard Sams, Indianapolis, Ind. 1987.
3. *Websters Ninth New Collegiate Dictionary,* 1985.
4. J. Hebrank and D. Wright, "Are Two Ears Necessary for Localization of Sound Sources in the Median Plane?," *Journal of the ASA,* V56N3, 1974, pp. 935–938.
5. Donald W. Matteson, *The Auto Radio (A Romantic Genealogy),* Thornridge Publishing, Jackson, Mich., 1987.
6. Natalie Cole, *Unforgettable,* compact disc, Elektra Records, 1991.
7. Frank Zappa, *Jazz from Hell,* compact disc, Barking Pumpkin Records, 1988.
8. Jehl, *Menlo Park Reminiscences,* 1937 and 1990, Henry Ford Museum/Dover.
9. Audio Engineering Society Centennial Booklet, *The Evolution of Recordings . . . From Cylinder to Video Disk,* 1977.
10. William F. Boyce, *Hi-Fi Stereo Handbook,* Howard Sams, Indianapolis, Ind., 1967.
11. Motorola Publication, *Introduction to the Motorola C-Quam System,* 1985.
12. *Stereophonic FM Broadcasting,* BTR, vol. 7, no. 2, July 1961.
13. R. Summerville, "Advances in Tackling FM Reception Problems," SAE 850022, Society of Automotive Engineers, Warrendale, Pa., 1986.
14. Philips Semiconductors, *Car Radio Design-in Guide,* Doc # 9398-706-42011.
15. B. Goldes, *Improved Test Generator for Radio Noise Blanker,* personal communication.
16. R. W. Landee, D. C. Davis, A. P. Albrecht, and L. J. Giacoletto, *Electronic Designers Handbook,* 2d ed., McGraw-Hill, New York, 1977.
17. D. Manquen, "Magnetic Recording," Chap. 27, in Ballou (ed.), *Handbook for Sound Engineers,* 2d ed., Howard Sams, Indianapolis, Ind., 1987.
18. *Publication 958-Digital Audio Interface, First Edition, 1989–03,* International Electrotechnical Commission (IEC).
19. G. Alexandrovich, "Recording and Playback," Chap. 25, in Ballou (ed.), *Handbook for Sound Engineers,* 2d ed., Howard Sams, Indianapolis, Ind., 1987.
20. "Digital Audio Input/Output Circuit (DAIO) TDA1315," Philips Semiconductors Data Sheet, 1993.
21. "Audio Local Area Network Transceiver Circuit (A-Lan) CS8425," Crystal Semiconductor Data Sheet, 1992.

22. E. Geddes, H. Blind, *The Equalized Sound Power Measurement Technique,* Audio Engineering Society, New York, 1989.

23. David L. Clark, *Effective Listening (Seminar Notes),* DLC Designs Publication/Seminar, Dearborn, Mich., 1990.

24. David L. Clark, Test Car, 1990.

25. Philips Semiconductors Internal Application Notes 901026R2, *RDS (Radio Data System).*

26. CENELEC European Committee for Standardization, *RDS Specification (EN 50 067).*

27. *Electronic Industries Association Publication,* May 26, 1993.

28. "Policy snags delay DAB," *Electronic Engineering Times,* Sept. 20, 1993.

29. M. Halbe, "DAB Receiver Technology and Implementation Considerations," *1st International Symposium on DAB,* 1992.

30. Philips Marketing Brochure, "*DCC Fundamentals—The New Digital Sound System.*"

31. David Clark, "DA/B/Xing DCC," *Audio Magazine,* April 1992.

32. Leonard Feldman, "The Mechanics of Sony's Minidisc," *Audio Magazine,* Dec. 1992.

33. Texas Instruments, TMS32010 Data Sheet, 1982.

34. Motorola, DSP56004 Data Sheet, 1993.

35. Robert W. Keyes, "The Future of the Transistor," *Scientific American,* June 1993.

ABOUT THE AUTHOR

Thomas Chrapkiewicz has been an applications engineer for Philips Semiconductors since 1993. As an analog design engineer from 1977 to 1983 at both ADM Technology (formerly Audio Designs and Manufacturing) and Harris Broadcast Products, he designed audio circuits and systems for broadcast, recording, and film applications. He then spent 10 years designing analog and digital signal-processing circuits for Ford Motor Co.

CHAPTER 26
MULTIPLEX WIRING SYSTEMS

Fred Miesterfeld
Chrysler Corporation

26.1   VEHICLE MULTIPLEXING

Production and proposed passenger vehicle multiplexing and data communications network systems will be thoroughly examined in this chapter. The systems covered are those methods that are relevant to the electronic engineer who has the assignment of applying multiplexing techniques to high-volume production. In passenger vehicle design, cost is the universal method of determining whether or not a design will be put into production. If a multiplex network design can be applied while delivering functional improvements at a system-cost saving, then this design is the most likely network design to be accepted.

The SAE Vehicle Network for Multiplexing and Data Communications (Multiplex) Committee has defined[1] three classes of vehicle data communication networks:

Class A.   A potential multiplex system usage where vehicle wiring is reduced by the transmission and reception of multiple signals over the same signal bus between nodes that would have ordinarily been accomplished by individual wires in a conventionally wired vehicle. The nodes used to accomplish multiplexed body wiring typically did not exist in the same or similar form in a conventionally wired vehicle.

Class B.   A potential multiplex system usage where data (e.g., parametric data values) are transferred between nodes to eliminate redundant sensors and other system elements. The nodes in this form of a multiplex system typically already existed as stand-alone modules in a conventionally wired vehicle.

Class C.   A potential multiplex system usage where high data rate signals, typically associated with real-time control systems, such as engine controls and antilock brakes, are sent over the signal bus to facilitate distributed control and to further reduce vehicle wiring.

The Class B network is intended to be a functional superset of the Class A network; i.e., the Class B bus must be capable of communications that would perform all of the functions of a Class A bus. This feature protects the use of the same bus for all Class A and Class B functions or an alternate configuration of both buses with a *gateway* device. In a similar manner, the Class C bus is intended as a functional superset of the Class B bus.

Generally, this section will deal only with the requirements for the lowest three layers of the seven-layer ISO open system interconnects (OSI) model (Ref. ISO 7498). These layers in descending order are the network layer, data link layer, and the physical layer.

26.1.1 Background of Vehicle Network Architectures

A wide variety of network topologies[2] can be envisioned by network designers. The message structure described in this section is very flexible and useful in exchanging information between network nodes. The following discussion describes two network architectures which are likely configurations that can use this message definition set: a single-network architecture and a multiple-network architecture.

The selection would be application-specific and, thus, it is the system designer's choice as to which network architectures to use. It should be noted that the hardware that supports these two message structures is generally not interchangeable. It is recommended that care be taken in choosing which message definition to use, because the selection is generally irreversible because of hardware limitations.

Header Selection.   The header field (header) is a one-, two-, or three-byte field within a frame and contains information about the message priority, message source, target address, message type, and in-frame response. The multiple network architecture is usually associated with the single-byte header protocol. Figure 26.1 (1) illustrates the header byte as the message identifier (ID), which is primarily used for functional "broadcast"-type messages and implicitly defines all the required information about the message. It is unnecessary to specify the source or destination of functional-type messages. Reception becomes the exclusive responsibility of the receiving node. Figure 26.1 (2) also illustrates header bytes, which are primarily used for physical-type messages, and has two bytes: the first is the ID and the second is the target address.

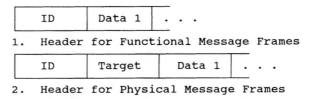

1.   Header for Functional Message Frames

2.   Header for Physical Message Frames

FIGURE 26.1   Single-byte header protocol.

The single-network architecture is usually associated with the multiple-byte header protocol, shown in Fig. 26.2. The first byte of the frame defines the priority and message types, functional or physical.

Priority/Type	Target	Source	Data 1	. . .

FIGURE 26.2   Multiple-byte header protocol.

Architecture Selection.   Consideration must be given by the network designer as to whether a single-network architecture or a multiple-network architecture is preferable for an application. For example, a multiple-network architecture could be based on one network optimized around data communication (Class B) protocol requirements, and another network optimized around sensor type (Class A) multiplexing requirements. The Class B network may be characterized such that low latency is a significant requirement of the protocol and where the short functional type of messages can most effectively be used. A Class A network could handle the vehicle's event-driven multiplexing requirements. See the next section on Class A networking for more information on Class A multiplexing considerations.

Without regard to either the header or architecture selection, in Class B communications the network consists of the interconnection of intelligent nodes such as an engine controller, a body computer, a vehicle instrument cluster, and other modules. Such a network normally does not significantly reduce the base vehicle wiring but provides an intermodule data communications capability for distributed processing. The data shared between modules may be repetitive in nature and sometimes requires handshaking between modules or acknowledgment of data reception. As a result of handling the repetitive data and response-type data, a network can be optimized around functional addressing. Functional addressing sends data on the network, which can be received by one or more nodes without regard to the physical location of the module but only by their "interest" in those specific functions. In general, the transmitting node does not care which, if any, nodes receive the data it is sending. When physical addressing is required in a data communications network (Class B), it is usually for vehicle maintenance purposes and can be easily handled without reducing network bandwidth.

The nature of Class A multiplexing requires the interconnection of limited intelligence nodes, often simply sensors or actuators. These Class A networks can significantly reduce the base vehicle wiring as well as potentially remove redundant sensors from the vehicle. The data shared between nodes in this case are generally event-driven in nature. In most vehicles, the number of event-driven signals predominates, but they are only needed infrequently. The message to "turn headlamps on," for example, can be easily seen as event-driven. Because these messages are infrequent (only sent once when the signal changes) they generally require acknowledgment, either within the same message or a separate handshake/response message.

The single-network architecture carries both the Class A and Class B messages on one network and the multiple-byte header has the advantage of having more bits available for use in assigning message identifiers, priorities, message types, etc. The characteristics of both time-critical and event-driven messages must be accommodated on a message-by-message basis. In general, this level of complexity will need the flexibility of the multiple-byte header structure. It should be clear that both network architectures must be cost effective for the application and the specific nodes on each network.

The multiple network architecture tends to separate the Class A messages from the Class B messages and optimize each network and node interface for the specific characteristics of each network class. The time-critical messages could be exchanged on one network, while the event-driven messages are sent on another. For example, the data communication (Class B) repetitive messages can be handled on one network and the sensor and control (Class A) multiplexing requirements on another network. This architecture requires both networks to work together to achieve the total vehicle network requirements. If information is needed between the multiple networks, care must be exercised to meet the needs of each of the networks. This concept of multiple networks is not limited to two, but can be extended to several separate networks if desired.

Class A Network. Class A multiplexing[3] is most appropriate for low-speed body wiring and control functions. The example most often used to illustrate the benefits of Class A multiplexing is the base exterior lighting circuit. However, this example is the hardest function to cost-justify. The base exterior lighting system is extremely simple and very low cost. A multiplex network applied to this lighting system could result in increased wiring complexity and cost. Data integrity in the lighting system can be a stringent requirement for Class A multiplexing; e.g., a single-bit error that results in headlights "off" when they should be "on." Adequate data integrity in a Class A multiplex network is a constraint and bit-error checking may be required.

In the future, the results could change if new features, such as low-current switching or lamp-outage warning, became a requirement or new lamp technology, such as smart bulbs, became a reality. In general, the addition of new features will play a major role as to when and how multiplexing will become a cost-effective solution.

Other Driving Forces.   The design of vehicles to minimize manufacturing complexity is a major force that will lead to architecture partitioning development. The properly developed multiplex architecture can be very effective in reducing the number of parts in the assembly plants and built-in testability can substantially reduce vehicle build test time.

Example Class A Systems.   To illustrate how a Class A multiplex network could be used to simplify the vehicle wiring situation, consider the vehicle theft alarm system shown in Fig. 26.3. Although this example does not represent the epitome in theft alarm features, it does illustrate the nonmultiplexed condition. The horn actuator and the sensor switches are all wired directly to the theft alarm module. The module is then armed by activating the dash arm switch. The module can be disarmed by either the driver door key switch, passenger door key switch, or the trunk key switch. When the module is armed, the horn is sounded when the hood, door, or trunk is tampered with.

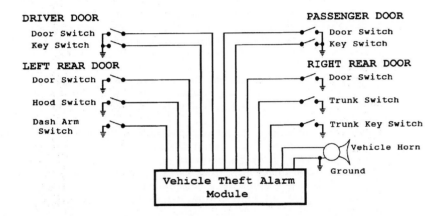

FIGURE 26.3   Vehicle theft alarm system.

The vehicle theft alarm system shown in Fig. 26.4 illustrates a near-optimal configuration of a Class A network. The sensors and actuators are integrated with the multiplexing electronics so that they can communicate over a single wire to the theft alarm module. The integration of electronics into the sensors and actuator improve sensor diagnostics because the sensor status and condition can be reported back to the controlling module. The integrity of the sensor status and condition can be linked to the mechanical operation of the sensor. This level of switch integrity cannot be achieved with normal switch-biasing methods. In a theft alarm system, there is an added benefit: the sensor condition can be used to set off the alarm and foil the tampering of a would-be thief.

The I/O requirements support T-tap connections, which can be highly automated in the production of wiring harnesses, reducing the wire bundle size and eliminating dual crimps. The configuration also supports the concept of adding sensors or actuators as the option requires without changing the theft alarm module configuration to support the optional features. This expandability feature allows the cost of the option to drive the system cost.

To show how this configuration is flexible and easily expandable, consider the example condition in which some versions of theft alarms are built as originally described, but an upscaled version is offered as an option in which the unit is armed by the driver locking the doors. To support this option, the dash arm switch would be eliminated and the driver door lock switch would be configured with the integrated switch multiplex at a different address. The same theft alarm module's software could then reconfigure itself without hardware modifications.

There are approximately seven sensors to every actuator in a real vehicle body system. This theft alarm system is typical with 10 sensors (switches) to one actuator (horn).

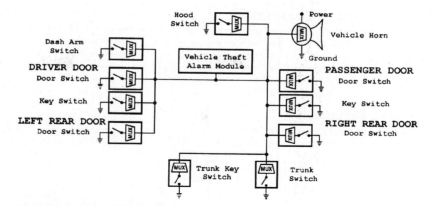

FIGURE 26.4   Multiplexed vehicle theft alarm system.

The sensors and multiplexing electronics can be integrated into the switch component. This configuration eliminates separate wiring and mounting of the multiplex module. Some component manufacturers have even been working on two wire (signal and ground) sensors in which the power to run the sensor has been supplied by the multiplex signal. For an example component, see Sec. 26.3.7. These sensors have been designed to include the multiplex circuit integrated with the Hall effect device in the same TO92 size package. The multiplexer portion is very small and requires approximately 300 logic gates.

The actuator driver and multiplexer can similarly be integrated into the horn or motor. This configuration also reduces wiring and mounting complexity. Actuators normally require more power then sensors and usually require three wires; signal, power, and ground. However, some manufacturers are developing a method to eliminate one of these wires by placing the signal on the power wire.

Class B Data Communications.   The vehicle system designer now has many architecture partitioning options. A prime example is when to integrate many features into a module or when to employ a dedicated node. Care must be taken or the partitioning strategy may not achieve optimal results. The issue is much more complex when vehicle multiplexing is involved in this partitioning strategy. The most popular networking strategy is the Class B single-network architecture. However, this architectural strategy does not always result in an optimal solution.

A hypothetical vehicle will be described to illustrate this point. Figure 26.5 illustrates the part of a data communications network that contains a body computer, an instrument cluster, and a message center. In this example, all the sensors that feed the network enter through the body computer.

As illustrated in Fig. 26.5, all sensors are wired directly to the body computer. This example shows that for a base vehicle with only a small amount of electronic content, where all the sensors are directly wired to the body computer, the wire bundle size and number of connector pins is attainable. As additional features are made standard, either by consumer demands or government regulations, it becomes more and more difficult to implement the required system. This added complexity is due to the tremendous number of interconnecting wires from sensors to the modules. The build complexity and troubleshooting problems make this option a limited solution for this partitioning strategy.

The Class B single-network architecture strategy would solve this complex problem by adding a sensor node and reducing the number of interconnecting wires. Conventional sensors are connected directly to the node which serves as a gateway to the other modules over the Class B data network. Figure 26.6 illustrates the dramatic reduction in the number of cir-

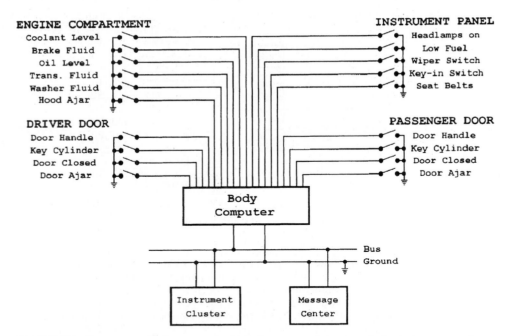

FIGURE 26.5   Data communications network with body computer, instrument cluster, and message center.

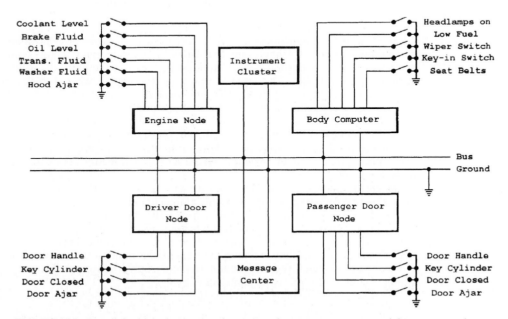

FIGURE 26.6   Data link with body computer, instrument cluster, message center, and three sensor nodes.

cuits required. This method is effective in reducing the number of sensor wires connected through "crunch points" such as the bulkhead or door hinge. This reduction in wiring, however, is obtained at the expense of three added sensor nodes.

Class B multiplexing is a very useful technique for reducing many of the problems encountered by the automotive system engineers. This section will demonstrate that in many situations the multiplex strategy, shown by Fig. 26.6, leads to a less than optimum system architecture. It is highly desirable to have a multiplexing architecture which would permit the use of smaller module connectors, reduce the number of wires crowding through the congested areas, and attain a solution without introducing more modules to mount, wire, and service.

Engine Compartment Node. In this hypothetical example, it may be desirable to integrate the node with the engine controller module, which would reduce module count and wiring circuits at the same time. The integration solution is not always possible because the engine controller already has an uncontrollably large module connector and would add a separate part just to cover an option.

Door Nodes. In this hypothetical example, the best location for the door node would be inside the door (See Fig. 26.7). By placement inside the door, the number of circuits through the door hinge is minimized, but without making further improvements the same wiring complexity inside the door still exists. These further improvements generally could integrate the electronics and mechanics into a single package.

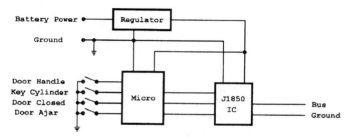

FIGURE 26.7 A driver door node.

General Node Concerns. General node concerns include the following:

- In order to achieve minimum cost, nodes tend to become application-specific and not generic because they usually can cover only one feature product.

- To cover more than one product, nodes tend to become intelligent and employ a microcomputer, and may negatively impact the system cost and complexity.

- Using conventional sensors remote from the node does not normally improve sensor diagnostics; e.g., the node cannot tell if the sensor switch is off or if the wire is disconnected. Refer to the previous section, "Example Class A Systems," for a discussion on switch integrity.

- The door node illustrated in Fig. 26.7, and nodes in general, can be effective in some wire bundle size and weight reduction but further improvements are possible with Class A sensor/actuator networking. The number of connector pins for the system can also be reduced with Class A networking.

Multiple Network Architecture. The multiple network architecture is the second strategy that solves many of these concerns. This architecture requires the development of many types of specialized network hardware components to efficiently handle each application. These components are connected together by a gateway on the Class B network for diagnostics purposes. Figure 26.8 illustrates this local area network (LAN) solution.

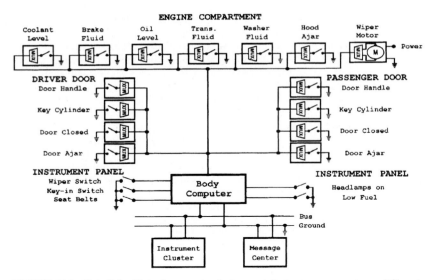

FIGURE 26.8 Data link with body computer, instrument cluster, message center, and Class A network for sensors.

Multiple network architecture strategy requires the integration of electronics into the sensors, actuators, and motors so that they can communicate over a single wire into the module that utilizes them. Since the sensor and actuator components contain the added multiplex electronics, the separate installation and wiring of the multiplex module is eliminated. Unlike the single-network architecture strategy, the integration of electronics into the sensors, actuators, and motors normally does improve sensor diagnostics because the sensor status and condition can be reported back to the controlling module. This method makes use of a Class A LAN without adding components to the vehicle system.

Figure 26.8 shows that the Class A LAN eliminates the need for the engine compartment node and two-door sensor module while still reducing wiring at the crunch points. The multiplex architecture shown in Fig. 26.8 significantly simplifies the same system shown in Fig. 26.6. This simplification is made possible by separating the Class B intermodule communications network from the Class A sensor-to-module communications.

The Class A LAN connects all the multiplexed components in parallel. The I/O requirements support T-tap connections, which can be highly automated in the production of wiring harnesses. This configuration reduces bundle size and eliminates dual crimps. The configuration also supports the concept of adding sensors or actuators, as the option requires, without changing the body computer configuration to support the option. This add-on feature allows the option to dictate the cost and not the cost of the added node dominating.

The two different Class A networks using multiplexed sensors are shown in Fig. 26.8 and Fig. 26.9 and illustrate a body computer flexibility trait that is not available in the other architectural approaches. The typical base vehicle using the Class A network is shown in Fig. 26.9. The body computer in the base, medium, and premium vehicle systems all have the wiper switch, seat belt switch, headlamps on, low fuel level, key-in ignition switch, Class A interface, and the Class B multiplex interface. This trait across option rates allows additional inputs to be connected without modifying the hardware in the body computer.

Unlike this hypothetical situation just used for illustration purposes, a real vehicle will have several actuators as well as sensors connected to the body computer. As it was previously discussed, there are approximately seven sensors to every actuator in a real vehicle body system. For illustrative purposes, 14 sensors and one actuator (wiper motor) were shown in this example. The principles shown, however, apply similarly to any number of actuators.

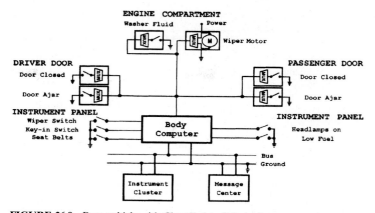

FIGURE 26.9   Base vehicle with Class B data link, body computer, instrument cluster, message center, and Class A network for sensors.

Class C Real-Time Control.   The Class C network is the least mature network, and consensus of opinion on requirements does not yet exist. Experts cannot agree on many facets and many of the requirements are controversial. Many automotive engineers believe that an adequate statistical latency achievable with a bit-by-bit arbitration-based media access protocol is sufficient for real-time distributed Class C multiplexing. Others believe a token-passing media access protocol is required because a maximum latency is guaranteed, because with an arbitration-based media access only a statistical maximum latency is achievable. There are still others who argue that both the arbitration-based and token-passing media access is not good enough for tightly looped distributed processing because both methods have too great a variation in latency time. They argue that a time-triggered media access method is required because the network variations in latency should not affect tightly looped processing times. Other factors such as required data rates and the physical media type also remain open. It is clear that more research and development is required to resolve these questions.

26.2   ENCODING TECHNIQUES

The data encoding technique[4] has a significant effect on the radiated EMI. In order to achieve the highest possible data rate, it is important to choose a data-encoding technique that has the fewest transitions per bit with the maximum amount of time between transitions and bit-synchronized so that invalid bit testing can be effective. PWM, for example, has two transitions per bit with ⅓ bit times between transitions. NRZ has a maximum of one transition per bit but is increased to provide for synchronization. Some of the disk drive encoding techniques such as modified frequency modulation (MFM) are synchronous with fewer than one transition per bit. (See Table 26.1 for a comparison chart of a selection of encoding techniques used in vehicle multiplexing.)

The variable column in the table describes an attribute whereby the transmission time for data byte is a variable quantity depending on the data value. VPWM and Bit-Stuf NRZ both have variable byte repetition rate (*data variability*).

Some of the bit-encoding techniques synchronize on transitions that fall on or within the bit boundaries. 10-bit NRZ, Bit-Stuf NRZ, and E-MAN all employ added transitions for synchronization (*clock synchronization*).

TABLE 26.1   Comparison of Multiplexing Bit-Encoding Techniques

	PWM	VPWM	10-Bit NRZ	Bit-Stuf NRZ	L-MAN	E-MAN	MFM
Variable	No	Yes	No	Yes	No	No	No
Synchronizing	Yes	Yes	No	No	Yes	No	Yes
Arbitrates	Yes	Yes	Yes	Yes	Yes	Yes	Yes
Transition/bit	2	1	≤1.25	≤1.015	≤2	≤1.25	≤1
Max data rate	7.1 K	11.2 K	13.5 K	16.6 K	8.4 K	13.5 K	16.8 K
dBV < PWM	Base	9	11	14	5	11	15
Oscillator tolerance	±29.2%	±29.2%	±5.1%	±9.7%	±29.2%	±9.7%	±10.7%
Integrity	Perfect	Good	Fair	Fair	Perfect	Fair	Superb

All of the encoding techniques considered are capable of bit-by-bit arbitration. This is not commonly recognized with some of the encoding techniques, e.g. MFM, and will be addressed in Sec. 26.2.7 (*arbitrates*). Bit-by-bit arbitration is calculated on the number of *transitions per bit* of data.

A suitable data-encoding technique should not generate excessive levels of EMI, and this consideration is a dominating challenge in making an encoding choice. The CISPR Standard* is usually considered adequate. This factor determines the *maximum allowable data rate* of the encoding technique, in order to maintain a level of EMI below the CISPR standard break point, i.e., −60 dBV at 500 kHz. The values predicted in Table 26.2 used the same technique described in the next section.

Equation (26.1) in Fig. 26.10 can be used to predict[5] the EMI levels radiated by a single wire in a vehicle wiring harness. The technique was used to calculate and plot a Fourier series of a sample trapezoid wave to determine the values given in Table 26.2. The calculations assumed a 10.4 Kbps data rate at a 42 percent factor of the minimum feature size (minimum pulse width) to determine the rise time. Consider the trapezoidal wave shown in Fig. 26.10. The shortest rise time (42 percent of shortest pulse width), shortest pulse time, and fastest repetition rate should yield the worst-case EMI in dBV. The actual measured EMI will be a few dBV better than the calculated dBV because the output driver frequency bandwidth does act as a low-pass filter [EMI below PWM (dBV < PWM)].

---

* CISPR/D/WG2 (Secretariat) 19 Sept 1989 Radiated Emissions Antenna & Probe Test Document has been generally interpreted by most RF engineers to specify a break point at 500 kHz of −60 dBV.

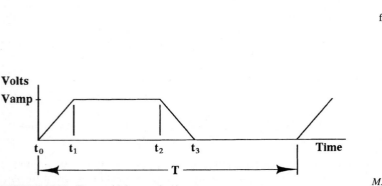

FIGURE 26.10   Trapezoidal wave shaping.

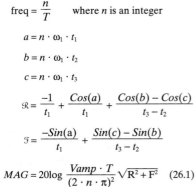

$$\omega_1 = \frac{2 \cdot \pi}{T}$$

$$\text{freq} = \frac{n}{T} \qquad \text{where } n \text{ is an integer}$$

$$a = n \cdot \omega_1 \cdot t_1$$

$$b = n \cdot \omega_1 \cdot t_2$$

$$c = n \cdot \omega_1 \cdot t_3$$

$$\mathcal{R} = \frac{-1}{t_1} + \frac{Cos(a)}{t_1} + \frac{Cos(b) - Cos(c)}{t_3 - t_2}$$

$$\mathcal{I} = \frac{-Sin(a)}{t_1} + \frac{Sin(c) - Sin(b)}{t_3 - t_2}$$

$$MAG = 20\log \frac{Vamp \cdot T}{(2 \cdot n \cdot \pi)^2} \sqrt{R^2 + F^2} \quad (26.1)$$

There are a number of hardware constraints that affect network synchronization and *oscillator tolerance*. The values given in Table 26.2 are calculated without considering these constraints because they are not generally considered a factor for evaluating encoding techniques. For all encoding techniques, the same nominal bit rates or average bit rate, as in the case of VPWM, was used. The small decrease in data rates for 10-Bit NRZ, Bit-Stuf NRZ, and E-MAN, due to the added bits for synchronization, is normally neglected; i.e., Baud rate was used.

The technique used by the receiver to detect a synchronizing transition plays a role in determining oscillator tolerance. Many different sampling or integration techniques could be used for a comparison, but for the sake of obtaining a reasonable judgment, for the encoding techniques under consideration, a very simple pulse width counter technique was assumed. A 12.5 percent of minimum pulse width (PW min) was assumed for variability in integration time (IT). The maximum time for synchronization was either the maximum pulse width (nominal) or time (nominal) between synchronization transitions.

Equation (26.2) in Fig. 26.11 yields the natural oscillator tolerance for the encoding technique. Figure 26.11 illustrates the maximum fast clock and minimum slow clock that can determine the logic value, either a "1" or a "0", for the symbol decoded by the symbol decoder. The IT is the time of uncertainty in determining the pulse width. The example demonstrated is for PWM encoding technique. All the other encoding techniques follow the same method. The actual tolerance would be affected by the application and the specific hardware used in the network. The variabilities introduced by the specific hardware will be needed to adjust parameters in Eq. (26.2) in order to find the final node oscillator tolerance.

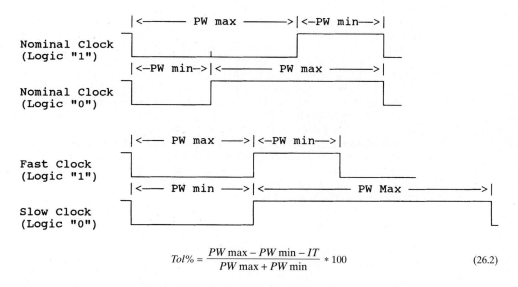

$$Tol\% = \frac{PW\max - PW\min - IT}{PW\max + PW\min} * 100 \tag{26.2}$$

FIGURE 26.11 Example of oscillator tolerance calculations.

There are generally three types of oscillators used with vehicle multiplex circuits: quartz crystal for very tight oscillator tolerances; ceramic resonators for low-cost, tight tolerances and fast startup time; and RC oscillators for very low cost and very fast startup time at a very loose oscillator tolerance.

The noise filter used is usually a digital filter or some type of sampling process. RC filters are usually not used because they are not precise enough. For all of the encoding techniques, a 12.5 percent of minimum pulse width was used for IT in calculating the oscillator tolerance.

In a single-wire network, ground offsets between nodes cause an added received pulse-width variability. This condition is especially acute when trapezoidal waveforms are used to reduce EMI. Figure 26.12 illustrates the pulse-width timing (T) variability introduced by ground offset. This pulse-width variability must be accounted for because it causes a reduction in minimum pulse width and an increase in maximum pulse width, thus having the effect of reducing oscillator tolerance.

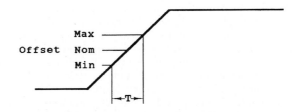

FIGURE 26.12   Ground offset on pulse-width timing.

The output drivers are the source of another pulse-width variability. The effect is the same as with ground offset only not nearly as acute. The problem is caused by line drivers used to permit arbitration having a longer delay time when going from the active to passive state than from a passive to active condition.

Data integrity is judged on a scale from poor, fair, good, superb, to perfect. Data integrity is generally considered to be affected by the EMI. The ambient levels of EMI in a vehicle are very low. This condition must remain in order to operate a communications receiver (consumer radio) in a vehicle. The problem is that very high levels of "bursty" noise for a short period at random intervals can completely disrupt multiplex communications for the duration of the noise. The only other effect of this bursty noise is a barely noticeable pop in the radio speaker. During these events, data integrity is compromised. The accepted practice for data communication (Class B) multiplexing is to simply detect this data corruption and throw out the full message rather than try to recover the data. This practice is acceptable because the amount of corrupted data compared to noncorrupted data is considered negligible, and/or can be retransmitted without causing bus bandwidth problems.

A thorough noise immunity study is very complex, and the criteria for judging would consider many factors. If something is known about the noise environment and the detector hardware, as is the case with the automotive situation, a study of data integrity may be useful. For the purpose of this discussion, assume that the criteria for judging which data-encoding method is acceptable is mainly dependent on its natural ability to detect corruption. Also, the corruption detection ability is often determined by the interface hardware capability and its message-handling protocol.

A number of validation tests can be performed on the message level. Bit-error algorithms such as a parity bit, checksum, or CRC are the most common test. Also, some protocols can perform message length by either message type or defining the message length in the data. These and other message level tests are independent of the bit-encoding method and should not influence data integrity of the bit-encoding technique.

The natural ability of the encoding technique to detect corruption is known as invalid bit detection. Usually three types of data integrity factors are considered for vehicle multiplexing because the effects of EMI environment are basically known:

1. *Low pass filtering.*   For this factor, the data bit is passed through a low pass filter, i.e., an integrator; the longer the shortest pulse duration, the more effective the filtering.

2. The bursty noise detection test checks for a short duration of EMI.

3. Two independent data bit tests confirm valid data. PWM, for example, has two unique sample periods per bit and both periods must complement each other.

26.2.1 Pulse-Width Modulation (PWM)

The PWM encoding technique[6] is composed of two sample periods or phases (T_1 and T_2) per bit, as shown by Fig. 26.13. PWM encoding has the advantage that the time per bit remains constant, but has the disadvantage of generating more EMI because it has two transitions per bit. This time per phase of PWM also affects the generated EMI noise and, to minimize the EMI effect, one phase time is usually defined to be two times the other phase time in duration.

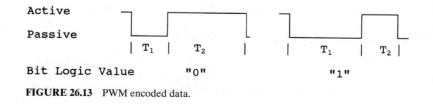

FIGURE 26.13   PWM encoded data.

Arbitration of PWM.   PWM has the ability to perform bit-by-bit arbitration. Figure 26.14 illustrates that a "0" bit dominates and takes priority when bit-by-bit arbitrating over a logic "1".

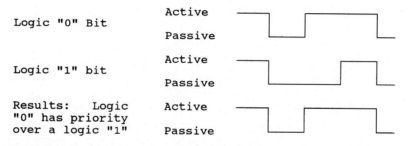

FIGURE 26.14   A logic "0" arbitrating with a logic "1".

Data Integrity of PWM.   Consider a hardware sampler that has the capability of detecting (1) transition and (2) phase (ϕ) every sample window, as shown in Fig. 26.15. The sampler starts sampling at a transition, then sequentially samples window 1, window 2, and then window 3. If a transition is not detected by window 3, then data has been corrupted and the message is thrown out. When this type of sampler is used for PWM encoded data the sampler would sample five windows per bit and yield dual transition and phase information per bit. The transition and

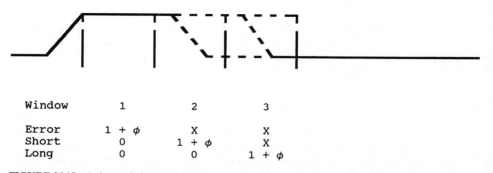

FIGURE 26.15   A three-window sampler.

phase information must be consistent for a correct PWM encoded data or corruption would be assumed and the message will be thrown out. If at any time a transition of either phase is detected in sample window 1, the data has been corrupted and the message is thrown out.

PWM encoding is judged to have very good "perfect" invalid bit-testing capabilities even though the effectiveness of the low-pass filter is poor. Otherwise, it has two of the three (e.g., dual periods confirmation of data and burst noise) validation tests. PWM is "perfect" encoding technique used in vehicle multiplexing when data integrity has the highest priority. However, this encoding technique has multiple transitions per bit and would not allow operation at data rates near the natural EMI limits for single-wire or twisted pair transmission media.

26.2.2   Variable Pulse-Width Modulation (VPWM)

VPWM (sometimes referred to as VPW modulation) is a variation of PWM. Normal PWM has two phases per bit as shown by Fig. 26.16. T_1 is illustrated as a passive short and T_2 as an active long. This combination is defined as a logic "0" bit. Notice that a logic "0" bit takes priority when arbitrating over the opposite pattern of a passive long and an active short.

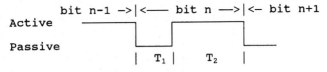

```
           bit n-1 ->|<—— bit n —>|<- bit n+1
  Active ———————|     |————|     |————
  Passive        |————|     |————|
                 |  T₁  |   T₂    |
```

FIGURE 26.16   A PWM encoded logic "0" bit.

One of the most attractive features of VPWM is that the pulse-width variability introduced by factors such as ground offset and output driver timing variabilities can be added to the pulse-width timing without severely reducing the oscillator tolerance.

Arbitration of VPWM.   VPWM encodes each phase as a data bit. Figure 26.17 illustrates a passive short arbitrating with a passive long. Figure 26.18 illustrates an active long arbitrating with an active short. In both cases, a logic "0" takes priority over a logic "1" bit. Therefore, arbitration using VPWM data encoding can be achieved.

A passive Short is defined as a logic "0" bit	Active Passive
A passive long is defined as a logic "1" bit	Active Passive
Results: A passive short has priority over a passive long	Active Passive

FIGURE 26.17   A passive short arbitrating with a passive long.

VPWM is utilized by SAE J1850; i.e., it uses a pulse width of 64 μs for a short and 128 μs for a long and approximates the same average data rate (10.4 Kbps) as regular PWM using a pulse width of 32 μs for a short and 64 μs for a long. The VPWM minimum pulse width for a short is 64 μs and permits a rise time of 16 μs for T as illustrated in Fig. 26.12. Compare this rise time to conventional PWM where a 32-μs short permits only an 8-μs rise time. The result of the proportionally longer rise time and wave shaping is an approximate 9-dBV improvement in EMI over PWM. The disadvantage of VPWM encoding is that the data rate per byte

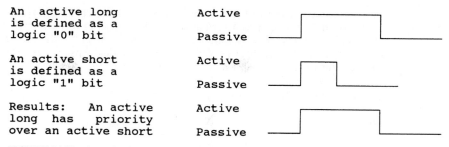

An active long
is defined as a
logic "0" bit

An active short
is defined as a
logic "1" bit

Results: An active
long has   priority
over an active short

FIGURE 26.18   An active long arbitrating with an active short.

transmitted will vary in time depending on the data value. The microcomputer interfacing transmitter/receiver polling rate with VPWM is required to be less than ≈ 512 μs per byte, whereas with PWM, less than ≈ 768 μs per byte is required.

Data Integrity of VPWM.   VPWM has good data integrity by sampling up to three times every pulse width as shown in Fig. 26.15. The sampler is designed to detect a transition and phase (ϕ) every sample window and have an average number of 2.5 samples per bit. If at any time a transition of either phase is detected in sample window 1, the data has been corrupted and the message is thrown out.

The sampling sequence is initiated by a transition of either phase. A short symbol is then sensed by not detecting a transition (0) in window 1 and detecting a transition $(1 + \phi)$ and proper phase in window 2. Sampling in window 3 is a "don't care" (X), because sampling is terminated and the procedure is repeated. Window 3 is actually window 1 on the next sampling sequence.

A long symbol is likewise sensed by not detecting a transition (0) in window 1 or 2 and detecting a transition $(1 + \phi)$ and proper phase in window 3.

The proper phase detection, when a transition is sensed, is used to ensure that the sequence does not get scrambled. It is also used to define which logic level, "1" or "0", has been received.

VPWM has been judged to have "good" data integrity because low-pass filtering of the data pulse width is good. Every transition is validated by an error-sampling window, and pulse duration measurements are validated by the proper phase test, i.e., two of the three invalid bit tests.

26.2.3   Standard 10-Bit NRZ

This is an asynchronous serial I/O (standard UART) 10 bits-per-byte of data. A start bit and a stop bit are added to provide data byte synchronization. The standard UART used in RS232 is bit-ordered least significant bit (LSB) first. Figure 26.19 illustrates this 10-bit NRZ waveform. Vehicle multiplex networks that use 10-bit NRZ make use of the available hardware that have this asynchronous I/O, i.e., the serial communications interface (SCI) available on many microcomputers.

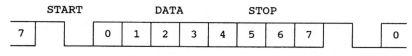

FIGURE 26.19   A 10-bit NRZ waveform (LSB first).

Arbitration of 10-Bit NRZ.   Figure 26.20 illustrates 28H from transmitter #1 arbitrating with 44H from transmitter #2. An active "0" is defined to win arbitration over a passive "1". Take note that bus has a 28H on it and, therefore, transmitter #2 shuts off its output when it tries to transmit bit #2. This loss of arbitration action is the usual method employed by all arbitrating protocols.

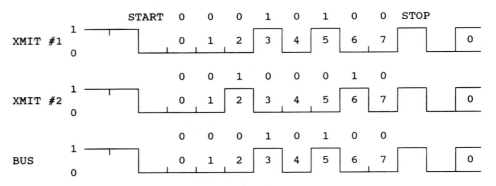

FIGURE 26.20   Arbitration of a 10-bit NRZ network.

Data Integrity of 10-Bit NRZ.   The bit-synchronized sampling technique used for PWM and VPWM could be used for 10-bit NRZ encoded data, but it would be much more complex because it could be guaranteed to synchronize only on the stop-to-start transition. It would not sample only one bit, it may have to sample all eight. The normal technique is to use a start bit detector to sense a valid start bit and then sample all eight of the data bits sequentially.

As with all decoding techniques, the data is passed through a low-pass filter. However, filtering for NRZ is very effective because of the long data pulse duration. 10-bit NRZ encoding has been judged to have "fair" data integrity, mainly because the addition of a transition between the stop bit and start bit is not unique in the sequence and the detector hardware could get scrambled. Adding an invalid bit detection for bursty noise between data bits would improve the data integrity, but it could not validate every bit.

26.2.4 Bit-Stuf NRZ

Bit-stuffing is another way of synchronizing NRZ encoded data. The concept is to insert a bit (i.e., two transitions) after a specified number (X) of bits of contiguous "1" or "0" bits and if the X + 1 bit is the same logical value as the other contiguous bits. The proper number of contiguous bits is chosen as a compromise between the oscillator tolerance and the generated EMI. The higher the number of contiguous bits before inserting a stuff-bit, the better the synchronizing oscillator tolerance must be, but the lower the EMI. There is also a receiver decoding complexity consideration with bit-stuf NRZ. Figure 26.21 illustrates waveform used by CAN for X = 5.

The number of stuff-bits in a frame is dependent on the data value, and the transmission time for a data byte is a variable quantity depending on this data value. A number of the factors used to evaluate bit-stuf NRZ require a knowledge of the average number of data bytes per stuff-bit (see Fig. 26.22). This average number can be derived because the nature of a data bit in a message has equal probability of being a "1" or "0".

Arbitration of Bit-Stuf NRZ.   As with all arbitrating encoding methods, the bit-stuf NRZ transmitter utilizes a driver that has an active state and a passive state, thereby supporting bit-by-bit arbitration.

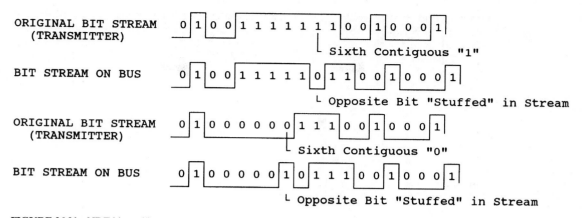

FIGURE 26.21   NRZ bit-stuffing.

The probability of there being a stuff-bit before B_i in the stuffing algorithm where X = 5 is as follows:

$$B_0, \; B_1 \bullet \bullet \; B_i \bullet \bullet \; B_{n-1}$$

$$p_i = \begin{cases} 0 & when \;\; i < 5 \\ 1/32 & when \;\; i = 5 \\ 1/64 & when \;\; i > 5 \end{cases}$$

$$F(N) = No. \; of \; BYTES/STUF$$

$$F(N) = \frac{N}{\displaystyle\sum_{i=0}^{n-1} p_i} \quad \begin{array}{l} where \\ n = No. \; of \; Bits \\ N = \frac{n}{8} = No. \; of \; Bytes \end{array}$$

$$\lim_{N \to \infty} \; F(N) = 8$$

$$F(12) = 8.348$$

FIGURE 26.22   Derivation of average number of stuff-bits.

Data Integrity Bit-Stuf NRZ.   The bit-synchronized six-window sampling technique illustrated in Fig. 26.23 could be used for bit-stuf NRZ encoded data and would be guaranteed to synchronize on the stuff-bit. It must accommodate sampling from one to five data bits sequentially. All bits of data prior to sampling a transition are assigned the same logic level as the level detected by transition and phase detector. If transition is detected in window #1, which is due to bursty noise, the message would be thrown out. This detector could somewhat improve the data integrity, but it could not validate every bit. As with all decoding techniques, the data is passed through a low-pass filter. However, filtering for NRZ is very effective because of the long data pulse duration.

Bit-Stuf NRZ encoding has been judged to have "fair" data integrity, mainly because the addition of a synchronizing stuff bit is not unique in the sequence and the detector hardware could get scrambled.

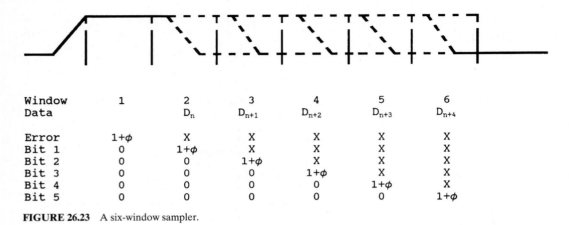

Window	1	2	3	4	5	6
Data		D_n	D_{n+1}	D_{n+2}	D_{n+3}	D_{n+4}
Error	$1+\phi$	X	X	X	X	X
Bit 1	0	$1+\phi$	X	X	X	X
Bit 2	0	0	$1+\phi$	X	X	X
Bit 3	0	0	0	$1+\phi$	X	X
Bit 4	0	0	0	0	$1+\phi$	X
Bit 5	0	0	0	0	0	$1+\phi$

FIGURE 26.23   A six-window sampler.

26.2.5   L-Manchester (L-MAN)

The L-MAN encoding technique is composed of two sample periods of opposite phases per bit, as shown by Fig. 26.24. L-MAN encoding has the advantage that the time per bit remains constant, but has the disadvantage of generating more EMI because it can have an average of one-and-a-half and maximum of two transitions per bit.

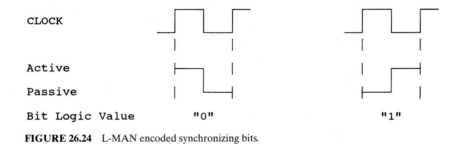

FIGURE 26.24   L-MAN encoded synchronizing bits.

A transition from active to passive level will be decoded as a logic "0" and a transition from passive to active level will be decoded as a logic "1". A synchronizing transition is always generated in the center of the bit period but may not be generated at the beginning of a bit period, depending on the data. As illustrated by Fig. 26.25, when there is a "0" to "1" or "1" to "0" data sequence the transition is not generated.

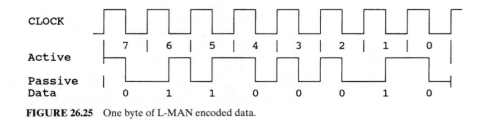

FIGURE 26.25   One byte of L-MAN encoded data.

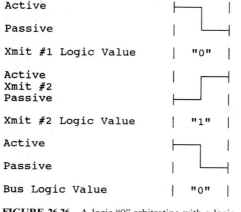

FIGURE 26.26 A logic "0" arbitrating with a logic "1".

Arbitration of L-MAN. Figure 26.26 illustrates how a logic "0" arbitrating with a logic "1" always wins arbitration. This situation is true because the active portion of the signal overrides the passive portion and also shuts off the output of the passive contender before it would become active.

Data Integrity of L-MAN. Consider a three-window sampler that has the capability of detecting a transition (1) and phase (ϕ) every sample window as shown in Fig. 26.15. The circuit starts sampling at a transition and then sequentially samples window 1, window 2, and then window 3. If a transition is not detected by window 3, then data has been corrupted and the message is thrown out. When this type of sampler is used for L-MAN encoded data, the sampler would sample four to five windows per bit and yield complementary transition and phase information per bit. If D_n and D_{n+1} have the same logic level—i.e., "1s" or "0s"—then a transition must not occur at the bit boundary or a corrupted data would be assumed and the message will be thrown out. If at any time a transition of either phase is detected in sample window 1, the data has been corrupted and the message is thrown out.

L-MAN encoding is judged to have very good "perfect" invalid bit-testing capabilities even though the effectiveness of the low-pass filter is poor. Otherwise, it has two of the three validation tests: dual validation of data by proper periods at the bit boundary and bursty noise test every bit. L-MAN has "perfect" encoding technique used in vehicle multiplexing when data integrity has the highest priority. However, this encoding technique has multiple transitions per bit and would not allow operation at data rates near the natural EMI limits for single-wire or twisted pair transmission media.

26.2.6 E-Manchester (E-MAN)

E-Manchester, or enhanced manchester, utilizes an L-Manchester encoded data bit for synchronization combined with three bits of NRZ encoded data bits. Figure 26.24 illustrates the L-Manchester synchronizing bit values and Fig. 26.27 is an illustration of four bits of E-MAN encoded data.

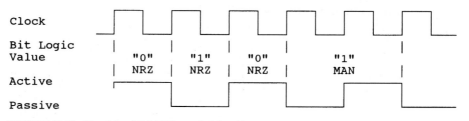

FIGURE 26.27 Four bits of E-MAN encoded data bits.

Arbitration of E-MAN. When arbitrating, an active (logic "0") takes priority over the opposite pattern (logic "1") for both the NRZ bits and the MAN encoded synchronization bit. This domination of a logic "0" over a logic "1" is easily understood for the NRZ encoded portion of an E-MAN encoded byte. The dominance of a logic "0" synchronization bit, which seems confusing, can be easily realized by considering the fact that the active portion of the signal overrides the passive portion and also shuts off the output of the passive contender before it would become active.

The main advantage of E-MAN over PWM or VPWM is that the shortest pulse width at 10.4 Kbps is $\approx$ 76.8 μs, and permits a 42 percent rise time of 32.3 μs compared to a 32 μs short and 13 μs rise time with conventional PWM. The result of the proportionally longer rise time and wave shaping is an approximate 11-dbV improvement in EMI over PWM. Another advantage of E-MAN over VPWM is that the data rate per byte transmitted is constant. The microcomputer transmitter/receiver polling rate with E-MAN is required to be a constant of less than $\approx$ 768 μs per byte.

Data Integrity of E-MAN.   If the same sampling technique is used for E-MAN as was used for the bit-stuf NRZ case, it is capable of detecting (1) a transition and (2) a phase (ϕ) every sample window. The E-MAN sampling hardware can sample up to six times every pulse width as shown in Fig. 26.23.

The sampling sequence is initiated by a transition of either phase. If there is a transition (1 + ϕ) in window 2, then the value of D_n is determined by the logic level and phase.

If there is a transition (1 + ϕ) in window 3 in the sampling sequence, then $D_n = D_{n+1}$ and is determined by the logic level and phase. If there is a transition (1 + ϕ) in window 4 in the sampling sequence, then $D_n = D_{n+1} = D_{n+2}$ and is determined by the logic level and phase.

If there is a transition (1 + ϕ) in window 5 in the sampling sequence, then $D_n = D_{n+1} = D_{n+2}$ and is determined by the logic level and phase. The value of D_{n+3} is determined by the phase (ϕ) because it is the L-MAN encoded bit and will be confirmed by a transition (1 + ϕ) in window 2 on the following sampling sequence.

If there is a transition (1 + ϕ) in window 6 in the sampling sequence, then $D_n = D_{n+1} = D_{n+2}$ and is determined by the logic level and phase. The value of D_{n+3} is determined by the phase (ϕ) because it is the L-MAN encoded bit.

The L-MAN encoded bit is not unique in the sequence and the detector hardware must keep track of where the L-MAN bit should be, because if a transition (1 + ϕ) for the L-MAN encoded bit falls in a window other than window 6, then the value of D_{n+3} is determined by the phase (ϕ) of the transition.

E-MAN encoding has been judged to have "fair" data integrity, mainly because the L-MAN encoded bit is not unique in the sequence and the detector hardware could get scrambled. If a transition is detected in window 1, an invalid bit was detected, which helps data integrity but it could not validate every bit. As with all decoding techniques, the data is passed through a low-pass filter. However, filtering for E-MAN is very effective because of the long data pulse duration.

26.2.7 Modified Frequency Modulation (MFM)

Modified frequency modulation (MFM), a modulation technique developed during the latter 1960s, was used in disk drives and is adaptable to vehicle multiplexing. The advantage of using the MFM encoding technique is that it would be synchronous with an average of 0.75 and a maximum of 1 transition per bit. The encoding technique permits a transition rise time that can be maximized and wave-shaped to significantly reduce EMI. Disk drives have a similar requirement where the modulation technique allows pulses to be recorded on a disk at maximum density. The diagram shown in Fig. 26.28 demonstrates one method of applying MFM encoding technique to a data communication network.

The rule for encoding simply causes a transition at the data time when the data at that time slot is a logic "1". A transition is also generated at the clock time slot when the data before and after the time slot was a logic "0" (or two "0"s in a row).

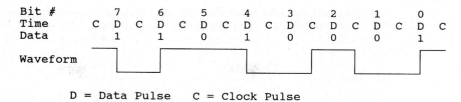

FIGURE 26.28   MFM encoded byte of data.

Arbitration of MFM.   A requirement for vehicle multiplexing is that the data from one device shall bit-by-bit arbitrate with the data from another device. The arbitration bit-ordering is defined MSB first, and 00H has the highest priority. To support arbitration, the output driver is defined and designed to have an active state that has priority over a passive state. Figure 26.29 demonstrates the four encoding rules that can be used to generate a waveform "A" that always wins arbitration.

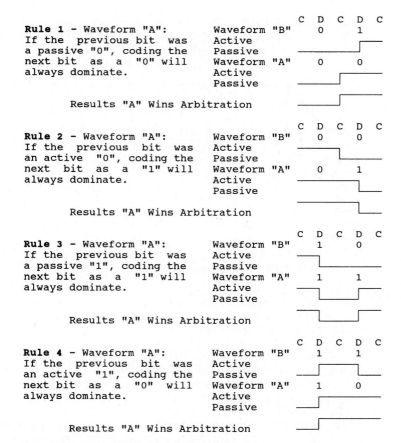

FIGURE 26.29   The four rules for winning arbitration.

Assume that the existence of four rules for winning arbitration demonstrates that it is possible to convert data into a form that will correctly arbitrate. This assumption means that data can be encoded into a different byte, which will have to be decoded back after arbitration. Applying the four rules, the process required to code a "0" in the original byte to win, and a "1" to lose, is: start with the MSB, move toward the LSB, i.e., left to right. When encoding, make sure all the "0s" encountered are of the type that will win arbitration, i.e., Rule 1 and 4. When a "1" is encountered make sure the type of "0" that will be following the previous bit will win arbitration over the "1" in the present bit, i.e., Rule 2 and 3. For each "1" encountered in a row, make sure the other byte that has the same bits up to that point, but now has a "0", will win arbitration with that "0".

Encoding and decoding of data into an MFM format can be accomplished by hardware in the interface circuit. A two-step process is required. First the data bytes to be transmitted must be translated into the correct form for arbitration using the rules illustrated by Fig. 26.28. The operation of the MFM encoder depends on a starting value of a dominant "1", which is provided by the start of frame (SOF).

After the data is translated into the correct form for arbitration, it can be encoded by the circuit. The data is then ready to be transmitted by the I/O. The received data requires the reverse sequence of first decoding by the circuit and then translation into the correct binary form. Translation can be accomplished by the circuit.

Data Integrity of MFM. The MFM encoding receiver samples up to four times every pulse width when starting at a data transition, and up to three times every pulse width when starting on a clock, as shown in Fig. 26.30.

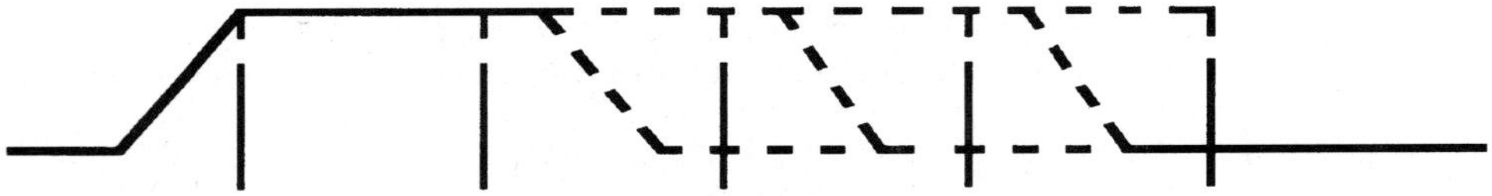

Window	1	2	3	4
Clock	D_n	C	D_{n+1}	
Data	C	D_n	C	D_{n+1}
Error	$1+\phi$	X	X	X
Bit 1	0	$1+\phi$	X	X
Bit 1½	0	0	$1+\phi$	X
Bit 2	0	0	0	$1+\phi$

FIGURE 26.30 MFM data integrity capability.

The sampling sequence is initiated by a transition of either phase. The sampler can detect a transition $(1 + \phi)$ of either phase in every sample window. The following sequences begin with a transition in a data window:

1. If next $1 + \phi$ in data window 1, then an error has been detected.
2. If next $1 + \phi$ in data window 2, then the value of $D_n = 1$.
3. If next $1 + \phi$ in data window 3, then the value of $D_n = 0$ and $D_{n+1} = 0$.
4. If next $1 + \phi$ in data window 4, then the value of $D_n = 0$ and $D_{n+1} = 1$.

The following sequences begin with a transition in a clock window:

1. If next $1 + \phi$ in clock window 1, then an error has been detected.
2. If next $1 + \phi$ in clock window 2, then the value of $D_n = 0$ and $D_{n+1} = 0$.

3. If next $1 + \phi$ in clock window 3, then the value of $D_n = 0$ and $D_{n+1} = 1$.

4. If next $1 + \phi$ in clock window 4, then an error has been detected.

MFM has been judged to have very good ("superb") data integrity because, as with VPWM encoding, every transition is validated by an error-sampling window and a proper phase test. Also, when transitions fall in windows 3 and 4 for data and in 2 and 3 for clock, the value of two data bits is sensed. One sampling confirms the previous, thus improving data integrity capability. With MFM decoding technique, the data is passed through a low-pass filter. However, filtering for MFM is very effective because of the long data pulse duration.

26.3 PROTOCOLS

Table 26.2 describes the protocol sections.[7] These descriptions appear in the order in which they are discussed for each protocol.

The following describes the *intent* of the various sections of the protocol characteristics.

The *application* section briefly identifies the applications for which the protocol was designed to serve: military, aircraft, industrial, land vehicles, and trucks. The *affiliation* section identifies the organization(s) that originally developed the protocol, specified the protocol, or which now endorse the protocol.

The *transmission media* section describes the physical medium generally associated or required by the given protocol: single-wire, dual-(parallel) wire, twisted pair, twisted pair with shield, dual twisted pair, and fiber optics.

The *physical interface* section describes the basic circuitry used to connect the nodes to the network. In some cases, the schematic of a typical interface may be shown. In others, a reference to a generally known interface technique may be made. This section may also include additional data about aspects of the interface not readily shown. An example would be that receiver nodes synchronize to the signal from a transmitting node, or that receiver nodes adjust their receiver clock to the received data signal.

The *bit encoding* section describes the way in which the logical bits, "1"s and "0"s, are translated into signals on the transmission medium by the physical interface (NRZ, PWM, and MANCHESTER).

The *network access* section describes the method used to award the communication network to one of the nodes for the transmission of a message: master/slave, token passing, and CSMA/CD.

The *message format* section describes the fields that make up the basic message(s) used in the protocol. This includes the order, name, and size of the fields.

The *handshaking* section describes the interaction of nodes within a network in order to effect a transfer of data. This may include such things as negative and positive acknowledgment, and in-message acknowledgment.

The *error detection management* section describes the types of errors the protocol detects and the recovery techniques it uses: wrong message length and CRC.

The *fault tolerance* section describes the ability of the protocol to continue operation, possibly at a degraded level, when various parts of the physical layer or medium of the network on which the protocol is operating fails (i.e., node connections are broken, bus wires are opened, bus wires are shorted to ground or to vehicle battery voltage).

The *data rate* section identifies the maximum data rate supported by the protocol.

The *framing overhead* section briefly shows the amount of nondata overhead, i.e., framing overhead, associated with the given protocol. If possible, the calculation of overhead is shown. Because some protocols offer significantly different message formats and/or message sizes, several overhead calculations may be necessary to give an accurate picture of the range of the protocol's overhead requirements.

TABLE 26.2 Protocol Descriptions

	A-BUS	CAN	D2B	SAE J1567 C²D	SAE J1850 PWM	SAE J1850 VPWM	SAE J2058 CSC	SAE J2106 token slot	TTP	VAN
SAE class	Class B & C	Class B & C	Class B	Class B	Class B	Class B	Class A	Class C	Class C	Class C
Affiliation	VW	Proposed ISO Bosch	Philips	Chrysler	SAE RP Ford	SAE RP Chrysler, GM	Chrysler	GM	University Wien Austria	Proposed ISO
Application	Auto in-vehicle	Auto in-vehicle	Audio/video	Auto in-vehicle	Auto in-vehicle	Auto in-vehicle	Auto in-vehicle	Auto in-vehicle	Auto in-vehicle	Auto in-vehicle
Transmission media	Single-wire	Twisted pair/fiber optic	Twisted pair	Twisted pair	Twisted pair	Single-wire	Single-wire	Twisted pair/fiber optic	Twisted pair/fiber optic	Twisted pair
Bit-encoding	NRZ	NRZ with bit-stuffing	PWM	10-bit NRZ	PWM	VPWM	Analog, NRZ, & PWM	NRZ with bit-stuffing	MFM	L-MAN E-MAN
Media access	Contention	Contention	Contention	Contention	Contention	Contention	Master/slave	Token slot	Time-triggered	Contention
Error detection	Bit only	CRC	Parity	Checksum	CRC	CRC	Parity	CRC	CRC	CRC
Data field length	2 bytes	0–8 bytes	2–128 bytes	1–6 bytes	0–8 bytes	0–8 bytes	1–32 bits	0–256 bytes	2–8 bytes	0–8 bytes
In-message acknowledge		Yes		Yes	Yes	Yes	Yes	Yes	Yes	
Maximum bit rate	500 Kbps	1 Mbps	100 Kbps	7.812 Kbps	41.6 Kbps	10.4 Kbps	1 Kbps	2 Mbps	1 Mbps	User definable
Maximum bus length	Not specified typical 30 m	Not specified typical >40 m	150 m	Not specified typical >30 m	40 m	40 m	Not specified typical >40 m	Not specified typical 30 m	Not specified typical 20 m	20 m
Maximum number of nodes	Not specified typical 32	Not specified typical >16	50	Not specified	Not specified	Not specified	Not specified	32 (transmit capability)	Not specified	16
Hardware available	Yes	Yes	Yes	Yes	Yes	Yes	Yes	No	No	Yes

The *latency* section describes the factors that affect the delay between the availability of a message to be transmitted and the beginning of the reception of that message by the intended receiver.

The *power reduction* section has general information about any modes of operation that require less power than normal operation. As a minimum, this section identifies the lower power level(s). It also includes a brief description of the criteria used in transitioning to the lower power mode(s) and to return to normal power mode. Some of this information may be device-version-specific and will be so identified.

26.3.1 Automotive Bit-Serial Universal Interface System (A-BUS)

Application/Affiliation.   Designed for automotive applications by Volkswagen AG.

Transmission Media.   Not specified. Single-wire suggested.

Physical Interface.   Not specified.

Bit Encoding.   NRZ with eight samples/bit, which means each sample is ⅛th the length of the bit. A valid bit has to have either four or six complementary samples (see Fig. 26.31). This choice of either 4 or 6 matching samples is a user selectable function.

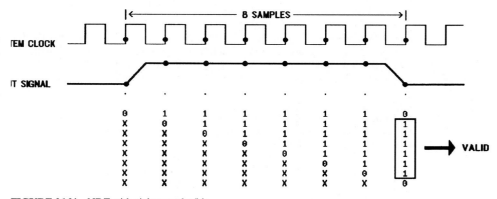

FIGURE 26.31 NRZ with eight samples/bit.

Network Access.   Network access is achieved by a contention process that occurs through the end of the identifier field using a nondestructive bit-by-bit arbitration operation.

Message Format.   Message length is constant and consists of 1 start bit, 1 bit (NC/DAT) indicating whether it is a data message or a command message, an 11-bit identifier, 16 bits of data, and 2 stop bits (STP0, STP1). Further detail is provided in Fig. 26.32. Two different types of messages are possible: the data message and the command message. Command messages may be used to ensure that a following command will not be accepted on the bus until the receiver has read the command. The ABUS IC can be programmed in a way that every following command will not be accepted on the bus until the master controller unit has read the command last received. In this case, no commands are lost.

Handshaking.   Negative acknowledgment by receiver after error is detected. Any receiving device that notices a protocol error notifies all other bus members by pulling down the STP1

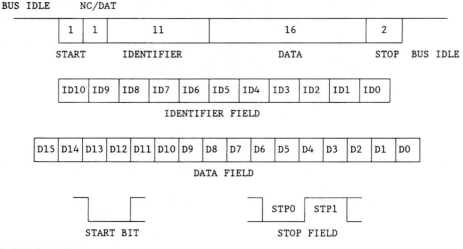

FIGURE 26.32 Message format.

bit. If the STP1 bit is low, the message is regarded as invalid by all members. There is no required or dedicated positive acknowledgment.

Error Detection Management.   The transmitter and receiver monitor the bus for errors. The transmitter reads its own message back from the bus and compares it with the message that it intended to send. The receiver detects four different types of code errors by sampling the bus and when it has not been possible to compare the samples.

Start-Bit Error.   This occurs when it has not been possible to generate a start bit at the beginning of the transmission process.

Transmit Error.   A transmit error is monitored when, during a message transmission, the value read back was not equal to the value sent out a total of Y times* consecutively between the arbitration and STP1 bit.

Receive Error.   A receive error is monitored when, during a message reception, an error has been detected a total of X times* consecutively prior to the STP1 bit.

Short Circuit.   This occurs when no logical "1" has been read for a period of 256 clock pulses after a high to low transition.

Fault Tolerance.   Not specified.

Data Rate.   Maximum specified bit rate = 500 Kbps.

Framing Overhead.   The message length is 31 bits; 16 of these are data. To transmit four bytes of data, two messages must be sent. Using the formula:

$$\frac{\text{OVERHEAD}}{\text{MESSAGE}} = \frac{\text{FRAMING}}{(\text{FRAMING} + \text{DATA})}$$

Approximate framing overhead/message calculated is: $(15+15)/((15+16)+(15+16))=48\%$.

---

* X and Y are programmable values (to 8, 16, and 32). In the present implementation, these error occurrences are stored in a status register and cause an interrupt. The sender tries to send a message for 8 to 32 times before it is recognized as an error.

Latency. The ABUS protocol uses nondestructive bit-by-bit arbitration in contention to determine bus access. In the case of two or more nodes beginning transmission simultaneously, the message with the highest priority will win the arbitration and continue transmission. As a result, the maximum latency for the highest priority message is the number of bits in the maximum length message multiplied by the time per bit. A 31-bit message will require 64 μs at 500 Kbps. Lower priority messages may encounter additional delay in the event that they lose arbitration. Their latency may be determined based on a statistical analysis of the system, bus load, priority, and other.

Power Reduction Mode.   The power consumption of the ABUS IC can be reduced by using the sleep mode. In this mode, the oscillator is turned off and the power consumption is reduced to 10 to 100 μA. The sleep mode is initiated by the host microprocessor. The IC will wake up either by a reset or by bus activity, but will go through a reset in either case. After the reset it will take about 50 ms for the oscillator to work properly; e.g., the first message works as an "alarm clock," which implies it is not received completely.

26.3.2   Controller Area Network (CAN)

Application/Affiliation.   Both standard (S) and extended (E) message formats are intended for automotive in-vehicle applications. An ISO draft standard and an SAE Information Report[8] have been published.

Transmission Media.   Not specified. Most of the announced production-intent systems use a wire-shielded or unshielded bus. Fiber optic systems using CAN have been demonstrated.

Physical Interface.   User defined. One specific implementation is defined in Bosch presentations and documents to ISO.

Bit Encoding.   NRZ (Nonreturn to Zero) with bit-stuffing (see Fig. 26.33). Logic level is constant for entire bit field, i.e., either "1" or "0", and bit of opposite state is inserted into bitstream by a transmitter if five contiguous bits of the same state are seen. Receivers remove the inserted bit from the bitstream, resulting in restoration of the original data stream. Implementations are programmable to allow either three or one samples per bit and specify the location of samples within a bit.

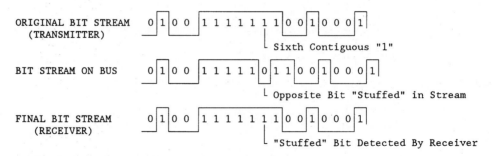

FIGURE 26.33 NRZ bit-stuffing.

Network Access. Contention using nondestructive bit-by-bit arbitration. Any node may transmit if the bus is idle. In the case of simultaneous transmissions, arbitration is resolved through the value in the identifier field. The message priority is defined in the identifier. Each message has a unique identifier, and, as a result, a unique priority. These identifiers/priorities are defined by the user, i.e., the system designer.

Message Format.   There are primarily three message types: data frame (see Fig. 26.34), remote frame (see Fig. 26.35), error frame (see Fig. 26.36), and overload frame (used in events where individual node has not had complete time to store message, see Fig. 26.37).

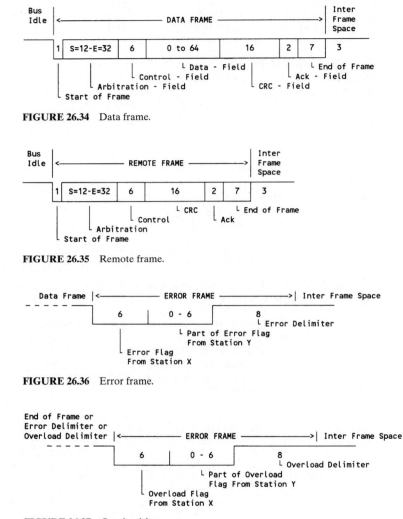

FIGURE 26.34   Data frame.

FIGURE 26.35   Remote frame.

FIGURE 26.36   Error frame.

FIGURE 26.37   Overload frame.

Handshaking.   Handshaking is provided within the message via either positive or negative acknowledgment. Positive acknowledgment is provided by a dedicated two-bit field in the message frame; one bit for acknowledgment and one bit for delimiter. All nontransmitting nodes will confirm uncorrupted message reception by transmitting a "dominant" bit in this dedicated field. As a result, the transmitting node receives confirmation that the message was received uncorrupted and does not have independent acknowledgments from individual nodes. Negative acknowledgment is provided through the error frame. See Fig. 26.34 for additional detail.

Error Detection Management. All nodes monitor all messages. If an error is detected within a message, then the node(s) detecting that error destroy that message by transmitting an error frame. The result of this error frame is that all nodes (including the transmitting node) know that an error has been detected within the present message. The transmitter will retransmit the message at its next opportunity through normal bus access arbitration. Error-checking is provided on CRC, message length, message format, and bit level and timing. The message length is specified in the control field.

Fault Tolerance. Protocol is intended to treat all node address faults in the same manner. Fault confinement is provided by each node constantly monitoring its performance with regard to successful and unsuccessful message transactions. Each node will act on its own bus status based on its individual history. As a result, graceful degradation allows a node transmitter to disconnect itself from the bus. If the bus media is severed or shorted, the ability to continue communications is dependent upon the condition and the physical interface used.

Data Rate. Bit rate of up to 1 Mbit/s.

Framing Overhead. Maximum message length, which is the maximum time between messages, is 111 bit times for standard format and 131 bit times for extended format, i.e., 111 and 131 μs at 1 Mbps. For the highest priority message, if a message has just begun and the message in question is queued up, the latency will be 111/131 μs, and 222/262 μs maximum until its transmission is complete.

The maximum time between messages with four bytes data is 79 bits for standard format and 99 bits for extended format. Please note that this includes interframe space. For a message transmitting four bytes of data, using the formula OVERHEAD/MESSAGE = FRAMING/(FRAMING + DATA), the approximate framing overhead/message calculated for standard format is 47/(47 + 32) = 59%. For eight data bytes, the approximate framing overhead/message calculated is 47/(47 + 64) = 42%. For extended format, it is 67/(67 + 32) = 68% and 67/(67 + 64) = 51%, and does not include bit-stuffing.

Latency. The CAN protocol uses nondestructive bit-by-bit arbitration in contention to determine bus access. In the case of two or more nodes beginning transmission simultaneously, the message with the highest priority will win the arbitration and continue transmission. As a result, the maximum latency for the highest priority message is the number of bits in the maximum length message multiplied by the time per bit. In other words, it will have 111 bit times or 111 μs at 1 Mbit/s for standard format and 131 bit times or 131 μs at 1 Mbit/s for extended format. In the event that they lose arbitration, lower priority messages may encounter additional delay. Their latency may be determined based on a statistical analysis of the system, i.e., bus load, priority, and other.

Power Reduction Mode. Not specified.

26.3.3 Digital Data Bus (D2B)

Application/Affiliation. Digital data bus is a product of Philips for use in audio/video communications, computer peripherals, and automotive.

Transmission Media

Twisted pair
Physical interface
Differential floating pair (see Fig. 26.38)

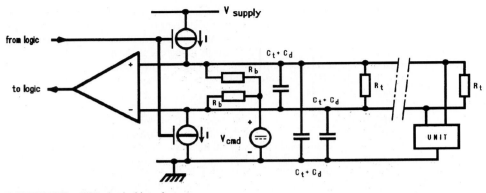

FIGURE 26.38   D2B physical interface.

Bit Encoding

Pulse-Width Modulation (PWM).   The general bit format is composed of four sections: the preparation period, the sync period, the data period, and the stop period. The duration of the periods and the bit is dependent on the speed of the bus and the type of the bit. The speed of the bus is determined during contention. Low speed is dominant. There are three speeds possible. The general bit format is shown in Fig. 26.39.

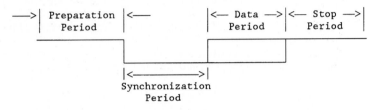

FIGURE 26.39   Pulse-width modulation bit format.

Network Access.   Access is achieved by contention using nondestructive prioritized bit-by-bit arbitration. Competing nodes arbitrate first on the mode in which the node will operate in a three-bit field, where low mode is dominant. All nodes in a common mode then arbitrate based on the unique address bits of the competing masters. Low address is dominant. The mode designates the speed at which the bus will operate during the message transfer. A unit may use the bus for one time slot. The amount of data transferred in the time slot depends on the speed mode determined during arbitration.

Message Format.   The frame consists of six fields. A parity bit follows the master, slave, control, and data fields. An acknowledge bit follows the slave field, control field, and the data field. An end-of-data bit follows each data byte. The total length of the frame is 47 bits. See Fig. 26.40 for the frame.

Handshaking.   Handshaking is accomplished with positive acknowledgment in the transfer message. No reply from the slave is interpreted as a negative acknowledgment. The master can retry the message provided time remains in the slot. During every transfer, there are three different acknowledge bits: after the slave address, after the control bits, and after each data byte.

   A master has the ability to lock a slave node to its address, having the effect of disabling the node from communicating with any other master on the network. This is done when a data

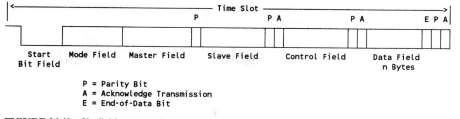

FIGURE 26.40 Six-field message format.

transfer exceeds the time slot and the master must arbitrate again for the bus to complete the data transfer.

Error Detection Management.   Error checking is performed through odd parity on the slave address, control field, and after each data byte. The acknowledge bit in the transfer message will not be transmitted by the addressed slave if there is a parity error, the speed mode is too high, there is a timing error, slave locked to another master, or the receive buffer is full.

Fault Tolerance.   Fault tolerance for nodes is not specified.

Data Rate.   The maximum bit rate is 1Mbps. Three different transmission speeds are allowed.

Framing Overhead.   The total frame size is 34 bits including interframe separation. In speed mode 1, 32 data bytes can be transferred from master to slave. Therefore, the percentage of overhead is $34/(34 + 256) = 11.7\%$.

Latency.   D2B allows for three different speed modes for transmission and arbitrates on the address of the competing nodes once in a speed mode. Therefore, a low-priority node may experience high latency times vs. the average. Latency is also affected by the ability of a master to lock a slave node; a locked node will not respond to any messages. In certain situations, this could degrade the overall performance of the system.

Power Reduction Modes.   Power reduction modes are available for the bus controllers.

26.3.4   Chrysler Collision Detection (C²D), SAE J1567

Application/Affiliation.   The serial communications network and bus interface special function integrated circuit[9] was developed by Chrysler Corporation and is supplied commercially by Harris Corporation. The interface IC was intended to provide a simple, yet reliable, data communications network between members of a distributed processing vehicle multiplex system. The communications protocol chosen minimizes the software support overhead requirement of the modules on the multiplex bus.

Transmission Media.   Conventional 120-ohm automotive dual twisted pair >1 twist/in.

Physical Interface.   The differential transceiver is a serial interface device which accepts digital signals and translates this information for transmission on a two-wire differential bus. The transmitter section, when transmitting, shall provide matched constant current sources to the bus "+" and bus "−" drivers (Refer to Fig. 26.41) sourcing and sinking current, respectively. When a logic "0" is supplied to the "transmit data" input, the differential amplifier shall cause the bus "+" driver to provide source current and the bus "−" driver to provide a matched current sink. A logic one at the transmit data input must cause the bus "+" and bus "−" drivers to simultaneously provide a high impedance state.

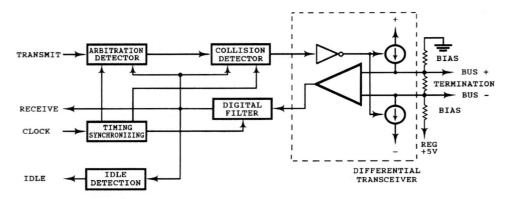

FIGURE 26.41 Simplified block diagram of network interface.

The wired OR action of the transmitting section allows more than one device to transmit at the same time, thus permitting data collisions. The nonsymmetrical action of the bus drivers will allow a transmission of a logic "0" from one device to overpower the transmission of a logic "1" from other devices. In this manner, two or more devices can simultaneously transmit and contend for the bus, each using a unique message ID byte. The winner is determined by the value or priority of the ID byte without losing bus time. A logic "0" bit in one message ID byte has priority over a logic "1" bit in another message ID byte.

The bus shall depend on external resistor and other components for bias and termination. Clamping diodes may be added to provide a high level of transient protection.

In addition to the transmission of data, the differential transceiver receives data at its bus "+" and bus "−" terminals. The received data is translated back into the standard digital logic levels by a differential amplifier. The microcomputer always receives the actual transmitted data and in this manner can test for loss of arbitration.

Bit Encoding.   The bit encoding chosen is standard 10-bit NRZ, an asynchronous serial I/O. A start bit and a stop bit is added to provide data byte synchronization. Figure 26.42 illustrates this 10-bit NRZ waveform. The interface makes use of the available hardware that has this asynchronous I/O, e.g., the serial communications interface (SCI) available on many microcomputers.

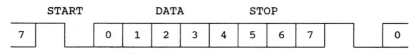

FIGURE 26.42   10-bit NRZ waveform (LSB first).

Network Access.   The network access method of resolving contention is by nondestructive bit-by-bit arbitration.

Message Format.   The message format shown in Fig. 26.43 will support a number of higher level protocols. Take note that idle periods, i.e., interbyte separations (IBS), are allowed between each byte of data. This permits the use of firmware control and direct connection to the host microcomputer's asynchronous serial I/O port.

```
(SOM),(id 1),(id 2),(data 1),(data 2)···(data n),(EOM)
```

1. SOM, defines start of message
2. id 1, 8 bit firmware addressing scheme
3. id 2, optional identifier
4. Data, may take any form, i.e., data value, CRC, checksum, number of
    bytes in message, acknowledgment, etc.
5. EOM, defines end of message (10 bits of Idle bus)

FIGURE 26.43 Frame format.

Handshaking.   The IC utilizes a low-cost serial universal interface to most microcomputers by three modes of operation that are supported in one device: SCI, SPI, and buffered SPI.

The circuits of the interface IC used when connected to the microcomputer SCI are basic to the operation of all the other modes of serial communications. Therefore, this mode will be explained first. The components of the device (See Fig. 26.41) include the following: a contention permitting differential transceiver, a collision detector, an arbitration detector, a digital filter, a bus idle detector, and a timing and synchronizing circuit.

For a contention permitting differential transceiver, see the "Physical Interface" section for details. With a collision detector, data collision detection occurs because the transceiver output is reflected back into its input. The data collision detector samples the transmitted signal and the received signal. The timing of this sampling is determined by the timing circuit. When the collision detector determines that a logic "1" bit is being transmitted, but a logic "0" bit is being received, the collision detector blocks the transmitted signal. In this way, the data collision detector will permit only the interface with the highest priority to continue transmitting. The collision detector action of blocking transmission is also reset by detection of bus idle (10 consecutive idle bits).

The arbitration detector works in conjunction with the timing and synchronizing circuit to arbitrate between the start of data to be transmitted with the start of a received message from the bus. The arbitration detector blocks a transmission that could corrupt a message that is already in progress. It also allows the device that starts transmission first, after a bus idle, to pass its data through the interface and out onto the bus. In all other nontransmitting devices, the arbitration detector blocks transmission of data until the detection of a bus idle condition. When more than one device wants to transmit at about the same time, greater than ¼ bit time, the arbitration detector will allow transmission on a first-come first-served basis. If data transmission from more than one device on the bus is attempted in near synchronism—i.e., less than or equal ¼ bit time—the arbitration detector will allow the transmission. However, the data collision detector will permit only the one with the highest priority to continue transmission. The arbitration detector is also reset by the detection of a bus idle.

A low-pass digital filter is placed between the transceiver and the received data output. This circuit functions to filter out any received EMI from the desired digital data signal before being processed by the other circuits of the interface.

The function of the bus idle detector circuit is to detect when the bus is idle (not active) or busy (active) and then feed this information back to the microcomputer. It accomplishes idle detection by sensing a received stop bit followed by 10 bits of continuous idle or logic "1"s. Normally, an active or busy period follows an idle period. The sensing of an active or busy bus is accomplished by detecting a start bit. During unusual conditions such as node startup, any transition from a logic "1" to a logic "0" that is maintained for a period longer than ¼ bit time sets the active or busy flag.

The timing and synchronizing circuit uses an external clock and establishes the synchronizing and Baud rate timing signal. This generator circuit first synchronizes on the negative edge of a start bit and then generates a timing signal at the center (½ bit time) of each bit. This timing signal is used by the arbitration and collision detector circuit for sampling received data. This timing signal is also used by the idle detection circuit to determine an idle bus.

Error Detection Management.   The normal method used to detect message data error is a firmware checksum scheme. Also, the correct number of bytes in a frame is validated by the microcomputer firmware and, in some applications, data byte overrun flags are utilized by the microcomputer hardware.

Fault Tolerance.   There is continued network operation when a node loses power or is disconnected from the bus.

Data Rate.   A 7812.5 Baud rate is recommended.

Framing Overhead.   The typical frame length is four bytes long. Framing consists of 4 start bits, 4 stop bits, 8 id bits, 8 checksum bits, and 10 end of message bits = 34 bits total framing, not including IBS. Data = 16 bits.

$$\frac{\text{OVERHEAD}}{\text{MESSAGE}} = \frac{\text{FRAMING}}{(\text{FRAMING} + \text{DATA})}$$

$$\frac{\text{OVERHEAD}}{\text{MESSAGE}} = \frac{34}{(34 + 16)} = 68\% \text{ not including IBS}$$

Latency.   In a nondestructive bit-by-bit arbitration scheme, a node will experience varying amounts of latency based on the priority of the message to be transmitted. When more than one device wants to transmit at the same time—i.e., less than ¼ bit time—the arbitration detector will allow transmission on a priority basis. If more than one device wants to transmit at about the same time—i.e., greater than ¼ bit time—the arbitration detector will allow transmission on a first-come first-served basis.

Power Reduction Mode.   This supports a "sleep state" under microcomputer control by a <10-μ source or sink from bus "+" or bus "−" of input leakage shutdown current.

26.3.5   Class B Data Communication Network Interface, SAE J1850 PWM

The SAE J1850 Standard[10] defines two versions of vehicle multiplex networks. This section covers the PWM encoded at 41.6 Kbps and the following section (26.3.6) discusses the VPWM data encoded at 10.4 Kbps version.

Application/Affiliation.   The Society of Automotive Engineers (SAE) developed a vehicle data network for Class B data communications. The latest revision, MAY94, is in publication.

Transmission Media.   The physical layer approach is a dual-wire voltage drive. The media for dual-wire is either a twisted or parallel wire pair.

Physical Interface.   A representative circuit diagram for the receiver/transmitter is shown in Fig. 26.44.

Bit Encoding

Pulse-Width Modulation.   A "1" bit and "0" bit are shown in Fig. 26.45. All bits are encoded in this manner except for a few unique symbols differentiated by the pulse timing. Some of the symbols include start of frame (SOF), end of data (EOD), and end of frame (EOF).

Network Access.   Nondestructive prioritized bit-by-bit arbitration.

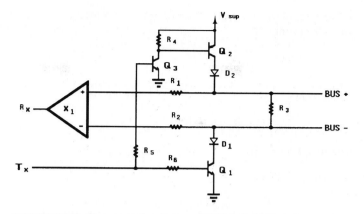

FIGURE 26.44   Representative diagram of PWM physical interface.

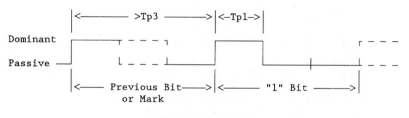

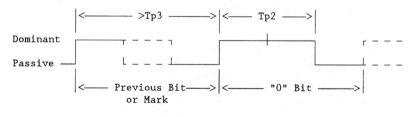

FIGURE 26.45   SAE J1850 PWM bit representation.

Message Format.   The maximum length for a frame is 101 bit times. The error detection byte is included in the data field at the discretion of the designer. Another possible use of the data field could be a message/address identifier. The response byte is explained more fully in the handshaking section following. Interframe spacing is nominally 2 bit times. The message frame is shown in Fig. 26.46.

Handshaking.   Acknowledgment is provided in the message frame using the response bytes. The response byte appears after the EOD. If an acknowledgment is not expected, a response byte will not be sent and the bus will remain in the passive state signifying an EOF. If the in-message acknowledge/response feature is active, then the response byte is an 8-bit acknowledge identifier or one or more response bytes followed by an ERR byte. One or more nodes may attempt to respond to the requesting node and arbitration will occur during the response time period.

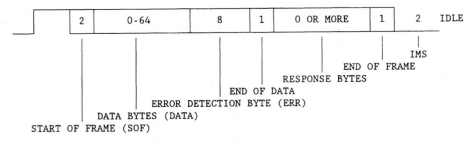

FIGURE 26.46   SAE J1850 PWM version message frame.

Error Detection Management.   Includes detection of invalid bit value and invalid message structure. An invalid bit or an invalid message will cause the receive process to be terminated until the next SOF. The in-message error detection field (ERR) uses an 8-bit CRC based on the polynomial $x^8 + x^4 + x^3 + x^2 + 1$.

Fault Tolerance.   Communications may be interrupted to/from a node when a node loses power, there is a bus short to ground, a bus short to battery, or a transceiver failure, but there shall be no damage to any other node. The remaining nodes are capable of communications when a node loses power, there is a transceiver failure, and for a loss of connection to network.

Data Rate.   The bit rate specified is 41.6 Kbps.

Framing Overhead.   The total length for the frame is 101 bit times and, for the overhead calculation, add two bits for IMS. The total length for the calculation becomes 103. The total allowed data is 80 bits for a one-byte form of header, a message identifier, and 64 bits for a three-byte form of header. The percentage of overhead is therefore $23/(80 + 23) = 22.3\%$ and $39/(64 + 39) = 37.9\%$.

Latency.   In a nondestructive bit-by-bit arbitration scheme, the highest priority message/address will gain access to the bus. In a message priority scheme, a node will experience varying amounts of latency based on the average priority of messages to be transmitted. A node in an address priority system will experience a delay proportional to the priority level of its address and the activity on the bus. An example of such a delay is a low-priority node, which will experience higher than average latency during periods of high bus loading.

Power Reduction Mode.   A node should enter a "sleep state" if the bus is idle for more than 500 ms. "Wake-up" occurs with any activity on the bus.

26.3.6   Class B Data Communication Network Interface, SAE J1850 VPWM

The SAE J1850 Standard[10] defines two versions of vehicle multiplex networks. This section covers the VPWM encoded data at 10.4 Kbps and the previous section (26.3.5) discusses the PWM encoded data at 41.6 Kbps version.

Application/Affiliation.   The Society of Automotive Engineers (SAE) developed a vehicle data network for communications. The latest revision, MAY94, is in publication.

Transmission Media.   The physical layer of the VPWM version defines a single-wire voltage drive. The media for single-wire is a single random lay wire.

Physical Interface.   The representative circuit diagram for the VPWM receiver/transmitter is shown in Fig. 26.47.

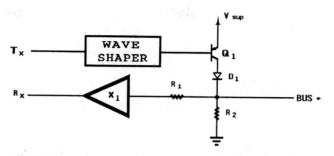

FIGURE 26.47   Representative diagram of a VPWM physical interface.

Bit Encoding.   Each bit or symbol in variable pulse-width encoding (except break) is defined by the time between two consecutive transitions and the level of the bus, dominant or passive. Therefore, there is one symbol per transition and one transition per symbol. The end of the previous symbol starts the current symbol.

The "1" and "0" Bits.   A "1" bit is either a long 128-μs passive pulse or a short 64-μs dominant pulse. Conversely, a "0" bit is either a short passive pulse or a long dominant pulse (see Fig. 26.48). The pulse widths change between passive and dominant bus states in order to accommodate the arbitration and priority requirements.

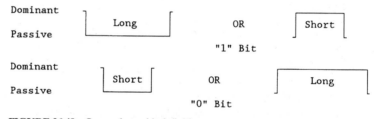

FIGURE 26.48   One and zero bit definitions.

The start of frame (SOF) is a dominant pulse, 200 μs in duration (see Fig. 26.49).

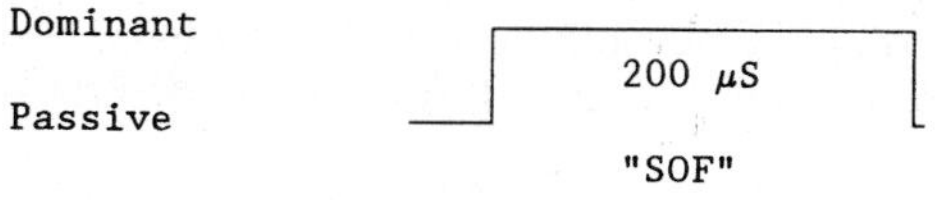

The end of data (EOD) is a passive pulse, 200 μs in duration (see Fig. 26.50).

The end of frame (EOF) is a passive pulse, 280 μs in duration (see Fig. 26.51).

The In-Frame Response Byte(s)/Normalization Bit.   The in-frame response is transmitted by the responder and begins after the

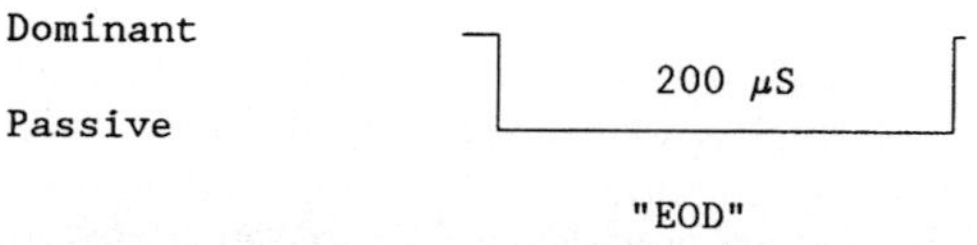

FIGURE 26.49   Start of frame (SOF) symbol.

FIGURE 26.50   End of data (EOD) symbol.

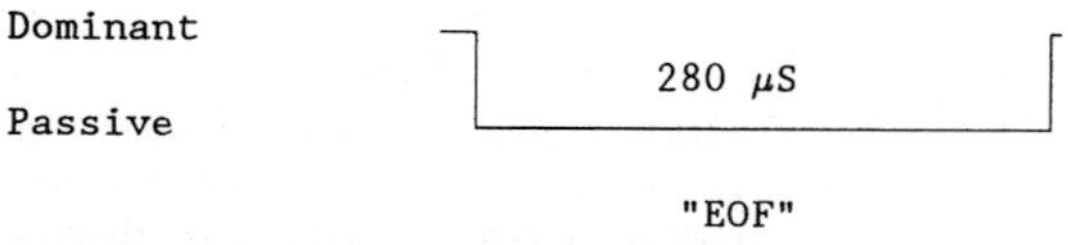

FIGURE 26.51   End of frame (EOF) symbol.

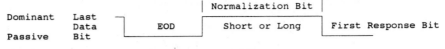

FIGURE 26.52 Normalization bit pulse-width modulation.

passive EOD symbol. For variable pulse-width modulation, the first bit of the in-frame response data is also passive. It is necessary to generate a normalization bit to follow the EOD symbol. The responding device generates the normalization bit prior to sending the IFR data. This normalization bit defines the start of the in-frame response and can take two forms. The first type is a dominant short period. The second type is a dominant long period and may be used to define an in-frame response with a CRC. Figure 26.52 illustrates the in-frame response using the normalization bit.

Network Access.   Network access is by nondestructive prioritized bit-by-bit arbitration.

Message Format.   The maximum length for a frame is 101 bit times. The error detection byte is included in the data field at the discretion of the designer. Another possible use of the data field could be a message/address identifier. The response byte is explained more fully in the handshaking section that follows. Interframe spacing is nominally 300 µs in duration bit times. The message frame is shown in Fig. 26.53.

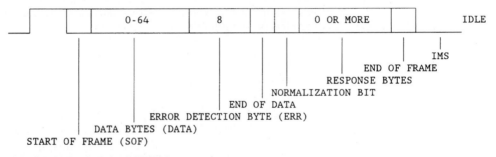

FIGURE 26.53 SAE J1850 VPWM message frame.

Handshaking.   Acknowledgment is provided in the message frame using the response bytes. The response byte appears after the EOD. If an acknowledgment is not expected, a response byte will not be sent and the bus will remain in the passive state signifying an EOF. If the in-message acknowledge/response feature is active, then the response byte is an 8-bit acknowledge identifier or one or more response bytes followed by an ERR byte. One or more nodes may attempt to respond to the requesting node and arbitration will occur during the response time period.

Error Detection Management.   Includes detection of bus out-of-range, invalid bit value, and invalid message structure. An invalid bit or an invalid message will cause the receive process to be terminated until the next SOF. The error detection field (ERR) uses an 8-bit CRC based on the polynomial: $x^8 + x^4 + x^3 + x^2 + 1$.

Fault Tolerance.   Communications may be interrupted to/from a node when a node loses power, there is a bus short to ground, a bus short to battery, or a transceiver failure, but there shall be no damage to any other node. The remaining nodes are capable of communications when a node loses power, there is a transceiver failure, and for a loss of connection to network.

Data Rate.   The bit rate specified is 10.4 Kbps.

Framing Overhead.   The total length for the frame is 101 bit times. For the overhead calculation, add 2 bits for IMS. The total length for the calculation becomes 103. The total allowed data is 80 bits for a one-byte form of Header (message identifier) and 64 bits for a three-byte form of header. The percentage of overhead is therefore $23/(80 + 23) = 22.3\%$ and $39/(64 + 39) = 37.9\%$.

Latency.   In a nondestructive bit-by-bit arbitration scheme, the highest priority message/address will gain access to the bus. In a message priority scheme, a node will experience varying amounts of latency based on the average priority of messages to be transmitted. A node in an address priority system will experience a delay proportional to the priority level of its address and the activity on the bus. For example, a low-priority node will experience higher than average latency during periods of high bus loading.

Power Reduction Mode.   A node should enter a sleep state if the bus is idle for more than 500ms. Wake-up occurs with any activity on the bus.

26.3.7   Chrysler Sensor and Control (CSC), SAE J2058

Application/Affiliation.   A proprietary multiplexing technique,[11] the Chrysler Sensor and Control (CSC) bus, yields the flexibility in expansion to meet the future demands of automotive customers. The CSC bus components were developed to provide simple, yet reliable, communication between a host-master module and its sensors and actuators. The scheme chosen provides the ability to communicate in both polling mode and direct addressing modes. This form of multiplexing will permit smaller module connectors and reduce the number of wires crowding through the congested areas without introducing more modules. The (CSC) bus is a style of multiplexing that meets these objectives and allows the design of the base vehicle while attaching the complete cost of optional features to the option.

Two CSC components are available as of this publication: (1) CSC bus two-pin, CSC Bus Hall Effect Sensors, Allegro P/N A3054U, and (2) Driver/Receiver Master Interface, Cherry Semiconductor, Automotive IC Data Book, P/N CS-8425 Hall-Effect Sensor.

Transmission Media.   The CSC network utilizes a single-wire random lay.

Physical Interface.   The output waveform of the driver/receiver master interface must be wave-shaped to limit the rise and fall time. Empirical vehicle testing has confirmed acceptable EMI levels if the waveform transients exceed 20 μs at data rates of 1 Kbps. The susceptibility to EMI is of greater concern. (See Fig. 26.54).

The preferred solution is to reference the CSC sensor at the driver/receiver master interface ground. This solution virtually eliminates this longitudinal noise current and, at the same time, significantly reduces the effects of ground offset voltage. In a production vehicle, returning the CSC sensor references to the master module usually does not add a wire circuit because these sensors originally had an independent ground wire return to the body or chassis. Further improvement to EMI susceptibility can be achieved by placing a small bypass capacitor across the CSC bus at the sensor.

Bit Encoding.   Continuous Polling Mode Sensor Multiplexing.   Figure 26.55 contains the typical voltage waveform used to communicate with multiplexed sensors. As illustrated, the sensors use current to respond back to the master that generates the voltage waveform. In this scheme, each sensor has an internal preprogrammed address. The voltage begins at a reset (zero volt) level and climbs to 6 V. This initial 6-V level provides power to the sensors. During

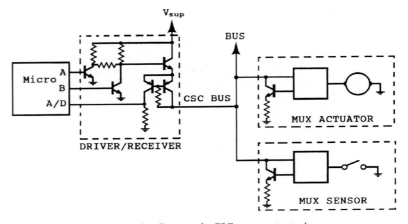

FIGURE 26.54   Representative diagram of a CSC sensor actuator bus.

this time, the master reads the amount of current required to keep the sensors powered. This current is called the sensor power current. At each change from 6 V to 9 V, a counter contained in the sensor is incremented. The sensors are addressed consecutively so this mode of CSC bus communication is called the *continuous polling mode*.

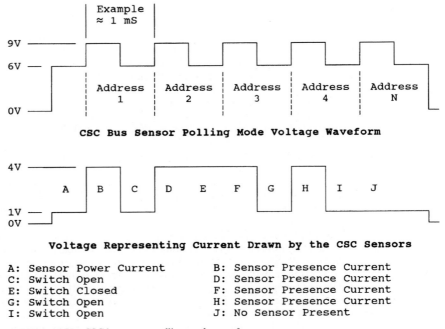

FIGURE 26.55   CSC bus sensor polling mode waveform.

While the voltage is at approximately 9 V, the sensors compare the value in their counter to their preprogrammed address. If a sensor detects a match between these two values, the sensor will increase the current drain on the CSC bus. This *response current* informs the master that a sensor has recognized its address. This condition remains until the voltage falls to about 6 V.

When the sensor being addressed detects that the voltage is below its threshold of about 7.5 V, it will determine the status of the sensing element, i.e., magnetic field detecting Hall effect sensor, optical sensor, or mechanical switch to ground. If the sensing element is active—i.e., a magnetic field is detected—light is detected, or a mechanical switch to ground is closed, the sensor continues to draw the response current so that the master can sense the sensor's status. If the sensing element is not active, response current will cease and only the sensor power current will be drawn.

Actuator Polling Multiplexing. This effort to control actuators utilizes the CSC bus multiplexing technique used as an extension of the sensor polling mode. A particular actuator is assigned an address, just as the sensor is assigned an address. Each actuator monitors the CSC bus to count the 6- to 9-V transitions in the same way as the sensor does. When the value in the counter of the actuator matches the actuator's address during the 6-V portion of the address, the actuator draws current to tell the master that the actuator is recognizing its address.

To activate an actuator output, the status must first be monitored by checking the current drawn during the second half of the address cycle. In contrast to the sensor polling scheme, which uses 6-V and 9-V levels only, the actuator multiplexing scheme adds a third 3-V level (see Fig. 26.56). During the second half of the address cycle, the level is driven to 3 V by the master when the output of the actuator is to be toggled. The actuator monitors the CSC bus during its address. If the actuator detects the 3-V level, a latch is set. The actuator does not change its output, because of noise considerations, after the first 3-V level is detected.

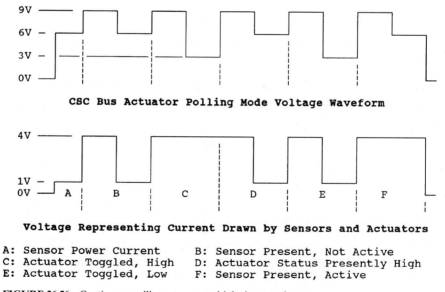

CSC Bus Actuator Polling Mode Voltage Waveform

Voltage Representing Current Drawn by Sensors and Actuators

A: Sensor Power Current   B: Sensor Present, Not Active
C: Actuator Toggled, High   D: Actuator Status Presently High
E: Actuator Toggled, Low   F: Sensor Present, Active

FIGURE 26.56 Continuous polling actuator multiplexing waveforms.

The actuator monitors the following polling cycle. If the second half of the actuator's address period in the very next polling cycle is 3 V then the actuator will toggle its output. Every subsequent polling cycle must contain the 6-V level during the actuator's address period for the output to remain constant. The current drawn by the actuator during this second half indicates the status of the output. When the output is to change state again, two consecutive polling cycles must contain 3-V levels during the second half of the actuator's address period.

Actuator Command Mode Multiplexing. In order to increase the flexibility of the communication scheme, the system designer has as an optional complementary actuator multiplexing capability. In order to provide all polling addresses to sensors and permit direct addressing of a particular actuator, a scheme was devised that complements the polling mode. This scheme has been called the *command mode, direct addressing,* or *control mode* of the CSC bus.

Instead of sequentially addressing the actuators as in the polled method, the master sends a 6-ms voltage signal to the actuators (Fig. 26.57). This waveform consists of transitions between 6 V and 3 V. The example 6-ms waveform is divided into six 1-ms bits and is called a 6-bit word. A 75%/25% pulse-width modulation technique is used to define the bit value. Each bit begins with a transition to 6 V. For example, a "1" bit is defined as 750 μs at 6 V and 250 μs at 3 V. A "0" bit is defined as 250 μs at 6 V and 750 μs at 3 V.

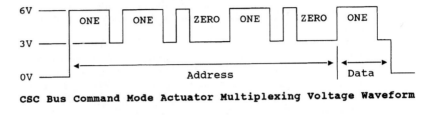

CSC Bus Command Mode Actuator Multiplexing Voltage Waveform

A, B, C, D, E, and G: Sensor Power Current
F: Actuator Response Current
H: Actuator Output Status High

Voltage Representing Current Drawn by Sensors and Actuators

FIGURE 26.57 CSC bus command mode actuator multiplexing waveform.

The first five bits of the 6-bit word are used to address the particular actuator and the sixth bit is used to control the state of the actuator's output. The master provides the voltage waveform. The CSC bus is initially at reset (≈0 V). From reset the voltage waveform is driven to 6 V. The waveform stays at 6 V for either 750 or 250 μs, depending on whether the bit is a "1" or a "0", respectively. The CSC bus then falls to 3 V for the remainder of the 1-ms bit period. During the 6-V portion of the first bit, the master monitors the current drawn by the components on the CSC bus. The master will use this current later as a reference to determine if an actuator has recognized its address.

All six bits are transmitted the same as just described. During the 3-V portion of the fifth and final address bit, the master can determine that an actuator has recognized its address by measuring the amount of current being drawn.

Network Access. The CSC bus utilizes a master-slave protocol. This protocol is appropriate because the master is usually the present major feature module and its associated sensors and actuators are the slaves. The feature module microcomputer is the host to the driver/receiver interface IC.

The CSC bus driver/receiver master interface integrated circuit contains the circuitry required to provide a DC offset square wave output. This output is controlled by two digital CMOS inputs: A and B. These two inputs are provided by a host microcomputer acting as the "brains" of the master control module. The IC is able to sense the CSC bus current and convert it to an analog voltage. This voltage is provided by the IC output for use by the micro-computer analog input.

Message Format. The network method for this communication system is a master-slave polling and/or direct address method. The master uses a voltage waveform to communicate to the sensors and actuators. A sensor is addressed through successive and ordered polling of each address (time slot or period) in ascending order.

```
<SOM>, Wake-Up Period, Addr 1, Addr 2, ..., Addr 32
```

An actuator may be controlled by either the polling mode shown or the direct address, command mode message below. The start of message (SOM) is defined as the rising edge from 0 to 6 V in the voltage waveform of Fig. 26.55.

```
<SOM>, <Five-Bit address>, <1 to N data bits>, {<parity bit>}
```

Handshaking. Both sensors and actuators respond to the master node when polled or directly addressed, with a response current informing the master that an address has been recognized.

Error Detection Management. Actuator data can be protected from unwanted actuation by a parity bit in the command message. The normal solution for eliminating EMI susceptibility that caused false sensor data is to software filter the data in the master control module.

In order to validate the proper addressing of a sensor or actuator in a noisy vehicle environment, the following procedure is suggested. If this current is not above the reference current measured, the sensor is not present or no actuator is listening. If two or more sensors or actuators are listening (determined by double the expected response current), the master can reset (output zero volts) the CSC bus. If the master detects that the sensor or actuator output is not in the correct state, the command can be repolled or resent.

Fault Tolerance. Handshaking between the master node and sensors allows operation and detection when sensors or actuators are removed from the network. The driver/receiver has a current limit that protects it from a bus short.

Data Rate. The data rate is determined by the master module software and need not be fixed. A rate of 1 Kbps is suggested.

Framing Overhead. The framing required time is equal to the data time therefore:

$$\frac{\text{OVERHEAD}}{\text{MESSAGE}} = \frac{\text{FRAMING}}{(\text{FRAMING} + \text{DATA})}$$

$$\frac{\text{OVERHEAD}}{\text{MESSAGE}} = \frac{1}{2} = 50\%$$

Latency. The master node is in control and can interrupt sensor or actuator polling to command an output to an actuator within a few milliseconds and 32 sensors can be polled within 32 ms, or a 1-Kbps rate.

Power Reduction Mode. The master node can control the power by not polling or addressing the network. The current draw will then be the sensor actuator standby power.

26.3.8 Token Slot Protocol, SAE J2106

Application/Affiliation.   General Motors developed protocol[12] for high-performance vehicle control and general information sharing.

Transmission Media.   Not specified. Electrical twisted pair or fiber optic media are recommended. Fiber optic token slot networks operating at 1 Mbps have been demonstrated.

Physical Interface.   Not specified. Multiple access to a logical common bus is required.

Bit Encoding.   NRZ (nonreturn to zero) with opposite logic level bit insertion (stuffing) after five contiguous bits of the same state. Receiving nodes detect and remove inserted bits.

Network Access.   The token passing bus network is open, peer-oriented, and multimaster. It is noncontention and uses a time slot token passing technique. See Fig. 26.58, 26.59, and 26.60.

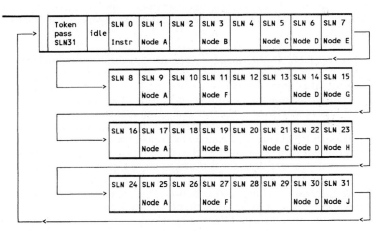

FIGURE 26.58   A typical token slot node assignment and slot sequence cycle pattern.

FIGURE 26.59   Token pass message format.

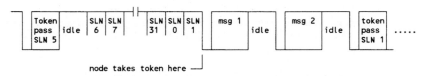

FIGURE 26.60   Typical token pass sequence.

The intent of this bus access protocol is to guarantee periodic opportunities for message transmission by each node on the bus. It is to also ensure that the bus remains operational when devices are dynamically added or deleted and it must provide for quick recovery from error conditions.

After a node has completed sending its message traffic, a sequenced scan of short, equal time intervals (slots) offer bus transmit privileges to the node slot owners as follows (see Fig. 26.59): A token pass message or a *bus jam* instructs all nodes to begin the token slot timing mode. Each node is assigned one or more specific time slots and will activate its transmitter to send a message during its slot only if it is operational and has message traffic to send. Otherwise, the token slot interval is allowed to pass. When the transmitter is activated, all other nodes recognize that the token has been taken and they enter the receive mode.

The new token owner next proceeds to send its message traffic (see Fig. 26.60). Token hold times are individually assigned to each node and are strictly limited to assure a system maximum message latency limit. Individual message transmit priorities are determined by each node's application and are not restricted by the data communications network.

A node concludes a transmit session by sending the token pass message that contains the current slot number (see Fig. 26.60). In the ensuing token slot sequence, the node that owns the next sequential slot number may take the token or let it pass. When the maximum slot number is reached, the sequence wraps around to slot 0 and continues until the slot is picked up or until the original token passer sees its slot, at which time a new token pass message is generated and the cycle begins again.

Message Format.   There are three basic message types which are distinguished by the 2-bit control field which is found in the first byte:

* *Token pass* (see Figs. 26.59 and 26.60).   This is a single-byte message which contains the message control field (2 bits), the current slot number (5 bits), and a single parity (even bit). It is followed by an idle line (8 bits) delimiter.
* *Data* (see Figs. 26.61 and 26.62).   This includes the message control field (2 bits), a message ID field (14 bits), up to 256 bytes of data, a 16-bit cyclic redundancy check (CRC) field, and a message delimiter bus idle line (8 bits). The message control field is used to request an "acknowledge" message response.

FIGURE 26.61   Token slot network general message framing.

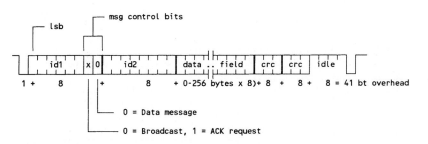

FIGURE 26.62   Token slot network data message format.

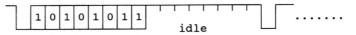

FIGURE 26.63   Token slot network acknowledge message format.

- *Acknowledge* (see Fig. 26.63).   This is a fixed, single-byte (Hex D5) message plus an 8-bit idle line delimiter (16 total bits). It is initiated by the previous data message control field.

Handshaking.   Any data message can be dynamically programmed to command an immediate returned acknowledge message from one receiving node. If after a short wait interval the requested acknowledge has not been received, the sender may retry and/or proceed to send other messages. Note that the responding node does not possess the token.

Error Detection Management.   Both the receiving and the transmitting nodes independently monitor transmissions on the bus. The transmitting node checks messages for a 1:1 received to transmitted bit correspondence. All nodes check for correct timing, CRC, intermessage gaps, and, if requested, an acknowledge message. Receiving nodes do not acknowledge erroneous messages.

The 16-bit CRC conforms to the CCITT standard and detects all single-bit errors, all parity errors, and all burst errors less than 17 bits long. For burst errors longer than 16 bits, the CRC misses 0.0015 percent of errors.

A transmitter detected *bus time out* (BTO) error occurs when the bus is idle for more than a complete token slot sequence period. When a BTO is detected, all nodes start a new token pass slot sequence beginning at slot 0.

Bus errors or collisions cause the detecting node to generate a bus jam signal, a dominant line for 8-bit times, before the end-of-message idle line. This declares the current operation or message invalid and instructs all nodes to start a new token pass slot sequence beginning at slot 0.

Fault Tolerance.   Each transmitting node monitors its own bus performance and fault history. Appropriate degraded mode operations are controlled by the node. The loss of any node or even a separated bus will not affect the continued bus operation by the remaining nodes.

Data Rate.   Data rate limit is specified at 2 MHz. However, the data rate is only limited by bus media bandwidth and future data rate growth is possible.

Framing Overhead.   The message framing overhead is summarized in Tables 26.3 and 26.4. See Fig. 26.64 for total message latency calculation methods.

TABLE 26.4   Token Slot Data Message Overhead*

Synchronization bit	1
ID	16
Data (system determined limit, e.g., 0–256 bytes)	var
CRC	16
Intermessage delimiter gap	8
Acknowledge response (if requested) + gap	16
Per message overhead—with ACK	57 bits
or per message overhead—without ACK	41 bits

* See Fig. 26.61, 26.62, and 26.63.

TABLE 26.3   Token Passing Slot Overhead in Bit Times (bt)*

Slot width (assume xmtr ON aqt mid slot = 2 bit)	2
Token pass message	8
Delimiter gap	8
Token pass overhead per node	18 bit

* See Fig. 26.59 and Fig. 26.60

<u>Token Slot Message Overhead (in bit times = bt)</u>:

```
Synchronization bit                              1
ID                                              16
Data (system determined limit - bytes)   (0-256 bytes)
CRC                                             16
Intermessage delimiter gap                       8
Acknowledge response (if requested) + gap       16
                                            ─────────
            Per message overhead - with ACK:    57 bt
    or      Per message overhead - without ACK: 41 bt
```

<u>Token Passing Slot Overhead</u>:

```
Slot width (assume xmtr on at mid slot = 1 bt)  1
Token Pass Message                              8
Delimiter gap                                   8
                                           ─────────
            Token pass overhead per node:  17  bt
```

<u>Summary of Loop Time Calculations</u>:

For P nodes sending an N message loop with M
total message data bytes:

```
Total message overhead (no ACK)          41N
Total token overhead                     17P
Total message data time (m x 8 bits)      8M
Unused slots =
   slot width x (max #slots - #usedslots) = 1(32-P)
                                        ──────────────────
        Total Loop Time             41N + 17P + 8M + 4(32-P)
```

<u>Example Token Slot Timing Calculation</u>

For 8 nodes sending a 16 message loop with 32 total
message data bytes (2 msgs x 2 bytes per node x 8 nodes):

```
Total message overhead (no ACK)    41x16 =      656
Total token overhead               17x8  =    + 136
                                           ──────────
                                                792
Total message data time (32 x 8 bits)    =    + 256
Unused slot time        (1x24)           =    +  24
                                           ──────────
                Total Loop Time (bt)         1072
```

Data-to-total time overhead efficiency: 256/1072 =   24.0%

FIGURE 26.64 Determination of token slot message latencies.

Latency.   The protocol is noncontention and deterministic. As such, message latencies in the token slot network are both predictable and bounded, which is a requirement for feedback control systems.

Factors that affect message latency times are discussed in the following. See Fig. 26.64 for methods of latency calculation and prediction.

The token loop time determines the interval between opportunities to transmit a message. It is defined as the total elapsed time between token possessions by a particular node. It includes all message traffic, token pass slot times, and all token hold times.

Token slot time length is important during the token pass sequence when each time slot must provide sufficient time for worst-case signal propagation delays in order to allow nodes to detect that the token has been taken.

Token hold time is the maximum number of bit times that each node is allowed to hold the token. All message IDs, data fields, CRCs, intermessage gaps, message synchronization bits, NRZ5 bit insertions, acknowledge messages or acknowledge time outs, and token pass messages must not exceed this limit. Each node monitors and controls this time to stay within its assigned limit.

Power Reduction Mode.   Not specified. Could be implemented.

26.3.9 Time Triggered Protocol (TTP)

Knowledge about the future (i.e., a priori knowledge) behavior of the TTP system is available to the system designer and is controlled by the progression of time.[13] For example, the point in time when a node is supposed to send a message can and must be determined by the real-time control algorithms and programmed into the module before release for production. The main advantage to TTP is to support high-speed distributed time-triggered real-time control of systems.

Application/Affiliation.   TTP was developed by the Institute for Technical Information, Technical University Wien, Austria, and is an integrated communications protocol for Class C in-vehicle applications that provides all services required for the implementation of a distributed fault-tolerant high-speed real-time control system.

Transmission Media.   A twisted pair or fiber optics is suggested for the transmission media.

Physical Interface.   The basic system I/O structure consists of nodes connected by two redundant physical interfaces to dual networks to protect for failures in cabling, contacts, connectors, etc. To tolerate a node failure, two nodes are connected in parallel. Four configurations are shown in Fig. 26.65.

Bit Encoding.   The bit encoding is not specified. However, modified frequency modulation (MFM) is suggested as the encoding technique because it has fewer than one transition per bit.

Network Access.   The network access is accomplished using a time division multiple access (TDMA) controlled by a global time base generated by time triggered protocol (TTP). A TDMA round is defined to be a complete cycle during which each vehicle module has been granted at least one sending access.

Message Format.   All information transmitted on a communications channel must be properly framed. A TTP frame consists of the following fields: start of frame (SOF), a control field, data field, and a CRC field. An interframe delimiter (IFD) exists between any two TTP frames. See Fig. 26.66.

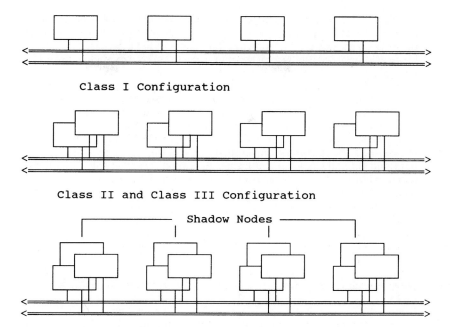

FIGURE 26.65 Fault-tolerant configurations.

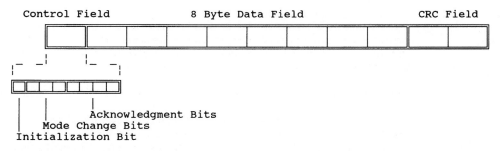

FIGURE 26.66 Typical frame format.

Start of Frame (SOF).   This identifies the beginning of a new frame.

Control Field.   The control field has three subfields.

Initialization Bit.   This specifies an initialization frame (I-frame) or a normal frame (N-frame). I-frames are required to initialize a node. The state of the communications controller node (i.e., C-state) consists of three fields: a node field, a time field, and a membership field. Typically, each one of these fields will have a length of two bytes, or 16 bits. When a node is initialized, these three fields are filled from the data field. N-frames are normal data frames containing the application data in the data field.

Mode Change Bits (3 bits).   If the initialization bit is unequal to zero, it allows the specification of seven successor modes to the current mode. Therefore, the protocol supports a rapid change from one mode to another mode, e.g., startup, normal operation, emergency, etc.

Acknowledgment Bits (4 bits). These bits contain an acknowledgment for the frames sent by the preceding vehicle module. The question of which module is the preceding module depends on the current membership. The length of the acknowledgment field makes it possible to acknowledge each one of the four frames sent by a module in a class III or Class IV configuration.

Data Field. The data field consists of the concatenation of one or more messages containing application data. The length of each message is statically defined in the mode definition. It is not necessary to carry a name field in the frame since the message name can be inferred from the mode field and the point in time of sending.

Cyclic Redundancy Check (CRC) Field. The CRC field has a length of two bytes. For N-frames, the CRC is calculated over the C-state of the controller concatenated with the control field and the data field of the frame. A normal frame is only accepted if the sender and receiver have identical C-states, i.e., if they agree on mode, time, and membership. Since the receiver knows a priori the time of sending of each frame, it is not necessary to carry the value of the send time in the frame.

Interframe Delimiter (IFD). The interframe delimiter is required for proper bit synchronization of sender and receiver.

Handshaking. As shown in Fig. 26.65, two nodes are connected in parallel to tolerate a node failure in replicated vehicle communications channels. These replicated channels perform the same state changes at about the same time and are synchronized to within a known precision by TTP.

Error Detection Management. TTP is based on the assumption that the communications channels have only omission failures and the nodes support the fail-silent abstraction; i.e., they either deliver correct results or no results at all, which helps to enforce error confinement at the system level. A sender attaches a CRC to each frame and a receiver can detect when a frame has been mutilated and discard the corrupted frame.

For correct operation, the node must assure, by use of space or time redundancy, that all internal failures of a node are detected and the node is turned off before an erroneous output message is transmitted. Moreover, a membership service is required to detect omission failures of incoming and outgoing communications links. This membership service is part of the protocol.

Fault Tolerance. With dual duplex buses and redundant node communications channels, the fault tolerance capability is excellent. Table 26.5 shows the fault tolerance capability achieved with the four class configurations shown in Fig. 26.65. The recovery interval for a transient event depends on the length of the transient blackout period and the time TTP takes to detect, monitor, and recover from a blackout. This time for TTP is in the millisecond range.

TABLE 26.5 Fault Tolerance Capability

Tolerance of	Class I	Class II	Class III	Class IV
Permanent node failure	0	1	1	2
Permanent bus failure	1	1	1	1
Transient node failure	0	1 per event	1 per event	1 per TDM round
Transient bus failure	1 of 2	1 of 2	3 of 4	3 of 4

Data Rate. The data rate is not specified, but 1 Mbps is suggested.

Framing Overhead. The length of SOF and IFD depends on the bus propagation delay, the quality of the clock synchronization, and bit-encoding method. For transmission speeds below

1 Mbit and a bus length below 20 m, the SOF = 1 and IFD = 3. The framing overhead is given by the following: OVERHEAD/MESSAGE = FRAMING/(FRAMING + DATA). For a message transmitting 4 bytes (32 bits) of data, using the formula: 28/(28 + 32) = 47%. For a message of 8 bytes (64 bits) of data, using the formula: 28/(28 + 64) = 30%. The total framing overhead is slightly higher to account for the periodic transmission of initialization frames.

Latency.   Given a 1-Mbit channel for eight nodes sending a 16-message loop with 32 total message data bytes, the TDMA round of TTP is 0.48 ms in Class I or Class II configuration. This is also the worst-case delay for a node switch. If a Class III or Class IV configuration with four replicated messages is selected, the TDMA round is doubled, i.e., just below 1 ms.

Power Reduction Mode.   The power reduction is not specified but could be specified as a mode of operation. The change to a power reduction could be done at any time.

26.3.10   Vehicle Area Network (VAN)

Application/Affiliation.   VAN (vehicle area network) is a multiplex bus protocol proposal being considered by the ISO Technical Committee 22/SC3/WG1.[14]

Transmission Media.   Twisted pair.

Physical Interface.   Transmission is on differential pair using current sources. An optional analog filter is provided to increase noise immunity. See Fig. 26.67.

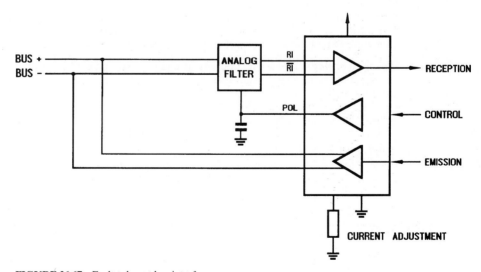

FIGURE 26.67   Fault-tolerant bus interface.

Bit Encoding.   Two different bit representations are allowed: L-Manchester and E-Manchester. The bit representation is selected by the user. When L-Manchester is selected, all the bits in the frame are Manchester encoded. E-Manchester will be NRZ encoded except for the last bit of each nibble. With E-Manchester idle, IMS, and SOF are NRZ encoded, and ACK is Manchester encoded. See Fig. 26.68 for an example of E-Manchester encoding.

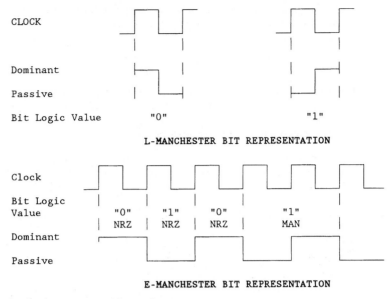

FIGURE 26.68 VAN bit encoding.

Network Access. Network access is by prioritized nondestructive bit-by-bit arbitration. Arbitration is resolved using the unique 12-bit identifier field at the start of the message. The format of this field is user-defined. VAN allows in-frame access based on a media access rank R. A node can access the frame, provided the previous R-1 bits of the arbitration field have been emitted and the previous time slot was recessive.

Message Format. The frame consists of eight fields. The start of frame (SOF) provides a common time reference that allows receiving nodes to correct their local clock. The start message bit initializes the frame. The two-byte frame identification field includes the unique 12-bit message identifier followed by three control bits and the remote transmission request bit (RTR). The RTR specifies if the frame includes data (0 bit) or if data is requested (1 bit). The RTR allows in-frame response immediately or later in a separate frame. The message frame is shown in Fig. 26.69.

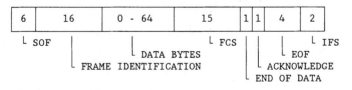

FIGURE 26.69 Single type frame format.

Handshaking. Message acknowledgment is achieved in one of two ways: no acknowledge or positive acknowledge, which means at least one station has received and accepted the message. If the receiving station cannot make an in-frame acknowledge, a separate acknowledge message must be sent later.

Error Detection Management. Methods of error detection include level monitoring, CRC, code violation detection, and frame check. Level monitoring is performed by the transmitting node. The transmitted bit levels are compared with the bit levels detected on the bus. Frame checking is performed through a 15-bit CRC code:

$$\frac{(x^8 + x^4 + x^3 + x^2 + 1)}{(x^7 + 1)}$$

Fault Tolerance.   Single-wire operation is possible with the differential drive scheme due to the ac-coupling if the other wire is shorted to ground, shorted to V_{batt}, or open circuited.

Data Rate.   The data rate is not specified.

Framing Overhead.   The total frame size (including data) is 109 bits. The total frame size includes start, stop, and idle bits. The maximum amount of data allowed in a frame is 64 bits. The percentage of overhead is therefore $45/(45 + 64) = 41.3\%$.

Latency.   As with all arbitration-based protocols, the latency amount varies depending on the priority of the message.

Power Reduction Mode.   Not specified.

26.4   SUMMARY AND CONCLUSIONS

Throughout the 20th century the auto industry has seen many changes. The electrical components in the horseless carriage were essentially a magneto ignition system. In the 1920s, the electric starter became popular but the first real use of the semiconductor in the auto industry was in the 1960s, first in electronic voltage regulators and then in brakerless ignition systems. Toward the end of the 1970s, the full engine control computer was in production. Then by the 1980s, consumers were demanding electronically controlled turbo, electronically driven instrument clusters, antilock brake systems, and navigation and trip computers. The electronic content of passenger vehicles had doubled by the 1990s.

26.4.1   The Future of Automotive Electronics

In the future, electronics will play an even larger roll. The automotive electronics field is presently going through a number of noteworthy changes. Integration, diagnostics, design for manufacturability, and system engineering are the buzzwords of the 1990s. The past add-a-feature, add-a-module mode of operation is replaced by integration. For example, the common practice is to package many of the feature items such as intermittent wipers and automatic door locks into a single module. The manufacturer will have a built-in diagnostics technique that can computer-verify that the product is functioning properly at the time of construction. Also, the dealer will have the capability of accurately and economically determining the failed module. Integration, diagnostics, and systems engineering promise higher quality, better performance, and lower cost for the manufacturer and the consumer.

26.4.2   The Class B Data Communications Network

The Class B data network is the main enabler and driving force to module integration and service diagnostics. The data network interconnects these integrated systems, allows the modules to communicate with each other, and provides for quick service and maintenance. These integrated systems must be coordinated to make sure that everything functions together properly. The Class B data communications network is applicable because most of these features will not require real-time control processing.

Electronics and vehicle multiplexing means more than just new innovative gadgets in a car. This relatively new field of automotive engineering is a highly developed technology that has the potential for enormous benefits to the consumer in that it promotes safety and provides convenient and useful features in the automobile. The data network and electronics should make it easier and more economical to manufacture a car, drive a car, and service a car.

Even though the electronic content will have doubled, the car of the mid 90s will be significantly easier to manufacture because there will be half the number of modules, due to feature content integration. The data network that interconnects these modules will also reduce the size and number of interconnecting cables and cut the number of circuits by 25 percent.

The objective of the industry is to deliver a quality, defect-free product to the customer. As previously illustrated, integration plays a major role in reducing the number of modules that can fail, the number of parts that can break and the number of interconnecting circuits that can fail, thereby substantially improving the reliability. The data network and built-in diagnostics also play a key role in verifying that the product is manufactured properly. Proper diagnostics is also accomplished more perfectly by computer during manufacturing, and reduces or eliminates the arduous task of manual verification on the assembly line.

The computerized vehicles of the future need logically acute ergonomics for the driver. Safety, reliability, ease of use, buttons that are easy to reach, and gages or dials that are easy to see can all be characterized as "slickness." Our neoteric generation of customers is rightfully demanding these innovations and world competition makes it a top priority.

At the heart of these ease-of-driving innovations is the data network that allows the various integrated modules to coordinate their activity so that the buttons that control the displays can be placed at the best ergonomic locations. The display is then located for convenient viewing while operating the vehicle.

With the aid of market research, the integrated module may be chosen to contain just the mix of features the customer desires. The data network can significantly simplify delivery of the required data to that module. This gives the customer greater freedom than ever to pick and choose a personally designed content in his new vehicle, thus promoting customer personalization and satisfaction.

The auto industry designs for reliability, but when things fail, the objective is to economically fix it right the first time. Vehicle multiplexing again plays a major role in allowing the service technician to communicate with each of the modules using a diagnostic tool through a centrally located diagnostic connector. This method uses the power of the computer in the vehicle and the diagnostic tool to walk the technician through the diagnostic flowchart to deliver the solution to the problem in a language the service technician can understand.

26.4.3   Class A Multiplexing

With all these benefits why is multiplexing taking so long? Over the last two decades the automotive component manufacturers of electronic equipment have been touting the virtues of Class A vehicle multiplexing (low-speed body wiring and control functions). Previously, articles were illustrated with dramatic pictures of the amount of wire that could be saved by multiplexing. Other articles projected immense cost savings and technical benefits to be derived through the utilization of vehicle multiplexing. Now 20 years later, few, if any, of these predictions have become a reality. Thus, the domestic vehicle manufacturers have not generally endorsed these concepts.

For years it was postulated that vehicle multiplexing would be practical once a semiconductor device was developed that would replace the relay and have the capability of driving lights and electric motors. The recently developed MOS power driver has this multiplexing potential. The semiconductor industry hopes that this device is the real breakthrough that will make Class A vehicle multiplexing a reality. However, with this development, the industry is only closer to a solution. The real situation is that Class A multiplexing is still not cost effective. A closer examination of the problems of Class A multiplexing from a vehicle manufacturers' perspective is warranted. The effectiveness of multiplexing must consider the following factors:

- The ability to reduce the average vehicle system cost
- The ability to allocate the cost of the option to the option
- Wiring reductions such as number of circuits and bundle size
- The support of built-in diagnostics for manufacturing and service
- Bus throughput (capacity) and how well the network architecture handles time-critical messages.
- Reductions in weight and ease of assembly

26.4.4 Comparison of Class A and B Data Networks

Is the Class B multiplexing situation any different than the Class A? A careful system cost analysis for Class B vehicle multiplexing shows that the added cost of the multiplexing electronic components is not offset by the cost savings in vehicle wiring harnesses. The condition is very similar to Class A data network leading one to adopt the theory that vehicle multiplexing by itself is not cost effective. The higher the cost of the electronic multiplexer, the larger the problem of finding effective cost offsets. Therefore, if the Class A data network is too complex it may not be cost effective.

There are other driving forces, such as increased content, packaging, and wire bundle size, that have the potential of outweighing the cost disadvantage. The situation with the Class B data network is much different. Class B vehicle multiplexing is the enabler to other cost-offsetting methods that are not possible with Class A multiplexing. Cost reductions such as module integration and diagnostics can be effectively used to more than offset the cost of the electronic multiplexer.

26.4.5 The SAE J1850 Standard

The SAE J1850 is a standard for a Class B data communications network. The entire automotive industry will benefit from the development of this data network. In the past, development of proprietary data networks inefficiently used scarce industry resources. Standardization will save manpower and resources, in both the semiconductor and automotive industry, and make the resources previously dedicated to proprietary data networks available for concentration on more competitive electronic developments.

The transition to an industry standard data network will be difficult and will take several years to accomplish effectively. The first introduction of the full industry standard vehicle multiplex network will be found on only luxury vehicles and then only after the system economics warrant support. Economics will play a major role in determining when the average vehicle, manufactured domestically or abroad, will have an industry standard data network. It will take the dedication and talent of electronic engineers in both the automotive and the semiconductor industries to develop the components that will meet the economic requirements. The development of a family of components is required to support the economical use on more than just the more expensive and luxury type vehicles. The application for data networks varies between manufacturers' product lines and there will be a need for different levels of industry standard data network interfaces to meet the full application requirements.

Acknowledgments

The author would like to thank the SAE support staff and all his colleagues on the Vehicle Networks for Multiplexing and Data Communications Standards Committee for their support in developing the original SAE documents from which the excerpts in this chapter originated. He would also like to thank Chrysler Corporation for its encouragement and use of its facilities. Without this material and support, this chapter would not have been possible.

GLOSSARY

This glossary contains generally accepted terminology for automotive electronic application. The terms may have additional definitions depending on usage in other disciplines.

Arbitration   The process of resolving which frame or in-frame response data continues to be transmitted when two or more nodes begin transmitting frames or in-frame response data simultaneously.

Arbitration detection   Refers to a contention-based arbitration circuit, whereby the contention created by simultaneous access of multiple nodes on the network is resolved in a bit-by-bit arbitration circuit by means of collision detection where dominant bits in the arbitration field survive without destruction and all others discontinue transmission. (See **Bit-by-bit arbitration** and **Collision detection**.)

Architecture   The organizational structure of a vehicle multiplex network, mainly referring to the application structure and communications protocol.

Balanced current I/O   An input/output circuit configuration in which signals are transmitted as currents that travel down one conductor and return on the other, and these currents are balanced, i.e., of equal magnitude.

Baud rate   A measurement or transfer rate; a number of discrete conditions or signal events per second.

Bipolar data   Data that is driven both positively and negatively from a common point such as a reference voltage or ground (0) potential.

Bit-by-bit arbitration   A contention-based arbitration, whereby the contention created by simultaneous access of multiple nodes on the network is resolved bit by bit. Bits may be represented as dominant or passive on the physical layer with dominant bits overriding passive ones in case of contention. The message with a dominant bit in the arbitration field survives without destruction and all others discontinue transmission. This procedure is repeated through all bits of the arbitration field.

Bit encoding   The smallest unit of information in the binary system of notation.

Bit rate   Bits per time during transmission, independent of bit representation.

Bit-stuf NRZ   The insertion of extra bits into an NRZ data stream to avoid the appearance of unintended control sequences for synchronization.

Bit synchronized   Transmission of a frame in which the data bits are transmitted with the transmitter and receiver bit transitions aligned in time (synchronized).

Broadcast type messages   The transmission of information to more than one receiver as differentiated from node-to-node communications.

Bus   Topology of a communications network where all nodes are reached by links, which allow transmission in both directions.

Bursty noise   Unwanted electromagnetic disturbances that are manifested as relatively short period barrages (bursts) at random or repetitive rates.

Checksum   An error-detecting code based on a simple eight-bit summation series of all the bytes in the frame that are to be checked.

Class A system   A multiplex system whereby vehicle wiring is reduced by the transmission and reception of multiple signals over the same signal bus between nodes that replaces the conventional wiring in vehicles. The nodes used to accomplish multiplexed body wiring typically did not exist in the same or similar form in a totally conventionally wired vehicle.

Class B system   A multiplex system whereby data (e.g., parametric data values) is transferred between nodes to eliminate redundant sensors and other system elements. The nodes in this form of a multiplex system typically already existed as stand-alone modules in a conventionally wired vehicle.

Class C system   A multiplex system whereby high data rate signals typically associated with real-time control systems, such as engine controls and antilock brakes, are sent over the signal bus to facilitate distributed control and to further reduce vehicle wiring.

Collision detection   Collision detection and bit-by-bit arbitration are sometimes used interchangeably and they both refer to a contention-based arbitration, in which the contention created by simultaneous access of multiple nodes on the network is resolved on a bit-by-bit arbitration basis utilizing a collision detection means. (See **Bit-by-bit arbitration**.)

Command mode   A mode of operation of a master-slave system in which the master node takes prompt control of the network to achieve the input and/or output function.

Common mode rejection ratio   The ratio of the common mode input voltage to output voltage commonly expressed in dBV, i.e., the extent to which a differential amplifier rejects an output when the same signal is applied to both inputs.

Contention process   A state of the bus in which data from two or more transmitters are simultaneously attempting to use a single shared network medium. A collision detection or arbitration process can be used to resolve the conflict.

Contiguous bits   A condition where a string of data bits is continuous and without dead time between bits.

Control field   A field in a frame which designates command information.

Control mode   Control mode and command mode are used interchangeably and refer to a mode of operation of a master-slave system in which the master node takes prompt control of the network to perform the input and/or output function.

Cyclic redundancy check (CRC)   An error-detecting code in which the code is defined to be the remainder resulting from dividing the bits to be checked in the frame by a predetermined binary number.

Data collision   A state of the bus in which two or more transmitters are turned on simultaneously to conflicting states.

Data consistency   A feature of communications in some multiplex wiring systems whereby it is determined and ensured that all required recipients of a message have received the message accurately before acting upon it simultaneously. This feature is desirable in, for example, ensuring that all four lamps are turned on at once or that all four brakes are energized simultaneously.

Data decoding technique   The process of retrieving a signal on the transmission medium that was encoded (e.g., NRZ, PWM, Manchester) back into the original logical, "1"s and "0"s bits.

Data encoding technique   Data bit encoding defines the way in which the logical bits, "1"s and "0"s, are translated into signals on the transmission medium by the physical interface (e.g., NRZ, PWM, Manchester).

Data field   Data (data field) are bytes between header bytes and error detection byte. Data and data field are sometimes used interchangeably and they both refer to a field within a frame that may include bytes with parameters pertaining to the message and/or secondary ID and/or extended addresses and/or test modes, which further define a particular message content being exchanged over the network.

Decibel volts (dBV)   A measure of the relative strength of two signals where the value is 20 times the log of the ratio of the voltage of the two signals.

Deterministic   A signal is said to be deterministic when the future behavior of the signal can be predicted precisely.

Differential receiver   The node receiver that contains a differential input. (See **Balanced current I/O.**)

Direct addressing mode   Direct addressing, control mode, and command mode are used interchangeably and they refer to a mode of operation of a master-slave system in which the master node takes prompt control of the network to perform the input and/or output function.

Dominant bit   A bit which wins arbitration when contending for the bus. For SAE J1850, a logic "0" is the dominant bit.

Driver   A solid state device used to transfer electrical power to the next stage, which may be another driver, an electrical load (power driver), a wire or cable (line driver), a display (display driver), etc.

Duplex bus   A multiplex bus where both transmission and reception occur simultaneously on the same network media. Also referred to as "full duplex."

Dynamic range   The difference between the overload level and the minimum acceptable signal level in a multiplex system, sometimes expressed in dBV.

Event-based   The attribute of transmission of data on a manually triggered event or on change of parametric value.

Event-driven   The attribute of an event-based network protocol.

Fault tolerance   Ability of a system to survive a certain number of failures while performing its required functions, but possibly with some degraded characteristics.

Frame   One complete transmission of information, which may or may not include an in-frame response. The frame is enclosed by the start of frame and end of frame symbols. For Class B networks, each frame contains of only one message. (See **Message** and **Message frame.**)

Framing overhead   The framing overhead defines the amount of nondata overhead associated with the given protocol, i.e., framing overhead.

Functional addressing   Functional addressing allows a message to be addressed or sent to one or more nodes on the network interested in that function. Functional addressing is intended for messages that may be of interest to more than a single node. For example, a vehicle speed message could be sent to all nodes requiring the vehicle speed using a functional address. Functional addressing is labeling of messages based on their operation code or data content.

Functional superset A Class C multiplex network is defined as a functional superset of Class B and Class A multiplex network, networks that have both physical and functional properties. As a functional superset, the network must be capable of communications that would perform all of the functions of the networks in that set.

Gate A minimum cell composed of transistors which form a circuit to perform a logic function such as NAND or NOR, and typically is used as a size or complexity measure of a component.

Gateway A node used to connect networks that use different protocols, as differentiated from a bridge. A gateway acts as a protocol converter.

Global address The predefined address or ID used as a broadcast to all nodes on the network.

Global time base A clock or timing device relating to, or involving, the entire vehicle network and providing the time base for the time-triggered protocol.

Ground offset Difference in voltage at a ground point as compared to a reference ground point. (See **Longitudinal noise**.)

Handshaking Defines the interaction of nodes within a network in order to effect a transfer of data. This may include such things as negative and positive acknowledgment and in-message acknowledgment.

Header field The header or header field, often used interchangeably, is a one- or three-byte field within a frame which directly or implicitly contains information about the message priority, message source and target addressing, message type, and in-frame response type.

Hexadecimal (Hex) A four-bit digital numbering system using 0, 1, ... A, B, C, D, E, and F to represent all the possible values of a decimal equivalent 0 to 15.

Identifier (ID) The primary ID identifies the target for this functional message and is the primary discriminator used to group functions into main categories.

Idle detection The capability of a circuit to detect the condition of a nondata period.

In-frame acknowledgment The form of the acknowledgment that is expected within that frame.

In-frame response (IFR) The form of the response that is expected within that frame. (See **Response**.)

Initialization Parameterization and eventual configuration of a system during startup.

Interbyte separation (IBS) A condition under which data bytes of an asynchronous serial transmission within a frame are disjoint or separate with variable amounts of dead time between bytes.

Interframe delimiter (IFD) Interframe delimiter (IFD), interframe separation (IFS), and interframe spacing are used interchangeably and refer to a condition under which the frames of an asynchronous serial transmission on a multiplex network are disjoint or separate with variable amounts of dead time between messages as a result of system clock tolerances in order to support synchronization of frames.

Invalid bit A detector system that determines when a data bit has deviated outside the established requirements.

Invalid message structure A detector system that determines when the message frame composition has deviated outside the established requirements.

Latency   The time required to transfer a message from the transmitting node measured from the moment it is prepared to send the message until it is correctly received by the targeted receiver. It may include a retry strategy delay if the initial exchange is not successful.

Line driver   A solid state device (driver) used to transfer electrical energy to a wire or cable communications medium (signal bus) performing the transmit portion of the transceiver function.

Local area network (LAN)   A local multiplex network that can serve a variety of devices. Typically in automotive systems it is used for collecting data from sensors and controlling actuators for one host module.

Longitudinal noise   Difference in voltage between two ground points as a result of ground offset electrical noise currents. (See **Ground offset**.)

Manchester (MAN)   A digital signaling technique in which there is a transition in the middle of each bit time. A "1" is encoded with a high level during the first half of the bit time and a "0" is encoded with a low level during the second half of the bit time. Therefore, there is a maximum of two transitions per bit time.

Master (node or module)   The master node and master module are used interchangeably and are defined as the device which controls the transfer of information on a multiplex network. (See **Master-slave**.)

Master-slave   A type of system whereby one node, a module, acts as a master or central unit and controls the actions of the other nodes designated as slaves or remote units.

Media access   The method used to award the communication network to one of the nodes for the transmission of a message, e.g., master slave, token passing, CSMA/CD.

Message   All of the data bytes contained in a frame. The message is what is left after the frame symbols have been removed from the frame. As such, the message is the sequence of bytes contained in the frame.

Message frame   A portion of a communication protocol within the message transfer specifying the arrangement and meaning of bits or bit fields in the sequence of transfer across the transmission medium. The message frame is what is left after the message has been removed from the frame.

Message latency   The time required by a system to access the medium so as to begin the delivery of information. Message latency is measured from the time that a node is ready to send specific information to the time of the start of the transmission of this information, which will ultimately be successful. Thus, the total time required to successfully send a desired message will be the sum of the message latency and the message transmission time.

Message source   An identifier that defines the physical origin of a frame of data.

Message transfer   The portion of the protocol dealing with the organization, meaning, and timing associated with the bits of data. Message transfer deals with what bits must be sent and when they must be sent to accomplish the transmission of a message.

Message type   A classification of the different categories or classes of messages, such as functional or physical.

Modified frequency modulation (MFM)   An encoding technique that defines two symmetrically spaced phases, data and clock, to a synchronizing signal. Modulating data causes transitions at these phases depending on the logic level.

Multiple-byte header protocol   A protocol that utilizes a number of bytes in the header field within a frame which directly contains information about the message priority, message source and target addressing, message type, and in-frame response type.

Multiplex bus (signal bus)   Multiplex bus and signal bus are sometimes used interchangeably and refer to the wiring serving all multiplex system nodes and includes the signal, power, and ground buses.

Multiplexing   The process of combining several messages for transmission over the same signal path. There are two widely used methods of multiplexing: time division and frequency division.

Negative acknowledgment   A control character on a communications network transmitted from a receiving point as a negative response to the reception of the message. The response signifies that the message was not received correctly.

Network   A system capable of supporting communications by three or more nodes.

Network access   Method used to award the communications network to one of the nodes for the transmission of a message.

Network topologies   The layout of elements capable of supporting communications by three or more nodes.

Node   Any subassembly of a multiplex system which communicates on the signal bus, i.e., a transceiver. In addition to modules, nodes may include other devices that contain the intelligence necessary to support these communications.

Nonreturn to zero (NRZ)   A data bit format in which the voltage or current value, which is typically voltage, determines the data bit value, i.e., one or zero.

Nondestructive bit-by-bit arbitration   Nondestructive bit-by-bit arbitration and bit-by-bit arbitration are used interchangeably and both refer to a contention-based arbitration, whereby the contention created by simultaneous access of multiple nodes on the network is resolved bit by bit. (See **Bit-by-bit arbitration**.)

Normalization bit   A VPW modulation bit symbol that follows an end of data symbol used to initialize an in-frame response with the proper phase.

OSI model   The open system interconnect (OSI) model defines a seven-layer model for a data communications network.

Parametric data values   A parameter is the variable quantity included in some messages. The parameter value, scaling, offset, units, transfer function, etc., are unique to each particular message.

Parity (odd or even)   The parity check bit is said to be odd or even when the simple sum of all the binary bits in the frame, including the check bit, is always odd or always even. (See **Parity bit**.)

Parity bit   A check bit appended to a frame composed of binary bits to make the simple sum of all the binary bits, including the check bit, always odd or always even.

Parity error   An error is determined when the locally calculated parity check bit disagrees with the parity check bit received in the frame.

Physical addressing   Labeling of messages for the physical address location of their source and/or destination(s). This is independent of their geographic location, connector pin, and/or wire identification assignments. The information in these messages are only of relevance to particular nodes, so the other nodes on the bus should ignore the message.

Physical layer The properties of the communications medium (signal bus) which can be determined by electrical measurements, such as voltages, currents, impedances, rise times, etc.

Poll The process by which a master device invites a slave device, such as a sensor or actuator, one at a time, to transmit data or to act on command.

Positive acknowledgment A control character on a communications network transmitted from a receiving point as a positive response to the reception of the message. The response signifies that the message was received correctly.

Priority Attribute of a message controlling its ranking during arbitration. A high priority increases the probability that a message wins the arbitration process.

Propagation delay The worst-case or maximum propagation time through a medium such as the circuits of an IC or a multiplex network.

Protocol A formal set of conventions or rules for the exchange of information between nodes, including the procedures for establishing and controlling transmissions on the multiplex signal bus (message administration) and the organization, meaning, and timing associated with the bits of data (message transfer).

Pulse-width variability The variations in pulse-width tolerances associated with variable pulse-width modulation caused by such things as ground offset and the bus driver.

Response A message or portion of a message initiated by a receiving node as a result of a message transmitted by a different node. A response can be an acknowledgment or response data, and it can be appended to the original message (immediate response) or a unique message (separate response).

Response current A system that utilizes change in current signal which is used to indicate whether a message has been received properly.

Response data A response to a message which provides the data or information requested in the message. This may be an in-frame response or a report to requested data.

Serial communications interface (SCI) A common microcomputer interface that provides a standard mark/space (NRZ) which produces one start bit, eight data bits, and one stop bit in a serial data format.

Shadow nodes A node in a time triggered protocol architecture which receives input messages but does not produce any output as long as the other two nodes of the network are operational. As soon as one of these other two nodes fails, the shadow node takes the time division multiple access (TDMA) slot from the failed node and produces output.

Single-byte header protocol A protocol that utilizes a single byte in the header field within a frame which implicitly contains information about the message priority, message source and target addressing, message type, and in-frame response type.

Single-wire random lay Refers to a transmission medium of a multiplex network that consists of a single conductor and a common return that is randomly placed in the wiring harness with all of the other vehicle circuits. The return conductor could be the vehicle chassis or a common ground conductor.

Sleep state (sleep mode) Sleep state and sleep mode are sometimes used interchangeably and refer to the behavior whereby a node is on a low-power consumption standby state waiting to be switched on by a frame or other activity. This is distinct from an off mode where there is no power consumption and it is disconnected from the power supply.

Start bit The bit encoded within an asynchronous transmission that synchronizes the receiver clock to terminate the end of that block or byte of data.

Stop bit   The bit encoded within an asynchronous transmission that synchronizes the receiver clock to the start of that block or byte of data.

Symbol   The individual elements that compose the message frame such as start of frame (SOF), end of data (EOD), end of frame (EOF), and CRC.

Synchronization   Procedure to ensure a desired timing for interrelated actions and/or processes.

System architecture   The organization of a multiplex system including, but not necessarily limited to, the location and ranking of logic or decision-making elements and the types and methods of communications between these elements.

T-tap connection   A splice in a wiring harness forming a "T" connection. This configuration is associated with an automated insulation displacement type connection at a connector.

Target address   The address of the node for which the message is intended. This address is usually the physical address of a particular node.

10-bit NRZ   A common microcomputer interface that provides a standard mark/space (NRZ) which produces a total of 10 bits, 1 start bit, 8 data bits, and 1 stop bit in a serial data format. [See **Serial communications interface (SCI)**]

Tightly looped distributed processing   A control strategy that acts within the actual time the physical events take place and whereby control elements are physically located in several different places.

Time-critical message   The attributes of a message that require action in a very short period of time bordering on real-time control requirements.

Time division multiple access (TDMA)   A general classification of multiplexing that utilizes time division multiplex protocols.

Time division multiplex protocol   A protocol in which the meaning of a piece of information on the signal bus is determined by its relationship, i.e., first, second, third, etc., to the start of the message or bitstream. In a time division multiplex protocol, data can be interleaved on a bit-by-bit, byte-by-byte, or block-by-block basis.

Time triggered media access   Bus access is controlled by a global time base which opens slots to data depending on the network protocol.

Time triggered protocol (TTP)   A real-time control system architecture where all system activities are triggered by the progression of real time. This distributed time triggered architecture requires clock synchronization by a global time base.

Token   The symbol of authority passed between nodes in a token-passing protocol. Possession of this symbol identifies the node currently in control of the medium.

Token-passing protocol   A node that has communicated passes the control of the bus, including the right to communicate to another node, at the end of the message via a token.

Token slot protocol   A protocol where bus access is controlled by a time base which opens a time slot to a number of nodes that, in turn, take control of the network when there is data to communicate to another node.

Transceiver   An electrical circuit which both transmits (line driver portion) and receives (line receiver portion).

Transitions (bit)   The process of changing from one voltage level to another voltage level.

Translated   The conversion from one binary number to another binary number in order to achieve correct bit-by-bit arbitration.

Trapezoidal waveforms   A sawtooth waveform superimposed onto a square wave.

Twisted pair   A transmission line consisting of two similar conductors that are insulated from each other and are twisted around each other to form a communications channel. The purpose for twisting the conductors around each other is to reduce the electric and magnetic field interaction with other conductors.

Variable pulse-width (VPW) modulation (VPWM)   A method of using both bus state and pulse width to encode bit information. This encoding technique is used to reduce the number of bus transitions for a given bit rate. One embodiment would define a "1" as a dominant short pulse or a passive long pulse while a "0" would be defined as a long dominant pulse or a short passive pulse. Since a message is composed of random "1"s and "0"s, general byte or message times cannot be predicted in advance.

Wake-up   The process of activating a node that is in the sleep state.

Wave-shaped   A technique of rounding the corners of a trapezoidal waveform in order to significantly minimize the EMI.

REFERENCES

1. "Glossary of Vehicle Networks for Multiplexing and Data Communications," SAE J1213 Part 1.
2. "Detailed Header Formats and Physical Address Assignments," SAE J2178 Part 1; "Network Architectures and Header Selection," Appendix A.
3. "Architecture Strategies," SAE J2057 Part 4.
4. "Network Access Methods," SAE J2056 Part 4 Draft.
5. "Media Choices," SAE J2056 Part 3.
6. Fred Miesterfeld, and Halter, Rick, Chrysler Corp., "Survey of Encoding Techniques for Vehicle Multiplexing," SAE 910715.
7. "Survey of Known Protocols," SAE J2056 Part 2.
8. "Inter Controller Area Network for In-Vehicle Applications," SAE J1583.
9. "Chrysler Collision Detection," SAE J1567.
10. "Class B Data Communications Network Interface," SAE J1850.
11. "Chrysler Sensor and Control," SAE J2058.
12. "Token Slot Network for Automotive Control," SAE J2106.
13. H. Kopetz, and Grunsteidl, G., TTP—"A Time Triggered Protocol for Automotive Applications," Research Report No. 16/1992, Institute for Technical Information, University Wien, Austria, Oct. 1992.
14. Vehicle Area Network: VAN Specification, Version 1.2, ISO/TC22/SC3/WG1.

ABOUT THE AUTHOR

Fred Miesterfeld is engineering supervisor of the advanced electronic development at Chrysler Corporation. A graduate of Johns Hopkins University with over 25 years of experience in automotive electronics, he has been an active member of various SAE Standards Committees since 1975. Presently, he is serving as chairman of the Vehicle Networks for Multiplexing and Data Communications Committee and previously has served as Secretary of the EMI Standards and Test Methods Committee.

P · A · R · T · 6

ELECTROMAGNETIC INTERFERENCE AND COMPATIBILITY

CHAPTER 27

ELECTROMAGNETIC STANDARDS AND INTERFERENCE

James P. Muccioli
EMC Consultant, JASTECH

27.1 SAE AUTOMOTIVE EMC STANDARDS

27.1.1 Overview

The Society of Automotive Engineers (SAE) has been involved in writing electromagnetic compatibility standards since 1957 with SAE-J551. In its original form, SAE-J551 was intended to protect "roadside receivers," particularly television, from vehicle ignition noise. There have been several revisions to SAE-J551 and new electromagnetic compatibility standards due to the evolution of digital electronics. With the implementation of digital electronic systems on vehicles, a new set of radio noise problems prompted a new standard to be written in 1987.

This chapter will review the Society of Automotive Engineers (SAE) Electromagnetic Compatibility (EMC) standards on both vehicle system level and component-level test methods. The Electromagnetic Radiation (EMR) and Electromagnetic Interference (EMI) Standards Committees are working together to cover all aspects of the EMC field and to develop test methods and limits relating to vehicle and other motorized equipment. Each of the committees has representation from automotive corporations, truck and bus corporations, suppliers, consumers, test houses, and government.

Presently, the Society of Automotive Engineers EMC Standards Committees are revising SAE J1113 and SAE J551 to create documents made up of multiple parts, covering all aspects of component and vehicle testing. SAE EMC standards are being harmonized with those of the International Standards Organization (ISO). The vehicle-level EMC standard, SAE J551, is divided into emissions test parts numbered 2 through 10 (Table 27.1) and immunity test parts numbered 11 through 20 (Table 27.2). The component-level EMC standard, SAE J1113, is divided into immunity test parts numbered 2 through 40 (Table 27.3) and emissions test parts numbered above 40 (Table 27.4). Part 1 of both documents contains an introduction and definitions. The SAE standards are structured to be living documents to accept changes and additions without the need to revise or renumber parts.

TABLE 27.1 EMC Emissions Tests for Vehicles—SAE J551

SAE J551 part	Bandwidth	Frequency range	Test distance	Comparable standard
2	Broadband	30 MHz—1 GHz	10 m	CISPR 12
3	Narrowband	10 kHz—1 GHz	3 m	CISPR TBD
4	Narrow & broad	150 kHz—1 GHz	1 m	CISPR TBD
5	Narrow & broad	20 kHz—1 GHz	10 m	CISPR TBD

TABLE 27.2 EMC Immunity Tests for Vehicles—SAE J551

SAE J551 part	Test type	Frequency range	Comparable standard
11	Off vehicle source	500 kHz—18 GHz	ISO 11451/2
12	On vehicle source	1.8 MHz—1.2 GHz	ISO 11451/3
13	Bulk current injection	1—400 MHz	ISO 11451/4
14	Reverberation chamber	200 MHz—18 GHz	None
15	Electrostatic discharge	N/A	ISO 10605
16	Transients	N/A	None
17	Power line magnetic field	60 Hz—30 kHz	None

TABLE 27.3 EMC Immunity Tests for Components—SAE J1113

SAE J1113 part	Test type	Frequency range	Comparable standard
2	Conducted immunity	30 Hz—250 kHz	None
3	Conducted immunity	100 kHz—400 MHz	ISO 11452/7
4	Bulk current injection	1—400 MHz	ISO 11452/4
11	Transients	N/A	ISO 7637-1
12	Coupled transients	N/A	ISO 7637-3
13	Electrostatic discharge	N/A	ISO 10605
21	Semi-anechoic chamber	30 MHz—18 GHz	ISO 11452/2
22	Power line magnetic	60 Hz—30kHz	None
23	RF stripline	10 kHz—1 GHz	ISO 11452/5
24	TEM cell	10 kHz—200 MHz	ISO 11452/3
25	Triplate	10 kHz—1 GHz	None
26	Power line E-field	60 Hz—30 kHz	None
27	Reverberation chamber	500 MHz—2 GHz	None

TABLE 27.4 EMC Emissions Tests for Components—SAE J1113

SAE J1113 part	Test type	Frequency range	Comparable standard
41	Narrowband	10 kHz—1 GHz	CISPR TBD
42	Transient	N/A	ISO 7637-1

27.1.2   SAE J551

Note: This section contains portions reprinted with permission from Draft SAE J551 ©1993 Society of Automotive Engineers, Inc.

SAE J551 combines all of the vehicle-level automotive-related EMC test methods for emissions and immunity tests into one document. The contents of the SAE J551 are as follows.

SAE J551/1 General and Definitions

Absorber lined chamber   A shielded room with absorbing material on its internal reflective surfaces (floor absorber material optional).

Amplitude modulation (AM)   The process by which the amplitude of a carrier wave is varied following a specific law. The result of that process is an AM signal.

Antenna correction factor   The factor that is applied to the voltage measured at the input connector of the measuring receiver to give the field strength at the antenna.

Antenna matching unit   A unit for matching the impedance of an antenna to that of the 50-ohm measuring receiver over the antenna measuring frequency range.

Artificial network (AN)   A network inserted in the supply leads of an apparatus to be tested which provides, in a given frequency range, a specified load impedance for the measurement of disturbance voltages and which isolates the apparatus from the power supply in that frequency range.

Bandwidth   The width of the frequency band over which a given characteristic of an equipment does not differ from its reference by more than a specified amount or ratio.

Broadband artificial network (BAN)   A network that presents a controlled impedance to the device under test over a specified frequency range while allowing the device under test to be interfaced to its support system. It is used in power, signal, and control lines.

Broadband emission   An emission which has a bandwidth greater than that of a particular measuring apparatus or receiver.

Bulk current   Total amount of common mode current in a harness.

Bulk current injection probe   A device for injecting current in a conductor without interrupting the conductor and without introducing significant impedance into the associated circuits.

Characteristic level   The controlling (or dominant) emission level experienced in each frequency subband. The characteristic level is the maximum measurement obtained for both antenna polarizations and for all the specified measurement positions of the vehicle or device. Known ambient signals shall not be considered part of the characteristic level.

Class   An arbitrary performance level agreed upon by the purchaser and the supplier and documented in the test plan.

Component continuous conducted emissions   The noise voltages/currents of a continuous nature existing on the supply or other wires of a component/module which may cause interference to reception in an on-board receiver.

Compression point   The input signal level at which the gain of the measuring system becomes nonlinear such that the indicated output deviates from an ideal receiving system's output by the specified increment in dB.

Coupling   A means or a device transferring power between systems.

Current (measuring) probe   A device for measuring the current in a conductor without interrupting the conductor and without introducing significant impedance into the associated circuits.

Degradation (of performance)   An undesired departure in the operational performance of any device, equipment, or system from its intended performance.

Device   A machine equipped with an internal combustion engine but not self-propelled. Devices include, but are not limited to, chain saws, irrigation pumps, and air compressors.

Directional coupler   A three- or four-port device consisting of two transmission lines coupled together in such a manner that a single traveling wave in any one transmission line will induce a single traveling wave in the other, the direction of propagation of the latter wave being dependent upon that of the former.

Disturbance suppression   Action which reduces or eliminates electrical disturbance.

Disturbance voltage; interference voltage   Voltage produced between two points on separate conductors by an electromagnetic disturbance, measured under specified conditions.

Electromagnetic compatibility (EMC)   The ability of an equipment or system to function satisfactorily in its electromagnetic environment without introducing intolerable electromagnetic disturbance to anything in that environment.

Electromagnetic disturbance   Any electromagnetic phenomenon which may degrade the performance of a device, equipment, or system or adversely affect living or inert matter.

Electromagnetic immunity (to a disturbance)   The ability of a device, equipment, or system to perform without degradation in the presence of an electromagnetic disturbance.

Electromagnetic interference (EMI)   Degradation of the performance of an equipment, transmission channel or system caused by an electromagnetic disturbance.

Electromagnetic radiation   The phenomena by which energy in the form of electromagnetic waves emanates from a source into space; energy transferred through space in the form of electromagnetic waves.

Forward power   Power supplied by the output of an amplifier (or generator) traveling towards the load.

Ground (reference) plane   A flat conductive surface whose potential is used as a common reference.

Ignition noise suppressor   That part of a high-voltage ignition circuit intended to limit the emission of impulsive ignition noise.

Immunity level   The maximum level of a given electromagnetic disturbance incident on a particular device, equipment, or system for which it remains capable of operating at a required degree of performance.

Impulse electric field strength   The root-mean-square value of the sinusoidally varying radiated electric field producing the same peak response in a bandpass system, antenna, and bandpass filter, produced by the unknown impulse electric field.

Impulse noise   Noise characterized by transient disturbances separated in time by quiescent intervals. The frequency spectrum of these disturbances must be substantially uniform over the useful pass band of the transmission system. The same source may produce impulse noise in one system and random noise in a different system (from ANSI/IEEE Std 100).

Impulsive ignition noise   The unwanted emission of electromagnetic energy, predominantly impulsive in content, arising from the ignition system within a vehicle or device.

Interference suppression   Action which reduces or eliminates electrical interference.

Measuring instrument impulse bandwidth   The maximum value of the output response envelope divided by the spectrum amplitude of an applied impulse.

Narrowband emission   An emission which has a bandwidth less than that of a particular measuring apparatus or receiver.

Net power   Forward power minus reflected power.

Peak detector   A detector, the output voltage of which is the peak value of the applied signal.

Polarization (of a wave or field vector)   The property of a sinusoidal electromagnetic wave or field vector defined at a fixed point in space by the direction of the electric field strength vector or of any field vector; when the direction varies with time, the property may be characterized by the locus described by the extremity of the considered field vector.

Quasi-peak detector   A detector having specified electrical time constants which, when regularly repeated identical pulses are applied to it, delivers an output voltage which is a fraction of the peak value of the pulses, the fraction increasing toward unity as the pulse repetition rate is increased.

Receiver terminal voltage (antenna voltage)   The voltage generated by a source of radio disturbance and measured in dB (μV) by a radio interference measuring receiver conforming to the requirements of CISPR Publications 16 or ANSI C63.2.

Reflected power   Power traveling toward the generator reflected by the load due to impedance mismatch between the transmission line and the load.

Resistive distributor brush   The resistive pick-up brush in an ignition distributor cap.

RF ambient (electromagnetic environment)   The totality of electromagnetic phenomena existing at a given location.

Shall   Used to express a command, i.e., conformance with the specific recommendation is mandatory and deviation is not permitted. The use of shall is not qualified by the fact that compliance with the standard is considered voluntary.

Shielded enclosure   A mesh or sheet metallic housing designed for the purpose of separating the internal from external electromagnetic environment.

Standing wave ratio (SWR); voltage standing wave ratio (VSWR)   The ratio, along a transmission line, of a maximum to an adjacent minimum magnitude of a particular field component of a standing wave.

Tracking generator   A narrowband radio frequency source synchronized to the instantaneous receive frequency of a scanning receiver or spectrum analyzer.

Transmission line system (TLS)   A transmission line system is a stripline or parallel plate or similar device to generate an E-field.

Vehicle   A self-propelled machine (excluding aircraft, rail vehicles, and boats over 10 m in length). Vehicles may be propelled by an internal combustion engine, electrical means, or both. Vehicles include, but are not limited to, mopeds, automobiles, trucks, agricultural tractors, snowmobiles, and small motorboats.

SAE J551/2 Performance Levels and Methods of Measurement of Electromagnetic Radiation from Vehicles and Devices, Broadband, 30 to 1000 MHz.   This document provides test procedures and recommended levels to assist engineers in the measurement of broadband electromagnetic radiation and control of radio interference.

SAE J551/3 Performance Levels and Methods of Measurement of Electromagnetic Radiation from Vehicles and Devices, Narrowband, 10 kHz to 1000 MHz.   This document covers methods of measuring incidental narrowband radiation from vehicles and devices and establishes performance levels intended to protect nearby communication and broadcast receivers.

SAE J551/4 Test Limits and Methods of Measurement of Radio Disturbance Characteristics from Vehicles and Devices, Narrowband, 150 kHz to 1000 MHz.   This document provides measurement techniques and test limits intended to protect radio receivers installed in a vehicle from disturbances produced by components/modules in the same vehicle.

SAE J551/5 Performance Levels and Methods of Measurement of Electromagnetic Radiation from Electric Vehicles, Broadband and Narrowband, 9 kHz to 1000 MHz.   This document provides electric vehicle test procedures and performance levels for the measurement of both radiated magnetic and electric field strengths.

SAE J551/11 Vehicle Electromagnetic Immunity—Off-Vehicle Source.   This document adopts ISO CD11451-2: Road Vehicles—Electrical Disturbances by Narrowband Radiated Electromagnetic Energy—Vehicle Test Methods—Part 2: Off-vehicle Radiation Source.

SAE J551/12 Vehicle Electromagnetic Immunity—On-board Transmitter Simulation.   This document adopts ISO CD11451-3: Road Vehicles—Electrical Disturbances by Narrowband Radiated Electromagnetic Energy—Vehicle Test Methods—Part 3: On-board Transmitter Simulation.

SAE J551/13 Vehicle Electromagnetic Immunity—Bulk Current Injection (BCI).   This document adopts ISO CD11451-4: Road Vehicles—Electrical Disturbances by Narrowband Radiated Electromagnetic Energy—Vehicle Test Methods—Part 4: Bulk Current Injection.

SAE J551/15 Vehicle Electromagnetic Immunity—Electrostatic Discharge (ESD).   This document adopts the portions of ISO TR10605 which pertain to ESD calibration and vehicle ESD testing.

27.1.3   SAE J1113

Note: This section contains portions reprinted with permission from Draft SAE J1113 ©1993 Society of Automotive Engineers, Inc.
SAE J1113 combines all of the module-level automotive-related EMC test methods for emissions and immunity tests into one document. The contents of the SAE J1113 are as follows.

SAE J1113/1 General and Definitions
Ambient Level   Those levels of radiated and conducted signal and noise existing at a specified test location and time when the test sample is not in operation. Atmospherics, interference from other sources, and circuit noise or other interference generated within the measuring set compose the ambient level.

Conducted emission   Desired or undesired electromagnetic energy which is propagated along a conductor.

Device under test (DUT)   The device whose immunity is being checked.

Electromagnetic compatibility (EMC)   The condition that enables equipment, subsystems, and systems (electronic, chemical, biological, etc.) to function without degradation from electromagnetic sources and without degrading the electromagnetic environment; i.e., it is the condition which allows the coexistence of different electromagnetic sources without significant change in performance of any one in the presence of any or all the other.

Emission   Electromagnetic energy propagated from a source by radiation or conduction.

Equipment under test (EUT)   The device or system whose immunity is being checked. Synonymous with DUT.

Field decay (voltage)   The exponentially decaying negative voltage transient such as developed by an automotive alternator when the field excitation is suddenly removed, as when the ignition switch is turned off.

Field strength   The term *field strength* shall be applied to either the electric or the magnetic component of the field, and may be expressed as V/m or A/m. When measurements are made in the far field and in free space, the power density in W/cm^2 may be obtained from field strengths approximately as (V/m)/377 or (A/m) × 377. When measurements are made in the near field and in free space, both the complex electric and magnetic vector components of the field must be fully defined. Power density may then be obtained by use of the Poynting vector.

Ground plane   A metal sheet or plate used as a common unipotential reference point for circuit returns and electrical or signal potential.

Immunity   A measure of electronic module or system tolerance to external electromagnetic fields. decaying posit

Load dump (voltage)   The exponentially live voltage transient developed by an automotive alternator, when disconnected suddenly from its load, while operating without a storage battery or with a discharged storage battery. Removal of the load, the resulting transient, or both in combination are commonly referred to as alternator load dump.

Radiated emission   Radiation- and induction-field components in space. (For the purpose of this document, induction fields are classed together with radiation fields.)

Spurious emission   Any unintentional electromagnetic emission from a device.

Susceptibility   The characteristic of an object that results in undesirable responses when subjected to electromagnetic energy.

Test plan   The specific document that details all tests and limits for the particular device in question.

SAE J1113/2 Conducted Immunity (30 Hz to 250 kHz).   This document provides the requirements for determining the immunity characteristics of automotive electronic equipment, subsystems, and systems to EM energy injected onto all leads over the frequency range of 30 Hz to 250 kHz. The method is applicable to all input, output, and power leads.

SAE J1113/3 Conducted Immunity (100 kHz to 400 MHz).   This document provides the requirements for determining the immunity characteristics of automotive electronic equipment, subsystems, and systems to electromagnetic energy injected onto all leads, including signal and power, over the frequency range 100 kHz to 400 MHz.

SAE J1113/4 Immunity to Radiated Electric Fields—Bulk Current Injection Method (1 to 400 MHz).   This document provides a test method for evaluating the immunity of automotive electrical/electronic devices to radiated electromagnetic fields coupled to the vehicle wiring harness. Bulk current injection (BCI) uses a current probe to inject RF current from 1 to 400 MHz into the wiring harness of automotive devices.

SAE J1113/11 Immunity to Conducted Transients on Power Leads.   This document provides the methods and apparatus to evaluate electronic devices for immunity to potential interference from conducted transients along battery feed or switched ignition inputs. The test apparatus specifications outlined in this procedure were developed for 12-V passenger cars and light trucks, 12-V heavy-duty trucks, and vehicles with 24-V systems.

SAE J1113/12 Electrical Interference by Conduction and Coupling—Coupling Clamp.   This document provides a common basis for the evaluation of devices and equipment in vehicles against transient transmission by coupling via lines other than the power supply lines. The test demonstrates the immunity of the instrument, device, or equipment to coupled fast transient disturbances, such as those caused by switching of inductive loads, relay contact bouncing, etc.

SAE J1113/13 Immunity to Electrostatic Discharge (ESD).   This document provides the test methods and procedures necessary to evaluate electrical components intended for automotive use to the threat of electrostatic discharges.

SAE J1113/21 Radiated Immunity Using an Absorber Lined Chamber—Far Field.   This document provides the test methods and procedures for testing electromagnetic immunity (off vehicle radiation sources) of electronic components for passenger cars and commercial vehicles. To perform this test method, the electronic module, along with the wiring harness (prototype or standard test harness) and peripheral devices, will be subjected to the electromagnetic disturbance generated inside an absorber-lined chamber.

SAE J1113/22 Immunity to Radiated Magnetic Fields from Power Lines.   This document provides the testing technique for determining the immunity of automotive electronic devices to magnetic fields generated by power transmission lines and generating stations.

SAE J1113/23 Radiated Immunity—Stripline Method.   This document provides recommended testing techniques for the determination of electric field immunity of an automotive electronic device when the device equipment harness is exposed to an interference RF field. This technique uses a stripline coupler from 10 kHz to 1 GHz and is limited to harnesses (and/or samples) which have a maximum height of equal to or less than one-third the stripline height.

SAE J1113/24 Radiated Immunity—Transverse Electromagnetic Mode (TEM) Cell.   This SAE document adopts ISO CD11452-3: Road Vehicles—Electrical Disturbances by Narrowband Electromagnetic Energy—Component Test Methods—Part 3: TEM Cell. It provides test methods and procedures for testing electromagnetic immunity of electronic components for passenger cars and commercial vehicles. The electromagnetic disturbance, considered in this part of ISO CD11452, will be limited to continuous narrowband electromagnetic fields.

SAE J1113/25 Radiated Immunity—Triplate Line Method.   This document provides testing techniques for the determination of electric field immunity of an automotive electronic device when the device equipment harness is exposed to an interference RF field. This technique uses a Tri-Plate Line (TPL) from 10 kHz to 1 GHz and is limited to components which have a maximum height of equal to or less than one-third the height between the driven element and the outer, grounded plates.

SAE J1113/26 Radiated Immunity—60 Hz E-field.   This document provides testing techniques using a parallel plate antenna and a low-current, high-voltage generator for the determination of electric field immunity of an automotive electronic device when the device and its equipment harness are exposed to a 60-Hz electric field.

SAE J1113/27 Immunity to Radiated Electromagnetic Fields (Reverberation) Method.   This document provides the reverberation test method to evaluate the immunity of electronic devices in the frequency range of 500 MHz to 2.0 GHz. The reverberation test data correlates with vehicle-level radiated immunity test data in the anechoic chamber and mobile transmitter sites.

SAE J1113/41 Test Limits and Methods of Measurement of Radio Disturbance Characteristics from Vehicle Components and Modules, Narrowband, 150 kHz to 1000 MHz.   This document provides test limits and procedures for the measurement of radio disturbances produced by components/modules in the same vehicle.

SAE J1113/42 Conducted Transient Emissions. This document provides a component-level test procedure to evaluate the automotive electrical and electronic components for conducted emissions of transients, and for other electromagnetic disturbances. The test apparatus specifications in this procedure were developed for components installed in 12-V passenger cars and light trucks.

27.2   IEEE STANDARDS RELATED TO EMC

Although some of the following standards were not developed in the EMC Society (EMCS), they were developed with EMCS input and coordination. (Following each item, the letters in parentheses are the initials of the developing society, and the numbers in square brackets are IEEE order numbers.)

27.2.1   IEEE Standard 139-1988

IEEE Recommended Practice for the Measurement of Radio Frequency Emission from Industrial, Scientific, and Medical (ISM) Equipment Installed on User's Premises. (EMCS) [SH12377]

27.2.2   IEEE Standard 140-1990

IEEE Recommended Practice for Minimization of Interference from Radio-Frequency Heating Equipment. (EMCS) [SH13581]

27.2.3   IEEE Standard 187-1990

IEEE Standard of Radio Receivers: Open Field Method of Measurement of Spurious Radiation from FM and Television Broadcast Receivers. (EMCS) [SH13698]

27.2.4   ANSI/IEEE Standard 211-1990

IEEE Standard Definitions of Terms for Radio Wave Propagation. (APS) [SH13904]

27.2.5   ANSI/IEEE Standard 213-1987

IEEE Standard Procedure for Measuring Conducted Emissions in the Range of 300 kHz to 25 MHz from Television and FM Broadcast Receivers to Power Lines. (EMCS) [SH12047]

27.2.6   IEEE Standard 291-1969 (Reaff 1981)

IEEE Standards Report on Measuring Field Strength in Radio Wave Propagation. (APS) [SH01800]

27.2.7   IEEE Standard 299-1991

IEEE Standard Method for Measuring the Effectiveness of Electromagnetic Shielding Enclosures. (EMCS) [SH14134]

27.2.8   IEEE Standard 368-1977

IEEE Recommended Practice for Measurement of Electrical Noise and Harmonic Filter Performance of High-Voltage Direct-Current Systems. (COMSOC) [SH07021]

27.2.9   ANSI/IEEE Standard 376-1975 (Reaff 1980)

IEEE Standard for the Measurement of Impulse Strength and Impulse Bandwidth. (EMCS) [SH03764]

27.2.10   ANSI/IEEE Standard 377-1980 (Reaff 1986)

IEEE Recommended Practice for Measurement of Spurious Emission from Land-Mobile Communication Transmitters. (EMCS) [SH07898]

27.2.11   ANSI/IEEE Standard 430-1986

IEEE Standard Procedures for the Measurement of Radio Noise from Overhead Power Lines and Substations. (PES) [SH10801]

27.2.12   ANSI/IEEE Standard 469-1988

IEEE Recommended Practice for Voice-Frequency Electrical-Noise Tests of Distribution Transformers. (COMSOC) [SH12328]

27.2.13   ANSI/IEEE Standard 473-1985

IEEE Recommended Practice for an Electromagnetic Site Survey (10 kHz to 10 GHz). (EMCS) [SH09134]

27.2.14   ANSI/IEEE Standard 475-1983

IEEE Measurement Procedure for Field Disturbance Sensors (RF Intrusion Alarm). (EMCS) [SH08433]

27.2.15   ANSI/IEEE Standard 518-1982 (Reaff 1990)

IEEE Guide for the Installation of Electrical Equipment to Minimize Noise Inputs to Controllers from External Sources. (IAS) [SH08813]

27.2.16   ANSI/IEEE Standard 539-1979

IEEE Standard Definitions and Terms Relating to Overhead Power Lines Corona and Radio Noise. (PES) [SH06882]

27.2.17   ANSI/IEEE Standard 539a-1984

Supplement to IEEE Standard 539-1979. (PES) [SH09530]

27.2.18   ANSI/IEEE Standard 644-1987

IEEE Standard Procedures for Measurement of Power Frequency Electric and Magnetic Fields from AC Power Lines. (PES) [SH10892]

27.2.19   ANSI/IEEE Standard 776-1987

IEEE Guide for Inductive Coordination of Electric Supply and Communication Lines. (COMSOC) [SH11239]

27.2.20   IEEE Standard 1027-1984

Draft Trial-Use Standard Method for Measuring the Magnetic Field Intensity Around a Telephone Receiver. (COMSOC) [SH09497]

27.3   THE ELECTROMAGNETIC ENVIRONMENT OF AN AUTOMOBILE ELECTRONIC SYSTEM

Note: Parts of this section were taken from the article of the same name by J. P. Muccioli and S. S. Awad published in the *IEEE Transactions on Electromagnetic Compatibility,* Aug. 1987.

This work was performed to study the electromagnetic environmental conditions in a typical midsize automobile with a high-power frequency modulation (FM) transmitter installed inside the vehicle. Different antenna locations were used to radiate the electromagnetic waves that were studied. The data obtained from the experimental results is presented and discussed.

27.3.1   Test Methodology

The levels of the electric field strength inside the vehicle depend on a number of factors. One basic factor is the size of the automobile. In this case, a midsize automobile was used for experimentation. The electromagnetic source was selected to be a 100-W FM transmitter operating on five frequencies: 25.04, 35.04, 39.04, 51.20, and 144.50 MHz. The transmitting antenna was placed at four different locations on the outer surface of the vehicle as shown in Fig. 27.1. The transmitter was placed on the passenger seat and was connected to the radiating antenna through a coaxial cable. The electromagnetic environment was mapped inside the vehicle with both doors closed, engine running at idle, and the driver seated in the left front seat. The electric field strength measurements were taken at 15 different locations inside the vehicle, as shown in Fig. 27.2. At each location, the electric field strength was measured once in a direction parallel to the transmitting antenna and once orthogonal to it.

An important factor that can influence the magnitude of the electric field strength is that of ground plane. For this test, the vehicle was placed outside in the open, on dry ground, and away from any other building or vehicles which could affect the electromagnetic environment inside.

27.3.2   Test Instrumentation

1. Field strength meter—IFI, EFS-1, frequency range 10 kHz to 220 MHz
2. Motorola Transmitter 90/100-W power amplifier
   a. Frequency 25.04 MHz @ 100 W
   b. Frequency 35.04 MHz @ 100 W

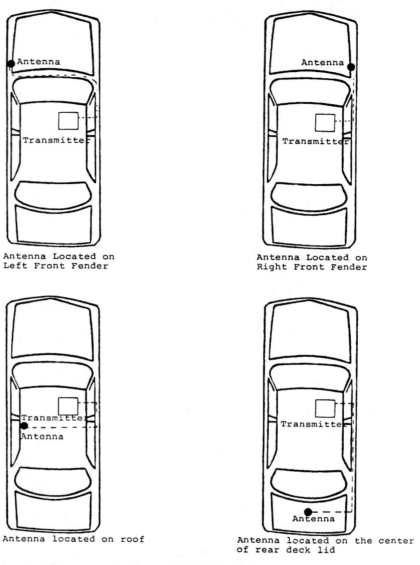

FIGURE 27.1 Antenna locations and coaxial cable routing.

    c. Frequency 39.04 MHz @ 100 W

    d. Frequency 51.20 Mhz @ 100 W

  3. Drake UV-3 FM transceiver, 160 W RF power amplifier, frequency 144.50 MHz @ 100 W

27.3.3 Summary

The results of the electric field measurements are shown in Table 27.5. For each of the four antenna locations, the electric field strength components (parallel and orthogonal to the

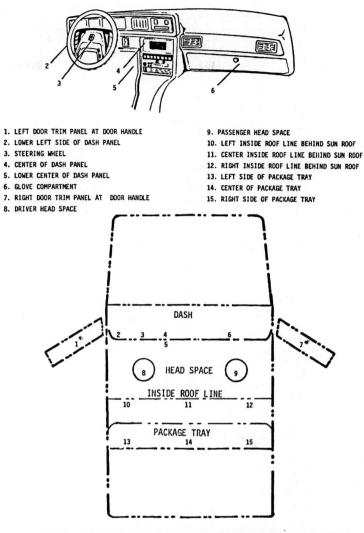

1. LEFT DOOR TRIM PANEL AT DOOR HANDLE
2. LOWER LEFT SIDE OF DASH PANEL
3. STEERING WHEEL
4. CENTER OF DASH PANEL
5. LOWER CENTER OF DASH PANEL
6. GLOVE COMPARTMENT
7. RIGHT DOOR TRIM PANEL AT DOOR HANDLE
8. DRIVER HEAD SPACE

9. PASSENGER HEAD SPACE
10. LEFT INSIDE ROOF LINE BEHIND SUN ROOF
11. CENTER INSIDE ROOF LINE BEHIND SUN ROOF
12. RIGHT INSIDE ROOF LINE BEHIND SUN ROOF
13. LEFT SIDE OF PACKAGE TRAY
14. CENTER OF PACKAGE TRAY
15. RIGHT SIDE OF PACKAGE TRAY

* NOTE: DOOR MEASUREMENTS WERE MADE AT ARM REST ABOVE DOOR HANDLE

FIGURE 27.2 Fifteen metered locations inside the vehicle.

antenna) are listed for the 15 different meter locations at various transmitting frequencies. From Table 27.5, the electric field environment inside the vehicle could be divided into three different groups:

1. Locations of electric field strengths greater than 150 V/m

    a. Left door trim panel at door handle

    b. Left inside roof line behind sunroof

    c. Right inside roof line behind sunroof

    d. Steering wheel

TABLE 27.5 Field Strength Data at Various Meter Locations

	Antenna location on vehicle: left front fender (driver side)									
	Frequency of transmitter 25.04 MHz @ 100 W		Frequency of transmitter 35.04 MHz @ 100 W		Frequency of transmitter 39.04 MHz @ 100 W		Frequency of transmitter 51.2 MHz @ 100 W		Frequency of transmitter 144.5 MHz @ 100 W	
Meter location	Field strength parallel to antenna	Field strength orthogonal to antenna	Field strength parallel to antenna	Field strength orthogonal to antenna	Field strength parallel to antenna	Field strength orthogonal to antenna	Field strength parallel to antenna	Field strength orthogonal to antenna	Field strength parallel to antenna	Field strength orthogonal to antenna
1	30 V/M	130 V/M	8 V/M	29 V/M	5 V/M	95 V/M	10 V/M	100 V/M	0 V/M	0 V/M
2	20 V/M	35 V/M	18 V/M	30 V/M	15 VLM	25 V/M	45 V/M	70 V/M	27 V/M	21 V/M
3	22 V/M	220 V/M	13 V/M	58 V/M	19 V/M	160 V/M	24 V/M	175 V/M	13 V/M	15 V/M
4	28 V/M	29 V/M	30 V/M	60 V/M	17 V/M	29 V/M	31 V/M	30 V/M	10 V/M	10 V/M
5	27 V/M	24 V/M	28 V/M	11 V/M	18 V/M	13 V/M	25 V/M	10 V/M	11 V/M	10 V/M
6	28 V/M	20 V/M	48 V/M	60 V/M	17 V/M	14 V/M	20 V/M	35 V/M	21 V/M	28 V/M
7	55 V/M	260 V/M	20 V/M	130 V/M	30 V/M	100 V/M	26 V/M	100 V/M	11 V/M	40 V/M
8	29 V/M	13 V/M	8 V/M	12 V/M	30 V/M	20 V/M	35 V/M	50 V/M	10 V/M	19 V/M
9	17 V/M	29 V/M	0 V/M	5 V/M	30 V/M	35 V/M	30 V/M	12 V/M	10 V/M	10 V/M
10	40 V/M	17 V/M	28 V/M	5 V/M	120 V/M	35 V/M	85 V/M	22 V/M	12 V/M	0 V/M
11	40 V/M	15 V/M	35 V/M	5 V/M	110 V/M	30 V/M	100 V/M	27 V/M	9 V/M	0 V/M
12	35 V/M	14 V/M	40 V/M	2 V/M	90 V/M	30 V/M	81 V/M	25 V/M	15 V/M	1 V/M
13	0 V/M	0 V/M	0 V/M	0 V/M	4 V/M	5 V/M	17 V/M	24 V/M	27 V/M	3 V/M
14	0 V/M	0 V/M	0 V/M	0 V/M	5 V/M	2 V/M	20 V/M	8 V/M	30 V/M	3 V/M
15	0 V/M	0 V/M	0 V/M	0 V/M	5 V/M	2 V/M	21 V/M	13 V/M	20 V/M	3 V/M
	Antenna location on vehicle: right front fender									
	Frequency of transmitter 25.04 MHz @ 100 W		Frequency of transmitter 35.04 MHz @ 100 W		Frequency of transmitter 39.04 MHz @ 100 W		Frequency of transmitter 51.2 MHz @ 100 W		Frequency of transmitter 144.5 MHz @ 100 W	
Meter location	Field strength parallel to antenna	Field strength orthogonal to antenna	Field strength parallel to antenna	Field strength orthogonal to antenna	Field strength parallel to antenna	Field strength orthogonal to antenna	Field strength parallel to antenna	Field strength orthogonal to antenna	Field strength parallel to antenna	Field strength orthogonal to antenna
1	5 V/M	70 V/M	1 V/M	30 V/M	2 V/M	32 V/M	12 V/M	58 V/M	0 V/M	5 V/M
2	2 V/M	5 V/M	18 V/M	19 V/M	14 V/M	17 V/M	90 V/M	85 V/M	5 V/M	10 V/M
3	0 V/M	18 V/M	5 V/M	70 V/M	15 V/M	90 V/M	55 V/M	115 V/M	5 V/M	2 V/M
4	10 V/M	11 V/M	15 V/M	28 V/M	14 V/M	40 V/M	8 V/M	73 V/M	15 V/M	52 V/M
5	5 V/M	5 V/M	19 V/M	18 V/M	16 V/M	13 V/M	8 V/M	10 V/M	12 V/M	12 V/M
6	13 V/M	30 V/M	52 V/M	55 V/M	30 V/M	35 V/M	11 V/M	15 V/M	10 V/M	18 V/M
7	12 V/M	180 V/M	14 V/M	140 V/M	5 V/M	50 V/M	18 V/M	220 V/M	5 V/M	11 V/M
8	2 V/M	0 V/M	11 V/M	11 V/M	35 V/M	13 V/M	20 V/M	8 V/M	20 V/M	5 V/M
9	1 V/M	10 V/M	16 V/M	20 V/M	30 V/M	24 V/M	35 V/M	8 V/M	11 V/M	11 V/M
10	14 V/M	1 V/M	110 V/M	27 V/M	80 V/M	26 V/M	48 V/M	16 V/M	20 V/M	5 V/M
11	17 V/M	2 V/M	100 V/M	16 V/M	80 V/M	30 V/M	53 V/M	11 V/M	18 V/M	5 V/M
12	18 V/M	8 V/M	100 V/M	23 V/M	75 V/M	23 V/M	62 V/M	13 V/M	17 V/M	5 V/M
13	8 V/M	8 V/M	5 V/M	5 V/M	3 V/M	3 V/M	10 V/M	8 V/M	24 V/M	10 V/M
14	8 V/M	8 V/M	5 V/M	5 V/M	5 V/M	1 V/M	10 V/M	3 V/M	30 V/M	3 V/M
15	10 V/M	35 V/M	5 V/M	5 V/M	3 V/M	2 V/M	8 V/M	5 V/M	14 V/M	5 V/M

2. Locations of electric field strengths between 50 and 150 V/m
   a. Center of dash panel
   b. Center of package tray
   c. Driver head space
   d. Glove compartment
   e. Lower center of dash panel

TABLE 27.5 Field Strength Data at Various Meter Locations (*Continued*)

Antenna location on vehicle: roof

Meter location	Frequency of transmitter 25.04 MHz @ 100 W		Frequency of transmitter 35.04 MHz @ 100 W		Frequency of transmitter 39.04 MHz @ 100 W		Frequency of transmitter 51.2 MHz @ 100 W		Frequency of transmitter 144.5 MHz @ 100 W	
	Field strength parallel to antenna	Field strength orthogonal to antenna	Field strength parallel to antenna	Field strength orthogonal to antenna	Field strength parallel to antenna	Field strength orthogonal to antenna	Field strength parallel to antenna	Field strength orthogonal to antenna	Field strength parallel to antenna	Field strength orthogonal to antenna
1	18 V/M	55 V/M	2 V/M	200 V/M	8 V/M	80 V/M	15 V/M	170 V/M	0 V/M	2 V/M
2	11 V/M	17 V/M	11 V/M	26 V/M	2 V/M	16 V/M	35 V/M	99 V/M	17 V/M	19 V/M
3	16 V/M	50 V/M	25 V/M	20 V/M	13 V/M	60 V/M	21 V/M	125 V/M	0 V/M	13 V/M
4	13 V/M	17 V/M	17 V/M	14 V/M	11 V/M	21 V/M	40 V/M	35 V/M	2 V/M	30 V/M
5	14 V/M	15 V/M	15 V/M	14 V/M	12 V/M	12 V/M	38 V/M	30 V/M	12 V/M	5 V/M
6	31 V/M	28 V/M	26 V/M	30 V/M	55 V/M	27 V/M	30 V/M	80 V/M	5 V/M	13 V/M
7	70 V/M	280 V/M	30 V/M	290 V/M	11 V/M	52 V/M	60 V/M	280 V/M	2 V/M	28 V/M
8	48 V/M	22 V/M	92 V/M	70 V/M	100 V/M	55 V/M	75 V/M	40 V/M	20 V/M	10 V/M
9	2 V/M	25 V/M	43 V/M	32 V/M	42 V/M	45 V/M	90 V/M	25 V/M	17 V/M	26 V/M
10	210 V/M	40 V/M	210 V/M	45 V/M	270 V/M	48 V/M	210 V/M	65 V/M	30 V/M	5 V/M
11	230 V/M	30 V/M	240 V/M	48 V/M	220 V/M	52 V/M	210 V/M	30 V/M	35 V/M	2 V/M
12	170 V/M	30 V/M	205 V/M	65 V/M	180 V/M	35 V/M	230 V/M	35 V/M	18 V/M	5 V/M
13	5 V/M	2 V/M	10 V/M	5 V/M	14 V/M	10 V/M	28 V/M	13 V/M	17 V/M	5 V/M
14	0 V/M	0 V/M	11 V/M	2 V/M	14 V/M	8 V/M	30 V/M	10 V/M	28 V/M	10 V/M
15	0 V/M	0 V/M	10 V/M	3 V/M	10 V/M	8 V/M	30 V/M	15 V/M	17 V/M	10 V/M

Antenna location on vehicle: center of rear deck lid

Meter location	Frequency of transmitter 25.04 MHz @ 100 W		Frequency of transmitter 35.04 MHz @ 100 W		Frequency of transmitter 39.04 MHz @ 100 W		Frequency of transmitter 51.2 MHz @ 100 W		Frequency of transmitter 144.5 MHz @ 100 W	
	Field strength parallel to antenna	Field strength orthogonal to antenna	Field strength parallel to antenna	Field strength orthogonal to antenna	Field strength parallel to antenna	Field strength orthogonal to antenna	Field strength parallel to antenna	Field strength orthogonal to antenna	Field strength parallel to antenna	Field strength orthogonal to antenna
1	2 V/M	31 V/M	0 V/M	45 V/M	15 V/M	100 V/M	10 V/M	180 V/M	0 V/M	2 V/M
2	2 V/M	5 V/M	24 V/M	40 V/M	30 V/M	75 V/M	45 V/M	55 V/M	0 V/M	13 V/M
3	5 V/M	45 V/M	22 V/M	110 V/M	14 V/M	150 V/M	20 V/M	280 V/M	2 V/M	18 V/M
4	2 V/M	5 V/M	43 V/M	40 V/M	10 V/M	24 V/M	30 V/M	15 V/M	5 V/M	30 V/M
5	2 V/M	0 V/M	30 V/M	30 V/M	5 V/M	16 V/M	50 V/M	30 V/M	2 V/M	2 V/M
6	20 V/M	30 V/M	5 V/M	1 V/M	100 V/M	78 V/M	10 V/M	12 V/M	1 V/M	1 V/M
7	21 V/M	200 V/M	55 V/M	300 V/M	150 V/M	>300 V/M	28 V/M	>300 V/M	5 V/M	35 V/M
8	22 V/M	11 V/M	0 V/M	11 V/M	50 V/M	18 V/M	58 V/M	27 V/M	2 V/M	11 V/M
9	14 V/M	68 V/M	22 V/M	2 V/M	92 V/M	52 V/M	68 V/M	52 V/M	2 V/M	10 V/M
10	100 V/M	21 V/M	5 V/M	13 V/M	150 V/M	20 V/M	150 V/M	45 V/M	40 V/M	13 V/M
11	110 V/M	18 V/M	5 V/M	18 V/M	180 V/M	27 V/M	130 V/M	30 V/M	38 V/M	8 V/M
12	140 V/M	24 V/M	10 V/M	16 V/M	175 V/M	26 V/M	160 V/M	30 V/M	28 V/M	10 V/M
13	12 V/M	5 V/M	27 V/M	2 V/M	23 V/M	5 V/M	35 V/M	11 V/M	45 V/M	9 V/M
14	23 V/M	8 V/M	40 V/M	3 V/M	40 V/M	5 V/M	45 V/M	12 V/M	60 V/M	20 V/M
15	10 V/M	5 V/M	24 V/M	0 V/M	25 V/M	5 V/M	25 V/M	18 V/M	30 V/M	28 V/M

    f. Lower left side of dash panel

    g. Passenger head space

  3. Locations of electric field strengths less than 50 V/m

    a. Left side of package tray

    b. Right side of package tray

The author acknowledges the editing assistance of Sandra Muccioli.

BIBLIOGRAPHY

Adams, J. W., H. E. Taggart, M. Kanda, and J. Shafer, "Electromagnetic Interference Radiative Measurements for Automotive Applications," Tech. Note 1014, Nat. Bur. Stand., Washington, DC, June 1979.

Bronaugh, E. L., and W. H. McGinnis, "Whole-Vehicle Electromagnetic Susceptibility Tests in Open-Area Test Sites: Applying SAE J1338," SAE Paper No. 830606.

ISO/TR 7637/0, 1-1984 (E), "Road Vehicles—Electrical Interference by Conduction and Coupling: Part 0, General, and Part 1, Vehicles with Nominal 12 V Supply Voltage—Electrical Transient Conduction Along Supply Lines Only," July 1, 1984.

Kinderman, J. C., et al., "Implementation of EMC Testing of Automotive Vehicles," SAE Paper No. 810333, Feb. 1981.

Nichols, F. J., and L. H. Hemming, "Recommendations and Design Guides for the Selection and Use of RF Shielded Anechoic Chamber in the 30-1000 MHz Frequency Range," *IEEE International Symposium on EMC,* Boulder, Col., Aug. 18–20, 1981, pp. 457–464.

SAE J1338, "Open Field Whole-Vehicle Radiated Susceptibility, 10 kHz-18 GHz, Electric Field," June 1981.

SAE J1448, "Electromagnetic Susceptibility Measurements of Vehicle Components Using TEM Cells, 14 kHz–200 MHz," Jan. 1984.

SAE J1507, "Anechoic Test Facility Radiated Susceptibility, 20 MHz–18 GHz, Electromagnetic Field," Jan. 1986.

SAE J1595, "Electrostatic Discharge Test For Vehicles," October 1988.

Tippet, J. C., "Modal Characteristics of Rectangular Coaxial Transmission Line," thesis submitted June 1978 for degree of Doctor of Philosophy to University of Colorado, Electrical Engineering Department, Boulder, Col.

Tippet, J. C., D. C. Chang, and M. L. Crawford, "An Analytical and Experimental Determination of the Cutoff Frequencies of Higher-order TE Modes in a TEM Cell," NBSIR 76-841, June 1976.

Vrooman, "An Indoor 60 Hz to 40 GHz Facility for Total Vehicle EMC Testing," SAE Paper No. 831011, June 1983.

ABOUT THE AUTHOR

James P. Muccioli has extensive experience in EMC design, analysis, and testing. His background includes 13 years of specialized EMC systems experience at Chrysler Corporation and United Technologies. He served on the faculty of Lawrence Technological University, teaching an undergraduate course on noise reduction techniques and a continuing education seminar on electronic system noise reduction. He teaches EMC seminars through his own consulting firm JASTECH and has authored several symposium papers on EMC and is a NARTE Certified EMC Engineer. He is an active member of SAE-J1113 and J-551 EMC committees (1984–present) and is chairperson of the SAE Integrated Circuit EMC Task Force (1991–present). He is an IEEE-Electromagnetic Compatibility Society Board of Directors member.

CHAPTER 28
ELECTROMAGNETIC COMPATIBILITY

James P. Muccioli
EMC Consultant, JASTECH

28.1 NOISE PROPAGATION MODES

28.1.1 Introduction

Before an engineer can design for EMC, he must first understand the paths where electromagnetic interference can affect electronic modules and how electromagnetic emissions from his module will affect other electronic modules. Noise propagation can be defined as conducted mode propagation and/or radiated emissions propagation.

28.1.2 Conducted Mode Propagation

Conducted mode propagation occurs when electromagnetic interference travels on the wiring harness connecting the noise source to the device affected, as shown in Fig. 28.1.

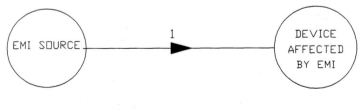

1 CONDUCTED MODE INTERFERENCE

FIGURE 28.1 Conducted mode propagation.

28.1.3 Radiated Emissions Propagation

Radiated emissions propagation occurs when the electromagnetic interference travels through free space (air) from a noise source to the device affected, as shown in Fig. 28.2.

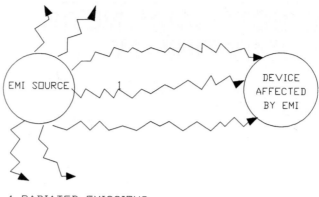

1 RADIATED EMISSIONS

FIGURE 28.2   Radiated emissions propagation.

28.1.4   Conducted and Radiated Propagation

Conducted and radiated propagation occurs when the electromagnetic interference travels on and radiates from the wiring harness connecting the noise source to the device affected, as shown in Fig. 28.3.

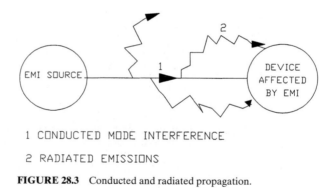

1 CONDUCTED MODE INTERFERENCE

2 RADIATED EMISSIONS

FIGURE 28.3   Conducted and radiated propagation.

28.1.5   Radiated and Conducted Propagation

Radiated and conducted propagation occurs when the electromagnetic interference travels through free space (air) from a noise source to the wiring harness of the device affected, as shown in Figure 28.4.

28.2   CABLING

28.2.1   Introduction

The use of wiring harnesses (transmission lines) in the presence of electromagnetic fields can cause unwanted noise energy to be induced onto signal-carrying conductors. Typical wiring

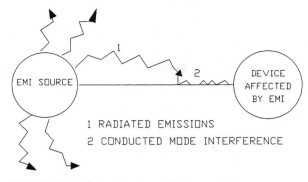

1 RADIATED EMISSIONS
2 CONDUCTED MODE INTERFERENCE

FIGURE 28.4   Radiated and conducted propagation.

harnesses in today's automobiles are made up of single, twisted pair, and coaxial type conductors. One of the biggest problems associated with using twisted pair and coaxial cables is an inappropriate method of termination. A test was performed to determine how termination affects them, and how they reject radiated interference.

28.2.2   Test Methodology

Using a stripline antenna, an E-field intensity of 50 V/m was maintained throughout the entire frequency range of the test. Figure 28.5 shows the test setup of the stripline antenna with relation to the cable under test and the ground plane. All cables used were 2 m in length and terminated with the same resistances. The cables were swept through a frequency range of 10 KHz to 100 MHz. Data points were selected at multiple decades of frequency.

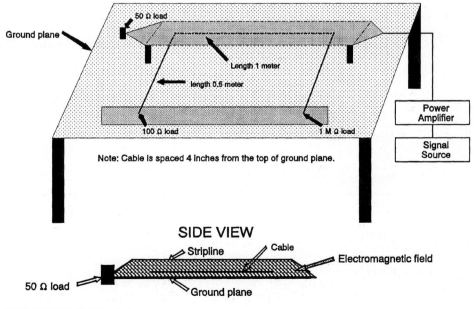

FIGURE 28.5   Stripline test setup.

28.2.3 Summary

Figure 28.6 shows the various cable configurations. Configurations A through F have both ends grounded, while configurations G through K have only one end grounded. The attenuation values for each cable configuration are shown in Table 28.1. Overall, cables with single-ended grounding offered more attenuation than cables with dual-ended grounding. This data should be used to get a feel for the different types of cable configurations. When the cable termination and load resistors are known, a test should be performed to verify the attenuation expected

TABLE 28.1 Attenuation in dB of Cable Configurations

Letter	10 kHz	50 kHz	100 kHz	1 MHz	10 MHz	100 MHz
A	0	0	0	0	0	0
B	0	0	0	0	0	−20
C	15	25	30	40	38	10
D	11	15	15	17	15	−10
E	8	8	7	13	10	20
F	8	12	15	27	28	20
G	40	44	46	56	38	51
H	20	15	15	15	10	−10
I	26	36	41	46	30	0
J	15	30	30	35	32	18
K	15	35	42	45	30	0

28.3 COMPONENTS

28.3.1 Capacitor

Capacitor Model.   A high-frequency capacitor model is needed for analyzing the effects due to electromagnetic compatibility. Figure 28.7 shows one way to model a high-frequency capacitor.

Capacitor EMC Guidelines.   Consider the frequency range, voltage rating, stability, temperature coefficient, and tolerance when choosing the dielectric type for the capacitance. The type of dielectric used in the capacitor will dictate the frequency range over which the capacitor will be most effective for filtering. Table 28.2 includes the relative losses (leakage) of dielectric types.

TABLE 28.2 Relative Losses of Dielectric Types

Dielectric type	Frequency range	Relative losses
Aluminum electrolytic	1 Hz–10 KHz	High
Tantalum electrolytic	1 Hz–10 KHz	High
Paper/mylar	100 Hz–5 MHz	Medium
High K-ceramic	1 KHz–100 MHz	Low
Plastic films	1 KHz–9 GHz	Low
Mica/glass/low-loss ceramic	5 KHz–10 GHz	Low

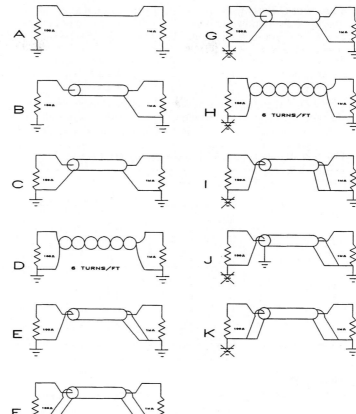

FIGURE 28.6   Cable configurations.

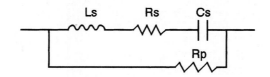

Cs = Series capacitance

Ls = Inductance due to lead length and capacitor structure

Rs = Effective series resistance and dissipation factor

Rp = Parallel leakage and volume resistivity of dielectric

FIGURE 28.7   Equivalent circuit for a capacitor.

Capacitor Quality Q Factor.   Quality factor Q of a capacitor is the ratio of the resonant frequency to the bandwidth between the frequencies on opposite sides of the resonance. The Q of a simple resonant circuit composed of a capacitance and inductances is given by the following equation:

$$Q = \frac{(Q_C \times Q_L)}{(Q_C + Q_L)}$$

where Q_C = the magnitude of the ratio of the capacitor susceptance to its effective shunt conductance at a specified frequency, and Q_L = the magnitude of the ratio of the inductor reactance to its effective series resistance at a specified frequency.

When Q is greater than 1, the capacitor impedance-versus-frequency model is as shown in Fig. 28.8. When Q is less than 1, the capacitor impedance-versus-frequency model is as shown in Fig. 28.9.

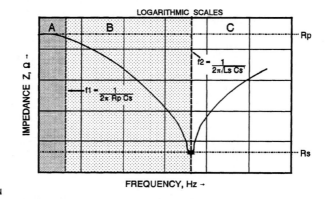

REGION

A   Capacitor impedance is primarily determined by parallel leakage and volume resistivity of the dielectric (Rp).

B   Capacitance (Cs) becomes the dominant with the impedance decreasing at -6 dB/octave.

★   Series resonance develops between Cs and Ls.

C   Series inductance (Ls) becomes dominant.

FIGURE 28.8   Capacitor impedance versus frequency when $Q > 1$.

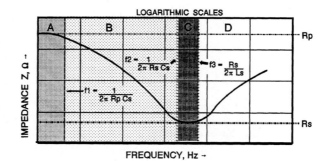

REGION

A   Capacitor impedance is primarily determined by parallel leakage and volume resistivity of the dielectric (Rp).

B   Capacitance (Cs) becomes the dominant with the impedance decreasing at -6 dB/octave.

C   Series resistance (Rs) causes the relatively flat characteristic between f2 and f3.

D   Series inductance (Ls) becomes dominant.

FIGURE 28.9   Capacitor impedance versus frequency when $Q < 1$.

The capacitor will self-resonate at some frequency dependent mainly upon the capacitive and inductive values of the capacitor itself, as shown in Figs. 28.8 and 28.9. Lead length is mainly responsible for the inductive element as depicted in the models. Excess length can reduce the resonant frequency significantly, hence reducing the operating frequency range.

Using a network analyzer, data in Table 28.3 was gathered on ceramic capacitors. The lower the value of the capacitor, the greater the effect the lead length will have on the self-resonate frequency.

TABLE 28.3 Capacitors Measured at Self-Resonate Frequencies

Capacitance	Self-resonate frequency at ¼″ leads	Self-resonate frequency at ½″ leads
1000 pF	35 MHz	32 MHz
500 pF	70 MHz	65 MHz
100 pF	150 MHz	120 MHz
50 pF	220 MHz	200 MHz
10 pF	500 MHz	350 MHz

28.3.2 Inductor

Inductor Model.   A high-frequency inductor model is needed for analyzing the effects due to electromagnetic compatibility. Figure 28.10 shows one way to model a high-frequency inductor.

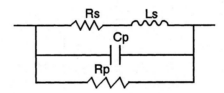

Ls = Series inductance

Rs = Series resistance from wire used in winding

Cp = Distributed capacitance between the windings

Rp = Core and winding resistance losses (including skin effect)
        at the resonant frequency

FIGURE 28.10   Equivalent circuit for an inductor.

Inductor EMC Guidelines.   EMC considerations for inductors include magnetic losses, mechanical stability, temperature coefficients, flux leakage, and dielectric losses. The shape of an inductor will determine some of its properties. An open core inductor, such as a cylinder, will have a large external magnetic field. A closed core inductor will confine most of the magnetic field. The toroid-shaped inductor has the maximum inductance per unit volume and low flux leakage. This is due to the fact that the toroid provides a closed circular path for magnetic flux, hence the external flux levels are very low. Figure 28.11 shows air core versus magnetic core inductors.

Inductor Quality Q Factor.   Quality factor Q of an inductor is the ratio of the resonant frequency to the bandwidth between the frequencies on opposite sides of the resonance. The Q of a simple resonant circuit composed of a capacitance and inductances is given by the following equation:

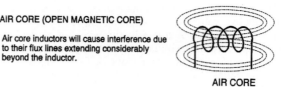

• AIR CORE (OPEN MAGNETIC CORE)

Air core inductors will cause interference due
to their flux lines extending considerably
beyond the inductor.

AIR CORE

• MAGNETIC CORE

Magnetic core inductors have small external
magnetic fields , since the flux remains
inside the magnetic core.

TOROIDAL

FIGURE 28.11   Air core versus magnetic core inductors.

$$Q = \frac{(Q_L \times Q_C)}{(Q_L + Q_C)}$$

where Q_L = the magnitude of the ratio of the inductor reactance to its effective series resistance at a specified frequency

Q_C = the magnitude of the ratio of the capacitor susceptance to its effective shunt conductance at a specified frequency

Figure 28.12 shows the inductor impedance versus frequency. An inductor has capacitance between each turn of the windings and leads. At some frequency, the inductor will become self-resonant, as shown in Fig. 28.12, due to its winding capacitance.

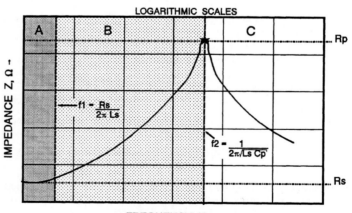

REGION

A   Inductor impedance is primarily determined by the winding dc resistance (Rs).

B   Inductance (Ls) becomes the dominant with the impedance increasing at +6 dB/octave.

★   Parallel resonance develops between Ls and Cp.

C   Parallel capacitance (Cp) becomes dominant.

FIGURE 28.12   Inductor impedance versus frequency.

28.3.3 Resistor

Resistor Model.   A high-frequency resistor model is needed for analyzing the effects due to electromagnetic compatibility. In Fig. 28.13, one way to model a high-frequency resistor is shown.

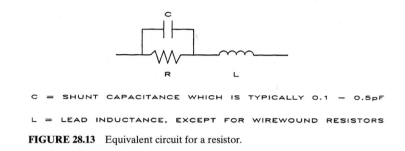

C = SHUNT CAPACITANCE WHICH IS TYPICALLY 0.1 — 0.5pF

L = LEAD INDUCTANCE, EXCEPT FOR WIREWOUND RESISTORS

FIGURE 28.13   Equivalent circuit for a resistor.

Resistor EMC Guidelines.   Consider the construction of the resistor before determining the transient handling capability and frequency characteristics. The resistor construction types are defined as carbon composition, chip (surface mount and leaded), film (thin and thick), and wirewound.

Transient Dissipation.   Carbon composition resistors are capable of handling large transients without degradation to the resistor value. Chip-type resistors are capable of handling moderate (less than 40 V) transients, making them suitable for most printed circuit board applications. Film-type resistors should be *avoided* for lines which encounter transients of significant power, since the film degrades after many transients and the resistor value will become lower. Wirewound resistors can dissipate repetitive, high-power, and high-peak transients without failure. The larger the diameter of the wire windings, the more effectively the transient can be dissipated

Resistor Noise.   In general, composition-type resistors produce the most electrical noise and wirewound resistors produce the least. Electrical noise in resistors manifests due to the thermal properties present in their construction. If a high-power and a low-power composition-type resistor are put in identical circuit conditions, the higher power resistor will produce less electrical noise. Because the noise produced by film-type resistors is less than that of composition types, they are used in small-signal or high-gain applications.

28.4   PRINTED CIRCUIT BOARD EMC CHECKLIST

1. Reduce radiated emissions and susceptibility by selecting the slowest possible switching speed (bandwidth) for the electronic devices.
2. Partition the PC-board.
   a. Bypass ground plane at I/O connector.
   b. Group regulators/power supplies near I/O connector.
   c. Place crystals/RC clock circuit directly next to ICs.
   d. Group same family of electronic devices together (interface, analog, low/medium/high-speed logic circuitry).

3. Single point the different types of ground circuits to I/O ground.
4. Bypass all lines at I/O connector.
   a. Reduce RF entering the PC-board by filtering at entrance.
   b. Reduce RF leaving the PC-board by filtering at exit.
5. Lay out the power distribution system.
   a. Low impedance power distribution system limits EMI.
   b. Power feed and return lines *must* be as close as possible to minimize impedance and loop sizes.
6. Decouple active components and power supply lines.
   a. Minimize instantaneous current draw on the power bus by placing a capacitor from the IC power to the IC ground.
   b. Calculate the size of capacitor required.
   c. Bulk decoupling capacitor (electrolytic typical 10–100 μF) is required at power entrance point.
7. Ground all unused IC input pins where possible.
   a. Reduce IC noise by lowering the ground impedance and eliminate unused IC pins from acting like antennas.
8. Design reverse voltage protection where needed.
   a. Diodes can be used to protect against reverse voltage damage.
9. Design clock line routing.
   a. Minimize clock line loop size.
   b. Clock line return path must be next to clock line.
10. Design PC-board jumper cables to minimize loop area by having return paths for all types of signal and power lines.
11. Autoroute the PC-board one partition group at a time with signal lines last.
12. Design metal housings to act as shields.

28.5 INTEGRATED CIRCUIT DECOUPLING—A KEY AUTOMOTIVE EMI CONCERN

Note: Parts of this section were taken from the paper of the same name presented by James P. Muccioli at the EMC/ESD International Conference in April 1992.

28.5.1 Abstract

Since the development of the first solid state engine control for automobiles, microcircuit technology has evolved with greater complexity, faster clock speeds, and smaller package size. Electromagnetic compatibility (EMC) has become a high priority in the design of electronic automotive modules. At the same time, the die size of CMOS technology has decreased from 9-micron process size (50-ns rise/fall time) to 0.8-micron process size (1.5-ns rise/fall time) in high-speed CMOS integrated circuits. To minimize the effect of EMC due to the faster rise/fall time, the design engineer must analyze the integrated circuit (IC) package and associated decoupling capacitor. This section will concentrate on how to analyze the decoupling capacitor requirements.

28.5.2 Introduction

Automotive electromagnetic emissions requirements and extreme cost constraints require the design engineer to be very innovative in addressing his EMI concerns. All components on the printed circuit board must be analyzed for effects and emissions contributed to the total radiated emissions from the electronic module. One source of noise on the printed circuit board is the integrated circuit. Choosing the right decoupling capacitor will limit the amount of electromagnetic emissions radiated from the integrated circuits on the printed circuit board. The decoupling capacitor, if not properly chosen for each integrated circuit, will contaminate the input/output lines in the form of ringing, overshooting, and/or undershooting.

28.5.3 Decoupling Capacitor Value

The decoupling capacitor supplies the instantaneous power required to the integrated circuit when switching from one of its transition states to another. When calculating the value for the decoupling capacitor, the following items must be considered:

1. Transient current of integrated circuit
2. Switching time of transition state
3. Allowable transient voltage drop in the supply voltage
4. Decoupling capacitor inductance due to lead length and capacitor structure
5. Printed circuit board trace inductance

Before the decoupling capacitor value can be determined, the design engineer must measure the rise/fall times of the various types of integrated circuits used on the printed circuit board. If the printed circuit board is using dual-source integrated circuits for production, the second source integrated circuits must also be measured and taken into account. After gathering this data, the switching frequency generated by the integrated circuit rise/fall time can be calculated by the formula:

$$f = \left[\frac{1}{\pi} \times t_r \right] \text{Hz} \tag{28.1}$$

where t_r = rise time/fall time in seconds

The value of the decoupling capacitor must satisfy two requirements:

1. The value of the decoupling capacitor must equal or exceed the minimum decoupling capacitor value required to supply enough power to meet the allowable transient voltage drop on the supply voltage.
2. The decoupling capacitor at this value must avoid self-resonance when instantaneous power is required for the integrated circuit.

The minimum value of the decoupling capacitor referred to in the first requirement (preceding) can be calculated by the formula:

$$C = \frac{(dI \times dt)}{dV} \tag{28.2}$$

where dI = current of transient (amps)
dt = switching time of transient (seconds)
dV = the transient voltage drop in the supply voltage (volts)

The self-resonant circuit referred to in the second requirement (see Fig. 28.14) is the combination of the capacitance and inductance between the decoupling capacitor and integrated circuit, resonating at the switching frequency generated by the integrated circuit. The inductance in the self-resonant circuit is the combination of inductances of the capacitor (L_C), the printed circuit board trace (L_{PCB}), and the integrated circuit lead frame (L_{IC}). The capacitance used for calculating the self-resonant circuit is the value of the capacitor C only (the capacitance value for the printed circuit board trace and the integrated circuit lead frame can be neglected because their values are negligible when compared to the decoupling capacitor value). The frequency of the self-resonant circuit can be calculated by the following formula:

$$f_c = \frac{1}{2\pi\sqrt{(L_{PCB} + L_{IC} + L_C)(C)}} \text{ Hz} \tag{28.3}$$

where L_{PCB} = inductance of printed circuit board trace (henrys)
   L_{IC} = inductance of integrated circuit lead frame (henrys)
   L_C = inductance of capacitor (henrys)
   C = capacitance value (farads)

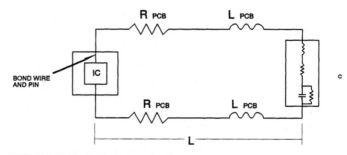

FIGURE 28.14   Self-resonant circuit.

If the second requirement is not met (the circuit becomes self-resonant), there will not be enough power to maintain the desired transient voltage drop.

When the design engineer analyzes the data from the three formulas and tries to meet the two requirements for a decoupling capacitor, the data will not always yield a solution.

The design engineer must also look at the decoupling capacitor placement (Fig. 28.15) and the various integrated circuit packages to determine if there are any differences in power and ground lead frame inductances.

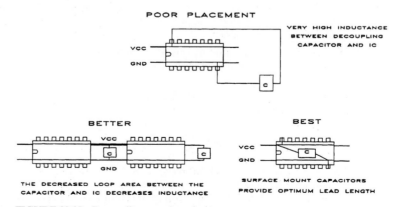

FIGURE 28.15   Decoupling capacitor placement.

The longest copper lead frame trace inductance values of various integrated circuits are not easily available. With the help of Mike Catherwood from Motorola, the following chart was created:

Package type	L_{max} (nH)
14 lead SOIC	1.81
16 lead SOIC	1.69
14 lead PDIP	3.93
16 lead PDIP	4.33
28 lead PDIP	8.72
20 lead PLCC	1.79
24 lead PLCC	2.45
44 lead PLCC	3.94
52 lead PLCC	4.06
68 lead PLCC	6.58
32 lead R-PLCC	1.89

This information is necessary for picking the lowest lead frame inductance for a specific IC package.

Sample Problem.   Find the decoupling capacitor value for a 74HCO4 14 lead PDIP hex inverter when assuming the following:

1. Supply voltage drop = 250 mV

2. Current of transient = 50 mA

3. Switching time of transient = rise/fall time of IC = 10 ns

Note: The smaller value of t_{TLH} or t_{THL}, taken from the IC specification sheet, can be used for t_r

4. Printed circuit board trace = 5 nH/cm

5. Printed circuit board trace length = 2 cm

6. Capacitor inductance = 1 nH

Solution.   The switching frequency generated by the IC rise/fall time can be calculated using Eq. (28.1):

$$f = [1/\pi \times t_r] \text{ Hz}$$
$$= 1/[\pi \times (1.0 \times 10^{-8})] \text{ Hz}$$
$$= 31\ 830\ 989 \text{ Hz}$$
$$= 31.8 \text{ MHz}$$

The minimum value of the decoupling capacitor referred to in the first requirement can be calculated using Eq. (28.2):

$$C = \frac{(dI \times dt)}{dV}$$
$$= [(5.0 \times 10^{-2}\text{A}) \times (1.0 \times 10^{-8}\text{s})]/2.5 \times 10^{-1}\text{V}$$
$$= 2.0 \times 10^{-9}\text{F}$$
$$= 2000 \text{ pF}$$

The frequency of the self-resonant circuit referred to in the second requirement can be calculated using Eq. (28.3):

$$f_c = \frac{1}{2\pi \left[(L_{PCB} + L_{IC} + L_C)(C) \right]^{1/2}}$$

$$= \frac{1}{2\pi \left[(2.0\ \text{cm})(5.0 \times 10^{-9}\text{H/cm}) + (2)(3.93 \times 10^{-9}\text{H}) + (1.0 \times 10^{-9}\text{H})(2.0 \times 10^{-9}\text{F}) \right]^{1/2}}$$

$$= 25{,}913{,}990\ \text{Hz}$$

$$= 25.9\ \text{MHz}$$

The second requirement is not met because the self-resonance of the capacitor combination (25.9 MHz) is lower in frequency than the integrated circuit switching frequency (31.8 MHz). If we change to a 14 lead SOIC package, the integrated circuit lead inductance is reduced to 1.81 nH per lead. Also, since the package is smaller, the printed circuit board trace length is reduced to 1 cm. The frequency of the self-resonant circuit is recalculated as shown:

$$f_c = \frac{1}{2\pi \sqrt{L_{PCB} + L_{IC} + L_C\ (C)}}$$

$$= \frac{1}{2\pi \sqrt{((1.0\ \text{cm})(5.0 \times 10^{-9}\ \text{H/cm}) + (2)(1.81 \times 10^{-9}\ \text{H}) + (1.0 \times 10^{-9}\ \text{H}))(2.0 \times 10^{-9}\ \text{F})}}$$

$$= 36{,}284{,}204\ \text{Hz}$$

$$= 36.3\ \text{MHz}$$

Therefore, by changing the IC package from PDIP to SOIC, we can meet both requirements.

28.5.4 Summary and Discussion

Decoupling capacitor values calculated using the formulas in this paper will not be optimal for every application due to lead frame and printed circuit board trace inductances. Integrated circuit manufacturers need to continue their search for ways to minimize the inductances in the power and ground leads. They should investigate supplying integrated circuits with decoupling capacitors internal to lead frame packages. Until the integrated circuit manufacturers can help the design engineer, the following items should be considered before a decoupling capacitor is chosen:

1. The larger the decoupling capacitor value, the lower the self-resonant frequency.
2. Too small a decoupling capacitor will not have sufficient charge storage for transient current needed by the integrated circuit.
3. Different integrated circuit package configurations will change the integrated circuit lead frame inductance.

28.6 IC PROCESS SIZE AFFECTS EMC

Note: Parts of this section were taken from the article of the same name by James P. Muccioli published in the June 1993 issue of *EMC Test & Design* magazine.

28.6.1 Abstract

This section focuses on how to measure the near-field radiated emissions generated by an integrated circuit. Testing was performed in a controlled manner that yields repeatable results using a miniature skin current probe. Integrated circuits are characterized by process size and its effect on radiated emissions.

28.6.2 Test Configuration

The devices under test (DUT) are all the same eight-bit microprocessor type with internal test ROM code. The only variable is the process size, which changes from 1.95 micron to 1.50 micron.

The DUT is in a standardized manufacturer IC test setup (Fig. 28.16) which is part of a ground plane to assure test repeatability. The DUT is powered by a low-impedance battery (alkaline) to assure that there is no possibility for conducted noise to interfere with or confuse the test results. The software for the programmable integrated circuit flows in a continuous loop and is part of the internal ROM.

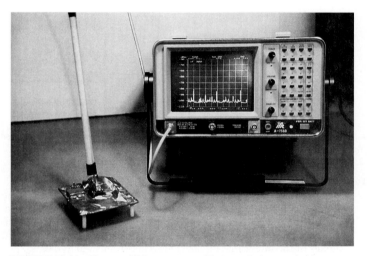

FIGURE 28.16   Picture of IC test setup with ground plane and skin current probe.

28.6.3 Test Methodology

The purpose for using a miniature skin current probe is to make quantitative measurements of currents (magnetic fields) generated by integrated circuits. The current probe can be used in a nonshielded room since only the magnetic fields related to the electromagnetic radiation potential of the integrated circuit affect the probe and it is relatively insensitive to stray electric fields.

The surface of the integrated circuit is mapped by orienting the probe for maximum sensitivity and then repeating the measurement after moving the probe to the next location. The skin current probe (Fischer Custom Communications, Inc. F-97) has a transfer impedance of 1 ohm ±20% from 70 MHz to greater than 1000 MHz as shown in Fig. 28.17.

The miniature skin current probe is in series with a 20-dB preamplifier (Mini-Circuits ZFL-1000LN) and is connected to a spectrum analyzer (IFR Systems, Inc. A-7550) as shown in Fig. 28.18. The system gain of the measuring equipment should be known with an accuracy

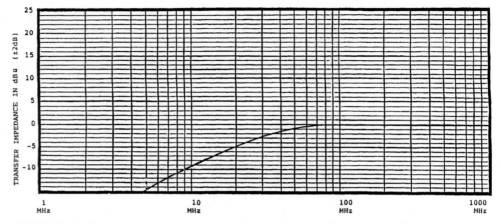

FIGURE 28.17   F-97 transfer impedance versus frequency. *(Courtesy of Fischer Custom Communications)*

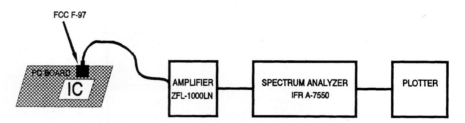

FIGURE 28.18   System test setup.

of ±0.5 dB. If the signals being measured by the skin current probe are within 6 dB of the system noise floor, then a smaller resolution bandwidth should be used on the spectrum analyzer.

The first measurement taken in each frequency band of the spectrum analyzer should be the ambient system level to assure that any ambient signals present are at least 6 dB below the signals of the integrated circuit. This is accomplished by taking the ambient measurement with the skin current probe placed on top of the integrated circuit in the measurement position with no power supply to the DUT. The DUT should be energized and a complete operational check of the integrated circuit test code performed to assure proper functioning of the device.

28.6.4   Test Results

Figures 28.19 and 28.20 show the system noise floor with the preamplifier and the F-97 probe. The frequency range of Fig. 28.19 is from 70 to 250 MHz with the center at 160 Mhz. The frequency range of Fig. 28.20 is from 250 to 500 MHz with the center at 375 MHz. The system noise floor from 70 to 500 MHz is below −120 dBm when the 20-dB gain is factored into the spectrum analyzer plot.

Figures 28.21 and 28.22 show the measured magnetic emissions of an eight-bit microprocessor with a 1.95-micron process size. The highest peak frequency from the microprocessor is at 72 MHz with a level corrected for preamp gain of −83.33 dBm.

Figures 28.23 and 28.24 show the measured magnetic emissions of an eight-bit microprocessor with a 1.50-micron process size. The highest peak frequency from the microprocessor is at 72 MHz with a corrected level of −86.00 dBm.

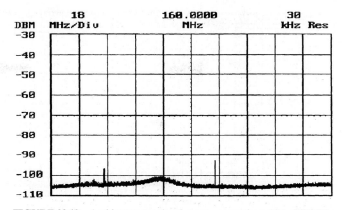

FIGURE 28.19   Ambient system level measurement from 70 to 250 MHz.

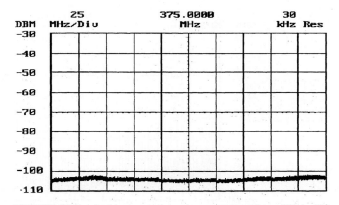

FIGURE 28.20   Ambient system level measurement from 250 to 500 MHz.

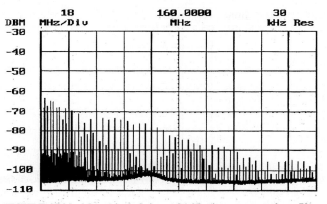

FIGURE 28.21   Magnetic emissions of 1.95-micron process from 70 to 250 MHz.

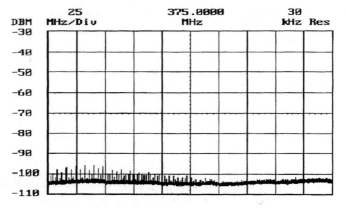

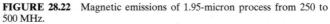

FIGURE 28.22   Magnetic emissions of 1.95-micron process from 250 to 500 MHz.

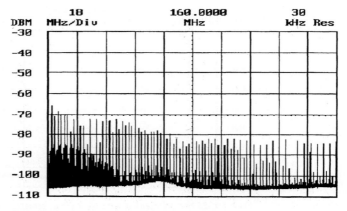

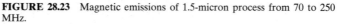

FIGURE 28.23   Magnetic emissions of 1.5-micron process from 70 to 250 MHz.

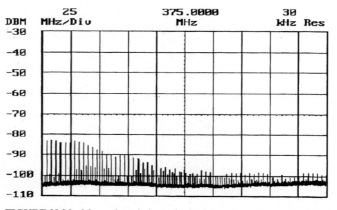

FIGURE 28.24   Magnetic emissions of 1.5-micron process from 250 to 500 MHz.

28.6.5 Summary and Discussion

When analyzing the data from Figs. 28.21, 28.22, 28.23, and 28.24, the following statements can be made:

1. The 1.95-micron process size magnetic emissions drop off faster than the 1.50-micron process size.
2. The 1.50-micron data has a more intense magnetic field between 70 and 115 MHz than the 1.95-micron data.
3. The amplitude of the 1.95-micron data is typically 10 to 15 dBm less than the 1.50-micron data after 200 MHz.

From the data analyzed, the author demonstrated that integrated circuit process size changes do have an effect on electromagnetic compatibility. The rise time of the integrated circuit is also affected by the process size change. The 1.95-micron process size has a rise time of 6.4 ns and the 1.50-micron process size has a rise time of 2.4 ns. Until the integrated circuit manufacturers can supply typical emission-level data with integrated circuit process size changes, the design engineer must make quantitative measurements of magnetic emissions from the integrated circuit.

The author acknowledges the editing assistance of Sandra Muccioli.

BIBLIOGRAPHY

Catherwood, Mike, "Designing for Electromagnetic Compatibility (EMC) with HCmos Microcontrollers," Motorola Semiconductor Application Note AN1050/D, 1989.

Catherwood, Mike, "HCMOS VLSI Design For EMC," *EMC/ESD International Conference Proceeding,* April 1992.

"Integrated Circuit Radiated Emissions Procedure from 1 MHz to 1000 MHz, Magnetic Field-loop probe," SAE IC-EMC task force draft document, Jan. 1993.

Keenan, Kenneth, *Decoupling and Layout of Digital Printed Circuits,* Pinellas Park, Florida, TKC, 1985.

Muccioli, James P., "Radiated Emissions of Very Large Scale Integrated Circuits," *IEEE International Symposium on Electromagnetic Compatibility,* Aug. 1990.

Ott, Henry W., *Noise Reduction Techniques in Electronic Systems,* 2d ed. John Wiley & Sons, New York, 1988.

Standler, Ronald B., *Protection of Electronic Circuits from Overvoltages,* John Wiley & Sons, New York, 1989.

Walker, Charles S., *Capacitance, Inductance and Crosstalk Analysis,* Artech House, Boston, 1990.

ABOUT THE AUTHOR

For information about the author, please refer to page 27.18.

P · A · R · T · 7

EMERGING TECHNOLOGIES

CHAPTER 29
NAVIGATION AIDS AND INTELLIGENT VEHICLE-HIGHWAY SYSTEMS*

Robert L. French
R. L. French & Associates

Autonomous navigation and route guidance systems with static databases are of considerable utility on a stand-alone basis. However, future versions will be linked to traffic management centers (TMC) by mobile data communications for maximum effectiveness. Automobile navigation technologies coupled with data communications also provide a basis for vehicle tracking and fleet management. These in-vehicle systems are viewed as a major subset of intelligent vehicle-highway systems (IVHS), a rapidly expanding worldwide movement to improve the efficiency, safety, and environmental aspects of road traffic through the application of information, communications, positioning, and control technologies.

29.1 BACKGROUND

Sophisticated vehicular navigation system concepts have become widely known only during the last decade. However, the historical roots of automobile navigation go much deeper.[1] The first vehicular navigation system was the "south-pointing chariot," a mechanical direction-keeping system developed by the Chinese around 200 to 300 A.D., almost 1000 years before the magnetic compass was invented. Its operation was based on the differential odometer phenomenon that, as a vehicle changes heading, the outer wheels travel further than the inner wheels by a distance that is a mathematical function of the change in heading.

Mechanical route guides for automobiles were introduced in the United States around 1910 to aid the drivers of early automobiles before roads were uniformly marked. These early devices incorporated the information of route maps in various forms including sequential instructions printed on a turntable, punched in a rotating disk, and printed on a moving tape, all driven by an odometer shaft in synchronization with distance traveled along the route.

For example, the 1910 Chadwick Road Guide rotated a metal disk in synchronization with distance traveled. The disk had holes spaced to coincide with decision points along the route

---

* As this book is going to press, the name "Intelligent Vehicle-Highway Systems" is being changed to "Intelligent Transportation Systems (ITS)" in the United States.

represented by the disk. An array of spring-loaded pins behind the slowly rotating disk was normally depressed, but when a punched hole traversed a pin, the pin released and raised a signal arm bearing a color-coded symbol indicating the action to be taken. In addition, a bell was sounded to draw the driver's attention to the signal.

The early mechanical route guidance systems faded out of the picture as roadside signs were standardized and became more plentiful by the 1920s. A resurgence of interest in route guidance occurred in the 1960s when ERGS (Electronic Route Guidance System) was researched by the U.S. Bureau of Public Roads.[2] Although ERGS was soon grounded from lack of Congressional support, it was followed in the 1970s by CACS (Comprehensive Automobile Control System) in Japan and by Autofahrer Leit-und Information System (ALI) in Germany.

Like ERGS, the CACS and ALI used real-time traffic information to compute best routes for downloading to on-board display equipment at strategically located proximity beacons. Thus, these early research and test projects, along with the evolution during the same era of advanced traffic management concepts for computerized control of area-wide traffic signals based on a centralized traffic database, set the stage for the much broader IVHS movements that started shaping up in Europe, Japan, and the United States in the mid-1980s.

Although comprehensive IVHS products and services, including data communication links between the traffic infrastructure and navigation-equipped vehicles, are not yet available, sophisticated autonomous navigation systems have been on the market in Japan since being introduced as a factory option by Toyota in 1987.[3] Approximately 500,000 had been sold by 1994, the year that OEM navigation systems were finally introduced in the United States and Europe.

29.2   AUTOMOBILE NAVIGATION TECHNOLOGIES

Positioning technologies are fundamental requirements of both vehicle navigation systems and vehicle tracking systems. Almost all vehicular navigation systems include dead reckoning with map matching as the main positioning technology, but most state-of-the-art systems also include a GPS (Global Positioning System) receiver now that the GPS satellite constellation is fully operational.

Map matching as well as route guidance must be supported by digital road maps. Another important supporting technology is mobile data communications for traffic and other traveler information. Although vehicle tracking systems may not require digital road maps aboard the vehicle (as is generally the case for navigation systems), they do require a mobile data communications link between the vehicle and dispatch office unless they use infrastructure-based integrated positioning and communications technologies. However, GPS and other radiopositioning technologies (e.g., Loran-C) are often used in conjunction with separate mobile communication systems for vehicle tracking.

29.2.1   Radiopositioning

Radiopositioning is the processing of special signals from one or more radio transmitters at known locations to determine the position of the receiving equipment. Although a number of radiopositioning technologies are potentially applicable, satellite-based GPS is by far the most popular.

GPS, which is operated by the U.S. Department of Defense, includes 24 satellites spaced in orbits such that a receiver can determine its position by simultaneously analyzing the travel time of signals from at least four satellites. GPS has the advantage of giving absolute position (albeit with an uncertainty of up to 100 m for civil receivers unless corrected by differential GPS). However, GPS alone is inadequate for automobile navigation because signal reception on roadways is sometimes blocked by buildings, foliage, etc. Nonetheless, GPS is very effective for automobile navigation when integrated with dead reckoning and map matching.

Proximity beacons provide another form of radiopositioning which is used in some vehicle navigation systems, particularly those that also use proximity beacons for communications purposes. Proximity beacons are devices installed at key intersections and other strategic roadside locations that communicate their location and/or other information to receivers in passing vehicles via very short-range radio, microwave, or infrared signals. The reception of a proximity beacon signal means that the receiving vehicle is within 50 m or so of the beacon, and provides an occasional basis for confirming vehicle position.

29.2.2 Dead Reckoning

Dead reckoning, the process of calculating location by integrating measured increments of distance and direction of travel relative to a known location, is used in virtually all vehicle navigation systems. Dead reckoning gives a vehicle's coordinates (X_n, Y_n) relative to earlier coordinates (X_o, Y_o):

$$X_n = X_o + \sum_1^n \Delta X_i = X_o + \sum_1^n \Delta l_i \sin \phi_i$$

$$Y_n = Y_o + \sum_1^n \Delta Y_i = Y_o + \sum_1^n \Delta l_i \cos \phi_i$$

where ϕ_i is the heading associated with l_i, the ith measured increment of travel as illustrated in Fig. 29.1. Dead reckoning for vehicle navigation thus requires sensors for measuring distance traveled and heading (or change in heading).

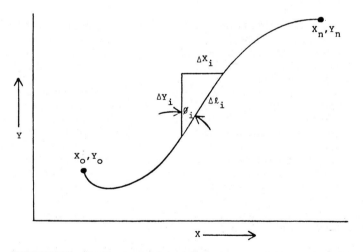

FIGURE 29.1 Dead-reckoning formulation.

Distance Sensors. Distance measurements for vehicle navigation systems are usually made with an electronic version of the odometer. Electronic odometers provide discrete signals from a rotating shaft or wheel, and a conversion factor is applied to obtain the incremental distance associated with each signal. Automobiles equipped with antilock braking systems (ABS) already have wheel sensors that may also serve as electronic odometers for navigation systems.

Odometers are subject to a number of error sources, some of which are systematic and may be corrected in the distance conversion process. The difference in the diameter of a new tire and a well-worn tire, for example, can contribute distance errors as high as 3 percent. The error in distance measurements increases by approximately 0.1 to 0.7 percent when vehicle speed is increased by 40 km/h due to the effect of centrifugal force on the tires, and a 10 psi change in tire pressure can induce an error of 0.25 to 1.1 percent.

Heading Sensors.   Vehicle heading may be measured directly with a magnetic compass, or indirectly by keeping track of heading relative to an initial heading by accumulating incremental changes in heading. A number of alternative means are available for measuring vehicle heading or heading changes. However, most have at least one drawback. As a result, it is a common practice to use two different types of sensors in combination to offset one another's weaknesses.

The magnetic compass's well-known accuracy problems due to anomalies in the earth's magnetic field are compounded when installed in a vehicle by induced fields which depend upon vehicle heading. Nonetheless, some form of magnetic compass is used in most vehicular navigation systems. Compact solid state flux-gate compasses with software processes for compensating errors resulting from both permanent and induced magnetism of the vehicle are popular in current systems.

In many applications, both a flux-gate compass and a differential odometer or a gyroscopic device are used along with a software filtering process that combines the outputs. Higher relative weight is placed on the differential odometer or gyro output for short-term changes in heading and on the compass output for longer-term trends in absolute heading.

A differential odometer consists of a pair of odometers, one each for the wheels on opposite ends of an axle. When a vehicle changes heading by an amount Θ as illustrated in Fig. 29.2, the outer wheel travels farther than the inner wheel by ΔD, which may be expressed in terms of heading change and vehicle width:

$$\Delta D = D_R - D_L = \Theta(R_R - R_L) = \Theta W$$

Thus $\Theta = \Delta D/W$.

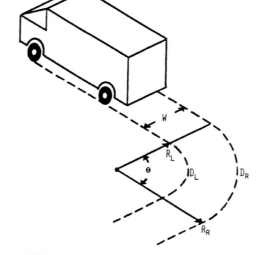

FIGURE 29.2   Differential odometer principle.

Several other types of heading-change sensors use some form of the gyroscopic principle. These range from traditional spinning devices and gas-jet sensors to vibrating bars and fiber optic gyros. Although more expensive than differential odometer sensors, they are much simpler to install. The fiber optic gyro started appearing in production automobile navigation systems in 1991. Finally, the more advanced forms of GPS receivers also support derivation of vehicle heading.

29.2.3   Digital Road Maps

Although a few route guidance systems use centrally located digital road map databases, the vast majority require an on-board database. The two basic approaches to digitizing maps are matrix encoding and vector encoding. A matrix-encoded map is essentially a digitized image in which each image element or pixel, as determined by an X-Y grid with arbitrary spacing, is defined by digital data-giving characteristics such as shade or color. In addition to requiring more data storage than vector encoding, matrix encoded maps are ill-suited for analytical treatment such as map matching or route finding.

The vector encoding approach applies mathematical modeling concepts to represent geometrical features such as roadways and boundaries in abstract form with a minimum of data.

FIGURE 29.3   Nodes and street segments of vector encoded map.

By considering each road or street as a series of straight lines and each intersection as a node, a map may be viewed as a set of interrelated nodes, lines, and enclosed areas as illustrated by Fig. 29.3.

Nodes may be identified by their coordinates (e.g., latitude and longitude). Additional nodes "shape points" are positioned along curves where the link between two intersections is not a straight line. Curves are thus approximated by a series of vectors connecting shape points, whereas a single vector directly connects the node points representing successive intersections if there are no curves in the connecting road segment.

The X-Y coordinates of node points may be encoded from maps or aerial photographs. The classic approach uses special work stations which record the coordinates of a given point when the cross hair of an instrument is placed over the point and a button pressed. This process has been automated in varying degrees. In some cases, the printed map is scanned to obtain a matrix image, which is then converted to vector form by software.

Various combinations of attributes associated with the encoded road network are included in digital map databases. Of particular importance are roadway classifications, street names, and address ranges between nodes. Map databases used with systems that give turn-by-turn route guidance also require traffic attributes such as turn restrictions by time of day and delineation of one-way streets. Directory and yellow pages information for selecting attractions, parking, restaurants, hotels, emergency facilities, etc., are commonly included.

29.2.4 Map Matching

Map matching is a type of artificial intelligence process used in virtually all vehicle navigation and route guidance systems that recognize a vehicle's location by matching the pattern of its apparent path (as approximated by dead reckoning and/or radiopositioning) with the road patterns of digital maps stored in computer memory. Most map-matching software may be classified as either semideterministic or probabilistic.[4]

Semideterministic.   This approach assumes that the equipped vehicle is essentially confined to a defined route or road network, and is designed to determine where the vehicle is along a route or within the road network. The concept may be illustrated by tracking the location of a vehicle over the simple route shown in Fig. 29.4*a* which defines a route from node A through nodes B, C, D, E and thence back to A in terms of instantaneous direction (ϕ) of travel versus cumulative distance (L) from the beginning as shown in Fig. 29.4*b*. Locations of nodes where direction changes occur (or could occur) are thus defined in terms of distance *L*. The solid line gives heading versus distance corresponding to the simple route. Alternative routes emanating from each node are indicated by dashed lines.

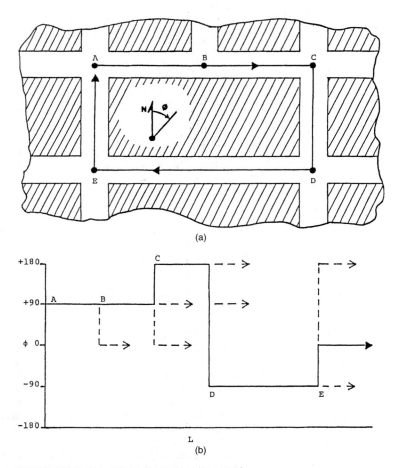

FIGURE 29.4   Simplified route and vector model.[4]

Figure 29.5 shows the kernel of a semideterministic algorithm in highly simplified form. Once initialized at a starting location ($\phi = 90°$ and $L = 0$ at Node A in the example), the algorithm, in effect, repeatedly asks, "Is the vehicle still on the route?" and "What is the present location along the route?" The vehicle is confirmed on the route if certain tests are satisfied. The location along the route is estimated by odometry, and error in the estimate is automatically removed at each node where it is determined that an expected change in heading actually occurs.

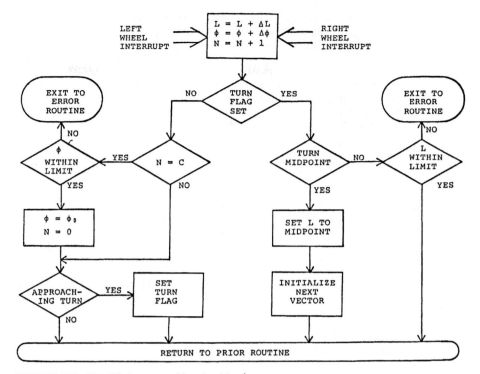

FIGURE 29.5   Simplified map-matching algorithm.[4]

The map-matching algorithm is driven by interrupts from differential odometer sensors installed on left and right wheels. The distance L from the beginning of a route segment is updated by adding an increment ΔL for each left wheel interrupt, and the vehicle heading ϕ is updated by adding an increment $\Delta \phi$ calculated from the difference in travel by the left and right wheels since the count N was last set to 0. As explained below, the N counter controls monitoring for unexpected heading changes occurring over relatively short distances.

Unless the turn flag is set to denote that the vehicle is approaching a distance L where a heading change should occur, count N is checked after each interrupt to determine if it has reached a limit C corresponding to an arbitrary amount of travel on the order of several meters. When the count limit C is reached, a test is made to determine if ϕ is within arbitrary limits (say ±5 degrees to allow for lane changes, slight road curvature, etc.). If so, ϕ is reset to ϕ_0 (the direction of the vector being traveled) and N is set to 0 to start another cycle of monitoring for unexpected heading changes.

In addition to verifying that the vehicle stays on the route between nodes, this process removes error in measured vehicle heading that accumulates while $0<N<C$. If the preceding test finds ϕ to be outside the limits, the vehicle is presumed to have turned off the route (perhaps into an unmapped driveway or parking lot) and other routines are called into play. For example, route recovery instructions could be issued.

When the vehicle approaches within an arbitrary distance (e.g., 75 m) of a node where a change in vehicle heading should occur, the turn flag is set and a route guidance instruction is issued, giving the direction of the turn and, if appropriate, the name of the next road. The algorithm then monitors for changes in ϕ to confirm that the midpoint of the expected turn is reached within an arbitrary limit (e.g., 10 m) of the value of L specified for the node, and afterwards to confirm that the turn is completed.

Upon reaching the midpoint, the current value of L is adjusted to that specified, thus removing any error in the measured distance accumulated since the last turn. If the expected turn is not confirmed within the allowed limits on distance $L,$ the vehicle is assumed to have missed the turn or to have taken an alternate turn (see dashed lines in Fig. 29.4b) and other routines may be called to identify the alternate route taken from the node.

The semideterministic algorithm concept outlined here may be extended to tracking a vehicle's location as it moves over arbitrary routes within a road network rather than following a preplanned route. As long as the vehicle stays on roadways defined by a vector-encoded digital map, the vehicle must exit each node via some vector. Thus, a map-matching algorithm can identify successive vectors traveled by measuring the direction of vehicle travel as it leaves each node and comparing the vehicle direction with that of various vectors emanating from the node.

Probabilistic.   An enhanced type of map-matching algorithm is required for tracking vehicles not presumed to be constrained to the roads. When the vehicle departs from the defined route or road network (e.g., into a parking lot), or appears to depart as a result of dead-reckoning error, the routine repeatedly compares the vehicle's dead-reckoned coordinates with those of the links surrounding the off-road area which encompasses the vehicle location in order to recognize where the vehicle returns to the road network. Unlike while traveling on defined roadways, map-matching adjustments do not prevent accumulation of dead-reckoning error. Thus, depending upon the distance traveled off road and the accuracy of the dead-reckoning sensors, there may be considerable uncertainty in vehicle coordinates, which could produce misleading conclusions when tested against the surrounding links.

Probabilistic map-matching algorithms minimize the potential of off-road errors by maintaining a running estimate of uncertainty in dead-reckoned location, which is considered in determining whether the vehicle is on a street. The estimate of location uncertainty is reduced each time it is deemed that the vehicle is on a street, but the uncertainty resumes growth in proportion to further vehicle travel until the next match occurs. Thus, a probabilistic algorithm repeatedly asks, "Where is the vehicle?," with no a priori presumption that it is on a road.

29.3   EXAMPLES OF NAVIGATION SYSTEMS

Figure 29.6 is a block diagram showing the major elements of a typical automobile navigation system. Distance and heading (or heading change) sensors are almost invariably included for dead-reckoning calculations which, in combination with map matching, form the basic platform for keeping track of vehicle location. However, dead reckoning with map matching has the drawback of occasionally failing due to dead-reckoning anomalies, extensive travel off mapped roads, ferry crossings, etc.

The *location sensor* indicated by dashed lines in Fig. 29.6 is an optional means of providing absolute location to avoid occasional manual reinitialization when dead reckoning with map matching fails. Although proximity beacons serve to update vehicle location in a few systems (particularly those that also use proximity beacons for data communication), most state-of-the-art systems use GPS receivers instead.

The recent evolution and present trends of automobile navigation and route guidance systems are illustrated by the following examples.

29.3.1   Etak Navigator™/Bosch Travelpilot™

The Etak, Inc. Navigator™ introduced in California in the mid-1980s was the first commercially available automobile navigation system to include digitized road maps, dead reckoning with

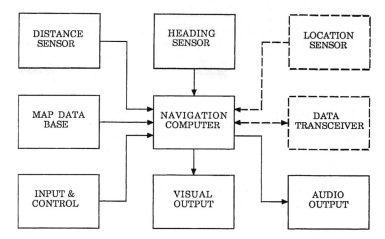

FIGURE 29.6 Typical components and subsystems of vehicle navigation system.

map matching, and an electronic map display. It used a flux-gate compass and differential odometer for dead reckoning. The equivalent of two printed city street maps were vector encoded and stored on 3.5-Mb digital cassettes for map matching and display purposes. Although sales were modest, the highly publicized Etak Navigator drew widespread attention to the concept of an electronic map display with icons showing current location and destination.

The Travelpilot, which is essentially a second generation of the Navigator, was jointly designed by Etak, Inc. and Bosch GmbH.[5] It was introduced in Germany in 1989 and in the United States two years later. One of the most conspicuous enhancements was the use of CD-ROM storage for digitized maps. The 640-Mb capacity permits the entire map of some countries to be stored on a single CD-ROM.

Like its predecessor, the Travelpilot displays a road map of the area around the vehicle, as illustrated by Fig. 29.7. The vehicle location and heading is indicated by the arrowhead icon below the center of the screen. The vertical bar at the right edge of the map indicates the dis-

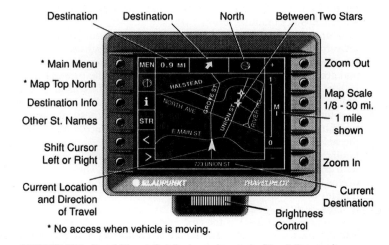

FIGURE 29.7 Bosch Travelpilot display and controls. (*Bosch literature*)

play scale which can be zoomed in to ⅛ mile for complete street detail or out to 30 miles to show only major highways. The map is normally oriented such that the direction in which the vehicle is heading points straight up on the display, thus allowing the driver to easily relate the map display to the view outside.

When parked, a menu accessible through the MEN button permits use of soft-labeled buttons in a scrolling scheme to enter destinations by street address, intersection, etc. Travelpilot uses a process called *geocoding* to locate an input destination and display it as a flashing star on the map. As illustrated in Fig. 29.7, a destination geocoded by street address is bracketed by two flashing stars when the map is zoomed in. In this case, the stars mark the block whose address range includes the street number of the destination. A line of information across the top of the map display indicates the crow-flight distance and points the direction from the vehicle's current location to the destination. Up to 100 input destinations may be stored for future use.

A submenu provides several methods for the driver to reset the vehicle's position on the map if the Travelpilot gets off track. The frequency with which the system requires reinitializing depends upon dead-reckoning anomalies and the completeness and accuracy of the map data for the area being driven. For example, map matching typically fails once in a thousand miles when operating in an environment like greater Los Angeles or North Texas. As for location accuracy the rest of the time (i.e., with map-matching operative), Travelpilot is claimed to have infinitesimal error relative to the map. The map-matching performance is compared to that of a servo-amplifier in which map-matching failure corresponds to loosing servo-lock to the map.

The Travelpilot hardware includes a V50 processor, ½-Mb DRAM, 64-Kb EPROM, and 8 Kb of nonvolatile RAM for storing vehicle location while the ignition is off, calibration factors, up to 100 saved destinations, etc. The Travelpilot may interact with other devices through an RS-232 serial port and an expansion card slot. For example, Travelpilots in 400 Los Angeles fire trucks and ambulances are connected by digital packet radio to the city's emergency control center. The emergency operators can monitor each vehicle's location and status, and can send destinations directly to a vehicle's Travelpilot for emergency dispatch.

29.3.2   Toyota Electro-Multivision

The Toyota Electro-Multivision has undergone numerous refinements since it was introduced in 1987 as the first sophisticated navigation system available as a factory option on automobiles sold in Japan. Except for a few features, it is representative of the more comprehensive models of navigation systems now available in Japan from almost all of the major automobile and electronics manufacturers.

Many Electro-Multivision features may be summarized with reference to those of the Travelpilot previously described in more detail. Both use dead reckoning and digitized maps stored on CD-ROM for display on a CRT screen with an icon representing present position, and are generally similar in their basic navigation features. However, a raster-scan color CRT rather than a vector-drawn monochromatic CRT is used in the Electro-Multivision. Also unlike Travelpilot, the Electro-Multivision map database includes yellow pages information such as the locations of facilities likely to be of interest to motorists.

The Electro-Multivision also serves as a reference atlas. In the original version, for example, a display shows a color map of all Japan with 16 superimposed rectangles. Touching a particular rectangle causes the map area it encompasses to zoom and fill the entire screen, again with grid lines superimposed to form 16 rectangles. Thus, a few touches of the screen takes the driver from an overview of the entire country down to major roads and landmarks in some quarter of Tokyo.

However, in spite of Electro-Multivision's sophisticated map-handling capabilities, map matching was not used in the first version because the digital maps then available for Japan did not contain sufficient detail at the city street level. In addition to detailed digital maps and map matching, subsequent versions of Electro-Multivision include a GPS receiver and a color

LCD rather than CRT display.[6] In 1991, a routing feature was added to calculate a suggested route to specified destinations and highlight the trace on the LCD map display. The most recent version[7] adds synthesized voice route guidance instructions.

As is the case for most other state-of-the-art navigation systems offered as factory-installed equipment in Japan, the Electro-Multivision navigation features are integrated with a full suite of entertainment features (e.g., AM-FM radio, tape cassette, audio CD player, color TV, etc.). In addition, the Electro-Multivision includes a CCD camera for rear vision on the LCD screen.

29.3.3 Oldsmobile Navigation/Information System

In January 1994, Oldsmobile announced its Navigation/Information System, the first navigation and route guidance system to be offered as a dealer-installed option from an automobile manufacturer in the United States. Initially sold only in California, the system was expected to be offered nationwide as digital map databases for other areas become available during 1994–1995.

The Oldsmobile system integrates a GPS receiver with dead reckoning and map matching. The dead-reckoning process uses gyroscopic and odometer inputs. A PCMCIA card is used for storing a map database which includes the locations of points of interest such as emergency services, restaurants, major retail stores, schools, office buildings, tourist attractions, etc. The major hardware modules of the system are shown in Fig. 29.8.

Destinations may be entered as specific street addresses or road intersections, or by selecting categories and scrolling through the points of interest included in the database. Routing criteria (e.g., avoiding expressways) may also be specified. The navigation computer then calculates the route and highlights it on a 4-in active matrix color LCD. Once underway, the distance to and direction of each turn is displayed on the screen and a voice prompt advises the driver as each turn is approached. A representative route guidance screen is shown in Fig. 29.9.

The Oldsmobile Navigation/Information system is supplied by Zexel USA Corp. and is an adaptation of Zexel's NAVMATE system which has been under development for several years specifically for the U.S. market.

29.3.4 TravTek Driver Information System

Whereas these examples of automobile navigation systems are already available in certain markets, TravTek was a functional prototype of a navigation-based in-vehicle traveler information system developed specifically for the TravTek IVHS operational field trial conducted for a one-year period ending in 1993 in Orlando, Florida. The field trial was a joint public sector-private sector project with the primary objective of obtaining field data on the acceptance and use by drivers of navigation and other information provided by comprehensive in-vehicle systems linked with traffic operations and other data centers.

The TravTek project used 100 General Motors automobiles equipped with the system shown schematically in Fig. 29.10 to provide navigation, route selection and guidance, real-time traffic information, local yellow pages and tourist information, and cellular phone service.[8] Most of the automobiles were made available to Orlando visitors through Avis Rent A Car for short-term trials and the rest were assigned to local drivers for extended periods. The American Automobile Association selected the test subjects and operated a TravTek Information and Services Center which could be accessed via cellular telephone.

TravTek navigation is based on a combination of dead reckoning and map matching, with a GPS receiver playing a "watchdog" role. TravTek's navigation function superimposes vehicle location on a map display screen, highlights suggested routes on the color CRT map display, and issues route guidance instructions via synthesized voice. Alternatively, turn-by-turn route guidance instructions may be displayed in the form of simplified graphics.

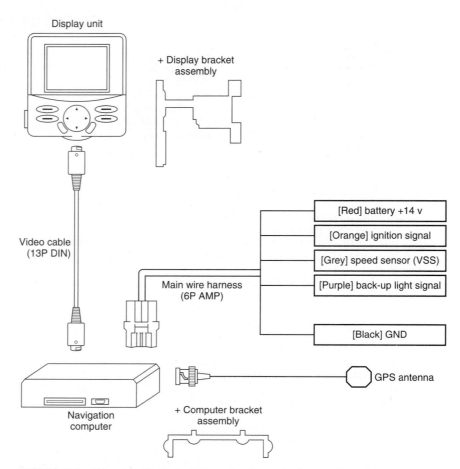

FIGURE 29.8   Oldsmobile Navigation/Information System hardware. (*Oldsmobile*)

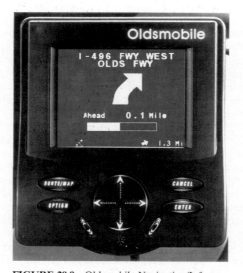

FIGURE 29.9   Oldsmobile Navigation/Information System route guidance screen. (*Oldsmobile*)

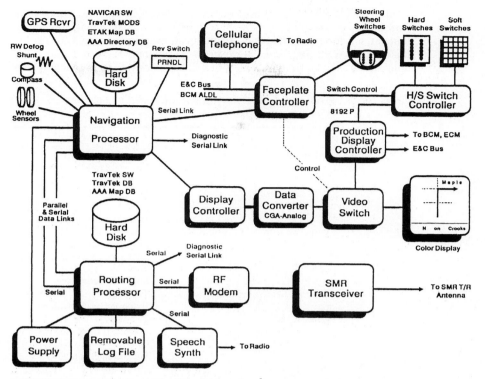

FIGURE 29.10   Architecture of TravTek vehicle system.[8]

Although functionally realistic, the TravTek in-vehicle system design used some features that would not typically appear in a production system. For example, rather than consolidated databases stored on a single CD-ROM or other data storage device, TravTek used separate map databases stored on separate hard disk drives for navigation processing and route guidance processing.[9]

However, compared to these examples of commercially available navigation and route guidance systems, TravTek's most distinct difference was the capability to superimpose information on current traffic conditions on the map display and to take traffic congestion levels into account in calculating recommended routes. The traffic information was received over a radio link from a special Traffic Management Center (TMC) operated by the City of Orlando in conjunction with the Federal Highway Administration and the Florida Department of Transportation. The TMC consolidated traffic data from various sources including "probe" data consisting of road segment travel times received via mobile radio from the TravTek vehicles themselves.

29.4   OTHER IVHS SYSTEMS AND SERVICES

A central aspect of IVHS (Intelligent Vehicle-Highway Systems) is the operation of advanced traffic management systems (e.g., the TravTek TMC outlined here) in conjunction with automobile navigation and route guidance systems. This requires the use of mobile data communication links between the infrastructure and in-vehicle systems. Although the United States, Europe, Japan, and other developed countries are now systematically pursuing IVHS development, selection of mobile data communication approaches remains under consideration as this handbook is prepared. However, it is generally expected that one or more of the approaches characterized in Table 29.1 will be selected for most geographical areas.

TABLE 29.1 Characteristics of Alternative Mobile Data Communication Approaches

Approach	Characteristics
FM sideband	One-way
	Low data rates
	Extended area coverage
Proximity beacon	One-way or two-way
	High data rates
	Spot area coverage
Inductive loop	One-way or two-way
	Low data rates
	Spot area coverage
Land mobile	Two-way
	Local area coverage
Specialized mobile radio	Two-way
	Extended area coverage
Cellular radio	Two-way
	Local/extended area coverage
Mobile satellite	One-way or two-way
	Wide area coverage
Meteor burst	Two-way
	Wide area coverage
	Involves time delays

The vast scope of IVHS is made easier to comprehend by subdivision into several interrelated and overlapping categories that have been used to structure the IVHS program in the United States: Advanced Traffic Management Systems (ATMS), Advanced Traveler Information Systems (ATIS), Advanced Vehicle Control Systems (AVCS), Commercial Vehicle Operations (CVO), Advanced Public Transportation Systems (APTS), and Advanced Rural Transportation Systems (ARTS).

29.4.1 Advanced Traffic Management Systems (ATMS)

ATMS includes freeway surveillance and incident detection, changeable message signs, electronic toll collection, and coordination of traffic signal timing over wide areas in response to real-time traffic conditions. Major elements of ATMS have been around for decades. The first computerized traffic signal control systems were developed in the 1960s, and approximately 200 computerized traffic signal control systems were in use in North America by the end of the 1980s. About 25 major freeway surveillance and control systems were in use, including many dating from the 1960s and 1970s. Electronic toll collection did not start experiencing significant implementation until the 1990s.

An additional ATMS function is to supply real-time traffic information (e.g., link travel times) over mobile data communication links to ATIS. The final selection of one or more communication links is unsettled because, among other things, their requirements (e.g., data rates) are highly dependent upon system architecture and the division of functions between infrastructure and in-vehicle equipment.

29.4.2   Advanced Traveler Information Systems (ATIS)

ATIS systems acquire, analyze, communicate, and present information to assist surface transportation travelers in moving from one location to another. Initially called ADIS (Advanced Driver Information Systems) by Mobility 2000 and essentially limited to navigation, route guidance, and traffic information presented by in-vehicle systems, ATIS concepts now also encompass the provision of transit schedules and connections to home, office, kiosk and handheld PPATIS (Portable ATIS) units as well as in-vehicle units. Vision enhancement devices for drivers also fall under the ATIS category.

Although PPATIS concepts are proliferating, most early ATIS market activity is expected to be what was originally called ADIS and will be centered on in-vehicle navigation and route guidance systems. A 1991 Delphi study by the University of Michigan forecasts some form of navigation incorporating GPS will be used in 5 percent of all vehicles sold annually by 2000 and in 50 percent by 2012. IVHS strategic planning assumes that manufacturers will sell 2.5 million vehicles annually with factory-installed ATIS by the year 2000.

The potential of the ATIS market is also illustrated by the fact that approximately 500,000 sophisticated automobile navigation systems had already been sold (mostly as factory options) in Japan by the end of 1993, even though they must operate autonomously because mobile communication links to ATMS traffic operations centers for enabling dynamic route adjustment according to traffic conditions have thus far been limited to developmental tests.

29.4.3   Advanced Vehicle Control Systems (AVCS)

Whereas ATIS assists drivers by providing information to facilitate efficient and safe operation, AVCS provides direct assistance with vehicle control. An existing example is ABS (antilock braking system). Other early forms of AVCS include obstacle detection and warning systems and intelligent cruise control. Intelligent cruise control automatically adjusts speed according to distance and speed of the vehicle being followed, and enables platooning concepts wherein closely spaced vehicles travel in groups to increase lane capacity and safety. AVCS may ultimately lead to fully automated chauffeuring.

Most of the more advanced forms of AVCS such as automatic lane keeping (lateral steering control) are still in the laboratory stage. Although driver warning, perception enhancement, and assistance/control systems are under active research and testing in the United States, Europe, and Japan, the most comprehensive demonstrations to date have been accomplished under Europe's PROMETHEUS program.

29.4.4   Commercial Vehicle Operations (CVO)

In addition to benefiting from ATMS, ATIS, and AVCS functions, commercial vehicle operations may be made more productive through additional IVHS functions. These include automatic vehicle location monitoring, computerized dispatch and fleet management systems for dynamic scheduling and routing, weigh-in-motion (WIM), automatic vehicle classification (AVC), automatic vehicle identification (AVI), on-board data acquisition computers, etc.

The earliest CVO applications were for managing critical urban fleets (e.g., police vehicles starting in the 1970s). However, extensive application of communication and location reporting schemes to long-distance trucking fleets got underway in the 1980s. Much of the present CVO activities (e.g., AVI, AVC, WIM) focus on this application with the objective of eliminating stops and regulatory paperwork now required when traveling from state to state.

29.4.5   Advanced Public Transportation Systems (APTS)

APTS encompasses some forms of CVO (e.g., automatic vehicle location reporting), as well as additional functions such as schedule monitoring for transit buses. APTS also includes

HOV (high-occupancy vehicle) lanes and instant car-pooling services. Although AVL implementation for transit buses was limited until the present generation of GPS-based systems started becoming available, extensive research and trials were conducted during the 1970s under auspices of the Urban Mass Transit Administration (recently renamed Federal Transit Administration). The use of AVL and communications technologies to monitor, control, and manage public transit continues to be a central thrust of APTS.

New APTS thrusts include making timely and accurate information on traffic conditions and on transit and ride-sharing alternatives readily available to travelers (especially commuters who normally drive alone) for pretrip planning. Another is to improve the customer interface through the use of integrated electronic fare systems such as smart cards valid for all transportation modes, and through the provision of real-time transit service information at homes, offices, and public places as well as at stops, aboard vehicles, etc. APTS also includes systems for controlling HOV access and enforcing proper usage.

29.4.6   Advanced Rural Transportation Systems (ARTS)

ARTS has the greatest overlap with other segments of the IVHS industry in that few, if any, additional functions or technologies are required. Instead, safety dominates rural IVHS planning with emphasis on in-vehicle safety advisory and warning systems, prevention of single-vehicle off-road accidents, prevention of passing accidents, warnings of animals on or near the roadway, vision enhancement, and Mayday calls from stranded vehicles. Although virtually all of these may evolve under other IVHS segments, ARTS communications considerations differ significantly from those of urban areas because lower population densities and fewer roads combined with greater distances among facilities require greater dependence upon wide-area communications.

REFERENCES

1. R. L. French, "Historical overview of automobile navigation technology," *Proceedings, 36th IEEE Vehicular Technology Conference,* Dallas, Texas, May 20–22, 1986, pp. 350–358.

2. D. A. Rosen, Mammano, F. J., and Favout, R., "An electronic route guidance system for highway vehicles," *IEEE Transactions on Vehicular Technology,* vol., VT-19, 1970, pp. 143–152.

3. R. L. French, "Evolution of automobile navigation in Japan," *Proceedings, 49th Annual Meeting of the Institute of Navigation,* Cambridge, Massachusetts, June 21–23, 1993, pp. 69–74.

4. R. L. French, "Map matching origins, approaches, and applications," *Proceedings, Second International Symposium on Land Vehicle Navigation,* Munster, Germany, July 4–7, 1989, pp. 93–116.

5. J. L. Buxton, Honey, S. K., Suchowerskyj, W. E., and Tempelhof, A., "The Travelpilot: a second-generation automotive navigation system," *IEEE Transactions on Vehicular Technology,*" vol. 40, no. 1, 1991, pp. 41–44.

6. K. Ishikawa, Ogawa, M., Azuma, S., and Ito, T., "Map navigation software of the Electro-Multivision of the '91 Toyota Soarer," *Proceedings, VNIS'91—Vehicular Navigation & Information Systems Conference,* vol. 1, Dearborn, Michigan, Oct. 20–23, 1991, pp. 463–473. [Also known as SAE Paper No. 912790.]

7. T. Ito, Azuma, K., and Sumiya, K., "Development of the new navigation system—Voice Route Guidance," Society of Automotive Engineers Paper No. 930554, 1993.

8. M. K. Krage, "The TravTek Driver Information System," *Proceedings, VNIS'91—Vehicular Navigation & Information Systems Conference,* vol. 2, Dearborn, Michigan, Oct. 20–23, 1991, pp. 739–748. [Also known as SAE Paper No. 912820.]

9. J. H. Rillings and Krage, M. K., "TravTek: an operational advanced driver information systems," *Proceedings of the 1992 International Congress on Transportation Electronics,* SAE P-260, 1992, pp. 461–472.

ABOUT THE AUTHOR

Robert L. French is a pioneer in automobile navigation and IVHS. He has been involved with navigation since 1969 and invented map-matching technology, now used in virtually all automobile navigation systems. He was commissioned in 1993 by IVHS America to serve as principal investigator leading an international team of experts in performing a comparative analysis of IVHS progress in the United States, Europe, and Japan. Early in 1994, he was selected by the U.S. Department of Transportation as one of 12 experts to serve on the technical review team for the three-year National IVHS System Architecture Development Program.

CHAPTER 30
ELECTRIC AND HYBRID VEHICLES

George G. Karady, Tracy Blake
Arizona State University

Raymond S. Hobbs
Arizona Public Service Company

Donald B. Karner
Electric Transportation Application

30.1 INTRODUCTION

Electric vehicle (EV) technology is under rapid development. Several different types of experimental vehicles are in operation in the United States and elsewhere. Each vehicle uses different technologies and systems. Most are converted from standard internal combustion engine vehicles (ICEV). Because EV technology is still in its infancy, trends and future development cannot be assessed. Only the present status and a possible outlook can be identified.

This chapter will present a description of the current technology available in EVs today and identify the areas where technological breakthroughs will be required to produce EVs that can successfully compete with the ICEV.

30.1.1 History of the EV

Electric vehicle development preceded the development of cars with internal combustion engines (ICE). Thomas Davenport built the first battery-powered car in the United States in 1835.[1] Easy control and starting of electric motors and a lack of gas stations promoted the use of battery-powered cars. However, fast development of the internal combustion engine and discovery of the electric starter motor halted development of EV technology. The use of electric vehicles was restricted to a small number of local delivery trucks and cars. An example is the U.S. Postal Service which used battery-powered trucks for mail delivery in New York City for several decades.

Increasing air pollution in the late 1960s prompted the development of experimental electric vehicles. But the automobile industry significantly reduced vehicular emissions, which again halted EV development. In the early 1970s, a gasoline shortage following the Arab oil embargos renewed interest in electric vehicles, but generated only a few inadequate vehicles.

The major problem with these EVs was their relatively small operating radius (traditional fuels have about a 20 times greater energy density than batteries).

Increased industry interest occurred recently when the California Air Resource Board (CARB) mandated that in California two percent of all new vehicles lighter than 1700 kg must produce zero tailpipe emissions by 1998.[2] The proportion of zero-emission vehicles must increase to five percent by 2001 and 10 percent by 2003. Other states in the Northeast are considering adopting similar regulations to improve air quality. Presently, electric vehicles are the only commercially feasible zero-emission vehicles.[3] This mandatory reduction of air pollution has promoted vigorous research programs in both the United States and abroad.[4] All major automobile manufacturers started programs in the late 1980s to manufacture viable electric vehicles by 1998.

30.1.2 Electric Vehicle Performance

The main focus of EV developmental programs is to produce cars that are competitive with present-day ICEVs. In order to demonstrate the present state-of-the-art technology, Table 30.1 shows the performance of the Solectria E-10 pickup trucks. The United States-made Solectria E-10 (Solectria Co., Arlington, Mass.) is commercially available and is typical of EVs on the market today, which allows for a direct comparison to ICE-powered pickup trucks.

TABLE 30.1   Performance Rating of the Solectria E-10 Pickup Truck

Performance parameter	Rating
System power	42 kW
Horsepower	56 HP
Torque	73 ft-lb
Gradeability	18%
Acceleration, 0–50 km/h	9 s
Top speed	100 km/h
Efficiency at 75 km/h	240 Wh/m
Curb weight	1680 kg
Range at 80 km/h	130 km
Payload (2 passengers +)	90 kg

The Solectria E-10 is powered by an ac induction motor with a direct-drive automatic transmission and a regenerative braking system. It has power-assisted brakes, power steering, an electric heater, and an on-board 2-kW 110-V battery charger. Typical ICEV pickup trucks have a range of 550 to 750 km and a top speed of 150+ km/h. The Solectria E-10 is a well-designed EV but with a top speed of 100 km/h and a range of 130 km, it does not compare very well to the ICEV pickup trucks.

A review of different electric vehicles has led to the assessment that present day EV performance is less than that of ICEVs. To demonstrate the status of EVs, major performance parameters are compared.

Range.   The major limitation of EV performance is the small operating range. An average ICEV travels 750 to 1100 km on a tank full of gas and refueling requires 5 to 10 minutes. The range of present-day electric vehicles is less than 150 km and the "refueling" (battery-charging) time is measured in hours. Statistical surveys indicate that the average car travels less than 50 km a day, which is well within the operating range of present-day EVs. The short range is due to the low energy density in the batteries. The specific energy density in a lead-acid battery varies between 30 and 35 Wh/kg, which is significantly less than the 12,000 Wh/kg energy density of standard automotive fuel. The practical operating range depends on the speed, driving pattern, weather (temperature), and battery condition (age).

Weight.   Because of the low energy density, electric cars are heavier than similar gas-powered vehicles. The specific weight of a small electric car is around 20 W/kg.

Speed.   The operating speed and acceleration of the EV is somewhat lower than today's ICEVs. This is particularly valid for highway driving. Although electric racing cars can run over 200 km/h for a short length of time, manufacturers normally limit the maximum speed of the electric vehicle to around 120 km/h. In general, the EV is well suited for city driving.

Acceleration.   Starting acceleration of today's EVs is comparable to that of ICEVs. However, acceleration of the EV at high speeds (from 110 km/h) and hill-climbing ability is significantly less than the present-day ICEVs.[4] A lack of high-end acceleration may produce safety problems during highway driving.

Cost.   Because of the low energy density in the batteries, lightweight construction and high efficiency will be required by the EV. To achieve high efficiency, the EV must have a low rolling resistance, low coefficient of drag (aerodynamic), and have a high efficiency air conditioning/heating unit. Simultaneously, the vehicle must be crashworthy. Most EVs use a large number of expensive power electronic components and microprocessors. Consequently, the initial cost of an EV is significantly higher than that of a gas-powered vehicle.

Expected operational costs of an EV should be less than a comparable ICEV. General Motors Corporation's Storm ICEV, with manual transmission, drives approximately 50 km on $1 worth of gasoline. The comparable General Motors Impact EV drives approximately 120 km on $1 worth of electricity, assuming the cost of electricity to be $0.12/kWh.[2]

Maintenance and Lifetime.   Wear of the EV's electric components is significantly less than the wear on the ICEV that is operating at high temperatures, is liquid cooled, and has many more moving parts. Therefore, maintenance requirements for the EV are significantly less and the useful lifetime of an electric vehicle is significantly longer than the ICEV. The only component that requires high maintenance and has a short life span is the battery. Currently, the lifetime of lead-acid batteries is only a few years. This led to the proposal that the batteries should be considered as a part of the operating expenses. Roadside service may charge the battery pack instead of quick charging.

In order to assess the status and feasibility of commercial use of electrical vehicles, Table 30.2 gives typical performance and technical data for electric vehicles currently under development.

30.1.3 Motivation to Use Electric Vehicles

Zero emissions of the EV is the main motivation for considering its use. Air pollution produced by ICEVs in large cities have reached critical levels. These levels can be decreased by reduction of emissions from internal combustion engines. Switching to electric-powered vehicles will reduce pollution levels but will increase the consumption of electricity, thereby increasing the air pollution produced by electric power generation. Considering only vehicle and power plant pollution, a switch to electric vehicles would practically eliminate carbon monoxide, ozone, and volatile organic compounds from the air. Carbon dioxide levels would be halved and nitrogen oxide levels would be cut by 20 to 25 percent, but sulfur dioxide levels would increase. Sulfur dioxide is a byproduct of coal-fired power plants. It is hoped that by the late 1990s, power plants will install equipment to reduce nitrogen oxide and sulfur dioxide emissions, which will reduce acid rain.

A second motivation for EV use would be in a reduction of dependency on imported oil. Only four percent of the electric energy generated in the United States uses petroleum-based fuels, while fuels for ICEVs are exclusively based on petroleum. A third advantage is that most electric cars will be charged at night during off-peak hours. This increases utilization of

TABLE 30.2 Selected Technical Data for Electric Vehicles.[2]

Vehicle	Developers	Type	Status	Battery	Range, km	Top speed, km/h	Comments
BMW E1/E2	BMW AG (Germany); Unique Mobility (U.S.)	4-passenger car	Concept; no production plans announced	Sodium/sulfur	240	120 (E1)	E1 uses a 32-kW permanent magnet dc motor
Ecostar	Ford Motor Co. (U.S.)	Minivan based on Ford's European Escort	80–100 were produced in 1993 and leased for 30 months	Sodium/sulfur	160	120 (governed)	Uses a three-phase, 56-kW ac induction motor integrated into front transaxle
Fiat Panda Elettra	Fiat SpA (Italy)	Passenger car	Production run of 500 planned	Lead/acid Nickel/cadmium	80 104 (city driving)	113	Uses a 9.2-kW series dc motor
GM Impact	GM, Aero-Vironment Inc. (U.S.)	2-seater sub-compact sports car	Commercial production in mid-1990s	Lead/acid	190 (at 90 km/h)	120 (governed)	Uses two 43-kW ac induction motors
G-Van	EPRI, General Motors Corp. (U.S.); Conceptor Industries Inc. (Canada)	Passenger/cargo van based on GM Vandura glider	About 100 in service in commercial fleets—mostly utilities	Lead/acid	96 (city driving)	83	Uses a 43-kW dc motor
LA 301	LADWP, SCE, Clean Air Transport (U.S.)	2-passenger, series hybrid car	Commercial production projected for 1993	Lead/acid Sodium/sulfur	96 154	97	Hybrid version with sodium/sulfur battery and auxiliary ICE has range of 240 km
Mercedes-Benz 190EV	Mercedes-Benz AG (Germany)	5-passenger, 4-door car	Research car	Sodium/nickel chloride	150	120	Uses two external-rotor dc motors
Nissan FEV	Nissan Motor Co. (Japan)	Passenger car	Concept; no production plans announced	Nickel/cadmium	160 at 72 km/h	120	Can accept a 40% charge in 6 min; has solar cells in roof to augment battery
Renault Zoom	Renault (France); Matra SA (France)	2-passenger car	Concept; production version under development	Nickel/cadmium	150	120	Wheelbase shortens from 1845–1245 mm for parking
Tepco Iza	Tokyo Electric Power Co. (Japan)	4-passenger car	Concept car; only one built	Nickel/cadmium	550 at 40 km/h	176	Has 25-kw brushless dc motor inside each wheel
TEVan	EPRI, Chrysler Corp., SCE (U.S.)	Passenger/cargo minivan based on Chrysler minivan glider	About 50 were produced in 1993	Nickel/iron	180	105	Uses a 46-kW dc motor
Volkswagen CityStromer	Volkswagen AG (Germany)	Passenger car	70 vehicles using lead/acid battery built and sold	Lead/acid Sodium/sulfur	140 120	104	Based on Jetta production vehicle

EPRI = Electric Power Research Institute; ICE = internal combustion engine; LADWP = Los Angeles Department of Water and Power; SCE = Southern California Edison Co.

existing power plants and reduces energy costs. Utilities intend to offer lower rates to charge vehicles during off-peak hours and penalties to those charging during peak hours. The United States government is considering tax credits to EV users, which will partially offset the higher purchase costs.

30.2 SYSTEM DESCRIPTION

An electric drive system has been used in almost every transportation application that ICEV has used, including light cars and vans to large city buses. Most EVs use the body and mechanical parts of commercially available ICEVs. Two examples are Ford Motor Company's Ecostar van and the Mercedes-Benz 190E sedan. General Motors' Impact sports coupe is one of the few EVs that has been specially designed as an EV. Figure 30.1 shows a block diagram and the major components of a typical EV.

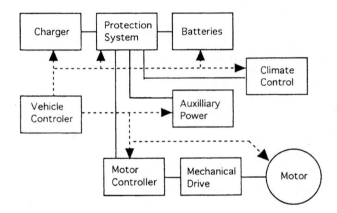

FIGURE 30.1 System-block diagram of a typical electric vehicle (EV).

The major components are:

1. *Charger.* It rectifies the ac network voltage for charging of the batteries.
2. *Protection system.* It consists of circuit breakers, relays, and fuses that are connected between the batteries and the rest of the electrical system and interrupt the supply in case of a fault.
3. *Motor.* EVs use both ac and dc motors.
4. *Motor controller.* This system controls the drive motor speed and torque. Both ac and dc drives are used.
5. *Mechanical drive system.* It consists of the transmission, differential, power steering, and so forth.
6. *Vehicle controller.* Most advanced EVs use a microprocessor-based controller that monitors the status of each of the major components and initiates control or protection actions as needed.
7. *Batteries.* The battery pack provides energy for the vehicle propulsion.
8. *Climate control system.* This system includes efficient air conditioning and heating systems.
9. *Auxiliary power.* It supplies the headlights, instrumentation, door opener, auxiliary motors (e.g., for the sunroof), power steering, etc.

The location of the major components depends upon vehicle type and construction. Several different arrangements are used by the EVs currently available.

EV technology is being developed at a fast pace. Several new types of vehicles are currently being tested. In some vehicles, the major components identified in Fig. 30.1 are combined. Some of the components, such as the protection system and auxiliary supply system, are similar to those used on standard ICEVs.

30.3 CHARGER AND PROTECTION SYSTEM

EVs can be charged overnight during off-peak hours or at a roadside station. The overnight slow charging takes 8 to 10 hours using a 240-V, 30-A connection. Quick charging requires several hundred amperes and takes 15 to 30 minutes. Today's EVs are equipped with slow chargers.

30.3.1 Chargers

The charger on an electric vehicle consists of a rectifier that converts the 240-V ac to the proper dc level required for charging. In most cases, this rectifier is mounted on the vehicle. However, it was proposed that the rectifier be installed in the charging station, where an advanced computer control would determine the charging voltage and the battery charge level. Subsequently, the computer will adjust the charging voltage to assure efficient and fast charging of the batteries.

The most simple technical solution is to use phase controlled rectifiers which control the charging rate by the delay of the device turn on. Figure 30.2 shows the connection diagram and typical voltage and current waveforms of a single-phase thyristor-controlled battery charger. Variance of the delay angle changes the average dc voltage and the charging current.

In some vehicles, the battery-charging circuit performs a dual role and is used to control motor current while the vehicle is being driven. The Ford Ecostar minivan uses this concept of a combined charger and drive controller. It can be built with high-power transistors, MOS-FETs, or insulated gate bipolar transistors (IGBTs). The circuit shown in Fig. 30.2 can be used as an inverter to drive ac motors or as a chopper to drive dc motors. A switching circuit is required to change from the charging mode to the drive (discharging) mode.

The connection between the vehicle and the charging station is currently under development. Two different systems have been proposed.[5] The first would use the transformer principle in which the ac system is connected to the vehicle charger through an inductive coupling, a transformer with two isolated coils. The coils are coupled with an iron core. The major advantage of this system is that the vehicle is not connected galvanically to the electrical network. This reduces the danger of touching energized parts or electrical accidents caused by ground faults. The separation of the vehicle from the network permits supplying of the inductive coupling from a higher voltage (480-V) three-phase system. This allows larger loads and suggests the use of the inductive coupling for quick-charging stations.

The second system connects the charging station to the vehicle charger through a metal plug similar to that used in outdoor appliances. Several different plug configurations are under development. The major requirements are that the plug has to be waterproof and touchproof, it has to withstand abuse and resist vandalism, it has to be energized only after it is connected to the vehicle charger, and damage of the plug should activate a protection system which would prevent energization.

30.3.2 Protection System

The battery and the electronic circuits must be protected against faults and short circuits. A short circuit in the car electric system discharges the battery. During a fault, the energy stored in the battery is converted to heat which can melt wires in the vehicle's electric system. Also,

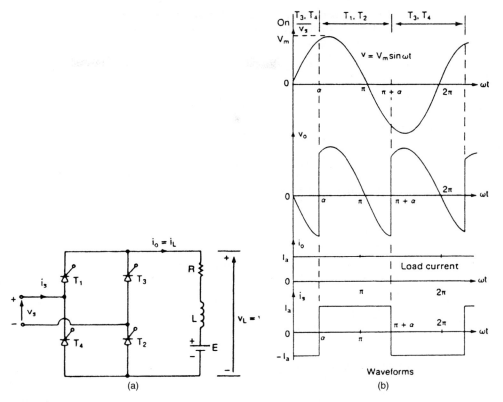

FIGURE 30.2   Thyristor-controlled battery charger: (*a*) connection diagram; (*b*) current and voltage waveforms.

a short circuit in a dc system may produce a large electric arc. Both the sudden heat generation and arcing endanger the life of the driver and passengers. Another problem is that the battery voltage in most EVs is between 100 and 200 V. In adverse conditions such as wet weather, this voltage level could cause electrocution.

Recognizing these problems, the manufacturers build electric vehicles with an ungrounded floating electrical system. The metal parts of the car's body are insulated from the electrical system and the tires insulate the car's body from the ground. In such a system, the first insulation fault between the electric system and the body will not produce battery discharge current. However, the second fault will short circuit the battery and endanger the operator. A possible fault scenario is a leakage path created by the conducting deposits produced by acid discharge from the battery. This conducting path can connect one terminal of the battery to the body, which is the first fault. Cable friction against body parts could cut the insulation, which may connect the conductor to the body of the vehicle and produces the second fault. This second fault will generate a short circuit. Figure 30.3 shows a schematic of the electric circuit and the current paths produced by the faults.

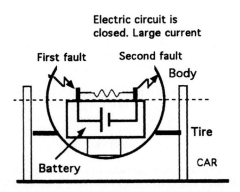

FIGURE 30.3   Effect of insulation faults in an EV.

Detection of the first insulation fault is very important. This may be achieved by a sensitive ground-fault protection circuit, which is similar to that used in bathrooms and kitchens in United States homes.

The second fault produces a short circuit which must be interrupted within milliseconds to prevent battery discharge. Fast-acting magnetic or electronic circuit breakers and/or fuses can provide adequate protection.

The operation of EVs in adverse conditions—snow, mud, and long inclines—may produce overloading of the electrical drive circuit and overheat the battery, motor, or cables. Overheating also reduces the life span of the insulation. The electronic drives have built-in overload protection but backup protection in the form of circuit breakers or fuses will prevent costly damage from fault conditions.

The electrical circuit backup protection used in most EVs consists of devices which are similar to those used in standard ICEVs. In addition to the breakers and fuses, microprocessor-based vehicle controllers are equipped with protection circuits, which provide primary protection by turning off systems which are affected by the fault.

The EV requires interlocks to assure safe operation.[4] The interlocks can be software-programmable in the vehicle control system or can be of the mechanical or relay type. Some of the frequently used interlocks are:

- *Charger interlock.*   Prevents the starting/driving of the vehicle when the charger is plugged in; disables the electric drive circuit while the charger is plugged in or operating.

- *Heater/air conditioner interlock.*   Disables the climate control system or switches it to the charger while the vehicle is being charged.

30.4   *MOTOR DRIVE SYSTEM*

The first electric vehicles used standard ac or dc motors but the required high efficiency and torque led to the development of special motors.

30.4.1   Motors

Important factors in choosing motors for EV applications include high efficiency, favorable torque characteristics, maintenance-free operation, and insensitivity to overload and contamination. Cost is also a major factor in motor selection.

AC Motors.   EVs which use an ac drive system use a three-phase induction motor which has a three-phase stator winding and squirrel cage rotor consisting of copper or aluminum bars installed in the slots of the iron core. The bars are short circuited at each end by a copper or aluminum ring.

Variable-frequency three-phase voltages supply the stator. The three-phase currents produce a rotating magnetic field which induces a current in the short-circuited rotor bars. The interaction between the rotor current and the magnetic flux produces the driving torque. Speed of the rotating magnetic field is determined by the frequency of the supply voltage and the motor construction. The rotor speed is always a few percent less than the speed of the magnetic field because the voltage induced in the rotor becomes zero if the motor and magnetic field speeds are equal.

Because of the squirrel cage rotor, these motors need very little maintenance. The sealed construction protects against spraying water and road mud. Motor efficiency varies with speed. As an example, a 7-kW motor has a maximum efficiency of 97 percent at 6000 rpm and 82 percent at 1500 rpm. The maximum speed of the same motor is around 15,000 rpm. The motor torque can be varied by reconfiguring the stator winding connections. The stator is delta-connected when the vehicle is at highway speed. The connection is switched to wye when a large amount of torque is needed for hill climbing or acceleration. The commercially available mechanical delta-wye switch can operate as a high-to-low gear shift.

DC Motors. EVs which have dc drive systems use series dc motors that have excellent speed-torque characteristics. Motor speed is proportional to the supply voltage, which simplifies the control circuit. The dc motors are less efficient than induction motors and the dc motor construction is more complicated because of the commutator. It requires regular maintenance and is sensitive to speeding and overloads. The dc motor maximum speed is less than the similarly rated induction motor. DC motors in an electric vehicle require a multispeed mechanical transmission.

The stator of a dc motor has poles with field windings. In a simple case, the rotor coils are connected in series and the end of each coil is connected to a commutator segment. The rotor winding is supplied by dc current through brushes connected to the commutator. The dc supply drives current through the field and the rotor windings, both of which generate a magnetic field. The interaction between these two fields generates a torque which tries to align the two fields. To assure continuous rotation, the commutator changes the direction of the coil current when it passes through the neutral zone.

Most dc motors are equipped with auxiliary poles, supplied by the rotor current, located close to the brushes. The poles reduce the magnetic field around the brushes to improve commutation.

The most suitable motor for electric vehicles is the series motor, where the field coil has low resistance and is connected in series with the rotor. This motor has a large starting torque but it decreases with increasing speed. This characteristic is suitable for urban driving but can produce problems on the highway. A lane change may require acceleration but the series motor torque is low at high speed. Some vehicles use compound motors, with a series and a separately excited field winding, which have higher torque at high speed.

The efficiency of series dc motors can be improved by replacing the current excited stator poles with permanent magnets. The expensive rare earth permanent magnets produce a higher magnetic field than the current excited coils, which leads to smaller and more efficient motors.

Brushless DC Motor. The brushless dc drive is basically a high-frequency ac synchronous drive. The motor consists of rotating permanent magnets and, typically, three or four sets of coils mounted on the stator. These coils are supplied by a dc current through electronic switches, where the coils are energized in sequence. At any given time, only one coil is energized. The rotation is generated by the force between the permanent magnet and the magnetic field generated by the energized coil. As an example, when coil one is energized, an attractive force develops between pole one and coil one. This force tries to align the energized coil with the permanent magnet. The alignment of the coil's field and the permanent magnet's field stops the rotation. To avoid this, before the field alignment occurs, the next coil is energized to maintain the driving force. The rotor position is monitored by a pickup coil. Switching time is determined by rotor position. The electronic switches energize the stator coils in a sequence to assure continuous motion. The sequential synchronous switching of the coils requires complicated electronic circuits to accurately measure the rotor position and activate the switches at the proper instants. The primary advantage of this drive is the elimination of brush friction and commutator arcing. The brushless dc motor has a higher efficiency and reliability than dc motors with brushes. Simultaneously, there is a significant increase in both the motor and the related electronics costs for the brushless dc motor. Its drives are particularly advantageous at constant high-speed driving. Most electric racing vehicles are built with brushless dc motors and drives.

Most vehicles's motors are mounted on the axle and connected to the wheels through fixed or variable ratio gears. An interesting experiment is the direct drive of the wheels with an in-wheel motor.

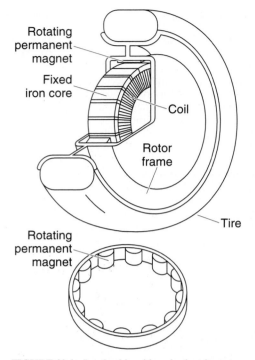

Rotating
permanent
magnet

Fixed
iron core

Coil

Rotor
frame

Tire

Rotating
permanent
magnet

FIGURE 30.4 In-wheel brushless dc electric motor.
(*Courtesy of Tokyo Electric Power Co.*)

Figure 30.4 shows the Tokyo Electric Company's in-wheel brushless dc motor. The rotating wheels with the tiers are equipped with an array of samarium-cobalt permanent magnets. The stator coils are installed on a stationary rim which is attached to the body of the car. Four motors have been used to drive an experimental car. The lack of gears makes the control of the four motors very difficult.

30.4.2 Motor Controller

The motor controller regulates the speed and torque of the electric motor, which drives the car. The motor controller also limits the motors' maximum current. Both ac and dc drive systems are used. The electric vehicle drive technology is changing continuously with the development of new electronic devices. Manufacturers are experimenting with different types of controllers that might be beneficial to EV design. The major requirements are smooth control of speed from zero to the maximum and the highest possible efficiency. Controllers should also have the capability of regenerative braking, forward-neutral-reverse control, overload/overheating protection, and production of a high starting torque.

Most dc drives use the traditional series dc motors with mechanical commutators. This well-tested motor is controlled by a simple electronic chopper (dc/dc converter). The dc motor efficiency can be improved by replacing the excitation coils with permanent magnets. However, the rare earth permanent magnets are expensive and difficult to manufacture because of the brittle nature of the material.

The latest motor development that has been incorporated into an EV is the electronically commutated brushless dc motor or ac synchronous motor, which eliminates the expense and high maintenance requirements of the mechanical commutator. These motors compete with inverter-driven ac motors. AC drives use variable-frequency inverters and three-phase induction motors. This technology is frequently used in the power industry. ac motors are inexpensive, more suitable for mass production, and are almost maintenance-free, but they do require complex electronic control circuits. Recent developments in high-power, high-current electronic devices like MOSfets and IGBTs will increase the power ratings and reduce the cost of inverters, which will increase the feasibility of using ac drives.

DC Drives.   The concept of a commutator-type series dc motor with regenerative braking is shown in Fig. 30.5. The motor speed is controlled by regulation of the armature voltage. The system consists of two transistors or IGBT switches. Each switch is shunted by a power diode to permit the circulation of inductive current and avoid high reverse voltages across the switching devices. The diode provides a path for the armature current when the switch is off. Switch T_1 operates as a chopper and regulates the average armature voltage. The motor speed is proportional to this voltage. When switch T_1 is closed, the battery drives current through the

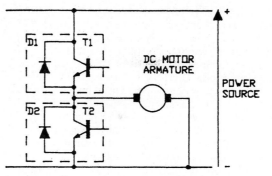

FIGURE 30.5 Concept of a commutator-type series dc motor drive.

motor. When T_1 is off, the motor current circulates through the diode D_2. The motor is driven only when the switch is on. The average armature dc voltage is proportional to the switch duty cycle, which is the ratio of the switch ON time and total switching period (ON time + OFF time). The motor speed is proportional to the armature voltage and, consequently, to the chopper duty cycle.

In the regenerative braking mode, T_1 is off. The motor operates as a dc generator and drives the current through diode D_1 back to the battery. This charging current is regulated by switch T_2. When T_2 is closed, the motor current will be diverted from the battery. The rate of recharging and braking action can be regulated by the duty cycle of switch T_2.

A more sophisticated double chopper circuit for compound dc motors is shown in Fig. 30.6. This circuit has been used in the Fiat Daily E2 van. The illustration shows the motor control cir-

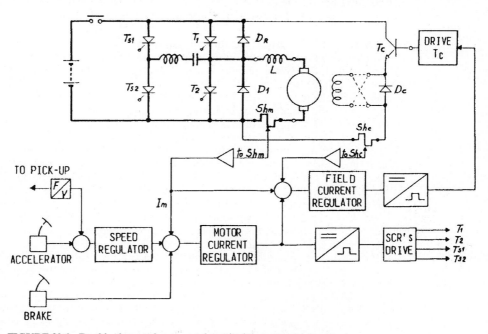

FIGURE 30.6 Double chopper for separately excited dc commutator motor.

cuit and the concept of the vehicle control. This vehicle uses a compound dc motor with a low resistance series and separate high-resistance field excitation windings. The former is connected in series with the armature while the field winding is separately excited. The armature voltage and current are controlled by a thyristor chopper, which is, in this case, a forced commutated thyristor bridge. Thyristor T_1 is turned on and off to regulate the motor armature current in drive mode. Thyristor T_2 is turned on and off to regulate the motor armature current in the regenerative braking mode. These thyristors are commutated by the discharge of the LC circuit through the auxiliary thyristors T_{s1} and T_{s2}. The diodes connected in parallel with thyristors T_1 and T_2 provide a path for the inductive motor current and eliminate the high reverse voltage. This circuit can be simplified by replacing the thyristors with high-current IGBTs.

The current of the separate field excitation winding is regulated by transistor Tc, which also operates as a chopper. The compound dc motor with the double chopper results in better speed and torque regulation.

Figure 30.6 also shows the concept of the vehicle control. Both the motor and the field excitation winding current, together with the motor speed, are monitored. The speed pickup signal and the accelerator pedal position activate the speed regulator. The speed regulator signal is compared with the motor current and the resulting signal activates the motor current regulator. The output signal of the regulator is converted to impulses that control the firing of the thyristors. A second control circuit is formed to regulate the field current. The motor current, motor current regulator output signal, and actual field currents are compared and the resulting signal controls the field current.

Brushless DC Drives. Brushless dc drives are the product of the latest developments in power electronics. The brushless dc motor[6] has permanent magnets on the rotor and coils in the stator. The elimination of the commutator from this dc motor made necessary the sensing of rotor position and sequential switching of the coils to the dc source to maintain rotation. The rotor position is sensed by a pickup coil. Each coil can be supplied either from the positive or the negative bus through a transistor switch. Each transistor is shunted by a diode to avoid high reverse voltages. The transistors are controlled from the control bus.

AC Drives. The ac drives use three-phase squirrel-cage induction motors supplied by a three-phase, voltage source, variable-frequency inverter using three-phase sine wave pulse-width modulation (PWM) voltage control. The motor speed is regulated by the variation of the supply voltage frequency. The change in voltage regulates the magnetic flux in the motor, which affects the motor torque and current. Regulation of the motor speed, torque, and current requires the simultaneous regulation of frequency and amplitude of the motor supply voltage. The most simple method is to maintain a constant supply voltage and frequency ratio. The voltage amplitude is controlled by pulse-width modulation (PWM).

The concept of ac motor regulation is shown in Fig. 30.7. The voltage source inverter consists of three parallel connected switching units. Each unit contains two switches connected in series. Each switch is built with a semiconductor device (transistor, IGBT, etc.) and a diode connected in parallel. The diode provides a path for the motor inductive current and eliminates dangerous reverse voltages across the switching devices.

The three-phase voltage, without PWM, is generated by the sequential operation of the switches. In each instance, three switches located in different branches, are turned on. As an example, switches Q_1, Q_2, and Q_3 can be turned on simultaneously. This connects the negative battery terminals to phase "c" and the positive terminals to phases "a" and "b." The simultaneous turn-on of switches Q_1, Q_4, and Q_6 is a prohibited combination because the simultaneous turn-on of Q_1 and Q_4 short circuits the battery. The turn-on of the switches is shifted from each other by 60 degrees and each switch conducts for 180 degrees. The turn-on gating signals are shown in Fig. 30.8. In each cycle, the switches are turned on in the following order: 123, 234, 345, 456, 561, and 612. It can be seen in Fig. 30.8 that this circuit produces square shape voltages and does not permit the regulation of the motor current. It can be regulated and circuit performance improved by using PWM when each switch is operated several times during each half cycle.

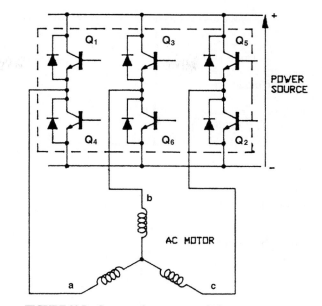

FIGURE 30.7 Concept of ac motor regulation.

The on and off time of the switch is determined by the comparison of a sinusoidal input signal with a triangular carrier signal. When the carrier amplitude is higher than the sine wave's amplitude, the switch is on; when it is lower, the switch is off. The described switch operation generates a pulse train of variable width at the terminals of the motor. The motor inductance integrates the variable-length voltage pulse train. Due to this integration effect, the variable-length pulse train drives a practically sinusoidal current through the motor. The widths of the output voltage pulses and the motor current are regulated by variation of the input sine wave amplitude. The described PWM method eliminates most of the harmonics from the motor current and results in a high-efficiency operation over a wide range of speeds. The expected peak efficiency is around 85 to 91 percent. These drives are particularly well suited for urban driving.

Switching Devices. The key component in both ac and dc drive systems is the semiconductor switching device. The device ratings for cars with a 40 to 50 kW drive and variable ratio transmission must be about 200 V and 250 A and for cars with fixed-ratio transmission, 400 to 600 V and 400 to 500 A.[7]

The advanced motor controllers should operate at a frequency between 10 and 20 kHz. High-frequency operation reduces the electronically generated audible noise. The disadvantage is the increase in switching losses and the generation of rf disturbances. The time of the transition from ON to OFF or OFF to ON state is important. The shorter transition time reduces the switching losses. Due to the wiring inductance, the fast switching may generate short duration overvoltages, which may be detrimental to the semiconductors. These overvoltages are controlled by selecting short leads and using filters or snubber circuits. The desired switching time is less than one microsecond.

Thyristor or Silicon Controlled Rectifier (SCR). SCRs have been used by the power industry for years in variable-speed drives. They have a large current-carrying capacity and high voltage ratings and relatively low voltage drop, but the current flow cannot be controlled after

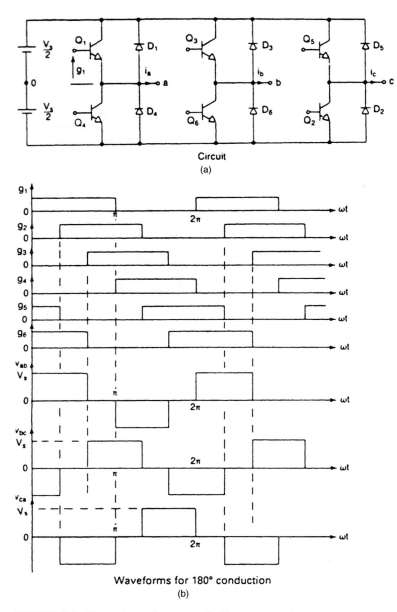

FIGURE 30.8 Three-phase voltage-controlled inverter operation.

firing. The turn-off requires cumbersome auxiliary circuits. In spite of these disadvantages, some EVs use SCRs.

Gate Turn-Off Thyristor (GTO). The gate turn-off thyristor can be turned off by a powerful gate signal. The problem is that the device can only operate at low frequencies (1 to 5 kHz) and the voltage drop is significantly higher than the SCR's voltage drop. Also, the firing and turn-off require large currents, which increase losses in the device.

Power Transistors. Both the voltage drop and the gain of power transistors are low. The low gain requires expensive gate drive systems. The transistors can operate in the required audio frequency range. The performance can be improved by connecting two transistors in a Darlington pair configuration. In this connection, the first transistor serves as an amplifier, which permits control of the device with low current. The Darlington connected transistors are sold as a unit at an attractive price. This is a frequently used circuit.

Power MOSFET. The MOSFET is a voltage-controlled device as compared to current-controlled (thyristor/transistor) and is designed for high-frequency operation. However, the saturation voltage drop and its temperature sensitivity limit the MOSFET application in power circuits.

Insulated Gate Bipolar Transistor (IGBT). The IGBT is a transistor which is controlled by a MOSFET. The IGBT requires low drive current, is suitable for high-frequency operation, and has a fast switching time. Disadvantages are that the device voltage drop and cost are higher than the Darlington transistor configuration. The large current capability and operating voltage, together with the low power drive circuit, makes the IGBT attractive for electric vehicles.

MOS-Controlled Thyristor (MCT). The MCT has a low voltage drop and can be turned on and off with a voltage signal (low switching losses). It can also be designed for high-voltage and high-current applications. This new device is very attractive for EVs.

The semiconductor industry frequently produces better and more powerful semiconductor switches which have potential for EV applications. The typical ratings of the most frequently used devices are shown in Table 30.3.[6]

30.4.3 Mechanical Drives

Lack of high-speed acceleration and the efficiency problems can be mitigated by the use of mechanical gears, similar to those used in today's ICEVs. The efficiency of an EV drive depends on the speed. Typically, ac drives operate at better than 80 percent efficiency in the range of 2000 to 12,000 rpm and the series dc drives in the 2000 rpm to 5000 rpm range. The brushless dc drives' efficiency is better than 85 percent in the 3000 to 8000 rpm range.

Another consideration is torque-speed characteristics. Most drives keep the motor torque more or less constant, in the 0 to 4000–5000 rpm range. However, at higher speeds, the torque begins to decline. This means that acceleration in the 65 to 105 km/h range is poor. This may create problems during highway driving.

These examples show that the efficient operation of electric drives requires more than 2000 to 3000 rpm, but the wheel speed at 105 km/h highway speed is only about 500 rpm. Frequent acceleration is characteristic of city driving, which requires high torque. In spite of the advancement in electronic drive technology, efficient EV operation requires mechanical gears to reduce motor speed. Typically, a gear ratio is between 4:1 and 8:1.

TABLE 30.3 Comparison of Power Switching Devices

	Darlington BJT	Power MOSFET	IGBT	MCT
Power capability	1200 V, 800 A	500 V, 50 A	1200 V, 400 A	600 V, 60 A
Gating	Current	Voltage	Voltage	Voltage
Conduction drop, V	1.9	3.2	3.2/1.7*	1.1
Switching frequency, kHz	10	100	20/40*	20
Reapplied dv/dt, V/μs	Limit for device loss and SOA	Limited by Miller effect	Limit for device loss	5000
Turn-on di/dt, A/μs	100	Very high	Very high	1000
Turn-on time	1.7 μs	90 ns	0.9 μs	1.0 μs
Turn-off time	5 μs	0.14 μs	1.4 μs/200 ns*	2.1 μs

* Second generation.

Multiratio Variable Drives. The multiratio variable drive utilizes present automotive technology, where motor speed is regulated with an automatic or manual transmission and the wheels are driven by a differential gear for further speed reduction. Most converted EVs use the same transmission and differential originally designed for the ICEV. In these vehicles, the internal combustion engine is replaced by an electric motor. However, the multiratio (manual transmission) variable gear is used in some of the cars designed specifically for electric operation. A typical example is the Fiat Panda Electric which has only a 9.2-kW motor with a manual four-speed transmission plus reverse gear. The multiratio variable-speed mechanical drives are used frequently in connection with series dc motor drives. These drives have a relatively narrow range of efficient operation. The multiratio gear permits the more accurate matching of the electric drive characteristics with different operating conditions.

Single-Ratio Drives. Some of the electric drives, like variable-frequency ac drives, have a broad range of efficient operation. A single-ratio reduction gear can match the drive characteristics with road conditions. Most vehicles designed for electric operation use this technique. The motor is mounted on the axle and the reduction gear is integrated with the motor. A typical example is the Ford Ecostar. In this vehicle, a 75-kW induction motor is mounted directly on the front transaxle.

An example of the integration of the motor and reduction gear is the transaxle-mounted motor[8] shown in Fig. 30.9. The maximum speed of the permanent magnet motor is 7500 rpm. A 7.5:1 ratio gear and a planetary differential, mounted on the motor, drives the wheels with a reduced speed. This transaxle arrangement matches the motor with road conditions.

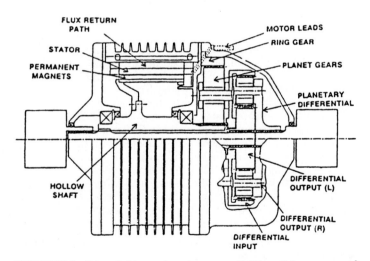

FIGURE 30.9 Integrated transaxle motor, gear, and differential arrangement.[8]

Direct Drives. The direct driving of the wheels by in-line motors is a desirable concept for EVs. An in-wheel drive eliminates gears and simplifies the mechanical construction of the vehicle, but it requires complicated electronic controls and sacrifices some vehicle performance. A typical example of in-wheel drive is shown in Fig. 30.4, where the motor is mounted directly on the wheel. The performance of direct drives can be improved by modifications to the motor connection by a switch. Typical solutions are a switch from delta to wye connection and a switch from series to parallel connection in a motor with two windings.

30.5 BATTERY

For the EV to become a viable option for transportation, the primary technological issue which must be improved upon is energy storage. Short range and long charging times have daunted EV design efforts since the early 1990s. The lead-acid battery, which has not improved much since the early EVs, is the only readily available and inexpensive battery technology available today.

In order to address the issues involved with the research and development of new battery technologies, major United States automobile manufacturers (Ford, Chrysler, and General Motors) created the United States Advanced Battery Consortium (USABC).[9] In 1992, the USABC working with the government began a $260 million project to develop more efficient energy storage systems for use in EVs. Since the lead-acid battery did not hold promise for EV use in the long run, its development was not addressed by USABC. But since lead-acid batteries are used extensively in current EV designs, another group—The Advanced Lead-Acid Battery Consortium (ALABC)—was formed to work with the government and industry in further development of lead-acid batteries for EVs.

30.5.1 EV Battery Requirements

EV batteries have the following requirements: high specific energy, high specific power, high efficiency, long cycle life, low cost, safety, reliability, maintenance free, reasonable recharge time, and recyclable materials. Since current batteries have deficiencies in many of the requirements, the motivation is strong to develop a battery that will meet most, if not all, of the requirements.

30.5.2 Battery Characteristics

Specific energy (energy density) is the most commonly used specification for batteries. It denotes the energy capacity per unit weight for a given battery, which normally relates to the driving range of the battery pack. To derive the specific energy, the total energy which can be removed from the battery for a given discharge profile is divided by the total weight of the battery. The ohmic losses (due to I^2R heating from internal resistance and contact resistances) and chemical energy losses represent energy which is stored in the battery during charging but not available during the discharge cycle. The energy efficiency is the ratio of the available energy for discharge to the total stored energy.

The specific power (power density) represents the maximum power that the battery can deliver, which is an indication of the battery's ability to perform under EV acceleration and hill climbing. Specific power will vary depending on the test parameters (DOD, current, age of batteries, etc.).

Table 30.4 lists characteristics of different battery technologies currently available and those under development.[6]

TABLE 30.4 Comparison of Battery Technologies (Relative to Lead-Acid)

Battery	Pb-acid	Ni-Fe	Ni-Cd	Ni-MH	Zn-Br	Na-S	Li-FeS2	Li-Poly
Relative energy density	1.0	1.5	1.6	1.7	2.2	2.5	4	4
Relative peak power density	1.0	1.2	1.9	2.1	0.6	1.1	4	3.5
Relative range	1.0	2.0	2.1	2.3	2.1	3.4	4	4
Energy efficiency, %	68	58	80	76	75	91	80	85

30.5.3 Battery Technologies

This section will cover battery technologies which are currently in use and those which are still under development.

Lead-Acid.   The lead-acid batteries are still the most commonly used for EVs today. Efforts are underway for the development of advanced lead-battery concepts for the short-term requirements of EV energy storage. A metal plate used in a liquid electrolyte configuration is the most inexpensive battery on the market today. Lead-acid batteries have a specific energy of about 35 Wh/kg and specific power of 93 W/kg.

Ni-Fe Battery.   Another metal plate in liquid electrolyte battery is the Ni-Fe battery which has a much longer cycle life than the lead-acid battery. The Ni-Fe battery is very robust but has a relatively small specific energy and specific power. It requires water to be added during each charging cycle (high maintenance), which means the battery cannot be sealed. Hydrogen release is also a problem and complicates the design of Ni-Fe battery equipped EV. The Ni-Fe battery is also expensive and has a specific energy of about 50 Wh/kg and a specific power of about 100 W/kg. Since the Ni-Fe battery has been extensively developed, it seems less likely that there will be a major breakthrough for its technology than for other newer technologies.

Ni-MH.   The nickel metal hydride batteries show promise for EV application. They use one nickel hydroxide electrode and one metal alloy electrode which has the property of being able to store hydrogen in the solid state. Typically the Ni-MH battery has specific energy and specific power of 54 Wh/kg and 174 W/kg, respectively. It also has a relatively long cycle life. The specific energy of one experimental Ni-MH battery is 81 Wh/kg.[2]

Zn-Br.   The Zn-Br battery uses carbon electrodes and pumps the electrolytes (zinc bromide/zinc bromide + bromine) to separate sides of the cell. Pumping of the electrolytes provides cooling and uniform plating of the electrode. The Zn-Br battery has a high energy density (72 Wh/kg), but a relatively low power density (53 W/kg). Because of the high energy density, the research will probably continue on the Zn-Br battery, but problems with low power density, higher cost (pumps, reservoirs, and lines), and the corrosive nature of the materials used will make it unlikely that this battery will be the long-term solution for EV use.

Na-S.   The sodium-sulphur battery does not have solid electrodes. It uses molten sodium (heated to 300 °C) as the electrode. The Na-S battery has a specific energy of 80 Wh/kg and a specific power of 100 W/kg. A distinct advantage of the Na-S technology is its long self-discharge time, which can be years. It comes about because the electrolyte is an insulator which allows only migration of sodium ions and not electrons. A long self-discharge time would be advantageous in any EV application where long periods must be tolerated without a recharge. High operating temperature and hazardous materials (sodium and sulphur) would require rigid packaging requirements (crashworthiness) for the Na-S battery, which would add substantially to the cost. Another drawback is the possibility of the molten sodium electrode solidifying after a period of nonoperation. The addition of heaters for the battery will also add additional cost. And continual solidifying and reheating of the electrode will eventually damage the battery.

Lithium-Based Technologies.   Lithium-based electrode batteries (lithium-iron sulfide, lithium-iron disulfide, and lithium-polymer) show promise for future EV use. Extensive research is underway. Heat dissipation during charging and discharging and manufacturing issues are fundamental problems which must be addressed.

30.5.4 Future of Battery Development

The USABC has projected goals for the development of new battery technologies. These goals have been divided into two categories: midterm and long-term. Table 30.5 lists the goals set by the USABC.[6]

TABLE 30.5 Midterm and Long-Term Objectives of the USABC

Criteria	Midterm	Long-Term
Primary criteria		
Power density, W/L	250	600
Specific power, W/kg (80% DOD/30 s)	150* (*200 desired)	400
Energy density, Wh/kg (C/3 discharge rate)	135	300
Specific energy, Wh/kg (C/3 discharge rate)	80* (*100 desired)	200
Cycle life, cycles	600 (5 years)	1000 (10 years)
Ultimate price, US$/kWh	<150	<100
Operating environment, °C	−30 to +65	−40 to +85
Recharge time, h	<6	3 to 6
Continuous discharge, % of rated energy capacity (no failure)	75	75
Secondary criteria		
Efficiency, % (C/3 discharge, 6 h charge)	75	80
Self-discharge	<15% in 48 h	<15% per month
Maintenance	Zero	Zero

30.6 VEHICLE CONTROL AND AUXILIARY SYSTEMS

30.6.1 Vehicle Controller

In addition to the motor drive, the EV has several other systems which must be monitored and controlled. Figure 30.10 shows the block diagram of a vehicle control system. It is divided into four major parts: motor controller, pedals, hand controls, and dashboards. The advanced system uses a microprocessor to monitor all subsystems. Quantities like temperature, speed, current, and voltage—which are relevant to the subsystem operation—are measured with transducers that convert operating conditions to analog signals. The signals are then digitized and supplied to the microprocessor. It evaluates the subsystem signals and sends out control signals. The microprocessor also shuts down the system in case of a fault. The vehicle controller also assures close to optimal operating conditions and optimal use of energy stored in the batteries. The batteries' condition is monitored and the available approximate mileage range is reported to the driver.

30.6.2 Climate Control System

The air conditioner and heating system consumes a considerable amount of power. The Ford Ecostar equipped with a 75-kW motor and its heater, for example, consumes 5 kW and its air conditioner, 6 kW.[2] This is particularly significant considering that the same vehicle requires about 8 kW of power when driven in accordance with the Federal Urban Driving Schedule. The use of the air conditioner or heater significantly reduces the vehicle range.

EV Air Conditioner.   A car's air conditioning system is designed to operate, typically, at outside temperatures of 44 °C and a relative humidity of 40 percent. The air conditioner cools the

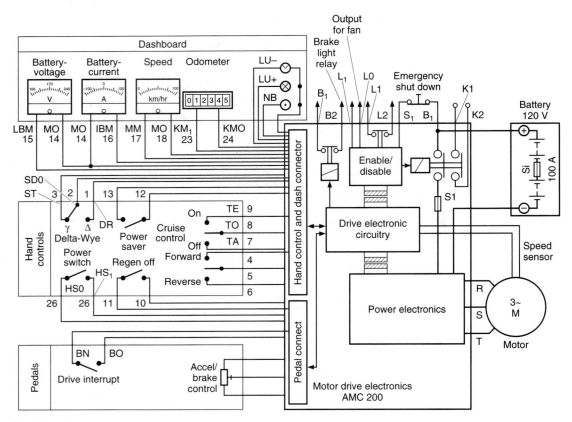

FIGURE 30.10   An electric vehicle control system.

inside of the vehicle to 27 °C and a relative humidity of 50 percent. The interior of the vehicle must be ventilated and this increases the air conditioning system heat load. The ANSI/ASHRAE 62-1981R "Ventilation for Acceptable Indoor Air Quality Code" requires 15 ft^3/min ventilation air per passenger. The finished car interior provides sufficient heat insulation, but EV side windows must be tinted and doors must be properly sealed to reduce heat loss.

A typical air conditioning system has relatively low efficiency, which reduces vehicle range considerably. Several research projects have dealt with the development of more efficient systems. The most promising concept is shown in Fig. 30.11. This system is built with a variable-speed compressor driven by a brushless dc motor. The compressor increases the coolant pressure and temperature. The coolant then expands in the expansion tube and evaporates in the evaporator, thus reducing its temperature. The evaporator coils cool the air, which is blown into the interior of the car. A variable-speed drive improves the air conditioner performance. Tests indicate, however, that better roof insulation, the use of wavelength-selective window tinting, and cooling of the parked vehicle by a small 20-W fan reduce the air conditioning thermal load and permit the use of a smaller and lighter unit.

EV Heating.   Current EVs use liquid fuel heaters, which are expensive and pollute the air, and the use of two fuels in a vehicle is not desirable. An alternative heating method is the use of the air conditioner as a heat pump, together with vehicle waste heat. In extreme conditions, the system can be supported by additional electric resistance heaters. Unfortunately, such a heating system also reduces vehicle range.

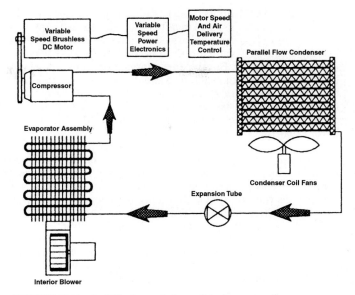

FIGURE 30.11   An EV advanced air conditioning system.[10]

30.6.3 Auxiliary Power

Proper operation of the vehicle requires an electric supply for power steering, power brakes, the headlights, turn indicators, etc. All these systems are well developed and optimized for ICEVs. Supply of the auxiliary equipment with more than 100-V batteries jeopardizes electric safety. Higher voltage requires better insulation and increases costs. Consequently, most electric vehicles have a 12-V auxiliary power supply and distribution system. One solution is a chopper, which charges a normal 12-V battery. Another solution is a constant voltage switching power supply like those used in the electronics industry.

30.7 INFRASTRUCTURE

The increasing use of ICEVs initiated the development of a highway system, the network of gas stations, the gas distribution system, and the increased production of high-quality grades of gasoline. Most of these facilities, except the gas supply and distribution, will be used by EVs. The electrical network is well developed, but the refueling of large numbers of vehicles may require an increase in network capacity.

30.7.1 Electric Network Reinforcement

The EV can be charged slowly overnight at the owner's home or it can be charged at charging stations at a much faster rate. The method of charging has a major effect on the electric system requirements.

Slow Charging.   EVs are charged from the local electric distribution system. The present concept[2] is that EVs will be charged at the owners home during off-peak hours (overnight).

This requires 5 to 10 hours from a 240-V, 30-A outlet. Also, credit card or coin-operated charging facilities will be installed in public parking lots and garages. These facilities will charge the vehicles with 30 to 50 A to provide a partial recharging while the vehicle is parked. Slow overnight charging will improve utilization of the electric network and does not require network reinforcement. But daytime charging of large numbers of EVs will increase the peak load and require both generation and distribution system improvement. The utilities will use time-of-day pricing, in which the night rate is significantly lower than the day rate. The use of interruptable tariffs may be considered. This would allow the utility to interrupt the vehicle charging by a remote signal during peak hours. It both cases, the customer is charged with a lower rate.

Quick-Charging.   In the future, high-capacity quick-charging stations will be available to the EV user. Quick-charging will require several hundred amperes and special equipment, which is currently under development. The large charging current will produce high peak loads on the local distribution system. To reduce these loads, the use of energy storage devices is being considered. These include batteries, flywheels, and superconducting magnetic storage systems. Quick-charging stations will not be designed to fully charge a discharged battery, but will provide an additional 110 to 160 km of driving range with a 10- to 30-min charge.

It can be visualized that quick-charging stations will be similar to today's gas stations. They will be located along highways where the electric distribution system is weak. The utility distribution system must be reinforced if quick-charging is to be used.

30.7.2   Harmonics and Power Factor

EV chargers are electronic devices that generate harmonics and consume reactive power. Expected operating conditions in a future slow-charging station can be estimated from the measurements performed during the APS Electric 500 Race in Phoenix, Arizona, in 1994. Figure 30.12 shows the supply cable current when 30 different vehicles were charging.[11] The maximum charging current per vehicle was limited by a circuit breaker to 50 A at 240 V. The figure shows severe harmonic distortion.

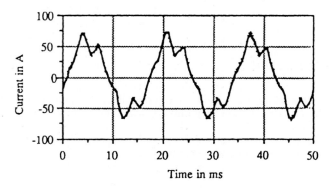

FIGURE 30.12   Charging current waveform at a slow-charging station.[11]

The measured power factor for the different chargers varied between 0.75 to 1. The cumulative distribution of the power factor at the supply cable shows that 50 percent of the chargers had a power factor less than 0.86.

The measured harmonic distortion factor was between 5 and 50 percent. The cumulative distribution of the harmonic distortion factor at the supply cable shows that 80 percent of the chargers operated with a distortion factor less than 30 percent.[11] The measured values are alarming and indicate the need for improvement.

Reactive power consumption can be reduced by the use of a voltage source type rectifier for charging. This circuit uses transistors instead of diodes or thyristors. The transistors are switched in such a way that the voltage and current are in phase. Another technique for reactive power control is to use phase correction capacitors.

The harmonic content of current in a charging station can be significant but it can be reduced by the use of pulse-width modulation (PWM) at the chargers. This method also requires transistors and a significantly more complicated control circuit. The current harmonic content in a charging station decreases as the number of vehicles being charged simultaneously increases. This is due to the phase shift between the harmonics being generated by the different types of chargers. The phase shift provides cancellation of harmonics.[11] Nevertheless, the harmonics generated by large numbers of EVs may produce significant problems for utilities.

30.7.3   Magnetic Field Generation

The current in an EV can be a few hundred amperes. It produces magnetic fields both inside and outside the EV. The magnetic field generated by the dc drives has both dc and ac components. The ac component is superimposed on the much higher dc component. The ac drive produces magnetic fields, which are distorted sine waves. The fundamental component is determined by the speed of the vehicle. The higher-frequency components up to the tenth harmonic are not negligible.

The highest magnetic field was measured during acceleration and regenerative braking. In this condition, the maximum field in the engine compartment was about 120 mG. The magnetic field in the passenger compartment was negligible due to the shielding effect of the car body.[12]

The magnetic field in a future charging station can be estimated from the measurements performed during the 1994 APS Electric 500 Race. The results indicate that the highest field around 50 mG was measured near the charging cables. The field 50 cm from the vehicles was between 20 and 30 mG.[13] Numbers suggest that the future charging station design has to consider the use of shielded cables and cable arrangements with low field emission.

30.8   HYBRID VEHICLES

The inherent low operating range of EVs suggests the building of hybrid vehicles with both electric and gas systems. Hybrid vehicles are equipped with an internal combustion engine and an electric motor drive and battery. In highway driving between cities, where the pollution is not critical, the car is driven by the internal combustion engine (ICE), which also charges the battery. In the city, the electric motor and drive are used. The operation can be improved by recharging the battery at night.

The two basic configurations for hybrid vehicles are series and parallel. Figure 30.13 shows two conceptual arrangements for hybrid vehicles.

30.8.1   Series Hybrid Drive

In a series hybrid drive, the ICE drives a generator, which charges the battery and supplies the electronically controlled motor. The electric motor propels the car. In this system, the ICE operates at constant speed with maximum efficiency. The vehicle is controlled electrically. The electric control simplifies the mechanical gears and differential. The disadvantage of this

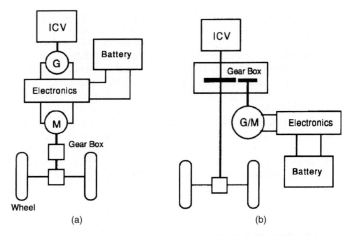

FIGURE 30.13 Two conceptual arrangements for hybrid vehicles: (*a*) series hybrid drive; (*b*) parallel hybrid drive.

arrangement is that both the ICE and the electric drive have to be rated to the maximum power. Another problem is low overall system efficiency.

30.8.2 Parallel Hybrid Drive

The parallel system consists of an ICE and an electric drive connected by a mechanical gear. The electric drive is built with a motor/generator, electronic control, and battery. The mechanical gear drives the wheels through a differential. In highway driving, the ICE propels the vehicle and charges the battery. The electric motor operates as a generator. In city driving, the battery and the electric motor drive the vehicle. During hill climbing or other conditions when the maximum power is needed, both engine and motor drive the vehicle. This arrangement results in better efficiency, less weight, and lower cost.

Hybrid vehicle technology is under development with several other arrangements which have been proposed and are being evaluated. Volkswagen built a city taxi[14] which performed well during a 100,000-km test. The problem with this vehicle is the weight. Today's lead acid batteries added 200 to 300 kg to the vehicle's weight.

GLOSSARY

Battery Self-contained electrochemical cell/cells or system which converts chemical energy to electrical energy in a reversible process.

Battery technologies Ni-Fe (nickel-iron), Ni-Cd (nickel-cadmium), Ni-MH (nickel-metal hydride), Zn-Br (zinc-bromine), Na-S (sodium-sulphur), $Li-FeS_2$ (lithium-iron disulfide), Li-Polymer (lithium-polymer).

Brush Conductor used to maintain an electric connection between the moving and stationary parts of a motor.

Capacity Energy storage capability of the battery.

Charge/discharge profile   Different charging/discharging schemes used for evaluation of a battery.

Commutator   Mechanical switch which transfers current from one coil to another at the proper instant.

Depth of discharge (DOD)   Percentage of capacity (ampere-hours) which has been removed from the battery.

Electric drive system   The motor, motor controller, and cabling used to drive an electric vehicle.

Electric vehicle (EV)   Automobile, truck, or any vehicle powered by rechargeable or non-rechargeable batteries and an electric motor.

Electrolyte   Medium in which current flows by movement of charged particles (ions).

Gear box   Gear that reduces the speed of a motor by connecting together different ratios of gears.

Inductive coupling   The association of two or more circuits by means of inductance mutual to the circuits.

Phase-controlled rectifier   A converter for conversion from ac to dc that varies the point within the cycle at which forward conduction is permitted to flow through the semiconductor elements.

Quick-charging   Charging batteries at a rate that will produce a 40 to 50 percent charge in about 15 minutes.

Regenerative braking   Capability of an electric drive to return the kinetic energy, stored in the velocity of the EV body, to the battery during braking.

Specific energy (energy density)   A battery's energy storage capability per unit weight (Wh/kg).

Specific power (power density)   Power delivery capability per unit weight of a battery (Wh/kg).

Squirrel-cage rotor   A rotor winding consisting of conducting bars connected by metal rings or bars at each end.

State of charge (SOC)   The battery level of charge can be stated as either DOD or SOC.

Transaxle   An axle that includes the differential and gear box.

REFERENCES

1. H. H. Braess and Regart, K. N., "Electrically propelled vehicles at BMW—experience to date and development trends," *Electrical Vehicles Design and Development,* SP-862, #910245, Society of Automotive Engineers Inc., Warrendale, Pa., Feb. 1991, pp. 53–62.

2. M. J. Riezenman, "Electric vehicles," *IEEE Spectrum,* Nov. 1992, pp. 18–24.

3. T. Moore, "Charging up for electric vehicles," *EPRI Journal,* June 1993, pp. 7–17.

4. P. Wuebben, Lloyd, A. C., and Leonard, J. H., "The future of electric vehicles in meeting the air quality challenge in southern California," *Electrical Vehicles Design and Development,* SP-817, #900580, Society of Automotive Engineers Inc., Warrendale, Pa. Feb. 1990, pp. 107–120.

5. S. Ohbe, "Determining component specifications for conventional on-road electric vehicles," SP-817, pp. 67–72 (see Ref. 4).

6. C. C. Chan, "An overview of electric vehicle technology," *Proceedings of the IEEE,* vol. 81, no. 9, Sept. 1993, pp. 1302–1313.

7. P. E. Morris and Adams, D. S., "Design considerations and component selection for volume-produced EV controllers," SP-817, pp. 85–97 (see Ref. 4).

8. W. M. Anderson and Cambier, C. S., "Integrated Electric Vehicle Drive," SP-862, pp. 63–68 (see Ref. 4).

9. "Electric vehicle research draws batteries of ChE's," *Chemical Engineering Progress,* Feb. 1993.

10. J. Dieckmann and Mallory, D., "Climate Control for Electric Vehicles," SP-862, pp. 101–110 (see Ref. 4).

11. G. G. Karady, Berisha, S. H., Blake, T., and Hobbs, R., "Power quality problems at electric vehicle's charging station," SP-1023, #940297, Society of Automotive Engineers Inc., Warrendale, Pa., Feb. 1994, pp. 31–37.

12. G. G. Karady, Berisha, S. H., Hobbs, R., and Demcko, J. A., "Electric vehicle magnetic field measurement," SP-984, #931790, Society of Automotive Engineers Inc., Warrendale, Pa., Aug. 1993, pp. 13–15.

13. G. G. Karady, Berisha, S. H., and Muralidhar, M., "Low frequency magnetic field generated at electric vehicles charging station," SP-1023, #940298, Society of Automotive Engineers Inc., Warrendale, Pa., Feb. 1994, pp. 39–45.

14. A. Kslberlah, "Electric hybrid drive for passenger car and taxis," SP-862, pp. 69–78 (see Ref. 4).

ABOUT THE AUTHORS

GEORGE G. KARADY is Salt River Project Chair Professor at Arizona State University, where he is responsible for the electric power education and performs research in power electronics and high-voltage engineering. He is the chairman of the IEEE Subcommittee on Lightning and Insulator and WG on Non-Ceramic Insulators. He is the author of more than 60 technical papers.

TRACY BLAKE is currently pursuing the Ph.D. in power engineering at Arizona State University. He previously worked as an electrical engineer for SYRE, a support service contractor to NASA. His research interests include HVDC and electric vehicle technology.

RAYMOND S. HOBBS is a senior research engineer in the R&D department at Arizona Public Service Co. He is the coauthor of several papers on electric vehicles and serves on the Electric Vehicle Infrastructure Working Committee of the Electric Power Research Institute.

DONALD B. KARNER is an independent consultant and president of Electric Transportation Applications, specializing in the infrastructure development required to support growth of electric vehicle use. He is project manager for the Safety of Electric Racing Vehicles Project, an effort to provide safety and logistical support to electric vehicle competitions.

CHAPTER 31
NOISE CANCELLATION SYSTEMS

Jeffrey N. Denenberg
Vice President of Engineering
Noise Cancellation Technologies, Inc.

Active noise cancellation is not a new idea. Creating a copy of the noise and using it to cancel the original dates back to the early part of this century. The first systems used a simple "delay and invert" approach and showed some promise, but the variability of real-world components limited their effectiveness.

In the mid-1970s, a major step forward took place with the application of adaptive filters to generate the antinoise. This greatly enhanced the effectiveness of the systems, because they could continuously adapt to changes in their external world as well as changes in their own components. A second breakthrough in the mid-1970s was the recognition that many noise sources, particularly those produced by man-made machines, exhibit periodic or tonal noise. This tonal noise allows a more effective solution, because each repetition of the noise is similar to the last and the predictability of the noise allows creation of an accurate antinoise signal.

Practical application of this approach still had to wait as the electronic technology available at that time was not sufficient for implementation of active noise cancellation systems. Now digital computer technology has evolved to the point where cost-effective digital signal processing (DSP) microcomputers can perform the complex calculations involved in noise cancellation. This advance has made it feasible to apply active noise cancellation at reasonable cost to previously difficult problems in low-frequency automotive noise and vibration.

31.1   NOISE SOURCES

Sources of noise and vibration exist throughout an automobile. One type of noise is due to turbulence and is, therefore, totally random and impossible to predict. This makes it a difficult noise to cancel unless the source of the noise is well understood.

Engineers like to look at signals, noise included, in the frequency domain. That is, "How is the noise energy distributed as a function of frequency?" These turbulent noises tend to distribute their energy evenly across the frequency spectrum and are, therefore, referred to as broadband noise. Examples of broadband noise in cars are wind and most road noise. A typical broadband noise spectrum is shown in Fig. 31.1.

A large number of noises are different. These narrowband noises concentrate most of their noise energy at specific frequencies. When the source of the noise is a rotating or repetitive machine such as an automobile engine, the noise frequencies are all multiples of a basic noise

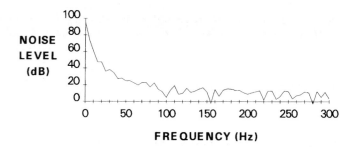

FIGURE 31.1   A typical broadband noise spectrum.

cycle and the noise is approximately periodic. The repetition rate of the noise cycle of a four-stroke automobile engine is two full revolutions (all cylinders firing). A typical narrowband noise spectrum is shown in Fig. 31.2.

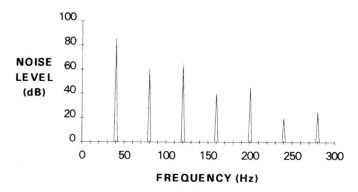

FIGURE 31.2   A typical narrowband noise spectrum.

Examples of sources of narrowband noise in automobiles include exhaust noise, along with broadband noise due to turbulence generated in the muffler; engine vibration, the major source of the "boom" in the passenger cabin; ventilation fans, again accompanied by broadband noise due to turbulent flow; and tire noise, with a regular tread pattern.

31.1.1   Noise Measurement

Any variation in air pressure is perceived by the human ear as sound. The pitch of the noise is related to the speed at which the pressure varies. As a reference, when the pressure fluctuates 440 times per second, the ear perceives it as the musical note "A" above middle "C." The intensity of the noise can be stated either in terms of the peak sound pressure level (SPL) or in terms of the noise power that varies proportionally with the square of the SPL.

Noise is usually measured in decibels and is defined as:

$$\text{Noise}_{dB} = 20 * \log_{10}[\text{SPL}/\text{SPL}_{ref}]$$

or equivalently,

$$\text{Noise}_{dB} = 10 * \log_{10}[(\text{noise power})/(\text{noise power}_{ref})]$$

where the reference (0 dB) is set as the softest 3-kHz tone that an average human can hear in a perfectly quiet environment.

An overall measure, commonly used in specifications, is A-weighted noise (dBA). It is adjusted to compensate for the fact that the average human ear has lower sensitivity at low and high frequencies at normal listening levels.

31.1.2 Passive Noise Control

The first line of defense against noise is good design. All machines should be well balanced. Symmetry in design and careful manufacturing can significantly reduce vibration and noise. Turbulence can be reduced by good aerodynamics. High "Q" resonances in structures and gas flows should be avoided.

The second line of defense is to absorb noise and vibration energy and control its propagation using passive materials. The use of sound-absorbing and rigid materials to reduce noise levels is an effective approach at high frequencies. Below 500 Hz, however, the cost, weight, and inefficiencies due to passive sound attenuation often make this approach ineffective or impractical. Another technique for noise control is required.

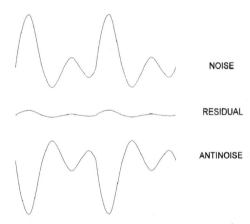

FIGURE 31.3 Relationships in time among noise, antinoise, and residual noise.

31.1.3 Noise Cancellation Technologies

Antinoise. The idea to create a copy of the noise and use it as antinoise to cancel the original dates back to the early part of this century. Figure 31.3 shows the relationship, in time, of a noise signal, an antinoise signal, and the residual noise that results when they meet. Note that active noise cancellation does not mask the noise; it removes a significant portion of the noise energy from the environment.

Digital Feed Forward. Digital feed forward is shown in Fig. 31.4 as used to reduce the noise in an air duct. This is the classic example application for active noise cancellation and is widely discussed in the technical literature. It is also the method to use to control blower noise in automotive ventilation systems and is discussed further in the applications section later in this chapter.

Referring to Fig. 31.4, a microphone is placed upstream in the duct to get a reference sample of the noise. The effect of the duct on the noise is modeled to produce an antinoise waveform at the output speaker. A residual microphone is placed downstream in the duct to determine how well the system is operating and the duct model is continuously adjusted to maintain peak cancellation. Feedback compensation is also required since the antinoise waveform also propagates backwards along the duct and makes the reference signal inaccurate. Incorrect feedback compensation results in unstable operation.

Systems that cancel broadband noise require causality (the reference signal must give a sufficiently advanced indication of the approaching noise). Noise that correlates with the reference will be canceled. Digital feed forward systems can readily achieve 6 to 10 dB (50 to 70% reduction in sound pressure level) in practical use.

Most active noise cancellation systems employ a variant of the LMS algorithm known as Filtered-X. The basic LMS algorithm correlates an error signal (the residual noise in this case)

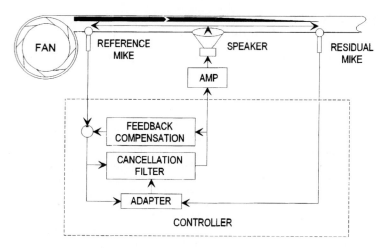

FIGURE 31.4 Feed forward cancellation system.

with a reference signal (called "X" by Widrow and Stearns, *Adaptive Signal Processing,* Prentice-Hall, 1985). The result is then multiplied by an adaptation rate constant and used to adjust the relevant parameter of the adaptive filter. This is done repeatedly for each filter parameter with the objective being convergence to an operation that minimizes the average power in the error signal.

In real-world systems, the LMS algorithm does not converge due to the delay and gain effects of the physical path taken by the antinoise signal. Using a compensation filter on the reference signal (hence, the name Filtered-X), restores stability and produces a well-behaved system.

Synchronous Feedback. The technique known as synchronous feedback, developed by G. B. B. Chaplin in the mid-1970s, is very effective on repetitive noise and does not rely on causality. Here, instead of the reference microphone, a tachometer signal is used to provide information on the rate of the noise. Since all of the repetitive noise energy is at harmonics (or multiples) of the machine's basic rotational rate, the DSP micrometer can dedicate its resources to canceling these known noise frequencies.

Figure 31.5 shows the configuration of such a system applied to reduce engine exhaust noise. Its basic operation is described in the applications context in the next section.

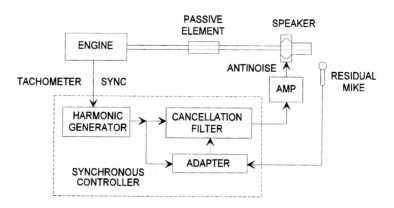

FIGURE 31.5 Narrowband noise cancellation (an active muffler).

31.2 APPLICATIONS

31.2.1 Canceling Exhaust Noise

The Passive Muffler.   Passive mufflers are now used to control exhaust noise in automobiles. There are three classes of these mufflers.
   Absorptive Mufflers.   These are the straight-through or "glass pack" mufflers that were used in the hot rods of the 50s. They consist of a length of pipe with holes wrapped by fiberglass (or other sound-absorbent material) which is then enclosed by a larger diameter pipe. Absorptive mufflers are very effective at high frequencies, reduce turbulence in the exhaust, and produce little or no back pressure. They have little effect, however, on the low-frequency tonal noise from the engine unless the muffler is made impractically large.
   Dispersive Mufflers.   These mufflers work by creating a tortuous path for the exhaust, dissipating some noise energy while spreading the remaining noise energy across frequencies through turbulent flow. A significant amount of exhaust gas pressure is created in this process. The backpressure decreases engine efficiency. Gas mileage is reduced (typically 5 percent in city driving and 1 percent in highway driving) and peak horsepower is wasted (up to 10 percent) pushing the exhaust gasses against the back pressure. Dispersive mufflers can be effective in noise reduction at low frequencies at a reasonable size but only at the cost of high backpressure. They can have less backpressure, but then can be impractically large and heavy.
   Reactive Mufflers.   Reactive mufflers use acoustical resonances to reflect noise energy back to the source. This technique is often used to handle a strong noise at a particular frequency. It is a good technique for fixed rpm engine noise, but does not deal effectively in automobiles where engine rpm (or temperature, since the speed of sound, nominally 1100 ft/s, changes with temperature) varies. Reactive mufflers do introduce some backpressure but much less than dispersive mufflers.
   The passive mufflers found in today's automobiles use a combination of dispersive and reactive techniques.

An Active Muffler System.   Figure 31.5 shows an active muffler system as it would be applied to an automotive engine exhaust. The passive element is a simple straight-through glass pack muffler (absorptive) that controls noise above 500 Hz. The active muffler is a speaker cabinet that is concentric to the exhaust pipe and outputs the antinoise in a ring around the end of the exhaust. The symmetry of the noise and antinoise sources in this arrangement provides for global cancellation of the low-frequency noise (at very low frequencies, a side-by-side arrangement can also work). A microphone in the exhaust sound field feeds back the residual noise (after cancellation) so that the adapter (usually an LMS adaption algorithm) can continuously adjust the cancellation to drive the residual noise toward zero at the noise frequencies. The tachometer signal drives a harmonic generator to internally provide pure tones at the harmonics of the engine's basic cycle (two full revolutions in a four-cycle engine). This sets up the whole system to concentrate its efforts on the noise from the engine.
   The cancellation algorithm is executed in a modern DSP computer that fits on one 250-cm^2 printed circuit board. Included on this board are:

- A digital signal processing computer (such as the ADSP-2101 from Analog Devices) capable of 10 million operations per second
- Two low-pass filters set at 500 Hz to avoid aliasing (the confusion of high-frequency signals with low-frequency signals due to sampling)
- An A/D converter to measure the noise remaining after cancellation
- A D/A converter to output the antinoise

   The electronic equipment also includes an audio power amplifier (100 W for a typical automobile exhaust system) to generate the required antinoise power. Since the antinoise is at low frequencies, a Class D switching amplifier should be used to further enhance energy efficiency. The total electronics package for a single-channel control system should be under $100 when produced in volume.

System Performance.   Active muffler systems can significantly attenuate exhaust noise. In steady state driving conditions, strong tonal components can be reduced by more than 25 dB with only a slight decrease in the attenuation level during rapid changes in driving conditions, such as gear shifting or sudden acceleration. The sound quality can also be managed by adjusting the attenuation level as a function of frequency, harmonic number, or engine conditions.

Current Status.   Active muffler systems for cars, busses, and trucks are currently under development by several companies. They have been demonstrated on production cars and passed life tests. Larger systems have been tested on trucks and busses and field trials were underway in 1993 on several metropolitan bus fleets in the United States and Canada. This is a viable technology that is going to be used in production vehicles in the middle of this decade due to the effective performance and fuel economy enhancements it provides in automotive designs.

31.2.2   Controlling Engine Vibration

Passive Vibration Control.   A primary consideration in modern automobile design is fuel economy. Automobile engines are therefore smaller and have fewer cylinders than the engines of a few years ago. Limiting this trend is the desire for a smooth-running car. It is difficult to balance the vibrational forces in an engine—especially the component at twice the engine rotational rate—with a small number of cylinders. One option is to use counter rotating shafts inside the engine that have a slight imbalance and spin at twice the engine rpm. The forces generated by the extra shaft can be designed to cancel the undesired vibration. The drawback to this approach is that it uses a significant percentage of the engine power (up to 10 percent has been estimated) by adding weight and friction losses.

Given that the engine vibrates, much design effort has gone into rubber engine mounts. Making the mount soft prevents engine vibration from propagating through the supporting members into the passenger compartment. The problem with soft mounts is that the engine is the heaviest single component in the car. If the engine is not firmly mounted, the handling characteristics of the automobile will suffer. The automotive designer is therefore left with a compromise among performance, economy, and comfort.

Active Engine Mounts.   A solution to the vibration problem is to provide an active mount that is compliant or soft only at the vibration frequencies. Here an active vibration control system dynamically adjusts the dimensions of each engine mount so that engine vibrations are isolated from the car chassis. Again, the energy needed by the electronics is much smaller than the energy that would be lost using the passive solution. A more energy-efficient car is the result.

Figure 31.6 shows synchronous cancellation applied to create an active engine isolation mount. The antivibration continuously works against the stiffness of the mount to keep the mount out of the way of the engine at harmonics of the vibration cycle. No vibration forces are then passed through the mount from the engine and the supporting frame is vibration free.

System Performance.   An active mount system can reduce peak vibrational components up to 25 dB. When applied to the major engine-mounting sites, active mounts significantly reduce vibration in the passenger compartment. They can also reduce secondary acoustical noise generated by vibrating surfaces in the passenger compartment—the major source of boom noise in cars.

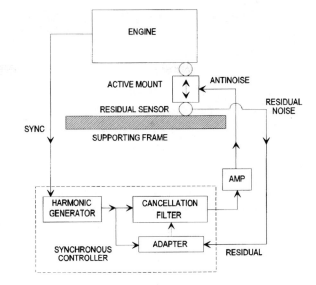

FIGURE 31.6   An active engine mount.

Current Status.   Active mounting systems have been demonstrated on several production vehicles and are under development for aircraft engines. The systems can also solve vibration and mounting problems in commercial and industrial rotating machines. The remaining technical hurdle before they are ready for the automotive market is to make certain that the mounts and their actuators can stand up to the harsh shock environment in the engine compartment. Active mounts should be ready for automotive production in the latter half of this decade.

31.2.3 Passenger Cab Quieting

The primary cabin noise that active noise cancellation technology can deal with is due to the engine. Many car designs are completed only to find that at some speeds there is a disturbing low-frequency boom noise in the cabin. This noise is caused by a resonance in the structure of the cabin and is difficult to deal with using sound-absorbent materials. The boom usually occurs between 90 and 150 Hz whenever one of the harmonics of the source noise moves into the bandwidth of a resonance in the cabin structure.

   The source of the noise can be either the exhaust or engine vibration passing through the mounts, vibrating cabin panels, and creating secondary noise in the cabin. The exhaust noise can be easily dealt with through the use of a good muffler and isolation of the exhaust pipes from the car body and frame. Engine vibration control is the job of the engine design and/or the mounting system but, as described earlier, it involves many tradeoffs.

   Most of the other noises in the cabin are broadband noise. They include road noise, wind noise, and blower noise. The technology to deal with zonal control of broadband noise is still in the research stage.

Passive Control.   Passive control of cabin noise is best done with sound and vibration absorbing materials. Fiber batting in door and ceiling panels is a significant help at higher frequencies. Vibration deadening panels (a laminate of steel and plastic) are quite effective but add significant cost to the vehicle.

   At low frequencies, car cabin dimensions are comparable to the wave length of the noise. It is therefore possible to match the sound field with an antinoise field that is generated by a small number of speakers. If a set of residual microphones is placed around the volume to be silenced, spaced less than ¼ wavelength apart, a multichannel noise cancellation control system can synthesize the required antinoise field. Figure 31.7 shows a general configuration and the resulting quiet zone.

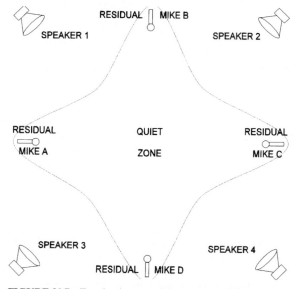

FIGURE 31.7   Zonal noise control for an automobile.

The algorithm is more complex than in single-channel applications since each residual microphone now "hears" antinoise from each of the antinoise speakers, and the electronic equipment is more expensive. This also occurs to a lesser extent for dual exhaust and multiple mount systems.

System Description.   Figure 31.8 shows a zonal noise control system adapted for use as an automotive cabin-quieting system. The four to six residual microphones are placed near normal passenger head positions in the roof liners, seat backs, and/or door panels. Extra microphones are used, since at some frequencies resonances in the cabin will place a null of the sound at some locations.

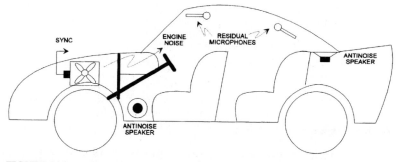

FIGURE 31.8   An automobile cabin-quieting system.

Four antinoise speakers are placed at convenient locations in the cabin. The existing sound system can be used to save money but care must then be taken to insure that the high-level antinoise tone does not create distortion in the amplifiers and speakers. This will usually require an upgrade in speaker quality, and separate low-frequency subwoofer speakers are desirable.

Proper design of a cabin-quieting system involves a careful analysis of cabin acoustics to determine proper speaker and microphone placement. It also depends on the existence of sufficient sound-absorbing materials in the cabin to limit the strength of resonances so that the mathematics of the algorithm do not require excessive precision.

System Performance.   Cabin-quieting systems can reduce the peak boom by up to 10 dB. This significantly enhances any vehicle that has a major boom problem.

Current Status.   Cabin-quieting systems have been installed and tested in a number of production cars. One model car with a cabin-quieting system was marketed in Japan in 1992. An aircraft manufacturer has announced the intention to market similar, but significantly larger, systems in its 1994 model turboprop aircraft. This is a currently viable technology to enhance automotive designs.

31.2.4   Controlling Blower Noise

Most of the noise from the heating/ventilation/air conditioning (HVAC) blower in cars is due to turbulent flow in the distribution ducts. This noise can be reduced through careful design of the ducts. Some guidelines follow:

- Reduced air velocity is the strongest factor in controlling turbulence. Larger duct cross sections and larger output ports should be used wherever possible.
- Duct liners made of sound-absorbing material can attenuate the higher-frequency noise.
- Discontinuities in the air flow should be eliminated. All turns should be smooth as any change in air flow direction or obstructions will generate additional turbulence and noise.

Passive controls can give 6 to 10 dB of improvement in the noise level and the successful use of active noise control for further reduction requires that attention be paid to passive controls first.

An Active Duct Silencer.   The feed forward cancellation system in Fig. 31.4 has already been described in the context of controlling broadband noise in an air duct. Implementation of a duct cancellation system requires a close interaction with the physical design of the air distribution system in the car. A successful system will result only after several design iterations between the group doing the cancellation system and the design group responsible for the cabin design.

A good duct cancellation system in these small ducts can reduce the noise by 10 to 15 dB from 50 Hz to 1 kHz. This results in a typical noise reduction in the dBA noise measurement of 4 to 6 dB.

Duct cancellation systems for commercial applications have been available for several years. The cost-effective (less than $50 system cost) application of this technology to home appliances has been announced and will see production in 1994. This is another viable application of active noise control in current automobile designs.

31.2.5   Active Suspension Systems

The technology used in an active suspension system is closely related to that used in active noise cancellation. For a description of active suspensions, see Chap. 17.

GLOSSARY

Active mount   The use of an actuator in a mounting system to continuously deform the mount so that no vibrational forces are passed through the mount at specific frequencies.

Adaptive filters   A signal-processing technique (usually digital) in which filter parameters are continuously modified to optimize some aspect of system performance.

Antinoise   sound that is identical to, but exactly opposite to, a disturbing sound. If heard alone, it would sound identical to the original noise, but it cancels the offending sound, thereby reducing the noise level.

Causality   In the real world you cannot have a result that precedes a cause. In an antinoise system that deals with broadband noise, the reference signal must be derived from a position in the system where noise that is correlated to the observed noise exists earlier in time.

Harmonic number   Narrowband sound, such as musical notes or noise from rotating machines, consists of a number of components at frequencies that are multiples of a fundamental frequency. The harmonic number is the ratio between the frequency of a particular component and the fundamental frequency.

LMS   The least mean squares measure of the error in a system.

Noise cycle   The repetitive cycle of a noise source. It is two revolutions in a four-stroke engine.

Residual noise   The noise that remains after the antinoise meets the noise.

Resonance   A phenomenon that occurs in low-loss systems where reflections reinforce the original energy. Energy storage in resonant structures can make noise problems much worse.

Sound field   The distribution of sound energy in a defined space. It can be quite complex when resonances are present.

SPL   The sound pressure level is the peak variation in air pressure due to a sound.

Subwoofer   A speaker that is designed to only produce sound below 200 Hz. A crossover filter is used to pass low-frequency energy to the subwoofer and all higher-frequency energy to other speakers.

Tonal noise   Noise that is made up of pure sinusoidal components with frequencies that are all multiples of a fundamental frequence.

Turbulence   The random mixing in an air flow that causes noise. A perfectly smooth flow is called laminar.

BIBLIOGRAPHY

Air Movement and Control Association, Inc., *Fans and Systems,* ACMA Publication 201-90, 1990.

Chaplin, G. B. B., "Anti-noise—the Essex breakthrough," *Chartered Mechanical Engineering,* vol. 30, 1983, pp. 41–47.

Denenberg, J., "Anti-noise," *IEEE Potentials,* vol. 11, no. 2, April 1992, pp. 36–40.

Eghtesadi, Kh., and H. G. Leventhal, "Comparison of active attenuators of noise in ducts," *Acoustics Letters,* vol. 4, no. 10, 1981, pp. 204–209.

Eghtesadi, Kh., and J. W. Gardner, "Experimental results of the nonrestrictive electronic muffler on internal combustion engines," *Acoustics Letters,* vol. 4, no. 4, 1990, pp. 70–73.

Eghtesadi, Kh., M. McLoughlin, and E. W. Ziegler, "Development of the simulation model of the multiple interacting sensors and actuators (MISACT) for an active control system," *Recent Advances in Active Control of Sound and Vibration,* C. A. Rogers and C. R. Fuller (eds.), Virginia Polytechnic Institute, April 15–17, 1991, pp. 246–257.

Lemme, H., and J. Denenberg, "Larm Kontra Larm," *Elektronic Magazine,* vol. 41, no. 19, Sept. 1992, pp. 42–48.

Mendat, D., et al, "Active control of centrifugal fan noise," *Fan Noise—An International INCE Symposium,* CETIM Senlis, France, Sept. 1–3, 1992, pp. 455–462.

Nelson, P. A., "Causal constraints in the active control of sound," *IEEE Conference on Acoustic Speech and Signal Processing,* vol. 1, April 1987.

Nelson, P., and S. Eliot, *Active Control of Sound,* Academic Press, 1992.

"Reducing the annoyance of noise," *Proceedings of NOISE-CON 90,* University of Texas at Austin, Oct. 1990.

Ross, C., "Quieter air travel takes off with active noise control technology," *Noise and Vibration Worldwide,* 1993.

Ross, Colin, "The control of noise inside passenger vehicles," *Recent Advances in Active Control of Sound and Vibration,* C. A. Rogers and C. R. Fuller (eds.), Virginia Polytechnic Institute, April 15–17, 1991, pp. 671–681.

Warneka, G. E., "Active attenuation of noise—the state of the art," *Noise Control Engineering Journal,* **18** (3), 1982, pp. 100–110.

Widrow, P., and S. D. Stearns, *Adaptive Signal Processing,* Prentice-Hall, 1985.

ABOUT THE AUTHOR

Jeffrey N. Denenberg has over 20 years of experience in the electronics, communications, and computer industries. He worked for Motorola, Bell Laboratories, and ITT prior to joining Noise Cancellation Technologies as vice president of engineering and chief technology officer. He holds 11 patents and is a Senior Member of the IEEE.

CHAPTER 32
FUTURE VEHICLE ELECTRONICS

Randy Frank and Salim Momin
Motorola Semiconductor Products

32.1 RETROSPECTIVE

Both the content and complexity of semiconductor technology for computing, power control sensing, communications, signal conditioning, and transient suppression is destined to increase in future vehicles. Therefore, this final chapter will tackle the difficult subjects of identifying potential technology developments and trends for future systems and consolidating previously mentioned development activities in areas relative to vehicle electronics. The terminology of the future generations of electronics (refer to the glossary at the end of this chapter) is a strong indication of how different emphasis will be placed in future vehicles.

Semiconductor technology is being applied to sensors in several automotive applications. Semiconductor technology is also at the heart of digital electronics including MCU (microcontroller unit), MPU (microprocessor unit), and DSP (digital signal processing) technology. Outputs of several systems have been controlled by power MOSFETs, smart power, and even IGBT (insulated gate bipolar technology) power devices. Communications, not only to the vehicle but from the vehicle, will cause major changes which will require high-frequency semiconductors. However, high-level digital electronics in MCU, MPU, and DSP will continue to determine the future of automotive electronics. Their growth from two MCUs per vehicle in 1980 to 14 per vehicle in 1990 and expected use of 35 per vehicle by 2000 will dominate automotive electronics content no matter which vehicle subsystem is involved.

32.2 IC TECHNOLOGY

Since the advent of integrated circuit (IC) technology, the automotive engineer has been designing more and more complex electronic modules—partially to meet government-mandated regulations for pollution control and fuel economy but also to provide increased performance and creature comforts. Table 32.1 is a summary of the control systems and subsystems being used or developed for modern vehicles. Transitions to higher levels of complexities are already underway as car companies worldwide migrate their engine management ECUs from 8-/16-bit microcontrollers to 32-/64-bit CISC/RISC based processors with more than one execution engine on-chip, such as Motorola's MC68332.

TABLE 32.1 Pervasiveness of Electronics in Modern Control Systems

Safety & chassis	Powertrain	Entertainment	Driver information	Convenience & body control
Traction control	Dynamic engine mount	Noise reduction systems	Digital & analog gauges	Multiplexed wiring
Antilock brakes	Electronic camshaft	Cellular radio/telephone	Engine diagnostic display	Intermodule network
Load-sense braking	Ignition timing	CD & optical disc players	Service reminders	Body system diagnostics
Air bag restraints	Spark distribution	CB radio	Digital clock	Smart power drivers
Dynamic ride control	Fuel delivery control	Digital audio tape	Trip computers	Antitheft device
Active suspension	Turbo control		Navigational computers	Climate control
Load leveling	Emissions monitor		Intelligent highways	Keyless entry
Electronic steering	Voltage regulator		Collision avoidance	Light reminder
	Alternator		Drowse/DWI alert	Memory seat
	Transmission shift			Sensory wipers
	On-board diagnostics			Auto door lock
	Operational adaptation			Headlight dimming
	Energy recovery			Window control
	Electronic muffler			
	Cruise control			

DSP technology is being used in audio and suspension control algorithms with new applications such as noise cancellation just on the horizon. Semiconductor technology, and specifically the integrated circuit, is the enabling technology. Thus, before we can discuss the future of automotive electronics, the future developments in semiconductor technology along with its critical success factors must be understood since they will have a profound impact not only on what systems get designed but, more importantly, on how they get designed.

The 1992 SIA Semiconductor Technology Workshop established a 15-year roadmap for key IC device characteristics such as feature size, chip size, defect density, power dissipation, and number of I/Os (Table 32.2). Based on this roadmap, the design engineers at the turn of the century will be dealing with ICs which will integrate 50 to 100 million transistors on a chip with clock speeds in excess of 250 MHz. This is based solely on extrapolation of today's technologies and does not take into account dramatic breakthroughs in technologies such as *quantum effect transistors,* which could increase device complexities by several orders of magnitude. There is already some work being done at the Massachusetts Institute of Technology and Texas Instrument R&D laboratories on *3-D quantum ICs* with complexities of 20 billion transistors. Today's more complex circuits have three to four metal layers, but future circuits will have six to seven metal layers for interconnect and power routing by the year 2005. Three-dimensional interconnections are key to denser electronic circuits. Thin circuits that can be lifted off an underlying substrate may allow not only faster circuits, but combinations of otherwise too-complex processes to be achieved and circuit placement in more varied packaging shapes including remote displays, sensors, or actuators.

TABLE 32.2 General Technology Roadmap

Characteristic	1992	1995	1998	2001	2004	2007
Feature size	0.5	0.35	0.25	0.18	0.12	0.1
Gates per chip	300K	800K	2M	5M	10M	20M
Wafer processing cost ($/cm^2)	$4.00	$3.90	$3.80	$3.70	$3.60	$3.50
Chip size (mm^2)	250	400	600	800	1000	1250
Wafer diameter (mm)	200	200	200–400	200–400	200–400	200–400
Defect density (defects/cm^2)	0.1	0.05	0.03	0.01	0.004	0.002
Number of interconnect levels	3	4–5	5	5–6	6	6–7
Power supply voltage (V)	5	3.3	2.2	2.2	1.5	1.5
No. of I/Os	500	750	1500	2000	3500	5000
Performance (MHz)	120	200	350	500	700	1000

Higher-speed electronics can generate high power levels, so design techniques to minimize the power or cope with the existing level of power dissipation are being pursued. Novel cooling methods using heat pipes enable self-contained cooling capability. Higher-temperature operating materials such as gallium arsenide (GaAS), silicon carbide (SiC), and diamond are also being investigated by automotive electronics manufacturers to solve the heat problem. The most critical technology required to turn the semiconductor technology roadmap into reality is CAD—computer-aided design.

32.2.1 Design Methodology/CAD

Design is the activity that turns underlying technologies into product solutions that satisfy society's needs. Design, coupled with a testing discipline to ensure quality, is the vehicle that generates revenues for the industries. Today, design activity is based on a loosely coupled, ad hoc collection of tools and techniques. The most successful companies use highly refined design methodologies that are dependent on vendor-supplied point tools and are heavily augmented by proprietary tools that encapsulate each company's accumulated design expertise. Use of these tools outside the company's design groups is next to impossible. Over the next 5 to 10 years the complexity of chips will grow so dramatically that new tools and techniques for IC design will be required. Coupled with continuing pressures on reduced product development cycle time, error-free designs, and affordable test procedures, these CAD tools for IC design will have to extend well into the systems development environment. Electronic design automation (EDA) will not only be a necessity but it will also be the only way of handling the prevailing levels of device and system complexities. Without the advanced level of technology tools, expected performance and reliability levels will not occur.

32.2.2 CPU Architecture

MPUs and MCUs in vehicle control systems have been developed around complex instruction set computer (CISC) architectures. The availability of larger, faster memory technologies allows RISC architecture with simpler instructions to achieve higher throughput and faster cycle times. RISC design philosophy includes:

1. Fixed length, consistently encoded instructions
2. A register-to-register (load/store) architecture with primitive addressing modes
3. Relatively simple instructions
4. A large orthogonal register file
5. Three-operand (nondestructive) instruction format

MPU chips are available in 1994 with floating-point performance of SPECfp92* of 85 at 80 MHz. Over 1.6 million transistors are integrated in a chip that is only 85 mm^2. This performance level is considerably above the highest-performing CISC architecture and utilizes less silicon area.

The core processor has increased from 8 to 16-bits and now 32-bits to handle the number of calculations that are required in complex engine control systems. The 32-bit CPUs can deliver at least 50 times higher processing capability than the 8-bit designs. ABS systems are increasingly using 16-bit machines to reduce the time required to compute wheel speed inputs from analog sensors and activate the appropriate brake solenoids. Air bags have increased from simple to more powerful 8-bit MCUs when the air bag system uses electronic sensors.

Single-chip programmable digital signal processor (DSP) technology is used when mathematically intense algorithms, real-time operation, and high-speed data sampling are required in the control system. DSP units have been designed into sophisticated audio entertainment, dynamic ride control, and noise cancellation systems. DSP units incorporate Harvard architecture similar to many MCUs and MPUs; extensive pipelining; dedicated hardware multiplier; special instructions not typically found in MCUs, such as multiply and accumulate (MAC); and fast instruction cycle times, less than 50 ns. DSP design can also be integrated into MCUs to provide similar functionality for systems.

It is important to note that automotive electronics manufacturers will benefit from higher levels of technology, but use of high-level electronics in the auto industry lags behind other segments, partially due to the design-in time and partially due to the cost. Only the level of performance necessary to solve the control problems that are expected to be encountered during the design life of the electronics is implemented. Figure 32.1 shows a general technology roadmap for one semiconductor manufacturer (Motorola) that provides detail for some of the elements of future semiconductors. The products that drive future technology are high-end microprocessors and fast static RAMs (SRAMs). However, other products, including logic, mixed-signal (analog/digital), sensors, and power devices, benefit from the improved process techniques and the tools that are developed to provide them.

GENERAL TECHNOLOGY ROADMAP
ULSI - HIGH PERFORMANCE LOGIC

	1990	1991	1992	1993	1994	1995	1996	1997	1998	1999	2000
SRAM	1Mb SRAM			4Mb SRAM		16Mb SRAM			64Mb SRAM		
Devices/MPU	1.5-2.5M		2-4M	3-5M	4-8M	5-11M	20-100M	20M - 500M			
Die Size	1.25 X 1.75cm			1.5 X 2.0cm			2.0 X 2.75cm				
Technology	HCMOS				HMOS/BiCMOS				BICMOS		
Voltage	5V			5/3.3V	3.3V/2.5V				2.5V/1.5V		
Min. Feature	0.80μm		0.65μm	0.50μm		0.40μm		0.30μm	0.25μm		0.15μm
Litho Tool	G-Line			I-Line			I-Line & Phase Shift Mask/DUV		X-Ray		
Materials	EPI/BL				EPI/BL/TRENCH				SOI		
Gate Oxide	150A				105A			80A		60A	
CMOS	N+POLY/LDD			N+/P+POLY With Silicide/LDD				Selective Silicon Elevated Source Drain			
Bipolar	Non-Self Aligned				Self Aligned				SiGe With Trench Isolation		
Contacts	Tapered				Straight-Walled, Filled						
Metallurgy	AL.Alloy			AL.Alloy M1,2,3,4					Copper		
Metal Layers	DLM		3LM			4LM			5-6 Level		

PRODUCTS	1Meg SRAM 68040/68050 88110/88410 683XX MCU	4 Meg SRAM 68060/68LP040 88120, PowerPC™ 683XXMCU	16 Meg SRAM 88130 RISC MCU PowerPC™	64 Meg SRAM Multi-Processors Large Cache

FIGURE 32.1 Operating frequencies/feature size/integration level.

32.2.3 Memory

As part of reduced vehicle development time, electronics module manufacturers need semiconductor suppliers to turn ROM circuits in shorter and shorter design time. Also, new memory types, such as flash memory, are required to allow manufacturers to reprogram when the memory is installed in the module and still be reliable under all vehicle operating modes for the remaining life of the vehicle. Future developments include the ability to reprogram at lower voltages: 5 V and even 3 V.

Figure 32.2 shows the increase in memory, throughput, functions, and inputs and outputs (I/O) since model year 1980 and an estimate for model year 2000. The most dramatic increase has occurred in the memory (RAM). Program memory (ROM) is also increasing. Memory in future MPUs will be limited more by the programmer's ability to generate the code than by the hardware's ability to store or process it—unless fundamental changes occur to the process of code generation.

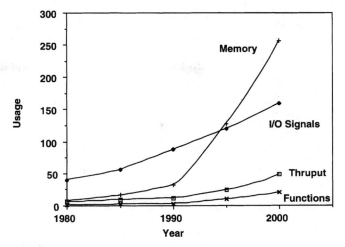

FIGURE 32.2   Automotive usage of microcontroller technology.

32.3   OTHER SEMICONDUCTOR TECHNOLOGIES

Semiconductor technology is also being applied to both the input and output side of the digital control to improve the performance of sensors and provide more efficient power switches. Both sensing and power devices are the focus of increased integration. The extent of integration depends on system constraints in the automobile in addition to the technology that is developed by semiconductor manufacturers. This section will discuss key items affecting future levels of system and component integration.

32.3.1   Micromachining and Microelectronics

Semiconductor technology is also being applied to manufacture mechanical structures in silicon that provide more reliability, higher accuracy, and higher functionality, while also lowering the cost of sensing for the automobile. Continued use of these techniques for more complex structures and combined sensors (e.g., pressure and temperature) will increase as university, government, and industry R&D technology is adapted by sensor and semiconductor manufacturers. Sensor technology has been identified as one of the key factors required to maintain leadership in automotive electronics.

Increased electronics will be used with these sensors either by simultaneously fabricating electronic circuitry with the mechanical structure or by packaging techniques such as multichip modules. Figure 32.3 shows a sensor technology migration path that ultimately has the sensor(s) fabricated directly on CMOS MCUs. While the cost of this final form may be several years away from the level necessary for automotive use, the technology capability can be demonstrated today. Intermediate forms of integration with CMOS memory components used for calibration and localized digital logic providing decisions are extremely likely within the near future (before 2000). The electronics system design will change as inherently digital signals, instead of analog, can be input directly to the MCU. These signals could be at the level that allows usage by several vehicle systems using a multiplex (MUX) bus. However, standards, such as SAE J1850, will be necessary to make the digital output transducers as readily available from many sources like today's analog output sensors.

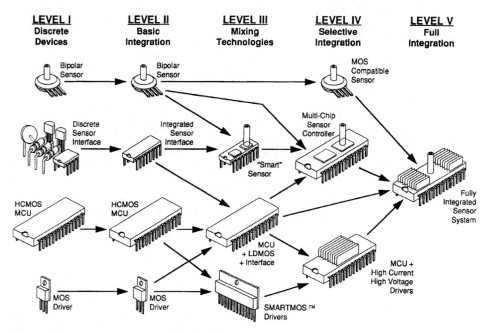

FIGURE 32.3   Sensor technology migration path.

32.3.2   Voltage Capability

In order to achieve high density in integrated circuits, the maximum voltage is being reduced from 5 to 3 V in computer and portable products. This level will be reduced even further as higher levels of integration require smaller and smaller geometries, and portable products are designed to operate at even lower voltage levels. Since this area is considerably larger than the automotive electronics area, it represents the mainstream of electronics technology. The automobile, however, operates from a 12-V battery today and is being pushed toward higher operating voltages to handle the ever-increasing loads that are part of every new vehicle system. Even the 12-V system has to deal with considerably higher voltage due to transients, including load dump. Electric vehicles will have a battery supply over 200 V. The requirement to withstand higher voltages reduces the efficiency of power semiconductors. Furthermore, the voltage extremes affect the choice of power devices and the level of integration that can be achieved. If the system voltage is increased to 24, 36, or 48 V, semiconductors will be among the system components that are significantly affected by the higher voltage.

32.3.3   Power Control

Depending on the vehicle, every 10 A of electric load reduces fuel economy by 0.3 to 0.5 miles per gallon. Design changes to cope with increased loads include:

- More energy-conserving designs
- Smarter power supplies that manage peak alternator-current demand
- Overvoltage transient protection from one central location, which is even more important if system voltage is increased
- Two 12-V batteries per system, especially on high-end vehicles

More efficient power devices are required to reduce overall vehicle power consumption and to reduce power dissipated in electronic modules. The on-resistance area product has been reduced nearly tenfold from the early 1980s to 1993, since the first use of power MOS-FETs on vehicles. Further improvements are made by reducing all of the resistive elements of the MOSFET, including metal connections to the package, starting material and cell structure. Figure 32.4 shows how the specific on-resistance can be reduced by using high-cell-density power MOSFETs and lower voltage ratings. Ignition coil drivers are high-voltage (greater than 350 V) applications on internal combustion vehicles where insulated gate bipolar transistors are more efficient than power MOSFETs or bipolar power transistors.

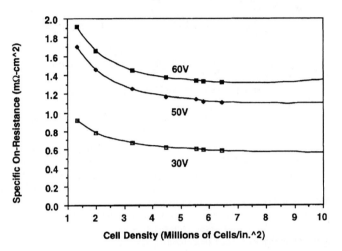

FIGURE 32.4 Power efficiency vs. voltage.

Merging power devices with control circuitry is also part of the integration that is occurring at an increasing rate as system complexity increases. Several design and processing techniques are used to merge these devices depending on the switch type and performance expectations. Table 32.3 provides some indication of differences in commonly used processes. Smart power, or power ICs are the terms that are generally used to describe these types of power devices.

The smart power approach to system design means that a number of circuit elements that would previously have been discrete components or the combination of a standard, or custom IC, and discrete output devices can be consolidated into one single device as illustrated in Fig. 32.5. This provides space saving, component reduction, total system cost reduction, improved performance, and increased reliability from the reduced number of interconnections. The choice of process technology has historically depended upon the type of control elements that were integrated. Some circuit elements, such as operational amplifiers (op amps), compara-

TABLE 32.3 Power ICs Attributes

Isolation process	Circuit components			Switch type		Complexity	Breakdown voltage
	Power MOSFET	CMOS	Bipolar	High side	Low side		
Self	Yes	Yes	No	Yes	No	Simple	Low
Junction	Yes	Yes	Yes	Yes	Yes	Medium	Medium
Dielectric	Yes	Yes	Yes	Yes	Yes	High	High

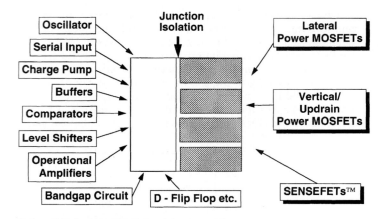

FIGURE 32.5   SMARTMOS™ technology cells.

tors, and regulators, are best implemented using a bipolar IC process. MOS circuitry handles logic, active filters (time delays), and current mirrors better than bipolar circuitry. Some circuits, such as A-D converters or power amplifiers, can be implemented equally well in either technology. A process that has both MOS and bipolar for the control circuitry does not have to sacrifice performance or features and, if it is combined with the appropriate output devices, it can handle the power control functions for a number of vehicle loads.

The need for increased diagnostics to meet legislated requirements, such as OBD-II, and to minimize time required to analyze vehicles experiencing faults is increasing the use and complexity of smart power devices. Power devices that can handle several amperes and operate at voltages in excess of 60 V have already been integrated into MCU processes. The number of loads that are controlled, the current and voltage rating of the output devices, and the power dissipation are factors that system designers must consider when evaluating the level of integration of power devices.

The three levels of power devices involved in automotive systems are power MOSFET, smart power IC with one or more power outputs, and MCU with integrated power devices. Integration in each of these levels and efficiency will improve in future systems. The ability to integrate memory components and transmit and receive digital signals at the power side of the control system is necessary in MUX systems. This also allows the system designer added flexibility in system partitioning.

32.3.4   Semiconductor Operation at High Temperatures

Increased operating temperatures are driving development for new materials such as GaAS (gallium arsenide) and other III-V, wide band gap, semiconductor materials, SiC (silicon carbide), and diamond films. Other wafer-level assembly techniques that can provide more reliable operation at high temperature, such as wafer-to wafer bonding and dielectric isolation, are part of today's semiconductor technologies that will be used in future vehicle electronics. As Chap. 5 pointed out, higher temperatures decrease reliability of electronic components. Therefore, improvements that allow higher temperature operation are being evaluated, and sometimes are a driving force for improving reliability. Some advanced materials, such as GaAs, also allow higher frequency operation or increased efficiency, providing additional incentive. The materials and techniques are being investigated for sensors, power, computing, and communication semiconductors. Their acceptance in one area could increase the effort to design and qualify similar technologies in other areas. However, at present these approaches are more expensive and would only be used if they solved a problem that had no alternative solution.

32.3.5 High-Frequency Semiconductors

Increasing communication to and from the vehicle requires radio frequency (RF) transistors to receive and transmit signals and data. High-frequency operation is required for cellular communications and sensing in systems such as near obstacle detection. Several technology choices exist in the RF front end of a communication product that must operate at 900 MHz as Fig. 32.6 demonstrates. Silicon competes with GaAS in the 1- to 2-GHz range, but in the 2- to 18-GHz range, GaAs is the only solution. In 3-V, high-frequency (1-GHz) operation, GaAs has an efficiency of 50 percent versus silicon bipolar's 40 percent or LDMOS's 43 percent. Chipset approaches are frequently used in the early phases of system design and can be cost effective alternatives to higher levels of integration. High-frequency designs for radio frequency are considerably different than high-speed digital processes, which limits the integration of these subsystems. The frequency range is much higher in RF circuits, frequently 800 MHz and higher. Mixed-signal technology in these designs means not only digital and analog but also RF must be processed. Circuit isolation is required to prevent unwanted coupling of signals which can range from 3 V peak-to-peak to less than 1 μ V peak-to-peak. RFIC (radio frequency integrated circuits) technology or MMIC (monolithic microwave integrated circuit), and MESFETs are part of the communications semiconductors that will be used in future vehicles.

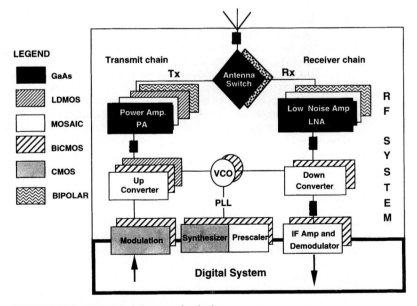

FIGURE 32.6   RF semiconductor technologies.

32.3.6 Semiconductor Packaging

Auto module manufacturers are using surface mount assembly techniques to improve reliability, reduce component size, and incorporate more functions in a given module form factor.

A number of SOIC packages are available for handling high-pin-count I/O in logic or high power in power ICs. Assembly techniques for surface-mount technology (SMT) also include flip chip, TAB (tape automated bonding), COB (chip on board), and bare die.

In many respects, the packaging requirements for highly integrated devices are similar to those for the full module. These include power distribution, signal distribution, heat dissipation, and circuit protection. In harsh applications, like the underhood mounting of automotive controls, hot and cold temperature extremes can result in severe damage to the electric connections in electronic components. Reducing the number of connections in a module, through the integration possible in a process like smart power ICs, reduces the number of potential failure points.

As more and more functionality is included in an IC design, the number of external components is reduced. This inherently lowers the number of solder joints that are required in a particular pc board layout. This can significantly reduce the potential for rejects in the surface-mount soldering operation. Unfortunately, in highly integrated silicon designs, packages are also required with power-dissipating capability and/or access to sense a mechanical input, such as a pressure port. These "combined" packaging problems have been solved at the module and not the semiconductor level. Smart power packaging engineers address the requirement for more complex I/O and higher power dissipation with increased lead count packages and integral heat-spreading capability. Sensor packaging engineers cope with increased media compatibility and higher pin count issues with new materials and unique attachment/access methods for pressure, acceleration, magnetic, or light sensing. Complex microcontrollers have high pin counts (≥ 256 pins) with close spacing and high coplanarity requirements. Still other silicon processing technologies are required to provide system glue-chips that provide interfaces that are not cost-effectively integrated in a particular time frame. As a result, three or more packaging roadmaps are pursued.

To achieve increased functionality without increased silicon complexity, available silicon technologies are being combined at the package level in packages based on semiconductor, not module manufacturer, assembly techniques. These multichip modules (MCMs) are being evaluated for automotive applications. There has been a decline in the use of the previously popular DIP (dual in-line plastic) package. Other through-hole packages, such as SIP (single in-line plastic) and PGA (pin grid array), will also not increase. New SMT approaches, such as BGA (ball grid array) packages, are the focus of present packaging development. For future highly-integrated components, packaging techniques must take into account more complex, system-level requirements, as well as SMT assembly requirements.

Testing is also a major consideration as more and more functionality is combined into one package. In some instances, the ability to provide fully functional, fully tested silicon die is required for products that are provided in packaged form today.

32.3.7 System-Level Integration

Increased integration is occurring to achieve increasingly more cost-effective systems. However, integration necessary to have all system components, MCU+power+sensor(s), on the same chip, can lead to mask levels that are well beyond the level necessary to obtain reasonable yields. Those components that would significantly add to the cost or detract from the performance must be partitioned as a separate system component. Integration can minimize some unwanted components, such as parasitic capacitances or lead inductances, but it can also lead to unexpected interaction of other circuit elements. Proven building blocks or modules increase the confidence that a new silicon design will work properly the first time.

System-level chips based on structured design approach are just starting to appear. For example, Motorola's CSIC, or Customer Specified Integrated Circuit, is a modular design approach that has over 150 developed combinations for solving a variety of 8-bit control problems. Figure 32.7 shows the concept of a System Chip™ integrated solution that combines input, output, and computation in a monolithic silicon chip. The MC68HC705V8 is an example of today's level of system integration. It is a necessary first step towards the more complex systems of tomorrow. This chip has an on-chip voltage regulator, a complete single-wire multiplex interface message data link controller, and various memory functions. The voltage regulator provides a regulated 5 V (±5 percent) from battery voltages between 7 and 26.5 V and can withstand alternator transients up to 40 V. As noted in Sec. 32.2.2, required cost-effectiveness by automotive electronics also applies to levels of integration. In a given time frame, higher levels of integration may be possible, but not cost effective. The ability to shift portions of the system from one unit to another, and partition the system for the most cost-effective approach in the most timely manner, is the goal of auto electronics manufacturers and the force behind approaches like Motorola's Seamless Silicon System™ methodology. This technique will allow common design rules for various silicon components, including MCUs, smart power and sensors, that will facilitate integration paths like the one shown in Fig. 32.3. However, when separate devices are determined to be more cost effective, the decision to have them as separate components will be a simple choice of the designer.

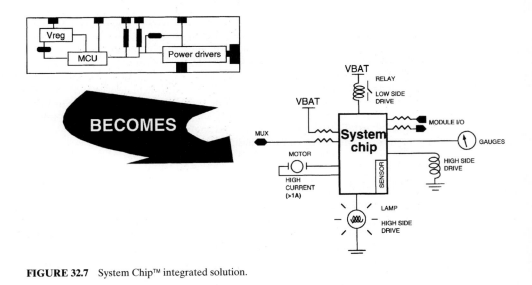

FIGURE 32.7   System Chip™ integrated solution.

32.4   *ENABLING THE FUTURE*

Driving forces for automotive manufacturers ultimately drive the electronic content of future vehicles. The major areas that impact electronics include meeting government regulations, environmental responsibility including recyclable materials, automotive manufacturing technology (and the transition from lean to agile manufacturing), improved security, increased safety to eliminate auto fatalities, reduced vehicle development time, high-efficiency 80-mpg super car, and the "personalized" car.

The first five items will be covered in more detail later in this section. The last three items on the list reflect key topics that are extremely timely and may not have appeared on a list developed in the 1980s.

United States manufacturers have gone on record with their goals of developing new vehicles in less time. In the mid-90s these goals are three years or less instead of the historical five years. Japanese manufacturers are already at the three-year design level and Chrysler has demonstrated the ability to design new vehicles in as little as 18 months. This will result in even shorter design cycles in the future. As a result, the more complex electronics that will be part of these systems must be designed and verified in even less time than in the early 90s. This will require even closer linkage between semiconductor suppliers and automotive electronics manufacturers not only in hardware but also in the tools and software area as well.

The goal of a high-efficiency super car that can achieve 80 mpg is among the changes that can suddenly shape the direction of future electronics. While continuously more fuel-efficient vehicles have been developed over the past 20 years, government support for a reach-out goal can reduce the R&D time for enabling technologies.

Personalization in an increasingly nonpersonal world is among the marketing strategies that can impact electronics. The memory and automatic adjustments that are possible with electronics are already used to preset seat position and favorite radio stations when the automatic door opener identifies the driver of a multiple-driver vehicle. Electronics is also an essential part of the features used to differentiate vehicles. Increased marketing and manufacturing approaches to customize vehicles will increase the amount and variety of electronics, and of course, semiconductors in the vehicle. An excellent example is an office-on-wheels that has cellular phone, FAX, and printing capabilities as key accessories.

Achieving the goals of the auto manufacturer will require that automotive electronics and semiconductor manufacturers work together to provide fewer boxes, higher levels of integration, increased reliability, cost reduction (system, component, and assembly), surface-mount components, electronic replacements for mechanical components (relays, sensors, etc.), and reduced hardware and software design/development time.

The systems approach must be applied to a specific vehicle system, to the vehicle itself, the vehicle as a part of the transportation system, and, ultimately, as part of society (i.e., ecology, and the use of resources). A further understanding of the forces that are driving automotive electronics is gained by reviewing the changes that will occur by implementing IVHS, increased safety, the potential for antitheft/security, issues driving the EPA, consumer demands, and the effect of other industries on automotive electronics.

32.4.1   Changes from IVHS

Worldwide efforts in intelligent vehicle-highway system (IVHS) will change the electronics in the vehicle and the way systems are configured (see Chap. 29). The goals of IVHS will determine the nature of hardware that is required: reducing traffic congestion; improving safety; enhancing mobility of travelers, especially the elderly and disabled; increasing the productivity of the transportation infrastructure; reducing energy use; reducing pollution; reducing capital and operating costs; increasing the viability of public transportation; responding more effectively to incidents; and increasing the ease and convenience of travel.

Achieving these goals will require several new vehicle and infrastructure systems and associated electronics to enable the control strategies. On the hardware side, sensors are the most critical enabling technology. However, software is predicted to be the most labor-intensive aspect of the development activities.

32.4.2   Safety

Harry Mathew, a vehicle safety expert at Arthur D. Little, has made several predictions based on the need for improved safety in vehicles. Implementation of technologies that are discussed today is shown in Table 32.4. These areas and timing can be compared to projected penetration of super-smart vehicle systems (SSVS) in Japan that are shown in Table 32.5.

The emphasis that government and consumers place on aspects of vehicle technology will determine which elements are exploited in production vehicles. For example, the reporting of safety performance of vehicles in 35-mph frontal crashes by the National Highway Traffic Safety Administration (NHTSA) is intended to be a more consumer-oriented look at the probability of injury. This could result in even greater focus being placed on air bags, especially dual air bags and their effectiveness in preventing injuries by auto manufacturers.

TABLE 32.4 Timing and Implementation of New Vehicle Systems

System/Technology	Timing
Air bags	Mandatory by 2010
Keyless entry	Widespread use by 2030
Remote control starting	Widespread use by 2030
Programmable position controls	Widespread use by 2030
Integrated traction control and ABS	2030
Addition of power steering to above	2060
IVHS	2050
Collision avoidance (radar & auto pilot)	Late 21st century

TABLE 32.5 Penetration of SSVS Technologies in Automobiles

SSVS technology	Phase I yr 2000	Phase II yr 2010	Phase III yr 2020
Obstacle detection	20%	50%	80%
Road geometry detection	10%	40%	40%
Collision warning	10%	60%	80%
Auto braking/steering		10%	60%
Pedestrian detection		10%	60%
Driver assistance		10%	60%
Auto lane following			10%
Accident reduction	4%	20%	43%

32.4.3 Antitheft/Security

Antitheft equipment is an area that has developed from aftermarket implementation of products into OEM level. Auto theft cost American consumers nearly $10 billion per year. NHSTA estimates that between 10 and 16 percent of auto thefts are by professional chop shops that strip and sell the parts. The effectiveness of antitheft systems against professional versus novice-level thieves is among the criteria that may have deterred their use by OEMs. However, electronic antitheft devices (see Chap. 24) are available that range from simple sensing and warning devices to cellular tracking systems with the ability to locate and disable the vehicle. For example, GM's Pass-Key™ system is offered as an OEM product and is expected to be installed on more than 40 percent of GM vehicles by 1995. Auto theft is a worldwide problem that varies in significance in other regions. This could be an area of increased usage and the target of integrated control strategy in the future for OEMs.

32.4.4 EPA Driving Forces

The top official in the EPA has the following issues to address:

- Finalize rules for on-board vapor recovery during refueling
- Monitor implementation of California's Low Emission Vehicle (LEV) program
- Determine whether Northeast states can adopt California's LEV standards
- Resolve third-car controversy (states adopting California LEV standards without California clean-fuel standards)
- Monitor phase-out of CFCs and phase-in of replacement coolants
- Finalize regulations for on-board diagnostic computers to monitor emission control systems
- Finalize rules for cold temperature carbon dioxide emissions controls
- Finalize rules for evaporative emission controls

The involvement of electronics and next-generation semiconductors to solve these problems has been discussed in several chapters.

32.4.5 Consumer Demands

A consumer survey of 1000 Southern California drivers indicated the following preferences for 1997 vehicle power sources with more than one choice possible: gasoline (34 percent), hybrid—electric and gasoline (29 percent), electric (26 percent), natural gas (16 percent), methanol (15 percent), diesel (4 percent), and don't know (7 percent). Satisfying these different vehicle preferences should be the target of manufacturers' product plans. Electric vehicles specifically require a broad range of semiconductor technology, some of which will be unique to the operating voltage of these vehicles. With growing concern for the environment, vehicle manufacturers can potentially segment their market and address a previously undefined customer.

Industry monitoring by groups like *Consumer Reports* of vehicle reliability can shift manufacturers' emphasis towards other items, such as owner satisfaction indices. Electronics has been recognized for its ability to provide more reliable automobiles in spite of the increased complexity.

32.4.6 Effect of Other Industries on Automotive Electronics

Looking outside the industry for technology driving forces can provide insight to avoid being blindsided by new approaches. Many of today's automotive controls result from the use of aerospace technology and displaced engineers during the 1970s. Today's use of military-developed technology, defense engineers, and national laboratories to develop next-generation hardware and software may change automotive systems. However, the computer industry is a prime mover of the highest level of integrated semiconductors and has over eight times the sales of automotive semiconductors. In the computer industry, the term *convergence* is being used to describe the merging of computing, communications, and consumer electronics that is occurring in new products aimed at highly portable computing.

The vehicle of the future could provide a docking/recharging station for a device that provides paging, cellular phone, digital notebook, calendar of events, personal tracking, FAX modem, and all the programs of a personal computer (pc), yet weighs only a few kilograms. The linkage of this unit to other vehicle systems could appeal to a new classification of automotive consumers. Manufacturers already have incorporated cellular phones into the steering wheel to provide a safer, more user-friendly means to dial. However, portable units that individuals will want to take to and from their vehicle will define new automotive products.

32.4.7 Software

Making the transition from one technology to the other and providing a transparent-to-the-driver feel for any future system will require extensive software. Three phases have been previously identified in the evolution of automotive electronics. Initial electronic components were diodes, transistors, and analog ICs in alternators, voltage regulators, AM-FM radios, and clocks. Phase II was the result of government regulations and enabled by the usage of microcontrollers in vehicle control systems. Phase III is marked by the use of smart peripherals, smart power drivers, and smart sensors, to bring the hardware closer to the capability of MCUs. The next phase will be the "software era," in which emphasis will be focused on standard open architecture; in-vehicle network backplane; factory, dealer, and consumer levels of configurability; neutral programming languages, and user-friendly software.

Advanced tools are required to deal with the increased level of software. From the semiconductor perspective, schematic capture, VHDL (VHSIC hardware description language) simulation, and synthesis generator tools are already used with products like field-programmable gate arrays (FPGAs). The extension of electronic design automation (EDA) software linking control system requirements to silicon design is necessary to complete the process. This is only one part of the software issues. Others are increased memory = increased development time, code reliability/ruggedness, code portability/upward compatibility, tools for code development, verification/testing aspects including tools, software—the "differentiator" for future systems, software design cycle time reduction, software independent of hardware, and digital and analog simulation.

Along with more complex hardware and software comes the need for improved testability to ensure that these more complex systems work the way they were designed. Powertrain vehicle personalization, IVHS, and hybrid vehicles are expected to be even more important to future automotive growth than air bags and antilock braking systems were in the early 90s. Testing is critical during assembly, at the end of line, and in service. Design for testability (DFT) methodology must be implemented at the beginning of the design process to satisfy the full range of test requirements. Techniques have been developed, including boundary scan and built-in self-test (BIST), that must be utilized. The IEEE JTAG (Joint Test Access Group) standard, OBD-II, and others that may be developed must be implemented to allow equipment manufacturers a common methodology for developing new equipment.

Today's high-end microprocessor designs already have clock rates that exceed 80 MHz and are capable of executing several millions of instructions per second (MIPs). To utilize this, and even greater, capability in future automotive products, automotive designers will have to spend far more time developing software than they did in the previous generations of products. This will require a different approach to software—one that starts with a formal software department dedicated to developing structured code. Sophisticated debug and system integration tools developed for the semiconductor industry must be implemented in a networked environment to support and facilitate a team approach to software.

In addition to digital simulation, complex analog systems also require analysis techniques beyond those used in today's vehicles. A simulator, such as Analogy's Saber™ simulator, can provide templates for various power supply topologies and evaluate virtual silicon prototypes in place of actual units to reduce cycle time and ensure adequate performance in production units.

EDA has been recognized for its ability to help vehicle manufacturers. Benefits that car makers are realizing include more effective and productive design engineers; parallel efforts in the design phase; simulation of more alternatives, early problem resolution, and optimization of final design; and the ability to incorporate more value-added electronic features for product differentiation.

The extent of interaction that must be analyzed and understood to provide future vehicle controls is extremely complex and will require several systems that simulate everything from vehicle combustion process to air bag deployment and driving simulation. Figure 32.8 shows a simple interrelation among the driver, his vehicle, and the environment. The ability to link together these systems and provide increased control to the driver will be the challenge for designers of future vehicles. This will require new semiconductor hardware, advanced development tools, and an unprecedented amount of software.

32.5 IMPACT ON FUTURE AUTOMOTIVE ELECTRONICS

Section 32.2.1 brought out the designer's role in future, sophisticated electronic systems. The enabling semiconductor technologies will be available. One potential system evolution path that could be taken to consolidate electronics in the passenger compartment is shown in Fig. 32.9. Given the level of complexity in the final stage, changes must be made in the way systems are designed.

A typical synthesis pipeline of today's design for digital electronics, which shows how an idea becomes a finished semiconductor product, is shown in Fig. 32.10. The RTL (register

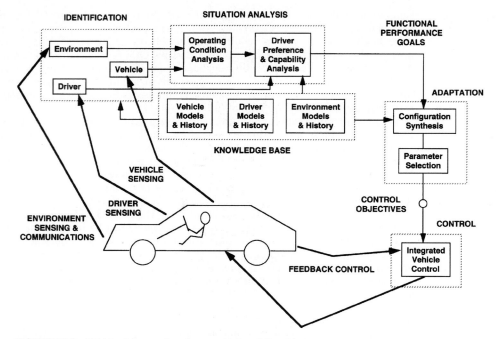

FIGURE 32.8 Vehicle, driver, and environment interrelationships.

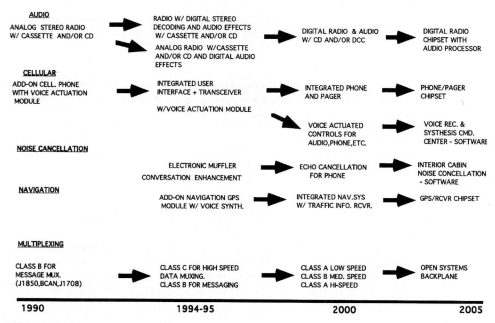

FIGURE 32.9 Audio, communication, navigation systems evolution.

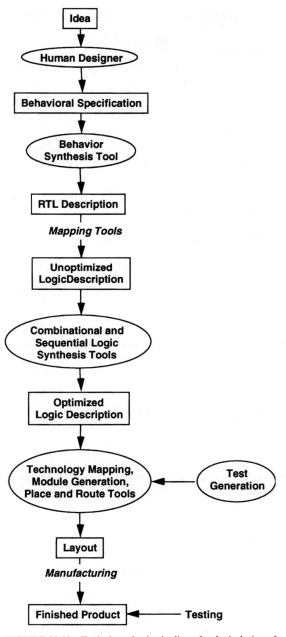

FIGURE 32.10   Typical synthesis pipeline of today's design of
VLSI silicon chip.

transfer level) description is the area where the functionality of the ALUs (arithmetic logic units) and buses are specified by the chip architect. The RTL description is an interconnection of predefined modules such as adders, multipliers, or finite state machines that comprise controllers. The sequential logic description that accomplishes the desired behavior of the system is performed by logic designer(s). Finally, circuit designers optimize the transistor-level design created by logic designers.

Challenges in automating this process include the need for a new breed of designer, the system architect, who will have to simultaneously deal with software and hardware systems; unified formalism for specifying, analyzing, and designing mixed software/hardware systems; and development of design automation software to aid system-level partitioning.

The leading edge in today's electronics is demonstrated by the totally automated development of silicon based on the use of behavior synthesis and high-level physical design tools. DSP ICs have already been developed using AutoCircuit behavioral synthesis technology from General Motors R & D Center and high-level physical tools developed by Cascade Design Automation. IC engineers at Delco Electronics used Verilog language to describe the DSP algorithms. After simulating the algorithms, AutoCircuit converted them into a Verilog list of datapath modules, such as adders, subtracters, ALUs, and state machines. The Verilog net lists were fed directly into Cascade's tools, which automatically compiled all of the datapath modules and synthesized the state machine control-logic modules. The Cascade tools placed and routed the modules, and extracted post-layout timing information for gate-level timing simulation.

This approach will be used extensively in the development of future ICs. In addition, the linkage of the system(s) performance simulation to silicon generating systems will be required.

32.5.1 Changing Role of the Automotive Electronics Designer

Software will drive IC technology. At the same time, the automotive engineer's role will change. Already this role has changed from that of a board-level designer using transistors to one using integrated circuits. Today, a systems approach is being pursued, but the systems have to be designed with a top-down methodology. Product development with system engineering guidance is shown in Fig. 32.11. This is today's approach and probably will not significantly change from the organizational side, except for a stronger role for software development. However, the activities performed by these functions must change through the use of more interactive tools. Starting with the total concept for the car, every module, every subsystem, every piece of electronic technology must be considered. Integration, system partitioning, design functionality, and distributed versus centralized intelligence are part of this approach. Audio system evolution, shown in Fig. 32.12, provides an excellent example of the transition. This figure will be examined closer in the next section.

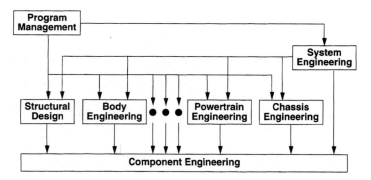

FIGURE 32.11 Product development with system engineering operation.

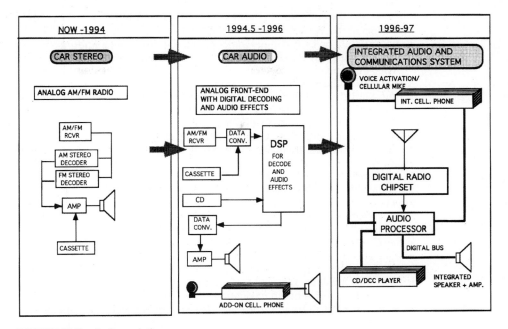

FIGURE 32.12   Audio evolution.

32.5.2   Potential System Architectures of the Future

It is apparent by now that the trend in automotive electronics is toward up-integration, with designers taking advantage of the compute power available, along with packaging technologies and adding more functionality to the modules. For example, engine management is being combined with cruise control and transmission control to form the powertrain controller. This trend is mainly driven by the need to reduce the cost of the modules—*value engineering* is the term being used, where value = function/cost. Value can be increased by either decreasing the cost of given functionality or by increasing functionality for the same cost. Integration then becomes a series of decisions or tradeoffs involving packaging, pc board, and semiconductor technologies. The designer continually makes cost/performance tradeoffs in selecting the technologies, and as technologies evolve, these tradeoffs must be updated.

So, given the technology scenario described earlier in this chapter, one can ask where will this evolution of up-integration end? Will everything eventually be integrated into a central control module? Or, given the trend in multiplexing, will ECUs be added ad infinitum, creating a distributed intelligence architecture? The answer is most probably "no" for both scenarios, and for several reasons, the key ones being cost effectiveness, reliability, heat dissipation, serviceability, and space requirements. The more likely scenario will be a combination of centralization and distributed intelligence where the centralization would be based along the lines of body, chassis and safety, powertrain, and audio/entertainment and communications. Within these centralized systems would be distributed intelligence based on multiplex wiring with smart sensors, switch decoders, and smart actuators all controlled by a central intelligence.

The strongest case for this scenario is the body system controller (refer to Table 32.1). Here functions such as door locks, interior dome lights, trunk lock, remote entry, antitheft alarm, electronic window lift, and electronic seat control with memory could all be centralized with multiplex wiring connecting the smart actuators (i.e., door locks, trunk release solenoids, etc.), switch decoders, and lamp and motor drivers. Another alternative to centralizing the whole car into one system could be partitioning the system into four systems controlling the four quadrants of the vehicle. The multiplex wiring within each quadrant linking the switches and actuators could be class A type, while the quadrants could be interlinked with a class B multiplex bus for diagnostic purposes and to provide a gateway into the driver information system.

The audio/entertainment system is probably the most interesting system from an architecture viewpoint because of how it has evolved, its uniqueness from the standpoint of standardization, and the possibilities that integrated semiconductor technology could provide. To understand the possibilities, let's examine how the radio has evolved. As shown in Fig. 32.12, the initial analog-based AM radio has integrated functions to include stereo (both AM and FM) and cassette or compact disc (CD) in the early 90s. Audio effects similar to ones found in home stereo systems are made possible with DSPs and are being offered on high-end vehicles today. With the availability of high-resolution, high-speed data conversion devices (e.g., 16- to 18-bit sigma-delta A/Ds and D/As), the radio will move from the analog domain to a digital domain, with the DSPs performing the task of AM/FM stereo decoding along with the audio effects.

A new dimension to the car audio system has been the addition of cellular phones. Instead of being an add-on aftermarket feature, the cellular phone is being integrated into the audio system. Bosch and Pioneer both have introduced stereo systems with the cellular phone integrated. This integration allows features such as automatic muting of the radio when a call comes in and better quality sound because the phone now uses the audio speakers instead of it's own tiny speaker. The next feature to be added to the audio system will be global positioning system (GPS) based navigation.

In the next few years all three functions—radio/audio, cellular phone, and GPS receivers—will be reduced to single-chip functions or chipsets. The system designer will then design a motherboard for an audio/phone/navigation system where each function could be offered simply by putting in the chipset—the plug-and-play concept similar to that used in the pc world. Taking this one step further, if all three functions were made available as a standard package, the system designer could take a total systems approach and develop one chip or chipset and implement the three functions in software. This would eliminate redundant computing power from the three-function chipsets scenario. This is possible because at any given time either the radio/audio system or the phone would be functioning, and the same hardware could handle the functions with context-switching software. Since the GPS receiver function is not time critical, it could be handled again by the same hardware on a cycle-stealing basis. Features such as voice recognition could also be added in software. The designer would need to develop an operating system to handle all the function switching and the user interface—perhaps, the automotive operating systems (AOS). Again, the analogy of the pc world is appropriate.

This would lead us to conclude that software is going to play an increasingly important role in future automotive electronics. Given that the capability of the semiconductor industry and the IC design tools will evolve, the differentiating factor will be software.

32.6 CONCLUSIONS

A universally accepted approach to electronics in all regions of the world does not appear very likely. Europe, North America, Japan, and other regions of the world have differences in use and design that are obvious in the electronic requirements. Europe may be the most likely to favor a backplane approach. In the United States, captive electronics support can provide individuality, but independent electronic suppliers in Europe support several different automotive customers in several countries with a wide range of requirements. Obviously, this requires standards that allow users to specify within the capabilities of several suppliers and still configure the functions that are required.

With rapid advances that are occurring in research, the technology of choice for semiconductors is a moving target which can change in the present design cycle time for vehicles. Problems for one approach can be solved, making it a viable alternative. Based on the kinds of systems that will drive future vehicle technology, and the potential for more drive power options—four- or two-stroke internal combustion, electric, hybrid and diesel—automobile manufacturers will continue to look to electronics and semiconductor technology to provide cost-effective solutions. Software will be the next frontier for semiconductor, electronics, and automotive manufacturers.

This chapter has described activities that are occurring or are likely to occur based on information that is widely discussed in public electronic and automotive forums. Several sources of new information that will provide an update or revise these projections can be found in:

- Semiconductor Industry Association (SIA) reports
- Proceedings of International Congress on Transportation Electronics (Convergence)
- University of Michigan Delphi Report (Rev. VII or later)
- Morgan Stanley research
- Hansen Report on automotive electronics, published monthly
- BIS strategic decisions
- Arthur D. Little reports
- *Inside IVHS,* published biweekly
- Automotive periodicals (e.g., *Automotive Engineering, Automotive Industries, Automotive News, Ward's Auto World*)
- Electronics periodicals (e.g., *EE Times, Electronic Design, Electronic Design News, IEEE Spectrum*)
- Other SAE or IEEE publications

SMARTMOS, Seamless Silicon System, System Chip, and SENSEFET are trademarks of Motorola, Inc. Saber is a trademark of Analogy, Inc. Pass-Key is a trademark of General Motors. All other trademarks are the property of their respective owners.

GLOSSARY

ASIC   Application-specific integrated circuit, an IC designed for a custom requirement, frequently a gate array or programmable logic device.

ATPG   Automation test program/pattern generator.

BIST   Built-in self-test, design technique that allows a chip to be tested for a guaranteed level of functionality.

CISC   Complex instruction set computer, standard computing approach as compared to RISC architecture.

Combinational technologies   Integrated mixed-signal, analog and digital technology.

DFT   Design for testability, methodology that takes test requirements into account early in the design process.

EPROM   Erasable programmable read-only memory, a semiconductor technique used for permanent storage but can be erased by ultraviolet light.

EEPROM   Electrically erasable programmable read-only memory, a semiconductor technique used for permanent storage. It can be reprogrammed in the system.

Engine (micro engine)   The computational portion of an IC.

Flash   Semiconductor memory, faster than EEPROM, that can be used for permanent storage and is easily electrically reprogrammed in the system.

Flops   Floating-point operations per second, a measurement of microprocessor performance.

FPGA   Field-programmable gate array, an IC that can be programmed.

Harvard architecture   On-chip program and data are in two separate spaces and are carried in parallel by two separate buses.

HDL   Hardware description language.

HLL   High-level language, a programming language that utilizes macro statements and instructions that closely resemble human language or mathematical notation to describe the problem to be solved or the procedure to be used.

Integration   The combination of previous levels of separate circuit designs.

Mechatronics   The combination of mechanical and electronic technology as in motor controls.

MESFET (metal semiconductor field effect transistor)   A high-frequency semiconductor device produced in GaAs semiconductor technology.

Micromachining   The chemical etching of mechanical structures in silicon, or other semiconductor material, usually to produce a sensor or actuator.

Mips   Millions of instructions per second, a measurement of microprocessor throughput.

Mixed-signal   The combination of analog and digital circuitry in a single semiconductor process.

Multiprocessing   The simultaneous execution of two or more instructions by a computer.

MCU   Microcontrol unit, or microcontroller unit, a semiconductor that has both a CPU, memory, and I/O capability on the same chip.

MMIC   Monolithic microwave integrated circuit, a high-frequency integrated circuit.

Partitioning   System design methodology that determines which portion of the circuit is integrated using a particular silicon process instead of completely integrating design using one process.

Pipeline   Bus structure within an MPU that allows concurrent operations to occur.

Protocol   The rules governing the exchange of data between networked elements.

RISC   Reduced instruction set computer, a CPU architecture which optimizes processing speed by the use of a smaller number of basic machine instructions.

Scalable   Ability of MCU or MPU architecture to be modified to meet the needs of several applications providing competitive price-performance points.

Silicon compiler   A tool that translates algorithms into a design layout for silicon.

SMD   Surface-mount device (see **SMT**).

SMT   Surface-mount technology, method of attaching components, both electrically and mechanically, to the surface of a conductive pattern.

SPECfp92   Floating-point benchmark test and rating (1992) for comparing microprocessor computing power.

SPECint92   Integer benchmark test and rating (1992) for comparing microprocessor computing power.

State machine   Logic circuitry that when clocked sequences through logical operations and can be a preprogrammed set of instructions or logic states.

SSVS   Super-smart vehicle systems, term used in Japan for vehicles with several new electronic systems, typically used in IVHS.

Submicron   Measurement of the geometries or critical spacing used for complex, highly integrated circuits.

Superscalar   The ability of an MPU to dispatch multiple instructions per clock from a conventional linear instruction stream.

Verilog   A hardware description language for behavior-level circuit design placed in public domain by Cadence Design Systems Inc.

VHDL   VHSIC Hardware Description Language, a hardware description language for behavior-level circuit design developed by the U.S. Department of Defense.

Von Neumann (architecture)   Program and data are carried sequentially on the same bus.

BIBLIOGRAPHY

"Behavior Synthesis Yields Working Silicon," *Electronic Design,* Dec. 2, 1993, p. 28.

Benson, M., R. Frank, J. Jandu, and M. Shaw, *Proceedings of Sensors Expo 1993,* Philadelphia, Pa., Oct. 26–28, 1993, pp. 133–143.

"Circuits don't need substrates at UCLA," Technology News section of *Solid State Technology,* Dec. 1993, pp. 18–19.

Devadas, S., "Microelectronic System Design Skills for the Year 2000 and Beyond," *Journal of Microelectronic Systems Integration,* vol. 1, no. 1, 1993, pp. 85–95.

"EDA: An Emerging Competitive Weapon," *The Hansen Report,* July/August 1992.

Faubert, R., "Mainstream logic designers need to master new hardware and software design skills," *IEEE Spectrum,* p. 57.

Fleming, William, "Automotive Electronics," *IEEE Vehicular Technology Society News,* May 1993, pp. 32–34.

Gates, M., "EPA nominee is tough on environment, open to ideas," *Automotive News,* July 26, 1993, p. 4.

Schilke, N. A., et al., "Integrated Vehicle Controls," *Proceedings of 1988 International Congress on Transportation Electronics,* IEEE 88CH2533-8, Dearborn, Mich., Oct. 17–18, 1988, pp. 97–106.

SIA Semiconductor Technology, Workshop Working Group Reports, San Jose, Calif., 1993.

"Systems Engineering: and Update," *Automotive Engineering,* Feb. 1992, pp. 65–66.

Wilhelm, R. V., E. M. Norppa, and K. D. Casey, "Voice of the Customer Linkages to Powertrain Controller Design," *Proceedings of 1992 International Congress on Transportation Electronics,* SAE, Warrendale, Pa., Oct., 1992, pp. 253–258.

ABOUT THE AUTHORS

RANDY FRANK (see biography at the end of Chap. 2).

SALIM MOMIN is director of market development, Automotive Segment, Semiconductor Product Systems, Motorola Inc. His main function is strategic marketing and technology planning. He started his career with Chrysler Corp., working on the first fuel-injected turbocharged engine. At Gulf & Western Mfg. Co., he developed electronic modules for the automotive industry. He holds two patents for his work at Chrysler.

Index

Index

ABOUT THE EDITOR

Ronald K. Jurgen recently retired as senior editor at *IEEE Spectrum*, where he specialized in automotive and consumer electronics. He performed a broad range of editorial functions for the magazine since its inception in 1964, including writing more than 100 articles. He also served as chief editor for *Spectrum*'s special issues devoted to a wide variety of automotive technology. A graduate of Rensselaer Polytechnic Institute, he was editor in chief of the book *Computers and Manufacturing Productivity* (IEEE Press, 1987).